CAMBRIDGE TEXTS
HISTORY OF PHIL(

ANTHONY ASHLEY COOPER,
THIRD EARL OF SHAFTESBURY
*Characteristics of Men,
Manners, Opinions, Times*

CAMBRIDGE TEXTS IN THE
HISTORY OF PHILOSOPHY

Series editors

KARL AMERIKS
Professor of Philosophy at the University of Notre Dame

DESMOND M. CLARKE
Professor of Philosophy at University College Cork

The main objective of Cambridge Texts in the History of Philosophy is to expand the range, variety and quality of texts in the history of philosophy which are available in English. The series includes texts by familiar names (such as Descartes and Kant) and also by less well-known authors. Wherever possible, texts are published in complete and unabridged form, and translations are specially commissioned for the series. Each volume contains a critical introduction together with a guide to further reading and any necessary glossaries and textual apparatus. The volumes are designed for student use at undergraduate and postgraduate level and will be of interest not only to students of philosophy, but also to a wider audience of readers in the history of science, the history of theology and the history of ideas.

For a list of titles published in the series, please see end of book.

ANTHONY ASHLEY COOPER, THIRD EARL OF SHAFTESBURY

Characteristics of Men, Manners, Opinions, Times

EDITED BY

LAWRENCE E. KLEIN

University of Nevada, Las Vegas

CAMBRIDGE UNIVERSITY PRESS

PUBLISHED BY THE PRESS SYNDICATE OF THE
UNIVERSITY OF CAMBRIDGE
The Pitt Building, Trumpington Street, Cambridge, United Kingdom

CAMBRIDGE UNIVERSITY PRESS
The Edinburgh Building, Cambridge, CB2 2RU, UK   http://www.cup.cam.ac.uk
40 West 20th Street, New York, NY 10011–4211, USA   http://www.cup.org
10 Stamford Road, Oakleigh, Melbourne 3166, Australia

First published 1999

Typeset in 10/12pt Ehrhardt [wv]

A catalogue record for this book is available from the British Library

ISBN 0 521 57022 0 hardback
ISBN 0 521 57892 2 paperback

Transferred to digital printing 2003

Contents

Acknowledgments

This edition of Shaftesbury's *Characteristics* has been supported by grants and other aid from several units of the University of Nevada, Las Vegas (UNLV): the History Department, the Office of Research and the University Fellowships and Grants Committee. The National Endowment for the Humanities provided a summer stipend in 1998 to support research in the British Library, London.

Producing this edition was facilitated by the technical assistance of the UNLV History Department staff, especially Jan Harris and Frances Honour, and several UNLV students, Mary Dowling, Gary Handley, Robert Kryger, James Murphey, and Stacie Pearl. Mary Wammack was an outstanding research assistant.

For suggestions about the Introduction, I am grateful to David Shields of the Citadel and Michael Prince of Boston University as well as my History colleagues, A. J. E. Bell, Gregory Brown and Chris Rasmussen. I also thank Douglas Den Uyl of the Liberty Fund in Indianapolis, Indiana, for inviting me to a conference in November 1998 on Shaftesbury where the discussion helped to direct my approach to the Introduction.

I am also extremely grateful to Desmond Clarke for inviting me to undertake this project and to him and Hilary Gaskin of Cambridge University Press for assistance (as well as patience) while I completed it.

Since the third Earl of Shaftesbury assumed a classically educated readership, *Characteristics* was laced with quotations in the original Greek and Latin. The translations provided here are the work of my colleague and friend, A. J. E. Bell. His participation in this project was an act of collegiality and friendship far beyond the call of duty: *quis nunc diligitur nisi conscius?*

Introduction

In 1711, Anthony Ashley Cooper, the third Earl of Shaftesbury (1671–1713), brought out an anthology of his previously published works. He had revised them and supplemented them with new writing, and he called the collection *Characteristics of Men, Manners, Opinions, Times*. In its optimistic assessment of an orderly cosmos, confidence in human sociability and fellow feeling, harmonization of ethical and aesthetic experience, emphases on liberty and toleration, and commitment to the role of philosophy in educating humanity, *Characteristics* found readers throughout the eighteenth century, in Britain and on the Continent.

Shaftesbury did not explain why he chose the particular title he gave to the collection, but the title does convey the fact that the work was diverse in its contents and, also, often concrete and topical in approach. It is hardly surprising that *Characteristics* has been of interest to a wide range of modern scholars. The text has been read to illuminate the histories of religion and irreligion, ethics and aesthetics, political discourse, painting, architecture, gardening, literature, scholarship and, most recently, gender – not to mention such big themes in the interpretation of the eighteenth century as the civilizing process, the Enlightenment, the public sphere and sensibility. *Characteristics* is indeed a fundamental work for understanding the intellectual and cultural aspirations and achievements of the eighteenth century (and, in some respects, of a period extending deep into the nineteenth century).[1]

Though the title may suggest a project almost sociological in nature, Shaftesbury certainly regarded it as a work of philosophy. We should take this claim seriously, although much of the work differed from the dominant style of philosophical discourse in its own era and in the philosophical tradition ever

---

[1] J. W. Burrow in *Whigs and Liberals: Continuity and Change in English Political Thought* (Oxford: Clarendon Press, 1988) presents 'the concept of politeness', developed in the post-1688 decades by the writers including Shaftesbury, Joseph Addison and Richard Steele, as 'the distinctively modern form of virtue', persuasive in Whig thinking through the 1870s.

vii

since. This introduction aims to explain, in the first place, what Shaftesbury meant by philosophy and how he tended to conflate philosophical with cultural and political reflection. His interpretation of the identity of philosophy helps, in turn, to explain why the book is so miscellaneous, both in its content and its form. Finally, because *Characteristics* is so miscellaneous, the introduction lays out the most important frames of reference through which Shaftesbury grasped the world.

The worldliness of philosophy

At the heart of *Characteristics* was the philosophical dialogue, 'The Moralists', which opened with a character bemoaning the current condition of philosophy. 'She is no longer active in the world nor can hardly, with any advantage, be brought upon the public stage. We have immured her, poor lady, in colleges and cells and have set her servilely to such works as those in the mines' (p. 232). We can be confident that this character voiced Shaftesbury's own opinion on the subject. His work aimed at nothing other than returning philosophy to the world, an aspiration that explains both the work's themes and its design.

What did philosophical worldliness mean? Most important, Shaftesbury thought that philosophy should make people effective participants in the world. It was a practical enterprise and, given the disabilities from which humans generally suffered, often a therapeutic one. Philosophy was neither an intellectual discipline for specialists nor a profession, according to Shaftesbury, but a wisdom that had to touch each thoughtful individual: 'If philosophy be, as we take it, the study of happiness, must not everyone, in some manner or other, either skilfully or unskilfully philosophize?' (p. 336).

This practical activity embraced the pursuit of moral self-knowledge and the process of moral self-transformation. Self-consciously seeking to re-animate a Socratic project, Shaftesbury repeatedly invoked the imperative to know oneself. At the same time, he was original in conceiving the pursuit of self-knowledge as a procedure of inner conversation. He elaborated extensively on the technique of talking to oneself, but he also used dialogic patterns throughout *Characteristics* to illustrate and underpin his point.

Self-knowledge through inner conversation was not an end in itself; rather, it helped the individual to refashion the self on a moral pattern. Shaftesbury emphasized the 'workmanship' that went into being a moral agent, the 'improvement' to which the self should aspire, and the creative energy required for the self to be its own 'author' (pp. 117, 332, 151): this emphasis on self-fashioning was one of many ways in which Shaftesbury's aesthetic propensities contributed to his moralism. Though the technique of self-fashioning might demand episodes of withdrawal and solitary ascetic discipline, the point was always to re-enter the world in a morally effective way, just as the moralists at the very end of the philosophical dialogue of that title, having acknowledged the cosmic framework of human endeavour, returned 'to the common affairs of life'.

Philosophical worldliness had another important value for Shaftesbury. He assumed that philosophy was embedded in history and culture – a position he adopted for several reasons. First, he believed that the Western philosophical tradition at its best insisted on the imperative of self-knowledge and self-transformation. He also believed that humans were naturally sociable and thus always already participants in processes of civilization. In addition, he believed that the development of moral sensibility was inextricably linked with that of aesthetic sensibility. Thus, while the core of Shaftesburian philosophy was a moral imperative of self-knowledge and character formation, Shaftesbury was really propagating a *paideia*, a programme of intellectual and aesthetic as well as ethical cultivation. This explains the proximity in his writing of philosophy and 'politeness', a contemporary expression for moral and cultural refinement: 'To philosophize, in a just signification, is but to carry good breeding a step higher', he wrote (p. 407). Shaftesbury's commitment to this broad programme of training also explains why so much of the material in *Characteristics* was historical and cultural commentary rather than strictly philosophical argumentation.

Finally, philosophical worldliness had a political resonance since Shaftesbury linked his *paideia* to a political programme. The contours of his moral thinking and his cultural sensibility fitted political preferences and priorities that were very much of his immediate world. In ways discussed below, Shaftesbury was a partisan in a world divided by parties. However, philosophical worldliness had a political significance beyond partisan allegiance: to be philosophical, for Shaftesbury, was to understand and orient oneself toward 'the public'.

Shaftesbury lived during events that allowed him to reconsider the status of monarchs, and, though his perspective was always aristocratic, he used resources within the ancient and English traditions to conceive what might take the place of the political culture of kings, courts and courtiers. Like other Europeans of the eighteenth century who were attempting to imagine a world without royal and ecclesiastical authoritarianism, Shaftesbury developed norms for conduct, conversation and limited conflict that could accommodate both liberty and order, both individual actualization and social responsibility. Perhaps his most important, and neglected, contribution to European reflection was his vision of civil society. Shaftesbury's moralism aimed to cultivate political subjectivities appropriate to civil society while his cultural commentary demonstrated the opportunities and pathologies that emerged from the complex relationship among manners, culture and power.

Though later thinkers tended to distinguish the spheres of ethics, culture and politics, Shaftesbury assumed their mutual inextricability. To insist on the worldliness of philosophy was to claim that philosophy had to be, all at once, oriented toward ethical practice, immersed in human history and culture, and committed to a political programme. As his writing conflated ethical, cultural and political matters, so his own persona conflated those of philosopher, poet and ideologist.[2]

The idiosyncrasies of the text

Shaftesbury's ambition for worldliness helps to explain the unusual form his philosophical writing took. *Characteristics* has never been an easy text for readers to get a grasp of, and philosophical commentators have often remarked on its intractability. It is, to be sure, long, somewhere in length between Thomas Hobbes' *Leviathan* and the Baron de Montesquieu's *Spirit of the Laws*: eighteenth-century editions appeared in three hefty volumes. More important, *Characteristics* is composite, both in its contents and in its form: it has ten component parts; these components explore a wide range of subject matters; and they are in different genres and styles.

This composite quality may suggest that *Characteristics* is not a work of any particular integrity. Nor is it surprising that scholars have often approached *Characteristics* in a selective manner. Philosophers, in particular, finding so much in the text that they do not recognize as philosophy, have known Shaftesbury primarily through extracts of *Characteristics*, often identified as the 'genuinely philosophical' parts, in anthologies devoted to 'the British moralists'.[3]

In part, this composite quality of *Characteristics* is explained by the circumstances of its production. It was not written as a whole but was in fact an anthology, representing, more or less, the complete works of Shaftesbury, gathered together and supplemented with new material. Although the idea for such an anthology came to him late, Shaftesbury had been working on its contents for most of his short adult life.

He began in the 1690s, drafting *An Inquiry Concerning Virtue*, which was first published in 1699. The *Inquiry* argued that goodness and virtue had real foundations in the nature of the human self and in its relations to a morally designed universe and that virtue was its own reward since its practice conduced to human happiness. The *Inquiry* advocated natural human sociability, as against theories of egoism, and a scheme of ethical value independent of religious institutions and teachings.

---

[2] This formulation is inspired by Douglas J. Den Uyl, 'Shaftesbury and the Modern Problem of Virtue', *Social Philosophy and Policy* 15 (1998): 275–316.

[3] For instance, L. A. Selby-Bigge, ed., *British Moralists* (Oxford: Clarendon Press, 1897); D. H. Monro, *A Guide to British Moralists* (London: William Collins Sons & Co., 1972); and J. B. Schneewind, *Moral Philosophy from Montaigne to Kant* (Cambridge: Cambridge University Press, 1990).

This work was formal philosophy, demonstrative in its aspiration to argue some of Shaftesbury's most important ethical convictions. However, when he included a revised version of this treatise in *Characteristics*, he repeatedly distanced himself from its form, though not its substance. The other components of *Characteristics* forthrightly presented themselves as alternative and less formal approaches to knowledge. In the decade that intervened between the initial publication of the *Inquiry* and its inclusion in *Characteristics*, it appears that Shaftesbury decided to shift the rhetorical grounds on which philosophy needed to fight its battles.[4]

On the one hand, he moved toward the more self-consciously literary form of the highly wrought philosophical dialogue, *The Moralists*, drafted in the early 1700s but published in much revised form in 1709.[5] *The Moralists* was a complex account of a number of conversations narrated by one of the participants. These conversations delineated Shaftesbury's notion of the worldly aims of modern philosophy while illustrating its dialogic practice. The principal substantive tasks of the work, however, were to fend off sceptical attacks on Shaftesbury's ethical realism while underpinning it with an aesthetic foundation. *The Moralists* argued the inseparability of ethical truth and aesthetic beauty. While this allowed Shaftesbury to develop a theistic cosmic vision of harmonious aesthetic and ethical order, it also provided a cosmic foundation for his more quotidian concerns with bodily comportments, discursive practices and aesthetic tastes.

On the other hand, Shaftesbury moved toward apparently more spontaneous, digressive, though no less self-conscious, forms of writing. The first of these was *A Letter Concerning Enthusiasm* (1708) (about which more will be said below). Stimulated by the appearance in London of a group of prophetically inspired Christians, the *Letter* both ridiculed religious delusion and recuperated imagination and feeling as fundamental to human experience. Shaftesbury's proposal that the most efficient means to disarm dangerously deluded people was good humour and tolerance, rather than shrill polemics and publicly orchestrated persecutions, made the *Letter* itself an object of critical comment.

---

4   The *Inquiry* itself underwent serious revision between the 1699 edition and the first edition of *Characteristics*. The two versions can now be read, side by side, in the Shaftesbury Standard Edition, Volume II, Part 2. See Further reading. See also David Walford's edition of the *Inquiry* (Manchester: Manchester University Press, 1977).

5   An early version of the dialogue was printed privately as *The Social Enthusiast* in 1704. *The Social Enthusiast* and 'The Moralists', as it appeared in the first edition of *Characteristics*, are printed on facing pages in the Shaftesbury Standard Edition, Volume II, Part 1. See Further reading. The complex evolution of this work is told in Horst Meyer, *Limae Labor: Untersuchungen zur Textgenese und Druckgeschichte von Shaftesburys 'The Moralists'* (Frankfurt am Main: Peter Lang, 1978). The work is interpreted brilliantly in Michael Prince, *Philosophical Dialogue in the British Enlightenment* (Cambridge: Cambridge University Press, 1996), pp. 23–73.

In response to several pamphlets attacking the *Letter*, Shaftesbury wrote *Sensus Communis, An Essay on the Freedom of Wit and Humour* (1709).[6] Here Shaftesbury's defence of good humour, tolerance and the benefits of open discussion led him to present conversation in a free society as the basis for moral and cultural improvement, or politeness. However, he went further, arguing that the premise for all such improvement was the possibility of human virtue, which he grounded in natural human sociability, the *sensus communis* or the sense of the common, to which he sought to provide a rich moral and civic definition.

At about the same time, Shaftesbury was writing *Soliloquy, or Advice to an Author*, which first appeared in 1710. As the main title indicated, this essay took up the conversational theme, already suggested in the *Letter* and enunciated in *Sensus Communis*, and redirected it. *Soliloquy* asserted the necessity of self-discourse in constituting moral subjectivity. In particular, however, authors, who should be the ethical moulders of a civilization, were in need of self-knowledge and self-discourse. This argument was supplemented with assessments of the roles of the social and political elite, of critics and, finally, of the people at large in the formation of a culture. We find here an elaborate and complex discussion of the dynamics and politics of culture, in which the themes of conversation, philosophy and liberty were interwoven.

It is hard to specify precisely when Shaftesbury decided to combine his several published writings into a collection. However, clearly it was not later than 1710 since *Characteristics* appeared in the spring of 1711. Its first volume comprised *A Letter Concerning Enthusiasm*, *Sensus Communis* and *Soliloquy*, each of which was modestly revised for its new appearance. The second volume of *Characteristics* contained *An Inquiry Concerning Virtue or Merit* in a considerably revised form and *The Moralists*. For the third volume, Shaftesbury wrote a new set of pieces, five highly discursive, even rambling, essays. In these 'Miscellaneous Reflections on the Preceding Treatises and Other Critical Subjects' (as they were identified on the title page of the third volume), Shaftesbury adopted the remarkable trope of assuming the voice of a commentator on the contents of *Characteristics*. The miscellanies of the third volume allowed Shaftesbury to bring some coherence to this assemblage: the five components of 'Miscellaneous Reflections' corresponded roughly to the first five treatises and provided a unifying gloss. Shaftesbury also took advantage of the opportunity offered by his anthology to knit the various pieces together

---

[6]   The pamphlets were: Mary Astell, *Bart'lemy Fair: Or an Enquiry after Wit* (1709), Edward Fowler, *Reflections upon A Letter Concerning Enthusiasm, to Lord **** (1709), and *Remarks upon the Letter Concerning Enthusiasm. In a Letter to a Gentleman* (1708). Both the 'Letter' and 'Sensus Communis' are helpfully presented in Richard B. Wolf, *An Old-Spelling Critical Edition of Shaftesbury's Letter Concerning Enthusiasm and Sensus Communis* (New York and London: Garland Publishing, Inc., 1988).

with hundreds of cross-referencing footnotes, directing readers to thematic continuities.[7]

However, it is a mistake to exaggerate the unity of *Characteristics*. Indeed, to proffer thematic summaries of the component treatises (in the manner just performed) goes against the grain of the text and violates the tone and style of much of the writing. Shaftesbury took great care to give *Characteristics* play, both in the sense of humour and playfulness and also in the sense of variety and open-endedness. Humour, playfulness, variety, open-endedness – these were Shaftesburian values, formal expressions of his aspiration to worldliness. It is important to understand how this worldly style served both rhetorical and cognitive purposes in *Characteristics*.

Shaftesbury's readership was gentlemanly. (In Shaftesbury's case, the gender bias of this expression is accurate since he was consistently dismissive of women as participants in civil society.) He wrote for members of the English upper orders, wealthy men who were probably but not necessarily landed, literate men who were educated but not necessarily learned. He wrote, in short, for men of the world, and humour, playfulness, variety and open-endedness recommended themselves as ways to reach them.

In justifying his approach, Shaftesbury constructed a picture of the English gentleman bored and bullied by clerics and academics (frequently the same persons in Shaftesbury's era). He regularly denigrated the clerical and the homiletic, the academic and the pedantic. He regarded sermons and lectures as notably unsuitable vehicles for edification, and often dismissed or ridiculed their characteristic traits: the formal, the systematic, the consistent, the methodical and the abstract. (He blamed the same traits for the sterility of much philosophical writing.) He condemned the style of the pulpit and the classroom as authoritarian or 'magisterial', a word that, in light of its Latin origin, *magister*, combined a reference to the schoolteacher with one to the magistrate. Indeed, *Characteristics* was a collection of rhetorical gambits aiming to represent a discursive practice distinct from that of the lecture or the sermon.

A more 'polite' approach was required. 'Politeness', referring to the conventions of good manners, conveyed the fundamental rhetorical necessity of making concessions to the knowledge, interests and attention spans of an audience. As well, the word 'polite' had a more idiomatic meaning at this time, referring to matters of refined conversation. Shaftesbury invoked the importance of regulating 'style or language by the standard of good company and people of the better sort' (p. 75). Replacing the magisterial with the polite man-

---

[7] In the second edition, further unity was provided by a set of emblematic engravings, commissioned by Shaftesbury to illustrate the work's main points: see Felix Paknadel, 'Shaftesbury's Illustrations of *Characteristics*', *Journal of the Warburg and Courtauld Institutes* 37 (1974): 290–312.

ner implied writing that was more informal, miscellaneous, conversational, open-ended and sceptical.

A philosophy that lectured or a moralism that hectored was in danger of sterility, leaving audiences bored and unmoved. However, it was more than unpersuasive: it posed serious cognitive problems.

For one thing, it violated the goals of philosophy. At the outset of *Soliloquy*, Shaftesbury discussed the art of giving advice in a way relevant to the practice of philosophy. The central quandary of giving advice was that an effort ostensibly devoted to the good of the advisee degenerated so easily into a means to celebrate the adviser or, worse, to establish the dominance of adviser over advisee. The challenge for the adviser, for the philosopher and, indeed, for all who would teach and edify, was how to create and encourage, and not undermine, the autonomy of the subject: philosophy had to create moral agents. (The magisterial approach, by contrast, induced passivity before authority.) The form of *Characteristics* was meant to meet this challenge, to make philosophers of readers and to ensure that, as philosophers, they would be morally intelligent agents in the world.

The magisterial approach also violated the limits of human knowledge, promising more than philosophy could, ought or needed to provide. The discursive practice to which Shaftesbury aspired was often sceptical. Endorsing the sceptical methodology of ancient schools and such moderns as Pierre Bayle,[8] he urged on his readers the open-ended quest for truth and the benefits to be derived from free exchange. Scepticism was an attribute of an active and questing philosophical comportment. At the same time, Shaftesbury's scepticism limited his patience with the technical pursuit of philosophical truth: he lacked confidence that extensive logical analysis produced significant answers. One of the most important grounds on which Shaftesbury rejected the 'cavils of philosophy' in his own time was its quixotic search for analytic precision in domains far from moral concern and, in any case, where precision was far from attainable. Thus, René Descartes was of much less interest to Shaftesbury as a sceptic than as a deluded seeker after certainty.[9]

---

[8] Pierre Bayle (1647–1706) was a French Protestant scholar and philosopher who, after the revocation of the Edict of Nantes, settled in Rotterdam. His most influential publication was the *Dictionnaire historique et critique* (1697) in which expository articles on religious, philosophical and historical topics were supplemented by notes and commentaries that challenged received opinions. His scepticism targeted especially Christian orthodoxies. Shaftesbury associated with Bayle during his stays in Rotterdam and left a tribute to him in a letter to John Darby, publisher of *Characteristics*, dated 2 February 1708, Public Record Office (PRO) 30/24/22/4, f.63 (Benjamin Rand, ed., *The Life, Unpublished Letters and Philosophical Regimen of Anthony, Earl of Shaftesbury* (London: Swan Sonnenschein, 1900) (referred to in this edition's notes as Rand, *Regimen*), pp. 385–6).

[9] The Frenchman René Descartes (1596–1650), famous for his sceptical methodology, was also the inventor of co-ordinate geometry and the central analytic genius of the seventeenth-century revolutions in physics and philosophy.

However, Shaftesbury was far from being a thorough sceptic. He had a pragmatic side which dismissed the possibility that human feelings and thoughts might not have a relation to a determinate reality. He responded to extreme scepticism with an animal faith in the senses, the feelings and their referents: 'I take my being upon trust' (p. 421). Moreover, he had no doubt about his most important metaphysical and ethical convictions. In *Characteristics*, he toyed with the persona of the dogmatist (p. 395), but he provided a more accurate assessment once in a letter: 'I am but few removes from mere scepticism, and, though I may hold some principles perhaps tenaciously, they are, however, so very few, plain, and simple that they serve to little purpose towards the great speculations in fashion with the world.'[10]

The principles to which he tenaciously held were the intelligence and order of the cosmos and the reality of human sociability. *Characteristics* was devoted to conveying these principles although they were only occasionally argued on an abstract plane and with analytic rigour. As Shaftesbury put it, 'it is in a manner necessary for one who would usefully philosophize, to have a knowledge in this part of philosophy sufficient to satisfy him that there is no knowledge or wisdom to be learnt from it' (p. 427). Thus, he readily abandoned 'the high road of demonstration' for 'the diverting paths of poetry or humour' (p. 425), where he hoped not only to encounter his gentlemanly reader but guide him on his way. Thus, the text of *Characteristics* moved back and forth between the ancient and the modern worlds and among the topics of morals and customs, politics and culture – 'men, manners, opinions, times'.

Shaftesbury's frames of reference

Modern politics

Shaftesbury was deeply attentive to public affairs during his life, and *Characteristics* testified to this political consciousness.

The memory of civil war and revolution in seventeenth-century Britain haunted Shaftesbury's era and was frequently invoked, especially at moments of political crisis: during the Exclusion movement of the late 1670s and early 1680s, at the Revolution of 1688, and in the partisan contests between Whig and Tory during the reign of Anne. Moreover, Shaftesbury's life was entirely contained within the span of Louis XIV's reign in France. In the English imagination, Louis embodied arbitrary government and the aspiration to universal monarchy. He also kept alive the spirit of persecution that had made possible

---

[10] See Shaftesbury to 'Tiresias', 29 November 1706, PRO 30/24/22/4, ff. 358–9 (Rand, *Regimen*, pp. 366–9).

an age of religious wars: as recently as 1685, Louis had revoked the Edict of Nantes, precipitating a flood of Protestant emigration from France.[11]

Against this background, Shaftesbury advocated liberty and constitutional government, which he contrasted with Continental absolutism. He attacked politicized religion and deformations of the religious spirit that menaced the body politic. He urged toleration and rational conversation, softened by good manners and good humour, as models of behaviour for civil society.

His invention of a normative design for modern political culture took off from the Revolution of 1688, the central public event during his life. The Revolution was a new beginning in a number of ways. To be sure, this was a political revolution in the House of Stuart: James II's proclivities toward abso-lutism and Catholicism inspired the aristocratic coup that replaced him with his Protestant daughter, Mary II, and her Dutch husband, William III. The Revolution brought with it the Toleration Act of 1689, which provided reli-gious freedom, at least for Protestants. It also brought wars with France, last-ing most of Shaftesbury's adult life, in which Britain acceded to a greater European role and a more self-consciously imperial identity.

More generally, the post-1688 era was one of growing prosperity, however unevenly distributed, marked by increasing consumption at many levels of soci-ety: as convenience and luxury achieved wider circulation in society, so too did 'taste' as an acknowledged capacity in human experience. This consumption fostered a burgeoning culture of print (facilitated by the lapse of censorship laws in 1695) and an elaboration of commercialized urban institutions – coffeehouses, theatres, assemblies, lectures, clubs – which offered expanded opportunities for sociability, cultural expression and political contestation. All told, Shaftesbury's lifetime witnessed an increasing sense of British leadership not just in European politics but also in European culture. Shaftesbury hailed these developments, articulating the ideal of politeness through which British cultural ambitions could be conveyed.[12]

---

[11] Shaftesbury had significant relations with a number of displaced Protestant intellectuals, aside from Pierre Bayle. These included: Pierre Coste (1668–1747), friend and correspondent of Shaftesbury, who translated much of John Locke's work into French; Pierre Desmaizeaux (1673–1745), who wrote, translated and edited numerous works of contemporary philosophy and scholarship as an intellectual broker in the European Republic of Letters; and Jean Le Clerc (1657–1736), a Genevan polymath, prolific writer on theology, philosophy, criticism and his-tory, and editor of several international periodicals concerning literature and scholarship. The intellectual world of these men, through which Shaftesbury passed, is presented in Anne Goldgar, *Impolite Learning: Conduct and Community in the Republic of Letters, 1680–1750* (New Haven and London: Yale University Press, 1995).

[12] Some basic works on these developments are: Ann Bermingham and John Brewer, eds., *The Consumption of Culture, 1600–1800* (London and New York: Routledge, 1995); Peter Borsay, *The English Urban Renaissance: Culture and Society in the Provincial Town, 1660–1770* (Oxford: Clarendon Press, 1989); John Brewer, *The Sinews of Power: War, Money and the English State, 1688–1783* (London: Unwin Hyman Ltd, 1989); Jonathan I. Israel, *The Anglo-Dutch Moment: Essays on the Glorious Revolution and its World Impact* (Cambridge: Cambridge University Press,

Envisioning the shape and norms of civil society was, for Shaftesbury, a deeply partisan project, however, and *Characteristics* cannot be understood without reference to his passionate, though nuanced, Whiggism and his unsubtle hostility to Toryism. His grandfather, the first Earl, achieved eminence during the Exclusion crisis as leader of the first Whigs, who orchestrated a pre-emptive strike against the future James II by trying to exclude him from the succession. For Tories, who defended the hereditary succession, the name 'Shaftesbury' evoked an image of moral and political monstrosity.[13]

The third Earl's early life was dominated by the famous grandfather, who arranged for him to be tutored by a political ally, the philosopher and Whig ideologist John Locke (see p. xxvii). After the Whig movement collapsed and the first Earl was exiled, Shaftesbury spent several uncomfortable years at Winchester school (a Tory stronghold), followed by more private tutoring and a Grand Tour of the Continent. He was abroad in 1688 but wrote home celebrating 'our late purges from those promoters of that interest [Tories] that was to have enslaved us to the horridest of all religions [Catholicism] and to the service of the usurpations and treacheries of that neighbouring crown that has aimed so long at the subjection of all Europe [France]'.[14]

After 1688, Whiggism was associated with support for the Revolution and its consequences. Whigs claimed to be the defenders of the English constitution, liberty, Protestantism and toleration. They attacked Bourbon power and argued the case for vigorous warfare against France. These positions are evident in *Characteristics*, where the Revolution of 1688 was depicted as a pivot in British history, preserving and extending liberty in public life by ensuring the rule of law and the balanced constitution of monarch and Parliament.

However, *Characteristics*' main contribution to Whiggish thinking was analysing the moral and cultural concomitants of politics: it is precisely by articulating for Whiggism a cultural ideology, a politics of manners and culture, that *Characteristics* approaches the status of political discourse. Much of the work was devoted to elaborating the positive connection between liberty and intellectual and cultural achievement, expressed in the proposition that 'all politeness is owing to liberty' (p. 31).

Likewise, Shaftesbury expressed his Whiggish suspicion of kings in an elaborate critique of the culture of royal courts. Shaftesbury accepted England's (and, after the Union with Scotland in 1707, Britain's) constitutional monarchs and only occasionally aired criticism (at least in print) of the pre-1688 Stuarts,

---

1991); and Kathleen Wilson, *The Sense of the People: Politics, Culture and Imperialism in England, 1715–1785* (Cambridge: Cambridge University Press, 1995).

[13] John Dryden (1631–1700), Poet Laureate from 1670 through the 1688 Revolution, gave this sentiment classic literary formulation in his depiction of the first Earl as Achitophel in *Absalom and Achitophel* (1681).

[14] Shaftesbury to the second Earl, 3 May 1689, PRO 30/24/21/229 (Rand, *Regimen*, pp. 275–80).

but he explicitly attacked Bourbon monarchy. He depicted the moral and cultural turpitude of the French Court where a mixture of thrusting egoism and craven submissiveness undermined any possibility for sociability or autonomy. (He assimilated other contemporary instances, as he saw them, of despotism, whether the sultan's in Turkey, the Mogul's in India, or the Pope's in Rome, to this model of Court culture.)

Shaftesbury's Whiggism also had an ecclesiastical dimension. The Whigs had been identified since their beginnings with the policy of toleration. Shaftesbury accepted the Church of England as a component of the constitution and supported the tolerant Low Churchmanship associated with such Whiggish clerics of the post-1688 period as John Tillotson and Gilbert Burnet. Meanwhile, he condemned the High Church wing of Anglicanism for what he identified as its spirit of bigotry and persecution. The decades of Shaftesbury's maturity saw a revitalization of High Church postures among Tories, encouraged by politicians such as Daniel Finch, second Earl of Nottingham, and clerics such as Francis Atterbury, and symbolized by the great controversy surrounding the sermons of Henry Sacheverell in 1709 and 1710. Against this background, Shaftesbury argued for broad religious and intellectual toleration in the context of a public sphere, a worldly domain of free and open discussion in which exchange and criticism advanced both truth and refinement.

For Shaftesbury as well as many Whigs, the concomitant of tolerationism was Erastianism, the commitment to the subordination of the Church to the State. He strongly disliked pretensions, which he discerned among the High Churchmen, to ecclesiastical independence in the political arena. Thus, he frequently attacked politicized clergymen, lavishing attention on the history of 'priestcraft'. This term had emerged in the middle of the seventeenth century to express alarm that, even among Protestants, clerics were liable to arrogate power in the manner of the Catholic hierarchy, thus undermining moral and political liberty.[15] (This hostility to the High Church fed his hostility to educational institutions, especially the universities, which, in his era, were branches of the established Church. He saw them, accurately, as hotbeds of High Church sentiment.)[16]

In his political and ecclesiastical views, Shaftesbury was the opponent of contemporary Tories, whom he identified with support of the pre-1688 Stuarts, High Church Anglicanism and France. In pursuing this partisan project through an examination of culture, Shaftesbury was highly aware that he was

---

[15] Mark Goldie, 'Priestcraft and the Birth of Whiggism', in Nicholas Phillipson and Quentin Skinner, eds., *Political Discourse in Early Modern Britain* (Cambridge: Cambridge University Press, 1993), pp. 209–31.

[16] Given his experience at Winchester School in the 1680s, his hostility to educational institutions also had an autobiographical explanation.

attempting to reverse the cultural associations of the two political allegiances: the Tories were traditionally conceded an intellectual and cultural precedence, 'their sovereignty in arts and sciences, their presidentship in letters, their Alma Maters and academical virtues' while the Whigs were dismissed as 'poor rival presbyterians . . . unpolite, unformed, without literature or manners'. The burden of *Characteristics* was to demonstrate how the Tories were not just 'corrupters merely of morals and public principles', but also 'the very reverse or antipodes of good breeding, scholarship, behaviour, sense and manners'.[17]

This strong emphasis on the cultural dimensions of Whiggism helps to explain Shaftesbury's relationship with John Baron Somers (1651–1716). Somers had impeccable political credentials: a lawyer, he was sympathetic to the Whigs of the 1670s, active in the events that precipitated James II's deposition, and a dominant figure during the 1690s, when he was a member of the Junto, the clique that led the Whigs in office and Parliament. He rose to be Lord Chancellor, but suffered severe political attack at the end of William III's reign and was out of office for most of Anne's. However, he was also an important patron and intellectual in his own right as well as president of the Royal Society. Shaftesbury addressed his 'Letter Concerning Enthusiasm' to Somers and, indeed, made a point of sending Somers dedicatory letters of respect and devotion along with most of his work, including the three volumes of *Characteristics*, before it was printed.

To claim politeness for the Whigs was a way to attack the Tories, but it also required reworking the Whig inheritance. Though a friend of Somers, Shaftesbury also associated, especially in the 1690s, with a group of younger Whigs critical of the compromises being made by Whig elders, such as Somers, who had moved to the centre of power, the Court, after 1688. These Real or Country Whigs included Robert Molesworth, John Toland, Andrew Fletcher, Walter Moyle, John Trenchard and Thomas Gordon.[18] Familiar with the writings of James Harrington, Niccolò Machiavelli and, of course, the ancients themselves, their political critique was informed by the tradition of civic humanism: they endorsed liberty, active participation, political virtue and republican institutions and investigated how these themes played themselves out in the political history of the ancient, medieval and modern worlds. Shaftesbury always retained a strong Country suspicion that anyone with power at Court was liable to corruption, substituting self-interest for public good as

---

[17] Shaftesbury to John Somers, 30 March 1711, PRO 30/24/22/4, ff. 153–66 (Rand, *Regimen*, pp. 430–2).

[18] On this circle, see Caroline Robbins, *The Eighteenth Century Commonwealthman* (Cambridge, MA: Harvard University Press, 1959), and A. B. Worden, Introduction to Edmund Ludlow, *A Voyce from the Watch Tower, Part Five: 1660–1662* (Camden Fourth Series, Volume 21, London: Royal Historical Society, 1978). When Shaftesbury served in the Commons of 1695–8, he pursued policies identified with Country Whiggism.

the basis for action. However, the civic tradition sometimes proposed that the best guarantee of civic virtue was economic and social simplicity: liberty and virtue had been safest, it was proposed, in the conditions of early Rome or of Gothic Europe.[19] Though a proponent of liberty and virtue, Shaftesbury was also an aesthete who favoured cultural sophistication. He therefore elaborated old, even ancient, commonplaces about the positive association of liberty and culture and he looked to cultivation as the best security for virtue.[20]

Humanistic scholarship

The European past, and especially the ancient world, provided Shaftesbury with a wealth of models, both positive and negative, for his critical and constructive efforts in conceptualizing the political dimensions of the modern era. Having been taught classics as a young scholar, he extended his command of ancient philosophy, history and literature throughout his life. He added to the library he inherited, avidly collecting editions of the classical texts, especially during sojourns on the Continent in 1698–9 and 1703: he seems, for instance, to have gathered some fifteen editions of the works of Horace.[21]

Characteristics was filled with classical citations, used for several purposes. The fact that Shaftesbury translated little of this material suggested the degree of learning he anticipated in his imagined reader. The text itself was ornamented with lines of literature, which he regarded as capable of conveying philosophical insight. He was drawn especially to the Roman satirists, Horace, Juvenal and Persius, who echoed both the urbanity and incisiveness to which he aspired. He also quoted historians, geographers and others, usually in footnotes, to construct pictures of the relevant aspects of the classical past. These included Herodotus, Strabo, Diodorus Siculus, Pausanias and many others. However, he only occasionally cited the ancient writers who were most influential in shaping his philosophical ideas and moral orientation: Plato and Xenophon, Epictetus and Marcus Aurelius. He barely cited Cicero, with whom he shared many attitudes. Thus, the citations, while significant devices, are not sufficient guides to the sources of his thinking; nor do they illuminate how much Shaftesbury was inspired by the forms of ancient literature (for instance, by *Phaedrus* and other Platonic dialogues in the constructing of 'The Moralists').

In mastering the ancient inheritance, Shaftesbury became a connoisseur not just of the classics but of the humanist scholarship that, during the preceding

---

[19] On the civic humanist tradition, see J. G. A. Pocock, *The Machiavellian Moment* (Princeton: Princeton University Press, 1975).
[20] On this commonplace in the eighteenth century, see Michael Meehan, *Liberty and Poetics in Eighteenth-Century England* (London: Croom Helm, 1986).
[21] A number of library lists survive in the Shaftesbury Papers: PRO 30/24/23/11, 30/24/23/12 and 30/24/27/14.

several centuries, had produced ever more accurate texts of ancient works and accurate pictures of ancient cultures (including those from which the classics of ancient Judaism and Christianity emanated). He deployed this material throughout *Characteristics*.[22] He cited numerous scholars, important in their day but not readily recognized in ours, including Daniel Heinsius, Isaac and Meric Casaubon, Claude Salmasius, Dionysius Lambinus, Joannes Harduinus, Isaac Vossius and many more. The underlying irony is that Shaftesbury, who so often attacked pedants, antiquarians and others for the inconsequence of their material and the inelegance of their style, was eager to display the scholarly evidence that supported his politically and philosophically inflected history of Western culture. To be a scholar was, in many ways, to be the opposite of a polite gentleman.[23] Yet, *Characteristics* strove for an elegant, gentlemanly and indeed polite form while offering obscure documentation for many of its points. In using footnotes extensively, Shaftesbury showed himself simultaneously playful with scholarly form and compulsive about scholarly erudition.[24]

Ancient culture

Shaftesbury's vision of antiquity mirrored the structure of his modern concerns about politics and culture. In Greece and Rome he found a model in which gentlemanly citizens discussed and advanced the good of Man and State while religion was reduced to a perfunctory civic cult. By contrast, ancient Egypt, infested with priests and superstitions, was the source of a pattern bequeathed first to the Hebrews and then, by long lines of filiation, to later Rome and the Catholic Middle Ages.

Within the ancient world, Shaftesbury was attracted most to ancient Greece, which he considered without rival in both politeness and liberty. He honoured the unique and supreme status of Homer, but was intellectually engaged by the political and cultural history of Greece, especially Athens, in the fifth and fourth centuries BC. He traced at length the process of refinement that accompanied the growth and defence of freedom between two encounters with 'universal monarchy', Persia's failed attempt to conquer Greece at the beginning of the fifth century and Macedonia's successful one in the middle of the fourth.

---

[22] This edition clarifies Shaftesbury's often cryptic references to humanistic scholarship by fleshing out and modernizing his citations.

[23] On this tension, see Steven Shapin, '"A Scholar and a Gentleman": The Problematic Identity of the Scientific Practitioner in Early Modern England', *History of Science* 29 (1991): 279–327, and, more extensively, *The Social History of Truth: Civility and Science in Seventeenth-Century England* (Chicago: University of Chicago Press, 1994).

[24] On the political and cultural history of footnotes, see Anthony Grafton, *The Footnote: A Curious History* (Cambridge, MA: Harvard University Press, 1997), which traces the footnote to the environment of Pierre Bayle.

In this interval, Greece developed not only participatory political institutions but, according to Shaftesbury, a culture based on public exchange and criticism. This public culture was an ingredient of the Greek political achievement since it was the arena in which the common good was determined. However, a public culture also contributed crucially to Greek cultural achievement since critical exchange about language and the arts led to that refinement of critical understanding and practice embodied in their literature and arts. In Aristotle and his successors, Shaftesbury found critical equipment and standards that mark his own discussion of literature and the arts with a strong concern for regularity, decorum and the imitation of nature.

In considering ancient cultures, Shaftesbury was particularly drawn to careers in which gentility, liberal education, philosophical insight and libertarian political commitments were conjoined. Among the Greeks, Xenophon (*c.* 430–*c.* 354 BC) was exemplary. He was a follower of Socrates and, after Socrates' fall, a champion of his memory and interpreter of his philosophical enterprise. However, Xenophon was also a defender of liberty and man of action: he joined the unsuccessful expedition of Prince Cyrus against the Persian Emperor and, after defeat, led the Greeks back to their homelands in the perilous journey recorded in Xenophon's own account, *Anabasis* (The expedition upland). Later, it is true, he was exiled from Athens, but the Spartans gave him an estate where for years he led the life of a country gentleman engaged in literary and philosophical pursuits. There he perfected what Shaftesbury called the 'simple' style, joining 'what was deepest and most solid in philosophy with what was easiest and most refined in breeding, and in the character and manner of a gentleman'. Thus, Xenophon united the roles of public servant and virtuous citizen with those of moral philosopher, elegant stylist and thorough gentleman.

Among the Romans, the poet Horace (65 BC–8 BC) most engaged Shaftesbury's attention. Like his contemporary, Virgil, Horace's career straddled the transition from Republic to Empire. Shaftesbury followed other civic humanists in directing attention to this process, in which republican liberty deteriorated, but, here as elsewhere, he was especially concerned to delineate its cultural concomitants. Shaftesbury was vexed by the figures of Octavius and Maecenas. Octavius, Augustus Caesar (63 BC–AD 14), came to dominate the Roman polity after the defeat of Antony and Cleopatra in 31 BC: Augustus was the destroyer of the Republic, but also a cultural patron whose support shaped the literature and arts of this great age. Maecenas (about 70 BC–8 BC) was friend, adviser and agent of the Emperor. Though presenting himself as luxurious and idle, the aristocratic Maecenas not only had considerable political acumen, but helped to create an Augustan age by bringing his own literary patronage to bear, especially on behalf of Virgil and Horace.

Virgil (70–19 BC) was, simply, the most celebrated of Augustan writers. Though humble and provincial in origin, he had a literary and philosophical education, which ultimately brought him to the attention of Maecenas. He was already a celebrated poet when he began work on the *Aeneid*, his great epic of Roman origins. Augustus took a strong interest in the writing of the *Aeneid*, which, in its patriotic evocation of the glorious Roman past, suggested the glories to be expected in the Augustan era. Shaftesbury, however, preferred to see the epic as the final efflorescence of republican culture.

Among *Characteristics*' numerous citations to writers both ancient and modern, Horace was by far the writer most frequently quoted, his verses providing apt, albeit sometimes dense and allusive, support for Shaftesbury's ideas. The 'best genius and most gentleman-like of Roman poets' (p. 146) was not born to gentility. He achieved it through a first-rate liberal education in Rome, which he furthered in Athens. To this, Horace added republican credentials, joining the army of Marcus Junius Brutus, conspirator against Julius Caesar and foe of Caesar's heirs Antony and Octavius. After Brutus' defeat at Philippi in 42 BC, Horace returned to Rome and, impoverished, he turned to writing poetry. He made the acquaintance of Virgil, which led him ultimately to the patronage of Maecenas. Henceforward, Horace was well connected in the social, political and literary circles of Rome, and he became a defender of Augustus' objectives and regime. He was rewarded with an estate north of Rome, his Sabine farm, which he idealized as a site of country retreat and literary endeavour. In this establishment, Shaftesbury could see Horace's resumption of his early principles and a reaction against the seductions of Court life in favour of independence and simplicity. In his urbanity, good humour and affability, Horace provided an appropriate ancient equivalent of the tone to which Shaftesbury aspired in *Characteristics*.

While granting Augustus credit for his cultural patronage, Shaftesbury condemned Augustus' imperial successors. He considered the reign of Augustus to have introduced an epoch of corruption and tyranny, epitomized in the turpitude of figures such as Nero (AD 37–68, Emperor, AD 54–68)

Precisely because of the enormities ascribed to Nero, Shaftesbury was drawn to interpret another intellectual career, that of Lucius Annaeus Seneca (*c.* 5 BC–AD 65), Nero's tutor and, after Nero's accession, a minister. From a wealthy and distinguished family, Seneca had a thorough education in rhetoric and philosophy before entering on a career in office. Though a serious and influential philosopher attracted to such stoic themes as tranquillity and providence, he was drawn into the disturbing realities of court politics. He was an accessory to the murder of Nero's mother, Agrippina, and later, accused of conspiring against Nero himself, he was allowed to kill himself. His death illustrated stoic dignity but, for Shaftesbury, his life dramatized the difficulty, as well as the value, of synthesizing worldly action with the philosophical frame of mind.

Like most humanists, Shaftesbury saw the imperial epoch as one of intellectual and cultural decline as well as political tyranny. He did, however, make exceptions for two imperial figures: the second-century Marcus Aurelius Antoninus on account of his philosophical writings (see p. xxvi) and the fourth-century Flavius Claudius Julianus (Julian the Apostate) on account of the toleration Shaftesbury discerned in his religious policies (p.375n).

In Shaftesbury's view, Roman decline paved the way for the Middle Ages, but the precedents for what went wrong were deep in the ancient world. *Characteristics* presented a remarkable account of ancient Egypt, where priests dominated both polity and culture by a mutually reinforcing mixture of economic and legal privileges and superstitious beliefs. According to Shaftesbury, they transmitted their priestcraft to the ancient Hebrews whose culture Shaftesbury reconstructed on the basis of both the Old Testament and seventeenth-century Biblical commentaries. In turn, later Roman paganism followed these 'oriental' examples by multiplying the number of religious officials, enhancing their material endowments and so proliferating superstitions – a pattern bequeathed to the Christian Middle Ages when, before expiring entirely, the Roman Empire was converted to Christianity.[25] Shaftesbury's Middle Ages were characterized by ecclesiastical domination, an absence of liberty, civic consciousness and public debate, and an accompanying lack of refinement in the verbal and visual arts, which Shaftesbury dismissed as 'Gothic'.

Ancient philosophy

Though Shaftesbury admired the Greco-Roman world for its political and cultural legacies, he was particularly taken by the status he imagined that philosophy occupied in it. Philosophy, not religion, was the central mode of understanding in classical antiquity. It was worldly, a component of gentlemanly education and a contributor to the public life of democratic and republican polities. Its content was civic and ethical in character.

Socrates loomed large in Shaftesbury's vision of ancient philosophy. Of course, since Socrates left no writings, Shaftesbury was dependent, as all commentators have been, on such sources as Plato's dialogues and Xenophon's *Memorabilia*. Immersing himself in this material, Shaftesbury planned a large work on Socrates for which his private papers contain an outline and notes.[26] Although Shaftesbury did not finish this work, *Characteristics* has much evidence of his interest in Socrates, who appeared repeatedly as the embodiment of a philosophy dedicated to the quest for self-knowledge and moral wisdom. Moreover, Socrates helped to underpin Shaftesbury's interest in philosophical

---

[25] See Lawrence E. Klein, 'Shaftesbury, Politeness and the Politics of Religion', in Phillipson and Skinner, eds., *Political Discourse in Early Modern Britain*, pp. 283–301.

[26] On this project, see Lawrence E. Klein, *Shaftesbury and the Culture of Politeness: Moral Discourse and Cultural Politics in Early Eighteenth-Century England* (Cambridge: Cambridge University Press, 1994), pp. 107–11.

worldliness since Socrates carried out his quest in public through a process of public conversation in the midst of the city-state.

Socrates, thus, provided a model for the project of philosophy as conceived by Shaftesbury. Indeed, *Characteristics* went so far as to trace the variety of ancient philosophy to Socratic origins. Platonism, Aristotelianism and cynicism were represented as stylistic or formal variations on Socratic themes: Plato and Aristotle took philosophy in new formal directions – toward the sublime and poetic in one case, toward the methodical and analytic in the other – but not in new substantive directions (pp. 113–15).

It is not surprising then that Shaftesbury also identified stoicism with Socratic philosophy. Crystallizing the history of philosophy in the ancient world, he once isolated 'two real distinct philosophies':

> the one derived from Socrates and passing into the old Academic, the Peripatetic and stoic; the other derived in reality from Democritus and passing into the Cyrenaic and Epicurean . . . The first therefore of these two philosophies recommended action, concernment in civil affairs, religion, etc.; the second derided all and advised inaction and retreat, and [with] good reason. For the first maintained that society, right and wrong was [*sic*] founded in nature and that nature had a meaning and was . . . well-governed and administered by one simple and perfect intelligence. The second, again, derided this and made Providence and Dame Nature not so sensible as a doting old woman. The first of these philosophies is to be called the civil, social, theistic; the second, the contrary.[27]

This distinction, as we will see, served Shaftesbury as a characterization of philosophy not just in the ancient world but in the modern world as well.

Shaftesbury's exposure to stoicism was primarily through his attentive reading of the later Roman stoics, of which he left a remarkable record. After serving vigorously in Parliament in the 1690s, his life took a sudden and unexpected shift in direction. At the age of twenty-seven, he withdrew from public affairs, leaving England for more than a year and setting up residence in Rotterdam for a life of privacy and study. Through Benjamin Furley (1636–1714), a Quaker businessman of advanced intellectual leanings and friend of Locke, he was connected to the local political and intellectual elite. However, his most important intellectual engagement during this period of self-exile was with the ancient stoics. His withdrawal from England seems to have reflected a spiritual, intellectual and, even, existential crisis, which is fully reflected in the notebooks he began keeping in 1698. These notebooks, which he labelled Ἀσκήματα (Exercises), explored his own moral quandaries, translating the ethical questions that he had considered already in a demonstrative manner in the 1699 edition of *An Inquiry Concerning Virtue* into a much more personal and

---

[27] Shaftesbury to Pierre Coste, 1 October 1706, PRO 30/24/22/7 (Rand, *Regimen*, pp. 355–66).

existential idiom. In this process, he read, recorded and engaged with stoic thought, especially that of the Roman stoics.

In Marcus Aurelius Antoninus (AD 121–80), Shaftesbury found a peer of Xenophon and Seneca: a man whose life combined upper-class pedigree, public action and philosophical preoccupation. Of aristocratic birth, he early achieved the favour of the Emperors Hadrian and his successor Antoninus Pius. His own reign as Emperor (161–80) was dominated by warfare which often required his presence at the margins of the Empire. However, his entire adult career was inspired by stoic philosophy, to which he gave eloquent expression in his *Meditations*, reflections compiled during his military campaigns. Marcus Aurelius had been influenced, meanwhile, by Epictetus (AD *c*.55–*c*.135), a freed Greek slave who started studying philosophy before his emancipation and, afterwards, taught a stoic philosophy in Rome and later in Greece. His teachings were collected by Arrian who also produced a well-known epitome of his wisdom, the *Enchiridion*. As the passage cited above suggests, these stoics of the imperial age offered Shaftesbury a number of themes: the importance of self-knowledge and moral discipline and autonomy; the participation of humans in ever larger schemes of civil, political and indeed cosmic association; and, ultimately, the order of the cosmos and the reality of virtue and beauty.

The counterpoint to these emphases Shaftesbury found in Epicureanism with its denial of world order and rejection of public service. Epicurus, who lived from about 342 to 271 BC, setting up his famous school in the Garden in Athens, makes several appearances in *Characteristics*. He was a Democritean atomist and a thorough materialist who believed the gods themselves were made up of atoms. The gods were remote from the world of men since they themselves were devoted to a lofty existence of ἀταραξία, *ataraxia*, a condition of serene impassiveness. The well-known Epicurean emphasis on pleasure was not hedonistic, but mainly negative, seeking to free the body and mind from disturbance and anxiety. This meant a withdrawal from the world of politics and business and even from marriage and reproduction in order to live in a quiet community of philosophical adepts. Since Epicurus' writings, said to be voluminous, hardly survived, Shaftesbury's knowledge of Epicurus was filtered through Lucretius (*c*.94–*c*.55 BC), of whom little is known except for his authorship of *On the Nature of Things*, a long didactic poem in six books expounding Epicurean views on the physical world and the moral dimensions of human life.

Modern philosophy

This excursion from Shaftesbury's politics through his response to the culture and especially the philosophy of the ancient world illuminates his engagements with the philosophy of his own era, which he regarded as a new manifestation of Epicureanism. The philosophical worldliness at which he aimed constituted a critique of the modern philosophical project.

At its broadest, Shaftesbury's dispute with contemporary philosophy concerned the nature of philosophy itself. The reader of *Characteristics* should observe how frequently and how extensively Shaftesbury undertook to define philosophy or to characterize its aims and methods. 'Philosophy' had many referents in this era: it applied not just to the scholastic inheritance still surviving in the universities, but also to new projects in natural philosophy itself or in epistemological mapping that were intended to facilitate the acquisition of sounder knowledge in the realms of nature.[28] Like much of the forward looking philosophy of the preceding century, Shaftesbury was breaking away from the formal, demonstrative and systematic pretensions of the inherited scholastic tradition. However, he also was criticizing many of the new philosophical initiatives of the same period. He was hostile to technical inquiry seeing in philosophy not a solution to metaphysical or epistemological quandaries but rather a vehicle for moral formation. As we have seen, he sought to revitalize philosophy's public capacity and revive those principles that had animated such philosophy in the ancient world.

The modern philosophy to which Shaftesbury was most attentive was the work of Thomas Hobbes and John Locke. Hobbes (1588–1679) responded to the sceptical crisis of the late sixteenth and early seventeenth centuries with a new initiative in demonstrative philosophy. Combining commitments to the analytic efficacy of geometry and the explanatory simplicity of materialism, Hobbes sought to demonstrate the links between nature, humans and society. Though Hobbes wrote many works, Shaftesbury confined his treatment of Hobbes to an attack on the pronouncements in *Leviathan*, first published in 1651.

Meanwhile, the third Earl of Shaftesbury grew up with an important personal tie to Locke (1632–1704), friend, assistant and dependant of the first Earl. Despite this close personal connection, the explicit statements of Shaftesbury's maturity reveal mostly intellectual hostility. Shaftesbury took issue with ideas in both the *Essay Concerning Human Understanding* (1689) and the second *Treatise of Government* (1690). If there is a Lockean resonance in Shaftesbury's thinking, it can be traced not to Locke's more famous works but to his views on mentorship and cultivation, crystallized in *Thoughts Concerning Education* (1693).

In the course of *Characteristics*, Shaftesbury recurred to two particular features of modern philosophy which seemed to him fundamentally Epicurean and thus counter to his Socratic/stoic enterprise.

---

[28] The philosophical bequest of the seventeenth century is surveyed in Daniel Garber and Michael Ayers, eds., *The Cambridge History of Seventeenth-Century Philosophy* (Cambridge: Cambridge University Press, 1998).

One was the nominalism of modern philosophy. Insisting on the trans-historical and transcultural reality of cosmic order and the moral principles woven into its fabric, Shaftesbury was alert to the suggestion that fundamental moral principles might be products of convention rather than structures of reality, the outcome of artifice rather than ingredients of nature. Thus, Shaftesbury read Hobbes unsympathetically, but not inaccurately, as a thorough nominalist: because, for Hobbes, human signs and their referents were entirely conventional, moral injunctions derived from custom or fiat. Similarly, Shaftesbury offered a selective but hardly perverse reading of Locke to emphasize the degree to which Locke, in the face of the diversity of moral opinion across cultures, relied on the commands of God (rather than the structure of nature) to ground ethical principles.

The second trait in modern philosophy to which Shaftesbury objected was philosophical egoism, which was consistent with the denial of ontological foundations for ethics or politics and with the methodological individualism espoused by its supporters. A conspicuous target in this regard was the contention that human self-regard made human action an enterprise in selfishness. Shaftesbury attributed such an outlook to Hobbes but also to expressions of a revived Augustinianism (as in the French Jansenists or such secularizing fellow travellers as the Duc de La Rochefoucauld): Bernard Mandeville's critical response to Shaftesbury derived from this standpoint.

A less conspicuous instance of the egoistic tenor of contemporary philosophy, to which Shaftesbury objected, was the commitment to analyses grounded on the ahistorical individual. Shaftesbury ridiculed the natural law tradition for resting a theory of society on the supposition of a natural condition of human atomism. From such a supposition, Hobbes had developed his argument for absolutism; but Locke argued for constitutional government on a similar basis. Shaftesbury sympathized with Locke's political beliefs but not his attempt to ground them on the consequences of a supposed natural state prior to society. A humanity prior to society was simply inconceivable if one insisted on natural human sociability. For Shaftesbury, humans were always already social, immersed in society, culture and history.

Though opposed to the figures who would in time occupy the apex of the philosophical canon, Shaftesbury derived support and inspiration from other recent writers. Many of them were, ironically, men of the Church. He cited such representatives of the latitudinarian strand of religious thinking as Jeremy Taylor and John Tillotson. The latitudinarians were committed to lowering the volume in religious dispute by shifting attention from narrow theological details to broad ethical concerns. They were thus more accepting of toleration than High Churchmen and more optimistic about the possibility of human goodness than Calvinists.

A tighter intellectual affiliation exists between Shaftesbury and the so-called

Cambridge Platonists. Shaftesbury's first publication, dating from the 1690s, was an edition of sermons by Benjamin Whichcote (1609–83), a London preacher usually counted among their number. In introducing a cleric who warmly endorsed the naturalness of human sociability and benevolence, Shaftesbury enunciated a theme he would elaborate later, the critique of selfishness underlying the writings of both Thomas Hobbes and Protestant divines.

Another Cambridge Platonist who influenced Shaftesbury was Ralph Cudworth (1617–88). Cudworth spent a long career at Cambridge and wrote profusely though only one principal work was published during his lifetime, the stupendous *True Intellectual System of the Universe* (1678). In its effort to justify theism against atheism while also discriminating among theisms that conduced toward or impeded morality, this volume paralleled Shaftesbury's simultaneous critique of Hobbes and utilitarian Christians. Moreover, certain key ideas of stoic derivation in Shaftesbury were supported by Cudworth and perhaps even cast by Shaftesbury in Cudworthian language.[29]

Modern enthusiasm

As much as Shaftesbury respected the latitudinarian clerics of the English Church, however, he was separated from them by a wide gulf. They were all committed to Church teachings which Shaftesbury opposed. The doctrine which he attacked most frequently in *Characteristics* was the promise of future rewards and punishments, which clashed with his search for an ethic, intrinsic to the design of the cosmos and of humanity, autonomous of religious prescription. In his view, the doctrine of future rewards and punishments reduced the spiritual orientation of the Christian to a high-minded condition of egoism, in which the Christian was coaxed to goodness through rational calculations of short- and long-term benefits.

Shaftesbury abandoned reliance on this doctrine and, indeed, on many defining features of Christianity, including sin, salvation and revelation, although he continued to endorse a significant role for a tolerant and charitable Church and the morally improving contributions of Christian traditions of benevolence. His ethic was grounded in ideas about cosmic intelligence and order which, though compatible with aspects of Christianity, were also easily detached from it.

It is important, however, to distinguish Shaftesbury from some contemporary deists and freethinkers. *Characteristics* ended with a peroration in defence of freethinking. Yet, Shaftesbury was careful here to acquiesce in the authority of a legitimate Church. Some deists were simply too radical for him. He had no truck with arguments liable to bring the entire social and cultural order

---

[29] J. A. Passmore, *Ralph Cudworth: An Interpretation* (Cambridge: Cambridge University Press, 1951), pp. 96–100. See also Further reading.

into question. More important, he objected to ideas that smacked of materialism and mechanism and, thus, in his view, tended toward atheism. While Shaftesbury was happy to admit that non-Christians (including atheists) were capable of virtue and that Christianity itself had unleashed many moral enormities, his own theism was fervent – at least, if we are to take the raptures of Theocles in 'The Moralists' as indicative of his spiritual experience.

Like Theocles, Shaftesbury was, by his own playful admission, an enthusiast. 'Enthusiasm' had played a most important role in English discussion of religion over the past half of a century. It was used to describe, in general, those who were extravagant in their religious expressions but, more specifically, those who made a false claim to inspiration and, with that, unwarranted independence from such anchors of faith as Scripture or the Church. In the polemically charged atmosphere of the period, the term functioned as a general aspersion of Puritanism or sectarianism, though the precise sense was only applicable to a small number of more radical Protestants.[30]

It was the appearance in London of just such a group that prompted Shaftesbury to write *A Letter Concerning Enthusiasm*. Though Louis XIV, in revoking the Edict of Nantes in 1685, had hoped to free France of its Huguenot population, Protestants remained, and in the early 1700s disturbances broke out between the authorities and a millennially-minded sect, known as the Camisards, in the remote Cevennes region of southern France. By 1706, several of these 'prophets' had arrived in London where, though condemned by the well-established Huguenot community, they attracted considerable attention through their detailed prophecies delivered often with dramatic bodily displays. The 'prophets' were joined in their activities by several Britons including John Lacy (b. 1664), a Londoner and man of means, whom Shaftesbury discussed in his *Letter*.[31]

Shaftesbury's *Letter* was only peripherally about the 'prophets' since its theme was enthusiasm and its burden to shift the term's meaning. The particular combination of imagination and passion that comprised enthusiasm was not, for Shaftesbury, confined to religious extremists but rather characteristic of a wide range of human creative, heroic and romantic activity. Indeed, it was

---

[30] The best summary of this discourse is Michael Heyd, *'Be Sober and Reasonable': The Critique of Enthusiasm in the Seventeenth and Early Eighteenth Centuries* (Leiden: E. J. Brill, 1995). For the term's eighteenth-century career, Lawrence E. Klein and Anthony J. La Vopa, eds., *Enthusiasm and Enlightenment in Europe, 1650–1850* (San Marino, CA: Huntington Library Press, 1998).

[31] The definitive study of this episode is Hillel Schwartz, *The French Prophets: The History of a Millenarian Group in Eighteenth-Century England* (Berkeley and Los Angeles: University of California Press, 1980). See also the bibliography of contemporary responses to the 'prophets' in Hillel Schwartz, *Knaves, Fools, Madmen and That Subtile Effluvium: A Study of the Opposition to the French Prophets in England, 1706–1710* (Gainesville, FL: University Presses of Florida, 1978).

an essential component of the philosopher's psychic equipment since it made available to him fundamental insights about the nature of the cosmos and its moral axes.

Ancient and modern

Shaftesbury lived during one of the set pieces of intellectual history, the so-called Battle of the Ancients and the Moderns. His high regard for the ancients and his deeply felt and informed classicism tend to make him look like an Ancient. Yet, his insistence on worldliness is a testament to his modernity. Though Ancients and Moderns did at times battle, the relation of the antique inheritance to modern demands in Shaftesbury's era was most often complex rather than polarized, collaborative rather than combative.[32] This, at any rate, was true in the case of Shaftesbury who deployed antiquity in a programme for modern philosophy, culture and politics.

In other ways, too, Shaftesbury yoked together unlikely pairs. He embraced hostility toward pedantry and also a fascination with erudition. He was sceptical yet deeply committed to beliefs about cosmic order and natural sociability. He urged the advantages and pleasures of open-ended conversation but argued that beauty was found in classical regularity. Finally, he demanded philosophical worldliness but retained a place for transcendence. While condemning the follies of enthusiasm and offering remedies for them, Shaftesbury absorbed enthusiasm into a philosophical programme for modernity. He significantly, even radically, demoted the role of the Judaeo-Christian God and so undermined the functions of the Church. Yet he resisted that undertow of disenchantment that, according to Max Weber, was beginning to drag on the European spirit. Indeed, the continuing possibility of enchantment, in the form of a modern enthusiasm, was perhaps what many of his Enlightenment readers, both in England and abroad, found worthwhile in his writing.

---

[32] Joseph Levine covers these relations exhaustively in *The Battle of the Books: History and Literature in the Augustan Age* (Ithaca and London: Cornell University Press, 1991).

Chronology

Further reading

Characteristics contains most of what Shaftesbury published during his life. However, an understanding of Shaftesbury can be enhanced by reference to his manuscripts, housed, for the most part, at the Public Record Office (PRO) at Kew, Surrey. Some of these have been published. Shaftesbury's stoic notebooks, the Ἀσκήματα, are included, in an incomplete and unreliable version, in Benjamin Rand, ed., *The Life, Unpublished Letters and Philosophical Regimen of Anthony, Earl of Shaftesbury* (London: Swan Sonnenschein, 1900) (referred to in this edition's notes as Rand, *Regimen*). A complete and highly informative version of the notebooks is in French, edited and translated by Laurent Jaffro, *Exercices* (Paris: Aubier, 1993). Benjamin Rand also edited the manuscripts and published components of Shaftesbury's projected companion to *Characteristics* in *Second Characters or the Language of Forms by the Right Honourable Anthony, Earl of Shaftesbury* (Cambridge: Cambridge University Press, 1914; repr. New York: Greenwood Press, 1969). Other materials from the Public Record Office are being published in the Standard Edition of Shaftesbury's *Complete Works*, under the general editorship of Gerd Hemmerich, Wolfram Benda and Ulrich Schödlbauer and published by Frommann-Holzboog (Stuttgart-Bad Canstatt, 1981–). This edition also contains variants for the several printed versions of *Characteristics* and its components, and much else of use to students of Shaftesbury.

The standard biography of Shaftesbury, which also does much to interpret his writings, is Robert Voitle, *The Third Earl of Shaftesbury, 1671–1713* (Baton Rouge and London: Louisiana State University Press, 1984).

Only a few books about Shaftesbury have been written in English during the twentieth century. Each provides a general orientation to Shaftesbury while approaching him from a different angle. Alfred O. Aldridge, 'Shaftesbury and the Deist Manifesto', *Transactions of the American Philosophical Society*, New Series 41 (1951), Part II: 297–385, emphasizes Shaftesbury's religious and ecclesiastical views, especially his deism. The most extensive treatment in a philosophical vein remains Stanley Grean, *Shaftesbury's Philosophy of Religion and Ethics: A Study in Enthusiasm* (Athens, OH: Ohio University Press, 1967). R. L. Brett's *The Third Earl of Shaftesbury: A Study in Eighteenth-Century Literary Theory* (London: Hutchinson's University Library, 1951) is another older and extensive treatment of both the intellectual content and literary form of *Characteristics*. For an interpretation that puts Shaftesbury in his social and political context, see Lawrence E. Klein, *Shaftesbury and the Culture of Politeness: Moral Discourse and Cultural Politics in Early Eighteenth-Century England* (Cambridge: Cambridge University Press, 1994).

Otherwise, Shaftesbury has to be approached through articles and chapters.

Shaftesbury figures as a political thinker and actor, in relation to differing contexts, in, among others: Caroline Robbins, *The Eighteenth-Century Commonwealthman* (New York: Athenaeum, 1968); Isaac Kramnick, *Bolingbroke and his Circle* (Cambridge, MA: Harvard University Press, 1968); and A. B. Worden's introduction to Edmund Ludlow, *A Voyce from the Watch Tower, Part Five: 1660–1662* (Camden Fourth Series, Volume 21, London: Royal Historical Society, 1978). The material on Shaftesbury in Justin Champion, *The Pillars of Priestcraft Shaken: The Church of England and its Enemies, 1660–1730* (Cambridge: Cambridge University Press, 1992), thoroughly revises the perspective of A. O. Aldridge, mentioned above.

For philosophers, Shaftesbury has always been associated with the tradition of thinking about the 'moral sense' for which one can see D. D. Raphael, *The Moral Sense* (London: Oxford University Press, 1947), and Robert Voitle, 'Shaftesbury's Moral Sense', *Studies in Philology* 52 (1955): 17–38. A more complex and rhetorically aware account is provided by Stephen Darwall, *The British Moralists and the Internal 'Ought', 1640–1740* (Cambridge: Cambridge University Press, 1995). Shaftesbury's philosophical setting is provided in Ernst Cassirer, *The Platonic Renaissance in England* (trans. James P. Pettegrove, Austin: University of Texas Press, 1953), and Frederick C. Beiser, *The Sovereignty of Reason: The Defense of Rationality in the Early English Enlightenment* (Princeton: Princeton University Press, 1996).

Shaftesbury's aesthetic views were explored in several classic articles by Jerome Stolnitz: 'On the Significance of Lord Shaftesbury in Modern Aesthetic Theory', *Philosophical Quarterly* 11 (1961): 97–113, and 'On the Origins of "Aesthetic Disinterestedness"', *Journal of Aesthetics and Art Criticism* 20 (1961): 131–43. More recently, Dabney Townsend has explored this territory in 'From Shaftesbury to Kant: The Development of the Concept of Aesthetic Experience', *Journal of the History of Ideas* 48 (1987): 287–306. A more historically situated account appears in Howard Caygill, *Art of Judgment* (Oxford: Basil Blackwell, 1989).

In keeping with his propensity to view theory as the agenda for practice, Shaftesbury was also an influential patron of art. Most immediately relevant are the allegorical engravings commissioned by Shaftesbury to ornament the second and subsequent editions of *Characteristics*: these are discussed by Felix Paknadel, 'Shaftesbury's Illustrations of *Characteristics*', *Journal of the Warburg and Courtauld Institutes* 37 (1974): 290–312. Contrasting views of Shaftesbury's importance for eighteenth-century art history are: John Barrell, *The Political Theory of Painting from Reynolds to Hazlitt* (New Haven and London: Yale University Press, 1986); David Solkin, *Painting For Money: The Visual Arts and the Public Sphere in Eighteenth-Century England* (New Haven and London: the Paul Mellon Centre for Studies in British Art by Yale University Press, 1992); and any number of works by Ronald Paulson in which Shaftesbury plays Ancient to Hogarth's Modern.

More current approaches from the direction of literary studies are: David Marshall, *The Figure of Theater* (New York: Columbia University Press, 1986); Robert Markley, 'Style as Philosophical Structure: The Contexts of Shaftesbury's *Characteristicks*', in Robert Ginzberg, ed., *The Philosopher as Writer: The Eighteenth Century* (Selinsgrove: Susquehanna University Press; London and Toronto: Associated Universities Press, 1987), pp. 140–54; Jack Prostko, '"Natural Conversation Set in View": Shaftesbury and Moral Speech', *Eighteenth-Century Studies* 23 (1989): 42–61; and Michael Prince, *Philosophical Dialogue in the British Enlightenment* (Cambridge: Cambridge University Press, 1996).

Finally, Shaftesbury has recently received considerable attention from students of the changing constructions of gender in this period: John Barrell, '"The Dangerous Goddess": Masculinity, Prestige and the Aesthetic in Early Eighteenth-Century Britain', in his *The Birth of Pandora and the Division of Knowledge* (London: Macmillan Press, 1992), pp. 63–87; Brian Cowan, 'Reasonable Ecstasies: Shaftesbury and the Language of Libertinism', *Journal of British Studies* 37 (1998): 111–38; and G. J. Barker Benfield, *The Culture of Sensibility: Sex and Society in Eighteenth-Century Britain* (Chicago and London: University of Chicago Press, 1992).

Note on the text

This edition of *Characteristics* is based on the British Library's copy of the second edition of 1714 (BL 231.g.1). *Characteristics* was first published in 1711, but, before his death in 1713, Shaftesbury made many revisions and corrections in preparation for the second edition. Shaftesbury's own copy of the 1711 edition, with manuscript notations and revisions, is also in the British Library (C.28.g.16) and has been consulted comprehensively in preparing this edition. A number of manuscripts in the Shaftesbury Papers, Public Record Office (PRO), Kew, Surrey, are devoted to this process of revision and have been consulted.

This edition diverges from the content of the 1714 edition in two significant respects: 'The Notion of the Historical Draught or Tablature of the Judgment of Hercules', written by Shaftesbury after the publication of the first edition, appeared in the second edition; so did a set of emblematic engravings, commissioned by Shaftesbury, to ornament and illustrate the text. It has not been possible to include either of these components of the 1714 edition here.

In keeping with the goals of Cambridge Texts in the History of Philosophy, spelling and punctuation have been modernized. In one or two instances, silent changes in syntax have been made to facilitate comprehensibility. However, in certain sections, significant alterations have been made in the format of the text. Given the importance of the themes of conversation and soliloquy in *Characteristics*, it is not surprising that Shaftesbury often presented ideas in various forms of dialogue. Accordingly, he instructed his printer to make his dialogic intent legible to the reader by a system of variable spacings between sentences. According to a manuscript note (I, 157) in Shaftesbury's copy of the 1711 edition: 'The marks which I have here put into the text are by way of caution to the compositor in this peculiar dialogue style, where the two parts, or different speaking parties should be neatly represented with obvious distinction to the eye. And therefore, in such a page as this, the distances between sentence and sentence should be made less than ordinary, that those which are between party and party may appear the greater.' (This remark is adjacent to the text of *Soliloquy* 1.1, where Shaftesbury asserts that 'we have each of us ourselves to practise [inner conversation] on' (p. 72).) I have taken this practice as a sanction to arrange such passages in the modern format and orthography for dialogue.

Shaftesbury's extensive quotation from Greek and Latin sources has all been translated along with a few quotations from French. All verse has been translated as prose, and the goal throughout has been literal and comprehensible rather than literary translation. When differences exist between the classical text used by Shaftesbury and modern readings, the text used by Shaftesbury has been translated. When Shaftesbury has included his own translation of a text, the translation appears in roman characters in quotation marks. When a text has been translated for this edition, it appears in italics. Translations from the Bible are rendered as they appear in the King James version.

Shaftesbury used a wide range of typographical and orthographical devices (capitalization, quotation marks, italics) for different effects. In general these have been eliminated although in certain places italics are used to convey intensification and in others quotation marks are used to mirror Shaftesbury's own practice of creating the effect of quotation.

Shaftesbury used footnotes extensively for purposes of citation, explanation and cross-reference. These footnotes, referenced with arabic numbers, are all included in this edition although they have been put in a consistent modern form. All notes referenced with letters, and all bracketed material in Shaftesbury's notes, are provided by the editor.

Characteristics of Men, Manners, Opinions, Times

Preface

If the author of these united tracts had been any friend to prefaces, he would probably have made his entrance after that manner in one or other of the five treatises formerly published apart.[A] But as to all prefatory or dedicatory discourse, he has told us his mind sufficiently in that treatise which he calls *Soliloquy*.[B] Being satisfied, however, that there are many persons who esteem these introductory pieces as very essential in the constitution of a work, he has thought fit, in behalf of his honest printer, to substitute these lines under the title of a preface and to declare 'that (according to his best judgment and authority) these presents ought to pass and be received, construed and taken as satisfactory in full, for all preliminary composition, dedication, direct or indirect application for favour to the public or to any private patron or party whatsoever, nothing to the contrary appearing to him from the side of truth or reason'. Witness his hand, this fifth day of December 1710.

A.A.C.A.N.A.AE.C.
M.D.C.L.X.X.I.[C]

[A] See Note on the text.
[B] See p. 104.
[C] These initials stand for 'Anthony Ashley Cooper, Count, born in the year of the Christian era 1671' in Latin.

3

A Letter Concerning Enthusiasm to My Lord *****^A

What prevents the man of mirth
from telling the truth?[1]

September 1707

My Lord,

Now you are returned to . . . . ., and, before the season comes which must engage you in the weightier matters of state, if you care to be entertained a while with a sort of idle thoughts, such as pretend only to amusement and have no relation to business or affairs, you may cast your eye slightly on what you have before you. And if there be anything inviting, you may read it over at your leisure.

It has been an established custom for poets, at the entrance of their work, to address themselves to some Muse, and this practice of the ancients has gained so much repute that even in our days we find it almost constantly imitated. I cannot but fancy, however, that this imitation, which passes so currently with other judgments, must at some time or other have stuck a little with your Lordship, who is used to examine things by a better standard than that of fashion or the common taste. You must certainly have observed our poets under a

---

^A 'Enthusiasm' derives from the Greek for 'possession by a god'. In the seventeenth century, the term referred, negatively, to the claim to be immediately inspired by God although it could also refer to other delusional claims and to intense religious emotionality. Shaftesbury used the term in these senses but also, in the course of the essay, gave the term a positive meaning, the 'sublime in human passions' (p. 27): see Introduction, p. xxx. The addressee was John Baron Somers, Whig statesman, intellectual and patron, for whom see Introduction, p. xix. On the circumstances of publication, see Introduction, p. xxx. The original 1708 edition, printed by John Morphew, contained the following 'to the reader': 'This letter must have been written, as plainly appears, about the middle or latter end of last summer and, in all probability, was designed to be kept private. But though it came afterwards to be seen abroad in several hands, the printer could not obtain his copy till very lately, or you had had it more in season' (p. 3).

[1] Horace, *Satires* 1.1.24–5.

4

remarkable constraint, when obliged to assume this character, and you have wondered perhaps why that air of enthusiasm, which sits so gracefully with an ancient, should be so spiritless and awkward in a modern. But, as to this doubt, your Lordship would have soon resolved yourself, and it could only serve to bring across you a reflection you have often made on many occasions besides, that truth is the most powerful thing in the world, since even fiction itself must be governed by it and can only please by its resemblance.[2] The appearance of reality is necessary to make any passion agreeably represented. And to be able to move others, we must first be moved ourselves, or at least seem to be so, upon some probable grounds. Now what possibility is there that a modern, who is known never to have worshipped Apollo or owned any such deity as the Muses, should persuade us to enter into his pretended devotion and move us by his feigned zeal in a religion out of date?[B] But as for the ancients, it is known they derived both their religion and polity from the Muses' art. How natural therefore must it have appeared in any, but especially a poet of those times, to address himself in raptures of devotion to those acknowledged patronesses of wit and science? Here the poet might with probability feign an ecstasy, though he really felt none, and, supposing it to have been mere affectation, it would look however like something natural and could not fail of pleasing.

But perhaps, my Lord, there was a further mystery in the case. Men, your Lordship knows, are wonderfully happy in a faculty of deceiving themselves whenever they set heartily about it. And a very small foundation of any passion will serve us not only to act it well, but even to work ourselves into it beyond our own reach. Thus, by a little affectation in love-matters and with the help of a romance or novel, a boy of fifteen or a grave man of fifty may be sure to grow a very natural coxcomb and feel the *belle passion*[C] in good earnest. A man of tolerable good nature who happens to be a little piqued may, by improving his resentment, become a very fury for revenge. Even a good Christian, who would needs be over-good and thinks he can never believe enough, may, by a small inclination well improved, extend his faith so largely as to comprehend in it not only all scriptural and traditional miracles, but a solid system of old wives' stories. Were it needful, I could put your Lordship in mind of an eminent, learned, and truly Christian prelate you once knew,

---

[B] In Greek mythology, the Muses were nine divine sisters, the children of Zeus (the Roman Jupiter or Jove) and Mnemosyne or Memory, who inspired the varieties of the arts and learning. Apollo, another child of Zeus, was, independently of the Muses, associated with the support of music and poetry; some ancient writers identified him, however, as leader of the Muses.

[C] The tender passion or love.

[2] See pp. 65-6, 448-9.

who could have given you a full account of his belief in fairies.[D] And this, methinks, may serve to make appear how far an ancient poet's faith might possibly have been raised together with his imagination.

But we Christians, who have such ample faith ourselves, will allow nothing to poor heathens. They must be infidels in every sense. We will not allow them to believe so much as their own religion, which we cry is too absurd to have been credited by any besides the mere vulgar. But if a reverend Christian prelate may be so great a volunteer in faith as, beyond the ordinary prescription of the catholic Church, to believe in fairies, why may not a heathen poet, in the ordinary way of his religion, be allowed to believe in Muses? For these, your Lordship knows, were so many divine persons in the heathen creed and were essential in their system of theology. The goddesses had their temples and worship, the same as the other deities, and to disbelieve the Holy Nine or their Apollo was the same as to deny Jove himself and must have been esteemed equally profane and atheistical by the generality of sober men. Now what a mighty advantage must it have been to an ancient poet to be thus orthodox and, by the help of his education and a good will into the bargain, to work himself up to the belief of a divine presence and heavenly inspiration? It was never surely the business of poets in those days to call revelation in question, when it evidently made so well for their art. On the contrary, they could not fail to animate their faith as much as possible when, by a single act of it well enforced, they could raise themselves into such angelical company.

How much the imagination of such a presence must exalt a genius we may observe merely from the influence which an ordinary presence has over men. Our modern wits are more or less raised by the opinion they have of their company, and the idea they form to themselves of the persons to whom they make their addresses. A common actor of the stage will inform us how much a full audience of the better sort exalts him above the common pitch. And you, my Lord, who are the noblest actor and of the noblest part assigned to any mortal on this earthly stage, when you are acting for liberty and mankind, does not the public presence, that of your friends and the well-wishers to your cause, add something to your thought and genius? Or is that sublime of reason and that power of eloquence, which you discover in public, no more than what you

---

[D] As early as the publication, at the Hague in 1709, of a French translation of the first edition of this work, the prelate was identified as Edward Fowler, bishop of Gloucester. However, he was not identified in any of the editions of *Characteristics* published by John Darby (those of 1711, 1714, 1723, 1727, 1732, 1737). Fowler (1632–1714) was a latitudinarian divine, appointed bishop of Gloucester in 1691. He has been identified as the author of *Reflections upon A Letter Concerning Enthusiasm, to my Lord **** (1709), one of the responses to the original publication of *A Letter Concerning Enthusiasm*; however, these *Reflections* do not indicate that the bishop took particular umbrage at this reference. It is known, however, that Fowler supplied stories of the supernatural to Henry More who included them in *Sadducismus Triumphatus, or Full and Plain Evidence Concerning Witches and Apparitions* (1681), his reworking of an earlier work by Joseph Glanvill. See A. Rupert Hall, *Henry More* (Oxford: Basil Blackwell, 1990), pp. 137–42.

are equally master of in private and can command at any time alone or with indifferent company or in any easy or cool hour? This indeed were more godlike; but ordinary humanity, I think, reaches not so high.

For my own part, my Lord, I have really so much need of some considerable presence or company to raise my thoughts on any occasion that, when alone, I must endeavour by strength of fancy to supply this want and, in default of a Muse, must inquire out some great man of a more than ordinary genius, whose imagined presence may inspire me with more than what I feel at ordinary hours. And thus, my Lord, have I chosen to address myself to your Lordship, though without subscribing my name, allowing you, as a stranger, the full liberty of reading no more than what you may have a fancy for, but reserving to myself the privilege of imagining you read all with particular notice, as a friend, and one whom I may justifiably treat with the intimacy and freedom which follows.

Section 2

If the knowing well how to expose any infirmity or vice were a sufficient security for the virtue which is contrary, how excellent an age might we be presumed to live in! Never was there in our nation a time known when folly and extravagance of every kind were more sharply inspected or more wittily ridiculed. And one might hope, at least, from this good symptom that our age was in no declining state since, whatever our distempers are, we stand so well affected to our remedies. To bear the being told of faults is in private persons the best token of amendment. It is seldom that a public is thus disposed. For where jealousy of state or the ill lives of the great people or any other cause is powerful enough to restrain the freedom of censure in any part, it in effect destroys the benefit of it in the whole. There can be no impartial and free censure of manners where any peculiar custom or national opinion is set apart, and not only exempted from criticism but even flattered with the highest art. It is only in a free nation, such as ours, that imposture has no privilege and that neither the credit of a court, the power of a nobility, nor the awfulness of a church can give her protection or hinder her from being arraigned in every shape and appearance. It is true, this liberty may seem to run too far. We may perhaps be said to make ill use of it. So everyone will say when he himself is touched and his opinion freely examined. But who shall be judge of what may be freely examined and what may not, where liberty may be used and where it may not? What remedy shall we prescribe to this in general? Can there be a better than from that liberty itself which is complained of? If men are vicious, petulant or abusive, the magistrate may correct them. But if they reason ill, it is reason still must teach them to do better. Justness of thought and style, refinement in manners, good breeding and politeness of every kind can come only from the trial and experience of what is best. Let but the search go freely on, and the right measure of every thing will soon be found. Whatever humour has got the start, if it be unnatural, it cannot hold, and the ridicule, if ill-placed at first, will certainly fall at last where it deserves.

I have often wondered to see men of sense so mightily alarmed at the approach of anything like ridicule on certain subjects, as if they mistrusted their own judgment. For what ridicule can lie against reason? Or how can any-one of the least justness of thought endure a ridicule wrong-placed? Nothing is more ridiculous than this itself. The vulgar, indeed, may swallow any sordid jest, any mere drollery or buffoonery, but it must be a finer and truer wit which takes with the men of sense and breeding. How comes it to pass, then, that we appear such cowards in reasoning and are so afraid to stand the test of ridicule? 'Oh,' say we, 'the subjects are too grave.' Perhaps so, but let us see first whether they are really grave or no, for, in the manner we may conceive them they may peradventure be very grave and weighty in our imagination, but very ridiculous and impertinent in their own nature. Gravity is of the very essence of imposture. It does not only make us mistake other things, but is apt perpetually almost to mistake itself. For even in common behaviour, how hard is it for the grave character to keep long out of the limits of the formal one? We can never be too grave if we can be assured we are really what we suppose. And we can never too much honour or revere anything for grave if we are assured the thing is grave, as we apprehend it. The main point is to know always true gravity from the false, and this can only be by carrying the rule constantly with us and freely applying it not only to the things about us but to ourselves. For if unhappily we lose the measure in ourselves, we shall soon lose it in everything besides. Now what rule or measure is there in the world, except in the considering of the real temper of things, to find which are truly serious and which ridiculous? And how can this be done unless by applying the ridicule to see whether it will bear?[3] But if we fear to apply this rule in anything, what security can we have against the imposture of formality in all things? We have allowed ourselves to be formalists[E] in one point, and the same formality may rule us as it pleases in all other.

It is not in every disposition that we are capacitated to judge of things. We must beforehand judge of our own temper and, accordingly, of other things which fall under our judgment. But we must never more pretend to judge of things, or of our own temper in judging them, when we have given up our preliminary right of judgment and, under a presumption of gravity, have allowed ourselves to be most ridiculous and to admire profoundly the most ridiculous things in nature, at least for ought we know. For having resolved

---

[E] In Shaftesbury's vocabulary, the formalist was the person who sustained his views through self-solemnity and what Shaftesbury regarded as the imposture of gravity.

[3] See pp. 29, 36.

never to try, we can never be sure. *Mirth, for the most part, cuts through weighty matters with greater firmness and ease than seriousness.*[4] This, my Lord, I may safely aver is so true in itself, and so well known for truth by the cunning formalists of the age, that they can better bear to have their impostures railed at, with all the bitterness and vehemence imaginable, than to have them touched ever so gently in this other way. They know very well that, as modes and fashions, so opinions, though ever so ridiculous, are kept up by solemnity, and that those formal notions, which grew up probably in an ill mood and have been conceived in sober sadness, are never to be removed but in a sober kind of cheerfulness and by a more easy and pleasant way of thought. There is a melancholy which accompanies all enthusiasm.[F] Be it love or religion (for there are enthusiasms in both), nothing can put a stop to the growing mischief of either, till the melancholy be removed and the mind at liberty to hear what can be said against the ridiculousness of an extreme in either way.

It was heretofore the wisdom of some wise nations to let people be fools as much as they pleased and never to punish seriously what deserved only to be laughed at and was, after all, best cured by that innocent remedy.[G] There are certain humours in mankind which of necessity must have vent. The human mind and body are both of them naturally subject to commotions, and, as there are strange ferments in the blood, which in many bodies occasion an extraordinary discharge, so in reason, too, there are heterogeneous particles which must be thrown off by fermentation. Should physicians endeavour absolutely to allay those ferments of the body and strike in the humours which discover themselves in such eruptions, they might, instead of making a cure, bid fair perhaps to raise a plague and turn a spring ague or an autumn surfeit into an epidemical malignant fever. They are certainly as ill physicians in the body politic who would needs be tampering with these mental eruptions and, under the specious pretence of healing this itch of superstition and saving souls from the contagion of enthusiasm, should set all nature in an uproar and turn a few innocent carbuncles into an inflammation and mortal gangrene.

We read in history that Pan, when he accompanied Bacchus in an expedition to the Indies, found means to strike a terror through a host of enemies by

[F]   Melancholy or melancholia, 'black bile', was one of four temperaments or humours in classical medical psychology (along with the sanguine, the choleric and the phlegmatic). It was also regarded as a mental disease. In both senses, it was long associated with enthusiasm. On the relation between melancholy and enthusiasm and for some of the psycho-physiological language on which Shaftesbury drew here, see Michael Heyd, *'Be Sober and Reasonable': The Critique of Enthusiasm in the Seventeenth and Early Eighteenth Centuries* (Leiden: E. J. Brill, 1995), pp. 44–71, 214–19.

[G]   As Shaftesbury made clear below, these 'wise nations' were the Greek and Roman polities of classical antiquity.

[4]   Horace, *Satires* 1.10.14–15.

the help of a small company, whose clamours he managed to good advantage among the echoing rocks and caverns of a woody vale. The hoarse bellowing of the caves, joined to the hideous aspect of such dark and desert places, raised such a horror in the enemy that, in this state, their imagination helped them to hear voices and doubtless to see forms too, which were more than human, while the uncertainty of what they feared made their fear yet greater and spread it faster by implicit looks than any narration could convey it.[5] And this was what in aftertimes men called a 'panic'. The story indeed gives a good hint of the nature of this passion, which can hardly be without some mixture of enthusiasm and horrors of a superstitious kind.

One may with good reason call every passion 'panic' which is raised in a multitude and conveyed by aspect or, as it were, by contact or sympathy. Thus, popular fury may be called 'panic' when the rage of the people, as we have sometimes known, has put them beyond themselves, especially where religion has had to do.[6] And in this state their very looks are infectious. The fury flies from face to face, and the disease is no sooner seen than caught. They who in a better situation of mind have beheld a multitude under the power of this passion, have owned that they saw in the countenances of men something more ghastly and terrible than at other times is expressed on the most passionate occasions. Such force has society in ill as well as in good passions, and so much stronger any affection is for being social and communicative.[7]

Thus, my Lord, there are many panics in mankind besides merely that of fear. And thus is religion also panic when enthusiasm of any kind gets up as oft, on melancholy occasions, it will. For vapours naturally rise and, in bad times especially, when the spirits of men are low, as either in public calamities or during the unwholesomeness of air or diet, or when convulsions happen in nature, storms, earthquakes or other amazing prodigies——at this season the panic must needs run high, and the magistrate of necessity give way to it. For to apply a serious remedy and bring the sword or *fasces*[ll] as a cure must make the case more melancholy and increase the very cause of the distemper. To forbid men's natural fears and to endeavour the overpowering them by other fears, must needs be a most unnatural method. The magistrate, if he be any artist, should have a gentler hand and, instead of caustics, incisions and amputations, should be using the softest balms, and, with a kind sympathy,

---

[ll] The symbol of the power of the Roman magistracy, a bundle of rods from which protruded the blade of an axe bound within.

[5] Polyaenus, *Stratagems* 1.2. [Bacchus, or Dionysus, was the focus of an ancient Greek cult in which worshippers pursued ecstasy through wild dancing, intoxication and other orgiastic behaviours. Pan was a deity associated with the fertility of flocks and could produce flock-like stampedes among humans, namely, 'panics'.]

[6] See pp. 23, 367n.

[7] See pp. 51, 201, 203–4, 212.

entering into the concern of the people and taking, as it were, their passion upon him, should, when he has soothed and satisfied it, endeavour, by cheerful ways, to divert and heal it.

This was ancient policy and, hence (as a notable author of our nation expresses it), it is necessary a people should have a 'public leading' in religion.[8] For to deny the magistrate a worship or take away a national church is as mere enthusiasm as the notion which sets up persecution. For why should there not be public walks as well as private gardens? Why not public libraries as well as private education and home tutors? But to prescribe bounds to fancy and speculation, to regulate men's apprehensions and religious beliefs or fears, to suppress by violence the natural passion of enthusiasm or to endeavour to ascertain it or reduce it to one species or bring it under any one modification is in truth no better sense, nor deserves a better character, than what the comedian declares of the like project in the affair of love: *You would do no more good than if you took pains to be methodically mad.*[9] Not only the visionaries and enthusiasts of all kinds were tolerated, your Lordship knows, by the ancients; but, on the other side, philosophy had as free a course and was permitted as a balance against superstition. And while some sects, such as the Pythagorean and latter Platonic, joined in with the superstition and enthusiasm of the times, the Epicurean, the Academic and others were allowed to use all the force of wit and raillery against it. And thus matters were happily balanced: reason had fair play; learning and science flourished. Wonderful was the harmony and temper which arose from all these contrarieties. Thus superstition and enthusiasm were mildly treated and, being let alone, they never raged to that degree as to occasion bloodshed, wars, persecutions and devastations in the world. But a new sort of policy, which extends itself to another world and considers the future lives and happiness of men rather than the present, has made us leap the bounds of natural humanity and, out of a supernatural charity, has taught us the way of plaguing one another most devoutly. It has raised an antipathy which no temporal interest could ever do and entailed upon us a mutual hatred to all eternity.[10] And now uniformity in opinion (a hopeful project!) is looked on as the only expedient against this evil. The saving of souls is now the heroic passion of exalted spirits and is become in a manner the chief care of the magistrate and the very end of government itself.

---

[8] Harrington. [James Harrington, 1611–77, was a political theorist best known for the propagation of republican ideas inspired by classical history and the writings of Machiavelli. His most important work was *The Commonwealth of Oceana* (1656). He used the expression 'public leading' in *The Art of Lawgiving* (1659) and *A System of Politics*, first published in John Toland's 1700 edition of Harrington, which Shaftesbury owned. See J. G. A. Pocock, ed., *The Political Works of James Harrington* (Cambridge: Cambridge University Press, 1977), pp. 678, 845.]

[9] Terence, *The Eunuch* 1.62–3.

[10] See pp. 364–5, 373.

If magistracy should vouchsafe to interpose thus much in other sciences, I am afraid we should have as bad logic as bad mathematics and, in every kind, as bad philosophy as we often have divinity in countries where a precise orthodoxy is settled by law. It is a hard matter for a government to settle wit. If it does but keep us sober and honest, it is likely we shall have as much ability in our spiritual as in our temporal affairs, and, if we can but be trusted, we shall have wit enough to save ourselves when no prejudice lies in the way. But if honesty and wit be insufficient for this saving work, it is in vain for the magistrate to meddle with it, since, if he be ever so virtuous or wise, he may be as soon mistaken as another man. I am sure the only way to save men's sense or preserve wit at all in the world is to give liberty to wit. Now wit can never have its liberty where the freedom of raillery is taken away, for against serious extravagances and splenetic humours there is no other remedy than this.

We have indeed full power over all other modifications of spleen. We may treat other enthusiasms as we please. We may ridicule love or gallantry or knight-errantry to the utmost, and we find that, in these latter days of wit, the humour of this kind, which was once so prevalent, is pretty well declined. The Crusades, the rescuing of Holy Lands and such devout gallantries are in less request than formerly. But, if something of this militant religion, something of this soul-rescuing spirit and saint-errantry, prevails still, we need not wonder when we consider in how solemn a manner we treat this distemper and how preposterously we go about to cure enthusiasm.

I can hardly forbear fancying that, if we had a sort of inquisition or formal court of judicature, with grave officers and judges, erected to restrain poetical licence and in general to suppress that fancy and humour of versification (but in particular that most extravagant passion of love, as it is set out by poets, in its heathenish dress of Venuses and Cupids), if the poets, as ringleaders and teachers of this heresy, were, under grievous penalties, forbid to enchant the people by their vein of rhyming, and if the people, on the other side, were, under proportionable penalties, forbid to hearken to any such charm or lend their attention to any love tale, so much as in a play, a novel or a ballad, we might perhaps see a new Arcadia arising out of this heavy persecution. Old people and young would be seized with a versifying spirit. We should have field-conventicles of lovers and poets. Forests would be filled with romantic shepherds and shepherdesses, and rocks resound with echoes of hymns and praises offered to the powers of love. We might indeed have a fair chance, by this management, to bring back the whole train of heathen gods and set our cold northern island burning with as many altars to Venus and Apollo as were formerly in Cyprus, Delos or any of those warmer Grecian climates.

Section 3
But, my Lord, you may perhaps wonder that, having been drawn into such a

serious subject as religion, I should forget myself so far as to give way to raillery and humour. I must own, my Lord, it is not merely through chance that this has happened. To say truth, I hardly care so much as to think on this subject, much less to write on it, without endeavouring to put myself in as good humour as is possible. People, indeed, who can endure no middle temper but are all air and humour, know little of the doubts and scruples of religion and are safe from any immediate influence of devout melancholy or enthusiasm, which requires more deliberation and thoughtful practice to fix itself in a temper and grow habitual. But be the habit what it will, to be delivered of it at so sad a cost as inconsiderateness or madness is what I would never wish to be my lot. I had rather stand all adventures with religion than endeavour to get rid of the thoughts of it by diversion. All I contend for is to think of it in a right humour, and that this goes more than halfway towards thinking rightly of it, is what I shall endeavour to demonstrate.

Good humour is not only the best security against enthusiasm but the best foundation of piety and true religion, for, if right thoughts and worthy apprehensions of the Supreme Being are fundamental to all true worship and adoration, it is more than probable that we shall never miscarry in this respect, except through ill humour only. Nothing beside ill humour, either natural or forced, can bring a man to think seriously that the world is governed by any devilish or malicious power. I very much question whether anything besides ill humour can be the cause of atheism. For there are so many arguments to persuade a man in humour that, in the main, all things are kindly and well disposed, that one would think it impossible for him to be so far out of conceit with affairs as to imagine they all ran at adventures and that the world, as venerable and wise a face as it carried, had neither sense nor meaning in it. This however I am persuaded of, that nothing beside ill humour can give us dreadful or ill thoughts of a Supreme Manager. Nothing can persuade us of sullenness or sourness in such a being, beside the actual sore feeling of somewhat of this kind within ourselves. And, if we are afraid of bringing good humour into religion or thinking with freedom and pleasantness on such a subject as God, it is because we conceive the subject so like ourselves and can hardly have a notion of majesty and greatness without stateliness and moroseness accompanying it.

This, however, is the just reverse of that character which we own to be most divinely good, when we see it, as we sometimes do, in men of highest power among us. If they pass for truly good, we dare treat them freely and are sure they will not be displeased with this liberty. They are doubly gainers by this goodness of theirs. For the more they are searched into and familiarly examined, the more their worth appears, and the discoverer, charmed with his success, esteems and loves more than ever, when he has proved this additional bounty in his superior and reflects on that candour and generosity he has experienced. Your Lordship knows more perhaps of this mystery than anyone. How else should you have been so beloved in power, and out of power so adhered to and still more beloved?[1]

Thank Heaven! there are even in our own age some such examples. In former ages there have been many such. We have known mighty princes and even emperors of the world who could bear unconcernedly not only the free censure of their actions, but the most spiteful reproaches and calumnies, even to their faces. Some perhaps may wish there had never been such examples found in heathens, but, more especially, that the occasion had never been given by Christians. It was more the misfortune indeed of mankind in general than of Christians in particular that some of the earlier Roman emperors were such monsters of tyranny and began a persecution, not on religious men merely, but on all who were suspected of worth or virtue. What could have been a higher honour or advantage to Christianity than to be persecuted by a Nero?[J] But better princes who came after were persuaded to remit these severe courses. It is true the magistrate might possibly have been surprised with the newness of a notion, which he might pretend, perhaps, did not only destroy the sacredness of his power, but treated him and all men as profane, impious and damned, who entered not into certain particular modes of worship, of which there had been formerly so many thousand instituted, all of them compatible and sociable till that time. However, such was the wisdom of some succeeding ministries that the edge of persecution was much abated, and even that prince, who was esteemed the greatest enemy of the Christian sect and who himself had been educated in it, was a great restrainer of persecution, and would allow of nothing further than a resumption of church lands and public schools, without any attempt on the goods or persons, even of those who branded the state religion and made a merit of affronting the public worship.[11]

It is well we have the authority of a sacred author in our religion to assure us that the spirit of love and humanity is above that of martyrs.[12] Otherwise, one might be a little scandalized, perhaps, at the history of many of our prim-

---

[1] Somers' power was at a peak during the reign of William III, when he was Lord Chancellor. However, with the Whigs generally, he lost power at the accession in 1702 of Anne, who had a particular animus against him.

[J] For Nero, see Introduction, p. xxiii. Though his reign began competently, it deteriorated, making him a symbol of criminal and immoral government. A fire burned much of Rome in AD 64 and, though rumours blamed Nero himself for the fire, he sought to assign responsibility to the Christians of Rome.

[11] See p. 375n. [The reference is to Flavius Claudius Julianus, known as Julian the Apostate, 331–63, Roman Emperor, 361–3. Although brought up a Christian, he underwent a 'pagan conversion'. During his brief reign, he sought to reverse the achievements of Christianity as Rome's official religion and revive the pagan cults.]

[12] 1 Corinthians 13.3.

itive confessors and martyrs, even according to our own accounts. There is hardly now in the world so good a Christian (if this be indeed the mark of a good one) who, if he happened to live at Constantinople or elsewhere under the protection of the Turks, would think it fitting or decent to give any disturbance to their mosque worship. And as good Protestants, my Lord, as you and I are, we should consider him as little better than a rank enthusiast, who, out of hatred to the Romish idolatry, should, in time of High Mass (where Mass perhaps was by law established) interrupt the priest with clamours or fall foul on his images and relics.

There are some, it seems, of our good brethren, the French Protestants, lately come among us, who are mightily taken with this primitive way.^{K} They have set afoot the spirit of martyrdom to a wonder in their own country, and they long to be trying it here, if we will give them leave and afford them the occasion – that is to say, if we will only do them the favour to hang or imprison them, if we will only be so obliging as to break their bones for them, after their country fashion, blow up their zeal and stir afresh the coals of persecution. But no such grace can they hitherto obtain of us. So hard-hearted we are that, notwithstanding their own mob are willing to bestow kind blows upon them and fairly stone them now and then in the open street, though the priests of their own nation would gladly give them their desired discipline and are earnest to light their probationary fires for them, we Englishmen, who are masters in our own country, will not suffer the enthusiasts to be thus used. Nor can we be supposed to act thus in envy to their phoenix sect, which it seems has risen out of the flames and would willingly grow to be a new church by the same manner of propagation as the old one, whose seed was truly said to be 'from the blood of the martyrs'.^{L}

But how barbarous still and more than heathenishly cruel are we tolerating Englishmen! For, not contented to deny these prophesying enthusiasts the honour of a persecution, we have delivered them over to the cruellest contempt in the world. I am told, for certain, that they are at this very time the subject of a choice droll or puppet-show at Bartholomew Fair.[13] There, doubtless, their strange voices and involuntary agitations are admirably well acted, by the motion of wires and inspiration of pipes. For the bodies of the prophets in their state of prophecy, being not in their own power but (as they say themselves) mere passive organs, actuated by an exterior force, have nothing

---

^{K} See Introduction, p. xxx.
^{L} Tertullian, *Apology* 50.13.

[13] Namely, in the year 1707. [Bartholomew Fair, though in its origins a commercial fair, had become an occasion for a variety of entertainments, including theatrical presentations. It was held annually around St Bartholomew's Day, 24 August, at Smithfield, just outside the walls of the City of London.]

natural or resembling real life in any of their sounds or motions, so that how awkwardly soever a puppet-show may imitate other actions, it must needs represent this passion to the life. And while Bartholomew Fair is in possession of this privilege, I dare stand security to our national Church that no sect of enthusiasts, no new venders of prophecy or miracles, shall ever get the start or put her to the trouble of trying her strength with them, in any case.

Happy it was for us, that when Popery had got possession, Smithfield was used in a more tragical way.[M] Many of our first reformers, it is feared, were little better than enthusiasts. And God knows whether a warmth of this kind did not considerably help us in throwing off that spiritual tyranny. So that had not the priests, as is usual, preferred the love of blood to all other passions, they might in a merrier way, perhaps, have evaded the greatest force of our reforming spirit. I never heard that the ancient heathens were so well advised in their ill purpose of suppressing the Christian religion in its first rise as to make use at any time of this Bartholomew Fair method. But this I am persuaded of, that had the truth of the Gospel been any way surmountable, they would have bid much fairer for the silencing it, if they had chosen to bring our primitive founders upon the stage in a pleasanter way than that of bearskins and pitch-barrels.[N]

The Jews were naturally a very cloudy people and would endure little raillery in anything, much less in what belonged to any religious doctrines or opinions.[14] Religion was looked upon with a sullen eye, and hanging was the only remedy they could prescribe for anything which looked like setting up a new revelation. The sovereign argument was 'Crucify, crucify!' But with all their malice and inveteracy to our Saviour and his apostles after him, had they but taken the fancy to act such puppet-shows in his contempt as at this hour the Papists are acting in his honour, I am apt to think they might possibly have done our religion more harm than by all their other ways of severity.

I believe our great and learned apostle found less advantage from the easy treatment of his Athenian antagonists than from the surly and cursed spirit of

---

[M] Smithfield was also the site of public executions for many centuries. In particular, some 200 Protestants were executed here during the reign of Mary I (Mary Tudor, 'Bloody Mary'), 1516–58, reigned 1553–8. 'Popery' here referred to her Catholicism.

[N] An allusion to Tacitus' description, *Annals* 15.44, of Nero's persecution of Christians after the fire of AD 64, during which some Christians, clothed in the skins of wild animals, were fed to dogs and others were burnt on the crosses on which they had been crucified.

[14] Our author having been censured for this and some following passages concerning the Jews, the reader is referred to the notes and citations on pp. 361–3, 387ff; see also pp. 126–7. [Shaftesbury was not alone among deists in finding fault with both ancient Hebrews and modern Jews, who were said to exemplify, among other things, theocracy, ritualism and dogmatism: see Todd M. Endelman, *The Jews of Georgian London 1714–1830: Tradition and Change in a Liberal Society* (Philadelphia: Jewish Publication Society of America, 1979), pp. 96–8.]

the most persecuting Jewish cities.[15] He made less improvement of the candour and civility of his Roman judges than of the zeal of the synagogue and vehemence of his national priests. Though when I consider this apostle as appearing either before the witty Athenians or before a Roman court of judicature in the presence of their great men and ladies, and see how handsomely he accommodates himself to the apprehensions and temper of those politer people, I do not find that he declines the way of wit or good humour, but, without suspicion of his cause, is willing generously to commit it to this proof and try it against the sharpness of any ridicule which might be offered.

But, though the Jews were never pleased to try their wit or malice this way against our Saviour or his apostles, the irreligious part of the heathens had tried it long before against the best doctrines and best characters of men which had ever arisen among them. Nor did this prove in the end any injury, but, on the contrary, the highest advantage to those very characters and doctrines, which, having stood the proof, were found so solid and just. The divinest man who had ever appeared in the heathen world was in the height of witty times and by the wittiest of all poets most abominably ridiculed in a whole comedy, written and acted on purpose.[O] But so far was this from sinking his reputation or suppressing his philosophy that they each increased the more for it, and he apparently grew to be more the envy of other teachers. He was not only contented to be ridiculed, but, that he might help the poet as much as possible, he presented himself openly in the theatre, that his real figure (which was no advantageous one) might be compared with that which the witty poet had brought as his representative on the stage. Such was his good humour! Nor could there be in the world a greater testimony of the invincible goodness of the man, or a greater demonstration that there was no imposture either in his character or opinions. For that imposture should dare sustain the encounter of a grave enemy is no wonder. A solemn attack, she knows, is not of such danger to her. There is nothing she abhors or dreads like pleasantness and good humour.

Section 4

In short, my Lord, the melancholy way of treating religion is that which, according to my apprehension, renders it so tragical and is the occasion of its acting in reality such dismal tragedies in the world. And my notion is that,

---

[O] Socrates, for whom see Introduction, p. xxiv, as mocked by Aristophanes, Greek comic playwright, *c.* 450–*c.* 385 BC, in *The Clouds*. The anecdote that follows was based on Aelian, *Miscellany* 2.13.

[15] What advantages he made of his sufferings and how pathetically his bonds and stripes were set to view and often pleaded by him to raise his character and advance the interest of Christianity, anyone who reads his epistles and is well acquainted with his manner and style may easily observe. [That is, St Paul.]

provided we treat religion with good manners, we can never use too much good humour or examine it with too much freedom and familiarity. For, if it be genuine and sincere, it will not only stand the proof but thrive and gain advantage from hence. If it be spurious or mixed with any imposture, it will be detected and exposed.

The melancholy way in which we have been taught religion makes us unapt to think of it in good humour. It is in adversity chiefly or in ill health, under affliction, or disturbance of mind, or discomposure of temper, that we have recourse to it, though in reality we are never so unfit to think of it as at such a heavy and dark hour. We can never be fit to contemplate anything above us when we are in no condition to look into ourselves and calmly examine the temper of our own mind and passions. For then it is we see wrath and fury and revenge and terrors in the Deity – when we are full of disturbances and fears within and have, by sufferance and anxiety, lost so much of the natural calm and easiness of our temper.

We must not only be in ordinary good humour, but in the best of humours and in the sweetest, kindest disposition of our lives, to understand well what true goodness is and what those attributes imply which we ascribe with such applause and honour to the Deity. We shall then be able to see best whether those forms of justice, those degrees of punishment, that temper of resentment and those measures of offence and indignation, which we vulgarly suppose in God, are suitable to those original ideas of goodness, which the same Divine Being, or Nature under him, has implanted in us and which we must necessarily presuppose, in order to give him praise or honour in any kind. This, my Lord, is the security against all superstition – to remember that there is nothing in God but what is God-like and that he is either not at all or truly and perfectly good. But when we are afraid to use our reason freely, even on that very question, 'whether he really be or not', we then actually presume him bad and flatly contradict that pretended character of goodness and greatness, while we discover this mistrust of his temper and fear his anger and resentment, in the case of this freedom of inquiry.

We have a notable instance of this freedom in one of our sacred authors. As patient as Job is said to be, it cannot be denied that he makes bold enough with God and takes his Providence roundly to task. His friends, indeed, plead hard with him and use all arguments, right or wrong, to patch up objections and set the affairs of Providence upon an equal foot. They make a merit of saying all the good they can of God at the very stretch of their reason, and sometimes quite beyond it. But this, in Job's opinion, is 'flattering God', 'accepting of God's person', and even 'mocking him'.[16] And no wonder. For what merit can there be in believing God or his Providence upon frivolous and weak grounds?

---

[16] Job 13.7–10.

What virtue in assuming an opinion contrary to the appearance of things, and resolving to hear nothing which may be said against it? Excellent character of the God of Truth! that he should be offended at us for having refused to put the lie upon our understandings, as much as in us lay, and be satisfied with us for having believed, at a venture and against our reason, what might have been the greatest falsehood in the world, for anything we could bring as a proof or evidence to the contrary!

It is impossible that any besides an ill-natured man can wish against the being of a God, for this is wishing against the public and even against one's private good too, if rightly understood. But if a man has not any such ill will to stifle his belief, he must have surely an unhappy opinion of God and believe him not so good by far as he knows himself to be, if he imagines that an impartial use of his reason, in any matter of speculation whatsoever, can make him run any risk hereafter, and that a mean denial of his reason and an affectation of belief in any point too hard for his understanding can entitle him to any favour in another world. This is being sycophants in religion, mere parasites of devotion. It is using God as the crafty beggars use those they address to, when they are ignorant of their quality.[17] The novices among them may innocently come out perhaps with a 'Good Sir!' or a 'Good Forsooth!'; but with the old stagers, no matter whom they meet in a coach, it is always 'Good your Honour!' or 'Good your Lordship!' or 'Your Ladyship!' For if there should be really a Lord in the case, we should be undone (say they) for want of giving the title, but, if the party should be no Lord, there would be no offence – it would not be ill taken.

And thus it is in religion. We are highly concerned how to beg right, and think all depends upon hitting the title and making a good guess. It is the most beggarly refuge imaginable, which is so mightily cried up and stands as a great maxim with many able men, that 'they should strive to have faith and believe to the utmost, because if, after all, there be nothing in the matter, there will be no harm in being thus deceived, but, if there be anything, it will be fatal for them not to have believed to the full'.[P] But they are so far mistaken that, while they have this thought, it is certain they can never believe either to their satisfaction and happiness in this world, or with any advantage of recommendation to another. For besides that our reason, which knows the cheat, will

---

[P] The 'maxim' here was a simplification of the so-called 'wager' on belief articulated by Blaise Pascal, French mathematician, scientist and moralist, 1623–62, in the fragment 'Infinity nothingness' [No. 680]: see Blaise Pascal, *Pensées and Other Writings*, trans. Honor Levi (Oxford and London: Oxford University Press, 1995), pp. 152–8. Various English writers, including John Locke, White Kennett and John Tillotson, adopted or echoed Pascal's arguments: see John Barker, *Strange Contrarieties: Pascal in England during the Age of Reason* (Montreal and London: McGill–Queen's University Press, 1975), pp. 50–2, 133–4.

[17] See pp. 391–2.

never rest thoroughly satisfied on such a bottom but turn us often adrift and toss us in a sea of doubt and perplexity, we cannot but actually grow worse in our religion, and entertain a worse opinion still of a Supreme Deity, while our belief is founded on so injurious a thought of him.

To love the public, to study universal good, and to promote the interest of the whole world, as far as lies within our power, is surely the height of goodness and makes that temper which we call 'divine'. In this temper, my Lord (for surely you should know it well), it is natural for us to wish that others should partake with us by being convinced of the sincerity of our example. It is natural for us to wish our merit should be known, particularly if it be our fortune to have served a nation as a good minister or, as some prince or father of a country, to have rendered happy a considerable part of mankind under our care. But if it happened that of this number there should be some so ignorantly bred and of so remote a province as to have lain out of the hearing of our name and actions or, hearing of them, should be so puzzled with odd and contrary stories told up and down concerning us that they knew not what to think, whether there were really in the world any such person as ourself, should we not, in good truth, be ridiculous to take offence at this? And should we not pass for extravagantly morose and ill-humoured if, instead of treating the matter in raillery, we should think in earnest of revenging ourselves on the offending parties who, out of their rustic ignorance, ill judgment or incredulity, had detracted from our renown?

How shall we say then? Does it really deserve praise to be thus concerned about it? Is the doing good for glory's sake so divine a thing? Or is it not diviner to do good even where it may be thought inglorious, even to the ungrateful and to those who are wholly insensible of the good they receive? How comes it then that what is so divine in us should lose its character in the Divine Being? And that according as the Deity is represented to us, he should more resemble the weak, womanish and impotent part of our nature than the generous, manly and divine?[18]

Section 5
One would think, my Lord, it were in reality no hard thing to know our own weaknesses at first sight and distinguish the features of human frailty with which we are so well acquainted. One would think it were easy to understand that provocation and offence, anger, revenge, jealousy in point of honour or power, love of fame, glory and the like, belong only to limited beings and are necessarily excluded a being which is perfect and universal. But if we have never settled with ourselves any notion of what is morally excellent, or if we cannot trust to that reason which tells us that nothing beside what is so can have place in

[18] See pp. 148, 467.

the Deity, we can neither trust to anything which others relate of him or which he himself reveals to us. We must be satisfied beforehand that he is good and cannot deceive us. Without this, there can be no real religious faith or confidence. Now, if there be really something previous to revelation, some antecedent demonstration of reason, to assure us that God is and, withal, that he is so good as not to deceive us, the same reason, if we will trust to it, will demonstrate to us that God is so good as to exceed the very best of us in goodness. And after this manner we can have no dread or suspicion to render us uneasy, for it is malice only, and not goodness, which can make us afraid.

There is an odd way of reasoning, but in certain distempers of mind very sovereign to those who can apply it, and it is this: 'There can be no malice but where interests are opposed. A universal being can have no interest opposite and therefore can have no malice.' If there be a general mind, it can have no *particular* interest; but the general good or good of the whole and its own private good must of necessity be one and the same. It can intend nothing besides, nor aim at any thing beyond, nor be provoked to anything contrary. So that we have only to consider whether there be really such a thing as a mind which has relation to the whole or not. For if unhappily there be no mind, we may comfort ourselves, however, that nature has no malice. If there be really a mind, we may rest satisfied that it is the best-natured one in the world. The last case, one would imagine, should be the most comfortable, and the notion of a common parent less frightful than that of forlorn nature and a fatherless world. Though, as religion stands among us, there are many good people who would have less fear in being thus exposed and would be easier perhaps in their minds if they were assured they had only mere chance to trust to. For nobody trembles to think there should be no God, but rather that there should be one. This however would be otherwise if Deity were thought as kindly of as Humanity, and we could be persuaded to believe that, if there really was a God, the highest goodness must of necessity belong to him, without any of those defects of passion, those meannesses and imperfections, which we acknowledge such in ourselves, which as good men we endeavour all we can to be superior to and which we find we every day conquer as we grow better.[19]

Methinks, my Lord, it would be well for us if, before we ascended into the higher regions of divinity, we would vouchsafe to descend a little into ourselves and bestow some poor thoughts upon plain honest morals.[20] When we had once looked into ourselves and distinguished well the nature of our own affections, we should probably be fitter judges of the divineness of a character

---

[19] 'For my own part', says honest Plutarch, 'I had rather men should say of me that "there neither is, nor ever was, such a one as Plutarch" than they should say that "there was a Plutarch, an unsteady, changeable, easily provokable and revengeful man"' (Plutarch, *Superstition* 10 [*Moralia* 169–70]). See p. 391.

[20] See pp. 354, 424n.

and discern better what affections were suitable or unsuitable to a perfect being. We might then understand how to love and praise when we had acquired some consistent notion of what was laudable or lovely. Otherwise we might chance to do God little honour when we intended him the most. For it is hard to imagine what honour can arise to the Deity from the praises of creatures who are unable to discern what is praiseworthy or excellent in their own kind.

If a musician were cried up to the skies by a certain set of people who had no ear in music, he would surely be put to the blush and could hardly, with a good countenance, accept the benevolence of his auditors, till they had acquired a more competent apprehension of him and could by their own senses find out something really good in his performance. Till this were brought about, there would be little glory in the case, and the musician, though ever so vain, would have little reason to be contented.

They who affect praise the most had rather not be taken notice of than be impertinently applauded. I know not how it comes about that He who is ever said to do good the most disinterestedly should be thought desirous of being praised so lavishly, and be supposed to set so high a rate upon so cheap and low a thing as ignorant commendation and forced applause.

It is not the same with goodness as with other qualities, which we may understand very well and yet not possess. We may have an excellent ear in music without being able to perform in any kind. We may judge well of poetry without being poets or possessing the least of a poetic vein. But we can have no tolerable notion of goodness, without being tolerably good. So that, if the praise of a divine being be so great a part of his worship, we should, methinks, learn goodness, were it for nothing else than that we might learn, in some tolerable manner, how to praise. For the praise of goodness from an unsound hollow heart must certainly make the greatest dissonance in the world.

Section 6
Other reasons, my Lord, there are, why this plain homespun philosophy of looking into ourselves may do us wondrous service in rectifying our errors in religion. For there is a sort of enthusiasm of second hand. And when men find no original commotions in themselves, no prepossessing panic which bewitches them, they are apt still, by the testimony of others, to be imposed on and led credulously into the belief of many false miracles. And this habit may make them variable and of a very inconstant faith, easy to be carried away with every wind of doctrine and addicted to every upstart sect or superstition. But the knowledge of our passions in their very seeds, the measuring well the growth and progress of enthusiasm, and the judging rightly of its natural force and what command it has over our very senses, may teach us to oppose more suc-

cessfully those delusions which come armed with the specious pretext of moral certainty and matter of fact.[21]

The new prophesying sect I made mention of above pretend, it seems, among many other miracles, to have had a most signal one, acted premeditatedly and with warning, before many hundreds of people, who actually give testimony to the truth of it.[Q] But I would only ask whether there were present, among those hundreds, any one person who, having never been of their sect or addicted to their way, will give the same testimony with them? I must not be contented to ask whether such a one had been wholly free of that particular enthusiasm but whether, before that time, he was esteemed of so sound a judgment and clear a head, as to be wholly free of melancholy and in all likelihood incapable of all enthusiasm besides. For, otherwise, the panic may have been caught, the evidence of the senses lost as in a dream, and the imagination so inflamed, as in a moment to have burnt up every particle of judgment and reason. The combustible matters lie prepared within and ready to take fire at a spark, but chiefly in a multitude seized with the same spirit.[22] No wonder if the blaze rises so of a sudden when innumerable eyes glow with the passion and heaving breasts are labouring with inspiration, when not the aspect only but the very breath and exhalations of men are infectious, and the inspiring disease imparts itself by insensible transpiration. I am not a divine good enough to resolve what spirit that was which proved so catching among the ancient prophets that even the profane Saul was taken by it.[23] But I learn from Holy Scripture that there was the *evil* as well as the *good* spirit of prophecy. And I find, by present experience as well as by all histories, sacred and profane, that the operation of this spirit is everywhere the same as to the bodily organs.

A gentleman, who has written lately in defence of revived prophecy and has since fallen himself into the prophetic ecstasies, tells us that 'the ancient prophets had the spirit of God upon them under ecstasy, with diverse strange gestures of body denominating them madmen (or enthusiasts) as appears evidently', says he, 'in the instances of Balaam, Saul, David, Ezekiel, Daniel, etc.'.[R] And he proceeds to justify this by the practice of the apostolic times and by

---

Q   Richard B. Wolf argues that the 'signal miracle' referred to Pierre Claris, who safely walked through fire in 1703: see *An Old–Spelling, Critical Edition of Shaftesbury's Letter Concerning Enthusiasm and Sensus Communis* (New York and London: Garland Publishing, Inc., 1988), pp. 118–21.

R   John Lacy in the preface to the second edition of *A Cry from the Desart, or Testimonials of the Miraculous Things Lately Come To Pass in the Cevennes* (London, 1707), a translation of François Maximilien Misson's *Théâtre sacré des Cevennes* (London, 1707), p. x. The parenthetical 'or enthusiasts' was Shaftesbury's insertion in an otherwise accurate quotation. On Lacy, see Introduction, p. xxx.

[21]   See pp. 355–6, 367–8.
[22]   See p. 367n.
[23]   See 1 Kings 22.2ff and 2 Chronicles 18.19ff. See also pp. 387–8.

the regulation which the Apostle himself applies to these seemingly irregular gifts, so frequent and ordinary (as our author pretends) in the primitive church on the first rise and spreading of Christianity.[24] But I leave it to him to make the resemblance as well as he can between his own and the apostolic way. I only know that the symptoms he describes, and which himself (poor gentleman!) labours under, are as heathenish as he can possibly pretend them to be Christian. And when I saw him lately under an agitation (as they call it), uttering prophecy in a pompous Latin style, of which, out of his ecstasy, it seems, he is wholly incapable,[S] it brought into my mind the Latin poet's description of the Sibyl, whose agonies were so perfectly like these: *Suddenly her expression, her colour, was not the same, her tresses did not remain trained; but her breast heaves and her heart swells madly with frenzy; and she appears greater and her utterance is not mortal. She is filled now with the breath of divinity, closer upon her.*[25] And again presently after: *Huge in her cave the prophetess raves as though she were able to shake out the mighty god from her breast: so much the more does he weaken her frenzied mouth, taming her wild breast, and fashion her by his grasp.*[26] Which is the very style of our experienced author: 'For the inspired', says he, 'undergo a probation, wherein the spirit, by frequent agitations, forms the organs, ordinarily for a month or two before utterance.'[T]

The Roman historian, speaking of a most horrible enthusiasm which broke out in Rome long before his days, describes this spirit of prophecy: *Men, as if possessed, would prophesy with fanatical convulsions of the body.*[27] The detestable things which are further related of these enthusiasts, I would not willingly transcribe. But the Senate's mild decree in so execrable a case, I cannot omit copying, being satisfied that, though your Lordship has read it before now, you can read it again and again with admiration: *For the future*, says Livy, *it was then ordered by decree of the Senate [that there be no Bacchanalia in Rome or in Italy].*

[S] According to Hillel Schwartz, *The French Prophets: The History of a Millenarian Group in Eighteenth-Century England* (Berkeley and Los Angeles: University of California Press, 1980), p. 93n, this encounter occurred on 5 July 1707. In Lacy's own account of his prophetical activities during the summer of 1707, he began making utterances in Latin in early July: *The Prophetical Warnings of John Lacy, Esq.* (London, 1707), pp. 56ff. He gave an account of his limited training in Latin in the preface to the same work, pp. ix–xi.

[T] Lacy's precise words, referring to the inspired members among the Cevennais refugees, were: 'Every one that is inspired, did undergo a preparation, wherein the Spirit (by agitations much more frequent in the beginning than afterwards) did form the organs, ordinarily for one, two or three months, before such person uttered anything as under inspiration': Lacy, *A Cry from the Desart*, p. xi.

[24] 1 Corinthians 14.

[25] Virgil, *Aeneid* 6.47–51. [The sibyls were prophetesses, each identified with a specific location, whose performances tended to the ecstatic. In Book VI, Aeneas encountered the Sibyl of Cumae near Naples. Her utterances were delivered from a cave and inscribed on palm leaves.]

[26] Virgil, *Aeneid* 6.77–80.

[27] Livy, *History of Rome* 39.13.12.

If anyone held such a rite to be customary and necessary and that he could not omit the rite without scruple and atonement, he was to make a profession before the urban praetor, and the praetor would consult the Senate. If it were permitted him, when there were no less than a hundred in the Senate, he should perform that rite, provided that no more than five were involved in the ritual and that there should be no common funds nor any master of the rites or priest.[28]

So necessary it is to give way to this distemper of enthusiasm that even that philosopher who bent the whole force of his philosophy against superstition appears to have left room for visionary fancy and to have indirectly tolerated enthusiasm. For it is hard to imagine that one who had so little religious faith as Epicurus should have so vulgar a credulity as to believe those accounts of armies and castles in the air and such visionary phenomena.[U] Yet he allows them, and then thinks to solve them by his *effluvia* and aerial looking-glasses, and I know not what other stuff – which his Latin poet, however, sets off beautifully, as he does all: *Many likenesses of things wander in many ways in all directions, delicate likenesses, like spider web or gold leaf, which easily join with one another in the breezes when they meet . . . And so we see centaurs and the limbs of Scyllas and the doggy face of a Cerberus and likenesses of those whose bones the earth embraces after death has come their way, since all kind of likenesses are borne about everywhere – some spontaneously come into being in the air itself and some are shed from all sorts of things.*[29]

It was a sign that this philosopher believed there was a good stock of visionary spirit originally in human nature. He was so satisfied that men were inclined to see visions that, rather than they should go without, he chose to make them to their hand. Notwithstanding he denied the principles of religion to be natural,[30] he was forced tacitly to allow there was a wondrous disposition in mankind towards supernatural objects and that, if these ideas were vain, they were yet in a manner innate, or such as men were really born to and could hardly by any means avoid. From which concession, a divine, methinks, might raise a good argument against him for the truth as well as the usefulness of religion. But so it is. Whether the matter of apparition be true or false, the symptoms are the same and the passion of equal force in the person who is vision-struck. The *Lymphatici*[V] of the Latins were the *Nympholepti*[W] of the Greeks. They were persons said to have seen some species of divinity as either

---

[U] For Epicurus, see Introduction, p. xxvi. In keeping with his materialism, he believed that physical objects gave off from their surfaces thin films of atoms – the *effluvia* of the next sentence – which impressed the organs of sentient beings such as humans.

[V] The panic-stricken.

[W] The nymph-possessed. Nymphs were female nature spirits.

[28] Livy, *History of Rome* 39.18.8–9.

[29] Lucretius, *On the Nature of Things*, 4.724–7, 732–6. [For Lucretius, see Introduction, p. xxvi.]

[30] See p. 54.

some rural deity or nymph, which threw them into such transports as overcame their reason. The ecstasies expressed themselves outwardly in quakings, tremblings, tossings of the head and limbs, agitations, and (as Livy calls them) fanatical throws or convulsions, extemporary prayer, prophecy, singing and the like. All nations have their lymphatics of some kind or another, and all churches, heathen as well as Christian, have had their complaints against fanaticism.

One would think the ancients imagined this disease had some relation to that which they called hydrophoby.[X] Whether the ancient lymphatics had any way like that of biting to communicate the rage of their distemper, I cannot so positively determine. But certain fanatics there have been since the time of the ancients who have had a most prosperous faculty of communicating the appetite of the teeth. For since first the snappish spirit got up in religion, all sects have been at it, as the saying is, 'tooth and nail',[Y] and are never better pleased than in worrying one another without mercy.

So far indeed the innocent kind of fanaticism extends itself that, when the party is struck by the apparition, there follows always an itch of imparting it and kindling the same fire in other breasts. For thus poets are fanatics too. And thus Horace either is, or feigns himself, lymphatic and shows what an effect the vision of the nymphs and Bacchus had on him: *I saw Bacchus teaching odes on distant crags – believe me, posterity! – and nymphs as his pupils . . . Evoe! my mind quakes at this recent fright and raves in disorder, my breast full of Bacchus!*[31] (as Heinsius reads).[Z]

No poet (as I ventured to say at first to your Lordship) can do anything great in his own way without the imagination or supposition of a divine presence, which may raise him to some degree of this passion we are speaking of. Even the cold Lucretius[32] makes use of inspiration, when he writes against it and is forced to raise an apparition of Nature, in divine form, to animate and conduct him in his very work of degrading nature and despoiling her of all her seeming wisdom and divinity: *Nurturing Venus, you who fills with your presence the ship-bearing sea, beneath the gliding stars of heaven, and the crop-bearing lands*

[X] For the ancient Greeks, hydrophobia was, literally, the fear of water, said to be caused by the bite of a mad, possessed or diseased dog. It corresponds to the modern rabies.

[Y] With all one's might.

[Z] In the original text, Shaftesbury misquoted the text of Ode 2.19 as it appeared in both Heinsius and Torrentius.

[31] Horace *Odes* 2.19.1–7. So again, *Satires* 1.5.97, where Horace wittily treats the people of Gnatia as lymphatics and enthusiasts, for believing a miracle of their priests. See Heinsius and Torrentius and the first quotation in n. 35. [Daniel Heinsius, 1580–1655, was a Dutch poet, orator and philologist whose commentary on Horace's works first appeared in 1610. Laevinus Torrentius, 1525–95, was bishop of Antwerp and a humanist scholar whose edition of Horace with commentary appeared in 1608. Shaftesbury owned copies of both editions.]

[32] See p. 352.

... Since you alone govern the nature of things, nor without you does anything come forth into the bright shores of light, nor without you does anything joyous or lovely come into being, you I am eager to be my comrade in the writing of verses which I attempt to compose On the Nature of Things for our noble Memmius.[33]

Section 7

The only thing, my Lord, I would infer from all this is that enthusiasm is wonderfully powerful and extensive, that it is a matter of nice judgment and the hardest thing in the world to know fully and distinctly since even atheism is not exempt from it.[34] For, as some have well remarked, there have been enthusiastical atheists. Nor can divine inspiration, by its outward marks, be easily distinguished from it. For inspiration is a real feeling of the Divine Presence and enthusiasm a false one. But the passion they raise is much alike. For when the mind is taken up in vision and fixes its view either on any real object or mere spectre of divinity, when it sees, or thinks it sees, anything prodigious and more than human, its horror, delight, confusion, fear, admiration or whatever passion belongs to it or is uppermost on this occasion, will have something vast, 'immane' and (as painters say) beyond life. And this is what gave occasion to the name of fanaticism, as it was used by the ancients in its original sense, for an apparition transporting the mind.

Something there will be of extravagance and fury when the ideas or images received are too big for the narrow human vessel to contain. So that 'inspiration' may be justly called 'divine enthusiasm', for the word itself signifies 'divine presence' and was made use of by the philosopher whom the earliest Christian Fathers called 'divine' to express whatever was sublime in human passions.[35] This was the spirit he allotted to heroes, statesmen, poets, orators, musicians and even philosophers themselves. Nor can we, of our own accord, forbear

---

[33] Lucretius, *On the Nature of Things* 1.2–4 and 1.21–6. [Gaius Memmius, a prominent Roman orator and politician of the first century BC, was the dedicatee of Lucretius' poem.]

[34] See pp. 365–6. [As Shaftesbury made clear in Miscellany II, Chapter 2, the idea that atheism itself was a symptom of enthusiasm had been explored by the Cambridge Platonists Henry More and Ralph Cudworth.]

[35] *Surely you know that, with foresight and clarity, the nymphs shall enthuse me. So many, and yet more, fine deeds I can tell you when madness comes from the gods*: Plato, *Phaedrus* 241E. *And we could especially say of the politicians that they are both god-like and enthused*: Plato, *Meno* 99D. *So I recognized, in short order, this too, in the case of the poets, that they compose what they compose not by wisdom but by a nature and being enthused, like the prophets and oracle deliverers*: Plato, *Apology* 22B. In particular as to philosophers, Plutarch tells us that it was the complaint of some of the four old Romans, when learning first came to them from Greece, that their youth grew enthusiastic with philosophy. For speaking of one of the philosophers of the Athenian embassy, he says, *[Carneades] cast a tremendous passion into the youth resulting in their abandoning other pleasures and pastimes to be enthused about philosophy*: Plutarch, *Marcus Cato* 22.3 [*Parallel Lives*].

ascribing to a noble enthusiasm whatever is greatly performed by any of these.[36] So that almost all of us know something of this principle. But to know it as we should do and discern it in its several kinds, both in ourselves and others, this is the great work and by this means alone we can hope to avoid delusion. For 'to judge the spirits whether they are of God',[AA] we must antecedently 'judge our own Spirit', whether it be of reason and sound sense, whether it be fit to judge at all by being sedate, cool and impartial, free of every biassing passion, every giddy vapour or melancholy fume. This is the first knowledge and previous judgment: 'To understand ourselves and know what spirit we are of.' Afterwards we may judge the spirit in others, consider what their personal merit is and prove the validity of their testimony by the solidity of their brain. By this means we may prepare ourselves with some antidote against enthusiasm. And this is what I have dared affirm is best performed by keeping to good humour. For otherwise the remedy itself may turn to the disease.

And now, my Lord, having after all, in some measure, justified enthusiasm and owned the word, if I appear extravagant in addressing to you after the manner I have done, you must allow me to plead an impulse. You must suppose me (as with truth you may) most passionately yours and, with the kindness which is natural to you on other occasions, you must tolerate your enthusiastic friend who, excepting only in the case of this over-forward zeal, must ever appear, with the highest respect,

My Lord,
Your Lordship's, etc.

[AA] 1 John 4.1.

[36] Of this passion in the nobler and higher sense, see more on pp. 191, 351–5.

Sensus Communis,[A] an Essay on the Freedom of Wit and Humour in a Letter to a Friend

Here presses the wolf, here the dog.[1]

Part I

Section 1

I have been considering, my friend, what your fancy was to express such a surprise as you did the other day when I happened to speak to you in commendation of raillery. Was it possible you should suppose me so grave a man as to dislike *all* conversation of this kind? Or were you afraid I should not stand the trial, if you put me to it, by making the experiment in *my own* case?

I must confess you had reason enough for your caution if you could imagine me at the bottom so true a zealot as not to bear the least raillery on my own opinions. It is the case, I know, with many. Whatever they think grave or solemn, they suppose must never be treated out of a grave and solemn way, though what another thinks so, they can be contented to treat otherwise and are forward to try the edge of ridicule against any opinions besides their own.

The question is whether this be fair or no, and whether it be not just and reasonable to make as free with our own opinions as with those of other people. For to be sparing in this case may be looked upon as a piece of selfishness. We may be charged perhaps with wilful ignorance and blind idolatry for having taken opinions upon trust and consecrated in ourselves certain idol-notions, which we will never suffer to be unveiled or seen in open light. They

---

[A] Literally, 'common sense'. The expression usually referred to sound practical judgment or to the synthetic sense that integrated the information gathered by the five senses. However, Shaftesbury's entire essay was aimed at interpreting this expression as 'the sense of the common', that is, the human aptitude for community and civility. See especially pp. 48–51 below. On the significance of *sensus communis*, see Hans-Georg Gadamer, *Truth and Method*, trans. William Glen-Doepel (London: Sheed and Ward, 1975), pp. 19–29.

[1] Horace, *Satires* 2.2.64.

may perhaps be monsters, and not divinities or sacred truths, which are kept thus choicely in some dark corner of our minds. The spectres may impose on us, while we refuse to turn them every way and view their shapes and complexions in every light. For that which can be shown only in a certain light is questionable. Truth, it is supposed, may bear *all* lights, and one of those principal lights, or natural mediums, by which things are to be viewed, in order to a thorough recognition, is ridicule itself, or that manner of proof by which we discern whatever is liable to just raillery in any subject. So much, at least, is allowed by all who at any time appeal to this criterion. The gravest gentlemen, even in the gravest subjects, are supposed to acknowledge this and can have no right, it is thought, to deny others the freedom of this appeal, while they are free to censure like other men and in their gravest arguments make no scruple to ask, 'Is it not ridiculous?'

Of this affair, therefore, I design you should know fully what my sentiments are. And by this means you will be able to judge of me whether I was sincere the other day in the defence of raillery, and can continue still to plead for those ingenious friends of ours who are often censured for their humour of this kind and for the freedom they take in such an airy way of conversation and writing.

Section 2
In good earnest, when one considers what use is sometimes made of this species of wit and to what an excess it has risen of late in some characters of the age, one may be startled a little and in doubt what to think of the practice or whither this rallying humour will at length carry us. It has passed from the men of pleasure to the men of business. Politicians have been infected with it, and the grave affairs of state have been treated with an air of irony and banter. The ablest negotiators have been known the notablest buffoons; the most celebrated authors, the greatest masters of burlesque.

There is indeed a kind of defensive raillery (if I may so call it) which I am willing to allow in affairs of whatever kind – when the spirit of curiosity would force a discovery of more truth than can conveniently be told. For we can never do more injury to truth than by discovering too much of it on some occasions. It is the same with understandings as with eyes: to such a certain size and make, just so much light is necessary and no more. Whatever is beyond brings darkness and confusion.

It is real humanity and kindness to hide strong truths from tender eyes. And to do this by a pleasant amusement is easier and civiller than by a harsh denial or remarkable reserve. But to go about industriously to confound men in a mysterious manner, and to make advantage or draw pleasure from that perplexity they are thrown into by such uncertain talk, is as unhandsome in a way of raillery as when done with the greatest seriousness or in the most solemn way of deceit. It may be necessary, as well now as heretofore, for wise men to speak in parables and with a double meaning, that the enemy may be amused and they only 'who have ears to hear may hear'.[B] But it is certainly a mean, impotent and dull sort of wit which amuses all alike and leaves the most sensible man and even a friend equally in doubt and at a loss to understand what one's real mind is upon any subject.

This is that gross sort of raillery which is so offensive in good company. And indeed there is as much difference between one sort and another as between fair dealing and hypocrisy, or between the genteelest wit and the most scurrilous buffoonery. But by freedom of conversation, this illiberal kind of wit will lose its credit. For wit is its own remedy. Liberty and commerce bring it to its true standard. The only danger is the laying an embargo. The same thing happens here as in the case of trade. Impositions and restrictions reduce it to a low ebb. Nothing is so advantageous to it as a free port.

We have seen in our own time the decline and ruin of a false sort of wit, which so much delighted our ancestors that their poems and plays as well as sermons were full of it. All humour had something of the quibble. The very language of the Court was punning. But it is now banished the Town and all good company, there are only some few footsteps of it in the Country, and it seems at last confined to the nurseries of youth as the chief entertainment of pedants and their pupils.[C] And thus, in other respects, wit will mend upon our hands and humour will refine itself, if we take care not to tamper with it and bring it under constraint by severe usage and rigorous prescriptions. All politeness is owing to liberty. We polish one another and rub off our corners and rough sides by a sort of amicable collision. To restrain this is inevitably to bring a rust upon men's understandings. It is a destroying of civility, good breeding and even charity itself, under pretence of maintaining it.

Section 3

To describe true raillery would be as hard a matter, and perhaps as little to the purpose, as to define good breeding. None can understand the speculation beside those who have the practice. Yet everyone thinks himself well-bred, and the formallest pedant imagines he can rally with a good grace and humour. I have known some of those grave gentlemen undertake to correct an author for defending the use of raillery and at the same time have upon every turn made use of that weapon, though they were naturally so very awkward at it. And this

---

[B] Matthew 11.15. This passage was used by Shaftesbury as an epigraph to his first publication, an edition, with an introduction, of sermons by Benjamin Whichcote. See Introduction, p. xxix.

[C] Shaftesbury here noted and commended the decline of the pun, so frequently used in Shakespeare, and of word play in general, so much a part of the metaphysical or baroque literary sensibility of the earlier seventeenth century.

I believe may be observed in the case of many zealots who have taken upon them to answer our modern free-writers.[D] The tragical gentlemen, with the grim aspect and mien of true inquisitors, have but an ill grace when they vouchsafe to quit their austerity and be jocose and pleasant with an adversary, whom they would choose to treat in a very different manner. For to do them justice, had they their wills, I doubt not but their conduct and mien would be pretty much of a piece. They would in all probability soon quit their farce and make a thorough tragedy. But at present there is nothing so ridiculous as this Janus-face[E] of writers, who with one countenance force a smile and with another show nothing beside rage and fury. Having entered the lists and agreed to the fair laws of combat by wit and argument, they have no sooner proved their weapon than you hear them crying aloud for help and delivering over to the secular arm.

There cannot be a more preposterous sight than an executioner and a merry Andrew[F] acting their part upon the same stage. Yet I am persuaded anyone will find this to be the real picture of certain modern zealots in their controversial writings. They are no more masters of gravity than they are of good humour. The first always runs into harsh severity and the latter into an awkward buffoonery. And thus between anger and pleasure, zeal and drollery, their writing has much such a grace as the play of humoursome children, who, at the same instant, are both peevish and wanton and can laugh and cry almost in one and the same breath.

How agreeable such writings are like to prove and of what effect towards the winning over or convincing those who are supposed to be in error, I need not go about to explain. Nor can I wonder, on this account, to hear those public lamentations of zealots that, while the books of their adversaries are so current, their answers to them can hardly make their way into the world or be taken the least notice of. Pedantry and bigotry are millstones able to sink the best book which carries the least part of their dead weight. The temper of the pedagogue suits not with the age. And the world, however it may be taught, will not be tutored. If a philosopher speaks, men hear him willingly while he keeps to his philosophy. So is a Christian heard while he keeps to his professed charity and meekness. In a gentleman we allow of pleasantry and raillery as being managed always with good breeding and never gross or clownish. But if a mere scholastic, entrenching upon all these characters and writing as it were by starts and rebounds from one of these to another, appears upon the whole

---

[D] On the controversies between the Church and its freethinking critics, see Justin Champion, *The Pillars of Priestcraft Shaken: The Church of England and its Enemies, 1660–1730* (Cambridge: Cambridge University Press, 1992).

[E] In Rome, Janus was a divine guardian of doors and gates, who presided over beginnings. He was represented with two faces, on the front and back of his head.

[F] A comic entertainer or clown.

as little able to keep the temper of Christianity as to use the reason of a philosopher or the raillery of a man of breeding, what wonder is it if the monstrous product of such a jumbled brain be ridiculous to the world?

If you think, my friend, that by this description I have done wrong to these zealot-writers in religious controversy, read but a few pages in any one of them (even where the contest is not abroad, but within their own pale) and then pronounce.

Section 4
But now that I have said thus much concerning authors and writings, you shall hear my thoughts, as you have desired, upon the subject of conversation and, particularly, a late one of a free kind, which you remember I was present at with some friends of yours, whom you fancied I should in great gravity have condemned.

It was, I must own, a very diverting one, and perhaps not the less so for ending as abruptly as it did, and in such a sort of confusion as almost brought to nothing whatever had been advanced in the discourse before. Some particulars of this conversation may not perhaps be so proper to commit to paper. It is enough that I put you in mind of the conversation in general. A great many fine schemes, it is true, were destroyed; many grave reasonings, overturned; but, this being done without offence to the parties concerned and with improvement to the good humour of the company, it set the appetite the keener to such conversations. And I am persuaded that, had Reason herself been to judge of her own interest, she would have thought she received more advantage in the main from that easy and familiar way than from the usual stiff adherence to a particular opinion.

But perhaps you may still be in the same humour of not believing me in earnest. You may continue to tell me I affect to be paradoxical in commending a conversation as advantageous to reason which ended in such a total uncertainty of what reason had seemingly so well established.

To this, I answer that, according to the notion I have of reason, neither the written treatises of the learned nor the set discourses of the eloquent are able of themselves to teach the use of it. It is the habit alone of reasoning which can make a reasoner. And men can never be better invited to the habit than when they find pleasure in it. A freedom of raillery, a liberty in decent language to question everything, and an allowance of unravelling or refuting any argument without offence to the arguer, are the only terms which can render such speculative conversations any way agreeable. For to say truth, they have been rendered burdensome to mankind by the strictness of the laws prescribed to them and by the prevailing pedantry and bigotry of those who reign in them and assume to themselves to be dictators in these provinces.

Am I always only to be a listener?[2] is as natural a case of complaint in divinity, in morals and in philosophy as it was of old the satirist's in poetry. Vicissitude is a mighty law of discourse and mightily longed for by mankind. In matter of reason, more is done in a minute or two by way of question and reply than by a continued discourse of whole hours. Orations are fit only to move the passions, and the power of declamation is to terrify, exalt, ravish or delight rather than satisfy or instruct. A free conference is a close fight. The other way, in comparison to it, is merely a brandishing or beating the air. To be obstructed therefore and manacled in conferences and to be confined to hear orations on certain subjects must needs give us a distaste and render the subjects so managed as disagreeable as the managers. Men had rather reason upon trifles, so they may reason freely and without the imposition of authority, than on the usefullest and best subjects in the world, where they are held under a restraint and fear.

Nor is it a wonder that men are generally such faint reasoners and care so little to argue strictly on any trivial subject in company, when they dare so little exert their reason in greater matters and are forced to argue lamely where they have need of the greatest activity and strength. The same thing therefore happens here as in strong and healthy bodies which are debarred their natural exercise and confined in a narrow space. They are forced to use odd gestures and contortions. They have a sort of action and move still, though with the worst grace imaginable. For the animal spirits in such sound and active limbs cannot lie dead or without employment.[G] And thus the natural free spirits of ingenious men, if imprisoned and controlled, will find out other ways of motion to relieve themselves in their constraint and, whether it be in burlesque, mimicry or buffoonery, they will be glad at any rate to vent themselves and be revenged on their constrainers.

If men are forbid to speak their minds seriously on certain subjects, they will do it ironically. If they are forbid to speak at all upon such subjects or if they find it really dangerous to do so, they will then redouble their disguise, involve themselves in mysteriousness and talk so as hardly to be understood, or at least not plainly interpreted, by those who are disposed to do them mischief. And thus raillery is brought more in fashion and runs into an extreme. It is the persecuting spirit has raised the bantering one, and want of liberty

[G] As the ancient theory of the humours became less convincing during the seventeenth century, greater emphasis in physiological psychology was placed on 'animal spirits', which provided a mechanistic and sometimes corpuscular explanation for the emotional manifestations of the soul. See Michael Heyd, *'Be Sober and Reasonable': The Critique of Enthusiasm in the Seventeenth and Early Eighteenth Centuries* (Leiden: E. J. Brill, 1995), pp. 191–210.

[2] Juvenal, *Satires* 1.1.

may account for want of a true politeness and for the corruption or wrong use of pleasantry and humour.

If in this respect we strain the just measure of what we call 'urbanity' and are apt sometimes to take a buffooning rustic air, we may thank the ridiculous solemnity and sour humour of our pedagogues; or, rather, they may thank themselves if they in particular meet with the heaviest of this kind of treatment. For it will naturally fall heaviest, where the constraint has been the severest. The greater the weight is, the bitterer will be the satire. The higher the slavery, the more exquisite the buffoonery.

That this is really so may appear by looking on those countries where the spiritual tyranny is highest. For the greatest of buffoons are the Italians and, in their writings, in their freer sort of conversations, on their theatres and in their streets, buffoonery and burlesque are in the highest vogue.[H] It is the only manner in which the poor cramped wretches can discharge a free thought. We must yield to them the superiority in this sort of wit. For what wonder is it if we who have more of liberty have less dexterity in that egregious way of raillery and ridicule?

Section 5

It is for this reason, I verily believe, that the ancients discover so little of this spirit, and that there is hardly such a thing found as mere burlesque in any authors of the politer ages. The manner indeed in which they treated the very gravest subjects was somewhat different from that of our days. Their treatises were generally in a free and familiar style. They chose to give us the representation of real discourse and converse by treating their subjects in the way of dialogue and free debate.[3] The scene was usually laid at table or in the public walks or meeting places, and the usual wit and humour of their real discourses appeared in those of their own composing. And this was fair. For without wit and humour, reason can hardly have its proof or be distinguished. The magisterial voice and high strain of the pedagogue commands reverence and awe. It is of admirable use to keep understandings at a distance and out of reach. The other manner, on the contrary, gives the fairest hold and suffers an antagonist to use his full strength hand to hand upon even ground.

It is not to be imagined what advantage the reader has when he can thus cope with his author, who is willing to come on a fair stage with him and exchange the tragic buskin[I] for an easier and more natural gait and habit. Grimace and tone are mighty helps to imposture. And many a formal piece of

H   On the link Shaftesbury made between tyranny and culture, see Introduction, p. xvii.
I   A thick-soled and therefore clumsy boot worn by actors of tragedy in ancient Greece.

3   See the following treatise, namely, *Soliloquy* 1.3.

sophistry holds proof under a severe brow which would not pass under an easy one. It was the saying of an ancient sage that 'humour was the only test of gravity, and gravity, of humour. For a subject which would not bear raillery was suspicious, and a jest which would not bear a serious examination was certainly false wit.'[4]

But some gentlemen there are so full of the spirit of bigotry and false zeal that, when they hear principles examined, sciences and arts inquired into, and matters of importance treated with this frankness of humour, they imagine presently that all professions must fall to the ground, all establishments come to ruin, and nothing orderly or decent be left standing in the world. They fear, or pretend to fear, that religion itself will be endangered by this free way, and are therefore as much alarmed at this liberty, in private conversation and under prudent management, as if it were grossly used in public company or before the solemnest assembly. But the case, as I apprehend it, is far different. For you are to remember, my friend, that I am writing to you in defence only of the liberty of the Club and of that sort of freedom which is taken among gentlemen and friends who know one another perfectly well. And that it is natural for me to defend liberty with this restriction, you may infer from the very notion I have of liberty itself.

It is surely a violation of the freedom of public assemblies for anyone to take the chair who is neither called nor invited to it. To start questions or manage debates, which offend the public ear, is to be wanting in that respect which is due to common society. Such subjects should either not be treated at all in public or in such a manner as to occasion no scandal or disturbance. The public is not, on any account, to be laughed at to its face or so reprehended for its follies as to make it think itself contemned. And what is contrary to good breeding is in this respect as contrary to liberty. It belongs to men of slavish principles to affect a superiority over the vulgar and to despise the multitude. The lovers of mankind respect and honour conventions and societies of men. And in mixed company and places where men are met promiscuously on account of diversion or affairs, it is an imposition and hardship to force them to hear what they dislike and to treat of matters in a dialect which many who are present have perhaps been never used to. It is a breach of the harmony of public conversation to take things in such a key as is above the common reach, puts others to silence, and robs them of their privilege of turn. But as to private society and what passes in select companies, where friends meet knowingly and with that very design of exercising their wit and looking freely into all subjects, I see no pretence for any-

---

[4] Gorgias Leontinus, in Aristotle, *Rhetoric* 3.18.7. [Gorgias of Leontini in Sicily, 485–380 BC, was an important sophistic thinker and stylist whose arrival in Athens as an ambassador in 427 helped shape the Athenian rhetorical tradition. A more accurate translation of the passage is: 'Gorgias said it was necessary to spoil the seriousness of opponents by jest and their jest by seriousness.']

one to be offended at the way of raillery and humour, which is the very life of such conversations, the only thing which makes good company and frees it from the formality of business and the tutorage and dogmaticalness of the Schools.

Section 6

To return therefore to our argument. If the best of our modern conversations are apt to run chiefly upon trifles, if rational discourses (especially those of a deeper speculation) have lost their credit and are in disgrace because of their formality, there is reason for more allowance in the way of humour and gaiety. An easier method of treating these subjects will make them more agreeable and familiar. To dispute about them will be the same as about other matters. They need not spoil good company or take from the ease or pleasure of a polite conversation. And the oftener these conversations are renewed, the better will be their effect. We shall grow better reasoners by reasoning pleasantly and at our ease, taking up or laying down these subjects as we fancy. So that, upon the whole, I must own to you, I cannot be scandalised at the raillery you took notice of, nor at the effect it had upon our company. The humour was agreeable and the pleasant confusion which the conversation ended in is at this time as pleasant to me upon reflection, when I consider that, instead of being discouraged from resuming the debate, we were so much the readier to meet again at any time and dispute upon the same subjects, even with more ease and satisfaction than before.

We had been a long while entertained, you know, upon the subject of morality and religion. And amid the different opinions started and maintained by several of the parties with great life and ingenuity, one or other would every now and then take the liberty to appeal to common sense. Everyone allowed the appeal and was willing to stand the trial. No one but was assured common sense would justify him. But when issue was joined and the cause examined at the bar, there could be no judgment given. The parties however were not less forward in renewing their appeal on the very next occasion which presented. No one would offer to call the authority of the court in question, till a gentleman, whose good understanding was never yet brought in doubt, desired the company, very gravely, that they would tell him what common sense was.

'If, by the word "sense", we were to understand opinion and judgment and, by the word "common", the generality or any considerable part of mankind, it would be hard', he said, 'to discover where the subject of common sense could lie. For that which was according to the sense of one part of mankind was against the sense of another. And if the majority were to determine common sense, it would change as often as men changed. That which was according to common sense today would be the contrary tomorrow, or soon after.'

But notwithstanding the different judgments of mankind in most subjects, there were some however in which it was supposed they all agreed and had the same thoughts in common. The question was asked still: where? 'For whatever was of any moment, it was supposed, might be reduced under the head of religion, policy or morals.

Of the differences in religion, there was no occasion to speak. The case was so fully known to all and so feelingly understood by Christians, in particular, among themselves. They had made sound experiment upon one another, each party in their turn. No endeavours had been wanting on the side of any particular sect. Whichever chanced to have the power failed not of putting all means in execution to make their private sense the public one. But all in vain. Common sense was as hard still to determine as Catholic or Orthodox. What with one was inconceivable mystery, to another was of easy comprehension. What to one was absurdity, to another was demonstration.

As for policy, what sense, or whose, could be called "common" was equally a question. If plain British or Dutch sense were right, Turkish and French sense must certainly be very wrong. And as mere nonsense as passive obedience[J] seemed, we found it to be the common sense of a great party among ourselves, a greater party in Europe and perhaps the greatest part of all the world besides.

As for morals, the difference, if possible, was still wider. For without considering the opinions and customs of the many barbarous and illiterate nations, we saw that even the few who had attained to riper letters and to philosophy could never as yet agree on one and the same system or acknowledge the same moral principles. And some even of our most admired modern philosophers had fairly told us that virtue and vice had, after all, no other law or measure than mere fashion and vogue.'[K]

It might have appeared perhaps unfair in our friends had they treated only the graver subjects in this manner and suffered the lighter to escape. For, in the gayer part of life, our follies are as solemn as in the most serious. The fault is we carry the laugh but half-way. The false earnest is ridiculed, but the false jest passes secure and becomes as errant deceit as the other. Our diversions, our plays, our amusements become solemn. We dream of happiness and possessions and enjoyments, in which we have no understanding, no certainty, and yet we pursue these as the best known and most certain things in the world. There is nothing so foolish and deluding as a partial scepticism.[5] For while the doubt is cast only on one side, the certainty grows so much stronger on the

---

[J] Passive obedience was a doctrine, enunciated throughout the later seventeenth and into the eighteenth century by divines of the Anglican Church, endorsing unqualified submission to the magistrate's commands regardless of their merit. It was a doctrine associated with the High Church Party in England and, thus, with the Tories.

[K] Shaftesbury ascribed this view to Thomas Hobbes and John Locke on the basis of the nominalism he discerned in their works. See Introduction, p. xxvii. Cf. Locke's *Essay Concerning Human Understanding* 2.28.7–13 for relevant expressions of Locke's.

[5] See p. 251.

other. While only one face of folly appears ridiculous, the other grows more solemn and deceiving.

But it was not thus with our friends. They seemed better critics, and more ingenious and fair in their way of questioning received opinions and exposing the ridicule of things. And if you will allow me to carry on their humour, I will venture to make the experiment throughout and try what certain knowledge or assurance of things may be recovered in that very way by which all certainty, you thought, was lost, and an endless scepticism introduced.

Part II

Section 1

If a native of Ethiopia were on a sudden transported into Europe and placed either at Paris or Venice at a time of Carnival, when the general face of mankind was disguised and almost every creature wore a mask, it is probable he would for some time be at a stand before he discovered the cheat, not imagining that a whole people could be so fantastical as, upon agreement at an appointed time, to transform themselves by a variety of habits and make it a solemn practice to impose on one another by this universal confusion of characters and persons. Though he might at first perhaps have looked on this with a serious eye, it would be hardly possible for him to hold his countenance when he had perceived what was carrying on. The Europeans, on their side, might laugh perhaps at this simplicity. But our Ethiopian would certainly laugh with better reason. It is easy to see which of the two would be ridiculous. For he who laughs and is himself ridiculous bears a double share of ridicule. However, should it so happen that in the transport of ridicule, our Ethiopian, having his head still running upon masks and knowing nothing of the fair complexion and common dress of the Europeans, should upon the sight of a natural face and habit, laugh just as heartily as before, would not he in his turn become ridiculous, by carrying the jest too far, when by a silly presumption he took nature for mere art and mistook perhaps a man of sobriety and sense for one of those ridiculous mummers?

There was a time when men were accountable only for their actions and behaviour. Their opinions were left to themselves. They had liberty to differ in these as in their faces. Everyone took the air and look which was natural to him. But in process of time it was thought decent to mend men's countenances and render their intellectual complexions uniform and of a sort. Thus the magistrate became a dresser and, in his turn, was dressed too, as he deserved, when he had given up his power to a new order of tire-men.[L] But, though in this extraordinary conjuncture it was agreed that there was only one certain and

[L] A tire-man is a person who assists at another's toilet, a valet or dresser.

true dress, one single peculiar air, to which it was necessary all people should conform, yet the misery was that neither the magistrate nor the tire-men themselves could resolve which of the various modes was the exact true one. Imagine now what the effect of this must needs be when men became persecuted thus on every side about their air and feature and were put to their shifts how to adjust and compose their mien, according to the right mode, when a thousand models, a thousand patterns of dress, were current and altered every now and then, upon occasion, according to fashion and the humour of the times. Judge whether men's countenances were not like to grow constrained and the natural visage of mankind, by this habit, distorted, convulsed and rendered hardly knowable.

But as unnatural or artificial as the general face of things may have been rendered by this unhappy care of dress and over-tenderness for the safety of complexions, we must not therefore imagine that all faces are alike besmeared or plastered. All is not fucus or mere varnish. Nor is the face of truth less fair and beautiful for all the counterfeit vizards which have been put upon her. We must remember the Carnival and what the occasion has been of this wild concourse and medley, who were the institutors of it, and to what purpose men were thus set awork and amused. We may laugh sufficiently at the original cheat and, if pity will suffer us, may make ourselves diversion enough with the folly and madness of those who are thus caught and practised on by these impostures. But we must remember withal our Ethiopian and beware, lest by taking plain nature for a vizard, we become more ridiculous than the people whom we ridicule. Now if a jest or ridicule thus strained be capable of leading the judgment so far astray, it is probable that an excess of fear or horror may work the same effect.

Had it been your fortune, my friend, to have lived in Asia at the time when the Magi by an egregious imposture got possession of the empire,[M] no doubt you would have had a detestation of the act, and perhaps the very persons of the men might have grown so odious to you that, after all the cheats and abuses they had committed, you might have seen them dispatched with as relentless an eye as our later European ancestors saw the destruction of a like politic body of conjurers, the Knights Templars, who were almost become an over-match for the civil sovereign.[6] Your indignation perhaps might have carried you to

---

[M] The Magi were leaders of the Zoroastrian religion of Persia, where they had great influence over political as well as religious matters. At the death of the Emperor Cambyses in 521 BC, one of the Magi usurped the throne, reigning briefly until overthrown himself by Darius I.

[6] See pp. 359–60. [The Knights Templars were members of a military and religious order founded in 1118 to contribute to the Crusades. Their name derived from their having been housed near the Temple of Solomon in Jerusalem, where they were supposed to guard the Holy Sepulchre and protect Christian pilgrims to the Holy Land. In time, they gained great financial and political power within Europe, which led to their suppression in 1312.]

propose the razing all monuments and memorials of these magicians. You might have resolved not to leave so much as their houses standing. But, if it had happened that these magicians in the time of their dominion had made any collection of books or compiled any themselves, in which they had treated of philosophy or morals or any other science or part of learning, would you have carried your resentment so far as to have extirpated these also, and condemned every opinion or doctrine they had espoused for no other reason than merely because they had espoused it? Hardly a Scythian, a Tartar or a Goth would act or reason so absurdly.^N Much less would you, my friend, have carried on this 'magophony', or priest-massacre, with such a barbarous zeal. For, in good earnest, to destroy a philosophy in hatred to a man implies as errant a Tartar-notion as to destroy or murder a man in order to plunder him of his wit and get the inheritance of his understanding.

I must confess indeed that, had all the institutions, statutes and regulations of this ancient hierarchy resembled the fundamental one of the Order itself,[7] they might with a great deal of justice have been suppressed; for one cannot, without some abhorrence, read that law of theirs: *For a Magus must be born of a mother and son.*[8]

But the conjurers (as we will rather suppose), having considered that they ought in their principle to appear as fair as possible to the world, the better to conceal their practice, found it highly for their interest to espouse some excellent moral rules and establish the very best maxims of this kind. They thought it for their advantage perhaps, on their first setting out, to recommend the greatest purity of religion, the greatest integrity of life and manners. They may perhaps too, in general, have preached up charity and good will. They may have set to view the fairest face of human nature and, together with their by-laws and political institutions, have interwoven the honestest morals and best doctrine in the world.

How therefore should we have behaved ourselves in this affair? How should we have carried ourselves towards this order of men at the time of the discovery of their cheat and ruin of their empire? Should we have fallen to work instantly with their systems, struck at their opinions and doctrines without distinction and erected a contrary philosophy in their teeth? Should we have flown at every religious and moral principle, denied every natural and social affection, and rendered men as much wolves as was possible to one another, while

---

^N Scythians, Tartars and Goths were all, at one time, nomadic peoples at the margins of Mediterranean or European civilization who, thus, served as figures of the barbarian.

[7] *But the Persians and particularly those that seem to practise wisdom, the Magi, they marry their mothers*: Sextus Empiricus, *Outlines of Pyrrhonism* 3.205.

[8] Catullus, *Poems* 90.3. [Shaftesbury identified this poem as No. 87 as it appeared in several contemporary editions.]

we described them such and endeavoured to make them see themselves by far more monstrous and corrupt than with the worst intentions it was ever possible for the worst of them to become?[9] – This, you will say, doubtless, would have been a very preposterous part and could never have been acted by other than mean spirits, such as had been held in awe and over-frighted by the Magi.[10]

And yet an able and witty philosopher of our nation was, we know, of late years so possessed with a horror of this kind that, both with respect to politics and morals, he directly acted in this spirit of massacre.[11] The fright he took upon the sight of the then governing powers, who unjustly assumed the authority of the people,[o] gave him such an abhorrence of all popular government and of the very notion of liberty itself that, to extinguish it for ever, he recommends the very extinguishing of Letters and exhorts princes not to spare so much as an ancient Roman or Greek historian. – Is not this in truth somewhat Gothic? And has not our philosopher in appearance something of the savage, that he should use philosophy and learning as the Scythians are said to have used Anacharsis and others for having visited the wise of Greece and learnt the manners of a polite people?[p]

His quarrel with religion was the same as with liberty. The same times gave him the same terror in this other kind. He had nothing before his eyes beside the ravage of enthusiasm and the artifice of those who raised and conducted that spirit. And the good sociable man, as savage and unsociable as he would make himself and all mankind appear by his philosophy, exposed himself during his life, and took the utmost pains that after his death we might be delivered from the occasion of these terrors. He did his utmost to show us that 'both in religion and morals we were imposed on by our governors', that 'there was nothing which by nature inclined us either way, nothing which naturally drew us to the love of what was without or beyond ourselves'[12] – though the love of such great truths and sovereign maxims, as he

---

[o] Hobbes published *Leviathan* in 1651 during the Commonwealth, after the Stuart Charles I had been executed, the English monarchy had been abolished, and Parliament had assumed power.

[p] Anacharsis was a legendary Scythian prince who is said to have travelled extensively in Greece during the sixth century BC, consorting with sages and learning Greek customs. He was put to death on his return to Scythia for attempting to introduce Greek cults to his own people.

[9] See pp. 55, 288.

[10] See p. 366n.

[11] Mr Hobbes, who thus expresses himself: 'By reading of these Greek and Latin authors, men from their childhood have gotten a habit (under a false show of liberty) of favouring tumults and of licentious controlling the actions of their sovereigns.' *Leviathan*, Part 2, Chapter 21. By this reasoning of Mr Hobbes, it should follow that there can never be any tumults or deposing of sovereigns at Constantinople or in Mogol. See again Part 2, Chapter 29, and Part 4, Chapter 46, and what he intimates to his prince in Part 2, Chapter 31, concerning this extirpation of ancient literature in favour of his Leviathan hypothesis and new philosophy. [For Hobbes, see Introduction, p. xxvii.]

[12] See p. 193.

imagined these to be, made him the most laborious of all men in composing systems of this kind for our use and forced him, notwithstanding his natural fear, to run continually the highest risk of being a martyr for our deliverance.

Give me leave therefore, my friend, on this occasion to prevent your seriousness, and assure you that there is no such mighty danger as we are apt to imagine from these fierce prosecutors of superstition, who are so jealous of every religious or moral principle. Whatever savages they may appear in philosophy, they are in their common capacity as civil persons as one can wish. Their free communicating of their principles may witness for them. It is the height of sociableness to be thus friendly and communicative.

If the principles, indeed, were concealed from us and made a mystery, they might become considerable. Things are often made so by being kept as secrets of a sect or party, and nothing helps this more than the antipathy and shyness of a contrary party. If we fall presently into horrors and consternation upon the hearing maxims which are thought poisonous, we are in no disposition to use that familiar and easy part of reason which is the best antidote. The only poison to reason is passion. For false reasoning is soon redressed where passion is removed. But if the very hearing certain propositions of philosophy be sufficient to move our passion, it is plain the poison has already gained on us, and we are effectually prevented in the use of our reasoning faculty.

Were it not for the prejudices of this kind, what should hinder us from diverting ourselves with the fancy of one of these modern reformers we have been speaking of? What should we say to one of these anti-zealots, who, in the zeal of such a cool philosophy, should assure us faithfully 'that we were the most mistaken men in the world to imagine there was any such thing as natural faith or justice? For that it was only force and power which constituted right. That there was no such thing in reality as virtue, no principle of order in things above or below, no secret charm or force of nature by which everyone was made to operate willingly or unwillingly towards public good, and punished and tormented if he did otherwise.'[Q]——Is not this the very charm itself? Is not the gentleman at this instant under the power of it?——'Sir! The philosophy you have condescended to reveal to us is most extraordinary. We are beholden to you for your instruction. But, pray, whence is this zeal in our behalf? What are we to you? Are you our father? Or, if you were, why this concern for us? Is there then such a thing as natural affection? If not, why all these pains, why all this danger on our account? Why not keep this secret to yourself? Of what advantage is it to you to deliver us from the cheat? The more are taken in it, the better. It is directly against your interest to undeceive us and let us know that only private interest governs you and that nothing nobler,

---

[Q] Shaftesbury ascribed such views to the 'cool philosophy', namely, Epicureanism, both ancient (as in Epicurus and Lucretius) and modern (as in Hobbes). See Introduction, pp. xxvi–xxvii.

or of a larger kind, should govern us whom you converse with. Leave us to ourselves and to that notable art by which we are happily tamed and rendered thus mild and sheepish. It is not fit we should know that by nature we are all wolves. Is it possible that one who has really discovered himself such should take pains to communicate such a discovery?'

Section 2

In reality, my friend, a severe brow may well be spared on this occasion, when we are put thus upon the defence of common honesty by such fair honest gentlemen, who are in practice so different from what they would appear in speculation. Knaves I know there are, in notion and principle as well as in practice, who think all honesty as well as religion a mere cheat and, by a very consistent reasoning, have resolved deliberately to do whatever by power or art they are able for their private advantage. But such as these never open themselves in friendship to others. They have no such passion for truth or love for mankind. They have no quarrel with religion or morals, but know what use to make of both upon occasion. If they ever discover their principles, it is only at unawares. They are sure to preach honesty and go to church.

On the other side, the gentlemen for whom I am apologising cannot however be called hypocrites. They speak as ill of themselves as they possibly can. If they have hard thoughts of human nature, it is a proof still of their humanity that they give such warning to the world. If they represent men by nature treacherous and wild, it is out of care for mankind, lest, by being too tame and trusting, they should easily be caught.

Impostors naturally speak the best of human nature that they may the easier abuse it. These gentlemen, on the contrary, speak the worst and had rather they themselves should be censured with the rest than that a few should by imposture prevail over the many. For it is opinion of goodness which creates easiness of trust and, by trust, we are betrayed to power, our very reason being thus captivated by those in whom we come insensibly to have an implicit faith.[13] But supposing one another to be by nature such very savages, we shall take care to come less in one another's power and, apprehending power to be insatiably coveted by all, we shall the better fence against the evil, not by giving all into one hand (as the champion of this cause would have us) but, on the contrary, by a right division and balance of power and by the restraint of good laws and limitations which may secure the public liberty.[R]

[R] A reference to Hobbes' defence of absolutism. The balance of power, a formulation deriving from the republican ideal of a mixed constitution that incorporated and balanced different segments of the polity, was assimilated to the English constitution with its components, King, Lords and Commons.

[13] See pp. 294, 387.

Should you therefore ask me whether I really thought these gentlemen were fully persuaded of the principles they so often advance in company, I should tell you that, though I would not absolutely arraign the gentlemen's sincerity, yet there was something of mystery in the case, more than was imagined. The reason, perhaps, why men of wit delight so much to espouse these paradoxical systems is not in truth that they are so fully satisfied with them, but in a view the better to oppose some other systems, which by their fair appearance have helped, they think, to bring mankind under subjection. They imagine that, by this general scepticism which they would introduce, they shall better deal with the dogmatical spirit which prevails in some particular subjects. And when they have accustomed men to bear contradiction in the main and hear the nature of things disputed at large, it may be safer (they conclude) to argue separately upon certain nice points in which they are not altogether so well satisfied. So that from hence, perhaps, you may still better apprehend why, in conversation, the spirit of raillery prevails so much, and notions are taken up for no reason besides their being odd and out of the way.[S]

Section 3

But let who will condemn the humour thus described, for my part I am in no such apprehension from this sceptical kind of wit. Men indeed may, in a serious way, be so wrought on and confounded by different modes of opinion, different systems and schemes imposed by authority, that they may wholly lose all notion or comprehension of truth. I can easily apprehend what effect awe has over men's understandings. I can very well suppose men may be frighted out of their wits, but I have no apprehension they should be laughed out of them. I can hardly imagine that in a pleasant way they should ever be talked out of their love for society or reasoned out of humanity and common sense. A mannerly wit can hurt no cause or interest for which I am in the least concerned, and philosophical speculations, politely managed, can never surely render mankind more unsociable or uncivilized. This is not the quarter from whence I can possibly expect an inroad of savageness and barbarity. And by the best of my observation, I have learned that virtue is never such a sufferer by being contested as by being betrayed. My fear is not so much from its witty antagonists, who give it exercise and put it on its defence, as from its tender nurses, who are apt to overlay it and kill it with excess of care and cherishing.

I have known a building which, by the officiousness of the workmen, has been so shored and screwed up on the side where they pretended it had a lean-

---

[S] Shaftesbury believed that both Hobbes and Locke were provoked to adopt 'paradoxical systems' in their attempt to extinguish 'the ghost of Aristotle', that is, the continuing power of scholastic habits in contemporary philosophy: Shaftesbury to James Stanhope, 7 November 1709, PRO 30/24/22/7, pp. 9–13 (Rand, *Regimen*, pp. 413–17).

ing, that it has at last been turned the contrary way and overthrown. There has something, perhaps, of this kind happened in morals. Men have not been contented to show the natural advantages of honesty and virtue. They have rather lessened these, the better, as they thought, to advance another foundation. They have made virtue so mercenary a thing and have talked so much of its rewards that one can hardly tell what there is in it, after all, which can be worth rewarding.[T] For to be bribed only or terrified into an honest practice bespeaks little of real honesty or worth. We may make, it is true, whatever bargain we think fit and may bestow in favour what overplus we please, but there can be no excellence or wisdom in voluntarily rewarding what is neither estimable nor deserving. And if virtue be not really estimable in itself, I can see nothing estimable in following it for the sake of a bargain.

If the love of doing good be not of itself a good and right inclination, I know not how there can possibly be such a thing as goodness or virtue. If the inclination be right, it is a perverting of it to apply it solely to the reward and make us conceive such wonders of the grace and favour, which is to attend virtue, when there is so little shown of the intrinsic worth or value of the thing itself.

I could be almost tempted to think that the true reason why some of the most heroic virtues have so little notice taken of them in our holy religion is because there would have been no room left for disinterestedness, had they been entitled to a share of that infinite reward which Providence has by revelation assigned to other duties. Private friendship and zeal for the public and our country are virtues purely voluntary in a Christian.[14] They are no essen-

---

[T] The rewards with which Shaftesbury was most concerned here were the future rewards along with future punishments promised in Christian doctrine.

[14] By private friendship no fair reader can here suppose is meant that *common* benevolence and charity which every Christian is obliged to show towards all men and, in particular, towards his fellow Christians, his neighbour, brother and kindred of whatever degree, but that *peculiar* relation, which is formed by a consent and harmony of minds by mutual esteem and reciprocal tenderness and affection and which we emphatically call a friendship. Such was that between the two Jewish heroes [David and Jonathan] mentioned below, whose love and tenderness was 'surpassing that of women' (2 Samuel 1.26). Such were those friendships described so frequently by poets, between Pylades and Orestes, Theseus and Pirithous, with many others. Such were those between philosophers, heroes and the greatest of men – between Socrates and Antisthenes, Plato and Dion, Epaminondas and Pelopidas, Scipio and Laelius, Cato and Brutus, Thrasea and Helvidius. And such there may have lately been and are still perhaps in our own age, though envy suffers not the few examples of this kind to be remarked in public. The author's meaning is indeed so plain of itself that it needs no explanatory apology to satisfy an impartial reader. As for others who object the singularity of the assertion as differing (they suppose) from what our Reverend Doctors in religion commonly maintain, they may read what the learned and pious Bishop Taylor says in his treatise of friendship: 'You [first] inquire', says he, 'how far a dear and a perfect friendship is authorized by the principles of Christianity? To this I answer that the word "friendship" in the sense we commonly mean by it is not so much as named in the New Testament, and our religion takes no notice of it. You think it strange, but read on before you spend so much as the beginning of a passion or a wonder upon it. There

tial parts of his charity. He is not so tied to the affairs of this life, nor is he obliged to enter into such engagements with this lower world as are of no help to him in acquiring a better. His conversation is in heaven. Nor has he occasion for such supernumerary cares or embarrassments here on earth as may obstruct his way thither or retard him in the careful task of working out his own salvation. If nevertheless any portion of reward be reserved hereafter for the generous part of a patriot, or that of a thorough friend, this is still behind the curtain and happily concealed from us that we may be the more deserving of it when it comes.

It appears indeed under the Jewish dispensation that each of these virtues had their illustrious examples and were in some manner recommended to us as honourable and worthy our imitation. Even Saul himself, as ill a prince as he is represented, appears, both living and dying, to have been respected and praised for the love he bore his native country. And the love which was so remarkable between his son and his successor gives us a noble view of a disinterested friendship, at least on *one* side.[U] But the heroic virtue of these persons had only the common reward of praise attributed to it and could not claim a future recompense under a religion which taught no future state nor exhibited any rewards or punishments, besides such as were temporal and had respect to the written law.

And thus the Jews as well as heathens were left to their philosophy, to be

---

is mention of "friendship of the world", and it is said to be "enmity with God", but the word is nowhere else named, or to any other purpose, in all the New Testament. It speaks of friends often, but by "friends" are meant our acquaintance, or our kindred, the relatives of our family or our fortune or our sect . . . and I think I have reason to be confident that the word "friend" (speaking of human intercourse) is no otherways used in the Gospels or Epistles or Acts of the Apostles.' And afterwards: 'Christian charity', says he, 'is friendship to all the world and, when friendships were the noblest things in the world, charity was little, like the sun drawn in at a chink or his beams drawn into the centre of a burning-glass, but Christian charity is friendship expanded like the face of the sun when it mounts above the Eastern hills.' In reality, the good bishop draws all his notions as well as examples of private friendship from the heathen world or from the times preceding Christianity. And, after citing a Greek author, he immediately adds: 'Of such immortal, abstracted, pure friendships, indeed there is no great plenty . . ., but they who are the same to their friend ἀπόπροθεν, when he is in another country or in another world, [these are they who] are fit to preserve the sacred fire for eternal sacrifices and to perpetuate the memory of those exemplary friendships of the best men, which have filled the world with history and wonder, for in no other sense but this can it be true that friendships are pure loves, regarding to do good more than to receive it. He that is a friend after death hopes not for a recompense from his friend and makes no bargain either for fame or love, but is rewarded with the conscience and satisfaction of doing bravely.' [Jeremy Taylor, *A Discourse of the Nature, Measure and Offices of Friendship* (London, 1657), pp. 3–4, 6, 81–2. Taylor, 1613–67, was an Anglican cleric, a royalist, a distinguished prose stylist and, toward the end of his life, bishop of Down and Connor in Ireland.]

U Saul was the first king of Israel, whose reign from *c.* 1020 to *c.* 1000 is related in the two books of Samuel. After the arrival of David at Saul's Court, a profound friendship arose between Saul's son, Jonathan, and David, who would succeed Saul on the throne.

instructed in the sublime part of virtue and induced by reason to that which was never enjoined them by command. No premium or penalty being enforced in these cases, the disinterested part subsisted, the virtue was a free choice, and the magnanimity of the act was left entire. He who would be generous had the means. He who would frankly serve his friend or country, at the expense even of his life, might do it on fair terms.[15] *Sweet and proper it is* was his sole reason.[16] It was inviting and becoming. It was good and honest. And that this is still a good reason and according to common sense, I will endeavour to satisfy you. For I should think myself very ridiculous to be angry with anyone for thinking me dishonest, if I could give no account of my honesty nor show upon what principle I differed from a knave.[17]

Part III

Section 1

The Roman satirist may be thought more than ordinarily satirical when, speaking of the nobility and Court, he is so far from allowing them to be the standard of politeness and good sense that he makes them in a manner the reverse: *For common sense is quite rare in that situation.*[18] Some of the most ingenious commentators, however, interpret this very differently from what is generally apprehended. They make this common sense of the poet, by a Greek derivation, to signify sense of public weal and of the common interest, love of the community or society, natural affection, humanity, obligingness, or that sort of civility which rises from a just sense of the common rights of mankind, and the natural equality there is among those of the same species.[19]

---

[15] 'Peradventure', says the Holy Apostle, 'for a good man one ['some' in the King James version] would even dare to die': Romans 5.7. This the apostle judiciously supposes to belong to human nature, though he is so far from founding any precept on it that he ushers his private opinion with a very dubious 'peradventure'.

[16] Horace, *Odes* 3.2.13. [The line continues: '. . . to die for one's fatherland'.]

[17] See pp. 60–1, 78–9.

[18] Juvenal, *Satires* 8.73.

[19] Namely, the two Casaubons, Isaac and Meric, [Claude] Salmasius and our English [Thomas] Gataker. See the first in *Historia Augusta* [with notes by Isaac Casaubon, Claude Salmasius and Janus Gruterus, Leiden, 1671], p. 402. The second in his comment on Book 1, Sections 13 and 16 in Meric Casaubon, ed., *Marcus Aurelius Antoninus . . . His Meditations* (London, 1634), pp. 16–18. Gataker on the same place [in his edition of Marcus Aurelius, Cambridge, 1652, pp. 31–2], and Salmasius in the same edition of the *Historia Augusta*, p. 403. The Greek word is κοινονοημοσύνη, which Salmasius interprets *the moderate, the usual and respected mind of a man, which takes thought for the communal good in some way and does not refer everything to its own advantage, and also has regard of those with whom it is engaged, thinking modestly and reasonably about itself. But, on the other hand, all the conceited and arrogant think that they are born only for themselves and their own benefits and, in favour of themselves, they disdain and neglect others. And these are those who can properly be said not to possess sensus communis. For so Juvenal understood 'sensus communis' in Satire 8. Galen calls 'philanthropy and goodness' what Marcus, speaking of*

And indeed, if we consider the thing nicely, it must seem somewhat hard in the poet to have denied wit or ability to a Court such as that of Rome, even under a Tiberius or a Nero.^V But, for humanity or sense of public good and the common interest of mankind, it was no such deep satire to question whether this was properly the spirit of a Court. It was difficult to apprehend what community subsisted among courtiers or what public between an absolute prince and his slave-subjects. And for real society, there could be none between such as had no other sense than that of private good.

Our poet therefore seems not so immoderate in his censure if we consider it is the heart, rather than the head, he takes to task when, reflecting on a Court education, he thinks it unapt to raise any affection towards a country and looks upon young princes and lords as the young masters of the world, who, being indulged in all their passions and trained up in all manner of licentiousness, have that thorough contempt and disregard of mankind, which mankind in a

---

himself, calls κοινονοημοσύνη *and, elsewhere, when he speaks about the same thing, 'moderation and good judgment', which is how Marcus expressed his gratitude to him [Galen] for accompanying him to the German war.* In the same manner, Isaac Casaubon, who says that Herodian calls this the *mean and equal measure: Indeed, Antoninus adds as though interpreting this saying, 'and the injunction to friends neither to dine with him at all nor necessarily to go off abroad with him'.* This, I am persuaded, is the *sensus communis* of Horace (*Satires* 1.3.66) which has been unobserved (as far as I can learn) by any of his commentators: it being remarkable withal that in this early satire of Horace, before his latter days and when his philosophy as yet inclined to the less rigid assertors of virtue, he puts this expression (as may be seen by the whole satire taken together) into the mouth of a Crispinus, or some ridiculous mimic of that severe philosophy, to which the coinage of the word κοινονοημοσύνη properly belonged. For so the poet again (*Satires* 1.4.77–8) uses the word *sensus*, speaking of those who without sense of manners or common society, without the least respect or deference to others, press rudely upon their friends and upon all company in general without regard to time or place or anything besides their selfish and brutish humour: *Not asking whether they do that without sense, whether they do it at an inopportune time. Obliviously,* as old [Dionysius] Lambinus interprets it, though without any other explanation, referring only to the *sensus communis* of Horace in that other satire [on p. 48 of his edition (Frankfurt, 1577) of Horace, which Shaftesbury owned]. Thus Seneca: *Thus you will avoid hatred from the offence by harming nobody gratuitously: from which sensus communis will protect you* (*Epistles* 105.4). And Cicero accordingly: *It is the business of justice not to harm men; of finer feeling, not to cause offence* (*On Duties* 1.28.99). It may be objected possibly, by some particularly versed in the philosophy above-mentioned, that the κοινὸς νοῦς to which the κοινονοημοσύνη seems to have relation is of a different meaning. But they will consider withal how small the distinction was in that philosophy between the ὑπόληψις and the vulgar αἴσθησις, how generally passion was by those philosophers brought under the head of opinion. And when they consider, besides this, the very formation of the word κοινονοημοσύνη upon the model of the other femalized virtues, the εὐγνωμοσύνη, σωφροσύνη, δικαιοσύνη, etc., they will no longer hesitate on this interpretation. — The reader may perhaps by this note see better why the Latin title of *Sensus Communis* has been given to this second treatise. He may observe, withal, how the same poet Juvenal uses the word *sensus* in *Satires* 15.133: *Sensus is the best part of us.*

^V Juvenal, *c.* AD 60–140, was a Roman satirical poet whose targets included the imperial Court. He was born long after the reign (AD 14–37) of the emperor Tiberius but he may have had direct experience of the worst phase of Nero's reign (AD 54–68).

manner deserves where arbitrary power is permitted and a tyranny adored: *So much for the young man whom tradition tells us was arrogant and conceited and full of his closeness to Nero.*[20]

A public spirit can come only from a social feeling or sense of partnership with humankind. Now there are none so far from being partners in this sense, or sharers in this common affection, as they who scarcely know an equal nor consider themselves as subject to any law of fellowship or community. And thus morality and good government go together. There is no real love of virtue without the knowledge of public good. And where absolute power is, there is no public.

They who live under tyranny and have learnt to admire its power as sacred and divine are debauched as much in their religion as in their morals. Public good, according to their apprehension, is as little the measure or rule of government in the universe as in the state. They have scarce a notion of what is good or just other than as mere will and power have determined. Omnipotence, they think, would hardly be itself, were it not at liberty to dispense with the laws of equity and change at pleasure the standard of moral rectitude.[21]

But notwithstanding the prejudices and corruptions of this kind, it is plain there is something still of a public principle, even where it is most perverted and depressed. The worst of magistracies, the mere despotic kind, can show sufficient instances of zeal and affection towards it. Where no other government is known, it seldom fails of having that allegiance and duty paid it which is owing to a better form. The Eastern countries and many barbarous nations have been and still are examples of this kind. The personal love they bear their prince, however severe towards them, may show how natural an affection there is towards government and order among mankind. If men have *really* no public parent, no magistrate in common, to cherish and protect them, they will still imagine they have such a one and, like new-born creatures who have never seen their dam, will fancy one for themselves and apply (as by nature prompted) to some like form for favour and protection. In the room of a true foster-father and chief, they will take after a false one and, in the room of a legal government and just prince, obey even a tyrant and endure a whole lineage and succession of such.

As for us Britons, thank Heaven, we have a better sense of government delivered to us from our ancestors. We have the notion of a public and a constitution, how a legislative and how an executive is modelled. We understand weight and measure in this kind and can reason justly on the balance of power and property. The maxims we draw from hence are as evident as those in mathematics. Our increasing knowledge shows us every day, more and more, what

---

[20] Juvenal, *Satires* 8.71–2.
[21] See p. 133.

common sense is in politics, and this must of necessity lead us to understand a like sense in morals, which is the foundation.

It is ridiculous to say there is any obligation on man to act sociably or honestly in a formed government and not in that which is commonly called the state of nature.[22] For, to speak in the fashionable language of our modern philosophy: 'Society being founded on a compact, the surrender made of every man's private unlimited right into the hands of the majority, or such as the majority should appoint, was of free choice and by a promise.' Now the promise itself was made in the state of nature, and that which could make a promise obligatory in the state of nature must make all other acts of humanity as much our real duty and natural part. Thus, faith, justice, honesty and virtue must have been as early as the state of nature or they could never have been at all. The civil union or confederacy could never make right or wrong if they subsisted not before. He who was free to any villainy before his contract will and ought to make as free with his contract when he thinks fit. The natural knave has the same reason to be a civil one and may dispense with his politic capacity as oft as he sees occasion. It is only his word stands in his way.——A man is obliged to keep his word. Why? Because he has given his word to keep it.——Is not this a notable account of the original of moral justice and the rise of civil government and allegiance?

Section 2

But to pass by these cavils of a philosophy which speaks so much of nature with so little meaning, we may with justice surely place it as a principle that, *if anything be natural in any creature or any kind, it is that which is preservative of the kind itself and conducing to its welfare and support*. If in original and pure nature it be wrong to break a promise or be treacherous, it is as truly wrong to be in any respect inhuman or any way wanting in our natural part towards human kind. If eating and drinking be natural, herding is so too. If any appetite or sense be natural, the sense of fellowship is the same. If there be anything of nature in that affection which is between the sexes, the affection is certainly as natural towards the consequent offspring and so again between the offspring themselves, as kindred and companions, bred under the same discipline and economy. And thus a clan or tribe is gradually formed, a public is recognized, and, besides the pleasure found in social entertainment, language and discourse, there is so apparent a necessity for continuing this good correspondency and union that to have no sense or feeling of this kind, no love of country, com-

---

[22] See pp. 282, 284. [Shaftesbury here criticized the categories and models of natural law theory, evident, among other places, in the political theories of Hobbes and Locke. On the natural law idiom, see Richard Tuck, *Natural Rights Theories: Their Origin and Development* (Cambridge: Cambridge University Press, 1979).]

munity or anything in common, would be the same as to be insensible even of the plainest means of self-preservation and most necessary condition of self-enjoyment.

How the wit of man should so puzzle this cause as to make civil government and society appear a kind of invention and creature of art, I know not. For my own part, methinks, this herding principle and associating inclination is seen so natural and strong in most men, that one might readily affirm it was even from the violence of this passion that so much disorder arose in the general society of mankind.

Universal good, or the interest of the world in general, is a kind of remote philosophical object. That greater community falls not easily under the eye. Nor is a national interest or that of a whole people or body politic so readily apprehended. In less parties, men may be intimately conversant and acquainted with one another. They can there better taste society and enjoy the common good and interest of a more contracted public. They view the whole compass and extent of their community, and see and know particularly whom they serve and to what end they associate and conspire. All men have naturally their share of this combining principle, and they who are of the sprightliest and most active faculties have so large a share of it that, unless it be happily directed by right reason, it can never find exercise for itself in so remote a sphere as that of the body politic at large. For here perhaps the thousandth part of those whose interests are concerned are scarce so much as known by sight. No visible band is formed, no strict alliance, but the conjunction is made with different persons, orders and ranks of men, not sensibly, but in idea, according to that general view or notion of a state or commonwealth.

Thus the social aim is disturbed for want of certain scope. The close sympathy and conspiring virtue is apt to lose itself for want of direction in so wide a field. Nor is the passion anywhere so strongly felt or vigorously exerted as in actual conspiracy or war in which the highest geniuses are often known the forwardest to employ themselves. For the most generous spirits are the most combining. They delight most to move in concert and feel, if I may say, in the strongest manner the force of the confederating charm.

It is strange to imagine that war, which of all things appears the most savage, should be the passion of the most heroic spirits. But it is in war that the knot of fellowship is closest drawn. It is in war that mutual succour is most given, mutual danger run, and common affection most exerted and employed. For heroism and philanthropy are almost one and the same. Yet by a small misguidance of the affection, a lover of mankind becomes a ravager; a hero and deliverer becomes an oppressor and destroyer.

Hence, other divisions among men. Hence, in the way of peace and civil government, that love of party and subdivision by cabal. For sedition is a kind of cantonizing already begun within the State. To cantonize is natural when the society grows vast and bulky, and powerful states have found other advantages in sending colonies abroad than merely that of having elbow room at home or extending their dominion into distant countries. Vast empires are in many respects unnatural, but particularly in this – that, be they ever so well constituted, the affairs of many must, in such governments, turn upon a very few, and the relation be less sensible and, in a manner, lost between the magistrate and people in a body so unwieldy in its limbs, and whose members lie so remote from one another and distant from the head.

It is in such bodies as these that strong factions are aptest to engender.[W] The associating spirits, for want of exercise, form new movements and seek a narrower sphere of activity when they want action in a greater. Thus we have wheels within wheels. And in some national constitutions (notwithstanding the absurdity in politics), we have one empire within another. Nothing is so delightful as to incorporate. Distinctions of many kinds are invented. Religious societies are formed. Orders are erected, and their interests espoused and served with the utmost zeal and passion. Founders and patrons of this sort are never wanting. Wonders are performed in this wrong social spirit by those members of separate societies. And the associating genius of man is never better proved than in those very societies which are formed in opposition to the general one of mankind and to the real interest of the State.

In short, the very spirit of faction, for the greatest part, seems to be no other than the abuse or irregularity of that social love and common affection which is natural to mankind. For the opposite of sociableness is selfishness. And of all characters, the thorough-selfish one is the least forward in taking party. The men of this sort are, in this respect, true men of moderation. They are secure of their temper and possess themselves too well to be in danger of entering warmly into any cause or engaging deeply with any side or faction.

Section 3

You have heard it, my friend, as a common saying that 'interest governs the world'.[X] But, I believe, whoever looks narrowly into the affairs of it will find

---

[W] Notwithstanding the partisan nature of later seventeenth- and early eighteenth-century English politics, conventional wisdom decried the presence of parties. Shaftesbury's observations on the naturalness of 'faction', therefore, went some way to transvaluating the term. See J. A. W. Gunn, *Factions No More* (London: Frank Cass, 1972), pp. 2–20.

[X] On ideas of interest in this period, see J. A. W. Gunn, *Politics and the Public Interest in the Seventeenth Century* (London and Toronto: Routledge & Kegan Paul and University of Toronto Press, 1969), and '"Interest Will Not Lie": A Seventeenth-Century Political Maxim', *Journal of the History of Ideas* 29 (1968): 551–64, especially 559, and Albert Hirschman, *The Passions and the Interests* (Princeton: Princeton University Press, 1977), pp. 31–55, especially 42–3. To the prominent later seventeenth-century divine, Edward Stillingfleet, it was 'interest that rules the world' (*Origines Sacrae, or A Rational Account of the Grounds of Christian Faith*, 1662, p. 471), and Sir Thomas Pope Blount published an essay on this theme in 1691.

that passion, humour, caprice, zeal, faction and a thousand other springs, which are counter to self-interest, have as considerable a part in the movements of this machine. There are more wheels and counterpoises in this engine than are easily imagined. It is of too complex a kind to fall under one simple view or be explained thus briefly in a word or two.^Y The studiers of this mechanism must have a very partial eye to overlook all other motions besides those of the lowest and narrowest compass. It is hard that, in the plan or description of this clockwork, no wheel or balance should be allowed on the side of the better and more enlarged affections, that nothing should be understood to be done in kindness or generosity, nothing in pure good nature or friendship or through any social or natural affection of any kind, when, perhaps, the mainsprings of this machine will be found to be either these very natural affections themselves or a compound kind derived from them and retaining more than one half of their nature.

But here, my friend, you must not expect that I should draw you up a formal scheme of the passions, or pretend to show you their genealogy and relation, how they are interwoven with one another or interfere with our happiness and interest.[23] It would be out of the genius and compass of such a letter as this to frame a just plan or model by which you might, with an accurate view, observe what proportion the friendly and natural affections seem to bear in this order of architecture.

Modern projectors,^Z I know, would willingly rid their hands of these natural materials and would fain build after a more uniform way. They would new-frame the human heart and have a mighty fancy to reduce all its motions, balances and weights to that one principle and foundation of a cool and deliberate selfishness. Men, it seems, are unwilling to think they can be so outwitted, and imposed on by nature, as to be made to serve her purposes rather than their own. They are ashamed to be drawn thus out of themselves and forced from what they esteem their true interest.

There has been in all times a sort of narrow-minded philosophers, who have thought to set this difference to rights by conquering nature in themselves. A primitive father and founder among these saw well this power of nature and understood it so far that he earnestly exhorted his followers neither to beget children nor serve their country.[24] There was no dealing with nature, it seems, while these alluring objects stood in the way. Relations, friends, countrymen,

---

^Y At this point, the French translator inserted a passage from Montaigne's essay, 'Of the Inconsistency of Our Actions': see n. 29.

^Z Promoters or undertakers of speculative businesses or other experimental though potentially rewarding enterprises.

[23] See the fourth treatise, namely, *An Inquiry Concerning Virtue* below.

[24] See p. 25 [regarding Epicurus]. See also pp. 193, 352–4.

laws, politic constitutions, the beauty of order and government, and the interest of society and mankind were objects which, he well saw, would naturally raise a stronger affection than any which was grounded upon the narrow bottom of mere *self*. His advice, therefore, not to marry nor engage at all in the public, was wise and suitable to his design. There was no way to be truly a disciple of this philosophy but to leave family, friends, country and society to cleave to it.——And, in good earnest, who would not if it were happiness to do so?——The philosopher, however, was kind in telling us his thought. It was a token of his fatherly love of mankind: *You, father, are the discoverer of things! You furnish us with a father's teachings!*[25]

But the revivers of this philosophy in latter days appear to be of a lower genius. They seem to have understood less of this force of nature and thought to alter the thing by shifting a name. They would so explain all the social passions and natural affections as to denominate them of the selfish kind.[26] Thus civility, hospitality, humanity towards strangers or people in distress is only a more deliberate selfishness. An honest heart is only a more cunning one, and honesty and good nature, a more deliberate or better-regulated self-love. The love of kindred, children and posterity is purely love of self and of one's own immediate blood, as if, by this reckoning, all mankind were not included, all being of one blood and joined by inter-marriages and alliances, as they have been transplanted in colonies and mixed one with another. And thus love of one's country and love of mankind must also be self-love. Magnanimity and courage, no doubt, are modifications of this universal self-love! For courage, says our modern philosopher, is 'constant anger',[27] and all men, says a witty poet, 'would be cowards if they durst'.[28]

That the poet and the philosopher both were cowards may be yielded perhaps without dispute. They may have spoken the best of their knowledge. But, for true courage, it has so little to do with anger that there lies always the strongest suspicion against it where this passion is highest. The true courage is the cool and calm. The bravest of men have the least of a brutal bullying insolence and, in the very time of danger, are found the most serene, pleasant and free. Rage, we know, can make a coward forget himself and fight. But what is done in fury or anger can never be placed to the account of courage. Were it otherwise, womankind might claim to be the stoutest sex,

[25] Lucretius, *On the Nature of Things* 3.9.9–10.
[26] See pp. 42, 288.
[27] 'Sudden courage', says Mr Hobbes, *Leviathan*, Part 1, Chapter 6, 'is anger.' Therefore courage considered as constant and belonging to a character must, in his account, be defined constant anger or anger constantly returning.
[28] Lord Rochester, *Satire against Man*. [John Wilmot, Earl of Rochester, 'A Satyr against Reason and Mankind', in David M. Vieth, ed., *The Complete Poems of John Wilmot, Earl of Rochester* (New Haven and London: Yale University Press, 1968), p. 100.]

for their hatred and anger have ever been allowed the strongest and most lasting.

Other authors there have been of a yet inferior kind, a sort of distributors and petty retailers of this wit, who have run changes and divisions without end upon this article of self-love.[29] You have the very same thought spun out a hundred ways and drawn into mottoes and devices to set forth this riddle, that 'act as disinterestedly or generously as you please, *self* still is at the bottom, and nothing else'. Now if these gentlemen who delight so much in the play of words, but are cautious how they grapple closely with definitions, would tell us only what self-interest was and determine happiness and good, there would be an end of this enigmatical wit.[30] For in this we should all agree – that happiness was to be pursued and in fact was always sought after. But, whether found in following nature and giving way to common affection or in suppressing it and turning every passion towards private advantage, a narrow self-end or the preservation of mere life, this would be the matter in debate between us. The question would not be 'who loved himself or who not?' but 'who loved and served himself the rightest and after the truest manner?'

It is the height of wisdom, no doubt, to be rightly selfish. And to value life, as far as life is good, belongs as much to discretion. But a wretched life is no wise man's wish. To be without honesty is, in effect, to be without natural affection or sociableness of any kind. And a life without natural affection, friendship or sociableness would be found a wretched one, were it to be tried. It is as these feelings and affections are intrinsically valuable and worthy that self-interest is to be rated and esteemed. A man is by nothing so much himself as by his temper and the character of his passions and affections. If he loses what is manly and worthy in these, he is as much lost to himself as when he loses his memory and understanding. The least step into villainy or baseness changes the character and value of a life. He who would preserve life at any rate must abuse himself more than anyone can abuse him. And if life be not a dear thing indeed, he who has refused to live a villain and has preferred death to a base action has been a gainer by the bargain.

[29] The French translator supposes with good reason that our author, in this passage, had an eye to those sentences or maxims which pass under the name of the Duc de La Rochefoucauld. He has added withal the censure of this kind of wit and of these maxims in particular by some authors of the same nation. The passages are too long to insert here though they are otherwise very just and entertaining. That which he has cited of old Montaigne is from the first chapter of the second essay. [See *Essai sur l'usage de la raillerie et de l'enjoument dans les conversations* (The Hague, 1710), pp. 103–5n, 114–16n, where the translator refers, in a note at this point, to Jean de la Bruyère's comment on La Rochefoucauld in the 'Discours sur Théophraste' at the outset of *Les caractères de Théophraste* and to the learned journal *Mémoires de Trévoux*. Montaigne's 'Of the Inconsistency of Our Actions' in the *Essais*, Book II, Chapter 1, is cited by the translator at an earlier point: see n. Y.]

[30] See pp. 170, 192–3, 196, 216–17ff.

Section 4

It is well for you, my friend, that in your education you have had little to do with the philosophy or philosophers of our days.[31] A good poet and an honest historian may afford learning enough for a gentleman, and such a one, while he reads these authors as his diversion, will have a truer relish of their sense and understand them better than a pedant with all his labours and the assistance of his volumes of commentators. I am sensible that of old it was the custom to send the youth of highest quality to philosophers to be formed. It was in their schools, in their company, and by their precepts and example that the illustrious pupils were inured to hardship and exercised in the severest courses of temperance and self-denial. By such an early discipline they were fitted for the command of others: to maintain their country's honour in war, rule wisely in the state, and fight against luxury and corruption in times of prosperity and peace. If any of these arts are comprehended in university learning, it is well. But, as some universities in the world are now modelled, they seem not so very effectual to these purposes, nor so fortunate in preparing for a right practice of the world or a just knowledge of men and things.[AA] Had you been thorough-paced in the ethics or politics of the Schools, I should never have thought of writing a word to you upon common sense or the love of mankind. I should not have cited the poet's *sweet and proper*.[32] Nor, if I had made a character for you, as he for his noble friend, should I have crowned it with his: *He is not afraid to die for dear friends or fatherland*.[33]

Our philosophy nowadays runs after the manner of that able sophister who said, 'Skin for skin: all that a man hath will he give for his life.'[34] It is orthodox divinity as well as sound philosophy with some men to rate life by the number and exquisiteness of the pleasing sensations. These they constantly set in opposition to dry virtue and honesty and, upon this foot, they think it proper to call all men fools who would hazard a life or part with any of these pleasing sensations, except on the condition of being repaid in the same coin and with good interest into the bargain. Thus, it seems, we are to learn virtue by usury and enhance the value of life and of the pleasures of sense in order to be wise and to live well.

But you, my friend, are stubborn in this point and, instead of being brought to think mournfully of death or to repine at the loss of what you may some-

---

[AA] Regarding Shaftesbury's attitude toward universities, see Introduction, p. xviii.

[31] Our author, it seems, writes at present as to a young gentleman chiefly of a Court breeding. See, however, his further sentiments more particularly in Treatise 3, namely, *Soliloquy*, p. 148n.

[32] See p. 48 [for this citation from Horace].

[33] Horace, *Odes* 4.9.51–2. [This was the final line in an ode praising Horace's contemporary, Marcus Lollius, who, Horace notwithstanding, had a reputation as a corrupt and rapacious imperial officer.]

[34] Job 2.4. [These were Satan's words in conversation with God.]

times hazard by your honesty, you can laugh at such maxims as these and divert yourself with the improved selfishness and philosophical cowardice of these fashionable moralists. You will not be taught to value life at their rate or degrade honesty as they do who make it only a name. You are persuaded there is something more in the thing than fashion or applause, that worth and merit are substantial and no way variable by fancy or will, and that honour is as much itself when acting by itself and unseen as when seen and applauded by all the world.

Should one who had the countenance of a gentleman ask me why I would avoid being nasty when nobody was present, in the first place I should be fully satisfied that he himself was a very nasty gentleman who could ask this question, and that it would be a hard matter for me to make him ever conceive what true cleanliness was. However, I might, notwithstanding this, be contented to give him a slight answer and say, 'It was because I had a nose.'

Should he trouble me further and ask again, 'What if I had a cold or what if naturally I had no such nice smell?', I might answer perhaps that 'I cared as little to see myself nasty as that others should see me in that condition'.

'But what if it were in the dark?'

'Why, even then, though I had neither nose nor eyes, my sense of the matter would still be the same: my nature would rise at the thought of what was sordid or, if it did not, I should have a wretched nature indeed and hate myself for a beast. Honour myself I never could while I had no better a sense of what *in reality* I owed myself, and what became me as a human creature.'

Much in the same manner have I heard it asked, 'Why should a man be honest in the dark?'

What a man must be to ask this question I will not say. But for those who have no better a reason for being honest than the fear of a gibbet or a jail, I should not, I confess, much covet their company or acquaintance. And if any guardian of mine who had kept his trust and given me back my estate when I came of age had been discovered to have acted thus through fear only of what might happen to him, I should, for my own part, undoubtedly continue civil and respectful to him, but, for my opinion of his worth, it would be such as the Pythian God had of his votary, who devoutly feared him and therefore restored to a friend what had been deposited in his hands: *Therefore he made restoration through fear, not morality, and, nevertheless, he proved the whole utterance of the oracle to be worthy of the shrine and true, extinguished as he was along with progeny and house.*[35]

I know very well that many services to the public are done merely for the sake of a gratuity, and that informers in particular are to be taken care of and sometimes made pensioners of state. But I must beg pardon for the particular

---

[35] Juvenal, *Satires* 13.204–6. [The Pythian God was Apollo, whose messages were received by the oracle at Delphi. The story to which Juvenal referred was told in Herodotus, *History* 6.86.]

thoughts I may have of these gentlemen's merit, and shall never bestow my esteem on any other than the voluntary discoverers of villainy and hearty prosecutors of their country's interest. And, in this respect, I know nothing greater or nobler than the undertaking and managing some important accusation, by which some high criminal of state or some formed body of conspirators against the public may be arraigned and brought to punishment through the honest zeal and public affection of a private man.

I know, too, that the mere vulgar of mankind often stand in need of such a rectifying object as the gallows before their eyes. Yet I have no belief that any man of a liberal education, or common honesty, ever needed to have recourse to this idea in his mind, the better to restrain him from playing the knave. And if a saint had no other virtue than what was raised in him by the same objects of reward and punishment in a more distant state, I know not whose love or esteem he might gain besides, but, for my own part, I should never think him worthy of mine. *If a slave says to me, 'I did not steal, I did not flee', I tell him, 'You have your reward – you are not being flogged.' 'I did not kill a man.' 'Then you won't feed the crows upon a cross.' 'I am good and honest.' My Sabine steward shakes his head and keeps on denying it.*[36]

Part IV

Section 1

By this time, my friend, you may possibly, I hope, be satisfied that, as I am in earnest in defending raillery, so I can be sober too in the use of it. It is in reality a serious study, to learn to temper and regulate that humour which nature has given us as a more lenitive remedy against vice, and a kind of specific against superstition and melancholy delusion. There is a great difference between seeking how to raise a laugh from everything and seeking in everything what justly may be laughed at. For nothing is ridiculous except what is deformed, nor is anything proof against raillery except what is handsome and just. And therefore it is the hardest thing in the world to deny fair honesty the use of this weapon, which can never bear an edge against herself and bears against everything contrary.

If the very Italian buffoons were to give us the rule in these cases, we should learn by them that, in their lowest and most scurrilous way of wit, there was nothing so successfully to be played upon as the passions of cowardice and avarice.[BB] One may defy the world to turn real bravery or generosity into ridicule. A glutton or mere sensualist is as ridiculous as the other two

---

[BB] Shaftesbury referred here to the Italian *commedia dell'arte*, improvised popular theatre of the early modern period, which used stock characters often representing standard vices and excesses.

[36] Horace, *Epistles* 1.16.46–9. [The Sabines were associated with strict morality.]

characters. Nor can an unaffected temperance be made the subject of contempt to any besides the grossest and most contemptible of mankind. Now these three ingredients make up a virtuous character, as the contrary three a vicious one. How therefore can we possibly make a jest of honesty?——To laugh *both* ways is nonsensical. And if the ridicule lie against sottishness, avarice and cowardice, you see the consequence. A man must be soundly ridiculous who, with all the wit imaginable, would go about to ridicule wisdom or laugh at honesty or good manners.

A man of thorough good breeding, whatever else he be, is incapable of doing a rude or brutal action.[37] He never deliberates in this case or considers of the matter by prudential rules of self-interest and advantage. He acts from his nature, in a manner necessarily and without reflection, and, if he did not, it were impossible for him to answer his character or be found that truly well-bred man on every occasion. It is the same with the honest man. He cannot deliberate in the case of a plain villainy. A 'plum' is no temptation to him. He likes and loves himself too well to change hearts with one of those corrupt miscreants, who among them gave that name to a round sum of money gained by rapine and plunder of the commonwealth.[CC] He who would enjoy a freedom of mind and be truly possessor of himself must be above the thought of stooping to what is villainous or base. He, on the other side, who has a heart to stoop must necessarily quit the thought of manliness, resolution, friendship, merit and a character with himself and others. But to affect these enjoyments and advantages together with the privileges of a licentious principle, to pretend to enjoy society and a free mind in company with a knavish heart, is as ridiculous as the way of children who eat their cake and afterwards cry for it. When men begin to deliberate about dishonesty and, finding it go less against their stomach, ask slily why they should stick at a good piece of knavery for a good sum, they should be told, as children, that they cannot eat their cake and have it.

When men indeed are become accomplished knaves, they are past crying for their cake. They know themselves and are known by mankind. It is not these who are so much envied or admired. The moderate kind are the more taking with us. Yet, had we sense, we should consider it is in reality the thorough profligate knave, the very complete unnatural villain alone, who can any way bid for happiness with the honest man. True interest is wholly on one side or the other. All between is inconsistency, irresolution, remorse, vexation and an ague fit, from hot to cold, from one passion to another quite contrary, a per-

---

[CC] In the early eighteenth century, 'plum' was a colloquialism for a large sum (in the order of £100,000) of the sort with which creditors of the State during the wars of the 1690s and other beneficiaries of the 1688 Revolution were said to be rewarded.

[37] See pp. 407–8,

petual discord of life and an alternate disquiet and self-dislike.[38] The only rest or repose must be through one determined, considerate resolution, which, when once taken, must be courageously kept, and the passions and affections brought under obedience to it, the temper steeled and hardened to the mind, the disposition to the judgment. Both must agree, else all must be disturbance and confusion. So that to think with one's self in good earnest, 'Why may not one do this *little* villainy or commit this *one* treachery, and but for *once*?', is the most ridiculous imagination in the world and contrary to common sense. For a common honest man, while left to himself and undisturbed by philosophy and subtle reasonings about his interest, gives no other answer to the thought of villainy than that he cannot possibly find in his heart to set about it or conquer the natural aversion he has to it. And this is natural and just.

The truth is, as notions stand now in the world with respect to morals, honesty is like to gain little by philosophy or deep speculations of any kind. In the main, it is best to stick to common sense and go no further. Men's first thoughts in this matter are generally better than their second, their natural notions better than those refined by study or consultation with casuists. According to common speech as well as common sense, 'honesty is the best policy', but, according to refined sense, the only well-advised persons as to this world are arrant knaves, and they alone are thought to serve themselves who serve their passions and indulge their loosest appetites and desires.——Such, it seems, are the wise and such the wisdom of this world!

An ordinary man talking of a vile action in a way of common sense says naturally and heartily, 'He would not be guilty of such a thing for the whole world.' But speculative men find great modifications in the case, many ways of evasion, many remedies, many alleviations. A good gift rightly applied, a right method of suing out a pardon, good almshouses and charitable foundations erected for right worshippers, and a good zeal shown for the right belief may sufficiently atone for one wrong practice, especially when it is such as raises a man to a considerable power, as they say, of doing good and serving the true cause.

Many a good estate, many a high station, has been gained upon such a bottom as this. Some crowns too may have been purchased on these terms, and some great emperors, if I mistake not, there have been of old, who were much assisted by these or the like principles and, in return, were not ungrateful to the cause and party which had assisted them.[39] The forgers of such morals have been amply endowed and the world has paid roundly for its philosophy since the original plain principles of humanity and the simple honest precepts of peace and mutual love have, by a sort of spiritual chemists, been so sublimated

---

[38] Our author's French translator cites, on this occasion, very aptly those verses of Horace, *Satires* 2.7.18–20: *The more resolutely he stayed the same in his vices, the less wretched he was and better off than he who struggles on a rope, now taut, now slack.*

[39] See pp. 372, 377.

as to become the highest corrosives and, passing through their alembics, have yielded the strongest spirit of mutual hatred and malignant persecution.

Section 2

But our humours, my friend, incline us not to melancholy reflections. Let the solemn reprovers of vice proceed in the manner most suitable to their genius and character. I am ready to congratulate with them on the success of their labours in that authoritative way which is allowed them. I know not, in the meanwhile, why others may not be allowed to ridicule folly and recommend wisdom and virtue, if possibly they can, in a way of pleasantry and mirth. I know not why poets, or such as write chiefly for the entertainment of themselves and others, may not be allowed this privilege. And if it be the complaint of our standing reformers that they are not heard so well by the gentlemen of fashion, if they exclaim against those airy wits who fly to ridicule as a protection and make successful sallies from that quarter, why should it be denied one, who is only a volunteer in this cause, to engage the adversary on his own terms and expose himself willingly to such attacks on the single condition of being allowed fair play in the same kind?

By 'gentlemen of fashion', I understand those to whom a natural good genius or the force of a good education has given a sense of what is naturally graceful and becoming. Some by mere nature, others by art and practice, are masters of an ear in music, an eye in painting, a fancy in the ordinary things of ornament and grace, a judgment in proportions of all kinds, and a general good taste in most of those subjects which make the amusement and delight of the ingenious people of the world. Let such gentlemen as these be as extravagant as they please or as irregular in their morals, they must at the same time discover their inconsistency, live at variance with themselves and in contradiction to that principle on which they ground their highest pleasure and entertainment.

Of all other beauties which virtuosos[DD] pursue, poets celebrate, musicians sing and architects or artists of whatever kind describe or form, the most delightful, the most engaging and pathetic, is that which is drawn from real life and from the passions. Nothing affects the heart like that which is purely from itself and of its own nature, such as the beauty of sentiments, the grace of actions, the turn of characters and the proportions and features of a human mind. This lesson of philosophy, even a romance, a poem or a play may teach

---

[DD] The word 'virtuoso' was applied to a learned or adept person in a wide range of areas including natural philosophy, philology, the arts and antiquities. It could be used, as in this instance, to refer to a lover of the arts or a man of taste; but elsewhere in *Characteristics* Shaftesbury used it as a derogatory term with reference to pedants, unworldly scholars or collectors of oddities. See Walter Houghton, 'The English Virtuoso in the Seventeenth Century', *Journal of the History of Ideas* 3 (1942): 51–73.

us, while the fabulous author leads us with such pleasure through the labyrinth of the affections and interests us, whether we will or no, in the passions of his heroes and heroines: *He pains my heart, he vexes, then soothes, he fills it with empty terrors like a Magus.*[40]

Let poets, or the men of harmony, deny, if they can, this force of nature or withstand this moral magic. They, for their parts, carry a double portion of this charm about them. For, in the first place, the very passion which inspires them is itself the love of numbers, decency and proportion, and this too, not in a narrow sense or after a selfish way (for who of them composes for himself?), but in a friendly social view for the pleasure and good of others, even down to posterity and future ages. And, in the next place, it is evident in these performers that their chief theme and subject, that which raises their genius the most and by which they so effectually move others, is purely manners and the moral part. For this is the effect and this the beauty of their art: in vocal measures of syllables and sounds to express the harmony and numbers of an inward kind and represent the beauties of a human soul by proper foils and contrarieties, which serve as graces in this limning and render this music of the passions more powerful and enchanting.

The admirers of beauty in the fair sex would laugh, perhaps, to hear of a moral part in their amours. Yet what a stir is made about a heart! What curious search of sentiments and tender thoughts! What praises of a humour, a sense, a *je ne sais quoi*[EE] of wit, and all those graces of a mind which these virtuoso-lovers delight to celebrate! Let them settle this matter among themselves and regulate, as they think fit, the proportions which these different beauties hold one to another. They must allow still, there is a beauty of the mind, and such as is essential in the case. Why else is the very air of foolishness enough to cloy a lover at first sight? Why does an idiot-look and manner destroy the effect of all those outward charms and rob the fair one of her power, though regularly armed in all the exactness of feature and complexion? We may imagine what we please of a substantial solid part of beauty, but, were the subject to be well criticized, we should find, perhaps, that what we most admired, even in the turn of *outward* features, was only a mysterious expression and a kind of shadow of something *inward* in the temper, and that when we were struck with a majestic air, a sprightly look, an Amazon bold grace or a contrary soft and gentle one, it was chiefly the fancy of these characters or qualities which wrought on us – our imagination being busied in forming beauteous shapes and images of this rational kind, which entertained the mind and held it in admiration, while other passions of a lower species were employed another way. The preliminary addresses, the declarations, the explanations, confidences,

---

[EE] 'I know not what', referring to an ineffable aspect of beauty or style.

[40] Horace, *Epistles* 2.1.211–13.

clearings, the dependence on something mutual, something felt by way of return, the *hope of the soul, trusting in returned affection*[FF] – all these become necessary ingredients in the affair of love and are authentically established by the men of elegance and art in this way of passion.

Nor can the men of cooler passions and more deliberate pursuits withstand the force of beauty in other subjects. Everyone is a virtuoso of a higher or lower degree. Everyone pursues a grace and courts a Venus of one kind or another.[41] The *Venustum*, the *Honestum*, the *Decorum*,[GG] of things will force its way. They who refuse to give it scope in the nobler subjects of a rational and moral kind will find its prevalency elsewhere, in an inferior order of things.[42] They who overlook the main springs of action and despise the thought of numbers and proportion in a life at large will, in the mean particulars of it, be no less taken up and engaged, as either in the study of common arts or in the care and culture of mere mechanic beauties. The models of houses, buildings and their accompanying ornaments, the plans of gardens and their compartments, the ordering of walks, plantations, avenues and a thousand other symmetries will succeed in the room of that happier and higher symmetry and order of a mind. The species of fair, noble, handsome, will discover itself on a thousand occasions and in a thousand subjects.[43] The spectre still will haunt us in some shape or other and, when driven from our cool thoughts and frighted from the closet, will meet us even at Court and fill our heads with dreams of grandeur, titles, honours and a false magnificence and beauty, to which we are ready to sacrifice our highest pleasure and ease, and for the sake of which we become the merest drudges and most abject slaves.

The men of pleasure, who seem the greatest contemners of this philosophical beauty, are forced often to confess her charms. They can as heartily as others commend honesty and are as much struck with the beauty of a generous part. They admire the thing itself, though not the means. And, if possible, they would so order it as to make probity and luxury agree. But the rules of harmony will not permit it. The dissonancies are too strong. However, the attempts of this kind are not unpleasant to observe. For, though some of the voluptuous are found sordid pleaders for baseness and corruption of every sort, yet others more generous endeavour to keep measures with honesty and, understanding pleasure better, are for bringing it under some rule. They condemn *this* manner; they praise *the other*. 'So far was right, but, farther, wrong.' 'Such a case was allowable, but such a one, not to be admitted.' They introduce a justice and an order in their

[FF] Horace, *Odes* 4.1.30.
[GG] The lovely, the honourable, the becoming.

[41] See p. 150.
[42] See p. 412.
[43] See pp. 353, 415–17.

pleasures. They would bring reason to be of their party, account in some manner for their lives and form themselves to some kind of consonancy and agreement. Or, should they find this impracticable on certain terms, they would choose to sacrifice their other pleasures to those which arise from a generous behaviour, a regularity of conduct and a consistency of life and manners: *And to learn by heart the measures and rhythms of the true life*.[44]

Other occasions will put us upon this thought but chiefly a strong view of merit in a generous character, opposed to some detestably vile one. Hence it is that among poets the satirists seldom fail in doing justice to virtue. Nor are any of the nobler poets false to this cause. Even modern wits, whose turn is all towards gallantry and pleasure, when bare-faced villainy stands in their way and brings the contrary species in view, can sing in passionate strains the praises of plain honesty.

When we are highly friends with the world, successful with the fair and prosperous in the possession of other beauties, we may perchance, as is usual, despise this sober mistress. But when we see, in the issue, what riot and excess naturally produce in the world, when we find that, by luxury's means and for the service of vile interests, knaves are advanced above us and the vilest of men preferred before the honestest,[45] we then behold virtue in a new light and, by the assistance of such a foil, can discern the beauty of honesty and the reality of those charms, which before we understood not to be either natural or powerful.

Section 3

And thus, after all, the most natural beauty in the world is honesty and moral truth. For all beauty is truth.[HH] True features make the beauty of a face and true proportions, the beauty of architecture as true measures, that of harmony and music. In poetry, which is all fable, truth still is the perfection. And whoever is scholar enough to read the ancient philosopher, or his modern copyists,[46] upon the nature of a dramatic and epic poem will easily understand this account of truth.[47]

[HH] On the resonance of this line with Keats's 'Ode on a Grecian Urn', see Harry M. Solomon, 'Shaftesbury's *Characteristics* and the Conclusion of "Ode on a Grecian Urn"', *Keats-Shelley Journal* 24 (1975): 89–101.

[44] Horace, *Epistles* 2.2.144.

[45] See pp. 468–9.

[46] The French translator [p. 162], no doubt, has justly hit our author's thought by naming in his margin the excellent Bossu, *Du poème épique*, who, in that admirable comment and explanation of Aristotle, has perhaps not only shown himself the greatest of the French critics but presented the world with a view of ancient literature and just writing beyond any other modern of whatever nation. [Shaftesbury owned the first edition of René Le Bossu, *Traité du poème épique* (Treatise on the epic poem), published in Paris in 1675. Le Bossu lived from 1631 to 1680.]

[47] See pp. 414–15, 448ff.

A painter, if he has any genius, understands the truth and unity of design and knows he is even then unnatural when he follows nature too close and strictly copies life. For his art allows him not to bring *all* nature into his piece but a *part* only. However, his piece, if it be beautiful and carries truth, must be a whole by itself, complete, independent and withal as great and comprehensive as he can make it. So that particulars, on this occasion, must yield to the general design and all things be subservient to that which is principal, in order to form a certain easiness of sight, a simple, clear and united view, which would be broken and disturbed by the expression of any thing peculiar or distinct.[48]

Now the variety of nature is such as to distinguish everything she forms by a peculiar original character, which, if strictly observed, will make the subject appear unlike to anything extant in the world besides. But this effect the good poet and painter seek industriously to prevent. They hate minuteness and are afraid of singularity, which would make their images, or characters, appear capricious and fantastical. The mere face-painter indeed has little in common with the poet, but, like the mere historian, copies what he sees and minutely

---

[48] The *ready apprehension*, as the great master of arts [Aristotle] calls it in his *Poetics*, Chapter 23, but particularly Chapter 7, where he shows 'that the τὸ καλόν, the beautiful or the sublime, in these above-mentioned arts, is from the expression of greatness with order, that is to say, exhibiting the principal or main of what is designed in the very largest proportions in which it is capable of being viewed. For when it is gigantic, it is in a manner out of sight and can be no way comprehended in that simple and *united* view. As, on the contrary, when a piece is of the miniature kind, when it runs into the detail and nice delineation of every little particular, it is, as it were, invisible, for the same reason, because the summary beauty, the whole itself, cannot be comprehended in that one united view, which is broken and lost by the necessary attraction of the eye to every small and subordinate part. In a poetic system, the same regard must be had to the memory, as in painting, to the eye. The dramatic kind is confined within the convenient and proper time of a spectacle. The epic is left more at large. Each work, however, must aim at vastness and be as great and of as long duration as possible, but so as to be comprehended (as to the main of it) by one easy glance or retrospect of memory. And this the Philosopher calls, accordingly, the *ready memorability*.' I cannot better translate the passage than as I have done in these explanatory lines. For besides what relates to mere art, the philosophical sense of the original is so majestic and the whole treatise so masterly that when I find even the Latin interpreters come so short, I should be vain to attempt anything in our own language. I would only add a small remark of my own, which may perhaps be noticed by the studiers of statuary and painting: that the greatest of the ancient as well as modern artists were ever inclined to follow this rule of the Philosopher and, when they erred in their designs or drafts, it was on the side of greatness by running into the unsizable and gigantic rather than into the minute and delicate. Of this, Michelangelo, the great beginner and founder among the moderns, and Zeuxis, the same among the ancients, may serve as instances. See Pliny, *Natural History* 35.60ff concerning Zeuxis and the notes of Father [Joannes] Harduinus in his edition [Paris, 1685], 5:200, on the words *Deprehenditur tamen Zeuxis* ['Nevertheless Zeuxis is seized']. And again Pliny himself upon Euphranor, in *Natural History* 35.128: *Skilful and exceedingly hardworking, he excelled in every field and remained always equal to himself. This man seems to have been the first to have represented fully the lofty qualities of heroes and to have attained a good sense of proportion, but he was rather too slight in dealing with whole bodies and rather too grand in heads and limbs. He also composed books about proportion and colours.* See p. 152n.

traces every feature and odd mark. It is otherwise with the men of invention and design. It is from the *many* objects of nature, and not from a *particular* one, that those geniuses form the idea of their work. Thus, the best artists are said to have been indefatigable in studying the best statues, as esteeming them a better rule than the perfectest human bodies could afford. And thus some considerable wits have recommended the best poems as preferable to the best of histories, and better teaching the truth of characters and nature of mankind.[49]

Nor can this criticism be thought high-strained. Though few confine them-selves to these rules, few are insensible of them. Whatever quarter we may give to our vicious poets or other composers of irregular and short-lived works, we know very well that the standing pieces of good artists must be formed after a more uniform way. Every just work of theirs comes under those natural rules of proportion and truth. The creature of their brain must be like one of nature's formation. It must have a body and parts proportionable, or the very vulgar will not fail to criticize the work when 'it has neither head nor tail'.[50] For so common sense (according to just philosophy) judges of those works which want the justness of a whole and show their author, however curious and exact in particulars, to be in the main a very bungler: *The point of the work is missed because he does not know how to fashion the whole.*[51]

Such is poetical and such (if I may so call it) graphical or plastic truth. Narrative or historical truth must needs be highly estimable, especially when we consider how mankind, who are become so deeply interested in the sub-ject, have suffered by the want of clearness in it. It is itself a part of moral truth. To be a judge in one requires a judgment in the other. The morals, the character and genius of an author must be thoroughly considered. And the his-torian or relater of things important to mankind must, whoever he be, approve himself many ways to us, both in respect of his judgment, candour and disin-terestedness before we are bound to take anything on his authority. And as for critical truth or the judgment and determination of what commentators, trans-lators, paraphrasts, grammarians and others have, on this occasion, delivered to us,[52] in the midst of such variety of style, such different readings, such inter-polations and corruptions in the originals, such mistakes of copyists, tran-scribers, editors and a hundred such accidents to which ancient books are subject, it becomes, upon the whole, a matter of nice speculation, considering withal that the reader, though an able linguist, must be supported by so many

---

[49] Thus the great Master himself in his *Poetics* [8.3] above cited: *Accordingly, poetics is more philo-sophic and more serious than history: for poetry speaks more about universal, whereas history, about particular matters.*

[50] See pp. 349, 448-9.

[51] Horace, *The Art of Poetry* 34. [Shaftesbury cited this passage mistakenly from one of Horace's epistles.]

[52] See pp. 471-2, 473ff.

other helps from chronology, natural philosophy, geography and other sciences.

And thus many previous truths are to be examined and understood in order to judge rightly of historical truth, and of the past actions and circumstances of mankind as delivered to us by ancient authors of different nations, ages, times and different in their characters and interests. Some moral and philosophical truths there are, withal, so evident in themselves, that it would be easier to imagine half mankind to have run mad and joined precisely in one and the same species of folly, than to admit anything as truth which should be advanced against such natural knowledge, fundamental reason and common sense.

This I have mentioned, the rather because some modern zealots appear to have no better knowledge of truth, nor better manner of judging it, than by counting noses. By this rule, if they can poll an indifferent number out of a mob, if they can produce a set of Lancashire noddles, remote provincial head-pieces or visionary assemblers to attest a story of a witch upon a broomstick and a flight in the air, they triumph in the solid proof of their new prodigy and cry, *The truth is great and it will prevail!*[II]

Religion, no doubt, is much indebted to these men of prodigy who, in such a discerning age, would set her on the foot of popular tradition and venture her on the same bottom with parish tales and gossiping stories of imps, goblins and demoniacal pranks, invented to fright children or make practice for common exorcists and 'cunning men'! For by that name, you know, country people are used to call those dealers in mystery who are thought to conjure in an honest way and foil the devil at his own weapon.

And now, my friend, I can perceive it is time to put an end to these reflections, lest by endeavouring to expound things any further, I should be drawn from my way of humour to harangue profoundly on these subjects. But should you find I had moralized in any tolerable manner according to common sense and without canting, I could be satisfied with my performance, such as it is, without fearing what disturbance I might possibly give to some formal censors of the age, whose discourses and writings are of another strain. I have taken the liberty, you see, to laugh upon some occasions and, if I have either laughed wrong or been impertinently serious, I can be content to be laughed at in my turn. If contrariwise I am railed at, I can laugh still, as before, and with fresh advantage to my cause. For though, in reality, there could be nothing less a laughing matter than the provoked rage, ill-will and fury of certain zealous gentlemen, were they armed as lately they have been known, yet, as the magistrate has since taken care to pare their talons, there is nothing very terrible in their encounter. On the contrary, there is something comical in the case. It brings to one's mind the fancy of those grotesque figures and dragon faces,

---

[II] 1 Esdras 4.41.

which are seen often in the frontispiece and on the cornerstones of old buildings. They seem placed there as the defenders and supporters of the edifice, but, with all their grimace, are as harmless to people without as they are useless to the building within. Great efforts of anger to little purpose serve for pleasantry and farce. Exceeding fierceness, with perfect inability and impotence, make the highest ridicule.

I am, dear friend,
Affectionately yours, etc.

Soliloquy, or Advice to an Author

No need to inquire outside yourself.[1]

Part I

Section 1

I have often thought how ill-natured a maxim it was, which, on many occasions, I have heard from people of good understanding, that, 'as to what related to private conduct, no one was ever the better for advice'. But, upon further examination, I have resolved with myself that the maxim might be admitted without any violent prejudice to mankind. For, in the manner advice was generally given, there was no reason, I thought, to wonder it should be so ill received. Something there was which strangely inverted the case and made the giver to be the only gainer. For, by what I could observe in many occurrences of our lives, that which we called giving advice was, properly, taking an occasion to show our own wisdom at another's expense. On the other side, to be instructed, or to receive advice on the terms usually prescribed to us, was little better than tamely to afford another the occasion of raising himself a character from our defects.

In reality, however able or willing a man may be to advise, it is no easy matter to make advice a free gift. For, to make a gift free indeed, there must be nothing in it which takes from another to add to ourself. In all other respects, to give and to dispense is generosity and goodwill, but to bestow wisdom is to gain a mastery which cannot so easily be allowed us. Men willingly learn whatever else is taught them. They can bear a master in mathematics, in music or in any other science, but not in understanding and good sense.

It is the hardest thing imaginable for an author not to appear assuming in this respect. For all authors at large are, in a manner, professed masters of understanding to the age. And, for this reason, in early days poets were looked

---

[1] Persius, *Satires* 1.7.

upon as authentic sages for dictating rules of life and teaching manners and good sense. How they may have lost their pretension, I cannot say. It is their peculiar happiness and advantage not to be obliged to lay their claim openly. And if, while they profess only to please, they secretly advise and give instruction, they may now perhaps, as well as formerly, be esteemed with justice the best and most honourable among authors.

Meanwhile, 'if dictating and prescribing be of so dangerous a nature in other authors, what must his case be who dictates to authors themselves?'

To this, I answer that my pretension is not so much to give advice as to consider of the way and manner of advising. My science, if it be any, is no better than that of a language-master or a logician.[A] For I have taken it strongly into my head that there is a certain knack or *legerdemain*[B] in argument, by which we may safely proceed to the dangerous part of advising and make sure of the good fortune to have our advice accepted if it be anything worth.

My proposal is to consider of this affair as a case of surgery. It is practice, we all allow, which makes a hand.

'But who, on this occasion, will be practised on? Who will willingly be the first to try our hand and afford us the requisite experience?'

Here lies the difficulty. For supposing we had hospitals for this sort of surgery and there were always in readiness certain meek patients who would bear any incisions and be probed or tented[C] at our pleasure, the advantage no doubt would be considerable in this way of practice. Some insight must needs be obtained. In time a hand too might be acquired but, in all likelihood, a very rough one, which would by no means serve the purpose of this latter surgery. For here, a tenderness of hand is principally requisite. No surgeon will be called who has not feeling and compassion. And where to find a subject in which the operator is likely to preserve the highest tenderness, and yet act with the greatest resolution and boldness, is certainly a matter of no slight consideration.

I am sensible there is in all considerable projects, at first appearance, a certain air of chimerical fancy and conceit, which is apt to render the projectors somewhat liable to ridicule. I would therefore prepare my reader against this prejudice by assuring him that in the operation proposed there is nothing which can justly excite his laughter or, if there be, the laugh perhaps may turn against him by his own consent and with his own concurrence, which is a specimen of that very art or science we are about to illustrate.

Accordingly, if it be objected against the above-mentioned practice and art of surgery, that 'we can nowhere find such a meek patient, with whom we can

---

[A] In the sense here of a master of λόγος, *logos*, of words, rather than a master of logic.
[B] Sleight of hand or conjuring, from 'lightness of touch'.
[C] Literally, treated with a tent, a piece of fabric inserted into a wound or natural orifice to keep it open.

in reality make bold and for whom nevertheless we are sure to preserve the greatest tenderness and regard', I assert the contrary and say, for instance, that 'we have each of us ourselves to practise on'.

'Mere quibble!', you will say, 'for who can thus multiply himself into two persons and be his own subject? Who can properly laugh at himself or find in his heart to be either merry or severe on such an occasion?'

Go to the poets, and they will present you with many instances. Nothing is more common with them than this sort of soliloquy. A person of profound parts, or perhaps of ordinary capacity, happens on some occasion to commit a fault. He is concerned for it. He comes alone upon the stage, looks about him to see if anybody be near, then takes himself to task without sparing himself in the least. You would wonder to hear how close he pushes matters and how thoroughly he carries on the business of self-dissection. By virtue of this soliloquy, he becomes two distinct persons. He is pupil and preceptor. He teaches and he learns. And, in good earnest, had I nothing else to plead in behalf of the morals of our modern dramatic poets, I should defend them still against their accusers for the sake of this very practice, which they have taken care to keep up in its full force. For whether the practice be natural or no in respect of common custom and usage, I take upon me to assert that it is an honest and laudable practice and that, if already it be not natural to us, we ought however to make it so by study and application.

'Are we to go therefore to the stage for edification? Must we learn our catechism from the poets and, like the players, speak aloud what we debate at any time with ourselves alone?' Not absolutely so, perhaps, though where the harm would be of spending some discourse and bestowing a little breath and clear voice purely upon ourselves, I cannot see. We might peradventure be less noisy and more profitable in company if at convenient times we discharged some of our articulate sound and spoke to ourselves *vivâ voce*[D] when alone. For company is an extreme provocative to fancy and, like a hotbed in gardening, is apt to make our imaginations sprout too fast. But, by this anticipating remedy of soliloquy, we may effectually provide against the inconvenience.

We have an account in history[E] of a certain nation who seem to have been extremely apprehensive of the effects of this frothiness or ventosity in speech, and were accordingly resolved to provide thoroughly against the evil. They carried this remedy of ours so far that it was not only their custom, but their religion and law, to speak, laugh, use action, gesticulate and do all in the same manner when by themselves as when they were in company. If you had stolen upon them unawares at any time when they had been by themselves, you might have found them in high dispute, arguing with themselves, reproving, coun-

---

[D] Orally, out loud.
[E] Xenophon, *Anabasis* 5.4.34.

selling, haranguing themselves, and in the most florid manner accosting their own persons. In all likelihood they had been once a people remarkably fluent in expression, much pestered with orators and preachers and mightily subject to that disease which has been since called 'the leprosy of eloquence', till some sage legislator arose among them who, when he could not oppose the torrent of words and stop the flux of speech by any immediate application, found means to give a vent to the loquacious humour and broke the force of the distemper by eluding it.

Our present manners, I must own, are not so well calculated for this method of soliloquy as to suffer it to become a national practice. It is but a small portion of this regimen which I would willingly borrow and apply to private use, especially in the case of authors. I am sensible how fatal it might prove to many honourable persons, should they acquire such a habit as this or offer to practise such an art within reach of any mortal ear. For it is well known we are not many of us like that Roman who wished for windows to his breast that all might be as conspicuous there as in his house, which, for that very reason, he had built as open as was possible. I would therefore advise our probationer upon his first exercise to retire into some thick wood or, rather, take the point of some high hill where, besides the advantage of looking about him for security, he would find the air perhaps more rarefied and suitable to the perspiration required, especially in the case of a poetical genius: *The entire troop of authors loves a grove and shuns cities.*[2]

It is remarkable in all great wits that they have owned this practice of ours, and generally described themselves as a people liable to sufficient ridicule for their great loquacity by themselves and their profound taciturnity in company. Not only the poet and philosopher, but the orator himself was wont to have recourse to our method. And the prince of this latter tribe may be proved to have been a great frequenter of the wood and river banks, where he consumed abundance of his breath, suffered his fancy to evaporate, and reduced the vehemence both of his spirit and voice. If other authors find nothing which invites them to these recesses, it is because their genius is not of force enough, or, though it be, their character, they may imagine, will hardly bear them out. For to be surprised in the odd actions, gestures or tones which are proper to such ascetics, I must own would be an ill adventure for a man of the world. But, with poets and philosophers, it is a known case: *Either the man is crazy or else he makes verses.*[3]

Composing and raving must necessarily, we see, bear a resemblance. And for those composers who deal in systems and airy speculations, they have vulgarly passed for a sort of prose poets. Their secret practice and habit has been

---

[2]   Horace, *Epistles* 2.2.77.
[3]   Horace, *Satires* 2.7.117.

as frequently noted: *They gnaw over their mutterings to themselves and their frenzied silences.*[4] Both these sorts are happily indulged in this method of evacuation. They are thought to act naturally and in their proper way when they assume these odd manners. But, of other authors, it is expected they should be better bred. They are obliged to preserve a more conversible habit, which is no small misfortune to them. For, if their meditation and reverie be obstructed by the fear of a nonconforming mien in conversation, they may happen to be so much the worse authors for being finer gentlemen. Their fervency of imagination may possibly be as strong as either the philosopher's or the poet's. But, being denied an equal benefit of discharge and withheld from the wholesome manner of relief in private, it is no wonder if they appear with so much froth and scum in public.

It is observable that the writers of memoirs and essays are chiefly subject to this frothy distemper. Nor can it be doubted that this is the true reason why these gentlemen entertain the world so lavishly with what relates to *themselves*. For having had no opportunity of privately conversing with themselves or exercising their own genius so as to make acquaintance with it or prove its strength, they immediately fall to work in a wrong place and exhibit on the stage of the world that practice which they should have kept to themselves, if they designed that either they or the world should be the better for their moralities. Who indeed can endure to hear an empiric[F] talk of his own constitution, how he governs and manages it, what diet agrees best with it and what his practice is with himself? The proverb, no doubt, is very just, 'physician, cure thyself!' Yet methinks one should have but an ill time to be present at these bodily operations. Nor is the reader in truth any better entertained when he is obliged to assist at the experimental discussions of his practising author, who all the while is in reality doing no better than taking his physic in public.

For this reason I hold it very indecent for anyone to publish his meditations, occasional reflections, solitary thoughts or other such exercises as come under the notion of this self-discoursing practice.[G] And the modestest title I can conceive for such works would be that of a certain author who called them his 'crudities'. It is the unhappiness of those wits who conceive suddenly, but without being able to go out their full time, that, after many miscarriages and

---

[F]   A quack doctor or a person who relies entirely on experiment.
[G]   In preceding decades, many works had had such titles, including: Joseph Henshaw, *Meditations, Miscellaneous, Holy and Humane* (1637); Henry Tubbe, *Meditations Divine and Moral* (1659); Robert Boyle, *Occasional Reflections upon Several Subjects* (1665) – which inspired Jonathan Swift's *Meditation on a Broomstick* (1710); Matthew Hale, *Contemplations, Moral and Divine* (1682); William Killigrew, *Midnight Thoughts* (1682); *The Artless Midnight Thoughts of a Gentleman at Court* (1684); *Divine Meditations* (1700); Charles Povey, *Meditations of a Divine Soul* (1705); and William Beveridge, *Private Thoughts upon Religion* (1709).

[4]   Persius, *Satires* 3.81.

abortions, they can bring nothing well-shapen or perfect into the world. They are not, however, the less fond of their offspring, which, in a manner, they beget in public. For so public-spirited they are that they can never afford themselves the least time to think in private for their own particular benefit and use. For this reason, though they are often retired, they are never by themselves. The world is ever of the party. They have their author-character in view, and are always considering how this or that thought would serve to complete some set of contemplations, or furnish out the commonplace book from whence these treasured riches are to flow in plenty on the necessitous world.

But if our candidates for authorship happen to be of the sanctified kind,[H] it is not to be imagined how much farther still their charity is apt to extend. So exceeding great is their indulgence and tenderness for mankind that they are unwilling the least sample of their devout exercise should be lost. Though there are already so many formularies and rituals appointed for this species of soliloquy, they can allow nothing to lie concealed which passes in this religious commerce and way of dialogue between them and their soul.

These may be termed a sort of pseudo-ascetics, who can have no real converse either with themselves or with Heaven, while they look thus asquint upon the world and carry titles and editions along with them in their meditations. And although the books of this sort, by a common idiom, are called 'good books', the authors, for certain, are a sorry race, for religious crudities are undoubtedly the worst of any. A saint-author of all men least values politeness.[5] He scorns to confine that spirit in which he writes to rules of criticism and profane learning. Nor is he inclined in any respect to play the critic on himself, or regulate his style or language by the standard of good company and people of the better sort. He is above the consideration of that which in a narrow sense we call 'manners'. Nor is he apt to examine any other faults than those which he calls 'sins', though a sinner against good breeding and the laws of decency will no more be esteemed a good author than will a sinner against grammar, good argument or good sense. And if moderation and temper are not of the party with a writer, let his cause be ever so good, I doubt whether he will be able to recommend it with great advantage to the world.

On this account, I would principally recommend our exercise of self-converse to all such persons as are addicted to write after the manner of holy advisers, especially if they lie under an indispensable necessity of being talkers or haranguers in the same kind. For to discharge frequently and vehemently in public is a great hindrance to the way of private exercise, which consists chiefly in control. But where, instead of control, debate or argument, the chief exercise of the wit consists in uncontrollable harangues and reasonings, which

---

[H]   That is, authors who were clerics or who at least engaged in religious polemic.

[5]   See pp. 439–40n.

must neither be questioned nor contradicted, there is great danger lest the party, through this habit, should suffer much by crudities, indigestions, choler, bile and particularly by a certain tumour or flatulency, which renders him of all men the least able to apply the wholesome regimen of self-practice. It is no wonder if such quaint practitioners grow to an enormous size of absurdity, while they continue in the reverse of that practice by which alone we correct the redundancy of humours and chasten the exuberance of conceit and fancy.

A remarkable instance of the want of this sovereign remedy may be drawn from our common 'great talkers', who engross the greatest part of the conversations of the world and are the forwardest to speak in public assemblies. Many of these have a sprightly genius, attended with a mighty heat and ebullition of fancy. But it is a certain observation in our science that they who are great talkers in company have never been any talkers by themselves, nor used to these private discussions of our home regimen, for which reason their froth abounds. Nor can they discharge anything without some mixture of it. But, when they carry their attempts beyond ordinary discourse and would rise to the capacity of authors, the case grows worse with them. Their page can carry none of the advantages of their person. They can no way bring into paper those airs they give themselves in discourse. The turns of voice and action with which they help out many a lame thought and incoherent sentence must here be laid aside, and the speech taken to pieces, compared together and examined from head to foot. So that, unless the party has been used to play the critic thoroughly upon himself, he will hardly be found proof against the criticisms of others. His thoughts can never appear very correct unless they have been used to sound correction by themselves, and been well formed and disciplined before they are brought into the field. It is the hardest thing in the world to be a good thinker without being a strong self-examiner and thorough-paced dialogist in this solitary way.

Section 2
But to bring our case a little closer still to morals, I might perhaps very justifiably take occasion here to enter into a spacious field of learning to show the antiquity of that opinion that 'we have each of us a daemon, genius, angel or guardian-spirit, to whom we were strictly joined and committed from our earliest dawn of reason or moment of our birth'.[1] This opinion, were it literally

---

[1] This word had a complex etymological history. In ancient Greece, a δαίμων, *daimon*, was an attendant personal deity (either good or bad), exemplified by the one with which Socrates claimed to hold discourse. This is the sense here. However, in early Christian times, the word came to be associated with an evil deity with powers far beyond the personal scope of the *daimon*. From this usage derived the English 'demon' – a sense in which Shaftesbury used the term elsewhere in *Characteristics*. In this edition, Shaftesbury's consistent spelling, 'daemon', is retained throughout.

true, might be highly serviceable, no doubt, towards the establishment of our system and doctrine. For it would infallibly be proved a kind of sacrilege or impiety to slight the company of so divine a guest and, in a manner, banish him our breast, by refusing to enter with him into those secret conferences by which alone he could be enabled to become our adviser and guide. But I should esteem it unfair to proceed upon such an hypothesis as this, when the very utmost the wise ancients ever meant by this daemon companion I conceive to have been no more than enigmatically to declare, that 'we had each of us a patient in ourself [sic]', that 'we were properly our own subject of practice' and that 'we then became due practitioners when, by virtue of an intimate recess, we could discover a certain duplicity of soul and divide ourselves into two parties'. One of these, as they supposed, would immediately approve himself a venerable sage and, with an air of authority, erect himself our counsellor and governor while the other party, who had nothing in him besides what was base and servile, would be contented to follow and obey.

According therefore as this recess was deep and intimate and the dual number practically formed in us, we were supposed to advance in morals and true wisdom. This, they thought, was the only way of composing matters in our breast and establishing that subordinacy which alone could make us agree with ourselves and be of a piece within. They esteemed this a more religious work than any prayers or other duty in the temple. And this they advised us to carry thither as the best offering which could be made: *Spiritual reconciliation of law and duty and mind's recesses pure.*[6]

This was, among the ancients, that celebrated Delphic inscription, 'Recognize yourself!', which was as much as to say, 'Divide yourself!' or 'Be two!'[J] For if the division were rightly made, all within would, of course, they thought, be rightly understood and prudently managed. Such confidence they had in this home-dialect of soliloquy! For it was accounted the peculiarity of philosophers and wise men to be able to hold themselves in talk. And it was their boast on this account that 'they were never less *alone* than when by *themselves*'. A knave, they thought, could never be by himself. Not that his conscience was always sure of giving him disturbance, but he had not, they supposed, so much interest with himself as to exert this generous faculty and raise himself a companion who, being fairly admitted into partnership, would quickly mend his partner and set his affairs on a right foot.

One would think there was nothing easier for us than to know our own minds and understand what our main scope was, what we plainly drove at and what

---

[J] Delphi was the site of a sanctuary, presided over by Apollo and sacred to all the Greeks. The oracle there delivered messages from Apollo to individuals and city-states about matters of ritual, policy and morality. The temple there was inscribed with two precepts: 'Know thyself' and 'Nothing too much'.

[6] Persius, *Satires* 2.73–4.

we proposed to ourselves, as our end, in every occurrence of our lives. But our thoughts have generally such an obscure implicit language that it is the hardest thing in the world to make them speak out distinctly. For this reason, the right method is to give them voice and accent. And this, in our default, is what the moralists or philosophers endeavour to do, to our hand, when, as is usual, they hold us out a kind of *vocal* looking-glass, draw sound out of our breast and instruct us to personate ourselves in the plainest manner. *Those thoughts he murmurs internally to himself and under his breath: 'Oh! a funeral for my uncle would be simply splendid!'*[7]

A certain air of pleasantry and humour, which prevails nowadays in the fashionable world, gives a son the assurance to tell a father he has lived too long and a husband the privilege of talking of his second wife before his first. But let the airy gentleman, who makes thus bold with others, retire a while out of company, and he scarce dares tell himself his wishes. Much less can he endure to carry on his thought, as he necessarily must, if he enters once thoroughly into himself and proceeds by interrogatories to form the home acquaintance and familiarity required. For thus, after some struggle, we may suppose him to accost himself:

'Tell me now, my honest heart, am I really honest and of some worth, or do I only make a fair show and am intrinsically no better than a rascal? As good a friend, a countryman or a relation as I appear outwardly to the world, or as I would willingly perhaps think myself to be, should I not in reality be glad they were hanged, any of them, or broke their necks who happened to stand between me and the least portion of an estate?'

'Why not, since it is *my interest?*'

'Should I not be glad therefore to help this matter forwards and promote my interest, if it lay fairly in my power?'

'No doubt, provided I were sure not to be punished for it.'

'And what reason has the greatest rogue in nature for not doing thus?'

'The same reason and no other.'

'Am I not then, at the bottom, the same as he?'

'The same: an arrant villain, though perhaps more a coward and not so perfect in my kind.'

'If interest therefore points me out this road, whither would humanity and compassion lead me?'

'Quite contrary.'

'Why therefore do I cherish such weaknesses? Why do I sympathize with others? Why please myself in the conceit of worth and honour, a character, a memory, an issue or a name? What else are these but scruples in my way?

---

[7] Persius, *Satires* 2.9–10.

Wherefore do I thus belie my own interest and, by keeping myself half-knave, approve myself a thorough fool?'

This is a language we can by no means endure to hold with ourselves, whatever raillery we may use with others. We may defend villainy or cry up folly before the world, but to appear fools, madmen or varlets to ourselves and prove it to our own faces that we are really such is insupportable. For so true a reverence has everyone for himself, when he comes clearly to appear before his close companion, that he had rather profess the vilest things of himself in open company than hear his character privately from his own mouth. So that we may readily from hence conclude that the chief interest of ambition, avarice, corruption and every sly insinuating vice is to prevent this interview and familiarity of discourse which is consequent upon close retirement and inward recess. It is the grand artifice of villainy and lewdness, as well as of superstition and bigotry, to put us upon terms of greater distance and formality with ourselves and evade our proving method of soliloquy. And, for this reason, how specious soever may be the instruction and doctrine of formalists, their very manner itself is a sufficient blind or *remora*[K] in the way of honesty and good sense.

I am sensible that, should my reader be peradventure a lover after the more profound and solemn way of love, he would be apt to conclude that he was no stranger to our proposed method of practice, being conscious to himself of having often made vigorous excursions into those solitary regions, abovementioned, where soliloquy is upheld with most advantage. He may chance to remember how he has many times addressed the woods and rocks in audible articulate sounds, and seemingly expostulated with himself in such a manner as if he had really formed the requisite distinction and had the power to entertain himself in due form. But it is very apparent that, though all were true we have here supposed, it can no way reach the case before us. For a passionate lover, whatever solitude he may affect, can never be truly by himself. His case is like the author's who has begun his courtship to the public and is embarked in an intrigue which sufficiently amuses and takes him out of himself. Whatever he meditates alone is interrupted still by the imagined presence of the mistress he pursues. Not a thought, not an expression, not a sigh, which is purely for himself – all is appropriated and all devoutly tendered to the object of his passion, insomuch that there is nothing ever so trivial or accidental of this kind which he is not desirous should be witnessed by the party whose grace and favour he solicits.

It is the same reason which keeps the imaginary saint or mystic from being capable of this entertainment. Instead of looking narrowly into his own nature and mind that he may be no longer a mystery to himself, he is taken up with the contemplation of other mysterious natures, which he can never explain or

[K] A delay or hindrance.

comprehend. He has the spectres of his zeal before his eyes and is as familiar with his modes, essences, personages and exhibitions of deity as the conjuror with his different forms, species and orders of genii or daemons. So that we make no doubt to assert that not so much as a recluse religionist, a votary or hermit was ever truly by himself. And thus since neither lover, author, mystic nor conjuror (who are the only claimants) can truly or justly be entitled to a share in this self-entertainment, it remains that the only person entitled is the man of sense, the sage or philosopher. However, since of all other characters we are generally the most inclined to favour that of a lover, it may not, we hope, be impertinent on this occasion to recite the story of an amour.

A virtuous young prince of a heroic soul, capable of love and friendship, made war upon a tyrant who was in every respect his reverse.[1] It was the happiness of our prince to be as great a conqueror by his clemency and bounty as by his arms and military virtue. Already he had won over to his party several potentates and princes who before had been subject to the tyrant. Among those who adhered still to the enemy, there was a prince who, having all the advantage of person and merit, had lately been made happy in the possession and mutual love of the most beautiful princess in the world. It happened that the occasions of the war called the new-married prince to a distance from his beloved princess. He left her secure, as he thought, in a strong castle far within the country, but in his absence the place was taken by surprise, and the princess brought a captive to the quarters of our heroic prince.

There was in the camp a young nobleman, favourite of the prince, one who had been educated with him and was still treated by him with perfect familiarity. Him he immediately sent for and, with strict injunctions, committed the captive princess to his charge, resolving she should be treated with that respect which was due to her high rank and merit. It was the same young lord who had discovered her disguised among the prisoners and learned her story, the particulars of which he now related to the prince. He spoke in ecstasy on this occasion, telling the prince how beautiful she appeared, even in the midst of sorrow, and, though disguised under the meanest habit, yet how distinguishable by her air and manner from every other beauty of her sex. But what appeared strange to our young nobleman was that the prince, during this whole relation, discovered not the least intention of seeing the lady or satisfying that curiosity which seemed so natural on such an occasion. He pressed him, but without success.

'Not see her, Sir!,' said he, wondering, 'when she is so handsome beyond what you have ever seen!'

'For that very reason', replied the prince, 'I would the rather decline the interview. For, should I, upon the bare report of her beauty, be so charmed as

---

[1] Xenophon, *Cyropaedia*, 5.1.1–18, 6.1.31–41.

to make the first visit at this urgent time of business, I may, upon sight, with better reason, be induced perhaps to visit her when I am more at leisure and so, again and again, till at last I may have no leisure left for my affairs.'

'Would you, Sir, persuade me then', said the young nobleman, smiling, 'that a fair face can have such power as to force the will itself and constrain a man in any respect to act contrary to what he thinks becoming him? Are we to hearken to the poets in what they tell us of that incendiary love and his irresistible flames? A real flame, we see, burns all alike. But that imaginary one of beauty hurts only those who are consenting. It affects no otherwise than as we ourselves are pleased to allow it. In many cases we absolutely command it, as where relation and consanguinity are in the nearest degree. Authority and law, we see, can master it. But it would be vain as well as unjust for any law to intermeddle or prescribe, were not the case voluntary and our will entirely free.'

'How comes it then', replied the prince, 'that, if we are thus masters of our choice and free at first to admire and love where we approve, we cannot afterwards as well cease to love whenever we see cause? This latter liberty you will hardly defend. For I doubt not you have heard of many who, though they were used to set the highest value upon liberty before they loved, yet afterwards were necessitated to serve in the most abject manner, finding themselves constrained and bound by a stronger chain than any of iron or adamant.'

'Such wretches', replied the youth, 'I have often heard complain who, if you will believe them, are wretched indeed, without means or power to help themselves. You may hear them in the same manner complain grievously of life itself. But though there are doors enough to go out of life, they find it convenient to keep still where they are. They are the very same pretenders who, through this plea of irresistible necessity, make bold with what is another's and attempt unlawful beds. But the law, I perceive, makes bold with them in its turn as with other invaders of property. Neither is it your custom, Sir, to pardon such offences. So that beauty itself, you must allow, is innocent and harmless and can compel no one to do anything amiss. The debauched compel themselves and unjustly charge their guilt on love. They who are honest and just can admire and love whatever is beautiful, without offering at anything beyond what is allowed. How then is it possible, Sir, that one of your virtue should be in pain on any such account or fear such a temptation? You see, Sir, I am sound and whole after having beheld the princess. I have conversed with her, I have admired her in the highest degree, yet am myself still and in my duty and shall be ever in the same manner at your command.'

'It is well,' replied the prince. 'Keep yourself so. Be ever the same man and look to your charge carefully, as becomes you. For it may so happen in the present posture of the war that this fair captive may stand us in good stead.'

With this the young nobleman departed to execute his commission and immediately took such care of the captive princess and her household that she seemed as perfectly obeyed and had everything which belonged to her in as great splendour now as in her principality and in the height of fortune. He found her in every respect deserving and saw in her a generosity of soul which was beyond her other charms. His study to oblige her and soften her distress made her in return desirous to express a gratitude, which he easily perceived. She showed on every occasion a real concern for his interest and, when he happened to fall ill, she took such tender care of him herself and by her servants that he seemed to owe his recovery to her friendship.

From these beginnings, insensibly and by natural degrees, as may easily be conceived, the youth fell desperately in love. At first he offered not to make the least mention of his passion to the princess, for he scarce dared tell it to himself. But afterwards he grew bolder. She received his declaration with an unaffected trouble and concern, spoke to him as a friend to dissuade him as much as possible from such an extravagant attempt. But when he talked to her of force, she immediately sent away one of her faithful domestics to the prince to implore his protection. The prince received the message with the appearance of more than ordinary concern, sent instantly for one of his first ministers and bid him go with that domestic to the young nobleman, and let him understand that 'force was not to be offered to such a lady; persuasion he might use, if he thought fit'.

The minister, who was no friend to the young nobleman, failed not to aggravate the message, inveighed publicly against him on this occasion, and to his face reproached him as a traitor and dishonourer of his prince and nation, with all else which could be said against him as guilty of the highest sacrilege, perfidiousness and breach of trust. So that in reality the youth looked upon his case as desperate, fell into the deepest melancholy and prepared himself for that fate which he thought he well deserved.

In this condition the prince sent to speak with him alone and, when he saw him in the utmost confusion, 'I find,' said he, 'my friend, I am now become dreadful to you indeed since you can neither see me without shame nor imagine me to be without resentment. But away with all those thoughts from this time forwards! I know how much you have suffered on this occasion. I know the power of love and am no otherwise safe myself than by keeping out of the way of beauty. It was I who was in fault; it was I who unhappily matched you with that unequal adversary and gave you that impracticable task and hard adventure, which no one yet was ever strong enough to accomplish.'

'In this, Sir,' replied the youth, 'as in all else, you express that goodness which is so natural to you. You have compassion and can allow for human frailty, but the rest of mankind will never cease to upbraid me. Nor shall I ever be forgiven, were I able to forgive myself. I am reproached by my nearest friends. I must be odious to all mankind wherever I am known. The least punishment I can think due to me is banishment forever from your presence.'

'Think not of such a thing forever', said the prince, 'but trust me. If you retire only for a while, I shall so order it that you shall soon return again with the applause even of those who are now your enemies, when they find what a considerable service you shall have rendered both to them and me.'

Such a hint was sufficient to revive the spirits of our despairing youth. He was transported to think that his misfortunes could be turned any way to the advantage of his prince: he entered with joy into the scheme the prince had laid for him and appeared eager to depart and execute what was appointed him. 'Can you, then,' said the prince, 'resolve to quit the charming princess?'

'Oh, Sir!,' replied the youth, 'well am I now satisfied that I have in reality within me two distinct separate souls. This lesson of philosophy I have learned from that villainous sophister Love. For it is impossible to believe that, having one and the same soul, it should be actually both good and bad, passionate for virtue and vice, desirous of contraries. No. There must of necessity be two, and, when the good prevails, it is then we act handsomely, when the ill, then basely and villainously. Such was my case. For lately the ill soul was wholly master. But now the good prevails by your assistance, and I am plainly a new creature with quite another apprehension, another reason, another will.'

Thus it may appear how far a lover by his own natural strength may reach the chief principle of philosophy and understand our doctrine of two persons in one individual self. Not that our courtier, we suppose, was able of himself to form this distinction justly and according to art. For could he have effected this, he would have been able to cure himself without the assistance of his prince. However, he was wise enough to see in the issue that his independency and freedom were mere glosses and resolution, a nose of wax. For let will be ever so free, humour and fancy, we see, govern it. And these, as free as we suppose them, are often changed we know not how, without asking our consent or giving us any account. If opinion be that which governs and makes the change, it is itself as liable to be governed and varied in its turn.[8] And by what I can observe of the world, fancy and opinion stand pretty much upon the same bottom. So that, if there be no certain inspector or auditor established within us to take account of these opinions and fancies in due form and minutely to animadvert upon their several growths and habits, we are as little like to continue a day in the same will as a tree, during a summer, in the same shape, without the gardener's assistance and the vigorous application of the shears and pruning knife.

As cruel a court as the Inquisition[M] appears, there must, it seems, be full as formidable a one erected in ourselves, if we would pretend to that uniformity

---

[M] Judicial apparatus within the Roman Catholic Church that aimed to detect and root out heresy, sometimes with the use of torture.

[8] See pp. 144–5, 422–3.

of opinion which is necessary to hold us to one will and preserve us in the same mind from one day to another. Philosophy, at this rate, will be thought perhaps little better than persecution, and a supreme judge in matters of inclination and appetite must needs go exceedingly against the heart. Every pretty fancy is disturbed by it; every pleasure interrupted by it. The course of good humour will hardly allow it, and the pleasantry of wit almost absolutely rejects it. It appears, besides, like a kind of pedantry to be thus magisterial with ourselves, thus strict over our imaginations and with all the airs of a real pedagogue to be solicitously taken up in the sour care and tutorage of so many boyish fancies, unlucky appetites and desires, which are perpetually playing truant and need correction.

We hope, however, that, by our method of practice and the help of the grand *arcanum*[N] which we have professed to reveal, this regimen or discipline of the fancies may not in the end prove so severe or mortifying as is imagined. We hope also that our patient (for such we naturally suppose our reader) will consider duly with himself that what he endures in this operation is for no inconsiderable end, since it is to gain him a will and ensure him a certain resolution by which he shall know where to find himself, be sure of his own meaning and design and, as to all his desires, opinions and inclinations, be warranted one and the same person today as yesterday and tomorrow as today.

This, perhaps, will be thought a miracle by one who well considers the nature of mankind and the growth, variation and inflection of Appetite and Humour. For Appetite, which is elder brother to Reason, being the lad of stronger growth, is sure, on every contest, to take the advantage of drawing all to his own side. And Will, so highly boasted, is at best merely a top or football between these youngsters, who prove very unfortunately matched, till the youngest, instead of now and then a kick or lash bestowed to little purpose, forsakes the ball or top itself and begins to lay about his elder brother. It is then that the scene changes. For the elder, like an arrant coward, upon this treatment, presently grows civil and affords the younger as fair play afterwards as he can desire.

And here it is that our sovereign remedy and gymnastic method of soliloquy takes its rise when, by a certain powerful figure of inward rhetoric, the mind apostrophizes its own fancies, raises them in their proper shapes and personages and addresses them familiarly, without the least ceremony or respect. By this means, it will soon happen that two formed parties will erect themselves within. For the imaginations or fancies being thus roundly treated are forced to declare themselves and take party. Those on the side of the elder brother Appetite are strangely subtle and insinuating. They have always the faculty to speak by nods and winks. By this practice they conceal half their

[N] Secret, mystery.

meaning and, like modern politicians, pass for deeply wise and adorn themselves with the finest pretexts and most specious glosses imaginable till, being confronted with their fellows of a plainer language and expression, they are forced to quit their mysterious manner and discover themselves mere sophisters and impostors, who have not the least to do with the party of reason and good sense.

Accordingly we might now proceed to exhibit, distinctly and in due method, the form and manner of this probation or exercise as it regards all men in general. But the case of authors in particular being, as we apprehend, the most urgent, we shall apply our rule in the first place to these gentlemen, whom it so highly imports to know themselves and understand the natural strength and powers as well as the weaknesses of a human mind. For without this understanding, the historian's judgment will be very defective, the politician's views very narrow and chimerical, and the poet's brain, however stocked with fiction, will be but poorly furnished as, in the sequel, we shall make appear. He who deals in characters must of necessity know his own, or he will know nothing. And he who would give the world a profitable entertainment of this sort should be sure to profit, first, by himself. For, in this sense, wisdom as well as charity may be honestly said 'to begin at home'. There is no way of estimating manners or apprising the different humours, fancies, passions and apprehensions of others without first taking an inventory of the same kind of goods within ourselves and surveying our domestic fund. A little of this home practice will serve to make great discoveries: *Live with yourself, and you'll know how modestly you are furnished.*[9]

Section 3

Whoever has been an observer of action and grace in human bodies must of necessity have discovered the great difference in this respect between such persons as have been taught by nature only and such as by reflection and the assistance of art have learned to form those motions which on experience are found the easiest and most natural. Of the former kind are either those good rustics who have been bred remote from the formed societies of men or those plain artisans and people of lower rank who, living in cities and places of resort, have been necessitated however to follow mean employments and wanted the opportunity and means to form themselves after the better models. There are some persons indeed so happily formed by nature herself that, with the greatest simplicity or rudeness of education, they have still something of a natural grace and comeliness in their action. And there are others of a better education who, by a wrong aim and injudicious affectation of grace, are of all people the farthest removed from it. It is undeniable, however, that the perfection of grace

---

[9] Persius, *Satires* 4.52.

and comeliness in action and behaviour can be found only among the people of a liberal education. And even among the graceful of this kind, those still are found the gracefullest who early in their youth have learned their exercises and formed their motions under the best masters.

Now such as these masters and their lessons are to a fine gentleman, such are philosophers and philosophy to an author. The case is the same in the fashionable and in the literate world. In the former of these, it is remarked that, by the help of good company and the force of example merely, a decent carriage is acquired, with such apt motions and such a freedom of limbs as on all ordinary occasions may enable the party to demean himself like a gentleman. But when, upon further occasion, trial is made in an extraordinary way, when exercises of the genteeler kind are to be performed in public, it will easily appear who of the pretenders have been formed by rudiments and had masters in private and who, on the other side, have contented themselves with bare imitation and learned their part casually and by rote. The parallel is easily made on the side of writers. They have at least as much need of learning the several motions, counterpoises and balances of the mind and passions as the other students, those of the body and limbs: *Of proper writing, wisdom is the beginning and the source. The Socratic texts will be able to show you the matter.*[10]

The gallant, no doubt, may pen a letter to his mistress as the courtier may a compliment to the minister, or the minister to the favourite above him, without going such vast depths into learning or philosophy. But for these privileged gentlemen, though they set fashions and prescribe rules in other cases, they are no controllers in the commonwealth of letters. Nor are they presumed to write to the age or for remote posterity. Their works are not of a nature to entitle them to hold the rank of authors or be styled writers by way of excellence in the kind. Should their ambition lead them into such a field, they would be obliged to come otherwise equipped. They who enter the public lists must come duly trained and exercised, like well-appointed cavaliers, expert in arms and well instructed in the use of their weapon and management of their steed. For to be well accoutred and well mounted is not sufficient. The horse alone can never make the horseman, nor limbs the wrestler or the dancer. No more can a genius alone make a poet, or good parts a writer in any considerable kind.

[10] Horace, *The Art of Poetry* 309–10. See even the dissolute Petronius' judgment of a writer: *If anybody wants success in stern art and applies his mind to great things, let him first have strength of character, following the law of frugality precisely. Nor should he care about the grim palace with its lofty aspect ... Nor should he sit as an applauder at a piece in the theatre, a slave to histrionics ... And presently filled with learning from the Socratic flock, let him loose the reins as a free man, and shake the weapons of mighty Demosthenes ... Gird up your soul for these good tasks, full so of the swelling torrent, pour forth your words from a heart dedicated to the Muses* [Petronius, *Satyricon* 5].

The skill and grace of writing is founded, as our wise poet tells us, in knowledge and good sense, and not barely in that knowledge which is to be learned from common authors or the general conversation of the world, but from those particular rules of art which philosophy alone exhibits.

The philosophical writings, to which our poet in his *Art of Poetry* refers, were in themselves a kind of poetry, like the mimes or personated pieces of early times, before philosophy was in vogue and when as yet dramatical imitation was scarce formed or, at least, in many parts, not brought to due perfection.[11] They were pieces which, besides their force of style and hidden numbers, carried a sort of action and imitation, the same as the epic and dramatic kinds. They were either real dialogues or recitals of such personated discourses, where the persons themselves had their characters preserved throughout, their manners, humours and distinct turns of temper and understanding maintained, according to the most exact poetical truth. It was not enough that these pieces treated fundamentally of morals and in consequence pointed out real characters and manners: they exhibited them alive and set the countenances and complexions of men plainly in view. And by this means they not only taught us to know others, but, what was principal and of highest virtue in them, they taught us to know ourselves.

The philosophical hero of these poems, whose name they carried both in their body and front, and whose genius and manner they were made to represent,[o] was in himself a perfect character, yet, in some respects, so veiled and in a cloud that to the unattentive surveyor he seemed often to be very different from what he really was, and this chiefly by reason of a certain exquisite and refined raillery which belonged to his manner and by virtue of which he could treat the highest subjects and those of the commonest capacity both together and render them explanatory of each other. So that, in this genius of writing, there appeared both the heroic and the simple, the tragic and the comic vein. However, it was so ordered that, notwithstanding the oddness or mysteriousness of the principal character, the under-parts or second characters showed human nature more distinctly and to the life. We might here, therefore, as in a looking-glass, discover ourselves and see our minutest features nicely delineated and suited to our own apprehension and cognizance. No one who was ever so little a while an inspector could fail of becoming acquainted with his own heart. And – what was of singular note in these magical glasses – it would happen that, by constant and long inspection, the parties accustomed to the practice would acquire a peculiar speculative habit, so as virtually to carry about with them a sort of pocket-mirror, always ready and in use.

[o] Namely, Socrates.

[11] See p. 114n. [Shaftesbury was referring primarily to Plato's dialogues. A mime was, in ancient Greece and Rome, a simple farcical drama including ludicrous representations and mimicry.]

In this, there were two faces which would naturally present themselves to our view: one of them, like the commanding genius, the leader and chief above-mentioned; the other like that rude, undisciplined and headstrong creature whom we ourselves in our natural capacity most exactly resembled. Whatever we were employed in, whatever we set about, if once we had acquired the habit of this mirror, we should, by virtue of the double reflection, distinguish ourselves into two different parties. And in this dramatic method, the work of self-inspection would proceed with admirable success.

It is no wonder that the primitive poets were esteemed such sages in their times since it appears they were such well-practised dialogists and accustomed to this improving method before ever philosophy had adopted it. Their mimes, or characterized discourses, were as much relished as their most regular poems and were the occasion perhaps that so many of these latter were formed in such perfection. For poetry itself was defined an imitation chiefly of men and manners and was that in an exalted and noble degree which in a low one we call mimicry. It is in this that the great mimographer, the father and prince of poets, excels so highly, his characters being wrought to a likeness beyond what any succeeding masters were ever able to describe.[12] Nor are his works, which are so full of action, any other than an artful series or chain of dialogues, which turn upon one remarkable catastrophe or event. He describes no qualities or virtues, censures no manners, makes no encomiums nor gives characters himself, but brings his actors still in view. It is they who show themselves. It is they who speak in such a manner as distinguishes them in all things from all others and makes them ever like themselves. Their different compositions and allays so justly made and equally carried on through every particle of the action give more instruction than all the comments or glosses in the world. The poet, instead of giving himself those dictating and masterly airs of wisdom, makes hardly any figure at all and is scarce discoverable in his poem. This is being truly *a master*. He paints so as to need no inscription over his figures to tell us what they are or what he intends by them. A few words let fall on any slight occasion, from any of the parties he introduces, are sufficient to denote their manners and distinct character. From a finger or a toe, he can represent to our thoughts the frame and fashion of a whole body. He wants no other help of art to personate his heroes and make them living. There was no more left for tragedy to do after him than to erect a stage and draw his dialogues and characters into scenes, turning, in the same manner, upon one principal action or event, with that regard to place and time which was suitable to a real

---

[12] *Homer deserves to be praised in many respects and especially because he alone of poets does not fail to understand what he ought to do. The poet should speak as little as possible as himself for he is not in this respect a mimetic poet: other poets themselves perform roles throughout the poem but represent mimetically few things and only occasionally*: Aristotle, *Poetics* 24.13–14.

spectacle. Even comedy itself was adjudged to this great master,[13] it being derived from those parodies, or mock-humours, of which he had given the specimen in a concealed sort of raillery intermixed with the sublime.[14]——A dangerous stroke of art! and which required a masterly hand, like that of the philosophical hero whose character was represented in the dialogue writings above-mentioned.

From hence possibly we may form a notion of that resemblance which on so many occasions was heretofore remarked between the prince of poets and the divine philosopher who was said to rival him and who, together with his contemporaries of the same school, wrote wholly in that manner of dialogue above-described. From hence too we may comprehend perhaps why the study of dialogue was heretofore thought so advantageous to writers and why this manner of writing was judged so difficult, which, at first sight, it must be owned, appears the easiest of any.

I have formerly wondered indeed why a manner, which was familiarly used in treatises upon most subjects with so much success among the ancients, should be so insipid and of little esteem with us moderns. But I afterwards perceived that, besides the difficulty of the manner itself and that mirror faculty which we have observed it to carry in respect of ourselves, it proves also of necessity a kind of mirror or looking-glass to the age. If so, it should of consequence, you will say, be the more agreeable and entertaining.

True, if the real view of ourselves be not perhaps displeasing to us.

But why more displeasing to us than to the ancients?

Because perhaps they could with just reason bear to see their natural countenances represented.

And why not we the same? What should discourage us? For are we not as handsome, at least in our own eyes?

Perhaps not, as we shall see when we have considered a little further what the force is of this mirror writing and how it differs from that more complaisant, modish way, in which an author, instead of presenting us with other natural characters, sets off his own with the utmost art and purchases his reader's favour by all imaginable compliancies and condescensions.

An author who writes in his own person has the advantage of being who or what he pleases. He is no certain man nor has any certain or genuine character, but suits himself on every occasion to the fancy of his reader, whom, as the fashion is nowadays, he constantly caresses and cajoles. All turns upon their two persons. And as in an amour or commerce of love-letters, so here the author has the privilege of talking eternally of himself, dressing and sprucing up him-

---

[13] See pp. 110n, 114n.

[14] Not only in his *Margites*, but even in his *Iliad* and *Odyssey*. [*Margites* was said to be a poem by Homer satirizing the fatuousness and pretentiousness of the poem's namesake.]

self while he is making diligent court and working upon the humour of the party to whom he addresses. This is the coquetry of a modern author, whose epistles dedicatory, prefaces and addresses to the reader are so many affected graces, designed to draw the attention from the subject towards himself and make it be generally observed not so much what he says as what he appears, or is, and what figure he already makes, or hopes to make, in the fashionable world.

These are the airs which a neighbouring nation[p] give themselves, more particularly in what they call their memoirs. Their very essays on politics, their philosophical and critical works, their comments upon ancient and modern authors, all their treatises are memoirs. The whole writing of this age is become indeed a sort of memoir-writing. Though in the real memoirs of the ancients, even when they wrote at any time concerning themselves, there was neither the 'I' nor 'thou' throughout the whole work. So that all this pretty amour and intercourse of caresses between the author and reader was thus entirely taken away.

Much more is this the case in dialogue. For here the author is annihilated, and the reader, being no way applied to, stands for nobody. The self-interesting parties both vanish at once. The scene presents itself as by chance and undesigned. You are not only left to judge coolly and with indifference of the sense delivered, but of the character, genius, elocution and manner of the persons who deliver it. These two are mere strangers, in whose favour you are no way engaged. Nor is it enough that the persons introduced speak pertinent and good sense at every turn. It must be seen from what bottom they speak, from what principle, what stock or fund of knowledge they draw, and what kind or species of understanding they possess. For the understanding here must have its mark, its characteristic note, by which it may be distinguished. It must be such and such an understanding, as when we say, for instance, 'such or such a face', since nature has characterized tempers and minds as peculiarly as faces. And for an artist who draws naturally, it is not enough to show us merely faces which may be called men's: every face must be a certain man's.

Now as a painter who draws battles, or other actions, of Christians, Turks, Indians or any distinct and peculiar people must of necessity draw the several figures of his piece in their proper and real proportions, gestures, habits, arms or at least with as fair resemblance as possible, so in the same manner that writer, whoever he be, among us moderns, who shall venture to bring his fellow moderns into dialogue, must introduce them in their proper manners, genius, behaviour and humour. And this is the mirror or looking-glass above-described.

For instance, a dialogue, we will suppose, is framed after the manner of our

[p] France.

ancient authors. In it a poor philosopher, of a mean figure, accosts one of the powerfullest, wittiest, handsomest and richest noblemen of the time as he is walking leisurely towards the temple.

'You are going then', says he, calling him by his plain name, 'to pay your devotions yonder at the temple?'

'I am so.'

'But with an air, methinks, as if some thought perplexed you.'

'What is there in the case which should perplex one?'

'The thought perhaps of your petitions and the consideration what vows you had best offer to the Deity.'

'Is that so difficult? Can anyone be so foolish as to ask of Heaven what is not for his good?'

'Not if he understands what his good is.'

'Who can mistake it if he has common sense and knows the difference between prosperity and adversity?'

'It is prosperity therefore you would pray for?'

'Undoubtedly.'

'For instance, that absolute sovereign, who commands all things by virtue of his immense treasures and governs by his sole will and pleasure, him you think prosperous and his state happy.'

While I am copying this (for it is no more indeed than a borrowed sketch from one of those originals before-mentioned),^Q I see a thousand ridicules arising from the manner, the circumstances and action itself, compared with modern breeding and civility. Let us therefore mend the matter if possible and introduce the same philosopher, addressing himself in a more obsequious manner, to 'his Grace', 'his Excellency', or 'his Honour', without failing in the least tittle of the ceremonial. Or let us put the case more favourably still for our man of letters. Let us suppose him to be incognito, without the least appearance of a character, which in our age is so little recommending. Let his garb and action be of the more modish sort in order to introduce him better and gain him audience. And with these advantages and precautions, imagine still in what manner he must accost this pageant of state, if at any time he finds him at leisure, walking in the fields alone and without his equipage. Consider how many bows and simpering faces! How many preludes, excuses, compliments! Now put compliments, put ceremony into a dialogue, and see what will be the effect!

This is the plain dilemma against that ancient manner of writing which we can neither well imitate nor translate, whatever pleasure or profit we may find in reading those originals. For what shall we do in such a circumstance? What if the fancy takes us and we resolve to try the experiment in modern subjects?

Q This is an adaptation of the opening of Plato's *Alcibiades* II.

See the consequence!——If we avoid ceremony, we are unnatural; if we use it and appear as we naturally are, as we salute and meet and treat one another, we hate the sight.——What is this but 'hating our own faces'? Is it the painter's fault? Should he paint falsely or affectedly, mix modern with ancient, join shapes preposterously and betray his art? If not, what medium is there? What remains for him but to throw away the pencil?——No more designing after the life, no more mirror writing or personal representation of any kind whatever.

Thus dialogue is at an end. The ancients could see their own faces, but we cannot.

And why this?

Why, but because we have less beauty, for so our looking-glass can inform us.

Ugly instrument! And for this reason to be hated.

Our commerce and manner of conversation, which we think the politest imaginable, is such, it seems, as we ourselves cannot endure to see represented to the life. It is here, as in our real portraitures, particularly those at full length, where the poor pencil-man is put to a thousand shifts while he strives to dress us in affected habits, such as we never wore, because, should he paint us in those we really wear, they would of necessity make the piece to be so much more ridiculous as it was more natural and resembling.

Thus much for antiquity and those rules of art, those philosophical sea-cards[R] by which the adventurous geniuses of the times were wont to steer their courses and govern their impetuous muse. These were the *chartae*[S] of our Roman master poet, and these the pieces of art, the mirrors, the exemplars he bids us place before our eyes: *You should handle Greek examples by night, you should handle them by day.*[15]

And thus poetry and the writer's art, as in many respects it resembles the statuary's and the painter's, so in this more particularly, that it has its original drafts and models for study and practice, not for ostentation, to be shown abroad or copied for public view. These are the ancient busts, the trunks of statues, the pieces of anatomy, the masterly rough drawings which are kept within, as the secret learning, the mystery and fundamental knowledge of the art. There is this essential difference however between the artists of each kind: that they who design merely after bodies and form the graces of this sort can never, with all their accuracy or correctness of design, be able to reform themselves or grow a jot more shapely in their persons. But for those artists who copy from another life, who study the graces and perfections of minds and are real masters of those rules which constitute this latter science, it is impossible

[R] A navigational map or chart of the sea.
[S] Texts.

[15] Horace, *The Art of Poetry* 268–9.

they should fail of being themselves improved and amended in their better part.

I must confess there is hardly anywhere to be found a more insipid race of mortals than those whom we moderns are contented to call poets for having attained the chiming faculty of a language with an injudicious random use of wit .and fancy. But for the man who truly and in a just sense deserves the name of poet, and who as a real master or architect in the kind can describe both men and manners and give to an action its just body and proportions, he will be found, if I mistake not, a very different creature. Such a poet is indeed a second Maker, a just Prometheus under Jove.[T] Like that sovereign artist or universal plastic nature,[U] he forms a whole, coherent and proportioned in itself, with due subjection and subordinacy of constituent parts. He notes the boundaries of the passions and knows their exact tones and measures, by which he justly represents them, marks the sublime of sentiments and action and distinguishes the beautiful from the deformed, the amiable from the odious. The moral artist who can thus imitate the Creator and is thus knowing in the inward form and structure of his fellow creature, will hardly, I presume, be found unknowing in *himself* or at a loss in those numbers which make the harmony of a mind. For knavery is mere dissonance and disproportion. And though villains may have strong tones and natural capacities of action, it is impossible that true judgment and ingenuity should reside where harmony and honesty have no being.[16]

[T] Prometheus was a Greek demi-god who as a cunning trickster repeatedly conflicted with Zeus, known to the Romans as Jupiter or Jove. However, Prometheus was also a master craftsman who was said to have created the first man and woman out of clay.

[U] 'Universal plastic nature', used here loosely to refer to divine powers of ordering, derived from language devised by Ralph Cudworth in *The True Intellectual System of the Universe* (1678) to provide an explanation for why the world was neither randomly organized nor mechanistic nor under the constant surveillance and immediate guidance of God. See J. A. Passmore, *Ralph Cudworth: An Interpretation* (Cambridge: Cambridge University Press, 1951), pp. 19–28.

[16] The maxim will hardly be disproved by fact or history, either in respect of philosophers themselves or others who were the great geniuses or masters in the liberal arts. The characters of the two best Roman poets [Virgil and Horace] are well known. Those of the ancient tragedians no less. And the great epic master [Homer], though of an obscurer and remoter age, was ever presumed to be far enough from a vile or knavish character. The Roman as well as the Grecian orator was true to his country and died in like manner a martyr for its liberty. And those historians who are of highest value were either in a private life approved good men or noted such by their actions in the public. As for poets in particular (says the learned and wise Strabo): 'Can we possibly imagine that the genius, power and excellence of a real poet consists in ought else than the just imitation of life in formed discourse and numbers? But how should he be that imitator of life while he himself knows not its measures nor how to guide himself by judgment and understanding? For we have not surely the same notion of the poet's excellence as of the ordinary craftsman's, the subject of whose art is senseless stone or timber, without life, dignity or beauty, while, the poet's art turning principally on men and manners, he has his virtue and excellence as poet naturally annexed to human excellence, and to the worth and dignity of man. Insomuch that it is impossible he should be a great and worthy poet, who is not first a worthy and good man.' Strabo, *Geography* 1.2.5. See pp. 125, 150, 156–7n, 442–3, 453, 457.

But having entered thus seriously into the concerns of authors and shown their chief foundation and strength, their preparatory discipline and qualifying method of self-examination, it is fit, before we disclose this mystery any further, we should consider the advantages or disadvantages our authors may possibly meet with from abroad, and how far their genius may be depressed or raised by any external causes arising from the humour or judgment of the world.

Whatever it be which influences in this respect must proceed either from the grandees and men in power, the critics and men of art, or the people themselves, the common audience and mere vulgar. We shall begin therefore with the grandees and pretended masters of the world, taking the liberty, in favour of authors, to bestow some advice also on these high persons, if possibly they are disposed to receive it in such a familiar way as this.

Part II

Section 1

As usual as it is with mankind to act absolutely by will and pleasure, without regard to counsel or the rigid method of rule and precept, it must be acknowledged nevertheless that the good and laudable custom of asking advice is still upheld and kept in fashion as a matter of fair repute and honourable appearance, insomuch that even monarchs, and absolute princes themselves, disdain not, we see, to make profession of the practice.[v]

It is, I presume, on this account that the royal persons are pleased on public occasions to make use of the noted style of 'we' and 'us'. Not that they are supposed to have any converse with themselves, as being endowed with the privilege of becoming plural and enlarging their capacity in the manner above-described. Single and absolute persons in government, I am sensible, can hardly be considered as any other than single and absolute in morals. They have no inmate-controller to cavil with them or dispute their pleasure. Nor have they, from any practice *abroad*, been able at any time to learn the way of being free and familiar with themselves *at home*. Inclination and will, in such as these, admit as little restraint or check in private meditation as in public company. The world, which serves as a tutor to persons of an inferior rank, is submissive to these royal pupils, who from their earliest days are used to see even

---

[v] On the role of this sort of advice literature in early modern political thought, see Quentin Skinner, *The Foundations of Modern Political Thought* (Cambridge: Cambridge University Press, 1979), I, 213–21, and on its relevance in the eighteenth century, see Dena Goodman, *Criticism in Action: Enlightenment Experiments in Political Writing* (Ithaca and London: Cornell University Press, 1989), pp. 6–15.

their instructors bend before them and hear everything applauded which they themselves perform.

For fear, therefore, lest their humour merely or the caprice of some favourite should be presumed to influence them when they come to years of princely discretion and are advanced to the helm of government, it has been esteemed a necessary decency to summon certain advisers by profession to assist as attendants to the single person and be joined with him in his written edicts, proclamations, letters-patent and other instruments of regal power. For this use, privy counsellors have been erected, who, being persons of considerable figure and wise aspect, cannot be supposed to stand as statues or mere ciphers in the government, and leave the royal acts erroneously and falsely described to us in the plural number, when at the bottom a single will or fancy was the sole spring and motive.

Foreign princes indeed have most of them that unhappy prerogative of acting unadvisedly and wilfully in their national affairs. But it is known to be far otherwise with the legal and just princes of our island. They are surrounded with the best of counsellors, the laws. They administer civil affairs by legal officers who have the direction of their public will and conscience, and they annually receive advice and aid in the most effectual manner from their good people. To this wise genius of our constitution, we may be justly said to owe our wisest and best princes, whose high birth or royal education could not alone be supposed to have given them that happy turn, since by experience we find that those very princes, from whose conduct the world abroad as well as we at home have reaped the greatest advantages, were such as had the most controverted titles and in their youth had stood in the remoter prospects of regal power and lived the nearest to a private life.[W]

Other princes we have had who, though difficult perhaps in receiving counsel, have been eminent in the practice of applying it to others. They have listed themselves advisers in form and, by publishing their admonitory works, have added to the number of those whom in this treatise we have presumed to criticize.[X] But our criticism being withal an apology for authors and a defence of the literate tribe, it cannot be thought amiss in us to join the royal with the plebeian penmen in this common cause.

It would be a hard case indeed should the princes of our nation refuse to countenance the industrious race of authors, since their royal ancestors and predecessors have had such honour derived to them from this profession. It is

[W] For example, Elizabeth I.
[X] For example, James I. See p. 96n.

to this they owe that bright jewel of their crown, purchased by a warlike prince who, having assumed the author and essayed his strength in the polemic writings of the School divines, thought it an honour on this account to retain the title of 'Defender of the Faith'.[Y]

Another prince, of a more pacific nature and fluent thought, submitting arms and martial discipline to the Gown and confiding in his princely science and profound learning, made his style and speech the nerve and sinew of his government. He gave us his works full of wise exhortation and advice to his royal son as well as of instruction to his good people, who could not without admiration observe their author-sovereign thus studious and contemplative in their behalf.[Z] It was then one might have seen our nation growing young and docile, with that simplicity of heart which qualified them to profit like a scholar-people under their royal preceptor. For with abundant eloquence he graciously gave lessons to his parliament, tutored his ministers and edified the greatest churchmen and divines themselves, by whose suffrage he obtained the highest appellations which could be merited by the acutest wit and truest understanding. From hence the British nations were taught to own in common a Solomon for their joint sovereign, the founder of their late completed Union. Nor can it be doubted that the pious treatise of self-discourse ascribed to the succeeding monarch contributed in a great measure to his glorious and never-fading title of Saint and Martyr.[AA]

However it be, I would not willingly take upon me to recommend this author-character to our future princes. Whatever crowns or laurels their renowned predecessors may have gathered in this field of honour, I should think that, for the future, the speculative province might more properly be committed to private heads. It would be a sufficient encouragement to the learned world and a sure earnest of the increase and flourishing of letters in our nation if its sovereigns would be contented to be the patrons of wit and vouchsafe to look graciously on the ingenious pupils of art. Or, were it the custom of their prime ministers to have any such regard, it would of itself be sufficient to change the face of affairs. A small degree of favour would ensure

---

[Y] In 1521, Henry VIII published *Assertio septem sacramentorum*, 'Defence of the Seven Sacraments', his attack on the heresies of Martin Luther. Henry dedicated the volume to Pope Leo X, who rewarded the monarch with the title 'Defender of the Faith', which he retained after the Reformation and passed on to his successors.

[Z] James I wrote *Basilikon Doron, or His Majesty's Instructions to His Dearest Son, Henry the Prince*, published in 1599, and, among other compositions for his subjects' benefit, *The True Law of Free Monarchies, or the Reciprocal and Mutual Duty betwixt a Free King and His Natural Subjects*, published in 1603. James was already James VI of Scotland when he inherited the English throne at the death of Elizabeth I in 1603. This regal union of the two nations was followed a century later by a parliamentary union in the Act of Union, 1707.

[AA] Charles I, Εἰκων Βασιλικη. *The Portraiture of His Sacred Majesty in His Solitude and Sufferings* (1649).

the fortunes of a distressed and ruinous tribe whose forlorn condition has helped to draw disgrace upon arts and sciences and kept them far off from that politeness and beauty in which they would soon appear if the aspiring genius of our nation were forwarded by the least care or culture.

There should not, one would think, be any need of courtship or persuasion to engage our grandees in the patronage of arts and letters. For, in our nation, upon the foot things stand and as they are likely to continue, it is not difficult to foresee that improvements will be made in every art and science. The Muses will have their turn and, with or without their Maecenases, will grow in credit and esteem as they arrive to greater perfection and excel in every kind.[BB] There will arise such spirits as would have credited their Court patrons, had they found any so wise as to have sought them out betimes and contributed to their rising greatness.

It is scarce a quarter of an age since such a happy balance of power was settled between our prince and people as has firmly secured our hitherto precarious liberties and removed from us the fear of civil commotions, wars and violence, either on account of religion and worship, the property of the subject, or the contending titles of the Crown.[CC] But, as the greatest advantages of this world are not to be bought at easy prices, we are still at this moment expending both our blood and treasure to secure to ourselves this inestimable purchase of our free government and national constitution.[DD] And as happy as we are in this establishment at home, we are still held in a perpetual alarm by the aspect of affairs abroad and by the terror of that power which, before mankind had well recovered the misery of those barbarous ages consequent to the Roman yoke, has again threatened the world with a universal monarchy and a new abyss of ignorance and superstition.[EE]

The British Muses, in this din of arms, may well lie abject and obscure, especially being as yet in their mere infant state. They have hitherto scarce arrived to anything of shapeliness or person. They lisp as in their cradles and their stammering tongues, which nothing beside their youth and rawness can excuse, have hitherto spoken in wretched pun and quibble. Our dramatic Shakespeare, our Fletcher, Jonson and our epic Milton preserve this style. And even a latter race, scarce free of this infirmity and aiming at a false sublime, with crowded simile and mixed metaphor (the hobby-horse and rattle of the

---

[BB] For the Muses, see p. 5n. For Maecenas, see Introduction, p. xxii.

[CC] That is, since the Revolution of 1688.

[DD] England had been at war with France for most of the years since the Revolution.

[EE] France was regularly criticized as seeking a universal monarchy. See Steven Pincus, *Protestantism and Patriotism: Ideologies and the Making of English Foreign Policy 1650–1668* (Cambridge: Cambridge University Press, 1996).

Muses), entertain our raw fancy and unpractised ear, which has not as yet had leisure to form itself and become truly musical.[17]

But those reverend bards, rude as they were according to their time and age, have provided us however with the richest ore. To their eternal honour they have withal been the first of Europeans who, since the Gothic model of poetry, attempted to throw off the horrid discord of jingling rhyme. They have asserted ancient poetic liberty and have happily broken the ice for those who are to follow them and who, treading in their footsteps, may at leisure polish our language, lead our ear to finer pleasure and find out the true rhythmus and harmonious numbers, which alone can satisfy a just judgment and muse-like apprehension.

It is evident our natural genius shines above that airy neighbouring nation,[FF] of whom, however, it must be confessed that, with truer pains and industry, they have sought politeness and studied to give the Muses their due body and proportion as well as the natural ornaments of correctness, chastity and grace of style. From the plain model of the ancients, they have raised a noble satirist.[18] In the epic kind their attempts have been less successful. In the dramatic they have been so happy as to raise their stage to as great perfection as the genius of their nation will permit.[GG] But the high spirit of tragedy can ill subsist where the spirit of liberty is wanting. The genius of this poetry consists in the lively representation of the disorders and misery of the great, to the end that the people and those of a lower condition may be taught the better to content themselves with privacy, enjoy their safer state and prize the equality and justice of their guardian laws. If this be found agreeable to the just tragic model, which the ancients have delivered to us, it will easily be conceived how little such a model is proportioned to the capacity or taste of those who, in a long series of degrees from the lowest peasant to the high slave of royal blood, are taught to idolize the next in power above them and think nothing so adorable as that unlimited greatness and tyrannic power, which is raised at their own expense and exercised over themselves.

It is easy, on the other hand, to apprehend the advantages of our Britain in this particular and what effect its established liberty will produce in everything which relates to art, when peace returns to us on these happy conditions. It was the fate of Rome to have scarce an intermediate age or single period of time between the rise of arts and fall of liberty. No sooner had that nation

---

[FF] France.
[GG] In the plays of Jean Racine, 1639–99, and Pierre Corneille, 1606–84.

[17] See p. 450.
[18] Boileau. [Nicolas Boileau-Despréaux, 1636–1711, was the author of a wide range of classically inspired verse satires which gained him many enemies but also the patronage of Louis XIV.]

begun to lose the roughness and barbarity of their manners and learn of Greece to form their heroes, their orators and poets on a right model than, by their unjust attempt upon the liberty of the world, they justly lost their own.[HH] With their liberty, they lost not only their force of eloquence but even their style and language itself. The poets who afterwards arose among them were mere unnatural and forced plants. Their two most accomplished, who came last and closed the scene, were plainly such as had seen the days of liberty and felt the sad effects of its departure.[II] Nor had these been ever brought in play, otherwise than through the friendship of the famed Maecenas, who turned a prince naturally cruel and barbarous to the love and courtship of the Muses.[19] These tutoresses formed in their royal pupil a new nature. They taught him how to charm mankind. They were more to him than his arms or military virtue and, more than Fortune herself, assisted him in his greatness and made his usurped dominion so enchanting to the world that it could see without regret its chains of bondage firmly riveted. The corrupting sweets of such a poisonous government were not indeed long-lived. The bitter soon succeeded. And, in the issue, the world was forced to bear with patience those natural and genuine tyrants who succeeded to this specious machine of arbitrary and universal power.

And now that I am fallen unawares into such profound reflections on the periods of government and the flourishing and decay of liberty and letters, I cannot be contented to consider merely of the enchantment which wrought so powerfully upon mankind when first this universal monarchy was established. I must wonder still more when I consider how, after the extinction of this Caesarean and Claudian family, and a short interval of princes raised and destroyed with much disorder and public ruin, the Romans should regain their perishing dominion and retrieve their sinking state by an after-race of wise and able princes successively adopted and taken from a private state to rule the empire of the world.[JJ] They were men who not only possessed the military virtues and supported that sort of discipline in the highest degree, but, as they sought the interest of the world, they did what was in their power to restore liberty and raise again the perishing arts and decayed virtue of mankind. But the season was now past! The fatal form of government was become too natural, and the world, which had bent under it and was become slavish and

---

[HH] This is a telegraphic account of a Whiggish version of Roman history in the second and first centuries BC: the expansion of Rome into the eastern Mediterranean brought greater cultural sophistication while also allowing social and political developments that destabilized the institutions of the Republic and led to the establishment of the Empire under Augustus from about 27 BC.

[II] Virgil and Horace.

[JJ] This account is designed to create a respectable role for the Antonines, especially Marcus Aurelius Antoninus. See Introduction, p. xxiv.

[19] See p. 121n. [On the prince, Augustus Caesar, and Maecenas, see Introduction, p. xxii.]

dependent, had neither power nor will to help itself. The only deliverance it could expect was from the merciless hands of the barbarians and a total dissolution of that enormous empire and despotic power, which the best hands could not preserve from being destructive to human nature. For even barbarity and Gothicism were already entered into arts before the savages had made any impression on the empire. All the advantage which a fortuitous and almost miraculous succession of good princes could procure their highly favoured arts and sciences, was no more than to preserve during their own time those perishing remains, which had for a while with difficulty subsisted after the decline of liberty.[20] Not a statue, not a medal, not a tolerable piece of architecture could show itself afterwards. Philosophy, wit and learning, in which some of those good princes had themselves been so renowned, fell with them, and ignorance and darkness overspread the world and fitted it for the chaos and ruin which ensued.

We are now in an age when liberty is once again in its ascendant. And we are ourselves the happy nation who not only enjoy it at home but, by our greatness and power, give life and vigour to it abroad and are the head and chief of the European league, founded on this common cause. Nor can it, I presume, be justly feared that we should lose this noble ardour or faint under the glorious toil, though, like ancient Greece, we should for succeeding ages be contending with a foreign power and endeavouring to reduce the exorbitancy of a Grand Monarch.[KK] It is with us at present as with the Roman people in those early days when they wanted only repose from arms to apply themselves to the improvement of arts and studies.[21] We should in this case need no ambitious monarch to be allured, by hope of fame or secret views of power, to give pensions abroad as well as at home and purchase flattery from every profession and science. We should find a better fund within ourselves and might, without such assistance, be able to excel by our own virtue and emulation.

Well it would be, indeed, and much to the honour of our nobles and princes, would they freely help in this affair and, by a judicious application of their bounty, facilitate this happy birth, of which I have ventured to speak in a prophetic style. It would be of no small advantage to them during their life and would, more than all their other labours, procure them an immortal memory. For they must remember that their fame is in the hands of penmen and that the greatest actions lose their force and perish in the custody of unable and mean writers.

[KK] A reference to the long antagonism between the ancient Greek city-states and the Persian empire.

[20] See pp. 107, 152n.

[21] *Not till late did the Roman stir his wits toward Greek texts, and, in the peace after the Punic wars, begin to ask what use could be made of Sophocles and Thespis and Aeschylus*: Horace, *Epistles* 2.1.161–3.

Let a nation remain ever so rude or barbarous, it must have its poets, rhapsoders, historiographers, antiquaries of some kind or other, whose business it will be to recount its remarkable transactions and record the achievements of its civil and military heroes. And, though the military kind may happen to be the farthest removed from any acquaintance with letters or the Muses, they are yet, in reality, the most interested in the cause and party of these remembrancers. The greatest share of fame and admiration falls naturally on the armed worthies. The great in council are second in the Muses' favour. But, if worthy poetic geniuses are not found nor able penmen raised to rehearse the lives and celebrate the high actions of great men, they must be traduced by such recorders as chance presents. We have few modern heroes who, like Xenophon or Caesar, can write their own commentaries.[LL] And the raw memoir-writings and unformed pieces of modern statesmen, full of their interested and private views, will in another age be of little service to support their memory or name, since already the world begins to sicken with the kind. It is the learned, the able and disinterested historian who takes place at last. And when the signal poet or herald of fame is once heard, the inferior trumpets sink in silence and oblivion.

But supposing it were possible for the hero or statesman to be absolutely unconcerned for his memory or what came after him, yet, for the present merely and during his own time, it must be of importance to him to stand fair with the men of letters and ingenuity and to have the character and repute of being favourable to their art. Be the illustrious person ever so high or awful in his station, he must have descriptions made of him in verse and prose under feigned or real appellations. If he be omitted in sound ode or lofty epic, he must be sung at least in doggerel and plain ballad. The people will needs have his effigies, though they see his person ever so rarely, and, if he refuses to sit to the good painter, there are others who, to oblige the public, will take the design in hand. We shall take up with what presents[MM] and, rather than be without the illustrious physiognomy of our great man, shall be contented to see him portraitured by the artist who serves to illustrate prodigies in fairs and adorn heroic sign-posts. The ill paint of this kind cannot, it is true, disgrace his excellence, whose privilege it is, in common with the royal issue, to be raised to this degree of honour and to invite the passenger or traveller by his signal representative. It is supposed in this case that there are better pictures current of

---

[LL] Xenophon, for whom see Introduction, p. xxii, provided an account of his military adventures in Asia Minor in *Anabasis*. Julius Caesar described his military exploits in the *Gallic Wars* and the *Civil Wars*.

[MM] According to a marginal note (I, 225) in Shaftesbury's copy of the 1711 edition (see Note on the text): 'The Expression of "We shall take up", I must confess, is somewhat coarse: But it is to be considered that this paragraph is plainly in the comic and ironical style, for which reason I alter nothing in it.'

the hero and that such as these are no true or favourable representations. But, in another sort of limning, there is great danger lest the hand should disgrace the subject. Vile encomiums and wretched panegyrics are the worst of satires and, when sordid and low geniuses make their court successfully in one way, the generous and able are aptest to revenge it in another.

All things considered as to the interest of our potentates and grandees, they appear to have only this choice left them: either wholly, if possible, to suppress letters or give a helping hand towards their support. Wherever the author-practice and liberty of the pen has in the least prevailed, the governors of the state must be either considerable gainers or sufferers by its means. So that it would become them either, by a right Turkish policy,[NN] to strike directly at the profession and overthrow the very art and mystery itself, or with alacrity to support and encourage it in the right manner by a generous and impartial regard to merit. To act narrowly or by halves, or with indifference and coolness, or fantastically and by humour, merely will scarce be found to turn to their account. They must do justice that justice may be done them in return. It will be in vain for our Alexanders to give orders that none besides a Lysippus should make their statue, nor any besides an Apelles should draw their picture. Insolent intruders will do themselves the honour to practise on the features of these heroes. And a vile Choerilus after all shall, with their own consent perhaps, supply the room of a deserving and noble artist.[OO]

In a government where the people are sharers in power but no distributers or dispensers of rewards, they expect it of their princes and great men that they should supply the generous part and bestow honour and advantages on those from whom the nation itself may receive honour and advantage. It is expected that they who are high and eminent in the state should not only provide for its necessary safety and subsistence but omit nothing which may contribute to its dignity and honour. The arts and sciences must not be left patronless. The public itself will join with the good wits and judges in the resentment of such a neglect. It is no small advantage, even in an absolute government, for a ministry to have wit on their side and engage the men of merit in this kind to be their well-wishers and friends. And in those states where ambitious leaders often contend for the supreme authority, it is a considerable advantage to the ill cause of such pretenders when they can obtain a name and interest with the men of letters. The good emperor Trajan, though himself no mighty scholar, had his due as well as an Augustus and was as highly

---

[NN] For Turkey, see Introduction, p. xviii.
[OO] The painter Apelles of Colophon and the sculptor Lysippus of Sicyon were outstanding artists of the later fourth century BC. According to Pliny, *Natural History* 7.125, Alexander the Great ordered that only Apelles should paint his picture and only Lysippus should cast him in bronze. The epic poet Choerilus was paid by Alexander to write verses flattering to the conqueror; thus, his name became a byword for the meretricious artist.

celebrated for his munificence and just encouragement of every art and virtue.[PP] And Caesar, who could write so well himself and maintained his cause by wit as well as arms, knew experimentally what it was to have even a Catullus his enemy and, though lashed so often in his lampoons, continued to forgive and court him.[QQ] The traitor knew the importance of this mildness. May none who have the same designs understand so well the advantages of such a conduct! I would have required only this one defect in Caesar's generosity to have been secure of his never rising to greatness or enslaving his native country. Let him have shown a ruggedness and austerity towards free geniuses, or a neglect or contempt towards men of wit, let him have trusted to his arms and declared against arts and letters, and he would have proved a second Marius or a Catiline of meaner fame and character.[RR]

It is, I know, the imagination of some who are called 'great men' that, in regard of their high stations, they may be esteemed to pay a sufficient tribute to letters, and discharge themselves as to their own part in particular, if they choose indifferently any subject for their bounty and are pleased to confer their favour either on some one pretender to art, or promiscuously to such of the tribe of writers whose chief ability has lain in making their court well and obtaining to be introduced to their acquaintance. This they think sufficient to install them patrons of wit and masters of the literate order. But this method will of any other the least serve their interest or design. The ill placing of rewards is a double injury to merit and, in every cause or interest, passes for worse than mere indifference or neutrality. There can be no excuse for making an ill choice. Merit in every kind is easily discovered when sought. The public itself fails not to give sufficient indication and points out those geniuses who want only countenance and encouragement to become considerable. An ingenious man never starves unknown, and great men must wink hard or it would be impossible for them to miss such advantageous opportunities of showing their generosity and acquiring the universal esteem, acknowledgments and good wishes of the ingenious and learned part of mankind.

Section 2

What judgment therefore we are to form concerning the influence of our grandees in matters of art and letters, will easily be gathered from the reflec-

---

[PP] Trajan, Marcus Ulpius Traianus, 53–117, was Roman emperor from 98 to 117 AD.

[QQ] Gaius Valerius Catullus, *c.* 84–*c.* 54 BC, was a lyric poet, most famous for his erotic verse, who was well connected in the highest literary and social circles of Rome. His satires strongly attacked Julius Caesar although a reconciliation was reported to have taken place.

[RR] Gaius Marius, 157–86 BC, was a Roman general whose ambitions led him to dominate the government in a tyranny that anticipated Julius Caesar's. Lucius Sergius Catilina, d. 62 BC, was a military man who turned to conspiracy and violence when his efforts in the usual constitutional routes were thwarted.

tions already made. It may appear from the very freedom we have taken in censuring these men of power, what little reason authors have to plead them as their excuse for any failure in the improvement of their art and talent. For, in a free country such as ours, there is not any order or rank of men more free than that of writers, who, if they have real ability and merit, can fully right themselves when injured and are ready furnished with means sufficient to make themselves considered by the men in highest power.

Nor should I suspect the genius of our writers or charge them with meanness and insufficiency on the account of this low-spiritedness which they discover, were it not for another sort of fear by which they more plainly betray themselves and seem conscious of their own defect. The critics, it seems, are formidable to them. The critics are the dreadful spectres, the giants, the enchanters, who traverse and disturb them in their works. These are the persecutors for whose sake they are ready to hide their heads, begging rescue and protection of all good people and flying in particular to the great, by whose favour they hope to be defended from this merciless examining race. 'For what can be more cruel than to be forced to submit to the rigorous laws of wit, and write under such severe judges as are deaf to all courtship and can be wrought upon by no insinuation or flattery to pass by faults and pardon any transgression of art?'

To judge indeed of the circumstances of a modern author by the pattern of his prefaces, dedications and introductions,[22] one would think that, at the moment when a piece of his was in hand, some conjuration was forming against him, some diabolical powers drawing together to blast his work and cross his generous design. He therefore rouses his indignation, hardens his forehead and, with many furious defiances and 'Avaunt[SS] Satans!', enters on his business, not with the least regard to what may justly be objected to him in a way of criticism, but with an absolute contempt of the manner and art itself.

I hate the unruly crowd, and I shun it[23] was in its time, no doubt, a generous defiance. The 'Avaunt!' was natural and proper in its place, especially where religion and virtue were the poet's theme. But with our moderns the case is generally the very reverse. And accordingly the defiance or 'Avaunt!' should run much after this manner:

'As for you vulgar souls, mere naturals, who know no art, were never admitted into the temple of wisdom nor ever visited the sanctuaries of wit or learning, gather yourselves together from all parts and hearken to the song or tale I am about to utter. But for you men of science and understanding, who have ears and judgment and can weigh sense, scan syllables and measure sounds,

---

[SS] Be gone!

[22] See pp. 147, 448, 455n.

[23] Horace, *Odes* 3.1.1.

you who by a certain art distinguish false thought from true, correctness from rudeness and bombast, and chaos from order and the sublime, away hence! or stand aloof! while I practise upon the easiness of those mean capacities and apprehensions, who make the most numerous audience and are the only competent judges of my labours.'

It is strange to see how differently the vanity of mankind runs in different times and seasons. It is at present the boast of almost every enterpriser in the Muses' art that, 'by his genius alone and a natural rapidity of style and thought, he is able to carry all before him', that 'he plays with his business, does things in passing at a venture and in the quickest period of time'. In the days of Attic[TT] elegance, as works were then truly of another form and turn, so workmen were of another humour and had their vanity of a quite contrary kind. They became rather affected in endeavouring to discover the pains they had taken to be correct. They were glad to insinuate how laboriously and with what expense of time they had brought the smallest work of theirs (as perhaps a single ode or satire, an oration or panegyric) to its perfection. When they had so polished their piece and rendered it so natural and easy that it seemed only a lucky flight, a hit of thought or flowing vein of humour, they were then chiefly concerned lest it should in reality pass for such and their artifice remain undiscovered. They were willing it should be known how serious their play was and how elaborate their freedom and facility that they might say, as the agreeable and polite poet, glancing on himself: *He will give the appearance of playing and yet he will be in torture.*[24] And: *So that anybody may hope the same for himself, may sweat a great deal and toil in vain, daring the same, so great is the power of order and correctness.*[25]

Such accuracy of workmanship requires a critic's eye. It is lost upon a vulgar judgment. Nothing grieves a real artist more than that indifference of the public which suffers work to pass uncriticized. Nothing, on the other side, rejoices him more than the nice view and inspection of the accurate examiner and judge of work. It is the mean genius, the slovenly performer, who knowing nothing of true workmanship, endeavours by the best outward gloss and dazzling show to turn the eye from a direct and steady survey of his piece.

What is there which an expert musician more earnestly desires than to perform his part in the presence of those who are knowing in his art? It is to the ear alone he applies himself – the critical, the nice ear. Let his hearers be of what character they please, be they naturally austere, morose or rigid – no matter, so they are critics, able to censure, remark and sound every accord and symphony. What is there mortifies the good painter more than when, amid his

[TT] Characteristic of classical Athens.

[24] Horace, *Epistles* 2.2.124.
[25] Horace, *The Art of Poetry* 242–4.

admiring spectators, there is not one present who has been used to compare the hands of different masters or has an eye to distinguish the advantages or defects of every style? Through all the inferior orders of mechanics, the rule is found to hold the same. In every science, every art, the real masters or proficients rejoice in nothing more than in the thorough search and examination of their performances by all the rules of art and nicest criticism. Why therefore (in the Muses' name!) is it not the same with our pretenders to the writing art, our poets and prose authors in every kind? Why in this profession are we found such critic-haters and indulged in this unlearned aversion, unless it be taken for granted that, as wit and learning stand at present in our nation, we are still upon the foot of empirics and mountebanks?[UU]

From these considerations I take upon me absolutely to condemn the fashionable and prevailing custom of inveighing against critics as the common enemies, the pests and incendiaries of the commonwealth of wit and letters. I assert, on the contrary, that they are the props and pillars of this building and that, without the encouragement and propagation of such a race, we should remain as Gothic architects as ever.

In the weaker and more imperfect societies of mankind, such as those composed of federate tribes or mixed colonies, scarce settled in their new seats, it might pass for sufficient good fortune if the people proved only so far masters of language as to be able to understand one another, in order to confer about their wants and provide for their common necessities.[26] Their exposed and indigent state could not be presumed to afford them either that full leisure or easy disposition which was requisite to raise them to any curiosity of speculation. They who were neither safe from violence nor secure of plenty were unlikely to engage in unnecessary arts. Nor could it be expected they should turn their attention towards the numbers of their language and the harmonious sounds which they accidentally emitted. But when, in process of time, the affairs of the society were settled on an easy and secure foundation, when debates and discourses on these subjects of common interest and public good were grown familiar, and the speeches of prime men and leaders were considered and compared together, there would naturally be observed not only a more agreeable measure of sound but a happier and more easy rangement of thoughts in one speaker than in another.

It may be easily perceived from hence that the goddess Persuasion must have been in a manner the mother of poetry, rhetoric, music and the other kindred arts. For it is apparent that, where chief men and leaders had the strongest interest to persuade, they used the highest endeavours to please. So that, in

[UU] Quack doctors and purveyors of remedies.

[26] As to this, and what remains of this section, see p. 396ff.

such a state or polity as has been described, not only the best order of thought and turn of fancy but the most soft and inviting numbers must have been employed to charm the public ear and to incline the heart by the agreeableness of expression.

Almost all the ancient masters of this sort were said to have been musicians. And tradition, which soon grew fabulous, could not better represent the first founders or establishers of these larger societies than as real songsters who, by the power of their voice and lyre, could charm the wildest beasts and draw the rude forests and rocks into the form of fairest cities.[vv] Nor can it be doubted that the same artists who so industriously applied themselves to study the numbers of speech must have made proportionable improvements in the study of mere sounds and natural harmony, which, of itself, must have considerably contributed towards the softening the rude manners and harsh temper of their new people.

If therefore it so happened in these free communities, made by consent and voluntary association, that after a while the power of one or of a few grew prevalent over the rest, if force took place and the affairs of the society were administered without their concurrence by the influence of awe and terror, it followed that these pathetic sciences and arts of speech were little cultivated since they were of little use. But where persuasion was the chief means of guiding the society, where the people were to be convinced before they acted, there elocution became considerable, there orators and bards were heard, and the chief geniuses and sages of the nation betook themselves to the study of those arts by which the people were rendered more treatable in a way of reason and understanding, and more subject to be led by men of science and erudition. The more these artists courted the public, the more they instructed it. In such constitutions as these, it was the interest of the wise and able that the community should be judges of ability and wisdom. The high esteem of ingenuity was what advanced the ingenious to the greatest honours. And they who rose by science and politeness in the higher arts could not fail to promote that taste and relish to which they owed their personal distinction and pre-eminence.

Hence it is that those arts have been delivered to us in such perfection by free nations, who, from the nature of their government as from a proper soil, produced the generous plants, while the mightiest bodies and vastest empires, governed by force and a despotic power, could, after ages of peace and leisure, produce no other than what was deformed and barbarous of the kind.

When the persuasive arts were grown thus into repute and the power of moving the affections become the study and emulation of the forward wits and aspiring geniuses of the times, it would necessarily happen that many geniuses

---

[vv] This tradition is expressed in Isocrates, *Nicocles or the Cyprians* 5–9, and in Cicero, *On Invention* 1.1.2–3.

of equal size and strength, though less covetous of public applause, of power or of influence over mankind, would content themselves with the contemplation merely of these enchanting arts. These they would the better enjoy, the more they refined their taste and cultivated their ear. For to all music there must be an ear proportionable. There must be an art of hearing found before the performing arts can have their due effect or anything exquisite in the kind be felt or comprehended. The just performers therefore in each art would naturally be the most desirous of improving and refining the public ear, which they could no way so well effect as by the help of those latter geniuses, who were in a manner their interpreters to the people, and who by their example taught the public to discover what was just and excellent in each performance.

Hence was the origin of critics, who, as arts and sciences advanced, would necessarily come withal into repute and, being heard with satisfaction in their turn, were at length tempted to become authors and appear in public. These were honoured with the name of sophists, a character which in early times was highly respected. Nor did the gravest philosophers, who were censors of manners and critics of a higher degree, disdain to exert their criticism in the inferior arts, especially in those relating to speech and the power of argument and persuasion.

When such a race as this was once risen, it was no longer possible to impose on mankind by what was specious and pretending. The public would be paid in no false wit or jingling eloquence. Where the learned critics were so well received and philosophers themselves disdained not to be of the number, there could not fail to arise critics of an inferior order who would subdivide the several provinces of this empire. Etymologists, philologists, grammarians, rhetoricians, and others of considerable note and eminent in their degree, would everywhere appear and vindicate the truth and justice of their art by revealing the hidden beauties which lay in the works of just performers and by exposing the weak sides, false ornaments and affected graces of mere pretenders. Nothing of what we call sophistry in argument or bombast in style, nothing of the effeminate kind or of the false tender, the pointed witticism, the disjointed thought, the crowded simile, or the mixed metaphor, could pass even on the common ear while the notaries, the expositors and prompters above-mentioned were everywhere at hand and ready to explode the unnatural manner.

It is easy to imagine that, amid the several styles and manners of discourse or writing, the easiest attained and earliest practised was the miraculous, the pompous or what we generally call the sublime. Astonishment is of all other passions the easiest raised in raw and unexperienced mankind. Children in their earliest infancy are entertained in this manner, and the known way of pleasing such as these is to make them wonder and lead the way for them in this passion by a feigned surprise at the miraculous objects we set before them. The best music of barbarians is hideous and astonishing sounds. And the fine sights

of Indians are enormous figures, various odd and glaring colours and whatever
of that sort is amazingly beheld with a kind of horror and consternation.

In poetry and studied prose, the astonishing part, or what commonly passes
for sublime, is formed by the variety of figures, the multiplicity of metaphors,
and by quitting as much as possible the natural and easy way of expression for
that which is most unlike to humanity or ordinary use.[27] This the prince of
critics assures us to have been the manner of the earliest poets, before the age
of Homer, or till such time as this father-poet came into repute, who deposed
that spurious race and gave rise to a legitimate and genuine kind. He retained
only what was decent of the figurative or metaphoric style, introduced the natural and simple, and turned his thoughts towards the real beauty of composition, the unity of design, the truth of characters and the just imitation of nature
in each particular.

The manner of this father-poet was afterwards variously imitated and divided
into several shares, especially when it came to be copied in dramatic. Tragedy
came first and took what was most solemn and sublime. In this part the poets
succeeded sooner than in comedy or the facetious kind, as was natural indeed
to suppose, since this was in reality the easiest manner of the two and capable
of being brought the soonest to perfection. For so the same prince of critics
sufficiently informs us.[28] And it is highly worth remarking what this mighty
genius and judge of art declares concerning tragedy: that whatever idea might
be formed of the utmost perfection of this kind of poem, it could in practice
rise no higher than it had been already carried in his time, 'having at length',

---

[27] *The mark of style is to be clear and not commonplace. The clearest style is made up of ordinary phrases
but it is commonplace . . . That which uses unfamiliar phrases is dignified and varies from familiar
idiom. By 'unfamiliar', I mean dialect and metaphor and lengthening and everything that is contrary
to what is ordinary. But if anyone composes entirely in this way, the result will be either obscurity or
gibberish; if he composes in metaphors, the result will be obscurity and, if in dialect words, gibberish:*
Aristotle, *Poetics* 22.1–4. This the same master critic explains further in his *Rhetoric* 3.1.9, where
he refers to these passages in his *Poetics: Since poets, although their utterances be silly, seemed to
have obtained a reputation because of style, a poetic style developed first . . . Even now many of the
uneducated think that such men express themselves most beautifully. But this is not so . . . For not even
composers of tragedy still use it in the same way, but, just as they have changed from tetrameters to
the iambic metre because this of all the other metres is most like speech, so too have they abandoned
all the words that are different from ordinary conversation . . . And even now those who compose hexa-
meters have abandoned them; consequently, it is ridiculous to imitate those who no longer themselves
use that manner of writing.* That, among the early reformers of this bombastic manner, he places
Homer as the chief, we may see easily in his *Poetics*, as particularly in that passage (24.3):
*Moreover, the thoughts and style should be attractive. Homer used all these and for the first time and
satisfactorily . . . In addition, they surpassed all poetry in style and thought.*

[28] *Tragedy originated in improvisation – and comedy too . . .*: Aristotle, *Poetics* 4:14. When he has
compared both this and tragedy together, he recapitulates in his next chapter (5.3): *Now, the
transformations of tragedy and those responsible for them are not obscure, but comedy was obscure
because of not being taken seriously from the beginning. And the archon [a chief magistrate] did not
give a chorus to a comedian until late . . .* See p. 398n.

says he, 'attained its ends and being apparently consummate in itself'.[29] But for comedy, it seems, it was still in hand. It had been already in some manner reduced, but, as he plainly insinuates, it lay yet unfinished, notwithstanding the witty labours of an Aristophanes and the other comic poets of the first manner, who had flourished a whole age before this critic.[WW] As perfect as were those wits in style and language, and as fertile in all the varieties and turns of humour, yet the truth of characters, the beauty of order and the simple imitation of nature were in a manner wholly unknown to them or, through petulancy or debauch of humour, were, it seems, neglected and set aside. A Menander had not as yet appeared, who arose soon after to accomplish the prophecy of our grand master of art and consummate philologist.[XX]

Comedy[30] had at this time done little more than what the ancient parodies[31] had done before it. It was of admirable use to explode the false sublime of early poets and such as in its own age were on every occasion ready to relapse into that vicious manner. The good tragedians themselves could hardly escape its lashes. The pompous orators were its never-failing subjects. Everything which

---

[WW] The Athenian playwright Aristophanes, *c.* 450–*c.* 385 BC, was the only practitioner of the Old Comedy whose works have survived. The Old Comedy was abusively satirical and highly personal.

[XX] Menander, 342–291 BC, also an Athenian, was the outstanding practitioner of the New Comedy, which was milder than the Old Comedy and devoted to the treatment of everyday life and manners.

[29] Aristotle, *Poetics* 4.15. So true a prophet as well as critic was this great man. For by the event it appeared that tragedy, being raised to its height by Sophocles and Euripides and no room left for further excellence or emulation, there were no more tragic poets besides these endured after the author's time. While comedy went on improving still to the second and third degree, tragedy finished its course under Euripides, whom, though our great author criticizes with the utmost severity in his *Poetics*, yet he plainly enough confesses to have carried the style of tragedy to its full height and dignity. For, as to the reformation which that poet made in the use of the sublime and figurative speech in general, see what our discerning author says in his *Rhetoric* 3.2.4–5, where he strives to show the impertinence and nauseousness of the florid speakers and such as understood not the use of the simple and natural manner. 'The just masters and right managers of the poetic or high style should learn', says he, 'how to conceal the manner as much as possible'. *Consequently it is necessary to conceal doing this and not to seem to speak artificially but naturally. For this is persuasive but that, the opposite, prompting suspicion, as though at a hostile plotter, just as at wines that have been mixed; and such was the case with Theodorus' voice contrasted with the other actors', for his voice seemed to be that of the speaker whereas the others' seemed alien. The trick is to pick one's words from customary usage which Euripides does and he was the pioneer.*

[30] *And just as Homer was especially a poet in serious matters [for he alone was not just a good but a dramatic poet in his mimetic representations], so too was he the first to mark out the outlines of comedy*: Aristotle, *Poetics* 4.12. No wonder if, in this descent, comedy came late. See pp. 89, 114n.

[31] The parodies were very ancient, but they were in reality no other than mere burlesque or farce. Comedy, which borrowed something from those humours as well as from the Phallica belowmentioned [see n. 35], was not, however, raised to any form or shape of art, as said above, till about the time of Aristophanes, who was of the first model and a beginner of the kind, at the same time that tragedy had undergone all its changes and was already come to its last perfection, as the grand critic has shown us and as our other authorities plainly evince.

might be imposing, by a false gravity or solemnity, was forced to endure the trial of this touchstone. Manners and characters, as well as speech and writings, were discussed with the greatest freedom. Nothing could be better fitted than this genius of wit to unmask the face of things and remove those *larvae*[YY] naturally formed from the tragic manner and pompous style which had preceded. *And he taught how to speak grandly and soar in the buskin. After these, Old Comedy arrived.*[32]

It was not by chance that this succession happened in Greece after the manner described, but rather through necessity and from the reason and nature of things.[33] For in healthy bodies, nature dictates remedies of her own and provides for the cure of what has happened amiss in the growth and progress of a constitution. The affairs of this free people being in the increase, and their ability and judgment every day improving as letters and arts advanced, they would of course find in themselves a strength of nature, which, by the help of good ferments and a wholesome opposition of humours, would correct in one way whatever was excessive or peccant,[ZZ] as physicians say, in another. Thus the florid and over-sanguine humour of the high style was allayed by something of a contrary nature. The comic genius was applied as a kind of caustic to those exuberances and funguses of the swollen dialect and magnificent manner of speech. But, after a while, even this remedy itself was found to turn into a disease, as medicines, we know, grow corrosive when the fouler matters on which they wrought are sufficiently purged and the obstructions removed. *But freedom fell into vice and violence, deserving to be regulated by law.*[34]

It is a great error to suppose, as some have done, that the restraining this licentious manner of wit by law was a violation of the liberty of the Athenian state, or an effect merely of the power of foreigners, whom it little concerned after what manner those citizens treated one another in their comedies, or what sort of wit or humour they made choice of for their ordinary diversions. If upon a change of government, as during the usurpation of the Thirty or when

---

[YY] Masks.

[ZZ] Causing disease, especially with reference to a bodily humour.

[32] Horace, *The Art of Poetry* 280–1. The immediate preceding verses [278–9] of Horace, after his having spoken of the first tragedy under Thespis, are: *After him [Thespis], Aeschylus was the inventor of the mask and the honourable robe, and he set his stages with modest planks.* Before the time of Thespis, tragedy indeed was said to be, as Horace calls it here (in a concise way), *a lowly kind.* It lay in a kind of chaos intermixed with other kinds and hardly distinguishable by its gravity and pomp from the humours which gave rise afterwards to comedy. But in a strict historical sense, as we find Plato speaking in his *Minos* 321, tragedy was of ancienter date and even of the very ancientest with the Athenians. His words are: *Tragedy is a thing of antiquity here, beginning not, as people think, with Thespis or Phrynichus, but, if you are willing to consider, you will find that it is a very ancient invention of this polis.*

[33] Of this subject, see more on pp. 396–7.

[34] Horace, *The Art of Poetry* 282–3. It follows: *The law was accepted and the chorus fell silent to its shame, having lost its right to injure* [283–4].

that nation was humbled at any time, either by a Philip, an Alexander or an Antipater, they had been forced against their wills to enact such laws as these, it is certain they would have soon repealed them when those terrors were removed (as they soon were) and the people restored to their former liberties.^^^ For notwithstanding what this nation suffered outwardly by several shocks received from foreign states, notwithstanding the dominion and power they lost abroad, they preserved the same government at home. And how passionately interested they were in what concerned their diversions and public spectacles, how jealous and full of emulation in what related to their poetry, wit, music and other arts, in which they excelled all other nations, is well known to persons who have any comprehension of ancient manners or been the least conversant in history.

Nothing therefore could have been the cause of these public decrees, and of this gradual reform in the commonwealth of wit, beside the real reform of taste and humour in the commonwealth or government itself. Instead of any abridgment, it was in reality an increase of liberty, an enlargement of the security of property, and an advancement of private ease and personal safety, to provide against what was injurious to the good name and reputation of every citizen. As this intelligence in life and manners grew greater in that experienced people, so the relish of wit and humour would naturally in proportion be more refined. Thus Greece in general grew more and more polite and, as it advanced in this respect, was more averse to the obscene buffooning manner. The Athenians still went before the rest and led the way in elegance of every kind. For even their first comedy was a refinement upon some irregular attempts which had been made in that dramatic way. And the grand critic shows us that, in his own time, the Phallica, or scurrilous and obscene farce, prevailed still and had the countenance of the magistrate in some cities of Greece, who were behind the rest in this reform of taste and manners.[35]

But what is yet a more undeniable evidence of this natural and gradual refinement of styles and manners among the ancients, particularly in what concerned their stage, is that this very case of prohibition and restraint happened among the Romans themselves, where no effects of foreign power or of a home tyranny

---

^^^The Thirty were the party of oligarchs who seized tyrannical power in Athens in 404 BC at the end of the Peloponnesian War and conducted an autocratic reign of terror until they were deposed the next year and the democracy was restored. Philip II, king of Macedon, 359–336 BC, established hegemony over the Greek city-states by 338 BC and bequeathed it to his son Alexander III, the Great, who used it as the basis for his conquests in Asia. Antipater, 397–319 BC, was a Macedonian general, servant of both Philip II and Alexander the Great, who, after the death of the latter, suppressed efforts by Greek city-states, including Athens, to liberate themselves from the Macedonians.

[35] Aristotle, *Poetics* 4.14: *And tragedy came out of those leading off the dithyramb; comedy, those leading off the phallic songs, which still to this day are enduring customs in many city-states.*

can be pretended. Their Fescennine and Atellan way of wit was in early days prohibited, and laws made against it for the public's sake and in regard to the welfare of the community, such licentiousness having been found in reality contrary to the just liberty of the people. *They were pained, vexed and bloodied by its bite. Even those untouched were concerned for the common condition: wherefore a law and penalty were enacted forbidding anyone from being libelled in verse.*[36]

In defence of what I have here advanced, I could, besides the authority of grave historians and chronologists,[37] produce the testimony of one of the wisest and most serious of ancient authors, whose single authority would be acknowledged to have equal force with that of many concurring writers. He shows us that this first-formed comedy and scheme of ludicrous wit was introduced upon the neck of the sublime.[38] The familiar airy muse was privileged as a sort of counter-pedagogue against the pomp and formality of the more solemn writers. And what is highly remarkable, our author shows us that, in philosophy itself, there happened almost at the very same time a like succession of wit and humour when, in opposition to the sublime philosopher and afterwards to his grave disciple and successor in the Academy,[39] there arose a comic philosophy in the person of another master and other disciples, who personally, as well as in their writings, were set in direct opposition to the former, not as differing in opinions or maxims but in their style and manner, in the turn of humour and method of instruction.[40]

It is pleasant enough to consider how exact the resemblance was between

---

[36] Horace, *Epistles* 2.1.150–4. [The Fescennine verses were ribald verse dialogues aimed at mocking weaknesses and vices and performed at harvest festivals and other celebratory occasions in earliest Rome. The *fabulae Atellanae* were improvised masked performances of coarse burlesque with stock characters, borrowed from the early Romans' Oscan neighbours. These spectacles were proscribed by Augustus.]

[37] To confirm what is said of this natural succession of wit and style, according to the several authorities above-cited in the immediate preceding notes, see Strabo, *Geography* 1.2.6: *Prose, that is to say, artistic prose, is an imitation of poetry. Poetic art first came forth and established a good reputation. Then, imitating it, abandoning metre but keeping the other poetic aspects, were the writers Cadmus and Pherecydes and Hecataeus and their followers. Then later writers, constantly taking away something of such qualities, brought prose down, as though from some great height, to its present form. In the same way, somebody might say that comedy takes its structure from tragedy and has been brought down from its poetic height to the prosaic, as it is now called.*

[38] *Tragedies were first brought on as reminders of events, and that these things do by nature occur, and so that you are not hurt on the greater stage of life by those things which, on the stage, might transport your soul . . . After tragedy, Old Comedy was brought on, which had an educative freedom of speech and which gave useful reminder of freedom from arrogance through its plain-spokenness. Somewhat similarly Diogenes inherited this tradition. After this, Middle Comedy and subsequently New Comedy . . .*: Marcus Aurelius, *Meditations* 11.6. *So ought to be one's practice throughout life, and one should, where matters seem to be wholly plausible, lay them bare and behold their shabbiness and remove the stuff upon which their pretension rests. Affectation cheats terribly and, when you convince yourself that you are busy, especially with serious things, then you are especially deluded. At any rate, see what Crates says about Xenocrates of all people!*: Marcus Aurelius, *Meditations* 6.13.

[39] See the citations immediately preceding.

[40] *Different only by a shirt*: Juvenal, *Satires* 13.122.

the lineage of philosophy and that of poetry as derived from their two chief founders or patriarchs, in whose loins the several races lay, as it were, enclosed. For as the grand poetic sire[41] was, by the consent of all antiquity, allowed to have furnished subject both to the tragic, the comic, and every other kind of genuine poetry, so the philosophical patriarch[BBB] in the same manner, containing within himself the several geniuses of philosophy, gave rise to all those several manners in which that science was delivered.

His disciple of noble birth and lofty genius, who aspired to poetry and rhetoric, took the *sublime* part and shone above his other condisciples.[42] He of mean birth and poorest circumstances, whose constitution as well as condition inclined him to the way we call *satiric*, took the reproving part, which in his better-humoured and more agreeable successor turned into the *comic* kind, and went upon the model of that ancient comedy which was then prevalent.[43] But another noble disciple, whose genius was towards action and who proved afterwards the greatest hero of his time, took the genteeler part and softer manner. He joined what was deepest and most solid in philosophy with what was easiest and most refined in breeding, and in the character and manner of a gentleman.[CCC] Nothing could be remoter than his genius was from the scholastic, the rhetorical or mere poetic kind. He was as distant, on one hand, from the sonorous, high and pompous strain as, on the other hand, from the ludicrous, mimical or satiric.

This[44] was that natural and simple genius of antiquity, comprehended by so few and so little relished by the vulgar. This was that philosophical Menander of earlier time, whose works one may wonder to see preserved from the same

---

[BBB] Socrates.

[CCC] Xenophon.

[41] See p. 110n. According to this Homerical lineage of poetry, comedy would naturally prove the drama of latest birth. For though Aristotle in the same place cites Homer's *Margites* as analogous to comedy, yet the *Iliad* and *Odyssey*, in which the heroic style prevails, having been ever highest in esteem, were likeliest to be first wrought and cultivated. [On *Margites*, see p. 89n.]

[42] His [Plato's] *Dialogues* were real poems (as has been shown above, p. 110n). This may easily be collected from the *Poetics* of the Grand Master. We may add what is cited by Athenaeus from another treatise of that author: *[Plato] utterly denigrated others, in the* Republic, *rejecting Homer and imitative poetics, but he himself wrote his dialogues in mimetic fashion, although not himself actually the inventor of the form, for, before him, Alexamenos of Teos invented the type of writing as Nicias of Nicaea and Sotion report. Aristotle in his work On Poets writes thus: 'Accordingly, shall we not say that the so-called mimes of Sophron are metrical works and imitations or those of Alexamenos of Teos, which were the first written Socratic dialogues?' The widely learned Aristotle bluntly declares that Alexamenos wrote dialogues before Plato*: Athenaeus, *The Deipnosophists* 11.505.

[43] According to the two citations, p. 113n. [Antisthenes and Diogenes. According to Diogenes Laertius, Socrates' successors were Plato, Xenophon and Antisthenes (2.47), the last of whom was succeeded in turn by Diogenes the Cynic (1.15; 6.2,15,21). Antisthenes in fact had no direct relation to the Cynics.]

[44] See p. 443.

fate, since, in the darker ages through which they passed, they might probably be alike neglected on the account of their like simplicity of style and composition.

There is, besides the several manners of writing above-described, another
of considerable authority and weight, which had its rise chiefly from the critical art itself and from the more accurate inspection into the works of preceding masters. The grand critic of whom we have already spoken was a chief and
leader in this order of penmen.[DDD] For, though the sophists of elder time had
treated many subjects methodically and in form, yet this writer was the first
who gained repute in the methodic kind. As the talent of this great man was
more towards polite learning and the arts than towards the deep and solid parts
of philosophy, it happened that in his school there was more care taken of other
sciences than of ethics, dialect or logic, which provinces were chiefly cultivated
by the successors of the Academy and Porch.[EEE]

It has been observed of this methodic or scholastic manner that it naturally
befitted an author who, though endowed with a comprehensive and strong
genius, was not in himself of a refined temper, blessed by the Graces or
favoured by any Muse, one who was not of a fruitful imagination, but rather
dry and rigid, yet withal acute and piercing, accurate and distinct. For the chief
nerve and sinew of this style consists in the clear division and partition of the
subjects. Though there is nothing exalting in the manner, it is naturally powerful and commanding and, more than any other, subdues the mind and
strengthens its determinations. It is from this genius that firm conclusions and
steady maxims are best formed, which, if solidly built and on sure ground, are
the shortest and best guides towards wisdom and ability in every kind, but, if
defective or unsound in the least part, must of necessity lead us to the grossest absurdities and stiffest pedantry and conceit.

Now, though every other style and genuine manner of composition has its
order and method as well as this which, in a peculiar sense, we call the *methodic*,
yet it is this manner alone which professes method, dissects itself in parts and
makes its own anatomy. The *sublime* can no way condescend thus or bear to
be suspended in its impetuous course. The *comic* or derisory manner is farther
still from making show of method. It is then, if ever, that it presumes to give
itself this wise air when its design is to expose the thing itself and ridicule the
formality and sophistry so often sheltered beneath it. The *simple* manner,

---

[DDD] Aristotle.
[EEE] The Academy was the school, established in the outskirts of Athens by Plato about 385 BC,
which survived for centuries. The Porch or Stoa was the school established by Zeno in a public hall in Athens about 300 BC, which gave its name to the stoic philosophy elaborated there.
Aristotle's own school took its name from Lyceum, its location in Athens, or the περίπατος,
peripatos, the covered walk in the buildings there.

which, being the strictest imitation of nature, should of right be the completest in the distribution of its parts and symmetry of its whole, is yet so far from making any ostentation of method that it conceals the artifice as much as possible, endeavouring only to express the effect of art under the appearance of the greatest ease and negligence. And even when it assumes the censuring or reproving part, it does it in the most concealed and gentle way.

The authors indeed of our age are as little capable of receiving as of giving advice in such a way as this, so little is the general palate formed as yet to a taste of real simplicity. As for the *sublime*, though it be often the subject of criticism, it can never be the manner or afford the means. The way of form and *method*, the didactive or perceptive manner, as it has been usually practised among us and as our ears have been long accustomed, has so little force towards the winning our attention that it is apter to tire us than the metre of an old ballad. We no sooner hear the theme propounded, the subject divided and subdivided (with 'first of the first' and so forth, as order requires), but instantly we begin a strife with nature, who otherwise might surprise us in the soft fetters of sleep, to the great disgrace of the orator and scandal of the audience. The only manner left in which criticism can have its just force among us is the ancient *comic*, of which kind were the first Roman miscellanies or satiric pieces, a sort of original writing of their own, refined afterwards by the best genius and politest poet of that nation,[FFF] who, notwithstanding, owns the manner to have been taken from the Greek comedy above-mentioned. And if our home wits would refine upon this pattern, they might perhaps meet with considerable success.

In effect, we may observe that in our own nation the most successful criticism or method of refutation is that which borders most on the manner of the earliest Greek comedy. The highly-rated burlesque poem, written on the subject of our religious controversies in the last age, is a sufficient token of this kind.[45] And that justly admired piece of comic wit, given us some time after by an author of the highest quality, has furnished our best wits in all their controversies, even in religion and politics as well as in the affairs of wit and learning, with the most effectual and entertaining method of exposing folly, pedantry, false reason and ill writing.[46] And without some such tolerated manner of criticism as this, how grossly we might have been imposed on, and should continue to be for the future, by many pieces of dogmatical rhetoric and pedantic wit, may easily be apprehended by those who know anything of the state

---

[FFF] Horace.

[45] *Hudibras* [by Samuel Butler, 1612–80. *Hudibras*, which appeared in three parts in 1662, 1663 and 1678, was a mock-heroic poem satirizing puritans of the Civil War period.]

[46] *The Rehearsal* [by George Villiers, second Duke of Buckingham, 1628–87. The play was first performed in 1671.] See pp. 455n and 457.

of letters in our nation, or are in the least fitted to judge of the manner of the common poets or formal authors of the times.

In what form or manner soever criticism may appear among us or critics choose to exert their talent, it can become none, besides the grossly superstitious or ignorant, to be alarmed at this spirit. For if it be ill-managed and with little wit, it will be destroyed by something wittier in the kind. If it be witty itself, it must of necessity advance wit.

And thus from the consideration of ancient as well as modern time, it appears that the cause and interest of critics is the same with that of wit, learning and good sense.

Section 3

Thus we have surveyed the state of authors as they are influenced from without, either by the frowns or favour of the great or by the applause or censure of the critics. It remains only to consider how the people, or world in general, stand affected towards our modern penmen and what occasion these adventurers may have of complaint or boast from their encounter with the public.

There is nothing more certain than that a real genius and thorough artist in whatever kind can never, without the greatest unwillingness and shame, be induced to act below his character and, for mere interest, be prevailed with to prostitute his art or science by performing contrary to its known rules. Whoever has heard anything of the lives of famous statuaries, architects or painters, will call to mind many instances of this nature. Or whoever has made any acquaintance with the better sort of mechanics, such as are real lovers of their art and masters in it, must have observed their natural fidelity in this respect. Be they ever so idle, dissolute or debauched, how regardless soever of other rules, they abhor any transgression in their art and would choose to lose customers and starve rather than, by a base compliance with the world, to act contrary to what they call the justness and truth of work.

'Sir,' says a poor fellow of this kind to his rich customer, 'you are mistaken in coming to me for such a piece of workmanship. Let who will make it for you as you fancy, I know it to be wrong. Whatever I have made hitherto has been true work. And neither for your sake or anybody's else shall I put my hand to any other.'

This is virtue, real virtue and love of truth, independent of opinion and above the world! This disposition, transferred to the whole of life, perfects a character and makes that probity and worth which the learned are often at such a loss to explain. For is there not a workmanship and a truth in actions? Or is the workmanship of this kind less becoming, or less worthy of our notice, that we should not in this case be as surly at least as the honest artisan, who has no other philosophy than what nature and his trade have taught him?

When one considers this zeal and honesty of inferior artists, one would wonder to see those who pretend to skill and science in a higher kind have so little regard to truth and the perfection of their art. One would expect it of our writers that, if they had real ability, they should draw the world to them and not meanly suit themselves to the world in its weak state. We may justly indeed make allowances for the simplicity of those early geniuses of our nation who, after so many barbarous ages, when letters lay yet in their ruins, made bold excursions into a vacant field to seize the posts of honour and attain the stations which were yet unpossessed by the wits of their own country. But since the age is now so far advanced, learning established, the rules of writing stated and the truth of art so well apprehended and everywhere confessed and owned, it is strange to see our writers as unshapen still and monstrous in their works as heretofore. There can be nothing more ridiculous than to hear our poets in their prefaces talk of art and structure, while in their pieces they perform as ill as ever and with as little regard to those professed rules of art as the honest bards, their predecessors, who had never heard of any such rules, or at least had never owned their justice or validity.

Had the early poets of Greece thus complimented their nation by complying with its first relish and appetite, they had not done their countrymen such service nor themselves such honour as we find they did by conforming to truth and nature. The generous spirits who first essayed the way had not always the world on their side, but soon drew after them the best judgments and soon afterwards the world itself. They forced their way into it and, by weight of merit, turned its judgment on their side. They formed their audience, polished the age, refined the public ear and framed it right, that in return they might be rightly and lastingly applauded. Nor were they disappointed in their hope. The applause soon came and was lasting, for it was sound. They have justice done them at this day. They have survived their nation and live, though in a dead language. The more the age is enlightened, the more they shine. Their fame must necessarily last as long as letters, and posterity will ever own their merit.

Our modern authors, on the contrary, are turned and modelled, as themselves confess, by the public relish and current humour of the times. They regulate themselves by the irregular fancy of the world and frankly own they are preposterous and absurd in order to accommodate themselves to the genius of the age. In our days the audience makes the poet, and the bookseller the author, with what profit to the public or what prospect of lasting fame and honour to the writer, let anyone who has judgment imagine.

But though our writers charge their faults thus freely on the public, it will, I doubt, appear from many instances that this practice is mere imposture, since those absurdities, which they are the aptest to commit, are far from being delightful or entertaining. We are glad to take up with what our language can afford us and, by a sort of emulation with other nations, are forced to cry up such writers of our own as may best serve us for comparison. But when we are out of this spirit, it must be owned, we are not apt to discover any great fondness or admiration of our authors. Nor have we any whom by mutual consent we make to be our standard. We go to plays as to other shows and frequent the theatre as the booth. We read epics and dramatics as we do satires and lampoons, for we must of necessity know what wit as well as what scandal is stirring. Read we must, let writers be ever so indifferent. And this perhaps may be some occasion of the laziness and negligence of our authors who, observing this need which our curiosity brings on us and making an exact calculation in the way of trade to know justly the quality and quantity of the public demand, feed us thus from hand to mouth, resolving not to over-stock the market or be at the pains of more correctness or wit than is absolutely necessary to carry on the traffic.

Our satire therefore is scurrilous, buffooning and without morals or instruction, which is the majesty and life of this kind of writing. Our encomium or panegyric is as fulsome and displeasing by its prostitute and abandoned manner of praise. The worthy persons who are the subjects of it may well be esteemed sufferers by the manner. And the public, whether it will or no, is forced to make untoward reflections when led to it by such satirizing panegyrists. For in reality the nerve and sinew of modern panegyric lies in a dull kind of satire which the author, it is true, intends should turn to the advantage of his subject, but which, if I mistake not, will appear to have a very contrary effect.

The usual method which our authors take when they would commend either a brother-author, a wit, a hero, a philosopher or a statesman, is to look abroad to find within the narrow compass of their learning some eminent names of persons who answered to these characters in a former time. These they are sure to lash, as they imagine, with some sharp stroke of satire. And when they have stripped these reverend personages of all their share of merit, they think to clothe their hero with the spoils. Such is the sterility of these encomiasts! They know not how to praise but by detraction. If a fair one is to be celebrated, Helen must in comparison be deformed, Venus herself degraded. That a modern may be honoured, some ancient must be sacrificed. If a poet is to be extolled, down with a Homer or a Pindar. If an orator or philosopher, down with Demosthenes, Tully, Plato. If a general of our army, down with any hero whatever of time past. 'The Romans knew no discipline! The Grecians never learned the art of war!'

Were there an art of writing to be formed upon the modern practice, this method we have described might perhaps be styled the Rule of Dispatch, or the Herculean Law, by which encomiasts, with no other weapon than their single club, may silence all other fame and place their hero in the vacant throne of honour.^{GGG} I would willingly however advise these celebrators to be a little more moderate in the use of this club-method. Not that I pretend to ask quarter for the ancients; but, for the sake merely of those moderns whom our panegyrists undertake to praise, I would wish them to be a little cautious of comparing characters. There is no need to call up a Publicola or a Scipio, an Aristides or a Cato, to serve as foils.^{IIIII} These were patriots and good generals in their time and did their country honest service. No offence to any who at present do the same. The Fabriciuses, the Aemiliuses, the Cincinnatuses^{III} (poor men!) may be suffered to rest quietly or, if their ghost should by this unlucky kind of enchantment be raised in mockery and contempt, they may perhaps prove troublesome in earnest and cast such reflections on our panegyrists and their modern patrons as may be no way for the advantage of either. The well-deserving ancients will have always a strong party among the wise and learned of every age. And the memory of foreign worthies, as well as those of our own nation, will with gratitude be cherished by the nobler spirits of mankind. The interest of the dead is not so disregarded but that, in case of violence offered them through partiality to the living, there are hands ready prepared to make sufficient reprisals.

It was in times when flattery grew much in fashion that the title of panegyric was appropriated to such pieces as contained only a profuse and unlimited praise of some single person. The ancient panegyrics were no other than merely such writings as authors of every kind recited at the solemn assemblies of the people. They were the exercises of the wits and men of letters who, as

---

^{GGG} The hero Hercules armed himself in one of his early exploits with a club cut from an olive tree on Mount Helicon. Later he scorned divine gifts of armour and weapons preferring the club with which he was often represented (for instance, in Paolo de Mattheis' *Judgment of Hercules* (1713), a painting commissioned by Shaftesbury).

^{IIIII} Publicola, or Publius Valerius, was traditionally one of the first Roman consuls at the overthrow of the monarchy in 509 BC. Scipio was a celebrated family of generals and statesmen during the Roman Republic: perhaps the greatest was Scipio Africanus Major (236–184 BC), who as consul invaded Africa and defeated the armies of Hannibal in 202 BC. Aristides, born about 520 BC, was an Athenian statesman and soldier who was a leader in the wars against Persia and whose name was a byword for honesty and integrity. Marcus Porcius Cato, 234–149 BC, was a Roman soldier and statesman associated with stern traditional morality.

^{III} Gaius Fabricius Luscinus was a Roman war hero, consul and censor in the early third century BC. Lucius Aemilius Paullus received the surname Macedonicus to celebrate his defeat of Perseus in 168 BC, which established Roman hegemony over Greece. Lucius Quinctius Cincinnatus was a fifth century BC Roman figure who was appointed dictator, led a successful military campaign and then resigned his dictatorship in order to return to the simple life of his farm. All three exemplified aspects of Roman civic virtue.

well as the men of bodily dexterity, bore their part at the Olympic and other national and panegyric games.[JJJ]

The British nation, though they have nothing of this kind ordained or established by their laws, are yet by nature wonderfully inclined to the same panegyric exercises. At their fairs and during the time of public festivals, they perform their rude Olympics and show an activity and address beyond any other modern people whatever. Their trials of skill, it is true, are wholly of the body, not of the brain. Nor is it to be wondered at, if being left to themselves and no way assisted by the laws or magistrate, their bodily exercises retain something of the barbarian character or, at least, show their manners[47] to hold more of Rome than Greece.[48] The gladiatorian and other sanguinary sports, which we allow our people, discover sufficiently our national taste. And the baitings and slaughter of so many sorts of creatures, tame as well as wild, for diversion merely, may witness the extraordinary inclination we have for amphitheatrical spectacles.

I know not whether it be from this killing disposition remarked in us that our satirists prove such very slaughter-men, and even our panegyric authors or encomiasts delight so much in the dispatching method above-described; but

---

[JJJ] Panegyrics were originally speeches composed for general gatherings or festivals such as the one at Olympia, Zeus's main sanctuary in Greece. These games, dating, according to legend, from 776 BC and held every four years, involved a range of athletic competitions as well as sacrifices, rituals and festivities.

[47] Whoever has a thorough taste of the wit and manner of Horace, if he only compares his epistle to Augustus (*Epistles* 2.1) with the secret character of that prince from Suetonius and other authors, will easily find what judgment that poet made of the Roman taste, even in the person of this sovereign and admired Roman prince, whose natural love of amphitheatrical spectacles and other entertainments (little accommodated to the interest of the Muses) is there sufficiently insinuated. The prince indeed was, as it is said above, p. 99, obliged in the highest degree to his poetical and witty friends for guiding his taste and forming his manners, as they really did with good effect and great advantage to his interest. Witness what even that flattering Court historian, Dion, relates of the frank treatment which that prince received from his friend Maecenas, who was forced to draw him from his bloody tribunal and murderous delight with the reproach of *Time in truth to arise, you butcher!* [Dion Cassius, *Roman History* 55.7.2] But Horace, according to his character and circumstances, was obliged to take a finer and more concealed manner, both with the prince and favourite. *Sly Horace touches every vice and finds his way to play around the depth of the heart – and his friend still laughs*: Persius, *Satires* 1.116–17. See p. 443n.

[48] We may add to this note what Tacitus or Quintilian remarks on the subject of the Roman taste: *Now indeed the vices peculiar and specific to this city seem to me to be conceived almost in the mother's womb – a theatrical taste and enthusiasms for gladiators and horses: how little room does a soul leave for decent arts when it is thus preoccupied and obsessed?*: *Dialogue on Orators* 29. [The authorship of this dialogue was long contested although now Tacitus, and not Quintilian, has generally been accepted as the author: see the introduction by Herbert W. Benario to *Tacitus' Agricola, Germany and Dialogue on Orators*, rev. edn (Norman, OK, and London: University of Oklahoma Press, 1991), pp. 7–9.]

sure I am that our dramatic poets stand violently affected this way, and delight to make havoc and destruction of every kind.[49]

It is alleged indeed by our stage-poets, in excuse for vile ribaldry and other gross irregularities, both in the fable and language of their pieces, that their success, which depends chiefly on the ladies, is never so fortunate as when this havoc is made on virtue and good sense and their pieces are exhibited publicly in this monstrous form. I know not how they can answer it to the fair sex to speak, as they pretend, experimentally and with such nice distinction of their audience. How far this excuse may serve them in relation to common amours and love adventures I will not take upon me to pronounce. But I must own I have often wondered to see our fighting plays become so much the entertainment of that tender sex.[50]

They who have no help from learning to observe the wider periods or revolutions of human kind, the alterations which happen in manners and the flux and reflux of politeness, wit and art, are apt at every turn to make the present age their standard, and imagine nothing barbarous or savage but what is contrary to the manners of their own time. The same pretended judges, had they flourished in our Britain at the time when Caesar made his first descent, would have condemned as a whimsical critic the man who should have made bold to censure our deficiency of clothing and laugh at the blue cheeks and party-coloured skins, which were then in fashion with our ancestors. Such must of necessity be the judgment of those who are only critics by fashion. But to a just naturalist or humanist, who knows the creature Man and judges of his growth and improvement in society, it appears evidently that we British men were as barbarous and uncivilized in respect of the Romans under a Caesar, as the Romans themselves were in respect of the Grecians when they invaded that nation under a Mummius.[KKK]

The noble wits of a Court education, who can go no farther back into antiquity than their pedigree will carry them, are able however to call to mind the different state of manners in some few reigns past, when chivalry was in such repute. The ladies were then spectators not only of feigned combats and martial exercises but of real duels and bloody feats of arms. They sat as umpires and judges of the doughty frays. These were the saint-protectresses to whom the champions chiefly paid their vows and to whom they recommended themselves by these gallant quarrels and elegant decisions of right and justice. Nor

---

[KKK] Lucius Mummius Achaicus was a Roman consul who defeated the Greek Achaean League in 147 BC. He was noted for his obliviousness to the value of the artistic treasures he sent from the defeated Corinth back to Rome.

[49] See p. 446.
[50] See p. 447.

is this spirit so entirely lost among us, but that even at this hour the fair sex inspire us still with the fancy of like gallantries. They are the chief subject of many such civil turmoils, and remain still the secret influencing constellation by which we are engaged to give and ask that satisfaction which is peculiar to the fine gentlemen of the age. For thus a certain gallant of our Court expressed the case very naturally, when, being asked by his friends why one of his established character for courage and good sense would answer the challenge of a coxcomb, he confessed, that 'for his *own* sex he could safely trust their judgment, but how should he appear at night before the maids of honour?'

Such is the different genius of nations and of the same nation in different times and seasons. For so, among the ancients, some have been known tender of the sex to such a degree as not to suffer them to expose their modesty by the view of masculine games or theatrical representations of any kind whatever.[51] Others, on the contrary, have introduced them into their amphitheatres and made them sharers in the cruellest spectacles.

But let our authors or poets complain ever so much of the genius of our people, it is evident we are not altogether so barbarous or Gothic as they pretend. We are naturally no ill soil and have musical parts which might be cultivated with great advantage if these gentlemen would use the art of masters in their composition. They have power to work upon our better inclinations, and may know by certain tokens that their audience is disposed to receive nobler subjects and taste a better manner than that which, through indulgence to themselves more than to the world, they are generally pleased to make their choice.

Besides some laudable attempts which have been made with tolerable success of late years towards a just manner of writing, both in the heroic and familiar style, we have older proofs of a right disposition in our people towards the

---

[51] *On the other hand, very many actions are seemly by our standards but considered base among the Greeks. What Roman would be ashamed to take his wife to a dinner party? Or whose mother [materfamilias] is not to be found in the front rooms and is not the object of attention? It is much different in Greece; for a woman is not admitted to a dinner party, unless it consists of close family, and she sits only in the interior part of the house, which is called 'the women's quarters', where no man goes unless he is closely related to her:* Cornelius Nepos, *On the Great Generals of Foreign Nations* Preface.6–7. See also Aelian, *Miscellany* 10.1, and the law in Pausanias, *Description of Greece* 5.6.7–8 (though the story in Aelian, better related as to the circumstances): *The law says to cast down from the rock women who have been caught getting into the Olympic games or who have even crossed the river Alphaeus on the days forbidden to women. However, they report that no woman was caught except Callipatira whom others call Pherenice. This widow disguised herself in a man's garb as an exercise coach and escorted her son Pisidorus to the competition. And when he was victorious, she leapt over the enclosure, where they keep the coaches apart, and her clothing was lost. Hence, she was recognized as a woman but charged with no crime. The judges gave her this indulgence because of the glory of her father, her brothers and her son, who all had left the Olympic games victorious. A law was passed that the coaches themselves should strip before entering the games.* [Shaftesbury quoted Pausanias not in the original Greek but in a Latin version, on which this translation is based.]

moral and instructive way. Our old dramatic poet may witness for our good ear and manly relish.[52] Notwithstanding his natural rudeness, his unpolished style, his antiquated phrase and wit, his want of method and coherence, and his deficiency in almost all the graces and ornaments of this kind of writing, yet, by the justness of his moral, the aptness of many of his descriptions and the plain and natural turn of several of his characters, he pleases his audience and often gains their ear without a single bribe from luxury or vice. That piece of his, which appears to have most affected English hearts and has perhaps been oftenest acted of any which have come upon our stage, is almost one continued moral: a series of deep reflections drawn from one mouth upon the subject of one single accident and calamity naturally fitted to move horror and compassion.[53] It may be properly said of this play, if I mistake not, that it has only one character or principal part. It contains no adoration or flattery of 'the sex',[l.l.l.] no ranting at the gods, no blustering heroism nor anything of that curious mixture of the fierce and tender which makes the hinge of modern tragedy and nicely varies it between the points of love and honour.

Upon the whole, since, in the two great poetic stations, the epic and dramatic, we may observe the moral genius so naturally prevalent, since our most approved heroic poem[54] has neither the softness of language nor the fashionable turn of wit but merely solid thought, strong reasoning, noble passion and a continued thread of moral doctrine, piety and virtue to recommend it, we may justly infer that it is not so much the public ear as the ill hand and vicious manner of our poets which needs redress.

And thus at last we are returned to our old article of advice: that main preliminary of self-study and inward converse which we have found so much wanting in the authors of our time. They should add the wisdom of the heart to the task and exercise of the brain, in order to bring proportion and beauty into their works. That their composition and vein of writing may be natural and free, they should settle matters in the first place with themselves. And having gained a mastery here, they may easily, with the help of their genius and a right use of art, command their audience and establish a good taste.

It is on *themselves* that all depends. We have considered their other subjects of excuse. We have acquitted the great men, their presumptive patrons, whom we have left to their own discretion. We have proved the critics not only an inoffensive but a highly useful race. And, for the audience, we have found it not so bad as might perhaps at first be apprehended.

It remains that we pass sentence on our authors after having precluded them

---

l.l.l. Shaftesbury's usage here, referring to women alone as 'the sex', was idiomatic.

[52] Shakespeare.
[53] *Hamlet.*
[54] Milton's *Paradise Lost.*

their last refuge. Nor do we condemn them on their want of wit or fancy, but of judgment and correctness, which can only be attained by thorough diligence, study and impartial censure of themselves. It is manners which is wanting.[55] It is a due sentiment of morals which alone can make us knowing, in order and proportion, and give us the just tone and measure of human passion.

So much the poet must necessarily borrow of the philosopher as to be master of the common topics of morality. He must at least be speciously honest and, in all appearance, a friend to virtue throughout his poem. The good and wise will abate him nothing in this kind. And the people, though corrupt, are, in the main, best satisfied with this conduct. *A play with attractive passages and characters nicely drawn, though lacking any charm, weight or art, delights the people more and holds them better than verses short on content and sweet-sounding fluff.*[56]

Part III

Section 1

It is esteemed the highest compliment which can be paid a writer, on the occasion of some new work he has made public, to tell him that 'he has undoubtedly surpassed himself'. And indeed when one observes how well this compliment is received, one would imagine it to contain some wonderful hyperbole of praise. For, according to the strain of modern politeness, it is not an ordinary violation of truth which can afford a tribute sufficient to answer any common degree of merit. Now it is well known that the gentlemen whose merit lies towards authorship are unwilling to make the least abatement on the foot of this ceremonial. One would wonder therefore to find them so entirely satisfied with a form of praise which in plain sense amounts to no more than a bare affirmative that 'they have in some manner differed from themselves and are become somewhat worse or better than their common rate'. For if the vilest writer grows viler than ordinary, or exceeds his natural pitch on either side, he is justly said to exceed or go beyond himself.

We find in the same manner that there is no expression more generally used in a way of compliment to great men and princes than that plain one, which is so often verified and may be safely pronounced for truth on most occasions, that 'they have acted like themselves and suitably to their own genius and character'. The compliment, it must be owned, sounds well. No one suspects it. For what person is there who in his imagination joins not something worthy and deserving with his true and native self, as often as he is referred to it and made to consider 'who he is'? Such is the natural affection of all mankind

[55] See pp. 93, 94, 150, 156n, 442–3, 453–4, 457.
[56] Horace, *The Art of Poetry* 319–22.

towards moral beauty and perfection that they never fail in making this presumption in behalf of themselves, that 'by nature they have something estimable and worthy in respect of others of their kind' and that 'their genuine, true and natural self is, as it ought to be, of real value in society and justly honourable for the sake of its merit and good qualities'. They conclude therefore they have the height of praise allotted them when they are assured by anyone that they have done nothing below themselves or that, in some particular action, they have exceeded the ordinary tenor of their character.

Thus is everyone convinced of the reality of a better self and of the cult or homage which is due to it. The misfortune is we are seldom taught to comprehend this self by placing it in a distinct view from its representative or counterfeit. In our holy religion, which for the greatest part is adapted to the very meanest capacities, it is not to be expected that a speculation of this kind should be openly advanced. It is enough that we have hints given us of a nobler self than that which is commonly supposed the basis and foundation of our actions. Self-interest is there taken as it is vulgarly conceived, though, on the other side, there are, in the most sacred characters, examples given us of the highest contempt of all such interested views, of a willingness to suffer without recompense for the sake of others, and of a desire to part even with life and being itself on account of what is generous and worthy.[57] But in the same manner as the celestial phenomena are in the sacred volumes generally treated according to common imagination and the then current system of astronomy and natural science, so the moral appearances are in many places preserved without alteration, according to vulgar prejudice and the general conception of interest and self-good. Our real and genuine self is sometimes supposed that ambitious one which is fond of power and glory, sometimes that childish one which is taken with vain show and is to be invited to obedience by promise of finer habitations, precious stones and metals, shining garments, crowns and other such dazzling beauties, by which another earth, or material city, is represented.

It must be owned that, even at that time when a greater and purer light disclosed itself in the chosen nation,[MMM] their natural gloominess appeared still by the great difficulty they had to know themselves or learn their real interest, after such long tutorage and instruction from above.[58] The simplicity of that people must certainly have been very great, when the best doctrine could not go down without a treat and the best disciples had their heads so running upon their loaves, that they were apt to construe every divine saying in a belly-sense, and thought nothing more self-constituent than that inferior receptacle.[59]

[MMM] The ancient Hebrews or Jews.

[57] Exodus 32.31–2, Romans 9.1–3.
[58] See pp. 16, 361–2, 387ff.
[59] Matthew 16.6–8.

Their taste in morals could not fail of being suitable to this extraordinary estimation of themselves. No wonder if the better and nobler self was left as a mystery to a people who, of all humankind, were the most grossly selfish, crooked and perverse. So that it must necessarily be confessed, in honour of their divine legislators, patriots and instructors, that they exceeded all others in goodness and generosity, since they could so truly love their nation and brethren, such as they were, and could have so generous and disinterested regards for those who were in themselves so sordidly interested and undeserving.

But whatever may be the proper effect or operation of religion, it is the known province of philosophy to teach us ourselves, keep us the self-same persons and so regulate our governing fancies, passions and humours as to make us comprehensible to ourselves and knowable by other features than those of a bare countenance. For it is not certainly by virtue of our face merely that we are ourselves. It is not we who change when our complexion or shape changes. But there is that which, being wholly metamorphosed and converted, we are thereby in reality transformed and lost.

Should an intimate friend of ours, who had endured many sicknesses and run many ill adventures while he travelled through the remotest parts of the East and hottest countries of the South, return to us so altered in his whole outward figure that, till we had for a time conversed with him, we could not know him again to be the same person, the matter would not seem so very strange nor would our concern on this account be very great. But should a like face and figure of a friend return to us with thought and humours of a strange and foreign turn, with passions, affections and opinions wholly different from anything we had formerly known, we should say, in earnest and with the greatest amazement and concern, that this was another creature and not the friend whom we once knew familiarly. Nor should we in reality attempt any renewal of acquaintance or correspondence with such a person, though perhaps he might preserve in his memory the faint marks or tokens of former transactions which had passed between us.

When a revolution of this kind, though not so total, happens at any time in a character, when the passion or humour of a known person changes remarkably from what it once was, it is to philosophy we then appeal. It is either the want or weakness of this principle which is charged on the delinquent. And on this bottom it is that we often challenge ourselves when we find such variation in our manners, and observe that it is not always the same self nor the same interest we have in view, but often a direct contrary one, which we serve still with the same passion and ardour. When from a noted liberality we change perhaps to as remarkable a parsimony, when from indolence and love of rest we plunge into business, or from a busy and severe character, abhorrent from the tender converse of the fair sex, we turn on a sudden to a contrary passion and become amorous or uxorious, we acknowledge the weakness and, charging our defect on the general want of philosophy, we say, sighing, 'Indeed, we none of us truly know ourselves.' And thus we recognize the authority and proper object of philosophy so far at least that, though we pretend not to be complete philosophers, we confess that, 'as we have more or less of this intelligence or comprehension of ourselves, we are accordingly more or less truly men and either more or less to be depended on in friendship, society and the commerce of life'.

The fruits of this science are indeed the fairest imaginable and, upon due trial, are found to be as well relished and of as good savour with mankind. But when, invited to the speculation, we turn our eyes on that which we suppose the tree, it is no wonder if we slight the gardenership and think the manner of culture a very contemptible mystery. 'Grapes', it is said, 'are not gathered from thorns, nor figs from thistles.'[60] Now, if in the literate world there be any choking weed, anything purely thorn or thistle, it is in all likelihood that very kind of plant which stands for philosophy in some famous Schools.[61] There can be nothing more ridiculous than to expect that manners or understanding should sprout from such a stock. It pretends indeed some relation to manners as being definitive of the natures, essences and properties of spirits, and some relation to reason as describing the shapes and forms of certain instruments employed in the reasoning art. But had the craftiest of men, for many ages together, been employed in finding out a method to confound reason and degrade the understanding of mankind, they could not, perhaps, have succeeded better than by the establishment of such a mock-science.

I knew once a notable enthusiast of the itinerant kind who, being upon a high spiritual adventure in a country where prophetic missions are treated as no jest, was, as he told me, committed a close prisoner and kept for several months where he saw no manner of light.[NNN] In this banishment from letters and discourse, the man very wittily invented an amusement much to his purpose and highly preservative both of health and humour. It may be thought perhaps that, of all seasons or circumstances, here was one the most suitable to our oft-mentioned practice of soliloquy, especially since the prisoner was one of those whom in this age we usually call philosophers, a successor of

---

[NNN] In his remarks on *Characteristics*, first published in 1715, Gottfried Wilhelm Leibniz identified this individual as Franciscus Mercurius van Helmont, *c.* 1614–98, physician and natural philosopher. He was working on a study of the 'natural' aspects of the Hebrew alphabet in the early 1660s while imprisoned by the Inquisition in Rome. He later published *Alphabeti vere naturalis hebraici brevissima delineatio* (A very brief sketch of the assuredly natural Hebrew alphabet) (1667).

[60] Matthew 7.16.
[61] See pp. 148–9, 232–3.

Paracelsus[ooo] and a master in the occult sciences. But as to a moral science or anything relating to self-converse, he was a mere novice. To work therefore he went after a different method. He tuned his natural pipes not after the manner of a musician, to practise what was melodious and agreeable in sounds, but to fashion and form all sorts of articulate voices the most distinctly that was possible. This he performed by strenuously exalting his voice and essaying it in all the several dispositions and configurations of his throat and mouth. And thus bellowing, roaring, snarling and otherwise variously exerting his organs of sound, he endeavoured to discover what letters of the alphabet could best design each species, or what new letters were to be invented to mark the undiscovered modifications. He found, for instance, the letter 'A' to be a most genuine character, an original and pure vowel, and justly placed as principal in the front of the alphabetic order. For having duly extended his under-jaw to its utmost distance from the upper and, by a proper insertion of his fingers provided against the contraction of either corner of his mouth, he experimentally discovered it impossible for human tongue under these circumstances to emit any other modification of sound than that which was described by this primitive character. The vowel 'O' was formed by an orbicular disposition of the mouth, as was aptly delineated in the character itself; the vowel 'U' by a parallel protrusion of the lips; the other vowels and consonants by other various collisions of the mouth and operations of the active tongue upon the passive gum or palate. The result of this profound speculation and long exercise of our prisoner was a philosophical treatise, which he composed when he was set at liberty. He esteemed himself the only master of voice and language on the account of this, his radical science and fundamental knowledge of sounds. But whoever had taken him to improve their voice or teach them an agreeable or just manner of accent or delivery would, I believe, have found themselves considerably deluded.

It is not that I would condemn as useless this speculative science of articulation. It has its place, no doubt, among the other sciences and may serve to grammar as grammar serves to rhetoric and to other arts of speech and writing. The solidity of mathematics and its advantage to mankind is proved by many effects in those beneficial arts and sciences which depend on it, though astrologers, horoscopers and other such are pleased to honour themselves with the title of 'mathematicians'. As for metaphysics and that which in the Schools is taught for logic or for ethics, I shall willingly allow it to pass for philosophy when by any real effects it is proved capable to refine our spirits, improve our understandings or mend our manners. But if the defining 'material' and 'immaterial substances' and distinguishing their properties and modes is recom-

---

[ooo] Paracelsus, or Theophrastus Bombast von Hohenheim, *c.* 1490–1541, was a German physician whose medical theories were based on a mystical application of Neoplatonic principles.

mended to us as the right manner of proceeding in the discovery of our own natures, I shall be apt to suspect such a study as the more delusive and infatuating on account of its magnificent pretension.[PPP]

The study of triangles and circles interferes not with the study of minds. Nor does the student, in the meanwhile, suppose himself advancing in wisdom or the knowledge of himself or mankind. All he desires is to keep his head sound as it was before. And well, he thinks indeed, he has come off if by good fortune there be no crack made in it. As for other ability or improvement in the knowledge of human nature or the world, he refers himself to other studies and practice. Such is the mathematician's modesty and good sense. But for the philosopher, who pretends to be wholly taken up in considering his higher faculties and examining the powers and principles of his understanding, if in reality his philosophy be foreign to the matter professed, if it goes beside the mark and reaches nothing we can truly call our interest or concern, it must be somewhat worse than mere ignorance or idiotism. The most ingenious way of becoming foolish is by a system. And the surest method to prevent good sense is to set up something in the room of it. The liker anything is to wisdom, if it be not plainly the thing itself, the more directly it becomes its opposite.

One would expect it of these physiologists and searchers of modes and substances that, being so exalted in their understandings and enriched with science above other men, they should be as much above them in their passions and sentiments. The consciousness of being admitted into the secret recesses of nature and the inward resources of a human heart should, one would think, create in these gentlemen a sort of magnanimity, which might distinguish them from the ordinary race of mortals. But if their pretended knowledge of the machine of this world and of their own frame is able to produce nothing beneficial either to the one or to the other, I know not to what purpose such a philosophy can serve, except only to shut the door against better knowledge and introduce impertinence and conceit with the best countenance of authority.

It is hardly possible for a student, but more especially an author, who has dealt in ideas and treated formally of the passions in a way of natural philosophy[QQQ] not to imagine himself more wise on this account and more knowing in his own character and the genius of mankind. But that he is mis-

---

[PPP] The distinction between 'material substance' and 'immaterial substance', usually rendered as 'corporeal' and 'incorporeal', arose in the context of scholastic philosophy to explain the difference between inanimate and living things. The language remained current in the seventeenth century as Cartesians, on one hand, and mechanists, on the other, tried to account for the difference between the body and the soul and their relations.

[QQQ] In early modern Europe, the passions were largely of interest to students of rhetoric, and treatises on them were often elaborations of Aristotle's *Rhetoric*. However, natural philosophers, such as René Descartes, whom Shaftesbury discussed below, came to turn their attention to them in the seventeenth century. See Susan James, *Passion and Action: The Emotions in Seventeenth-Century Philosophy* (Oxford: Clarendon Press, 1997).

taken in his calculation, experience generally convinces us, none being found more impotent in themselves, of less command over their passions, less free from superstition and vain fears, or less safe from common imposture and delusion than the noted headpieces of this stamp. Nor is this a wonder. The speculation in a manner bespeaks the practice. There needs no formal deduction to make this evident. A small help from our familiar method of soliloquy may serve turn, and we may perhaps decide this matter in a more diverting way by confronting this super-speculative philosophy with a more practical sort, which relates chiefly to our acquaintance, friendship and good correspondence with ourselves.

On this account it may not be to my reader's disadvantage if, forgetting him for a while, I apply chiefly to myself and, as occasion offers, assume that self-conversant practice which I have pretended to disclose. It is hoped therefore he will not esteem it as ill breeding if I lose the usual regard to his presence. And should I fall insensibly into one of the paroxysms described and, as in a sort of frenzy, enter into high expostulation with myself, he will not surely be offended with the free language or even with the reproaches he hears from a person who only makes bold with whom he may.

If a passenger should turn by chance into a watchmaker's shop and, thinking to inform himself concerning watches, should inquire of what metal or what matter each part was composed, what gave the colours or what made the sounds, without examining what the real use was of such an instrument or by what movements its *end* was best attained and its perfection acquired, it is plain that such an examiner as this would come short of any understanding in the real nature of the instrument. Should a philosopher, after the same manner, employing himself in the study of human nature, discover only what effects each passion wrought upon the body, what change of aspect or feature they produced and in what different manner they affected the limbs and muscles, this might possibly qualify him to give advice to an anatomist or a limner but not to mankind or to himself, since, according to this survey, he considered not the real operation or energy of his subject, nor contemplated the man, *as real man and as a human agent*, but as a watch or common machine.

'The passion of fear', as a modern philosopher informs me, 'determines the spirits to the muscles of the knees, which are instantly ready to perform their motion by taking up the legs with incomparable celerity in order to remove the body out of harm's way.'[62]——Excellent mechanism! But whether the knocking together of the knees be any more the cowardly symptom of flight than the chattering of the teeth is the stout symptom of resistance, I shall not

---

[62] Monsieur Descartes in his treatise of the passions. [Shaftesbury translated loosely here Descartes' discussion in *Les passions de l'âme* (The passions of the soul) 1.36, first published in 1649. On Descartes, see Introduction, p. xiv.]

take upon me to determine. In this whole subject of inquiry, I shall find nothing of the least *self*-concernment. And I may depend upon it that, by the most refined speculation of this kind, I shall neither learn to diminish my fears or raise my courage. This, however, I may be assured of: that it is the nature of fear as well as of other passions to have its increase and decrease as it is fed by opinion and influenced by custom and practice.

These passions, according as they have the ascendancy in me and differ in proportion with one another, affect my character and make me different with respect to myself and others. I must, therefore, of necessity find redress and improvement in this case, by reflecting justly on the manner of my own motion as guided by affections which depend so much on apprehension and conceit. By examining the various turns, inflections, declensions and inward revolutions of the passions, I must undoubtedly come the better to understand a human breast, and judge the better both of others and myself. It is impossible to make the least advancement in such a study without acquiring some advantage from the regulation and government of those passions on which the conduct of a life depends.

For instance, if superstition be the sort of fear which most oppresses, it is not very material to inquire, on this occasion, to what parts or districts the blood or spirits are immediately detached or where they are made to rendezvous. For this no more imports me to understand than it depends on me to regulate or change. But, when the grounds of this superstitious fear are considered to be from opinion, and the subjects of it come to be thoroughly searched and examined, the passion itself must necessarily diminish as I discover more and more the imposture which belongs to it.

In the same manner, if vanity be from opinion and I consider how vanity is conceived, from what imaginary advantages and inconsiderable grounds, if I view it in its excessive height as well as in its contrary depression, it is impossible I should not in some measure be relieved of this distemper. *Do you swell with love of praise? There are sure remedies . . . There are words and sayings with which you can soften this affliction and put aside a great deal of the disease.*[63]

The same must happen in respect of anger, ambition, love, desire and the other passions from whence I frame the different notion I have of interest. For, as these passions veer, my interest veers, my steerage varies and I make alternately now this, now that, to be my course and harbour. The man in anger has a different happiness from the man in love. And the man lately become covetous has a different notion of satisfaction from what he had before, when he was liberal. Even the man in humour has another thought of interest and advantage than the man out of humour or in the least disturbed. The examination, therefore, of my humours and the inquiry after my passions must necessarily

---

[63] Horace, *Epistles* 1.1.34–6. [Shaftesbury shifted the order of these lines.]

draw along with it the search and scrutiny of my opinions and the sincere consideration of my *scope* and *end*.[64] And thus the study of human affection cannot fail of leading me towards the knowledge of *human nature* and of *myself*.

This is the philosophy which by nature has the pre-eminence above all other science or knowledge. Nor can this surely be of the sort called 'vain' or 'deceitful', since it is the only means by which I can discover vanity and deceit.[65] This is not of that kind which depends on genealogies or traditions,[66] and ministers' questions and vain jangling.[67] It has not its name, as other philosophies, from the mere subtlety and nicety of the speculation but, by way of excellence, from its being superior to all other speculations, from its presiding over all other sciences and occupations, teaching the measure of each and assigning the just value of everything in life. By this science, religion itself is judged, spirits are searched, prophecies proved, miracles distinguished, the sole measure and standard being taken from moral rectitude and from the discernment of what is sound and just in the affections. For if the tree is known only by its fruits,[68] my first endeavour must be to distinguish the true taste of fruits, refine my palate and establish a just relish in the kinds. So that to bid me judge authority by morals, while the rule of morals is supposed dependent on mere authority and will,[69] is the same in reality as to bid me see with my eyes shut, measure without a standard and count without arithmetic.

And thus philosophy, which judges both of herself and of everything besides, discovers her own province and chief command, teaches me to distinguish between her person and her likeness, and shows me her immediate and real self by that sole privilege of teaching me to know myself and what belongs to me. She gives to every inferior science its just rank, leaves some to measure sounds, others to scan syllables, others to weigh vacuums and define spaces and extensions, but reserves to herself her due authority and majesty, keeps her state and ancient title of *Vitae Dux, Virtutis Indagatrix*[RRR] and the rest of those just appellations which of old belonged to her when she merited to be apostrophized, as she was, by the Orator: *You were the discoverer of laws, you are the teacher of morality and discipline . . . A single day spent well and following your precepts is to be preferred to an eternity of error!*[70] Excellent mistress!

[RRR] Guide of life, Lucretius, *On the Nature of Things* 2.172; investigatress of virtue, Cicero, *Tusculan Disputations* 5.5.

[64] See *An Inquiry Concerning Virtue*.
[65] Colossians 2.8.
[66] Titus 3.9.
[67] I Timothy, 1.4, 1.6, 6.20.
[68] Luke, 6.43–4, Matthew 7.16. See pp. 267, 294.
[69] See p. 50.
[70] Cicero, *Tusculan Disputations* 5.2.5.

But easy to be mistaken while so many handmaids wear as illustrious apparel, and some are made to outshine her far in dress and ornament.

In reality, how specious a study, how solemn an amusement is raised from what we call 'philosophical speculations', 'the formation of ideas, their compositions, comparisons, agreement, and disagreement'!^{sss}

What can have a better appearance or bid fairer for genuine and true philosophy?

Come on then. Let me philosophize in this manner if this be indeed the way I am to grow wise. Let me examine my ideas of space and substance. Let me look well into matter and its modes if this be looking into myself, if this be to improve my understanding and enlarge my mind. For of this I may soon be satisfied. Let me observe, therefore, with diligence what passes here, what connection and consistency, what agreement or disagreement I find within, 'whether, according to my present ideas, that which I approve this hour, I am like to approve as well the next and, in case it be otherwise with me, how or after what manner I shall relieve myself, how ascertain my ideas and keep my opinion, liking and esteem of things the same'. If this remains unsolved, if I am still the same mystery to myself as ever, to what purpose is all this reasoning and acuteness? Wherefore do I admire my philosopher or study to become such a one myself?

Today things have succeeded well with me, consequently my ideas are raised. 'It is a fine world! All is glorious! Everything delightful and entertaining! Mankind, conversation, company, society – what can be more desirable?' Tomorrow comes disappointment, crosses, disgrace. And what follows? 'O miserable mankind! Wretched state! Who would live out of solitude? Who would write or act for such a world?' Philosopher! where are thy ideas? Where is truth, certainty, evidence, so much talked of? It is here surely they are to be maintained if anywhere. It is here I am to preserve some just distinctions and adequate ideas, which, if I cannot do a jot the more by what such a philosophy can teach me, the philosophy is in this respect imposing and delusive. For whatever its other virtues are, it relates not to me myself, it concerns not the man, nor any otherwise affects the mind than by the conceit of knowledge and the false assurance raised from a supposed improvement.

Again, what are my ideas of the world, of pleasure, riches, fame, life? What judgment am I to make of mankind and human affairs? What sentiments am I to frame? What opinions? What maxims? If none at all, why do I concern myself in speculations about my ideas? What is it to me, for instance, to know what kind of idea I can form of space? 'Divide a solid body of whatever dimension', says a renowned modern philosopher, 'and it will be impossible for the parts to move within the bounds of its superficies, if there be not left

^{sss} This is the language of John Locke's *Essay Concerning Human Understanding*, 2.11–12.

in it a void space as big as the least part into which the said body is divided.'[71] ——

Thus the Atomist or Epicurean pleading for a vacuum. The Plenitudinarian, on the other side, brings his fluid in play and joins the idea of body and extension.[TTT]

'Of this', says one, 'I have clear ideas.'

'Of this', says the other, 'I can be certain.'

'And what', say I, 'if in the whole matter there be no certainty at all?'

For mathematicians are divided, and mechanics proceed as well on one hypothesis as on the other. My mind, I am satisfied, will proceed either way alike, for it is concerned on neither side.

'Philosopher! Let me hear concerning what is of some moment to me. Let me hear concerning life, what the right notion is and what I am to stand to upon occasion that I may not, when life seems retiring or has run itself out to the very dregs, cry "Vanity!", condemn the world and, at the same time, complain that "life is short and passing!"' For why so short indeed if not found sweet? Why do I complain both ways? Is vanity, mere vanity, a happiness? Or can misery pass away too soon?

This is of moment to me to examine. This is worth my while. If, on the other side, I cannot find 'the agreement or disagreement of my ideas' in this place, if I can come to nothing certain here, what is all the rest to me? What signifies it how I come by my ideas or how compound them, which are simple and which complex? If I have a right idea of life now, when perhaps I think slightly of it and resolve with myself that 'it may easily be laid down on any honourable occasion of service to my friends or country', teach me how I may preserve *this* idea or, at least, how I may get safely rid of it that it may trouble me no more nor lead me into ill adventures. Teach me how I came by such an opinion of worth and virtue, what it is which at one time raises it so high and at another time reduces it to nothing, how these disturbances and fluctuations happen, 'by what innovation, what composition, what intervention of other ideas'.

If this be the subject of the philosophical art, I readily apply to it and embrace the study. If there be nothing of this in the case, I have no occasion for this sort of learning, and am no more desirous of knowing how I form or compound those ideas which are marked by words, than I am of knowing how and by what motions of my tongue or palate I form those articulate sounds, which I can full as well pronounce without any such science or speculation.

[TTT] The Plenitudinarian here is Descartes.

[71] These are the words of the particular author cited. [Locke, *An Essay Concerning Human Understanding*, 2.13.22. The quotation is not precise.]

Section 2

But here it may be convenient for me to quit myself a while in favour of my reader, lest, if he prove one of the uncourteous sort, he should raise a considerable objection in this place. He may ask perhaps 'why a writer for self-entertainment should not keep his writings to himself without appearing in public or before the world'.

In answer to this I shall only say that, for appearing in public or before the world, I do not readily conceive what our worthy objector may understand by it. I can call to mind, indeed, among my acquaintance, certain merchant-adventurers in the letter-trade who, in correspondence with their factor-book-seller, are entered into a notable commerce with the world. They have, directly and in due form of preface and epistle dedicatory, solicited the public and made interest with friends for favour and protection on this account. They have ventured, perhaps, to join some great man's reputation with their own, having obtained his permission to address a work to him on presumption of its passing for something considerable in the eyes of mankind. One may easily imagine that such patronized and avowed authors as these would be shrewdly disappointed if the public took no notice of their labours. But, for my own part, it is of no concern to me what regard the public bestows on my amusements, or after what manner it comes acquainted with what I write for my private entertainment, or by way of advice to such of my acquaintance as are thus desperately embarked.

It is requisite that my friends who peruse these advices should read them in better characters than those of my own handwriting. And, by good luck, I have a very fair hand offered, which may save me the trouble of re-copying and can readily furnish me with as many handsome copies as I would desire for my own and friends' service. I have not indeed forbidden my amanuensis[UUU] the making as many as he pleases for his own benefit. What I write is not worth being made a mystery. And if it be worth anyone's purchasing, much good may it do the purchaser. It is a traffic I have no share in, though I accidentally furnish the subject matter.

And thus am I nowise more an author for being in print. I am conscious of no additional virtue, or dangerous quality, from having lain at any time under the weight of that alphabetic engine called the Press. I know no conjuration in it either with respect to Church or State. Nor can I imagine why the machine should appear so formidable to scholars and renowned clerks, whose very mystery and foundation depends on the letter-manufacture. To allow benefit of clergy and to restrain the press seems to me to have something of cross-purpose in it. I can hardly think that the quality of what is written can be altered by the manner of writing, or that there can be any harm in a quick way

[UUU] A person who copies manuscripts, a literary assistant.

of copying fair and keeping copies alike. Why a man may not be permitted to write with iron as well as quill, I cannot conceive, or how a writer changes his capacity by this new dress any more than by the wearing of woven stockings after having worn no other manufacture than the knit.

So much for my reader, if perchance I have any besides the friend or two above-mentioned. For, being engaged in morals and induced to treat so rigorous a subject as that of self-examination, I naturally call to mind the extreme delicacy and tenderness of modern appetites in respect of the philosophy of this kind. What distaste possibly may have arisen from some medicinal doses of a like nature administered to raw stomachs at a very early age, I will not pretend to examine. But whatever manner in philosophy happens to bear the least resemblance to that of catechism cannot, I am persuaded, of itself prove very inviting. Such a smart way of questioning ourselves in our youth has made our manhood more averse to the expostulatory discipline. And though the metaphysical points of our belief are by this method, with admirable care and caution, instilled into tender minds, yet the manner of this anticipating philosophy may make the after-work of reason and the inward exercise of the mind at a riper age proceed the more heavily and with greater reluctance.

It must needs be a hard case with us, after having passed so learned a childhood and been instructed in our own and other higher 'natures', 'essences', 'incorporeal substances', 'personalities' and the like, to condescend at riper years to ruminate and con over this lesson a second time. It is hard, after having, by so many pertinent interrogatories and decisive sentences, declared who and what we are, to come leisurely, in another view, to inquire concerning our real self and end, the judgment we are to make of interest, and the opinion we should have of advantage and good, which is what must necessarily determine us in our conduct and prove the leading principle of our lives.

Can we bear looking anew into these mysteries? Can we endure a new schooling after having once learned our lesson from the world?

Hardly, I presume. For by the lesson of this latter school and according to the sense I acquire in converse with prime men, should I at any time ask myself, 'What governed me?', I should answer readily, 'My interest.'

'But what is interest? And how governed?'

'By opinion and fancy.'

'Is everything therefore my interest which I fancy such? Or may my fancy possibly be wrong?'

'It may.'

'If my fancy of interest therefore be wrong, can my pursuit or aim be right?'

'Hardly so.'

'Can I then be supposed to hit, when I know not, in reality, so much as how to aim?'

My chief interest, it seems, therefore, must be to get *an aim* and know certainly where my happiness and advantage lies.

'Where else can it lie than in my pleasure, since my advantage and good must ever be pleasing, and what is pleasing can never be other than my advantage and good?'

'Excellent! Let fancy therefore govern and interest be what we please. For if that which pleases us be our good because it pleases us, anything may be our interest or good.[72] Nothing can come amiss. That which we fondly make our happiness at one time, we may as readily unmake at another. No one can learn what real good is. Nor can anyone upon this foot be said to understand his interest.'

Here, we see, are strange embroils!

But let us try to deal more candidly with ourselves and frankly own that pleasure is no rule of good,[73] since, when we follow pleasure merely, we are disgusted and change from one sort to another, condemning that at one time which at another we earnestly approve, and never judging equally of happiness while we follow passion and mere humour.

A lover, for instance, when struck with the idea or fancy of his enjoyment, promises himself the highest felicity if he succeeds in his new amour.——He succeeds in it, finds not the felicity he expected, but promises himself the same again in some other.——The same thing happens: he is disappointed as before, but still has faith.——Wearied with this game, he quits the chase, renounces the way of courtship and intrigue, and detests the ceremony and difficulty of the pleasure.——A new species of amours invites him. Here too he meets the same inquietude and inconstancy.——Scorning to grow sottish and plunge in the lowest sink of vice, he shakes off his intemperance, despises gluttony and riot and hearkens to ambition. He grows a man of business and seeks authority and fame.——*With what knot can I hold Proteus who ever changes faces?*[74]

Lest this therefore should be my own case, let me see whether I can control my fancy and fix it, if possible, on something which may hold good.——When I exercise my reason in moral subjects, when I employ my affection in friendly and social actions, I find I can sincerely enjoy myself. If there be a pleasure therefore of this kind, why not indulge it? Or what harm would there be, supposing it should grow greater by indulgence? If I am lazy and indulge myself in the languid pleasure, I know the harm and can foresee the drone. If I am luxurious, I know the harm of this also and have the plain prospect of the sot. If avarice be my pleasure, the end I know is being a miser. But if honesty be my delight, I know no other consequence from indulging

---

[72] See pp. 250, 423.
[73] See p. 151. [On pleasure and Epicureanism, see Introduction, p. xxvi.]
[74] Horace, *Epistles* 1.1.90.

such a passion than that of growing better natured, and enjoying more and more the pleasures of society. On the other hand, if this honest pleasure be lost by knavish indulgence and immorality, there can hardly be a satisfaction left of any kind, since good nature and social affection are so essential even to the pleasures of a debauch.[75]

If therefore the only pleasure I can freely and without reserve indulge be that of the honest and moral kind, if the rational and social enjoyment be so constant in itself and so essential to happiness, why should I not bring my other pleasures to correspond and be friends with it, rather than raise myself other pleasures which are destructive of this foundation and have no manner of correspondency with one another?

Upon this bottom, let me try how I can bear the assault of fancy and maintain myself in my moral fortress against the attacks which are raised on the side of corrupt interest and a wrong self.

When the idea of pleasure strikes I ask myself, 'Before I was thus struck by the idea, was anything amiss with me?'

'No.'

'Therefore, remove the idea and I am well.'

'But having this idea such as I now have, I cannot want the thing without regret.'

'See therefore which is best: either to suffer under this want till the idea be removed or, by satisfying the want, confirm not only this idea but all of the same stamp!'

In reality, has not every fancy a like privilege of passing, if any single one be admitted upon its own authority? And what must be the issue of such an economy if the whole fantastic crew be introduced and the door refused to none? What else is it than this management which leads to the most dissolute and profligate of characters? What is it, on the contrary, which raises us to any degree of worth or steadiness, besides a direct contrary practice and conduct? Can there be strength of mind, can there be command over oneself, if the ideas of pleasure, the suggestions of fancy, and the strong pleadings of appetite and desire are not often withstood, and the imaginations soundly reprimanded and brought under subjection?

Thus it appears that the method of examining our ideas is no pedantic practice. Nor is there anything ungallant in the manner of thus questioning the Lady Fancies, which present themselves as charmingly dressed as possible to solicit their cause and obtain a judgment by favour of that worse part and corrupt self to whom they make their application.

It may be justly said of these that they are very powerful solicitresses. They never seem to importune us, though they are ever in our eye and meet us

[75] See p. 212.

whichever way we turn. They understand better how to manage their appearance than by always throwing up their veil and showing their faces openly in a broad light, to run the danger of cloying our sight or exposing their features to a strict examination. So far are they from such forwardness that they often stand as at a distance, suffering us to make the first advance and contenting themselves with discovering a side-face, or bestowing now and then a glance in a mysterious manner as if they endeavoured to conceal their persons.

One of the most dangerous of these enchantresses appears in a sort of dismal weed, with the most mournful countenance imaginable, often casting up her eyes and wringing her hands, so that it is impossible not to be moved by her till her meaning be considered and her imposture fully known. The airs she borrows are from the tragic muse Melpomene. Nor is she in her own person any way amiable or attractive. Far from it. Her art is to render herself as forbidding as possible, that her sisters may by her means be the more alluring. And if, by her tragic aspect and melancholy looks, she can persuade us that Death (whom she represents) is such a hideous form, she conquers in behalf of the whole fantastic tribe of wanton, gay and fond desires. Effeminacy and cowardice instantly prevail. The poorest means of life grow in repute when the ends and just conditions of it are so little known, and the dread of parting with it raised to so high a degree. The more eagerly we grasp at life, the more impotent we are in the enjoyment of it. By this avidity, its very lees and dregs are swallowed. The ideas of sordid pleasure are advanced. Worth, manhood, generosity and all the nobler opinions and sentiments of honest good and virtuous pleasure disappear and fly before this Queen of Terrors.

It is a mighty delight which a sort of counter-philosophers take in seconding this phantom, and playing her upon our understandings whenever they would take occasion to confound them. The vicious poets employ this spectre too on their side though after a different manner. By the help of this tragic actress, they gain a fairer audience for the luxurious fancies and give their Eratos[vvv] and other playsome Muses a fuller scope in the support of riot and debauch. The gloomy prospect of death becomes the incentive to pleasures of the lowest order. Ashes and shade, the tomb and cypress, are made to serve as foils to luxury. The abhorrence of an insensible state makes mere vitality and animal sensation highly cherished. *Indulge your inner self: let us pluck sweet pleasures, yours is the life you live, you will become ash and ghost and a tale to be told.*[76] It is no wonder if luxury profits by the deformity of this spectre-opinion. She supports her interest by this childish bugbear and, like a mother by her infant, is hugged so much the closer by her votary as the fear presses him and grows importunate. She invites him to live fast, according to her best measure of life.

[vvv] Erato was the Muse of lyric poetry.

[76] Persius, *Satires* 5.151–2.

And well she may. Who would not willingly make life pass away as quickly as was possible, when the nobler pleasures of it were already lost or corrupted by a wretched fear of death? The intense selfishness and meanness, which accompanies this fear, must reduce us to a low ebb of enjoyment and, in a manner, bring to nothing that main sum of satisfactory sensations by which we vulgarly rate the happiness of our private condition and fortune.

But see! A lovely form advances to our assistance, introduced by the prime Muse, the beauteous Calliope![WWW] She shows us what real beauty is and what those numbers are which make life perfect and bestow the chief enjoyment. She sets virtue before our eyes and teaches us how to rate life from the experience of the most heroic spirits. She brings her sisters Clio and Urania to support her.[XXX] From the former she borrows whatever is memorable in history and ancient time to confront the tragic spectre, and show the fixed contempt which the happiest and freest nations, as well as single heroes and private men worthy of any note, have ever expressed for that impostress. From the latter she borrows what is sublimest in philosophy to explain the laws of nature, the order of the universe, and represent to us the justice of accompanying this amiable administration. She shows us that, by this just compliance, we are made happiest and that the measure of a happy life is not from the fewer or more suns we behold, the fewer or more breaths we draw or meals we repeat, but from the having once lived well, acted our part handsomely and made our exit cheerfully and as became us.

Thus we retain on virtue's side the noblest party of the Muses. Whatever is august among those sisters appears readily in our behalf. Nor are the more jocund ladies wanting in their assistance when they act in the perfection of their art, and inspire some better geniuses in this kind of poetry. Such were the nobler lyrics and those of the latter and more refined comedy of the ancients. The Thalias, the Polyhymnias, the Terpsichores, the Euterpes[YYY] willingly join their parts and, being alike interested in the cause of numbers, are with regret employed another way, in favour of disorder. Instead of being made sirens to serve the purposes of vice, they would with more delight accompany their elder sisters and add their graces and attractive charms to what is most harmonious, muse-like and divine in human life. There is this difference only between these and the more heroic dames: that they can more easily be perverted and take the vicious form. For who of any genius or masterly command in the poetic art could think of bringing the epic or tragic muse to act the pander, or be subservient to effeminacy and cowardice? It is not against death, hazards or toils that tragedy and the heroic fable are pointed. It is not mere life which is

---

[WWW] Calliope was the Muse of heroic poetry.

[XXX] Clio was the Muse of history; Urania, of astronomy.

[YYY] Thalia was the Muse of comedy; Polyhymnia, of sacred song; Terpsichore, of dance; and Euterpe, of music.

here exalted or has its price enhanced. On the contrary, its calamities are exposed, the disorders of the passions set to view, fortitude recommended, honour advanced, the contempt of death placed as the peculiar note of every generous and happy soul, and the tenacious love of life as the truest character of an abject wretch. *Is it really so pitiable to die?*[77]

It is not to be imagined how easily we deal with the deluding apparitions and false ideas of happiness and good, when this frightful spectre of misery and ill is after this manner well laid and by honest magic conjured down, so as not to give the least assistance to the other tempting forms. This is that occult science or sort of counter-necromancy which, instead of ghastliness and horror, inspires only what is gentle and humane and dispels the imposing phantoms of every kind. He may pass undoubtedly for no mean conjurer who can deal with spirits of this sort.——But hold!——Let us try the experiment in due form and draw the magic circle. Let us observe how the inferior imps appear when the head goblin is securely laid. ——

See! The enchantress Indolence presents herself in all the pomp of ease and lazy luxury. She promises the sweetest life and invites us to her pillow, enjoins us to expose ourselves to no adventurous attempt, and forbids us any engagement which may bring us into action.

'Where, then, are the pleasures which ambition promises and love affords? How is the gay world enjoyed? Or are those to be esteemed no pleasures which are lost by dullness and inaction?'

'But Indolence is the highest pleasure.'

'To live and not to feel!'

'To feel no trouble.'

'What good then?'

'Life itself.'

'And is this properly to live? Is sleeping, life? Is this what I should study to prolong?'

Here the fantastic tribe itself seems scandalized. A civil war begins. The major part of the capricious dames range themselves on Reason's side and declare against the languid siren. Ambition blushes at the offered sweet. Conceit and Vanity take superior airs. Even Luxury itself, in her polite and elegant humour, reproves the apostate-sister and marks her as an alien to true pleasure.

'Away, thou drowsy phantom! Haunt me no more. For I have learned from better than thy sisterhood that life and happiness consist in action and employment.'

But here a busy form solicits us: active, industrious, watchful, and despising pains and labour. She wears the serious countenance of virtue but with

[77] Virgil, *Aeneid* 12.646.

features of anxiety and disquiet. What is it she mutters? What looks she on with such admiration and astonishment?——Bags! Coffers! Heaps of shining metal!

'What! For the service of luxury? For her these preparations? Art thou then her friend, grave Fancy? Is it for her thou toilest?'

'No, but for provision against want.'

'But, Luxury apart, tell me now: hast thou not already a competence?'

'It is good to be secure against the fear of starving.'

'Is there then no death beside this? No other passage out of life? Are other doors secured if this be barred? Say, Avarice! thou emptiest of phantoms, is it not vile cowardice thou servest? What further have I then to do with thee, thou doubly vile dependant, when once I have dismissed thy patroness and despised her threats?'

Thus, I contend with Fancy and Opinion[78] and search the mint and foundry of imagination. For here the appetites and desires are fabricated. Hence they derive their privilege and currency. If I can stop the mischief here and prevent false coinage, I am safe.

'Idea! Wait a while till I have examined thee, whence thou art and to whom thou retainest. Art thou of Ambition's train? Or dost thou promise only Pleasure? Say! What am I to sacrifice for they sake? What honour? What truth? What manhood?——What bribe is it thou bringest along with thee? Describe the flattering object but without flattery, plain, as the thing is, without addition, without sparing or reserve. Is it wealth? Is it a report? a title? or a female? Come not in a troop, ye Fancies! Bring not your objects crowding to confound the sight. But let me examine your worth and weight distinctly. Think not to raise accumulative happiness. For if separately you contribute nothing, in conjunction you can only amuse.'

While I am thus penning a soliloquy in form, I cannot forbear reflecting on my work. And, when I view the manner of it with a familiar eye, I am readier, I find, to make myself diversion on this occasion than to suppose myself in good earnest about a work of consequence.

'What! Am I to be thus fantastical? Must I busy myself with phantoms, fight with apparitions and chimeras?'

'For certain, or the chimeras will be beforehand with me, and busy themselves so as to get the better of my understanding.'

'What! Talk to myself like some madman, in different persons and under different characters?'

'Undoubtedly, or it will be soon seen who is a *real* madman and changes character in earnest, without knowing how to help it.'

---

[78] See pp. 422ff.

This indeed is but too certain: that, as long as we enjoy a mind, as long as we have appetites and sense, the fancies of all kinds will be hard at work; and, whether we are in company or alone, they must range still and be active. They must have their field. The question is whether they shall have it wholly to themselves or whether they shall acknowledge some controller or manager. If none, it is this, I fear, which leads to madness. It is this, and nothing else, which can be called madness or loss of reason. For if Fancy be left judge of anything, she must be judge of all. Everything is right, if anything be so, because I fancy it.

'The house turns round. The prospect turns.'

'No, but my head turns indeed. I have a giddiness; that is all. Fancy would persuade me thus and thus, but I know better.'

It is by means therefore of a controller and corrector of Fancy that I am saved from being mad. Otherwise, it is the house turns when I am giddy. It is things which change, for so I must suppose, when my passion merely or temper changes.

'But I was out of order. I dreamt.'

'Who tells me this?'

'Who besides the correctress by whose means I am in my wits, and without whom I am no longer myself.'

Every man indeed who is not absolutely beside himself must of necessity hold his fancies under some kind of discipline and management. The *stricter* this discipline is, the more the man is rational and in his wits. The *looser* it is, the more fantastical he must be and the nearer to the madman's state. This is a business which can never stand still. I must always be winner or loser at the game. Either I work upon my fancies or they on me. If I give quarter, they will not. There can be no truce, no suspension of arms between us. The one or the other must be superior and have the command. For if the fancies are left to themselves, the government must of course be theirs. And then, what difference between such a state and madness?

The question therefore is the same here as in a family or household when it is asked, 'Who rules?' or 'Who is master?'

Learn by the voices. Observe who speaks aloud in a commanding tone, who talks, who questions, or who is talked with and who questioned. For if the servants take the former part, they are the masters, and the government of the house will be found such as naturally may be expected in these circumstances.

How stands it therefore in my own economy, my principal province and command? How stand my fancies? How deal they with me? Or do I take upon me rather to deal with them? Do I talk, question, arraign? Or am I talked with, arraigned and contented to hear without giving a reply? If I vote with Fancy, resign my opinion to her command and judge of happiness and misery as she judges, how am I myself?[79]

He who in a plain imagines precipices at his feet, impending rocks over his head, fears bursting clouds in a clear sky, cries 'Fire!', 'Deluge!', 'Earthquake!', or 'Thunder!' when all is quiet: does he not rave? But one whose eyes seemingly strike fire by a blow, one whose head is giddy from the motion of a ship after having been newly set ashore, or one who from a distemper in his ear hears thundering noises, can readily redress these several apprehensions and is by this means saved from madness.

A distemper in my eye may make me see the strangest kind of figures. And when cataracts and other impurities are gathering in that organ, flies, insects and other various forms seem playing in the air before me. But, let my senses err ever so widely, I am not on this account beside myself, nor am I out of my own possession while there is a person left within who has power to dispute the appearances and redress the imagination.

I am accosted by ideas and striking apprehensions, but I take nothing on their report. I hear their story and return them answer as they deserve. Fancy and I are not all one. The disagreement makes me my own. When, on the contrary, I have no debate with her, no controversy, but take for happiness and misery, for good and ill, whatever she presents as such, I must then join voices with her and cry, 'Precipice!', 'Fire!', 'Cerberus!', 'Elysium!' ——

Sandy deserts, flowery fields,
Seas of milk, and ships of amber!

A Grecian prince who had the same madness as Alexander and was deeply struck with the fancy of conquering worlds was ingeniously shown the method of expostulating with his Lady Governess when, by a discreet friend and at an easy hour, he was asked little by little concerning his design and the final purpose and promised good which the flattering dame proposed to him. The story is sufficiently noted. All the artifice employed against the prince was a well-managed interrogatory of 'What next?' Lady Fancy was not aware of the design upon her but let herself be wormed out by degrees. At first she said the prince's design was only upon a tract of land, which stood out like a promontory before him and seemed to eclipse his glory. A fair rich island, which was close by, presented itself next and, as it were, naturally invited conquest. The opposite coast came next in view. Then the continent on each side the larger sea. And then (what was easiest of all and would follow of course) the dominion both of sea and land.

[79] See pp. 422ff.

'And what next?', replied the friend. 'What shall we do when we are become thus happy and have obtained our highest wish?'

'Why then we will sit down peaceably and be good company over a bottle.'

'Alas, Sir! What hinders us from doing the same where we now are? Will our humour or our wine grow better? Shall we be more secure or at heart's ease? What you may possibly lose by these attempts is easy to conceive. But which way you will be a gainer, your own fancy, you see, cannot so much as suggest.'

Fancy in the meanwhile carried her point, for she was absolute over the monarch, and had been too little talked to by herself to bear being reproved in company. The prince grew sullen, turned the discourse, abhorred the profanation offered to his sovereign empress, delivered up his thoughts to her again with deep devotion and fell to conquering with all his might. The sound of victory rung in his ears. Laurels and crowns played before his eyes.———What was this beside giddiness and dream? Appearances uncorrected? 'Worlds dancing'? 'Phantoms playing'? 'Seas of milk, and ships of amber!'

It is easy to bring the hero's case home to ourselves and see, in the ordinary circumstances of life, how love, ambition and the gayer tribe of fancies, as well as the gloomy and dark spectres of another sort, prevail over our mind. It is easy to observe how they work on us when we refuse to be beforehand with them, and bestow repeated lessons on the encroaching sorceresses. On this it is that our offered advice and method of soliloquy depends. And whether this be of any use towards making us either wiser or happier, I am confident it must help to make us wittier and politer. It must, beyond any other science, teach us the turns of humour and passion, the variety of manners, the justness of characters and truth of things, which, when we rightly understand, we may naturally describe. And on this depends chiefly the skill and art of a good writer. So that, if to write well be a just pretence to merit, it is plain that writers who are apt to set no small value on their art must confess there is something valuable in this self-examining practice and method of inward colloquy.

As for the writer of these papers (as modern authors are pleased modestly to style themselves), he is contented, for his part, to take up with this practice barely for his own proper benefit, without regard to the high function or capacity of author. It may be allowed him in this particular to imitate the best genius and most gentleman-like of Roman poets. And, though by an excess of dullness, it should be his misfortune to learn nothing of this poet's wit, he is persuaded he may learn something of his honesty and good humour: *When my comfy couch or portico has welcomed me, I do not fail myself: 'This is the better course; this way I shall live better; so I shall delight the friends I meet.'* ... *With lips tight closed these are my debates with myself.*[80]

Section 3

We are now arrived to that part of our performance where it becomes us to cast our eye back on what has already passed. The observers of method generally make this the place of recapitulation. Other artists have substituted the practice of apology or extenuation. For the anticipating manner of prefatory discourse is too well known to work any surprising effect in the author's behalf, 'preface' being become only another word to signify excuse. Besides that the author is generally the most straitened in that preliminary part, which on other accounts is too apt to grow voluminous. He therefore takes the advantage of his corollary or winding-up, and ends pathetically by endeavouring in the softest manner to reconcile his reader to those faults which he chooses rather to excuse than to amend.

General practice has made this a necessary part of elegance, hardly to be passed over by any writer. It is the chief stratagem by which he engages in personal conference with his reader, and can talk immoderately of himself with all the seeming modesty of one who is the furthest from any selfish views or conceited thoughts of his own merit. There appears such a peculiar grace and ingenuity in the method of confessing laziness, precipitancy, carelessness, or whatever other vices have been the occasion of the author's deficiency, that it would seem a pity, had the work itself been brought to such perfection as to have left no room for the penitent party to enlarge on his own demerits. For from the multiplicity of these, he finds a subject to ingratiate himself with his reader, who doubtless is not a little raised by this submission of a confessing author and is ready, on these terms, to give him absolution and receive him into his good grace and favour.

In the gallant world, indeed, we easily find how far a humility of this kind prevails. They who hope to rise by merit are likeliest to be disappointed in their pretensions. The confessing lover, who ascribes all to the bounty of the fair one, meets his reward the sooner for having studied less how to deserve it. For merit is generally thought presumptuous and supposed to carry with it a certain assurance and ease with which a mistress is not so well contented. The claim of well-deserving seems to derogate from the pure grace and favour of the benefactress, who then appears to herself most sovereign in power and

---

[80] Horace, *Satires* 1.4.133–8. And again: *Wherefore I speak with myself so and silently recollect: if no amount of moisture were to stop your thirst you would tell the tale to the doctors: seeing that the more you gained the more you desire, do you not dare to make confession to someone? . . . You are not greedy: fine! what then? Have your other vices already gone with that one? is your heart free of empty ambition? is it free of fear of death and anger?*: Horace, *Epistles* 2.2.145–8, 205–7.

likeliest to be obeyed without reserve, when she bestows her bounty where there is least title or pretension.

Thus a certain adoration of the sex, which passes in our age without the least charge of profaneness or idolatry, may, according to vulgar imagination, serve to justify these gallant votaries in the imitation of the real religious and devout. The method of self-abasement[81] may perhaps be thought the properest to make approaches to the sacred shrines, and the entire resignation of merit, in each case, may be esteemed the only ground of well-deserving. But what we allow to Heaven or the fair should not, methinks, be made a precedent in favour of the world. Whatever deference is due to that body of men whom we call readers, we may be supposed to treat them with sufficient honour if, with thorough diligence and pains, we endeavour to render our works perfect and leave them to judge of the performance as they are able.

However difficult or desperate it may appear in any artist to endeavour to bring perfection into his work, if he has not at least the idea of perfection to give him aim, he will be found very defective and mean in his performance. Though his intention be to please the world, he must nevertheless be, in a manner, above it and fix his eye upon that consummate grace, that beauty of nature, and that perfection of numbers which the rest of mankind, feeling only by the effect while ignorant of the cause, term the *je ne sais quoi*, the unintelligible or the 'I know not what', and suppose to be a kind of charm or enchantment of which the artist himself can give no account.

But here I find I am tempted to do what I have myself condemned. Hardly can I forbear making some apology for my frequent recourse to the rules of common artists, to the masters of exercise, to the academies of painters, statuaries, and to the rest of the virtuoso tribe.*ZZZ* But in this I am so fully satisfied I have reason on my side that, let custom be ever so strong against me, I had rather repair to these inferior schools to search for truth and nature than to some other places where higher arts and sciences are professed.

I am persuaded that to be a virtuoso, so far as befits a gentleman, is a higher step towards the becoming a man of virtue and good sense than the being what in this age we call a scholar.[82] For even rude nature itself, in its primitive

---

ZZZ On virtuosi, see p. 62n.

[81] See p. 20.

[82] It seems indeed somewhat improbable that, according to modern erudition and as science is now distributed, our ingenious and noble youths should obtain the full advantage of a just and liberal education by uniting the scholar part with that of the real gentleman and man of breeding. Academies for exercises, so useful to the public and essential in the formation of a genteel and liberal character, are unfortunately neglected. Letters are indeed banished, I know not where, in distant cloisters and unpractised cells, as our poet has it, confined to the commerce and mean 'fellowship' of 'bearded boys'. The sprightly arts and sciences are severed from philosophy, which consequently must grow dronish, insipid, pedantic, useless and directly

simplicity, is a better guide to judgment than improved sophistry and pedantic learning. The *they are so knowing that they know nothing at all*[AAAA] will ever be applied by men of discernment and free thought to such logic, such principles, such forms and rudiments of knowledge as are established in certain schools of literature and science. The case is sufficiently understood even by those unwilling to confess the truth of it. Effects betray their causes. And the known turn and figure of those understandings, which sprout from nurseries of this kind, give a plain idea of what is judged on this occasion. It is no wonder if, after so wrong a ground of education, there appears to be such need of redress and amendment from that excellent school which we call 'the World'. The mere amusements of gentlemen are found more improving than the profound researches of pedants. And, in the management of our youth, we are forced to have recourse to the former as an antidote against the genius peculiar to the latter. If the formalists of this sort were erected into patentees with a sole commission of authorship, we should undoubtedly see such writing in our days as would either wholly wean us from all books in general, or at least from all such as were the product of our own nation under such a subordinate and conforming government.

However this may prove, there can be no kind of writing which relates to men and manners where it is not necessary for the author to understand poetical and moral truth, the beauty of sentiments, the sublime of characters, and

---

opposite to the real knowledge and practice of the world and mankind. Our youth accordingly seem to have their only chance between two widely different roads, either that of pedantry and school learning, which lies amid the dregs and most corrupt part of ancient literature, or that of the fashionable illiterate world, which aims merely at the character of the fine gentleman and takes up with the foppery of modern languages and foreign wit. The frightful aspect of the former of these roads makes the journey appear desperate and impracticable. Hence that aversion so generally conceived against a learned character, wrong turned and hideously set out under such difficulties and in such seeming labyrinths and mysterious forms. As if a Homer or a Xenophon imperfectly learned in raw years might not afterwards in a riper age be studied as well in a capital city and amid the world as at a college or country town! Or as if a Plutarch, a Tully or a Horace could not accompany a young man in his travels at a Court or (if occasion were) even in a camp! The case is not without precedent. Leisure is found sufficient for other reading of numerous modern translations and worse originals of Italian and French authors, who are read merely for amusement. The French indeed may boast of some legitimate authors of a just relish, correct and without any mixture of the affected or spurious kinds: the false tender or the false sublime; the conceited jingle; or the ridiculous point. They are such geniuses as have been formed upon the natural model of the ancients and willingly own their debt to those great masters. But for the rest, who draw from another fountain, as the Italian authors in particular, they may be reckoned no better than the corrupters of true learning and erudition and can indeed be relished by those alone whose education has unfortunately denied them the familiarity of the noble ancients and the practice of a better and more natural taste. See pp. 128, 232–3.

[AAAA] Terence, *The Woman of Andros* Prologue.17.

carry in his eye the model or exemplar of that natural grace which gives to every action its attractive charm.[83] If he has naturally no eye or ear for these interior numbers, it is not likely he should be able to judge better of that exterior proportion and symmetry of composition which constitutes a legitimate piece.

Could we once convince ourselves of what is in itself so evident, that *in the very nature of things there must of necessity be the foundation of a right and wrong taste, as well in respect of inward characters and features as of outward person, behaviour and action,*[84] we should be far more ashamed of ignorance and wrong judgment in the former than in the latter of these subjects. Even in the arts, which are mere imitations of that outward grace and beauty, we not only confess a taste but make it a part of refined breeding to discover, amid the many false manners and ill styles, the true and natural one, which represents the real beauty and Venus of the kind.[85] It is the like moral grace and Venus which, discovering itself in the turns of character and the variety of human affection, is copied by the writing artist. If he knows not this Venus, these graces, nor was ever struck with the beauty, the decorum of this inward kind, he can neither paint advantageously after the life nor in a feigned subject where he has full scope. For never can he, on these terms, represent merit and virtue or mark deformity and blemish.[86] Never can he with justice and true proportion assign the boundaries of either part or separate the distant characters. The schemes must be defective, and the drafts confused, where the standard is weakly established and the measure out of use. Such a designer, who has so little feeling of these proportions, so little consciousness of this excellence or these perfections, will never be found able to describe a perfect character or, what is more according to art, express the effect and force of this perfection from the result of various and mixed characters of life.[87] And thus the sense of inward numbers, the knowledge and practice of the social virtues, and the familiarity and favour of the moral graces are essential to the character of a deserving artist and just favourite of the Muses. Thus are the arts and virtues mutually friends and thus the science of virtuosos and that of virtue itself become, in a manner, one and the same.

One who aspires to the character of a man of breeding and politeness is careful to form his judgment of arts and sciences upon right models of perfection. If he travels to Rome, he inquires which are the truest pieces of architecture,

[83] See p. 93.
[84] See pp. 408, 414.
[85] See pp. 64, 415–17n.
[86] See p. 93.
[87] See pp. 448–9n.

the best remains of statues, the best paintings of a Raphael or a Carracci.[BBBB]
However antiquated, rough or dismal they may appear to him at first sight, he
resolves to view them over and over till he has brought himself to relish them
and finds their hidden graces and perfections. He takes particular care to turn
his eye from everything which is gaudy, luscious and of a false taste. Nor is he
less careful to turn his ear from every sort of music besides that which is of
the best manner and truest harmony.

It were to be wished we had the same regard to a right taste in life and manners. What mortal being, once convinced of a difference in inward character
and of a preference due to one kind above another, would not be concerned to
make his own the best? If civility and humanity be a taste, if brutality, insolence, riot be in the same manner a taste, who, if he could reflect, would not
choose to form himself on the amiable and agreeable rather than the odious
and perverse model? Who would not endeavour to force nature as well in this
respect as in what relates to a taste or judgment in other arts and sciences? For
in each place the force on nature is used only for its redress. If a natural good
taste be not already formed in us, why should not we endeavour to form it,
and become natural? ——

'I like! I fancy! I admire!'

'How?'

'By accident, or as I please.'

'No. But I *learn* to fancy, to admire, to please, as the subjects themselves
are deserving and can bear me out. Otherwise, I like at this hour but dislike
the next. I shall be weary of my pursuit and, upon experience, find little pleasure in the main, if my choice and judgment in it be from no other rule than
that single one, *because I please.*[88] Grotesque and monstrous figures often please.
Cruel spectacles and barbarities are also found to please and, in some tempers,
to please beyond all other subjects. But is this pleasure right? And shall I follow it if it presents? Not strive with it or endeavour to prevent its growth or
prevalency in my temper?——How stands the case in a more soft and flattering kind of pleasure?——Effeminacy pleases me. The Indian figures, the Japan
work, the enamel strikes my eye. The luscious colours and glossy paint gain
upon my fancy. A French or Flemish style is highly liked by me at first sight,

---

[BBBB] Rome was the ultimate destination of the English gentleman on the Grand Tour, for which
see Jeremy Black, *The British Abroad: The Grand Tour in the Eighteenth Century* (New York:
St Martin's Press, 1992), and Andrew Wilton and Ilaria Bignamini, *Grand Tour: The Lure of
Italy in the Eighteenth Century* (London: Tate Gallery, 1996). In Shaftesbury's art criticism,
Raphael (Raffaello Sanzio, 1483–1520) and the Carracci (Lodovico, 1555–1618, Agostino,
1557–1602, and Annibale, 1560–1609) were among the few modern painters to merit recognition.

[88] See pp. 138, 150.

and I pursue my liking.^{CCCC} But what ensues?——Do I not forever forfeit my good relish? How is it possible I should thus come to taste the beauties of an Italian master or of a hand happily formed on nature and the ancients? It is not by wantonness and humour that I shall attain my end and arrive at the enjoyment I propose. The art itself is severe, the rules rigid.[89] And if I expect the knowledge should come to me by accident or in play, I shall be grossly deluded and prove myself, at best, a mock-virtuoso or mere pedant of the kind.'

Here therefore we have once again exhibited our moral science in the same method and manner of soliloquy as above. To this correction of humour and formation of a taste, our reading, if it be of the right sort, must principally

---

CCCC Such judgments were abundant in Shaftesbury's writings on art. For instance: 'But this assert: that neither Jew, Egyptian, nor Chinese polite . . . If polite: show me a picture, a statue, coin, proportion, nature. But Arabesque! Japan! Indian! Savage. Monstrous.' See Benjamin Rand, *Second Characters or the Language of Forms by the Right Honourable Anthony, Earl of Shaftesbury* (Cambridge: Cambridge University Press, 1914; repr., New York: Greenwood Press, 1969), p. 104.

89 Thus, Pliny [in Book 35 of *Natural History*], speaking with a masterly judgment of the dignity of the then declining art of painting, shows it to be not only severe in respect of the discipline, style, design, but of the characters and lives of the noble masters, not only in the effect but even in the very materials of the art, the colours, ornaments and particular circumstances belonging to the profession: *Antidotus was the pupil of Euphranor . . . he was more careful than prolific and restrained in his colours* [35.40.130], *To Nicias is compared and sometimes preferred Athenion of Maronea, a pupil of Glaucion of Corinth, who is more sombre in his colour and yet more delightful in his sombreness, so that his erudition shines out in the picture itself . . . If he had not died in youth, nobody would be compared to him* [35.40.134], *Aristolaus, the son and pupil of Pausias, was among the very restrained painters* [35.40.137], *A recent painter, Amulius* [Famulus according to current readings], *was grave and restrained . . . He used to paint for only a few hours a day and yet did so with gravity, always wearing a toga even on scaffolding* [35.37.120]. One of the mortal symptoms upon which Pliny pronounces the sure death of this noble art, not long survivor to him, was what belonged in common to all the other perishing arts after the fall of liberty, I mean, the luxury of the Roman Court and the change of taste and manners naturally consequent to such a change of government and dominion. This excellent, learned and polite critic represents to us the false taste springing from the Court itself and from that opulence, splendour and affectation of magnificence and expense proper to the place. Thus, in the statuary and architecture then in vogue, nothing could be admired beside what was costly in the mere matter or substance of the work. Precious rock, rich metal, glittering stones and other luscious ware, poisonous to art, came every day more into request and were imposed as necessary materials on the best masters. It was in favour of these Court beauties and gaudy appearances that all good drawing, just design and truth of work began to be despised. Care was taken to procure from distant parts the most gorgeous splendid colours of the most costly growth and composition, not such as had been used by Apelles and the great masters, who were justly severe, loyal and faithful to their art. This newer colouring our critic calls 'the florid kind'. The materials were too rich to be furnished by the painter but were bespoke or furnished at the cost of the person who employed him [35.11.30]. The other he calls the 'austere kind'. And thus, says he, 'the cost, and not the life and art, is studied' [35.32.50]. He shows, on the contrary, what care Apelles took to subdue the florid colours by a darkening varnish [35.36.97]. And he says just before, of some of the finest pieces of Apelles, 'that they were wrought in four colours only'. So great and venerable was *simplicity* held among the ancients and so certain was the ruin of all true elegance in life or art where this mistress was once quitted or contemned! See pp. 66n, 100.

contribute. Whatever company we keep, or however polite and agreeable their characters may be with whom we converse or correspond, if the authors we read are of another kind, we shall find our palate strangely turned their way. We are the unhappier in this respect for being scholars if our studies be ill chosen. Nor can I, for this reason, think it proper to call a man well-read who reads many authors, since he must of necessity have more ill models than good and be more stuffed with bombast, ill fancy and wry thought than filled with solid sense and just imagination.

But notwithstanding this hazard of our taste from a multiplicity of reading, we are not, it seems, the least scrupulous in our choice of subject. We read whatever comes next us. What was first put into our hand when we were young serves us afterwards for serious study and wise research when we are old. We are, many of us, indeed, so grave as to continue this exercise of youth through our remaining life. The exercising authors of this kind have been above-described in the beginning of this treatise.[90] The manner of exercise is called meditation, and is of a sort so solemn and profound that we dare not so much as thoroughly examine the subject on which we are bid to meditate. This is a sort of task-reading, in which a taste is not permitted. How little soever we take of this diet, it is sufficient to give full exercise to our grave humour and allay the appetite towards further research and solid contemplation. The rest is holiday, diversion, play and fancy. We reject all rule as thinking it an injury to our diversions to have regard to truth or nature, without which, however, nothing can be truly agreeable or entertaining, much less instructive or improving. Through a certain surfeit taken in a wrong kind of serious reading,[91] we apply ourselves, with full content, to the most ridiculous. The more remote our pattern is from anything moral or profitable, the more freedom and satisfaction we find in it. We care not how Gothic or barbarous our models are, what ill-designed or monstrous figures we view or what false proportions we trace or see described in history, romance or fiction. And thus our eye and ear is lost. Our relish or taste must of necessity grow barbarous while barbarian customs, savage manners, Indian wars and wonders of the *terra incognita*[DDDD] employ our leisure hours and are the chief materials to furnish out a library.

These are in our present days what books of chivalry were in those of our forefathers. I know not what faith our valiant ancestors may have had in the stories of their giants, their dragons and St. Georges. But, for our faith, indeed, as well as our taste in this other way of reading, I must confess I cannot consider it without astonishment.

[DDDD]Unknown land, unexplored region.

[90] See pp. 74–5.
[91] See pp. 34–5.

It must certainly be something else than incredulity which fashions the taste and judgment of many gentlemen, whom we hear censured as atheists for attempting to philosophize after a newer manner than any known of late. For my own part, I have ever thought this sort of men to be in general more credulous, though after another manner, than the mere vulgar. Besides what I have observed in conversation with the men of this character, I can produce many anathematized authors who, if they want a true Israelitish faith, can make amends by a Chinese or Indian one. If they are short in Syria or the Palestine, they have their full measure in America or Japan. Histories of Incas or Iroquois, written by friars and missionaries, pirates and renegades, sea captains and trusty travellers, pass for authentic records and are canonical with the virtuosos of this sort. Though Christian miracles may not so well satisfy them, they dwell with the highest contentment on the prodigies of Moorish and pagan countries. They have far more pleasure in hearing the monstrous accounts of monstrous men and manners than the politest and best narrations of the affairs, the governments and lives of the wisest and most polished people.[EEEE]

It is the same taste which makes us prefer a Turkish history to a Grecian or a Roman, an Ariosto to a Virgil, and a romance or novel to an *Iliad*.[FFFF] We have no regard to the character or genius of our author, nor are so far curious as to observe how able he is in the judgment of facts or how ingenious in the texture of his lies. For facts unably related, though with the greatest sincerity and good faith, may prove the worst sort of deceit. And mere lies, judiciously composed, can teach us the truth of things beyond any other manner.[92] But to amuse ourselves with such authors as neither know how to lie nor tell truth discovers a taste which, methinks, one should not be apt to envy. Yet so enchanted we are with the travelling memoirs of any casual adventurer that, be his character or genius what it will, we have no sooner turned over a page or two than we begin to interest ourselves highly in his affairs. No sooner has he taken shipping at the mouth of the Thames, or sent his baggage before him to Gravesend or Buoy in the Nore, than straight our attention is earnestly taken up. If in order to his more distant travels he takes some part of Europe in his way, we can with patience hear of inns and ordinaries, passage boats and

---

[EEEE] In a letter of 3 June 1709, Shaftesbury referred to 'credulous Mr. Locke, with his Indian, barbarian stories of wild nations that have no such idea [of order and divine cosmic administration] (as travellers, learned authors! and men of truth! and great philosophers! have informed him): *Several Letters Written by a Noble Lord to a Young Man at the University* (London, 1716), pp. 39–40. Locke used such material in the *Essay Concerning Human Understanding*, among other places, at 1.3.9 and 1.4.8.

[FFFF] Ludovico Ariosto, 1474–1533, was an Italian poet whose *Orlando Furioso* was a highly episodic and often fantastic epic.

[92] The greatest of critics says of the greatest poet, when he extols him the highest, 'that above all others Homer understood how to lie': Aristotle, *Poetics* 24.18. See p. 448–9n.

ferries, foul and fair weather, with all the particulars of the author's diet, habit of body, his personal dangers and mischances on land and sea. And thus, full of desire and hope, we accompany him till he enters on his great scene of action and begins by the description of some enormous fish or beast. From monstrous brutes he proceeds to yet more monstrous men. For in this race of authors he is ever completest and of the first rank who is able to speak of things the most unnatural and monstrous.

This humour our old tragic poet seems to have discovered.[93] He hit our taste in giving us a Moorish hero, full-fraught with prodigy, a wondrous story-teller! But, for the attentive part, the poet chose to give it to womankind. What passionate reader of travels or student in the prodigious sciences can refuse to pity that fair lady, who fell in love with the miraculous Moor? Especially considering with what suitable grace such a lover could relate the most monstrous adventures and satisfy the wondering appetite with the most wondrous tales, wherein, says the hero-traveller:

> . . . of antres vast and deserts idle . . .,
> It was my hint to speak . . .
> And of the cannibals that each other eat,
> The anthropophagi, and men whose heads
> Do grow beneath their shoulders. These [things] to hear
> Would Desdemona seriously incline.[GGGG]

Seriously, it was a woeful tale, unfit, one would think, to win a tender fair one! It is true, the poet sufficiently condemns her fancy and makes her, poor lady, pay dearly for it in the end. But why, among his Greek names, he should have chosen one which denoted the lady 'superstitious',[HHHH] I cannot imagine, unless, as poets are sometimes prophets too, he should figuratively, under this dark type, have represented to us that about a hundred years after his time the fair sex of this island should, by other monstrous tales, be so seduced as to turn their favour chiefly on the persons of the taletellers and change their natural inclination for fair, candid and courteous knights into a passion for a mysterious race of black enchanters, such as of old were said to 'creep into houses' and 'lead captive silly women'.

It is certain there is a very great affinity between the passion of superstition and that of tales. The love of strange narrations and the ardent appetite towards unnatural objects has a near alliance with the like appetite towards the supernatural kind, such as are called prodigious and of dire omen. For so the mind

---

[GGGG] *Othello* 1.3.140–6. An antre is a cave. Anthropophagi are man-eaters.

[HHHH] Shaftesbury was not alone in relating Desdemona's name to the Greek word for 'superstitious', though it could as well be related to the word for 'wretched'.

[93] Shakespeare.

forebodes on every such unusual sight or hearing. Fate, destiny or the anger of Heaven seems denoted and, as it were, delineated by the monstrous birth, the horrid fact or dire event. For this reason the very persons of such relaters or taletellers, with a small help of dismal habit, suitable countenance and tone, become sacred and tremendous in the eyes of mortals who are thus addicted from their youth. The tender virgins, losing their natural softness, assume this tragic passion, of which they are highly susceptible, especially when a suitable kind of eloquence and action attends the character of the narrator. A thousand Desdemonas are then ready to present themselves and would frankly resign fathers, relations, countrymen and country itself to follow the fortunes of a hero of the black tribe.

But whatever monstrous zeal or superstitious passion the poet might foretell, either in the gentlemen, ladies or common people of an after age, it is certain that, as to books, the same Moorish fancy, in its plain and literal sense, prevails strongly at this present time. Monsters and monster lands were never more in request, and we may often see a philosopher or a wit run a tale-gathering in those 'idle deserts' as familiarly as the silliest woman or merest boy.

One would imagine that our philosophical writers, who pretend to treat of morals, should far outdo mere poets in recommending virtue and representing what was fair and amiable in human actions.[94] One would imagine, that if they

---

[94] Considering what has been so often said on this subject of philosophy, learning and the sister arts, after that ancient model which has since been so much corrupted, it may not be amiss perhaps to hear the confession of one of the greatest and most learned of moderns upon this head: *Of course, they would agree with the wise men of old that poetry shares quarters with the most restrained philosophy. We see that they have played down all concern for character, which truly is philosophy, in certain little fussy disputes, in sophistic fluff, in childish quibblings, in hurtful parrotings of dialectic, of which even in their own time Euphrades and Themistius complained, and so they abandon the heights of wisdom! Of course, the virility of Persius' eloquence or his recondite erudition will capture those for whom clinging tenaciously to an old-fashioned barbarity and basking in complete ignorance of antiquity seems quite preferable to laying claim to literature, which once had been snuffed out by a similar stupidity, but which in living memory of our forefathers, by the great grace of immortal God, was brought back to light from the deep depths of human oblivion, to be reappropriated and claimed for our prestige before posterity . . . Indeed, Arrian writes that Epictetus, that very wise old man, charged with impiety towards God those who in their studies of philosophy spurned the power of expression, as though it were a trivial business, since, a divine man [Socrates] said, 'It is the mark of an impious man to dishonour the blessings that come from God.' Behold German philosophy! Behold the golden voice! No less memorable is the prophecy of the outstanding philosopher Synesius, confirmed by the sad outcome of events, which was issued by himself long before, when he saw that the guiding principle for studies was similarly being undermined by his contemporaries. Arguing against those who brought to the studies of most holy theology childish babble and sophistry instead of solid erudition, he issued this almost oracular pronouncement: 'There is danger', he said, 'that these men shall fall into some abyss of nonsense and be corrupted.' Would that there had been no trust in this oracle! But certainly the invasions of the Goths and the Alans offered an opportunity for that depravity, both of this queen of sciences and all others, which happened afterwards; but the more accurate and true cause of that depravity was the undermining of the principles of study and education in the liberal disciplines and ignorance of both languages and the better, universal litera-*

turned their eye towards remote countries, of which they affect so much to speak, they should search for that simplicity of manners and innocence of behaviour which has been often known among mere savages before they were corrupted by our commerce and, by sad example, instructed in all kinds of treachery and inhumanity. It would be of advantage to us to hear the causes of this strange corruption in ourselves, and be made to consider of our deviation from nature and from that just purity of manners which might be expected, especially from a people so assisted and enlightened by religion. For who would not naturally expect more justice, fidelity, temperance and honesty from Christians than from Mohammedans or mere pagans? But so far are our modern moralists from condemning any unnatural vices or corrupt manners, whether in our own or foreign climates, that they would have vice itself appear as natural as virtue and, from the worst examples, would represent to us that 'all actions are naturally indifferent', that 'they have no note or character of good or ill in themselves but are distinguished by mere fashion, law, or arbitrary decree'. Wonderful philosophy, raised from the dregs of an illiterate mean kind, which was ever despised among the great ancients and rejected by all men of action or sound erudition but, in these ages, imperfectly copied from the original and, with much disadvantage, imitated and assumed in common both by devout and undevout attempters in the moral kind!

Should a writer upon music, addressing himself to the students and lovers of the art, declare to them that 'the measure or rule of harmony was caprice or will, humour or fashion', it is not very likely he should be heard with great attention or treated with real gravity. For harmony is harmony by nature, let men judge ever so ridiculously of music. So is symmetry and proportion founded still in nature, let men's fancy prove ever so barbarous or their fashions ever so Gothic in their architecture, sculpture or whatever other designing art. It is the same case where life and manners are concerned. Virtue has the same fixed standard. The same numbers, harmony and proportion will have place in morals and are discoverable in the characters and affections of mankind,

---

ture . . . *Nevertheless, not of course to that end have great men transmitted to posterity the precepts and examples of virtues, entrusted to memory, so that in contrast to the inane delights of the ears, or the empty parading of a useless erudition, we might recognize them for what they are; rather that by their endless toils they might arouse us to dig out and bring into action the seeds of what is right and honourable; when we inherited by nature these seeds, although they were hedged about by vices, they were not completely obliterated, but, save for the coming of a better civilization, they lie hid in our souls as if buried deep within some ditch. To this stand witness all those many volumes, which they have consumed, about the moral discipline of philosophy. The great band of Greek and Roman poets has the same goal but takes different routes. The number of types of poets (and they are numberless) is almost matched by the zigzaggings and meanderings of the paths that lead them there:* Isaac Casaubon in the preface, sigs. aiii^v–av^v, to his edition and commentary on Persius' *Satires* (Paris, 1605). See pp. 85–6, 93, 128, 133–4, 148–51, 365, 372–3, 439n.

in which are laid the just foundations of an art and science superior to every other of human practice and comprehension.

This, I suppose therefore, is highly necessary that a writer should comprehend. For things are stubborn and will not be as we fancy them or as the fashion varies, but as they stand in nature. Now whether the writer be poet, philosopher or of whatever kind, he is in truth no other than a copyist after nature. His style may be differently suited to the different times he lives in or to the different humour of his age or nation: his manner, his dress, his colouring may vary. But if his drawing be uncorrect or his design contrary to nature, his piece will be found ridiculous when it comes thoroughly to be examined. For nature will not be mocked. The prepossession against her can never be very lasting. Her decrees and instincts are powerful, and her sentiments inbred. She has a strong party abroad and as strong a one within ourselves. And when any slight is put upon her, she can soon turn the reproach and make large reprisals on the taste and judgment of her antagonists.

Whatever philosopher, critic or author is convinced of this prerogative of nature will easily be persuaded to apply himself to the great work of reforming his taste, which he will have reason to suspect if he be not such a one as has deliberately endeavoured to frame it by the just standard of nature. Whether this be his case, he will easily discover by appealing to his memory, for custom and fashion are powerful seducers, and he must of necessity have fought hard against these to have attained that justness of taste which is required in one who pretends to follow nature. But if no such conflict can be called to mind, it is a certain token that the party has his taste very little different from the vulgar. And on this account he should instantly betake himself to the wholesome practice recommended in this treatise. He should set afoot the powerfullest faculties of his mind and assemble the best forces of his wit and judgment in order to make a formal descent on the territories of the heart, resolving to decline no combat nor hearken to any terms till he had pierced into its inmost provinces and reached the seat of empire. No treaties should amuse him, no advantages lead him aside. All other speculations should be suspended, all other mysteries resigned, till this necessary campaign was made and these inward conflicts learned, by which he would be able to gain at least some tolerable insight into himself and knowledge of his own natural principles.

It may here perhaps be thought that, notwithstanding the particular advice we have given in relation to the forming of a taste in natural characters and manners, we are still defective in our performance while we are silent on supernatural cases, and bring not into our consideration the manners and characters delivered us in Holy Writ. But this objection will soon vanish when we consider that there can be no rules given by human wit to that which was never humanly conceived but divinely dictated and inspired.

For this reason, it would be in vain for any poet or ingenious author to form his characters after the models of our sacred penmen.[95] And whatever certain critics may have advanced concerning the structure of a heroic poem of this kind, I will be bold to prophesy that the success will never be answerable to expectation.

It must be owned that in our sacred history we have both leaders, conquerors, founders of nations, deliverers and patriots who, even in a human sense, are no way behind the chief of those so much celebrated by the ancients. There is nothing in the story of Aeneas which is not equalled or exceeded by a Joshua or a Moses. But, as illustrious as are the acts of these sacred chiefs, it would be hard to copy them in just heroic. It would be hard to give to many of them that graceful air which is necessary to render them naturally pleasing to mankind, according to the idea men are universally found to have of heroism and generosity.

Notwithstanding the pious endeavours which, as devout Christians, we may have used in order to separate ourselves from the interest of mere heathens and infidels, notwithstanding the true pains we may have taken to arm our hearts in behalf of a chosen people against their neighbouring nations of a false religion and worship, there will be still found such a partiality remaining in us towards creatures of the same make and figure with ourselves as will hinder us from viewing with satisfaction the punishments inflicted by human hands on such aliens and idolaters.

In mere poetry and the pieces of wit and literature, there is a liberty of thought and easiness of humour indulged to us in which, perhaps, we are not so well able to contemplate the divine judgments and see clearly into the justice of those ways, which are declared to be so far from our ways and above our highest thoughts or understandings. In such a situation of mind we can hardly endure to see heathen treated as heathen, and the faithful made the executioners of the divine wrath. There is a certain perverse humanity in us which inwardly resists the divine commission, though ever so plainly revealed. The wit of the best poet is not sufficient to reconcile us to the campaign of a Joshua or the retreat of a Moses by the assistance of an Egyptian loan.[IIII] Nor will it be possible, by the Muses' art, to make the royal hero appear amiable in human eyes who found such favour in the eye of Heaven.[JJJJ] Such are mere human

---

[IIII]   Joshua assumed the leadership of the Hebrews on the death of Moses and went on to conquer Canaan (as related in *Joshua*). Before departing Egypt, Moses advised the Hebrews to borrow gold and silver from the Egyptians, which they did: Exodus 11.2, 12.35.

[JJJJ]   David.

[95]   See pp. 439n.

hearts that they can hardly find the least sympathy with that only one which had the character of being after the pattern of the Almighty's.[KKKK]

It is apparent, therefore, that the manners, actions and characters of sacred writ are no wise the proper subject of other authors than divines themselves. They are matters incomprehensible in philosophy; they are above the pitch of the mere human historian, the politician or the moralist, and are too sacred to be submitted to the poet's fancy when inspired by no other spirit than that of his profane mistresses, the Muses.

I should be unwilling to examine rigorously the performance of our great poet, who sung so piously the Fall of Man.[96] The war in Heaven and the catastrophe of that original pair, from whom the generations of mankind were propagated, are matters so abstrusely revealed and with such a resemblance of mythology that they can more easily bear what figurative construction or fantastic turn the poet may think fit to give them. But should he venture further into the lives and characters of the patriarchs, the holy matrons, heroes and heroines of the chosen seed, should he employ the sacred machine, the exhibitions and interventions of divinity according to Holy Writ to support the action of his piece, he would soon find the weakness of his pretended orthodox muse and prove how little those divine patterns were capable of human imitation, or of being raised to any other majesty or sublime than that in which they originally appear.

The theology or theogony[LLLL] of the heathens could admit of such different turns and figurative expressions as suited the fancy and judgment of each philosopher or poet. But the purity of our faith will admit of no such variation. The Christian theology, the birth, procedure, generation and personal distinction of the Divinity, are mysteries only to be determined by the initiated or ordained, to whom the State has assigned the guardianship and promulgation of the divine oracles. It becomes not those who are uninspired from Heaven and uncommissioned from earth to search with curiosity into the original of those holy rites and records by law established. Should we make such an attempt, we should in probability find the less satisfaction the further we presumed to carry our speculations. Having dared once to quit the authority and direction of the law, we should easily be subject to heterodoxy and error when we had no better warrant left us for the authority of our sacred symbols than the integrity, candour and disinterestedness of their compilers and registers. How great that candour and disinterestedness may have been, we have no other histories to inform us than those of their own licensing or composing.

[KKKK] Jesus.

[LLLL] An account of the origin or genealogy of the gods.

[96] John Milton [in *Paradise Lost*].

But busy persons, who officiously search into these records, are ready even from hence to draw proofs very disadvantageous to the fame and character of this succession of men. And persons moderately read in these histories are apt to judge no otherwise of the temper of ancient councils than by that of later synods and modern convocations.

When we add to this the melancholy consideration of what disturbances have been raised from the disputes of this kind, what effusion of blood, what devastations of provinces, what shock and ruin of empires have been occasioned by controversies founded on the nicest distinction of an article relating to these mysteries, it will be judged vain in any poet or polite author to think of rendering himself agreeable or entertaining while he makes such subjects as these to be his theme.

But though the explanation of such deep mysteries and religious duties be allotted as the peculiar province of the sacred order, it is presumed, nevertheless, that it may be lawful for other authors to retain their ancient privilege of instructing mankind in a way of pleasure and entertainment. Poets may be allowed their fictions and philosophers their systems. It would go hard with mankind should the patentees for religion be commissioned for all instruction and advice relating to manners or conversation. The stage may be allowed to instruct as well as the pulpit. The way of wit and humour may be serviceable as well as that of gravity and seriousness, and the way of plain reason as well as that of exalted revelation. The main matter is to keep these provinces distinct and settle their just boundaries. And on this account it is that we have endeavoured to represent to modern authors the necessity of making this separation justly and in due form.

It would be somewhat hard, methinks, if religion, as by law established, were not allowed the same privilege as heraldry.[97] It is agreed on all hands that particular persons may design or paint, in their private capacity, after what manner they think fit, but they must blazon only as the public directs. Their lion or bear must be figured as the science appoints, and their supporters and crest must be such as their wise and gallant ancestors have procured for them. No matter whether the shapes of these animals hold just proportion with nature. No matter though different or contrary forms are joined in one. That which is denied to painters or poets is permitted to heralds. Naturalists may, in their separate and distinct capacity, inquire as they think fit into the real existence and natural truth of things, but they must by no means dispute the authorized forms. Mermaids and griffins were the wonder of our forefathers and, as such, delivered down to us by the authentic traditions and delineations above-mentioned. We ought not so much as to criticize the features or dimensions of a

[97] See pp. 369, 435, 480.

Saracen's face, brought by our conquering ancestors from the holy wars, nor pretend to call in question the figure or size of a dragon, on which the history of our national champion and the establishment of a high order and dignity of the realm depends.[MMMM]

But as worshipful as are the persons of the illustrious heralds (Clarenceux, Garter and the rest of those eminent sustainers of British honour and antiquity),[NNNN] it is to be hoped that in a more civilized age, such as at present we have the good fortune to live in, they will not attempt to strain their privileges to the same height as formerly. Having been reduced by law or settled practice from the power they once enjoyed, they will not, it is presumed, in defiance of the magistrate and civil power, erect anew their stages and lists, introduce the manner of civil combat, set us to tilt and tournament and raise again those defiances and mortal frays of which their order were once the chief managers and promoters.

To conclude: the only method, which can justly qualify us for this high privilege of giving advice, is in the first place to receive it ourselves with due submission where the public has vouchsafed to give it us by authority. And if in our private capacity we can have resolution enough to criticize ourselves and call in question our high imaginations, florid desires and specious sentiments, according to the manner of soliloquy above-prescribed, we shall, by the natural course of things, as we grow wiser, prove less conceited and introduce into our character that modesty, condescension and just humanity which is essential to the success of all friendly counsel and admonition. An honest home-philosophy must teach us the wholesome practice within ourselves. Polite reading, and converse with mankind of the better sort, will qualify us for what remains.

[MMMM] St George, associated with the slaying of a dragon, was made patron of England and the Order of the Garter by Edward III.

[NNNN] Heralds were originally messengers who bore the distinctive arms of their masters as signs of office. In time, they gained a supervisory role over the design and use of arms and were organized into a college, whose members included the Garter King of Arms and the Clarenceux King of Arms.

An Inquiry Concerning Virtue or Merit

Putting play aside, let us turn to serious things.[1]

Book I

Part I

Section 1

Religion and virtue appear in many respects so nearly related that they are generally presumed inseparable companions. And so willing we are to believe well of their union that we hardly allow it just to speak or even think of them apart. It may however be questioned whether the practice of the world in this respect be answerable to our speculation. It is certain that we sometimes meet with instances which seem to make against this general supposition. We have known people who, having the appearance of great zeal in religion, have yet wanted even the common affections of humanity and shown themselves extremely degenerate and corrupt. Others, again, who have paid little regard to religion and been considered as mere atheists, have yet been observed to practise the rules of morality and act in many cases with such good meaning and affection towards mankind as might seem to force an acknowledgment of their being virtuous. And, in general, we find mere moral principles of such weight that, in our dealings with men, we are seldom satisfied by the fullest assurance given us of their zeal in religion till we hear something further of their character. If we are told that a man is religious, we still ask, 'What are his morals?' But, if we hear at first that he has honest moral principles and is a man of natural justice and good temper, we seldom think of the other question, 'Whether he be religious and devout?'

This has given occasion to inquire *what honesty or virtue is considered by itself, and in what manner it is influenced by religion, how far religion necessarily implies*

---

[1] Horace, *Satires* 1.1.27.

virtue, and whether it is a true saying that 'it is impossible for an atheist to be vir-
tuous or share any real degree of honesty or merit'.[A]

And here it cannot justly be wondered at if the method of explaining things should appear somewhat unusual, since the subject matter has been so little examined and is of so nice and dangerous speculation. For so much is the religious part of mankind alarmed by the freedom of some late pens, and so great a jealousy is raised everywhere on this account, that, whatever an author may suggest in favour of religion, he will gain little credit in the cause if he allows the least advantage to any other principle. On the other side, the men of wit and raillery, whose pleasantest entertainment is in the exposing the weak sides of religion, are so desperately afraid of being drawn into any serious thoughts of it that they look upon a man as guilty of foul play who assumes the air of a free writer and at the same time preserves any regard for the principles of natural religion. They are apt to give as little quarter as they receive and are resolved to think as ill of the morals of their antagonists as their antagonists can possibly think of theirs. Neither of them, it seems, will allow the least advantage to the other. It is as hard to persuade one sort that there is any virtue in religion as the other that there is any virtue out of the verge of their particular community. So that, between both, an author must pass his time ill who dares plead for religion and moral virtue without lessening the force of either but, allowing to each its proper province and due rank, would hinder their being made enemies by detraction.

However it be, if we would pretend to give the least new light or explain anything effectually within the intended compass of this inquiry, it is necessary to take things pretty deep and endeavour by some short scheme to represent the original of each opinion, whether natural or unnatural, relating to the Deity. And if we can happily get clear of this thorny part of our philosophy, the rest, it is hoped, may prove more plain and easy.

Section 2

In the whole of things, or in the universe, either all is according to a good order and the most agreeable to a general interest, or there is that which is otherwise and might possibly have been better constituted, more wisely contrived and with more advantage to the general interest of beings or of the whole.

If everything which exists be according to a good order and for the best,

---

[A] The most prominent writer to raise these questions recently was Pierre Bayle in *Pensées diverses sur la comète*, published in 1683 and translated in 1708 as *Miscellaneous Reflections Occasioned by the Comet Which Appeared in December 1680* (which Shaftesbury owned). On Bayle, see Introduction, p. xiv. On the debate about religion and virtue, see John Redwood, *Reason, Ridicule and Religion: The Age of Enlightenment in England* (Cambridge, MA: Harvard University Press, 1976), pp. 29–35.

then, of necessity, there is no such thing as real ill in the universe, nothing ill with respect to the whole.

Whatsoever then is so as that it could not really have been better, or anyway better ordered, is perfectly good. Whatsoever in the order of the world can be called ill must imply a possibility in the nature of the thing to have been better contrived or ordered. For, if it could not, it is perfect and as it should be.

Whatsoever is *really* ill, therefore, must be caused or produced either by design (that is to say, with knowledge and intelligence) or, in defect of this, by hazard and mere chance.

If there be anything ill in the universe from design, then that which disposes all things is no one good designing principle. For either the one designing principle is itself corrupt or there is some other in being which operates contrarily and is ill.

If there be any ill in the universe from mere chance, then a designing principle or mind, whether good or bad, cannot be the cause of all things. And consequently if there be supposed a designing principle who is the cause only of good but cannot prevent the ill which happens from chance or from a contrary ill design, then there can be supposed in reality no such thing as a superior good design or mind, other than what is impotent and defective, for not to correct or totally exclude that ill of chance or of a contrary ill design must proceed either from impotency or ill will.

Whatsoever is superior in any degree over the world or rules in nature with discernment and a mind is what, by universal agreement, men call 'god'. If there are several such superior minds, they are so many gods, but, if that single or those several superiors are not in their nature necessarily good, they rather take the name of 'daemon'.[B]

To believe therefore that everything is governed, ordered or regulated for the best by a designing principle or mind, necessarily good and permanent, is to be a perfect theist.

To believe nothing of a designing principle or mind nor any cause, measure or rule of things but chance, so that in nature neither the interest of the whole nor of any particulars can be said to be in the least designed, pursued or aimed at, is to be a perfect atheist.

To believe no one supreme designing principle or mind, but rather two, three or more (though in their nature good), is to be a polytheist.

To believe the governing mind or minds not absolutely and necessarily good nor confined to what is best, but capable of acting according to mere will or fancy, is to be a daemonist.

There are few who think always consistently or according to one certain

---

[B] On 'daemon', see p. 76n.

hypothesis upon any subject so abstruse and intricate as the cause of all things and the economy or government of the universe. For it is evident in the case of the most devout people, even by their own confession, that there are times when their faith hardly can support them in the belief of a supreme wisdom, and that they are often tempted to judge disadvantageously of a providence and just administration in the whole.

That alone, therefore, is to be called a man's opinion which is, of any other, the most habitual to him and occurs upon most occasions. So that it is hard to pronounce certainly of any man that he is an atheist, because, unless his whole thoughts are at all seasons and on all occasions steadily bent against all supposition or imagination of design in things, he is no perfect atheist. In the same manner, if a man's thoughts are not at all times steady and resolute against all imagination of chance, fortune or ill design in things, he is no perfect theist. But if anyone believes more of chance and confusion than of design, he is to be esteemed more an atheist than a theist, from that which most predominates or has the ascendant. And in case he believes more of the prevalence of an ill designing principle than of a good one, he is rather a daemonist and may be justly so called from the side to which the balance of his judgment most inclines.

All these sorts both of daemonism, polytheism, atheism and theism may be mixed.[2] Religion excludes only perfect atheism. Perfect daemonists undoubtedly there are in religion because we know whole nations who worship a devil or fiend, to whom they sacrifice and offer prayers and supplications, in reality on no other account than because they fear him. And we know very well that, in some religions, there are those who expressly give no other idea of God than of a being arbitrary, violent, causing ill and ordaining to misery, which in effect is the same as to substitute a daemon or devil in his room.

Now since there are these several opinions concerning a superior power and since there may be found perhaps some persons who have no formed opinion

---

[2] As thus:
1. Theism with daemonism (as when the one chief mind or sovereign being is, in the believer's sense, divided between a good and an ill nature by being the cause of ill as well as good, or, otherwise, when two distinct and contrary principles subsist – one the author of all good, the other of all ill).
2. Daemonism with polytheism (as when there is not one but several corrupt minds who govern, which opinion may be called polydaemonism).
3. Theism with atheism (as when chance is not excluded, but God and chance divide).
4. Daemonism with atheism (as when an evil daemon and chance divide).
5. Polytheism with atheism (as when many minds and chance divide).
6. Theism (as it stands in opposition to daemonism and denotes goodness in the superior deity) with polytheism (as when there are more principal minds than one, but agreeing in good, with one and the same will and reason).
7. The same theism or polytheism with daemonism (as when the same system of deity or corresponding deities subsist, together with a contrary principle or with several contrary principles or governing minds).
8. Or with daemonism and atheism (as when the last case is, together with chance).

at all upon this subject, either through scepticism, negligence of thought or confusion of judgment, the consideration is how any of these opinions or this want of any certain opinion may possibly consist with virtue and merit or be compatible with an honest or moral character.

Part II

Section 1

When we reflect on any ordinary frame or constitution, either of art or nature, and consider how hard it is to give the least account of a particular part without a competent knowledge of the whole, we need not wonder to find ourselves at a loss in many things relating to the constitution and frame of nature herself. For to what end in nature many things, even whole species of creatures, refer or to what purpose they serve will be hard for anyone justly to determine. But to what end the many proportions and various shapes of parts in many creatures actually serve, we are able, by the help of study and observation, to demonstrate with great exactness.

We know that every creature has a private good and interest of his own, which nature has compelled him to seek by all the advantages afforded him within the compass of his make. We know that there is in reality a right and a wrong state of every creature, and that his right one is by nature forwarded and by himself affectionately sought. There being therefore in every creature a certain interest or good, there must be also a certain end to which everything in his constitution must naturally refer. To this end, if anything either in his appetites, passions or affections, be not conducing but the contrary, we must of necessity own it ill to him. And in this manner he is ill with respect to himself as he certainly is with respect to others of his kind when any such appetites or passions make him anyway injurious to them. Now if, by the natural constitution of any rational creature, the same irregularities of appetite which make him ill to others make him ill also to himself, and if the same regularity of affections which causes him to be good in one sense causes him to be good also in the other, then is that goodness by which he is thus useful to others a real good and advantage to himself. And thus virtue and interest may be found at last to agree.

Of this we shall consider particularly in the latter part of our inquiry. Our first design is to see if we can clearly determine what that quality is to which we give the name of 'goodness' or 'virtue'.

Should a historian or traveller describe to us a certain creature of a more solitary disposition than ever was yet heard of – one who had neither mate nor fellow of any kind, nothing of his own likeness towards which he stood well-affected or inclined, nor anything without or beyond himself for which he had the least passion or concern – we might be apt to say perhaps, without much hesitation, that this was doubtless a very melancholy creature, and that in this unsociable and sullen state he was like to have a very disconsolate kind of life. But if we were assured that, notwithstanding all appearances, the creature enjoyed himself extremely, had a great relish of life and was in nothing wanting to his own good, we might acknowledge, perhaps, that the creature was no monster nor absurdly constituted as to himself. But we should hardly, after all, be induced to say of him that he was a good creature.

However, should it be urged against us that, such as he was, the creature was still perfect in himself and therefore to be esteemed good ('For what had he to do with others?'), in this sense, indeed, we might be forced to acknowledge that he was a good creature, if he could be understood to be absolute and complete in himself, without any real relation to anything in the universe besides. For should there be anywhere in nature a system of which this living creature was to be considered as a part, then could he nowise be allowed good while he plainly appeared to be such a part as made rather to the harm than good of that system or whole in which he was included.

If therefore, in the structure of this or any other animal, there be anything which points beyond himself and by which he is plainly discovered to have relation to some other being or nature besides his own, then will this animal undoubtedly be esteemed a part of some other system. For instance, if an animal has the proportions of a male, it shows he has relation to a female. And the respective proportions both of the male and female will be allowed, doubtless, to have a joint relation to another existence and order of things beyond themselves. So that the creatures are both of them to be considered as parts of another system, which is that of a particular race or species of living creatures, who have some one common nature or are provided for by some one order or constitution of things subsisting together and co-operating towards their conservation and support.

In the same manner, if a whole species of animals contribute to the existence or well-being of some other, then is that whole species, in general, a part only of some other system.

For instance, to the existence of the spider that of the fly is absolutely necessary. The heedless flight, weak frame and tender body of this latter insect fits and determines him as much a prey as the rough make, watchfulness and cunning of the former fits him for rapine and the ensnaring part. The web and wing are suited to each other. And in the structure of each of these animals, there is as apparent and perfect a relation to the other as, in our own bodies, there is a relation of limbs and organs or as, in the branches or leaves of a tree, we see a relation of each to the other and all, in common, to one root and trunk.

In the same manner are flies also necessary to the existence of other creatures, both fowls and fish. And thus are other species or kinds subservient to one another as being parts of a certain system and included in one and the same order of beings.

So that there is a system of all animals: an animal order or economy according to which the animal affairs are regulated and disposed.

Now, if the whole system of animals, together with that of vegetables and all other things in this inferior world, be properly comprehended in one system of a globe or earth and if, again, this globe or earth itself appears to have a real dependence on something still beyond, as, for example, either on its sun, the galaxy or its fellow-planets, then is it in reality a part only of some other system. And if it be allowed that there is in like manner a system of all things and a universal nature, there can be no particular being or system which is not either good or ill in that general one of the universe, for, if it be insignificant and of no use, it is a fault or imperfection and consequently ill in the general system.

Therefore, if any being be wholly and really ill, it must be ill with respect to the universal system, and then the system of the universe is ill or imperfect. But if the ill of one private system be the good of others, if it makes still to the good of the general system (as when one creature lives by the destruction of another, one thing is generated from the corruption of another, or one planetary system or vortex may swallow up another), then is the ill of that private system no real ill in itself, more than the pain of breeding teeth is ill in a system or body which is so constituted that, without this occasion of pain, it would suffer worse by being defective.

So that we cannot say of any being that it is wholly and absolutely ill, unless we can positively show and ascertain that what we call 'ill' is nowhere good besides, in any other system or with respect to any other order or economy whatsoever.

But were there in the world any entire species of animals destructive to every other, it may be justly called an ill species as being ill in the animal system. And if in any species of animals, as in men, for example, one man is of a nature pernicious to the rest, he is in this respect justly styled an ill man.

We do not, however, say of anyone that he is an ill man because he has the plague spots upon him, or because he has convulsive fits which make him strike and wound such as approach him. Nor do we say, on the other side, that he is a good man when, having his hands tied up, he is hindered from doing the mischief he designs or (which is in a manner the same) when he abstains from executing his ill purpose through a fear of some impending punishment or through the allurement of some exterior reward.

So that, in a sensible creature, that which is not done through any affection at all makes neither good nor ill in the nature of that creature, who then only is supposed good when the good or ill of the system to which he has relation is the immediate object of some passion or affection moving him.

Since it is therefore by affection merely that a creature is esteemed good or ill, natural or unnatural, our business will be to examine which are the good and natural and which the ill and unnatural affections.

Section 2

In the first place, then, it may be observed that, if there be an affection towards any subject considered as private good, which is not really such but imaginary, this affection, as being superfluous and detracting from the force of other requisite and good affections, is in itself vicious and ill, even in respect of the private interest or happiness of the creature.

If there can possibly be supposed in a creature such an affection towards self-good as is actually, in its natural degree, conducing to his private interest and at the same time inconsistent with the public good, this may indeed be called still a vicious affection. And, on this supposition, a creature cannot really be good and natural in respect of his society or public without being ill and unnatural towards himself.[3] But if the affection be then only injurious to the society when it is immoderate and not so when it is moderate, duly tempered and allayed, then is the immoderate degree of the affection truly vicious, but not the moderate. And, thus, if there be found in any creature a more than ordinary self-concernment or regard to private good, which is inconsistent with the interest of the species or public, this must in every respect be esteemed an ill and vicious affection. And this is what we commonly call selfishness and disapprove so much in whatever creature we happen to discover it.[4]

On the other side, if the affection towards private or self-good, however selfish it may be esteemed, is in reality not only consistent with public good but in some measure contributing to it, if it be such, perhaps, as for the good of the species in general every individual ought to share, it is so far from being ill or blameable in any sense that it must be acknowledged absolutely necessary to constitute a creature good. For, if the want of such an affection as that towards self-preservation be injurious to the species, a creature is ill and unnatural as well through this defect as through the want of any other natural affection. And this no one would doubt to pronounce, if he saw a man who minded not any precipices which lay in his way nor made any distinction of food, diet, clothing or whatever else related to his health and being. The same would be averred of one who had a disposition which rendered him averse to any commerce with womankind, and of consequence unfitted him through illness of temper, and not merely through a defect of constitution, for the propagation of his species or kind.

[3] See pp. 193, 225ff.
[4] See p. 56.

Thus the affection towards self-good may be a good affection or an ill one. For if this private affection be too strong, as when the excessive love of life unfits a creature for any generous act, then is it undoubtedly vicious; and, if vicious, the creature who is moved by it is viciously moved and can never be otherwise than vicious in some degree when moved by that affection. Therefore, if through such an earnest and passionate love of life a creature be accidentally induced to do good, as he might be upon the same terms induced to do ill, he is no more a good creature for this good he executes than a man is the more an honest or good man either for pleading a just cause or fighting in a good one for the sake merely of his fee or stipend.

Whatsoever therefore is done which happens to be advantageous to the species through an affection merely towards self-good, does not imply any more goodness in the creature than as the affection itself is good. Let him, in any particular, act ever so well, if at the bottom it be that selfish affection alone which moves him, he is in himself still vicious. Nor can any creature be considered otherwise when the passion towards self-good, though ever so moderate, is his real motive in the doing that to which a natural affection for his kind ought by right to have inclined him.

And indeed whatever exterior helps or succours an ill-disposed creature may find to push him on towards the performance of any one good action, there can no goodness arise in him till his temper be so far changed that in the issue he comes in earnest to be led by some immediate affection, directly and not accidentally, to good and against ill.

For instance, if one of those creatures supposed to be by nature tame, gentle and favourable to mankind be, contrary to his natural constitution, fierce and savage, we instantly remark the breach of temper and own the creature to be unnatural and corrupt. If at any time afterwards the same creature, by good fortune or right management, comes to lose his fierceness and is made tame, gentle and treatable, like other creatures of his kind, it is acknowledged that the creature thus restored becomes good and natural. Suppose now that the creature has indeed a tame and gentle carriage but that it proceeds only from the fear of his keeper, which, if set aside, his predominant passion instantly breaks out, then is his gentleness not his real temper, but, his true and genuine nature or natural temper remaining just as it was, the creature is still as ill as ever.

Nothing therefore being properly either goodness or illness in a creature, except what is from natural temper, *a good creature is such a one as by the natural temper or bent of his affections is carried primarily and immediately, and not secondarily and accidentally, to good and against ill.* And an ill creature is just the contrary, namely, *one who is wanting in right affections of force enough to carry him directly towards good and bear him out against ill or who is carried by other affections directly to ill and against good.*

When in general all the affections or passions are suited to the public good or good of the species, as above-mentioned, then is the natural temper entirely good. If, on the contrary, any requisite passion be wanting or if there be any one supernumerary or weak or anyway disserviceable or contrary to that main end, then is the natural temper, and consequently the creature himself, in some measure corrupt and ill.

There is no need of mentioning either envy, malice, forwardness or other such hateful passions to show in what manner they are ill and constitute an ill creature. But it may be necessary perhaps to remark that, even as to kindness and love of the most natural sort, such as that of any creature for its offspring, if it be immoderate and beyond a certain degree, it is undoubtedly vicious. For thus over-great tenderness destroys the effect of love, and excessive pity renders us incapable of giving succour. Hence the excess of motherly love is owned to be a vicious fondness; over-great pity, effeminacy and weakness; over-great concern for self-preservation, meanness and cowardice; too little, rashness; and none at all or that which is contrary, namely, a passion leading to self-destruction, a mad and desperate depravity.

Section 3

But to proceed from what is esteemed mere goodness and lies within the reach and capacity of all sensible creatures, to that which is called virtue or merit and is allowed to man only:

In a creature capable of forming general notions of things, not only the outward beings which offer themselves to the sense are the objects of the affection, but the very actions themselves and the affections of pity, kindness, gratitude and their contraries, being brought into the mind by reflection, become objects. So that, by means of this reflected sense, there arises another kind of affection towards those very affections themselves, which have been already felt and have now become the subject of a new liking or dislike.

The case is the same in the mental or moral subjects as in the ordinary bodies or common subjects of sense. The shapes, motions, colours and proportions of these latter being presented to our eye, there necessarily results a beauty or deformity, according to the different measure, arrangement, and disposition of their several parts.[5] So in behaviour and actions, when presented to our understanding, there must be found, of necessity, an apparent difference, according to the regularity or irregularity of the subjects.

The mind, which is spectator or auditor of other minds, cannot be without its eye and ear so as to discern proportion, distinguish sound and scan each sentiment or thought which comes before it. It can let nothing escape its censure. It feels the soft and harsh, the agreeable and disagreeable in the affections, and

[5] See p. 326.

finds a foul and fair, a harmonious and a dissonant, as really and truly here as in any musical numbers or in the outward forms or representations of sensible things. Nor can it withhold its admiration and ecstasy, its aversion and scorn, any more in what relates to one than to the other of these subjects.[6] So that to deny the common and natural sense of a sublime and beautiful in things will appear an affectation merely to anyone who considers duly of this affair.[7]

Now as in the sensible kind of objects the species or images of bodies, colours and sounds are perpetually moving before our eyes and acting on our senses, even when we sleep, so, in the moral and intellectual kind, the forms and images of things are no less active and incumbent on the mind, at all seasons, and even when the real objects themselves are absent.

In these vagrant characters or pictures of manners, which the mind of necessity figures to itself and carries still about with it, the heart cannot possibly remain neutral but constantly takes part one way or other. However false or corrupt it be within itself, it finds the difference, as to beauty and comeliness, between one heart and another, one turn of affection, one behaviour, one sentiment and another and, accordingly, in all disinterested cases, must approve in some measure of what is natural and honest and disapprove what is dishonest and corrupt.

Thus the several motions, inclinations, passions, dispositions and consequent carriage and behaviour of creatures in the various parts of life, being in several views or perspectives represented to the mind, which readily discerns the good and ill towards the species or public, there arises a new trial or exercise of the heart, which must either rightly and soundly affect what is just and right and disaffect what is contrary or corruptly affect what is ill and disaffect what is worthy and good.

And in this case alone it is we call any creature worthy or virtuous, when it can have the notion of a public interest and can attain the speculation or science of what is morally good or ill, admirable or blameable, right or wrong. For though we may vulgarly call an ill horse vicious, yet we never say of a good one, nor of any mere beast, idiot or changeling, though ever so good-natured, that he is worthy or virtuous.

So that if a creature be generous, kind, constant, compassionate, yet if he cannot reflect on what he himself does or sees others do so as to take notice of what is worthy or honest and make that notice or conception of worth and honesty to be an object of his affection, he has not the character of being virtuous. For, thus and no otherwise, he is capable of having a sense of right or wrong, a sentiment or judgment of what is done through just, equal and good affection or the contrary.

[6] See pp. 327–9.
[7] See pp. 43–4, 352–3.

Whatsoever is done through any unequal affection is iniquitous, wicked and wrong. If the affection be equal, sound and good, and the subject of the affection such as may with advantage to society be ever in the same manner prosecuted or affected, this must necessarily constitute what we call equity and right in any action. For wrong is not such action as is barely the cause of harm (since at this rate a dutiful son, aiming at an enemy but, by mistake or ill chance, happening to kill his father, would do a wrong), but, when anything is done through insufficient or unequal affection (as when a son shows no concern for the safety of a father or, where there is need of succour, prefers an indifferent person to him), this is of the nature of wrong.

Neither can any weakness or imperfection in the senses be the occasion of iniquity or wrong if the object of the mind itself be not at any time absurdly framed nor anyway improper, but suitable, just and worthy of the opinion and affection applied to it. For if we will suppose a man who, being sound and entire both in his reason and affection, has nevertheless so depraved a constitution or frame of body that the natural objects are, through his organs of sense, as through ill glasses, falsely conveyed and misrepresented, it will be soon observed, in such a person's case, that, since his failure is not in his principal or leading part, he cannot in himself be esteemed iniquitous or unjust.

It is otherwise in what relates to opinion, belief or speculation. For, as the extravagance of judgment or belief is such that in some countries even monkeys, cats, crocodiles and other vile or destructive animals have been esteemed holy and worshipped even as deities, should it appear to anyone of the religion or belief of those countries that to save such a creature as a cat, preferably to a parent, was right and that other men who had not the same religious opinion were to be treated as enemies till converted, this would be certainly wrong and wicked in the believer, and every action, grounded on this belief, would be an iniquitous, wicked and vicious action.

And thus whatsoever causes a misconception or misapprehension of the worth or value of any object, so as to diminish a due or raise any undue, irregular or unsocial affection, must necessarily be the occasion of wrong. Thus he who affects or loves a man for the sake of something which is reputed honourable but which is in reality vicious is himself vicious and ill. The beginnings of this corruption may be noted in many occurrences as when an ambitious man, by the fame of his high attempts, a conqueror or a pirate by his boasted enterprises, raises in another person an esteem and admiration of that immoral and inhuman character which deserves abhorrence. It is then that the hearer becomes corrupt, when he secretly approves the ill he hears. But, on the other side, the man who loves and esteems another, as believing him to have that virtue which he has not but only counterfeits, is not on this account either vicious or corrupt.

A mistake therefore in fact, being no cause or sign of ill affection, can be no cause of vice. But a mistake of right, being the cause of unequal affection, must of necessity be the cause of vicious action in every intelligent or rational being.

But as there are many occasions where the matter of right may even to the most discerning part of mankind appear difficult and of doubtful decision, it is not a slight mistake of this kind which can destroy the character of a virtuous or worthy man. But when, either through superstition or ill custom, there come to be very gross mistakes in the assignment or application of the affection, when the mistakes are either in their nature so gross, or so complicated and frequent, that a creature cannot well live in a natural state nor with due affections compatible with human society and civil life, then is the character of virtue forfeited.

And thus we find how far worth and virtue depend on a knowledge of right and wrong and on a use of reason sufficient to secure a right application of the affections, that nothing horrid or unnatural, nothing unexemplary, nothing destructive of that natural affection by which the species or society is upheld, may on any account or through any principle or notion of honour or religion be at any time affected or prosecuted as a good and proper object of esteem. For such a principle as this must be wholly vicious and whatsoever is acted upon it can be no other than vice and immorality. And thus if there be anything which teaches men either treachery, ingratitude or cruelty, by divine warrant or under colour and presence of any present or future good to mankind, if there be anything which teaches men to persecute their friends through love or to torment captives of war in sport or to offer human sacrifice or to torment, macerate or mangle themselves in a religious zeal before their god or to commit any sort of barbarity or brutality as amiable or becoming, be it custom which gives applause or religion which gives a sanction, this is not nor ever can be virtue of any kind or in any sense but must remain still horrid depravity, notwithstanding any fashion, law, custom or religion which may be ill and vicious itself but can never alter *the eternal measures and immutable independent nature of worth and virtue*.[8]

Section 4
Upon the whole, as to those creatures who are only capable of being moved by sensible objects, they are accordingly good or vicious as the sensible affections stand with them. It is otherwise in creatures capable of framing rational objects of moral good. For in one of this kind, should the sensible affections stand ever so much amiss, yet, if they prevail not because of those

---

[8] See pp. 11–12, 387, 391.

other rational affections spoken of, it is evident the temper still holds good in the main and the person is with justice esteemed virtuous by all men.

More than this, if by temper anyone is passionate, angry, fearful, amorous, yet resists these passions and, notwithstanding the force of their impression, adheres to virtue, we say commonly in this case that 'the virtue is the greater', and we say well, though, if that which restrains the person and holds him to a virtuous-like behaviour be no affection towards goodness or virtue itself but towards private good merely, he is not in reality the more virtuous, as has been shown before. But this still is evident, that, if voluntarily and without foreign constraint an angry temper bears or an amorous one refrains, so that neither any cruel nor immodest action can be forced from such a person, though ever so strongly tempted by his constitution, we applaud his virtue above what we should naturally do if he were free of this temptation and these propensities. At the same time, there is nobody will say that a propensity to vice can be an ingredient in virtue or any way necessary to complete a virtuous character.

There seems therefore to be some kind of difficulty in the case, but it amounts only to this. If there be any part of the temper in which ill passions or affections are seated while in another part the affections towards moral good are such as absolutely to master those attempts of their antagonists, this is the greatest proof imaginable that a strong principle of virtue lies at the bottom and has possessed itself of the natural temper. Whereas if there be no ill passions stirring, a person may be indeed more cheaply virtuous, that is to say, he may conform himself to the known rules of virtue without sharing so much of a virtuous principle as another. Yet if that other person, who has the principle of virtue so strongly implanted, comes at last to lose those contrary impediments supposed in him, he certainly loses nothing in virtue, but, on the contrary, losing only what is vicious in his temper, is left more entire to virtue and possesses it in a higher degree.

Thus is virtue shared in different degrees by rational creatures, such at least as are called rational, but who come short of that sound and well-established reason which alone can constitute a just affection, a uniform and steady will and resolution. And thus vice and virtue are found variously mixed and alternately prevalent in the several characters of mankind. For it seems evident from our inquiry that, how ill soever the temper or passions may stand with respect either to the sensible or the moral objects, however passionate, furious, lustful or cruel any creature may become, however vicious the mind be or whatever ill rules or principles it goes by, yet, if there be any flexibleness or favourable inclination towards the least moral object, the least appearance of moral good (as if there be any such thing as kindness, gratitude, bounty or compassion), there is still something of virtue left, and the creature is not wholly vicious and unnatural.

Thus a ruffian who, out of a sense of fidelity and honour of any kind, refuses to discover his associates and, rather than betray them, is content to endure torments and death has certainly some principle of virtue, however he may misapply it. It was the same case with that malefactor who, rather than do the office of executioner to his companions, chose to keep them company in their execution.

In short, as it seems hard to pronounce of any man that 'he is absolutely an atheist', so it appears altogether as hard to pronounce of any man that 'he is absolutely corrupt or vicious', there being few, even of the horridest villains, who have not something of virtue in this imperfect sense. Nothing is more just than a known saying that 'it is as hard to find a man wholly ill as wholly good' because, wherever there is any good affection left, there is certainly some goodness or virtue still in being.

And having considered thus of virtue, what it is in itself, we may now consider how it stands with respect to the opinions concerning a deity, as above-mentioned.

Part III

Section 1
The nature of virtue consisting, as has been explained, in a certain just disposition or proportionable affection of a rational creature towards the moral objects of right and wrong, nothing can possibly in such a creature exclude a principle of virtue or render it ineffectual, except what:

1. either takes away the natural and just sense of right and wrong;
2. or creates a wrong sense of it;
3. or causes the right sense to be opposed by contrary affections.

On the other side, nothing can assist or advance the principle of virtue except what either in some manner nourishes and promotes a sense of right and wrong, or preserves it genuine and uncorrupt, or causes it, when such, to be obeyed, by subduing and subjecting the other affections to it.

We are to consider, therefore, how any of the above-mentioned opinions on the subject of a deity may influence in these cases or produce either of these three effects.

1. As to the first case, the taking away the natural sense of right and wrong.
It will not surely be understood that by this is meant the taking away the notion of what is good or ill in the species or society. For of the reality of such a good and ill, no rational creature can possibly be insensible. Everyone discerns and owns a public interest and is conscious of what affects his fellowship or com-

munity. When we say, therefore, of a creature that 'he has wholly lost the sense of right and wrong', we suppose that, being able to discern the good and ill of his species, he has at the same time no concern for either nor any sense of excellency or baseness in any moral action relating to one or the other. So that except merely with respect to a private and narrowly confined self-good, it is supposed there is in such a creature no liking or dislike of manners, no admiration or love of anything as morally good nor hatred of anything as morally ill, be it ever so unnatural or deformed.

There is in reality no rational creature whatsoever who knows not that, when he voluntarily offends or does harm to anyone, he cannot fail to create an apprehension and fear of like harm and consequently a resentment and animosity in every creature who observes him. So that the offender must needs be conscious of being liable to such treatment from everyone as if he had in some degree offended all.

Thus offence and injury are always known as punishable by everyone, and equal behaviour (which is therefore called merit) as rewardable and well-deserving from everyone. Of this even the wickedest creature living must have a sense. So that, if there be any further meaning in this sense of right and wrong, if in reality there be any sense of this kind which an absolute wicked creature has not, it must consist in a real antipathy or aversion to injustice or wrong and in a real affection or love towards equity and right for its own sake and on the account of its own natural beauty and worth.

It is impossible to suppose a mere sensible creature originally so ill-constituted and unnatural as that, from the moment he comes to be tried by sensible objects, he should have no one good passion towards his kind, no foundation either of pity, love, kindness or social affection. It is full as impossible to conceive that a rational creature, coming first to be tried by rational objects and receiving into his mind the images or representations of justice, generosity, gratitude or other virtue, should have no liking of these or dislike of their contraries, but be found absolutely indifferent towards whatsoever is presented to him of this sort. A soul, indeed, may as well be without sense as without admiration in the things of which it has any knowledge. Coming therefore to a capacity of seeing and admiring in this new way, it must needs find a beauty and a deformity as well in actions, minds and tempers as in figures, sounds or colours. If there be no real amiableness or deformity in moral acts, there is at least an imaginary one of full force. Though perhaps the thing itself should not be allowed in nature, the imagination or fancy of it must be allowed to be from nature alone. Nor can anything besides art and strong endeavour, with long practice and meditation, overcome such a natural prevention or prepossession of the mind in favour of this moral distinction.[9]

[9] See pp. 325–6, 329.

Sense of right and wrong therefore being as natural to us as natural affection itself, and being a first principle in our constitution and make, there is no speculative opinion, persuasion or belief which is capable immediately or directly to exclude or destroy it. That which is of original and pure nature, nothing beside contrary habit and custom (a second nature) is able to displace. And this affection being an original one of earliest rise in the soul or affectionate part, nothing beside contrary affection, by frequent check and control, can operate upon it so as either to diminish it in part or destroy it in the whole.

It is evident in what relates to the frame and order of our bodies that no particular odd mien or gesture, which is either natural to us and consequent to our make or accidental and by habit acquired, can possibly be overcome by our immediate disapprobation or the contrary bent of our will ever so strongly set against it. Such a change cannot be effected without extraordinary means and the intervention of art and method, a strict attention and repeated check. And, even thus, nature we find is hardly mastered but lies sullen and ready to revolt on the first occasion. Much more is this the mind's case in respect of that natural affection and anticipating fancy, which makes the sense of right and wrong. It is impossible that this can instantly or without much force and violence be effaced or struck out of the natural temper, even by means of the most extravagant belief or opinion in the world.

Neither theism, therefore, nor atheism nor daemonism nor any religious or irreligious belief of any kind being able to operate immediately or directly in this case, but indirectly, by the intervention of opposite or of favourable affections casually excited by any such belief, we may consider of this effect in our last case, where we come to examine the agreement or disagreement of other affections with this natural and moral one which relates to right and wrong.

Section 2
2. *As to the second case, namely, the wrong sense or false imagination of right and wrong.*
This can proceed only from the force of custom and education in opposition to nature, as may be noted in those countries where, according to custom or politic institution, certain actions naturally foul and odious are repeatedly viewed with applause and honour ascribed to them. For thus it is possible that a man, forcing himself, may eat the flesh of his enemies not only against his stomach but against his nature and think it nevertheless both right and honourable as supposing it to be of considerable service to his community and capable of advancing the name and spreading the terror of his nation.

But to speak of the opinions relating to a deity and what effect they may have in this place. As to atheism, it does not seem that it can directly have any effect at all towards the setting up a false species of right or wrong. For, notwithstanding a man may, through custom or by licentiousness of practice favoured by atheism, come in time to lose much of his natural moral sense, yet it does not seem that atheism should of itself be the cause of any estimation or valuing of anything as fair, noble and deserving, which was the contrary. It can never, for instance, make it be thought that the being able to eat man's flesh or commit bestiality is good and excellent in itself. But this is certain, that, by means of corrupt religion or superstition, many things the most horridly unnatural and inhuman come to be received as excellent, good and laudable in themselves.

Nor is this a wonder. For wherever anything in its nature odious and abominable is by religion advanced as the supposed will or pleasure of a supreme deity, if in the eye of the believer it appears not indeed in any respect the less ill or odious on this account, then must the deity of necessity bear the blame and be considered as a being naturally ill and odious, however courted and solicited through mistrust and fear. But this is what religion, in the main, forbids us to imagine. It everywhere prescribes esteem and honour in company with worship and adoration. Whensoever therefore it teaches the love and admiration of a deity who has any apparent character of ill, it teaches at the same time a love and admiration of that ill and causes that to be taken for good and amiable which is in itself horrid and detestable.

For instance, if Jupiter be he who is adored and reverenced and if his history represents him amorously inclined and permitting his desires of this kind to wander in the loosest manner, it is certain that his worshippers, believing this history to be literally and strictly true, must of course be taught a greater love of amorous and wanton acts.[c] If there be a religion which teaches the adoration and love of a god whose character it is to be captious and of high resentment, subject to wrath and anger, furious, revengeful and revenging himself when offended on others than those who gave the offence, and if there be added to the character of this god a fraudulent disposition, encouraging deceit and treachery among men, favourable to a few, though for slight causes, and cruel to the rest, it is evident that such a religion as this being strongly enforced must of necessity raise even an approbation and respect towards the vices of this kind and breed a suitable disposition, a capricious, partial, revengeful and deceitful temper. For even irregularities and enormities of a heinous kind must in many cases appear illustrious to one who considers them in a being admired and contemplated with the highest honour and veneration.

This indeed must be allowed, that, if in the cult or worship of such a deity there be nothing beyond common form, nothing beside what proceeds from mere example, custom, constraint or fear, if there be, at the bottom, no real heartiness, no esteem or love implied, the worshipper perhaps may not be much

---

[c] In mythology, Jupiter, especially when identified with the Greek Zeus, had numerous sexual encounters with females, both immortal and mortal, ranging from seduction to rape.

misled as to his notion of right and wrong. If in following the precepts of his supposed god or doing what he esteems necessary towards the satisfying of such his deity, he is compelled only by fear and, contrary to his inclination, performs an act which he secretly detests as barbarous and unnatural, then has he an apprehension or sense still of right and wrong and, according to what has been already observed, is sensible of ill in the character of his god, however cautious he may be of pronouncing anything on this subject or so thinking of it as to frame any formal or direct opinion in the case. But if by insensible degrees, as he proceeds in his religious faith and devout exercise, he comes to be more and more reconciled to the malignity, arbitrariness, partiality or revengefulness of his believed deity, his reconciliation with these qualities themselves will soon grow in proportion, and the most cruel, unjust and barbarous acts will, by the power of this example, be often considered by him not only as just and lawful but as divine and worthy of imitation.

For whoever thinks there is a god and pretends formally to believe that he is just and good must suppose that there is independently such a thing as justice and injustice, truth and falsehood, right and wrong, according to which he pronounces that God is just, righteous and true. If the mere will, decree or law of God be said absolutely to constitute right and wrong, then are these latter words of no significance at all. For thus, if each part of a contradiction were affirmed for truth by the Supreme Power, they would consequently become true. Thus, if one person were decreed to suffer for another's fault, the sentence would be just and equitable. And, thus, in the same manner, if arbitrarily and without reason some beings were destined to endure perpetual ill and others as constantly to enjoy good, this also would pass under the same denomination. But to say of anything that it is just or unjust on such a foundation as this is to say nothing or to speak without a meaning.

And thus it appears that where a real devotion and hearty worship is paid to a supreme being who in his history or character is represented otherwise than as really and truly just and good, there must ensue a loss of rectitude, a disturbance of thought and a corruption of temper and manners in the believer. His honesty will of necessity be supplanted by his zeal, while he is thus unnaturally influenced and rendered thus immorally devout.

To this we[D] need only add that, as the ill character of a god does injury to

---

D 'I' in the first edition. According to a manuscript note in Shaftesbury's copy of the 1711 edition (see Note on the text): 'This treatise being, in respect of style and genius of writing, such as it is characterized in Miscellany V [p. 460 in this edition] and in other passages, where the difference is shown between this didactic, methodic manner and the miscellaneous kind or that of epistle or dialogue, it becomes our author to suppress wholly the word "I" and "me", &c., in this treatise, which is of the former (namely, the didactic, methodic) kind. Nor is it a sufficient expedient in this case to change the singular word "I" into the plural "We", unless the manner of using this latter be such withal as seemingly to take in the reader into the party with the author and as a fellow-student and inquirer together with him.'

the affections of men and disturbs and impairs the natural sense of right and wrong, so, on the other hand, nothing can more highly contribute to the fixing of right apprehensions and a sound judgment or sense of right and wrong than to believe a god who is ever and on all accounts represented such as to be actually a true model and example of the most exact justice and highest goodness and worth. Such a view of divine providence and bounty extended to all and expressed in a constant good affection towards the whole must of necessity engage us, within our compass and sphere to act by a like principle and affection. And having once the good of our species or public in view as our end or aim, it is impossible we should be misguided by any means to a false apprehension or sense of right or wrong.

As to this second case, therefore, religion, according as the kind may prove, is capable of doing great good or harm, and atheism nothing positive in either way. For however it may be indirectly an occasion of men's losing a good and sufficient sense of right and wrong, it will not, as atheism merely, be the occasion of setting up a false species of it, which only false religion or fantastical opinion, derived commonly from superstition and credulity, is able to effect.

Section 3
3. Now as to the last case, the opposition made by other affections to the natural sense of right and wrong.
It is evident that a creature having this sort of sense or good affection in any degree must necessarily act according to it, if it happens not to be opposed either by some settled sedate affection towards a conceived private good or by some sudden, strong and forcible passion, as of lust or anger, which may not only subdue the sense of right and wrong, but the very sense of private good itself, and overrule even the most familiar and received opinion of what is conducing to self-interest.

But it is not our business in this place to examine the several means or methods by which this corruption is introduced or increased. We are to consider only how the opinions concerning a deity can influence one way or another.

That it is possible for a creature capable of using reflection to have a liking or dislike of moral actions, and consequently a sense of right and wrong, before such time as he may have any settled notion of a god, is what will hardly be questioned, it being a thing not expected, or anyway possible, that a creature such as man, arising from his childhood slowly and gradually to several degrees of reason and reflection, should at the very first be taken up with those speculations or more refined sort of reflections about the subject of God's existence.

Let us suppose a creature who, wanting reason and being unable to reflect, has, notwithstanding, many good qualities and affections, as love to his kind, courage, gratitude or pity. It is certain that, if you give to this creature a reflecting faculty, it will at the same instant approve of gratitude, kindness and pity, be taken with any show or representation of the social passion, and think nothing more amiable than this or more odious than the contrary. And this is to be capable of virtue and to have a sense of right and wrong.

Before the time, therefore, that a creature can have any plain or positive notion one way or other concerning the subject of a god, he may be supposed to have an apprehension or sense of right and wrong, and be possessed of virtue and vice in different degrees, as we know by experience of those who, having lived in such places and in such a manner as never to have entered into any serious thoughts of religion, are nevertheless very different among themselves, as to their characters of honesty and worth: some being naturally modest, kind, friendly and consequently lovers of kind and friendly actions; others, proud, harsh, cruel and consequently inclined to admire rather the acts of violence and mere power.

Now as to the belief of a deity and how men are influenced by it, we may consider, in the first place, on what account men yield obedience and act in conformity to such a supreme being. It must be either in the way of his power, as presupposing some disadvantage or benefit to accrue from him, or in the way of his excellency and worth, as thinking it the perfection of nature to imitate and resemble him.

If, as in the first case, there be a belief or conception of a deity who is considered only as powerful over his creature and enforcing obedience to his absolute will by particular rewards and punishments and if on this account, through hope merely of reward or fear of punishment, the creature be incited to do the good he hates or restrained from doing the ill to which he is not otherwise in the least degree averse, there is in this case, as has been already shown, no virtue or goodness whatsoever. The creature, notwithstanding his good conduct, is intrinsically of as little worth as if he acted in his natural way, when under no dread or terror of any sort. There is no more of rectitude, piety or sanctity in a creature thus reformed than there is meekness or gentleness in a tiger strongly chained or innocence and sobriety in a monkey under the discipline of the whip. For, however orderly and well those animals, or man himself upon like terms, may be induced to act, while the will is neither gained nor the inclination wrought upon, but awe alone prevails and forces obedience, the obedience is servile, and all which is done through it merely servile. The greater degree of such a submission or obedience is only the greater servility, whatever may be the object. For whether such a creature has a good master or an ill one, he is neither more nor less servile in his own nature. Be the master or superior ever so perfect or excellent, yet the greater submission caused in this case, through this sole principle or motive, is only the lower and more abject servitude and implies the greater wretchedness and meanness in the creature who has those passions of self-love so predominant and is in his temper so vicious and defective, as has been explained.

As to the second case, if there be a belief or conception of a deity who is considered as worthy and good and admired and reverenced as such, being understood to have, besides mere power and knowledge, the highest excellence of nature, such as renders him justly amiable to all and if in the manner this sovereign and mighty being is represented, or as he is historically described, there appears in him a high and eminent regard to what is good and excellent, a concern for the good of all and an affection of benevolence and love towards the whole, such an example must undoubtedly serve, as above explained, to raise and increase the affection towards virtue and help to submit and subdue all other affections to that alone.

Nor is this good effected by example merely. For where the theistical belief is entire and perfect, there must be a steady opinion of the superintendency of a supreme being, a witness and spectator of human life, and conscious of whatsoever is felt or acted in the universe, so that in the perfectest recess or deepest solitude there must be One still presumed remaining with us, whose presence singly must be of more moment than that of the most august assembly on earth. In such a presence it is evident that as the shame of guilty actions must be the greatest of any, so must the honour be of well-doing, even under the unjust censure of a world. And in this case it is very apparent how conducing a perfect theism must be to virtue and how great deficiency there is in atheism.

What the fear of future punishment and hope of future reward, added to this belief, may further contribute towards virtue, we come now to consider more particularly. So much in the meanwhile may be gathered from what has been said above, that neither this fear nor hope can possibly be of the kind called good affections, such as are acknowledged the springs and sources of all actions truly good. Nor can this fear or hope, as above intimated, consist in reality with virtue or goodness, if it either stands as essential to any moral performance or as a considerable motive to any act, of which some better affection ought alone to have been a sufficient cause.

It may be considered withal that, in this religious sort of discipline, the principle of self-love, which is naturally so prevailing in us, being no way moderated or restrained but rather improved and made stronger every day by the exercise of the passions in a subject of more extended self-interest, there may be reason to apprehend lest the temper of this kind should extend itself in general through all the parts of life. For, if the habit be such as to occasion in every particular a stricter attention to self-good and private interest, it must insensibly diminish the affections towards public good or the interest of society and introduce a certain narrowness of spirit, which, as some pretend, is peculiarly observable in the devout persons and zealots of almost every religious persuasion.

This too must be confessed: that, if it be true piety to love God for his own sake, the over-solicitous regard to private good expected from him must of necessity prove a diminution of piety. For while God is beloved only as the cause of private good, he is no otherwise beloved than as any other instrument or means of pleasure by any vicious creature. Now the more there is of this violent affection towards private good, the less room is there for the other sort towards goodness itself or any good and deserving object, worthy of love and admiration for its own sake, such as God is universally acknowledged, or at least by the generality of civilized or refined worshippers.

It is in this respect that the strong desire and love of life may also prove an obstacle to piety as well as to virtue and public love. For the stronger this affection is in anyone, the less will he be able to have true resignation or submission to the rule and order of the Deity. And if that which he calls resignation depends only on the expectation of infinite retribution or reward, he discovers no more worth or virtue here than in any other bargain of interest: the meaning of his resignation being only this, that 'he resigns his present life and pleasures conditionally for that which he himself confesses to be beyond an equivalent: eternal living in a state of highest pleasure and enjoyment'.

But, notwithstanding the injury which the principle of virtue may possibly suffer by the increase of the selfish passion in the way we have been mentioning, it is certain, on the other side, that the principle of fear of future punishment and hope of future reward, how mercenary or servile soever it may be accounted, is yet in many circumstances a great advantage, security and support to virtue.

It has been already considered that, notwithstanding there may be implanted in the heart a real sense of right and wrong, a real good affection towards the species or society, yet, by the violence of rage, lust or any other counter-working passion, this good affection may frequently be controlled and overcome. Where therefore there is nothing in the mind capable to render such ill passions the objects of its aversion and cause them earnestly to be opposed, it is apparent how much a good temper in time must suffer and a character by degrees change for the worse. But if religion, interposing, creates a belief that the ill passions of this kind, no less than their consequent actions, are the objects of a deity's animadversion, it is certain that such a belief must prove a seasonable remedy against vice and be in a particular manner advantageous to virtue. For a belief of this kind must be supposed to tend considerably towards the calming of the mind, and disposing or fitting the person to a better recollection of himself, and to a stricter observance of that good and virtuous principle which needs only his attention to engage him wholly in its party and interest.

And as this belief of a future reward and punishment is capable of supporting those who through ill practice are like to apostatize from virtue, so, when by ill opinion and wrong thought the mind itself is bent against the honest course and debauched even to an esteem and deliberate preference of a vicious one, the belief of the kind mentioned may prove on this occasion the only relief and safety.

A person, for instance, who has much of goodness and natural rectitude in his temper, but withal so much softness or effeminacy as unfits him to bear poverty, crosses or adversity, if by ill fortune he meets with many trials of this kind, it must certainly give a sourness and distaste to his temper and make him exceedingly averse to that which he may falsely presume the occasion of such calamity or ill. Now if his own thoughts or the corrupt insinuations of other men, present it often to his mind that 'his honesty is the occasion of this calamity' and that, 'if he were delivered from this restraint of virtue and honesty, he might be much happier', it is very obvious that his esteem of these good qualities must in proportion diminish every day as the temper grows uneasy and quarrels with itself. But if he opposes to this thought the consideration that 'honesty carries with it, if not a present, at least a future, advantage, such as to compensate that loss of private good which he regrets', then may this injury to his good temper and honest principle be prevented, and his love or affection towards honesty and virtue remain as it was before.

In the same manner, where instead of regard or love there is rather an aversion to what is good and virtuous (as, for instance, where lenity and forgiveness are despised and revenge highly thought of and beloved), if there be this consideration added, that 'lenity is, by its rewards, made the cause of a greater self-good and enjoyment than what is found in revenge', that very affection of lenity and mildness may come to be industriously nourished and the contrary passion depressed. And thus temperance, modesty, candour, benignity and other good affections, however despised at first, may come at last to be valued for their own sakes, the contrary species rejected, and the good and proper object beloved and prosecuted, when the reward or punishment is not so much as thought of.

Thus in a civil state or public we see that a virtuous administration and an equal and just distribution of rewards and punishments is of the highest service, not only by restraining the vicious and forcing them to act usefully to society, but by making virtue to be apparently the interest of everyone, so as to remove all prejudices against it, create a fair reception for it and lead men into that path which afterwards they cannot easily quit. For thus a people raised from barbarity or despotic rule, civilized by laws, and made virtuous by the long course of a lawful and just administration, if they chance to fall suddenly under any misgovernment of unjust and arbitrary power, they will on this account be the rather animated to exert a stronger virtue in opposition to such violence and corruption. And even where, by long and continued arts of a prevailing tyranny, such a people are at last totally oppressed, the scattered seeds of virtue will for a long time remain alive, even to a second generation, before the utmost force of misapplied rewards and punishments can bring them to the abject and compliant state of long-accustomed slaves.

But though a right distribution of justice in a government be so essential a cause of virtue, we must observe in this case that it is example which chiefly influences mankind and forms the character and disposition of a people. For a virtuous administration is in a manner necessarily accompanied with virtue in the magistrate. Otherwise it could be of little effect and of no long duration. But where it is sincere and well established, there virtue and the laws must necessarily be respected and beloved. So that, as to punishments and rewards, their efficacy is not so much from the fear or expectation which they raise as from a natural esteem of virtue and detestation of villainy, which is awakened and excited by these public expressions of the approbation and hatred of mankind in each case. For in the public executions of the greatest villains, we see generally that the infamy and odiousness of their crime and the shame of it before mankind contribute more to their misery than all besides and that it is not the immediate pain, or death itself, which raises so much horror either in the sufferers or spectators, as that ignominious kind of death which is inflicted for public crimes and violations of justice and humanity.

And as the case of reward and punishment stands thus in the public, so, in the same manner, as to private families. For slaves and mercenary servants, restrained and made orderly by punishment and the severity of their master, are not on this account made good or honest. Yet the same master of the family using proper rewards and gentle punishments towards his children teaches them goodness and, by this help, instructs them in a virtue which afterwards they practise upon other grounds and without thinking of a penalty or bribe. And this is what we call a liberal education and a liberal service, the contrary service and obedience, whether towards God or man, being illiberal and unworthy of any honour or commendation.

In the case of religion, however, it must be considered that, if by the hope of reward be understood the love and desire of virtuous enjoyment or of the very practice and exercise of virtue in another life, the expectation or hope of this kind is so far from being derogatory to virtue that it is an evidence of our loving it the more sincerely and for its own sake. Nor can this principle be justly called selfish, for, if the love of virtue be not mere self-interest, the love and desire of life for virtue's sake cannot be esteemed so. But if the desire of life be only through the violence of that natural aversion to death, if it be through the love of something else than virtuous affection or through the unwillingness of parting with something else than what is purely of this kind, then is it no longer any sign or token of real virtue.

Thus, a person loving life for life's sake and virtue not at all may, by the promise or hope of life and fear of death or other evil, be induced to practise virtue and even endeavour to be truly virtuous by a love of what he practises. Yet neither is this very endeavour to be esteemed a virtue. For though he may intend to be virtuous, he has not become so for having only intended or aimed at it through love of the reward. But as soon as he has come to have any affection towards what is morally good and can like or affect such good for its own sake, as good and amiable in itself, then is he in some degree good and virtuous, and not till then.

Such are the advantages or disadvantages which accrue to virtue from reflection upon private good or interest. For though the habit of selfishness and the multiplicity of interested views are of little improvement to real merit or virtue, yet there is a necessity for the preservation of virtue, that it should be thought to have no quarrel with true interest and self-enjoyment.

Whoever, therefore, by any strong persuasion or settled judgment, thinks in the main that 'virtue causes happiness and vice misery' carries with him that security and assistance to virtue which is required. Or though he has no such thought nor can believe virtue his real interest, either with respect to his own nature and constitution or the circumstances of human life, yet, if he believes any supreme powers concerned in the present affairs of mankind, immediately interposing in behalf of the honest and virtuous against the impious and unjust, this will serve to preserve in him, however, that just esteem of virtue which might otherwise considerably diminish. Or should he still believe little of the immediate interposition of providence in the affairs of this present life, yet, if he believes a god dispensing rewards and punishment to vice and virtue in a future, he carries with him still the same advantage and security, while his belief is steady and nowise wavering or doubtful.

For it must be observed that an expectation and dependency so miraculous and great as this must naturally take off from other inferior dependencies and encouragements. Where infinite rewards are thus enforced and the imagination strongly turned towards them, the other common and natural motives to goodness are apt to be neglected and lose much by disuse. Other interests are hardly so much as computed while the mind is thus transported in the pursuit of a high advantage and self-interest so narrowly confined within ourselves. On this account, all other affections towards friends, relations or mankind are often slightly regarded as being worldly and of little moment in respect of the interest of our soul. And so little thought is there of any immediate satisfaction arising from such good offices of life, that it is customary with many devout people zealously to decry all temporal advantages of goodness, all natural benefits of virtue, and, magnifying the contrary happiness of a vicious state, to declare that, 'except only for the sake of future reward and fear of future punishment, they would divest themselves of all goodness at once and freely allow themselves to be most immoral and profligate'. From whence it appears that in some respects there can be nothing more fatal to virtue than the weak and uncertain belief of a future reward and punishment.[10] For the stress being laid wholly here, if this foundation come to fail, there is no further prop or security to men's morals. And thus virtue is supplanted and betrayed.

Now as to atheism, though it be plainly deficient and without remedy in the case of ill judgment on the happiness of virtue, yet it is not, indeed, of necessity the cause of any such ill judgment. For without an absolute assent to any hypothesis of theism, the advantages of virtue may possibly be seen and owned and a high opinion of it established in the mind. However, it must be confessed that the natural tendency of atheism is very different.

It is in a manner impossible to have any great opinion of the happiness of virtue without conceiving high thoughts of the satisfaction resulting from the generous admiration and love of it, and nothing beside the experience of such a love is likely to make this satisfaction credited. The chief ground and support therefore of this opinion of 'happiness in virtue' must arise from the powerful feeling of this generous moral affection and the knowledge of its power and strength. But this is certain, that it can be no great strengthening to the moral affection, no great support to the pure love of goodness and virtue, to suppose there is neither goodness nor beauty in the whole itself nor any example or precedent of good affection in any superior being. Such a belief must tend rather to the weaning the affections from anything amiable or self-worthy and to the suppressing the very habit and familiar custom of admiring natural beauties or whatever in the order of things is according to just design, harmony and proportion. For how little disposed must a person be to love or admire anything as orderly in the universe who thinks the universe itself a pattern of disorder? How unapt to reverence or respect any particular subordinate beauty of a part, when even the whole itself is thought to want perfection and to be only a vast and infinite deformity?

Nothing indeed can be more melancholy than the thought of living in a distracted universe, from whence many ills may be suspected and where there is nothing good or lovely which presents itself, nothing which can satisfy in contemplation or raise any passion besides that of contempt, hatred or dislike. Such an opinion as this may by degrees embitter the temper and not only make the love of virtue to be less felt but help to impair and ruin the very principle of virtue, namely, natural and kind affection.

Upon the whole, whoever has a firm belief of a god whom he does not merely call good but of whom in reality he believes nothing beside real good, nothing beside what is truly suitable to the exactest character of benignity and goodness – such a person, believing rewards or retributions in another life, must believe them annexed to real goodness and merit, real villainy and baseness, and not to any accidental qualities or circumstances, in which respect they

[10] See p. 45–6.

cannot properly be styled rewards or punishments, but capricious distributions of happiness or unhappiness to creatures. These are the only terms on which the belief of a world to come can happily influence the believer. And on these terms, and by virtue of this belief, man perhaps may retain his virtue and integrity, even under the hardest thoughts of human nature, when either by any ill circumstance or untoward doctrine he is brought to that unfortunate opinion of 'virtue's being naturally an enemy to happiness in life'.

This, however, is an opinion which cannot be supposed consistent with sound theism. For whatever be decided as to a future life or the rewards and punishments of hereafter, he who, as a sound theist, believes a reigning mind, sovereign in nature and ruling all things with the highest perfection of goodness as well as of wisdom and power, must necessarily believe virtue to be naturally good and advantageous. For what could more strongly imply an unjust ordinance, a blot and imperfection in the general constitution of things, than to suppose virtue the natural ill and vice the natural good of any creature?

And now, last of all, there remains for us to consider a yet further advantage to virtue, in the theistical belief above the atheistical. The proposition may at first sight appear over-refined and of a sort which is esteemed too nicely philosophical. But after what has been already examined, the subject perhaps may be more easily explained.

There is no creature, according to what has been already proved, who must not of necessity be ill in some degree by having any affection or aversion in a stronger degree than is suitable to his own private good or that of the system to which he is joined. For in either case the affection is ill and vicious. Now if a rational creature has that degree of aversion which is requisite to arm him against any particular misfortune and alarm him against the approach of any calamity, this is regular and well. But if after the misfortune has happened, his aversion continues still, and his passion rather grows upon him while he rages at the accident and exclaims against his private fortune or lot, this will be acknowledged both vicious in present and for the future, as it affects the temper and disturbs that easy course of the affections on which virtue and goodness so much depend. On the other side, the patient enduring of the calamity and the bearing up of the mind under it must be acknowledged immediately virtuous and preservative of virtue. Now, according to the hypothesis of those who exclude a general mind, it must be confessed there can nothing happen in the course of things to deserve either our admiration and love or our anger and abhorrence. However, as there can be no satisfaction at the best in thinking upon what atoms and chance produce, so upon disastrous occasions and under the circumstances of a calamitous and hard fortune, it is scarce possible to prevent a natural kind of abhorrence and spleen, which will be entertained and kept alive by the imagination of so perverse an order of things. But in another hypothesis, that of perfect theism, it is understood that 'whatever the order of the world produces is in the main both just and good'. Therefore in the course of things in this world, whatever hardship of events may seem to force from any rational creature a hard censure of his private condition or lot, he may by reflection nevertheless come to have patience and to acquiesce in it. Nor is this all. He may go further still in this reconciliation and, from the same principle, may make the lot itself an object of his good affection, while he strives to maintain this generous fealty and stands so well disposed towards the laws and government of his higher country.

Such an affection must needs create the highest constancy in any state of sufferance, and make us in the best manner support whatever hardships are to be endured for virtue's sake. And as this affection must of necessity cause a greater acquiescence and complacency with respect to ill accidents, ill men and injuries, so of course it cannot fail of producing still a greater equality, gentleness and benignity in the temper. Consequently the affection must be a truly good one, and a creature the more truly good and virtuous by possessing it. For whatsoever is the occasion or means of more affectionately uniting a rational creature to his part in society and causes him to prosecute the public good or interest of his species with more zeal and affection than ordinary is undoubtedly the cause of more than ordinary virtue in such a person.

This too is certain, that the admiration and love of order, harmony and proportion, in whatever kind, is naturally improving to the temper, advantageous to social affection, and highly assistant to virtue, which is itself no other than the love of order and beauty in society. In the meanest subjects of the world, the appearance of order gains upon the mind and draws the affection towards it. But if the order of the world itself appears just and beautiful, the admiration and esteem of order must run higher and the elegant passion or love of beauty, which is so advantageous to virtue, must be the more improved by its exercise in so ample and magnificent a subject. For it is impossible that such a divine order should be contemplated without ecstasy and rapture since, in the common subjects of science and the liberal arts, whatever is according to just harmony and proportion is so transporting to those who have any knowledge or practice in the kind.[11]

Now if the subject and ground of this divine passion be not really just or adequate (the hypothesis of theism being supposed false), the passion still in itself is so far natural and good as it proves an advantage to virtue and goodness, according to what has been above-demonstrated. But if, on the other side, the subject of this passion be really adequate and just (the hypothesis of theism being real and not imaginary), then is the passion also just and becomes absolutely due and requisite in every rational creature.

[11] See pp. 317–8, 320, 351–2.

Hence we may determine justly the relation which virtue has to piety, the first being not complete but in the latter, since where the latter is wanting, there can neither be the same benignity, firmness or constancy, the same good composure of the affections or uniformity of mind.

And thus the perfection and height of virtue must be owing to the belief of a god.

Book II

Part I

Section 1

We have considered what virtue is and to whom the character belongs. It remains to inquire 'what obligation is there to virtue, or what reason to embrace it?'

We have found that, to deserve the name of good or virtuous, a creature must have all his inclinations and affections, his dispositions of mind and temper, suitable and agreeing with the good of his kind or of that system in which he is included and of which he constitutes a part. To stand thus well affected and to have one's affections right and entire not only in respect of oneself but of society and the public: this is rectitude, integrity or virtue. And to be wanting in any of these, or to have their contraries, is depravity, corruption and vice.

It has been already shown that, in the passions and affections of particular creatures, there is a constant relation to the interest of a species or common nature. This has been demonstrated in the case of natural affection, parental kindness, zeal for posterity, concern for the propagation and nurture of the young, love of fellowship and company, compassion, mutual succour and the rest of this kind. Nor will anyone deny that this affection of a creature towards the good of the species or common nature is as proper and natural to him as it is to any organ, part or member of an animal body, or mere vegetable, to work in its known course and regular way of growth. It is not more natural for the stomach to digest, the lungs to breathe, the glands to separate juices or other entrails to perform their several offices, however they may by particular impediments be sometimes disordered or obstructed in their operations.

There being allowed therefore in a creature such affections as these towards the common nature or system of the kind, together with those other which regard the private nature or self-system, it will appear that in following the first of these affections, the creature must on many occasions contradict and go against the latter. How else should the species be preserved? Or what would signify that implanted natural affection by which a creature through so many difficulties and hazards preserves its offspring and supports its kind?

It may therefore be imagined, perhaps, that there is a plain and absolute opposition between these two habits or affections. It may be presumed that the pursuing the common interest or public good through the affections of one kind must be a hindrance to the attainment of private good through the affections of another. For it being taken for granted that hazards and hardships of whatever sort are naturally the ill of the private state and it being certainly the nature of those public affections to lead often to the greatest hardships and hazards of every kind, it is presently inferred that 'it is the creature's interest to be without any public affection whatsoever'.

This we know for certain, that all social love, friendship, gratitude or whatever else is of this generous kind does by its nature take place of the self-interesting passions, draws us out of ourselves and makes us disregardful of our own convenience and safety. So that, according to a known way of reasoning on self-interest, that which is of a social kind in us should of right be abolished.[12] Thus, kindness of every sort, indulgence, tenderness, compassion and, in short, all natural affection should be industriously suppressed and, as mere folly and weakness of nature, be resisted and overcome, that, by this means, there might be nothing remaining in us which was contrary to a direct self-end, nothing which might stand in opposition to a steady and deliberate pursuit of the most narrowly confined self-interest.

According to this extraordinary hypothesis, it must be taken for granted that 'in the system of a kind or species, the interest of the private nature is directly opposite to that of the common one, the interest of particulars directly opposite to that of the public in general'.

A strange constitution in which it must be confessed there is much disorder and untowardness unlike to what we observe elsewhere in nature! As if, in any vegetable or animal body, the part or member could be supposed in a good and prosperous state as to itself when under a contrary disposition and in an unnatural growth or habit as to its whole.

Now, that this is in reality quite otherwise, we shall endeavour to demonstrate, so as to make appear that 'what men represent as an ill order and constitution in the universe, by making moral rectitude appear the ill and depravity the good or advantage of a creature, is in nature just the contrary', that 'to be well affected towards the public interest and one's own is not only consistent but inseparable', and that 'moral rectitude or virtue must accordingly be the advantage and vice the injury and disadvantage of every creature'.

Section 2
There are few perhaps who, when they consider a creature void of natural affection and wholly destitute of a communicative or social principle, will

[12] See pp. 42, 54–6.

suppose him at the same time either tolerably happy in himself or as he stands abroad, with respect to his fellow-creatures or kind. It is generally thought that such a creature as this feels slender joy in life and finds little satisfaction in the mere sensual pleasures which remain with him after the loss of social enjoyment and whatever can be called humanity or good nature. We know that to such a creature as this it is not only incident to be morose, rancorous and malignant, but that, of necessity, a mind or temper thus destitute of mildness and benignity must turn to that which is contrary and be wrought by passions of a different kind. Such a heart as this must be a continual seat of perverse inclinations and bitter aversions, raised from a constant ill humour, sourness and disquiet. The consciousness of such a nature, so obnoxious to mankind and to all beings which approach it, must overcloud the mind with dark suspicion and jealousy, alarm it with fears and horror and raise in it a continual disturbance, even in the most seeming fair and secure state of fortune and in the highest degree of outward prosperity.

This, as to the complete immoral state, is what, of their own accord, men readily remark. Where there is this absolute degeneracy, this total apostasy from all candour, equity, trust, sociableness or friendship, there are few who do not see and acknowledge the misery which is consequent. Seldom is the case misconstrued when at worst. The misfortune is, we look not on this depravity nor consider how it stands in less degrees. The calamity, we think, does not of necessity hold proportion with the injustice or iniquity, as if to be absolutely immoral and inhuman were indeed the greatest misfortune and misery, but that to be so in a little degree should be no misery nor harm at all! Which to allow is just as reasonable as to own that it is the greatest ill of a body to be in the utmost manner distorted and maimed, but that to lose the use only of one limb or to be impaired in some one single organ or member is no inconvenience or ill worthy the least notice.

The parts and proportions of the mind, their mutual relation and dependency, the connection and frame of those passions which constitute the soul or temper, may easily be understood by anyone who thinks it worth his while to study this inward anatomy. It is certain that the order or symmetry of this inward part is, in itself, no less real and exact than that of the body. However, it is apparent that few of us endeavour to become anatomists of this sort. Nor is anyone ashamed of the deepest ignorance in such a subject. For though the greatest misery and ill is generally owned to be from disposition and temper, though it is allowed that temper may often change and that it actually varies on many occasions, much to our disadvantage, yet how this matter is brought about we inquire not. We never trouble ourselves to consider thoroughly by what means or methods our inward constitution comes at any time to be impaired or injured. The *solutio continui*,[E] which bodily surgeons talk of, is never applied in this case by surgeons of another sort. The notion of a whole and parts is not apprehended in this science. We know not what the effect is of straining any affection, indulging any wrong passion or relaxing any proper and natural habit or good inclination. Nor can we conceive how a particular action should have such a sudden influence on the whole mind as to make the person an immediate sufferer. We suppose rather that a man may violate his faith, commit any wickedness unfamiliar to him before, engage in any vice or villainy, without the least prejudice to himself or any misery naturally following from the ill action.

It is thus we hear it often said, 'Such a person has done ill indeed, but what is he the worse for it?' Yet, speaking of any nature thoroughly savage, cursed and inveterate, we say truly, 'Such a one is a plague and torment to himself.' And we allow that, 'through certain humours or passions and from temper merely, a man may be completely miserable, let his outward circumstances be ever so fortunate'. These different judgments sufficiently demonstrate that we are not accustomed to think with much coherency on these moral subjects and that our notions in this respect are not a little confused and contradictory.

Now if the fabric of the mind or temper appeared such to us as it really is, if we saw it impossible to remove hence any one good or orderly affection or introduce any ill or disorderly one without drawing on, in some degree, that dissolute state, which at its height is confessed to be so miserable, it would then undoubtedly be confessed that, since no ill, immoral or unjust action could be committed without either a new inroad and breach on the temper and passions or a farther advancing of that execution already begun, whoever did ill or acted in prejudice of his integrity, good nature or worth, would of necessity act with greater cruelty towards himself than he who scrupled not to swallow what was poisonous or who with his own hands should voluntarily mangle or wound his outward form or constitution, natural limbs or body.

Section 3
It has been shown before that no animal can be said properly to act otherwise than through affections or passions, such as are proper to an animal. For in convulsive fits, where a creature strikes either himself or others, it is a simple mechanism, an engine or piece of clockwork, which acts and not the animal.

Whatsoever therefore is done or acted by any animal as such is done only through some affection or passion, as of fear, love or hatred moving him.

And as it is impossible that a weaker affection should overcome a stronger, so it is impossible but that where the affections or passions are strongest in the

---

[E] 'Interruption of continuity', a medical expression referring to the separation from each other of parts of the body which are normally joined together.

main and form in general the most considerable party, either by their force or number, thither the animal must incline, and, according to this balance, he must be governed and led to action.

The affections or passions which must influence and govern the animal are either:

1. the *natural affections*, which lead to the good of the public; or
2. the *self affections*, which lead only to the good of the private; or
3. such as are neither of these nor tending either to any good of the public or private, but contrariwise, and which may therefore be justly styled *unnatural affections*.

So that according as these affections stand, a creature must be virtuous or vicious, good or ill.

The latter sort of these affections, it is evident, are wholly vicious. The two former may be vicious or virtuous according to their degree.

It may seem strange, perhaps, to speak of natural affections as too strong or of self affections as too weak. But to clear this difficulty we must call to mind what has been already explained, that natural affection may, in particular cases, be excessive and in an unnatural degree, as when pity is so overcoming as to destroy its own end and prevent the succour and relief required or as when love to the offspring proves such a fondness as destroys the parent and consequently the offspring itself. And, notwithstanding it may seem harsh to call that unnatural and vicious which is only an extreme of some natural and kind affection, yet it is most certain that, wherever any single good affection of this sort is over-great, it must be injurious to the rest and detract in some measure from their force and natural operation. For a creature possessed with such an immoderate degree of passion must of necessity allow too much to that one and too little to others of the same character and equally natural and useful as to their end. And this must necessarily be the occasion of partiality and injustice while only one duty or natural part is earnestly followed and other parts or duties neglected, which should accompany it and perhaps take place and be preferred.

This may well be allowed true in all other respects, since even religion itself, considered as a passion, not of the selfish but nobler kind, may in some characters be strained beyond its natural proportion and be said also to be in too high a degree. For as the end of religion is to render us more perfect and accomplished in all moral duties and performances, if by the height of devout ecstasy and contemplation we are rather disabled in this respect and rendered more unapt to the real duties and offices of civil life, it may be said that religion indeed is then too strong in us. For how, possibly, can we call this superstition while the object of the devotion is acknowledged just and the faith orthodox? It is only the excess of zeal which in this case is so transporting as to render the devout person more remiss in secular affairs and less concerned for the inferior and temporal interests of mankind.

Now, as in particular cases, public affection, on the one hand, may be too high, so private affection may, on the other hand, be too weak. For if a creature be self-neglectful and insensible of danger or if he want such a degree of passion in any kind as is useful to preserve, sustain or defend himself, this must certainly be esteemed vicious in regard of the design and end of nature. She herself discovers this in her known method and stated rule of operation. It is certain that her provisionary care and concern for the whole animal must at least be equal to her concern for a single part or member. Now to the several parts she has given, we see, proper affections, suitable to their interest and security, so that even without our consciousness they act in their own defence and for their own benefit and preservation. Thus, an eye, in its natural state, fails not to shut together of its own accord, unknowingly to us, by a peculiar caution and timidity, which, if it wanted, however we might intend the preservation of our eye, we should not in effect be able to preserve it by any observation or forecast of our own. To be wanting therefore in those principal affections which respect the good of the whole constitution must be a vice and imperfection as great surely in the principal part, the soul or temper, as it is in any of those inferior and subordinate parts to want the self-preserving affections which are proper to them.

And thus the affections towards private good become necessary and essential to goodness. For though no creature can be called good or virtuous merely for possessing these affections, yet, since it is impossible that the public good or good of the system can be preserved without them, it follows that a creature really wanting in them is in reality wanting in some degree to goodness and natural rectitude and may thus be esteemed vicious and defective.

It is thus we say of a creature, in a kind way of reproof, that he is too good when his affection towards others is so warm and zealous as to carry him even beyond his part or when he really acts beyond it, not through too warm a passion of that sort, but through an over-cool one of another or through want of some self-passion to restrain him within due bounds.

It may be objected here that the having the natural affections too strong (where the self affections are overmuch so) or the having the self affections defective or weak (where the natural affections are also weak) may prove upon occasion the only cause of a creature's acting honestly and in moral proportion. For, thus, one who is to a fault regardless of his life may with the smallest degree of natural affection do all which can be expected from the highest pitch of social love or zealous friendship. And, thus, on the other hand, a creature excessively timorous may, by as exceeding a degree of natural affection, perform whatever the perfectest courage is able to inspire.

To this it is answered that, whenever we arraign any passion as too strong or complain of any as too weak, we must speak with respect to a certain constitution or economy of a particular creature or species. For if a passion, leading to any right end, be only so much the more serviceable and effectual for being strong, if we may be assured that the strength of it will not be the occasion of any disturbance within nor of any disproportion between itself and other affections, then consequently the passion, however strong, cannot be condemned as vicious. But if to have all the passions in equal proportion with it be what the constitution of the creature cannot bear, so that only some passions are raised to this height while others are not nor can possibly be wrought up to the same proportion, then may those strong passions, though of the better kind, be called excessive; for, being in unequal proportion to the others and causing an ill balance in the affection at large, they must of course be the occasion of inequality in the conduct and incline the party to a wrong moral practice.

But to show more particularly what is meant by the economy of the passions from instances in the species or kinds below us:[13] As for the creatures who have no manner of power or means given them by nature for their defence against violence nor anything by which they can make themselves formidable to such as injure or offend them, it is necessary they should have an extraordinary degree of fear but little or no animosity, such as might cause them to make resistance or incline them to delay their flight. For in this their safety lies, and, to this, the passion of fear is serviceable, by keeping the senses on the watch and holding the spirits in readiness to give the start.

And thus timorousness and an habitual strong passion of fear may be according to the economy of a particular creature, both with respect to himself and to the rest of his species. On the other hand, courage may be contrary to his economy and therefore vicious. Even in one and the same species, this is by nature differently ordered with respect to different sexes, ages and growths. The tamer creatures of the grazing kind, who live in herds, are different from the wilder, who herd not but live in pairs only, apart from company, as is natural and suitable to their rapacious life. Yet is there found, even among the former inoffensive kind, a courage proportionable to their make and strength. At a time of danger, when the whole herd flies, the bull alone makes head against the lion or whatever other invading beast of prey and shows himself conscious of his make. Even the female of this kind is armed, we see, by nature, in some degree, to resist violence, so as not to fly a common danger. As for a hind or doe or any other inoffensive and mere defenceless creature, it is no way unnatural or vicious in them, when the enemy approaches, to desert their offspring and fly for safety. But for creatures who are able to make resistance and are by nature armed offensively, be they of the poorest insect kind, such as bees or wasps, it is natural to them to be roused with fury and, at the haz-

---

[13] See pp. 213, 282–3, 429ff.

ard of their lives, oppose any enemy or invader of their species. For by this known passion in the creature, the species itself is secured when by experience it is found that the creature, though unable to repel the injury, yet voluntarily exposes his life for the punishment of the invader and suffers not his kind to be injured with impunity. And of all other creatures, man is in this sense the most formidable since, if he thinks it just and exemplary, he may, possibly in his own or in his country's cause, revenge an injury on anyone living and, by throwing away his own life (if he be resolute to that degree), is almost certain master of another's, however strongly guarded. Examples of this nature have often served to restrain those in power from using it to the utmost extent and urging their inferiors to extremity.

Upon the whole, it may be said properly to be the same with the affections or passions in an animal constitution as with the cords or strings of a musical instrument. If these, though in ever so just proportion one to another, are strained beyond a certain degree, it is more than the instrument will bear: the lute or lyre is abused, and its effect lost. On the other hand, if, while some of the strings are duly strained, others are not wound up to their due proportion, then is the instrument still in disorder and its part ill performed. The several species of creatures are like different sorts of instruments. And, even in the same species of creatures, as in the same sort of instrument, one is not entirely like the other nor will the same strings fit each. The same degree of strength which winds up one and fits the several strings to a just harmony and consort may in another burst both the strings and instrument itself. Thus, men who have the liveliest sense and are the easiest affected with pain or pleasure have need of the strongest influence or force of other affections, such as tenderness, love, sociableness, compassion, in order to preserve a right balance within and to maintain them in their duty and in the just performance of their part, while others, who are of a cooler blood or lower key, need not the same allay or counterpart nor are made by nature to feel those tender and endearing affections in so exquisite a degree.

It might be agreeable, one would think, to inquire thus into the different tunings of the passions, the various mixtures and allays by which men become so different from one another. For as the highest improvements of temper are made in humankind, so the greatest corruptions and degeneracies are discoverable in this race. In the other species of creatures around us, there is found generally an exact proportionableness, constancy and regularity in all their passions and affections, no failure in the care of the offspring or of the society to which they are united, no prostitution of themselves, no intemperance or excess in any kind. The smaller creatures, who live as it were in cities (as bees and ants), continue the same train and harmony of life, nor are they ever false to those affections which move them to operate towards their public good. Even those creatures of prey who live the farthest out of society maintain, we see, such a conduct towards one another as is exactly suitable to the good of their own species, while man, notwithstanding the assistance of religion and the direction of laws, is often found to live in less conformity with nature and, by means of religion itself, is often rendered the more barbarous and inhuman. Marks are set on men; distinctions formed; opinions decreed under the severest penalties; antipathies instilled, and aversions raised in men against the generality of their own species. So that it is hard to find in any region a human society which has human laws. No wonder if in such societies it is so hard to find a man who lives naturally and as a man.

But having shown what is meant by a passion's being in too high or in too low a degree and that to have any natural affection too high or any self affection too low, though it be often approved as virtue, is yet, strictly speaking, a vice and imperfection, we come now to the plainer and more essential part of vice and which alone deserves to be considered as such, that is to say:

1. when either the public affections are weak or deficient; or
2. the private and self affections too strong; or
3. that such affections arise as are neither of these nor in any degree tending to the support either of the public or private system.

Otherwise than thus, it is impossible any creature can be such as we call ill or vicious. So that, if once we prove that it is really not the creature's interest to be thus viciously affected but contrariwise, we shall then have proved that *it is his interest to be wholly good and virtuous*, since in a wholesome and sound state of his affections, such as we have described, he cannot possibly be other than sound, good and virtuous in his action and behaviour.

Our business, therefore, will be to prove:

1. that *to have the natural, kindly or generous affections strong and powerful towards the good of the public is to have the chief means and power of self-enjoyment* and that *to want them is certain misery and ill*;
2. that *to have the private or self affections too strong or beyond their degree of subordinacy to the kindly and natural is also miserable*; and
3. that *to have the unnatural affections, namely, such as are neither founded on the interest of the kind or public nor of the private person or creature himself, is to be miserable in the highest degree*.

Part II

Section 1
To begin therefore with this proof, that *to have the natural affections, such as are founded in love, complacency, good-will and in a sympathy with the kind or species, is to have the chief means and power of self-enjoyment* and that *to want*

them is certain misery and ill, we may inquire first what those are which we call pleasures or satisfactions, from whence happiness is generally computed. They are, according to the common distinction, either satisfactions and pleasures of the body or of the mind.

That the latter of these satisfactions are the greatest is allowed by most people and may be proved by this: that whenever the mind, having conceived a high opinion of the worth of any action or behaviour, has received the strongest impression of this sort and is wrought up to the highest pitch or degree of passion towards the subject, at such time it sets itself above all bodily pain as well as pleasure and can be no way diverted from its purpose by flattery or terror of any kind. Thus we see Indians, barbarians, malefactors and even the most execrable villains, for the sake of a particular gang or society or through some cherished notion or principle of honour or gallantry, revenge or gratitude, embrace any manner of hardship and defy torments and death. Whereas, on the other hand, a person being placed in all the happy circumstances of outward enjoyment, surrounded with everything which can allure or charm the sense and being then actually in the very moment of such a pleasing indulgence, yet no sooner is there anything amiss within, no sooner has he conceived any internal ail or disorder, anything inwardly vexatious or distempered, than instantly his enjoyment ceases, the pleasure of sense is at an end, and every means of that sort becomes ineffectual and is rejected as uneasy and subject to give distaste.

The pleasures of the mind being allowed, therefore, superior to those of the body, it follows that *whatever can create in any intelligent being a constant flowing series or train of mental enjoyments or pleasures of the mind is more considerable to his happiness than that which can create to him a like constant course or train of sensual enjoyments or pleasures of the body.*

Now the mental enjoyments are either actually the very natural affections themselves in their immediate operation, or they wholly in a manner proceed from them and are no other than their effects.

If so, it follows that, the natural affections duly established in a rational creature being the only means which can procure him a constant series or succession of the mental enjoyments, they are the only means which can procure him a certain and solid happiness.

Now, in the first place, to explain how much the natural affections are in themselves the highest pleasure and enjoyments, there should methinks be little need of proving this to anyone of humankind who has ever known the condition of the mind under a lively affection of love, gratitude, bounty, generosity, pity, succour or whatever else is of a social or friendly sort. He who has ever so little knowledge of human nature is sensible what pleasure the mind perceives when it is touched in this generous way. The difference we find between solitude and company, between a common company and that of friends, the reference of almost all our pleasures to mutual converse, and the dependence they have on society either present or imagined – all these are sufficient proofs in our behalf.

How much the social pleasures are superior to any other may be known by visible tokens and effects. The very outward features, the marks and signs which attend this sort of joy, are expressive of a more intense, clear and undisturbed pleasure than those which attend the satisfaction of thirst, hunger and other ardent appetites. But more particularly still may this superiority be known from the actual prevalence and ascendancy of this sort of affection over all besides. Wherever it presents itself with any advantage, it silences and appeases every other motion of pleasure. No joy, merely of sense, can be a match for it. Whoever is judge of both the pleasures will ever give the preference to the former. But to be able to judge of both, it is necessary to have a sense of each. The honest man indeed can judge of sensual pleasure and knows its utmost force. For neither is his taste nor sense the duller but, on the contrary, the more intense and clear on the account of his temperance and a moderate use of appetite. But the immoral and profligate man can by no means be allowed a good judge of social pleasure, to which he is so mere a stranger by his nature.

Nor is it any objection here that in many natures the good affection, though really present, is found to be of insufficient force. For where it is not in its natural degree, it is the same indeed as if it were not or had never been. The less there is of this good affection in any untoward creature, the greater the wonder is that it should at any time prevail, as in the very worst of creatures it sometimes will. And if it prevails but for once in any single instance, it shows evidently that, if the affection were thoroughly experienced or known, it would prevail in all.

Thus the charm of kind affection is superior to all other pleasure since it has the power of drawing from every appetite or inclination. And thus in the case of love to the offspring and a thousand other instances, the charm is found to operate so strongly on the temper as, in the midst of other temptations, to render it susceptible of this passion alone, which remains as the master-pleasure and conqueror of the rest.

There is no one who, by the least progress in science or learning, has come to know barely the principles of mathematics but has found that in the exercise of his mind on the discoveries he there makes, though merely of speculative truths, he receives a pleasure and delight superior to that of sense. When we have thoroughly searched into the nature of this contemplative delight, we shall find it of a kind which relates not in the least to any private interest of the creature, nor has for its object any self-good or advantage of the private system. The admiration, joy or love turns wholly upon what is exterior and foreign to ourselves. And though the reflected joy or pleasure which arises from the notice of this pleasure once perceived may be interpreted as self-passion or interested regard, yet the original satisfaction can be no other than what results from the love of truth, proportion, order and symmetry in the things without. If this be the case, the passion ought in reality to be ranked with natural affection. For having no object within the compass of the private system, it must either be esteemed superfluous and unnatural, as having no tendency towards the advantage or good of anything in nature, or it must be judged to be what it truly is, *a natural joy in the contemplation of those numbers, that harmony, proportion and concord, which supports the universal nature and is essential in the constitution and form of every particular species or order of beings.*[14]

But this speculative pleasure, however considerable and valuable it may be or however superior to any motion of mere sense, must yet be far surpassed by virtuous motion and the exercise of benignity and goodness, where, together with the most delightful affection of the soul, there is joined a pleasing assent and approbation of the mind to what is acted in this good disposition and honest bent. For where is there on earth a fairer matter of speculation, a goodlier view or contemplation, than that of a beautiful, proportioned and becoming action? Or what is there relating to us of which the consciousness and memory is more solidly and lastingly entertaining?

We may observe that in the passion of love between the sexes, where, together with the affection of a vulgar sort, there is a mixture of the kind and friendly, the sense or feeling of this latter is in reality superior to the former, since often through this affection, and for the sake of the person beloved, the greatest hardships in the world have been submitted to and even death itself voluntarily embraced without any expected compensation. For where should the ground of such an expectation lie? Not here in this world, surely, for death puts an end to all. Nor yet hereafter, in any other, for who has ever thought of providing a heaven or future recompense for the suffering virtue of lovers?

We may observe, withal, in favour of the natural affections, that it is not only when joy and sprightliness are mixed with them that they carry a real enjoyment above that of the sensual kind. The very disturbances which belong to natural affection, though they may be thought wholly contrary to pleasure, yield still a contentment and satisfaction greater than the pleasures of indulged sense. And where a series or continued succession of the tender and kind affections can be carried on, even through fears, horrors, sorrows, griefs, the emotion of the soul is still agreeable. We continue pleased even with this melancholy aspect or sense of virtue. Her beauty supports itself under a cloud and in the midst of surrounding calamities. For thus, when by mere illusion, as in a tragedy, the passions of this kind are skilfully excited in us, we prefer the entertainment to any other of equal duration. We find by ourselves that the mov-

[14] See p. 351–2.

ing our passions in this mournful way, the engaging them in behalf of merit and worth and the exerting whatever we have of social affection and human sympathy is of the highest delight and affords a greater enjoyment in the way of thought and sentiment than anything besides can do in a way of sense and common appetite. And after this manner it appears *how much the mental enjoyments are actually the very natural affections themselves.*

Now, in the next place, to explain how they proceed from them as their natural effects, we may consider first that the effects of love or kind affection, in a way of mental pleasure, are *an enjoyment of good by communication, a receiving it, as it were, by reflection or by way of participation in the good of others, and a pleasing consciousness of the actual love, merited esteem or approbation of others.*

How considerable a part of happiness arises from the former of these effects will be easily apprehended by one who is not exceedingly ill-natured. It will be considered how many the pleasures are of sharing contentment and delight with others, of receiving it in fellowship and company and gathering it, in a manner, from the pleased and happy states of those around us, from accounts and relations of such happinesses, from the very countenances, gestures, voices and sounds, even of creatures foreign to our kind, whose signs of joy and contentment we can anyway discern. So insinuating are these pleasures of sympathy, and so widely diffused through our whole lives, that there is hardly such a thing as satisfaction or contentment of which they make not an essential part.

As for that other effect of social love, namely, the consciousness of merited kindness or esteem, it is not difficult to perceive how much this avails in mental pleasure and constitutes the chief enjoyment and happiness of those who are, in the narrowest sense, voluptuous. How natural is it for the most selfish among us to be continually drawing some sort of satisfaction from a character, and pleasing ourselves in the fancy of deserved admiration and esteem? For though it be mere fancy, we endeavour still to believe it truth and flatter ourselves all we can with the thought of merit of some kind and the persuasion of our deserving well from some few at least with whom we happen to have a more intimate and familiar commerce.

What tyrant is there, what robber or open violator of the laws of society, who has not a companion or some particular set, either of his own kindred or such as he calls friends, with whom he gladly shares his good, in whose welfare he delights and whose joy and satisfaction he makes his own? What person in the world is there who receives not some impressions from the flattery or kindness of such as are familiar with him? It is to this soothing hope and expectation of friendship that almost all our actions have some reference. It is this which goes through our whole lives and mixes itself even with most of our vices. Of this, vanity, ambition and luxury have a share and many other disorders of our life partake. Even the unchastest love borrows largely from this source. So that were pleasure to be computed in the same way as other things commonly are, it might properly be said that out of these two branches, namely, community or participation in the pleasures of others and belief of meriting well from others, would arise more than nine-tenths of whatever is enjoyed in life. And thus, in the main sum of happiness, there is scarce a single article but what derives itself from social love and depends immediately on the natural and kind affections.

Now such as causes are, such must be their effects. And therefore as natural affection or social love is perfect or imperfect, so must be the content and happiness depending on it.

But lest any should imagine with themselves that an inferior degree of natural affection or an imperfect partial regard of this sort can supply the place of an entire, sincere and truly moral one, lest a small tincture of social inclination should be thought sufficient to answer the end of pleasure in society and give us that enjoyment of participation and community which is so essential to our happiness, we may consider, first, that partial affection, or social love in part, without regard to a complete society or whole, is in itself an inconsistency and implies an absolute contradiction. Whatever affection we have towards anything besides ourselves, if it be not of the natural sort towards the system or kind, it must be of all other affections the most dissociable and destructive of the enjoyments of society. If it be really of the natural sort and applied only to some one part of society or of a species but not to the species or society itself, there can be no more account given of it than of the most odd, capricious or humoursome passion which may arise. The person, therefore, who is conscious of this affection can be conscious of no merit or worth on the account of it. Nor can the persons on whom this capricious affection has chanced to fall be in any manner secure of its continuance of force. As it has no foundation or establishment in reason, so it must be easily removable and subject to alteration without reason. Now the variableness of such sort of passion, which depends solely on capriciousness and humour and undergoes the frequent successions of alternate hatred and love, aversion and inclination, must of necessity create continual disturbance and disgust, give an allay to what is immediately enjoyed in the way of friendship and society and, in the end, extinguish in a manner the very inclination towards friendship and human commerce. Whereas, on the other hand, entire affection (from whence integrity has its name) as it is answerable to itself, proportionable and rational, so it is irrefragable, solid and durable. And as, in the case of partiality or vicious friendship, which has no rule or order, every reflection of the mind necessarily makes to its disadvantage and lessens the enjoyment, so, in the case of integrity, the consciousness of just behaviour towards mankind in general casts a good reflection on each friendly affection in particular and raises the enjoyment of friendship still the higher in the way of community or participation above-mentioned.

And in the next place, as partial affection is fitted only to a short and slender enjoyment of those pleasures of sympathy or participation with others, so neither is it able to derive any considerable enjoyment from that other principal branch of human happiness, namely, consciousness of the actual or merited esteem of others. From whence should this esteem arise? The merit, surely, must in itself be mean, while the affection is so precarious and uncertain. What trust can there be to a mere casual inclination or capricious liking? Who can depend on such a friendship as is founded on no moral rule but fantastically assigned to some single person or small part of mankind, exclusive of society and the whole?

It may be considered, withal, as a thing impossible that they who esteem or love by any other rule than that of virtue should place their affection on such subjects as they can long esteem or love. It will be hard for them, in the number of their so beloved friends, to find any in whom they can heartily rejoice or whose reciprocal love or esteem they can sincerely prize and enjoy. Nor can those pleasures be sound or lasting which are gathered from a self-flattery and false persuasion of the esteem and love of others who are incapable of any sound esteem or love. It appears therefore how much the men of narrow or partial affection must be losers in this sense and of necessity fall short in this second principal part of mental enjoyment.

Meanwhile, entire affection has all the opposite advantages. It is equal, constant, accountable to itself, ever satisfactory and pleasing. It gains applause and love from the best and, in all disinterested cases, from the very worst of men. We may say of it, with justice, that it carries with it a consciousness of merited love and approbation from all society, from all intelligent creatures and from whatever is original to all other intelligence. And if there be in nature any such original, we may add that the satisfaction which attends entire affection is full and noble in proportion to its final object, which contains all perfection, according to the sense of theism above-noted. For this, as has been shown, is the result of virtue. And to have this entire affection or integrity of mind is to live according to nature and the dictates and rules of supreme wisdom. This is morality, justice, piety and natural religion.

But lest this argument should appear perhaps too scholastically stated and in terms and phrases which are not of familiar use, we may try whether possibly we can set it yet in a plainer light.

Let anyone, then, consider well those pleasures which he receives, either in private retirement, contemplation, study and converse with himself or in mirth, jollity and entertainment with others, and he will find that they are wholly founded in an easy temper, free of harshness, bitterness or distaste, and in a mind or reason well composed, quiet, easy within itself and such as can freely bear its own inspection and review. Now such a mind and such a temper, which fit and qualify for the enjoyment of the pleasures mentioned, must of necessity be owing to the natural and good affections.

As to what relates to temper, it may be considered thus. There is no state of outward prosperity or flowing fortune where inclination and desire are always satisfied, fancy and humour pleased. There are almost hourly some impediments or crosses to the appetite, some accidents or other from without or something from within, to check the licentious course of the indulged affections. They are not always to be satisfied by mere indulgence. And when a life is guided by fancy only, there is sufficient ground of contrariety and disturbance. The very ordinary lassitudes, uneasinesses and defects of disposition in the soundest body, the interrupted course of the humours or spirits in the healthiest people and the accidental disorders common to every constitution are sufficient, we know, on many occasions to breed uneasiness and distaste. And this in time must grow into a habit where there is nothing to oppose its progress and hinder its prevailing on the temper. Now the only sound opposite to ill humour is natural and kind affection. For we may observe that, when the mind upon reflection resolves at any time to suppress this disturbance already risen in the temper and sets about this reforming work with heartiness and in good earnest, it can no otherwise accomplish the undertaking than by introducing into the affectionate part some gentle feeling of the social and friendly kind, some enlivening motion of kindness, fellowship, complacency or love, to allay and convert that contrary motion of impatience and discontent.

If it be said, perhaps, that, in the case before us, religious affection or devotion is a sufficient and proper remedy, we answer that it is according as the kind may happily prove. For, if it be of the pleasant and cheerful sort, it is of the very kind of natural affection itself; if it be of the dismal or fearful sort,[15] if it brings along with it any affection opposite to manhood, generosity, courage or free thought, there will be nothing gained by this application, and the remedy will, in the issue, be undoubtedly found worse than the disease. The severest reflections on our duty and the consideration merely of what is by authority and under penalties enjoined will not by any means serve to calm us on this occasion. The more dismal our thoughts are on such a subject, the worse our temper will be, and the readier to discover itself in harshness and austerity. If perhaps by compulsion or through any necessity or fear incumbent, a different carriage be at any time affected or different maxims owned, the practice at the bottom will be still the same. If the countenance be composed, the heart, however, will not be changed. The ill passion may for the time be withheld from breaking into action, but will not be subdued or in the least debilitated against the next occasion. So that in such a breast as this, whatever devotion there may be, it is likely there will in time be little of an easy spirit or good temper remaining and, consequently, few and slender enjoyments of a mental kind.

[15] See pp. 17–20, 387–8, 391–2.

If it be objected, on the other hand, that, though in melancholy circumstances ill humour may prevail, yet, in a course of outward prosperity and in the height of fortune, there can nothing probably occur which should thus sour the temper and give it such disrelish as is suggested, we may consider that the most humoured and indulged state is apt to receive the most disturbance from every disappointment or smallest ail. And if provocations are easiest raised and the passions of anger, offence and enmity are found the highest in the most indulged state of will and humour, there is still the greater need of a supply from social affection to preserve the temper from running into savageness and inhumanity. And this, the case of tyrants and most unlimited potentates, may sufficiently verify and demonstrate.

Now as to the other part of our consideration, which relates to a mind or reason well composed and easy within itself, upon what account this happiness may be thought owing to natural affection, we may possibly resolve ourselves after this manner. It will be acknowledged that a creature such as man, who from several degrees of reflection has risen to that capacity which we call reason and understanding, must in the very use of this his reasoning faculty be forced to receive reflections back into his mind of what passes in itself as well as in the affections or will – in short, of whatsoever relates to his character, conduct or behaviour amid his fellow creatures and in society. Or should he be of himself unapt, there are others ready to remind him and refresh his memory in this way of criticism. We have all of us remembrances enough to help us in this work. Nor are the greatest favourites of fortune exempted from this task of self-inspection. Even flattery itself, by making the view agreeable, renders us more attentive this way and ensnares us in the habit. The vainer any person is, the more he has his eye inwardly fixed upon himself and is after a certain manner employed in this home survey. And when a true regard to ourselves cannot oblige us to this inspection, a false regard to others and a fondness for reputation raises a watchful jealousy and furnishes us sufficiently with acts of reflection on our own character and conduct.

In whatever manner we consider of this, we shall find still that every reasoning or reflecting creature is by his nature forced to endure the review of his own mind and actions and to have representations of himself and his inward affairs constantly passing before him, obvious to him and revolving in his mind. Now as nothing can be more grievous than this is to one who has thrown off natural affection, so nothing can be more delightful to one who has preserved it with sincerity.

There are two things which to a rational creature must be horridly offensive and grievous, namely, to have the reflection in his mind of any unjust action or behaviour, which he knows to be naturally odious and ill-deserving, or of any foolish action or behaviour, which he knows to be prejudicial to his own interest or happiness.

The former of these is alone properly called conscience, whether in a moral or religious sense. For to have awe and terror of the Deity does not, of itself, imply conscience. No one is esteemed the more conscientious for the fear of evil spirits, conjurations, enchantments or whatever may proceed from any unjust, capricious or devilish nature. Now to fear God any otherwise than as in consequence of some justly blameable and imputable act is to fear a devilish nature, not a divine one. Nor does the fear of hell or a thousand terrors of the Deity imply conscience, unless where there is an apprehension of what is wrong, odious, morally deformed and ill-deserving. And where this is the case, there conscience must have effect, and punishment of necessity be apprehended, even though it be not expressly threatened.

And thus religious conscience supposes moral or natural conscience. And though the former be understood to carry with it the fear of divine punishment, it has its force however from the apprehended moral deformity and odiousness of any act with respect purely to the divine presence and the natural veneration due to such a supposed being. For in such a presence the shame of villainy or vice must have its force, independently on that further apprehension of the magisterial capacity of such a being and his dispensation of particular rewards or punishments in a future state.

It has been already said that no creature can maliciously and intentionally do ill without being sensible at the same time that he deserves ill. And, in this respect, every sensible creature may be said to have conscience. For with all mankind and all intelligent creatures, this must ever hold, that 'what they know they deserve from everyone, that they necessarily must fear and expect from all'. And thus suspicions and ill apprehensions must arise, with terrors both of men and of the Deity. But besides this, there must in every rational creature be yet further conscience, namely, from sense of deformity in what is thus ill-deserving and unnatural and from a consequent shame or regret of incurring what is odious and moves aversion.

There scarcely is or can be any creature whom consciousness of villainy, as such merely, does not at all offend nor anything opprobrious or heinously imputable move or affect. If there be such a one, it is evident he must be absolutely indifferent toward moral good or ill. If this indeed be his case, it will be allowed he can be no way capable of natural affection; if not of that, then neither of any social pleasure or mental enjoyment as shown above, but, on the contrary, he must be subject to all manner of horrid, unnatural and ill affection. So that to want conscience, or natural sense of the odiousness of crime and injustice, is to be most of all miserable in life; but where conscience or sense of this sort remains, there, consequently, whatever is committed against it must of necessity, by means of reflection, as we have shown, be continually shameful, grievous and offensive.

A man who in a passion happens to kill his companion relents immediately on the sight of what he has done. His revenge is changed into pity, and his hatred turned against himself. And this merely by the power of the object. On this account he suffers agonies. The subject of this continually occurs to him, and of this he has a constant ill remembrance and displeasing consciousness. If on the other side we suppose him not to relent or suffer any real concern or shame, then, either he has no sense of the deformity of crime and injustice, no natural affection, and consequently no happiness or peace within, or, if he has any sense of moral worth or goodness, it must be of a perplexed and contradictory kind. He must pursue an inconsistent notion, idolize some false species of virtue and affect as noble, gallant or worthy that which is irrational and absurd. And how tormenting this must be to him is easy to conceive. For never can such a phantom as this be reduced to any certain form. Never can this Proteus[F] of honour be held steady to one shape. The pursuit of it can only be vexatious and distracting. There is nothing beside real virtue, as has been shown, which can possibly hold any proportion to esteem, approbation or good conscience. And he who, being led by false religion or prevailing custom, has learnt to esteem or admire anything as virtue which is not really such must either, through the inconsistency of such an esteem and the perpetual immoralities occasioned by it, come at last to lose all conscience and so be miserable in the worst way or, if he retains any conscience at all, it must be of a kind never satisfactory or able to bestow content. For it is impossible that a cruel enthusiast or bigot, a persecutor, a murderer, a bravo, a pirate or any villain of less degree, who is false to the society of mankind in general and contradicts natural affection, should have any fixed principle at all, any real standard or measure, by which he can regulate his esteem or any solid reason by which to form his approbation of any one moral act. And thus the more he sets up honour or advances zeal, the worse he renders his nature and the more detestable his character. The more he engages in the love or admiration of any action or practice as great and glorious, which is in itself morally ill and vicious, the more contradiction and self-disapprobation he must incur. For there being nothing more certain than this, that no natural affection can be contradicted, nor any unnatural one advanced, without a prejudice in some degree to all natural affection in general, it must follow that, inward deformity growing greater by the encouragement of unnatural affection, there must be so much the more subject for dissatisfactory reflection, the more any false principle of honour, any false religion or superstition prevails.

So that whatever notions of this kind are cherished or whatever character affected, which is contrary to moral equity and leads to inhumanity through a false conscience or wrong sense of honour, serve only to bring a man the more under the lash of real and just conscience, shame and self-reproach. Nor can

---

[F]   Proteus was a minor Greek deity capable of assuming many different shapes and characters.

anyone who, by any pretended authority, commits one single immorality be able to satisfy himself with any reason why he should not at another time be carried further into all manner of villainy, such perhaps as he even abhors to think of. And this is a reproach which a mind must of necessity make to itself upon the least violation of natural conscience in doing what is morally deformed and ill-deserving, though warranted by any example or precedent amongst men or by any supposed injunction or command of higher powers.

Now, as for that other part of conscience, namely, the remembrance of what was at any time unreasonably and foolishly done in prejudice of one's real interest or happiness, this dissatisfactory reflection must follow still and have effect wheresoever there is a sense of moral deformity contracted by crime and injustice. For even where there is no sense of moral deformity as such merely, there must be still a sense of the ill merit of it with respect to God and man. Or, though there were a possibility of excluding forever all thoughts or suspicions of any superior powers, yet, considering that this insensibility towards moral good or ill implies a total defect in natural affection and that this defect can by no dissimulation be concealed, it is evident that a man of this unhappy char- acter must suffer a very sensible loss in the friendship, trust and confidence of other men and, consequently, must suffer in his interest and outward happiness. Nor can the sense of this disadvantage fail to occur to him when he sees, with regret and envy, the better and more grateful terms of friendship and esteem on which better people live with the rest of mankind. Even therefore where natural affection is wanting, it is certain still that by immorality, necessarily happening through want of such affection, there must be disturbance from conscience of this sort, namely, from sense of what is committed imprudently and contrary to real interest and advantage.

From all this we may easily conclude how much our happiness depends on natural and good affection. For, if the chief happiness be from the mental pleasures and the chief mental pleasures are such as we have described and are founded in natural affection, it follows that *to have the natural affections is to have the chief means and power of self-enjoyment, the highest possession and happiness of life.*

Now as to the pleasures of the body and the satisfactions belonging to mere sense, it is evident they cannot possibly have their effect or afford any valuable enjoyment otherwise than by the means of social and natural affection.

To live well has no other meaning with some people than to eat and drink well. And methinks it is an unwary concession we make in favour of these pretended 'good livers' when we join with them in honouring their way of life with the title of 'living fast', as if they lived the fastest who took the greatest pains to enjoy least of life. For, if our account of happiness be right, the greatest enjoyments in life are such as these men pass over in their haste and have scarce ever allowed themselves the liberty of tasting.

But, as considerable a part of voluptuousness as is founded in the palate and as notable as the science is which depends on it, one may justly presume that the ostentation of elegance, and a certain emulation and study how to excel in this sumptuous art of living, goes very far in the raising such a high idea of it as is observed among the men of pleasure. For were the circumstances of a table and company, equipages, services and the rest of the management withdrawn, there would be hardly left any pleasure worth acceptance, even in the opinion of the most debauched themselves.

The very notion of a debauch, which is a sally into whatever can be imagined of pleasure and voluptuousness, carries with it a plain reference to society or fellowship. It may be called a surfeit or excess of eating and drinking but hardly a debauch of that kind, when the excess is committed separately, out of all society or fellowship. And one who abuses himself in this way is often called a sot, but never a debauchee. The courtesans and even the commonest of women who live by prostitution know very well how necessary it is that everyone whom they entertain with their beauty should believe there are satisfactions reciprocal and that pleasures are no less given than received. And were this imagination to be wholly taken away, there would be hardly any of the grosser sort of mankind who would not perceive their remaining pleasure to be of slender estimation.

Who is there can well or long enjoy anything when alone and abstracted perfectly, even in his very mind and thought, from everything belonging to society? Who would not, on such terms as these, be presently cloyed by any sensual indulgence? Who would not soon grow uneasy with his pleasure, however exquisite, till he had found means to impart it and make it truly pleasant to him by communicating and sharing it at least with some one single person? Let men imagine what they please, let them suppose themselves ever so selfish or desire ever so much to follow the dictates of that narrow principle by which they would bring nature under restraint, nature will break out and, in agonies, disquiets and a distempered state, demonstrate evidently the ill consequence of such violence, the absurdity of such a device and the punishment which belongs to such a monstrous and horrid endeavour.

Thus, therefore, not only the pleasures of the mind but even those of the body depend on natural affection insomuch that, where this is wanting, they not only lose their force but are in a manner converted into uneasiness and disgust. The sensations which should naturally afford contentment and delight produce rather discontent and sourness and breed a wearisomeness and restlessness in the disposition. This we may perceive by the perpetual inconstancy and love of change so remarkable in those who have nothing communicative or friendly in their pleasures. Good fellowship, in its abused sense, seems indeed to have something more constant and determining. The company supports the humour. It is the same in love. A certain tenderness and generosity of affection supports the passion, which otherwise would instantly be changed. The perfectest beauty cannot, of itself, retain or fix it. And that love which has no other foundation but relies on this exterior kind is soon turned into aversion. Satiety, perpetual disgust and feverishness of desire attend those who passionately study pleasure. They best enjoy it who study to regulate their passions. And by this they will come to know how absolute an incapacity there is in anything sensual to please or give contentment, where it depends not on something friendly or social, something conjoined and in affinity with kind or natural affection.

But before we conclude this article of social or natural affection, we may take a general view of it and bring it once for all into the scale to prove what kind of balance it helps to make within and what the consequence may be of its deficiency or light weight.[16]

There is no one of ever so little understanding in what belongs to a human constitution who knows not that, without action, motion and employment, the body languishes and is oppressed, its nourishment turns to disease, the spirits unemployed abroad help to consume the parts within, and nature, as it were, preys upon herself. In the same manner, the sensible and living part, the soul or mind, wanting its proper and natural exercise, is burdened and diseased. Its thoughts and passions, being unnaturally withheld from their due objects, turn against itself and create the highest impatience and ill humour.

In brutes and other creatures who have not the use of reason and reflection, at least not after the manner of mankind, it is so ordered in nature that, by their daily search after food and their application either towards the business of their livelihood or the affairs of their species or kind, almost their whole time is taken up, and they fail not to find full employment for their passion according to that degree of agitation to which they are fitted and which their constitution requires.[17] If any one of these creatures be taken out of his natural laborious state and placed amid such a plenty as can profusely administer to all his appetites and wants, it may be observed that, as his circumstances grow thus luxuriant, his temper and passions have the same growth. When he comes at any time to have the accommodations of life at a cheaper and easier rate than was at first intended him by nature, he is made to pay dear for them in another way, by losing his natural good disposition and the orderliness of his kind or species.

This needs not to be demonstrated by particular instances. Whoever has the least knowledge of natural history or has been an observer of the several breeds of creatures and their ways of life and propagation will easily understand this difference of orderliness between the wild and the tame of the same species.

[16] See pp. 198–200.
[17] See pp. 198–200, 282–3, 429ff.

The latter acquire new habits and deviate from their original nature. They lose even the common instinct and ordinary ingenuity of their kind, nor can they ever regain it while they continue in this pampered state, but, being turned to shift abroad, they resume the natural affection and sagacity of their species. They learn to unite in stricter fellowship and grow more concerned for their offspring. They provide against the seasons and make the most of every advantage given by nature for the support and maintenance of their particular species against such as are foreign and hostile. And thus, as they grow busy and employed, they grow regular and good. Their petulancy and vice forsakes them with their idleness and ease.

It happens with mankind that, while some are by necessity confined to labour, others are provided with abundance of all things by the pains and labour of inferiors. Now, if among the superior and easy sort there be not something of fit and proper employment raised in the room of what is wanting in common labour and toil, if, instead of an application to any sort of work such as has a good and honest end in society, as letters, sciences, arts, husbandry, public affairs, economy or the like, there be a thorough neglect of all duty or employment, a settled idleness, supineness and inactivity, this of necessity must occasion a most relaxed and dissolute state: it must produce a total disorder of the passions and break out in the strangest irregularities imaginable.

We see the enormous growth of luxury in capital cities, such as have been long the seat of empire. We see what improvements are made in vice of every kind where numbers of men are maintained in lazy opulence and wanton plenty. It is otherwise with those who are taken up in honest and due employment and have been well inured to it from their youth. This we may observe in the hardy remote provincials, the inhabitants of smaller towns and the industrious sort of common people, where it is rare to meet with any instances of those irregularities which are known in courts and palaces and in the rich foundations of easy and pampered priests.

Now if what we have advanced concerning an inward constitution be real and just, if it be true that nature works by a just order and regulation as well in the passions and affections as in the limbs and organs which she forms, if it appears withal that she has so constituted this inward part that nothing is so essential to it as exercise and no exercise so essential as that of social or natural affection, it follows that, where this is removed or weakened, the inward part must necessarily suffer and be impaired. Let indolence, indifference or insensibility be studied as an art or cultivated with the utmost care, the passions thus restrained will force their prison and, in one way or other, procure their liberty and find full employment. They will be sure to create to themselves unusual and unnatural exercise where they are cut off from such as is natural and good. And thus in the room of orderly and natural affection, new and unnatural must be raised and all inward order and economy destroyed.

One must have a very imperfect idea of the order of nature in the formation and structure of animals to imagine that so great a principle, so fundamental a part as that of natural affection, should possibly be lost or impaired without any inward ruin or subversion of the temper and frame of mind.

Whoever is the least versed in this moral kind of architecture will find the inward fabric so adjusted and the whole so nicely built that the barely extending of a single passion a little too far or the continuance of it too long is able to bring irrecoverable ruin and misery. He will find this experienced in the ordinary case of frenzy and distraction, when the mind, dwelling too long upon one subject, whether prosperous or calamitous, sinks under the weight of it and proves what the necessity is of a due balance and counterpoise in the affections. He will find that in every different creature and distinct sex there is a different and distinct order, set or suit of passions, proportionable to the different order of life, the different functions and capacities assigned to each. As the operations and effects are different, so are the springs and causes in each system. The inside work is fitted to the outward action and performance. So that where habits or affections are dislodged, misplaced or changed, where those belonging to one species are intermixed with those belonging to another, there must of necessity be confusion and disturbance within.

All this we may observe easily by comparing the more perfect with the imperfect natures, such as are imperfect from their birth by having suffered violence within in their earliest form and inmost matrix. We know how it is with monsters, such as are compounded of different kinds or different sexes. Nor are they less monsters who are misshapen or distorted in an inward part. The ordinary animals appear unnatural and monstrous when they lose their proper instincts, forsake their kind, neglect their offspring and pervert those functions or capacities bestowed by nature. How wretched must it be, therefore, for man, of all other creatures, to lose that sense and feeling which is proper to him as a man and suitable to his character and genius? How unfortunate must it be for a creature whose dependence on society is greater than any others to lose that natural affection by which he is prompted to the good and interest of his species and community? Such indeed is man's natural share of this affection, that he, of all other creatures, is plainly the least able to bear solitude. Nor is anything more apparent than that there is naturally in every man such a degree of social affection as inclines him to seek the familiarity and friendship of his fellows. It is here that he lets loose a passion and gives reins to a desire which can hardly by any struggle or inward violence be withheld or, if it be, is sure to create a sadness, dejection and melancholy in the mind. For whoever is unsociable and voluntarily shuns society or commerce with the world must of necessity be morose and ill-natured. He, on the other side, who is withheld by force or accident, finds in his temper the ill effects of this restraint. The inclination, when suppressed, breeds discontent and, on the contrary, affords a healing and enlivening joy when acting at its liberty and with full scope, as we may see particularly when, after a time of solitude and long absence, the heart is opened, the mind disburdened and the secrets of the breast unfolded to a bosom friend.

This we see yet more remarkably instanced in persons of the most elevated stations, even in princes, monarchs and those who seem by their condition to be above ordinary human commerce and who affect a sort of distant strangeness from the rest of mankind. But their carriage is not the same towards all men. The wiser and better sort, it is true, are often held at a distance, as unfit for their intimacy or secret trust. But, to compensate this, there are others substituted in their room who, though they have the least merit and are perhaps the most vile and contemptible of men, are sufficient, however, to serve the purpose of an imaginary friendship and can become favourites in form.[G] These are the subjects of humanity in the great. For these we see them often in concern and pain; in these they easily confide; to these they can with pleasure communicate their power and greatness, be open, free, generous, confiding, bountiful, as rejoicing in the action itself, having no intention or aim beyond it, and their interest, in respect of policy, often standing a quite contrary way. But where neither the love of mankind nor the passion for favourites prevails, the tyrannical temper fails not to show itself in its proper colours and to the life, with all the bitterness, cruelty and mistrust which belong to that solitary and gloomy state of uncommunicative and unfriendly greatness. Nor needs there any particular proof from history or present time to second this remark.

Thus it may appear how much natural affection is predominant, how it is inwardly joined to us and implanted in our natures, how interwoven with our other passions and how essential to that regular motion and course of our affections on which our happiness and self-enjoyment so immediately depend.

And thus we have demonstrated that *as, on one side, to have the natural and good affections is to have the chief means and power of self-enjoyment, so, on the other side, to want them is certain misery and ill.*

Section 2

We are now to prove that, *by having the self-passions too intense or strong, a creature becomes miserable.*

In order to this, we must, according to method, enumerate those home-affections which relate to the private interest or separate economy of the creature, such as love of life, resentment of injury, pleasure or appetite towards nourishment and the means of generation, interest or desire of those conve-

---

[G] Shaftesbury here raised the image of the royal favourite, the treasured although often unworthy recipient of a monarch's trust and generosity. Among the Stuart monarchs, the most notorious example was James I's affection for the beautiful but muddle-headed George Villiers, first Duke of Buckingham, 1592–1628.

niences by which we are well provided for and maintained, emulation or love of praise and honour, indolence or love of ease and rest. These are the affections which relate to the private system and constitute whatever we call interestedness or self-love.

Now these affections, if they are moderate and within certain bounds, are neither injurious to social life nor a hindrance to virtue, but, being in an extreme degree, they become cowardice, revengefulness, luxury, avarice, vanity and ambition, sloth, and, as such, are owned vicious and ill with respect to human society. How they are ill also with respect to the private person and are to his own disadvantage as well as that of the public, we may consider as we severally examine them.

If there were any of these self-passions which for the good and happiness of the creature might be opposed to natural affection and allowed to over-balance it, the desire and love of life would have the best pretence. But it will be found perhaps that there is no passion which, by having much allowed to it, is the occasion of more disorder and misery.

There is nothing more certain or more universally agreed than this, that 'life may sometimes be even a misfortune and misery'. To enforce the continuance of it in creatures reduced to such extremity is esteemed the greatest cruelty. And though religion forbids that anyone should be his own reliever, yet, if by some fortunate accident death offers of itself, it is embraced as highly welcome. And on this account the nearest friends and relations often rejoice at the release of one entirely beloved, even though he himself may have been so weak as earnestly to decline death and endeavour the utmost prolongment of his own ineligible state.

Since life, therefore, may frequently prove a misfortune and misery and since it naturally becomes so by being only prolonged to the infirmities of old age, since there is nothing, withal, more common than to see life over-valued and purchased at such a cost as it can never justly be thought worth, it follows evidently that the passion itself, namely, the love of life and abhorrence or dread of death, if beyond a certain degree and over-balancing in the temper of any creature, must lead him directly against his own interest, make him, upon occasion, become the greatest enemy to himself and necessitate him to act as such.

But though it were allowed the interest and good of a creature, by all courses and means whatsoever, in any circumstances or at any rate, to preserve life, yet would it be against his interest still to have this passion in a high degree. For it would by this means prove ineffectual and no way conducing to its end. Various instances need not be given. For what is there better known than that at all times an excessive fear betrays to danger instead of saving from it? It is impossible for anyone to act sensibly and with presence of mind, even in his own preservation and defence, when he is strongly pressed by such a passion. On all extraordinary emergencies, it is courage and resolution saves while cowardice robs us of the means of safety and not only deprives us of our defensive faculties but even runs us to the brink of ruin and makes us meet that evil which of itself would never have invaded us.

But were the consequences of this passion less injurious than we have represented, it must be allowed still that in itself it can be no other than miserable, if it be misery to feel cowardice and be haunted by those spectres and horrors which are proper to the character of one who has a thorough dread of death. For it is not only when dangers happen and hazards are incurred, that this sort of fear oppresses and distracts. If it in the least prevails, it gives no quarter so much as at the safest, stillest hour of retreat and quiet. Every object suggests thought enough to employ it. It operates when it is least observed by others and enters at all times into the pleasantest parts of life so as to corrupt and poison all enjoyment and content. One may safely aver that, by reason of this passion alone, many a life, if inwardly and closely viewed, would be found to be thoroughly miserable, though attended with all other circumstances which in appearance render it happy. But when we add to this the meannesses and base condescensions occasioned by such a passionate concern for living, when we consider how by means of it we are driven to actions we can never view without dislike and forced by degrees from our natural conduct into still greater crookednesses and perplexity, there is no one surely so disingenuous as not to allow that life in this case becomes a sorry purchase and is passed with little freedom or satisfaction. For how can this be otherwise while everything which is generous and worthy, even the chief relish, happiness and good of life, is for life's sake abandoned and renounced?

And thus it seems evident that to have this affection of desire and love of life too intense, or beyond a moderate degree, is against the interest of a creature and contrary to his happiness and good.

There is another passion very different from that of fear and which in a certain degree is equally preservative to us and conducing to our safety. As that is serviceable in prompting us to shun danger, so is this in fortifying us against it and enabling us to repel injury and resist violence when offered. It is true that, according to strict virtue and a just regulation of the affections in a wise and virtuous man, such efforts towards action amount not to what is justly styled passion or commotion. A man of courage may be cautious without real fear, and a man of temper may resist or punish without anger. But in ordinary characters there must necessarily be some mixture of the real passions themselves, which, however, in the main, are able to allay and temper one another. And thus anger in a manner becomes necessary. It is by this passion that one creature offering violence to another is deterred from the execution while he observes how the attempt affects his fellow and knows by the very signs which accompany this rising motion that, if the injury be carried further, it will not pass easily or with impunity. It is this passion, withal, which, after violence and hostility executed, rouses a creature in opposition and assists him in returning like hostility and harm on the invader. For, thus, as rage and despair increase, a creature grows still more terrible and, being urged to the greatest extremity, finds a degree of strength and boldness unexperienced till then and which had never risen except through the height of provocation.

As to this affection therefore, notwithstanding its immediate aim be indeed the ill or punishment of another, yet it is plainly of the sort of those which tend to the advantage and interest of the self-system, the animal himself, and is withal in other respects contributing to the good and interest of the species. But there is hardly need we should explain how mischievous and self-destructive anger is, if it be what we commonly understand by that word, if it be such a passion as is rash and violent in the instant of provocation or such as imprints itself deeply and causes a settled revenge and an eager vindictive pursuit. No wonder indeed that so much is done in mere revenge and under the weight of a deep resentment when the relief and satisfaction found in that indulgence is no other than the assuaging of the most torturous pain and the alleviating the most weighty and pressing sensation of misery. The pain of this sort, being for a while removed or alleviated by the accomplishment of the desire in the ill of another, leaves indeed behind it the perception of a delicious ease and an overflowing of soft and pleasing sensation. Yet is this, in truth, no better than the rack itself. For whoever has experienced racking pains can tell in what manner a sudden cessation or respite is used to affect him. From hence are those untoward delights of perverseness, forwardness and an envenomed malignant disposition acting at its liberty. For this is only a perpetual assuaging of anger perpetually renewed. In other characters, the passion arises not so suddenly or on slight causes but being once moved is not so easily quieted. The dormant fury, revenge, being raised once and wrought up to her highest pitch, rests not till she attains her end and, that attained, is easy and reposes, making our succeeding relief and ease so much the more enjoyed as our preceding anguish and incumbent pain was of long duration and bitter sense. Certainly, if among lovers and in the language of gallantry, the success of ardent love is called the assuaging of a pain, this other success may be far more justly termed so. However soft or flattering the former pain may be esteemed, this latter surely can be no pleasing one; nor can it be possibly esteemed other than sound and thorough wretchedness, a grating and disgustful feeling, without the least mixture of anything soft, gentle or agreeable.

It is not very necessary to mention the ill effects of this passion in respect of our minds or bodies, our private condition or circumstances of life. By these particulars we may grow too tedious. These are of the moral sort of subjects, joined commonly with religion and treated so rhetorically and with such enforced repetition in public as to be apt to raise the satiety of mankind. What has been said may be enough perhaps to make this evident that to be subject to such a passion as we have been mentioning is in reality to be very unhappy and that the habit itself is a disease of the worst sort, from which misery is inseparable.

Now as to luxury and what the world calls pleasure, were it true, as has been proved the contrary, that the most considerable enjoyments were those merely of the sense and were it true, withal, that those enjoyments of the sense lay in certain outward things capable of yielding always a due and certain portion of pleasure, according to their degree and quality, it would then follow that the certain way to obtain happiness would be to procure largely of these subjects, to which happiness and pleasure were thus infallibly annexed. But however fashionably we may apply the notion of 'good living', it will hardly be found that our inward faculties are able to keep pace with these outward supplies of a luxuriant fortune. And if the natural disposition and aptness from within be not concurring, it will be in vain that these subjects are thus multiplied from abroad and acquired with ever so great facility.

It may be observed in those who by excess have gained a constant nauseating and distaste that they have nevertheless as constant a craving or eagerness of stomach. But the appetite of this kind is false and unnatural as is that of thirst arising from a fever or contracted by habitual debauch. Now the satisfactions of the natural appetite, in a plain way, are infinitely beyond those indulgences of the most refined and elegant luxury. This is often perceived by the luxurious themselves. It has been experienced in people bred after the sumptuous way and used never to wait but to prevent appetite so that, when by any new turn of life they came to fall into a more natural course or, for a while, as on a journey or a day of sport came accidentally to experience the sweet of a plain diet, recommended by due abstinence and exercise, they have with freedom owned that it was then they received the highest satisfaction and delight which a table could possibly afford.

On the other side, it has been as often remarked in persons accustomed to an active life and healthful exercise that, having once thoroughly experienced this plainer and more natural diet, they have upon a following change of life regretted their loss and undervalued the pleasures received from all the delicacies of luxury in comparison with those remembered satisfactions of a preceding state. It is plain that, by urging nature, forcing the appetite and inciting sense, the keenness of the natural sensations is lost. And though through vice or ill habit the same subjects of appetite may every day be sought with greater ardour, they are enjoyed with less satisfaction. Though the impatience of abstaining be greater, the pleasure of indulgence is really less. The palls or nauseatings which continually intervene are of the worst and most hateful kind of sensation. Hardly is there anything tasted which is wholly free from this ill relish of a surfeited sense and ruined appetite, so that, instead of a constant and flowing delight afforded in such a state of life, the very state itself is in reality a sickness and infirmity, a corruption of pleasure and destructive of every natural and agreeable sensation. So far is it from being true that in this licentious course we enjoy life best or are likely to make the most of it.

As to the consequences of such an indulgence, how fatal to the body, by diseases of many kinds, and to the mind, by sottishness and stupidity – this needs not any explanation.

The consequences as to interest are plain enough. Such a state of impotent and unrestrained desire, as it increases our wants, so it must subject us to a greater dependence on others. Our private circumstances, however plentiful or easy they may be, can less easily content us. Ways and means must be invented to procure what may administer to such an imperious luxury as forces us to sacrifice honour to fortune and runs us out into all irregularity and extravagance of conduct. The injuries we do ourselves by excess and unforbearance are then surely apparent when, through an impotence of this sort and an impossibility of restraint, we do what we ourselves declare to be destructive to us. But these are matters obvious of themselves. And from less than what has been said, it is easy to conclude that luxury, riot and debauch are contrary to real interest and to the true enjoyment of life.

There is another luxury superior to the kind we have been mentioning and which in strictness can scarce be called a self-passion, since the sole end of it is the advantage and promotion of the species. But, whereas all other social affections are joined only with a mental pleasure and founded in mere kindness and love, this has more added to it and is joined with a pleasure of sense. Such concern and care has nature shown for the support and maintenance of the several species that, by a certain indigence and kind of necessity of their natures, they are made to regard the propagation of their kind. Now whether it be the interest or good of the animal to feel this indigence beyond a natural and ordinary degree, is what we may consider.

Having already said so much concerning natural and unnatural appetite, there needs less to be said on this occasion. If it be allowed that to all other pleasures there is a measure of appetite belonging, which cannot possibly be exceeded without prejudice to the creature, even in his very capacity of enjoying pleasure, it will hardly be thought that there is no certain limit or just boundary of this other appetite of the amorous kind. There are other sorts of ardent sensations accidentally experienced, which we find pleasant and acceptable while they are held within a certain degree but which, as they increase, grow oppressive and intolerable. Laughter provoked by titillation grows an excessive pain, though it retains still the same features of delight and pleasure. And though in the case of that particular kind of itch which belongs to a distemper named from that effect, there are some who, far from disliking the sensation, find it highly acceptable and delightful (yet it will hardly be reputed such among the more refined sort, even of those who make pleasure their chief study and highest good).

Now if there be in every sensation of mere pleasure a certain pitch or degree of ardour, which by being further advanced comes the nearer to mere rage and fury, if there be indeed a necessity of stopping somewhere and determining on some boundary for the passion, where can we fix our standard or how regulate ourselves but with regard to nature, beyond which there is no measure or rule of things? Now nature may be known from what we see of the natural state of creatures and of man himself when unprejudiced by vicious education.

Where happily anyone is bred to a natural life, inured to honest industry and sobriety and unaccustomed to anything immoderate or intemperate, he is found to have his appetites and inclinations of this sort at command. Nor are they on this account less able to afford him the pleasure or enjoyment of each kind. On the contrary, as they are more sound, healthy and uninjured by excess and abuse, they must afford him proportionate satisfaction. So that were both these sensations to be experimentally compared, that of a virtuous course which belonged to one who lived a natural and regular life and that of a vicious course which belonged to one who was relaxed and dissolute, there is no question but judgment would be given in favour of the former without regard to consequences and only with respect to the very pleasure of sense itself.

As to the consequences of this vice with respect to the health and vigour of the body, there is no need to mention anything. The injury it does the mind, though less noticed, is yet greater. The hindrance of all improvement, the wretched waste of time, the effeminacy, sloth, supineness, the disorder and looseness of a thousand passions through such a relaxation and enervating of the mind, are all of them effects sufficiently apparent when reflected on.

What the disadvantages are of this intemperance in respect of interest, society and the world and what the advantages are of a contrary sobriety and self-command would be to little purpose to mention. It is well known there can be no slavery greater than what is consequent to the dominion and rule of such a passion. Of all other, it is the least manageable by favour or concession and assumes the most from privilege and indulgence. What it costs us in the modesty and ingenuity of our natures and in the faith and honesty of our characters is as easily apprehended by anyone who will reflect. And it will from hence appear that there is no passion which in its extravagance and excess more necessarily occasions disorder and unhappiness.

Now as to that passion which is esteemed peculiarly interesting, as having for its aim the possession of wealth and what we call a settlement or fortune in the world, if the regard towards this kind be moderate and in a reasonable degree, if it occasions no passionate pursuit nor raises any ardent desire or appetite, there is nothing in this case which is not compatible with virtue and even suitable and beneficial to society. The public as well as private system is advanced by the industry which this affection excites. But if it grows at length into a real passion, the injury and mischief it does the public is not greater than that which it creates to the person himself. Such a one is in reality a self-oppressor and lies heavier on himself than he can ever do on mankind.

How far a coveting or avaricious temper is miserable needs not surely be explained. Who knows not how small a portion of worldly matters is sufficient for a man's single use and convenience and how much his occasions and wants might be contracted and reduced if a just frugality were studied and temperance and a natural life came once to be pursued with half that application, industry and art which is bestowed on sumptuousness and luxury? Now if temperance be in reality so advantageous and the practice as well as the consequences of it so pleasing and happy, as has been before expressed, there is little need, on the other side, to mention anything of the miseries attending those covetous and eager desires after things which have no bounds or rule as being out of nature, beyond which there can be no limits to desire. For where shall we once stop when we are beyond this boundary? How shall we fix or ascertain a thing wholly unnatural and unreasonable? Or what method, what regulation, shall we set to mere imagination or the exorbitancy of fancy in adding expense to expense or possession to possession?

Hence that known restlessness of covetous and eager minds in whatever state or degree of fortune they are placed, there being no thorough or real satisfaction but a kind of insatiableness belonging to this condition. For it is impossible there should be any real enjoyment except in consequence of natural and just appetite. Nor do we readily call that an enjoyment of wealth or of honour when through covetousness or ambition the desire is still forward and can never rest satisfied with its gains. But against this vice of covetousness, there is enough said continually in the world, and in our common way of speaking 'a covetous and a miserable temper has, in reality, one and the same signification'.

Nor is there less said abroad as to the ills of that other aspiring temper, which exceeds an honest emulation or love of praise and passes the bounds even of vanity and conceit. Such is that passion which breaks into an enormous pride and ambition. Now if we consider once the ease, happiness and security which attend a modest disposition and quiet mind, such as is of easy self-command, fitted to every station in society and able to suit itself with any reasonable circumstances whatever, it will, on the first view, present us with the most agreeable and winning character. Nor will it be found necessary after this to call to mind the excellence and good of moderation, or the mischief and self-injury of immoderate desires and conceited fond imagination of personal advantage in such things as titles, honours, precedencies, fame, glory or vulgar astonishment, admiration and applause.

This too is obvious, that, as the desires of this kind are raised and become impetuous and out of our command, so the aversions and fears of the contrary part grow proportionably strong and violent and the temper accordingly suspicious, jealous, captious, subject to apprehensions from all events and incapable of bearing the least repulse or ordinary disappointment. And hence it may be concluded that all rest and security as to what is future, and all peace, contentedness and ease as to what is present, is forfeited by the aspiring passions of this emulous kind and by having the appetites towards glory and outward appearance thus transporting and beyond command.

There is a certain temper placed often in opposition to those eager and aspiring aims of which we have been speaking. Not that it really excludes either the passion of covetousness or ambition, but because it hinders their effects and keeps them from breaking into open action. It is this passion which, by soothing the mind and softening it into an excessive love of rest and indolence, renders high attempts impracticable and represents as insuperable the difficulties of a painful and laborious course towards wealth and honours. Now though an inclination to ease and a love of moderate recess and rest from action be as natural and useful to us as the inclination we have towards sleep, yet an excessive love of rest, and a contracted aversion to action and employment, must be a disease in the mind equal to that of a lethargy in the body.

How necessary action and exercise are to the body may be judged by the difference we find between those constitutions which are accustomed and those which are wholly strangers to it, and by the different health and complexion which labour and due exercise create in comparison with that habit of body we see consequent to an indulged state of indolence and rest. Nor is the lazy habit ruinous to the body only. The languishing disease corrupts all the enjoyments of a vigorous and healthy sense and carries its infection into the mind, where it spreads a worse contagion. For however the body may for a while hold out, it is impossible that the mind in which the distemper is seated can escape without an immediate affliction and disorder. The habit begets a tediousness and anxiety, which influences the whole temper and converts the unnatural rest into an unhappy sort of activity, ill humour and spleen, of which there has been enough said above, where we considered the want of a due balance in the affections.

It is certain that, as in the body, when no labour or natural exercise is used, the spirits which want their due employment turn against the constitution and find work for themselves in a destructive way, so in a soul or mind unexercised, and which languishes for want of proper action and employment, the thoughts and affections, being obstructed in their due course and deprived of their natural energy, raise disquiet and foment a rancorous eagerness and tormenting irritation. The temper from hence becomes more impotent in passion, more incapable of real moderation, and, like prepared fuel, readily takes fire by the least spark.

As to interest, how far it is here concerned, how wretched that state is in which by this habit a man is placed towards all the circumstances and affairs of life when at any time he is called to action, how subjected he must be to all inconveniences, wanting to himself and deprived of the assistance of others while, being unfit for all offices and duties of society, he yet of any other person most needs the help of it as being least able to assist or support himself – all this is obvious. And thus it is evident that to have this over-biassing inclination towards rest, this slothful, soft or effeminate temper, averse to labour and employment, is to have an unavoidable mischief and attendant plague.

Thus have we considered the self-passions and what the consequence is of their rising beyond a moderate degree. These affections, as self-interesting as they are, can often, we see, become contrary to our real interest. They betray us into nasty misfortunes and into the greatest of unhappinesses, that of a profligate and abject character. As they grow imperious and high, they are the occasion that a creature in proportion becomes mean and low. They are original to that which we call selfishness and give rise to that sordid disposition of which we have already spoken. It appears there can be nothing so miserable in itself, or so wretched in its consequence, as to be thus impotent in temper, thus mastered by passion and, by means of it, brought under the most servile subjection to the world.

It is evident, withal, that, as this selfishness increases in us, so must a certain subtlety and feignedness of carriage which naturally accompanies it. And thus the candour and ingenuity of our natures, the ease and freedom of our minds, must be forfeited, all trust and confidence in a manner lost, and suspicions, jealousies and envies multiplied. A separate end and interest must be every day more strongly formed in us, generous views and motives laid aside, and the more we are thus sensibly disjoined every day from society and our fellows, the worse opinion we shall have of those uniting passions which bind us in strict alliance and amity with others. Upon these terms we must of course endeavour to silence and suppress our natural and good affections since they are such as would carry us to the good of society against what we fondly conceive to be our private good and interest, as has been shown.

Now, if these selfish passions, besides what other ill they are the occasion of, are withal the certain means of losing us our natural affections, then, by what has been proved before, it is evident that *they must be the certain means of losing us the chief enjoyment of life and raising in us those horrid and unnatural passions and that savageness of temper, which makes the greatest of miseries and the most wretched state of life*, as remains for us to explain.

Section 3

The passions, therefore, which in the last place we are to examine, are those which lead neither to a public nor a private good and are neither of any advantage to the species in general nor the creature in particular. These, in opposition to the social and natural, we call the unnatural affections.

Of this kind is that unnatural and inhuman delight in beholding torments and in viewing distress, calamity, blood, massacre and destruction with a peculiar joy and pleasure. This has been the reigning passion of many tyrants and barbarous nations, and belongs in some degree to such tempers as have thrown off that courteousness of behaviour which retains in us a just reverence of mankind and prevents the growth of harshness and brutality. This passion enters not where civility or affable manners have the least place. Such is the nature of what we call good breeding that, in the midst of many other corruptions, it admits not of inhumanity or savage pleasure. To see the sufferance of an enemy with cruel delight may proceed from the height of anger, revenge, fear and other extended self-passions, but to delight in the torture and pain of other creatures indifferently, natives or foreigners, of our own or of another species, kindred or no kindred, known or unknown, to feed as it were on death and be entertained with dying agonies – this has nothing in it accountable in the way of self-interest or private good, above-mentioned, but is wholly and absolutely unnatural as it is horrid and miserable.

There is another affection nearly related to this, which is a gay and frolicsome delight in what is injurious to others, a sort of wanton mischievousness and pleasure in what is destructive, a passion which, instead of being restrained, is usually encouraged in children so that it is indeed no wonder if the effects of it are very unfortunately felt in the world. For it will be hard, perhaps, for anyone to give a reason why that temper, which was used to delight in disorder and ravage when in a nursery, should not afterwards find delight in other disturbances and be the occasion of equal mischief in families, among friends and in the public itself. But of this passion there is not any foundation in nature, as has been explained.

Malice, malignity or ill will, such as is grounded on no self-consideration and where there is no subject of anger or jealousy nor anything to provoke or cause such a desire of doing ill to another – this also is of that kind of passion.

Envy too, when it is such as arises from the prosperity or happiness of another creature no ways interfering with ours, is of the same kind of passion.

There is also among these a sort of hatred of mankind and society, a passion which has been known perfectly reigning in some men and has had a peculiar name given to it.[18] A large share of this belongs to those who have long indulged themselves in a habitual moroseness, or who by force of ill nature and ill breeding have contracted such a reverse of affability and civil manners that to see or meet a stranger is offensive. The very aspect of mankind is a disturbance to them and they are sure always to hate at first sight. The distemper of

---

[18] Misanthropy.

this kind is sometimes found to be in a manner national, but peculiar to the more savage nations and a plain characteristic of uncivilized manners and barbarity. This is the immediate opposite to that noble affection which in ancient language was termed hospitality, namely, extensive love of mankind and relief of strangers.[19]

We may add likewise to the number of the unnatural passions all those which are raised from superstition (as before-mentioned) and from the customs of barbarous countries, all which are too horrid and odious in themselves to need any proof of their being miserable.

There might be other passions named, such as unnatural lusts in foreign kinds or species with other perversions of the amorous desire within our own. But as to these depravities of appetite, we need add nothing here after what has been already said on the subject of the more natural passion.

Such as these are the only affections or passions we can strictly call unnatural, ill and of no tendency so much as to any separate or private good. Others indeed there are which have this tendency but are so exorbitant and out of measure, so beyond the common bent of any ordinary self-passion and so utterly contrary and abhorrent to all social and natural affection that they are generally called and may be justly esteemed, unnatural and monstrous.

Among these may be reckoned such an enormous pride or ambition, such an arrogance and tyranny, as would willingly leave nothing eminent, nothing free, nothing prosperous in the world, such an anger as would sacrifice everything to itself, such a revenge as is never to be extinguished nor ever satisfied without the greatest cruelties, such an inveteracy and rancour as seeks, as it were, occasion to exalt itself and lays hold of the least subject, so as often to make the weight of its malevolence fall even upon such as are mere objects of pity and compassion.

Treachery and ingratitude are in strictness mere negative vices and, in themselves, no real passions, having neither aversion nor inclination belonging to them, but are derived from the defect, unsoundness or corruption of the affections in general. But when these vices become remarkable in a character and arise in a manner from inclination and choice, when they are so forward and active as to appear of their own accord, without any pressing occasion, it is apparent they borrow something of the mere unnatural passions and are derived from malice, envy and inveteracy, as explained above.

It may be objected here that these passions, unnatural as they are, carry still a sort of pleasure with them and that, however barbarous a pleasure it be, yet still it is a pleasure and satisfaction which is found in pride or tyranny, revenge, malice or cruelty exerted. Now if it be possible in nature that anyone can feel

[19] See p. 404n.

a barbarous or malicious joy otherwise than in consequence of mere anguish and torment, then may we perhaps allow this kind of satisfaction to be called pleasure or delight. But the case is evidently contrary. To love and to be kind, to have social or natural affection, complacency and good will, is to feel immediate satisfaction and genuine content. It is in itself original joy, depending on no preceding pain or uneasiness and producing nothing beside satisfaction merely. On the other side, animosity, hatred and bitterness is original misery and torment, producing no other pleasure or satisfaction than as the unnatural desire is for the instant satisfied by something which appeases it. How strong soever this pleasure therefore may appear, it only the more implies the misery of that state which produces it. For as the cruellest bodily pains do by intervals of assuagement produce, as has been shown, the highest bodily pleasure, so the fiercest and most raging torments of the mind do, by certain moments of relief, afford the greatest of mental enjoyments to those who know little of the truer kind.

The men of gentlest dispositions and best of tempers have at some time or other been sufficiently acquainted with those disturbances, which at ill hours even small occasions are apt to raise. From these slender experiences of harshness and ill humour, they fully know and will confess the ill moments which are passed when the temper is ever so little galled or fretted. How must it fare, therefore, with those who hardly know any better hours in life and who, for the greatest part of it, are agitated by a thorough active spleen, a close and settled malignity and rancour? How lively must be the shocks of disappointment, the stings of affront and the agonies of a working antipathy against the multiplied objects of offence? Nor can it be wondered at if, to persons thus agitated and oppressed, it seems a high delight to appease and allay for the while those furious and rough motions by an indulgence of their passion in mischief and revenge.

Now as to the consequences of this unnatural state in respect of interest and the common circumstances of life, upon what terms a person who has in this manner lost all which we call 'nature' can be supposed to stand in respect of the society of mankind, how he feels himself in it, what sense he has of his own disposition towards others and of the mutual disposition of others towards himself – this is easily conceived.

What enjoyment or rest is there for one who is not conscious of the merited affection or love but, on the contrary, of the ill will and hatred of every human soul? What ground must this afford for horror and despair? What foundation of fear and continual apprehension from mankind and from superior powers? How thorough and deep must be that melancholy which, being once moved, has nothing soft or pleasing from the side of friendship to allay or divert it? Wherever such a creature turns himself, whichever way he casts his eye, everything around must appear ghastly and horrid, everything hostile and, as it were, bent against a private and single being, who is thus divided from everything and at defiance and war with the rest of nature.

It is thus, at last, that a mind becomes a wilderness, where all is laid waste, everything fair and goodly removed and nothing extant beside what is savage and deformed. Now if banishment from one's country, removal to a foreign place or anything which looks like solitude or desertion, be so heavy to endure, what must it be to feel this inward banishment, this real estrangement from human commerce, and to be after this manner in a desert and in the horridest of solitudes, even when in the midst of society? What must it be to live in this disagreement with everything, this irreconcilableness and opposition to the order and government of the universe?

Hence it appears that the greatest of miseries accompanies that state which is consequent to the loss of natural affection and that *to have those horrid, monstrous and unnatural affections is to be miserable in the highest degree.*

Conclusion

Thus have we endeavoured to prove what was proposed in the beginning. And since, in the common and known sense of vice and illness, no one can be vicious or ill except either by the deficiency or weakness of natural affections, or by the violence of the selfish, or by such as are plainly unnatural, it must follow that, if each of these are pernicious and destructive to the creature, insomuch that his completest state of misery is made from hence, *to be wicked or vicious is to be miserable and unhappy.*

And since every vicious action must in proportion, more or less, help towards this mischief and self-ill, it must follow that *every vicious action must be self-injurious and ill.*

On the other side, the happiness and good of virtue has been proved from the contrary effect of other affections, such as are according to nature and the economy of the species or kind. We have cast up all those particulars from whence, as by way of addition and subtraction, the main sum or general account of happiness is either augmented or diminished. And, if there be no article exceptionable in this scheme of moral arithmetic, the subject treated may be said to have an evidence as great as that which is found in numbers or mathematics. For let us carry scepticism ever so far, let us doubt, if we can, of everything about us, we cannot doubt of what passes within ourselves. Our passions and affections are known to us. They are certain, whatever the objects may be on which they are employed. Nor is it of any concern to our argument how these exterior objects stand – whether they are realities or mere illusions, whether we wake or dream. For ill dreams will be equally disturbing, and a good dream, if life be nothing else, will be easily and happily passed. In this dream of life, therefore, our demonstrations have the same force, our balance and economy hold good and our obligation to virtue is in every respect the same.

Upon the whole there is not, I presume, the least degree of certainty wanting in what has been said concerning the preferableness of the mental pleasures to the sensual, and even of the sensual, accompanied with good affection and under a temperate and right use, to those which are no ways restrained nor supported by anything social or affectionate.

Nor is there less evidence in what has been said of the united structure and fabric of the mind and of those passions which constitute the temper or soul and on which its happiness or misery so immediately depend. It has been shown that in this constitution the impairing of any one part must instantly tend to the disorder and ruin of other parts and of the whole itself, through the necessary connection and balance of the affections, that those very passions through which men are vicious are of themselves a torment and disease; and that whatsoever is done which is knowingly ill must be of ill consciousness and, in proportion as the act is ill, must impair and corrupt social enjoyment and destroy both the capacity of kind affection and the consciousness of meriting any such. So that neither can we participate thus in joy or happiness with others nor receive satisfaction from the mutual kindness or imagined love of others, on which, however, the greatest of all our pleasures are founded.

If this be the case of moral delinquency and if the state which is consequent to this defection from nature be of all other the most horrid, oppressive and miserable, it will appear that to yield or consent to anything ill or immoral is a breach of interest and leads to the greatest ills and that, on the other side, everything which is an improvement of virtue or an establishment of right affection and integrity is an advancement of interest and leads to the greatest and most solid happiness and enjoyment.

Thus the wisdom of what rules and is first and chief in nature has made it to be according to the private interest and good of everyone to work towards the general good, which, if a creature ceases to promote, he is actually so far wanting to himself and ceases to promote his own happiness and welfare. He is on this account directly his own enemy, nor can he any otherwise be good or useful to himself than as he continues good to society and to that whole of which he is himself a part. So that virtue, which of all excellencies and beauties is the chief and most amiable, that which is the prop and ornament of human affairs, which upholds communities, maintains union, friendship and correspondence amongst men, that by which countries, as well as private families, flourish and are happy, and for want of which everything comely, conspicuous, great and worthy must perish and go to ruin – that single quality, thus beneficial to all society and to mankind in general, is found equally a happiness and good to each creature in particular and is that by which alone man can be happy and without which he must be miserable.

And thus virtue is the good and vice the ill of everyone.

The Moralists, a Philosophical Rhapsody, Being a Recital of Certain Conversations on Natural and Moral Subjects

To search for truth among the groves of the Academy.[1]

Part I

Section 1
Philocles to Palemon

What mortal, if he had never chanced to hear your character, Palemon, could imagine that a genius fitted for the greatest affairs and formed amid courts and camps, should have so violent a turn towards philosophy and the schools? Who is there could possibly believe that one of your rank and credit in the fashionable world should be so thoroughly conversant in the learned one, and deeply interested in the affairs of a people so disagreeable to the generality of mankind and humour of the age?

I believe, truly, you are the only well-bred man who would have taken the fancy to talk philosophy in such a circle of good company as we had round us yesterday, when we were in your coach together in the park. How you could reconcile the objects there to such subjects as these was unaccountable. I could only conclude that either you had an extravagant passion for philosophy, to quit so many charms for it, or that some of those tender charms had an extravagant effect, which sent you to philosophy for relief.

In either case, I pitied you, thinking it a milder fate to be, as I truly was for my own part, a more indifferent lover. It was better, I told you, to admire beauty and wisdom a little more moderately. It was better, I maintained, to engage so cautiously as to be sure of coming off with a whole heart and a fancy as strong as ever towards all the pretty entertainments and diversions of the

[1] Horace, *Epistles* 2.2.45.

231

world. For these, methought, were things one would not willingly part with for a fine romantic passion of one of those gentlemen whom they called 'virtuosi'.[A]

The name I took to belong in common to your lover and philosopher, no matter what the object was, whether poetry, music, philosophy or the fair. All who were enamoured any way were in the same condition. You might perceive it, I told you, by their looks, their admiration, their profound thoughtfulness, their waking ever and anon as out of a dream, their talking still of one thing, and scarce minding what they said on any other subject. Sad indications!

But all this warning served not to deter you. For you, Palemon, are one of the adventurous, whom danger rather animates than discourages. And now nothing less will satisfy you than to have our philosophical adventures recorded. All must be laid before you and summed in one complete account to remain, it seems, as a monument of that unseasonable conversation, so opposite to the reigning genius of gallantry and pleasure.

I must own, indeed, it has become fashionable in our nation to talk politics in every company and mix the discourses of state affairs with those of pleasure and entertainment. However, it is certain we approve of no such freedom in philosophy. Nor do we look upon politics to be of her province or in the least related to her. So much have we moderns degraded her, and stripped her of her chief rights.

You must allow me, Palemon, thus to bemoan philosophy since you have forced me to engage with her at a time when her credit runs so low. She is no longer active in the world nor can hardly, with any advantage, be brought upon the public stage. We have immured her, poor lady, in colleges and cells and have set her servilely to such works as those in the mines. Empirics and pedantic sophists are her chief pupils. The school syllogism and the elixir are the choicest of her products. So far is she from producing statesmen as of old that hardly any man of note in the public cares to own the least obligation to her. If some few maintain their acquaintance and come now and then to her recesses, it is as the disciple of quality came to his lord and master, 'secretly, and by night'.[B]

But as low as philosophy is reduced, if morals be allowed belonging to her, politics must undeniably be hers. For to understand the manners and constitutions of men in common, it is necessary to study man in particular and know the creature as he is in himself, before we consider him in company as he is interested in the state or joined to any city or community. Nothing is more familiar than to reason concerning man in his confederate state and national

[A] On virtuosi, see p. 62n.
[B] Possibly a reference to the high-standing Pharisee Nicodemus who came to Jesus 'by night': John 3.2.

relation, as he stands engaged to this or that society by birth or naturalization; yet to consider him as a citizen or commoner of the world, to trace his pedigree a step higher and view his end and constitution in nature itself, must pass, it seems, for some intricate or over-refined speculation.

It may be properly alleged perhaps, as a reason for this general shyness in moral inquiries, that the people to whom it has principally belonged to handle these subjects have done it in such a manner as to put the better sort out of countenance with the undertaking. The appropriating this concern to mere scholastics has brought their fashion and air into the very subject. There are formal set-places where, we reckon, there is enough said and taught on the head of these graver subjects. We can give no quarter to anything like it in good company. The least mention of such matters gives us a disgust and puts us out of humour. If learning comes across us, we count it pedantry; if morality, it is preaching.

One must own this, however, as a real disadvantage of our modern conversations, that by such a scrupulous nicety they lose those masculine helps of learning and sound reason. Even the fair sex, in whose favour we pretend to make this condescension, may with reason despise us for it and laugh at us for aiming at their peculiar softness. It is no compliment to them to affect their manners and be effeminate. Our sense, language and style, as well as our voice and person, should have something of that male feature and natural roughness by which our sex is distinguished. And whatever politeness we may pretend to, it is more a disfigurement than any real refinement of discourse to render it thus delicate.

No work of wit can be esteemed perfect without that strength and boldness of hand which gives it body and proportions. A good piece, the painters say, must have good muscling as well as colouring and drapery. And surely no writing or discourse of any great moment can seem other than enervated when neither strong reason, nor antiquity, nor the records of things, nor the natural history of man, nor anything which can be called knowledge, dares accompany it, except perhaps in some ridiculous habit, which may give it an air of play and dalliance.

This brings to my mind a reason I have often sought for: why we moderns, who abound so much in treatises and essays, are so sparing in the way of dialogue,[2] which heretofore was found the politest and best way of managing even the graver subjects. The truth is it would be an abominable falsehood and belying of the age to put so much good sense together in any one conversation as might make it hold out steadily and with plain coherence for an hour's time till any one subject had been rationally examined.

To lay colours, to draw or describe, against the appearance of nature and

[2] See pp. 87–92, 461ff.

truth, is a liberty neither permitted the painter nor the poet. Much less can the philosopher have such a privilege, especially in his own case. If he represents his philosophy as making any figure in conversation, if he triumphs in the debate and gives his own wisdom the advantage over the world's, he may be liable to sound raillery and possibly be made a fable of.

It is said of the lion that, being in civil conference with the man, he wisely refused to yield the superiority of strength to him when, instead of fact, the man produced only certain figures and representations of human victories over the lion kind. These masterpieces of art the beast discovered to be wholly of human forgery, and from these he had good right to appeal. Indeed, had he ever in his life been witness to any such combats as the man represented to him in the way of art, possibly the example might have moved him. But old statues of a Hercules, a Theseus or other beast-subduers could have little power over him while he neither saw nor felt any such living antagonist capable to dispute the field with him.[C]

We need not wonder, therefore, that the sort of moral painting, by way of dialogue, is so much out of fashion and that we see no more of these philosophical portraitures nowadays. For where are the originals or what, though you, Palemon, or I, by chance, have lighted on such a one and pleased ourselves with the life? Can you imagine it should make a good picture?

You know, too, that in this academic philosophy I am to present you with, there is a certain way of questioning and doubting which no way suits the genius of our age. Men love to take party instantly. They cannot bear being kept in suspense. The examination torments them. They want to be rid of it upon the easiest terms. It is as if men fancied themselves drowning whenever they dare trust to the current of reason. They seem hurrying away – they know not whither – and are ready to catch at the first twig. There they choose afterwards to hang, though ever so insecurely, rather than trust their strength to bear them above water. He who has got hold of an hypothesis, how slight soever, is satisfied. He can presently answer every objection and, with a few terms of art, give an account of everything without trouble.

It is no wonder if in this age the philosophy of the alchemists prevails so much since it promises such wonders and requires more the labour of hands than brains.[D] We have a strange fancy to be creators, a violent desire at least to know the knack or secret by which nature does all. The rest of our philoso-

---

[C] The hero Hercules had many encounters with lions and other creatures in the course of his legendary career. Theseus, the hero of Athens, was partly modelled on the figure of Hercules and likewise was said to have defeated numerous beasts.

[D] Alchemy was in general the chemistry of the medieval and early modern periods although it was associated, in particular, with the aim of transmuting base metals, such as lead, into the noble ones of gold and silver. Shaftesbury's usage here is general and could refer to such a pioneer of modern chemistry as Robert Boyle.

phers only aim at that in speculation which our alchemists aspire to in practice. For with some of these it has been actually under deliberation how to make man by other media than nature has hitherto provided. Every sect has a recipe. When you know it, you are master of nature, you solve all her phenomena,[3] you see all her designs and can account for all her operations. If need were, you might perchance, too, be of her laboratory and work for her: at least, one would imagine the partisans of each modern sect had this conceit. They are all Archimedeses in their way and can make a world upon easier terms than he offered to move one.[E]

In short, there are good reasons for our being thus superficial and consequently thus dogmatical in philosophy. We are too lazy and effeminate and, withal, a little too cowardly, to dare doubt. The decisive way best becomes our manners. It suits as well with our vices as with our superstition: whichever we are fond of is secured by it. If in favour of religion we have espoused an hypothesis on which our faith, we think, depends, we are superstitiously careful not to be loosened in it. If, by means of our ill morals, we are broken with religion, it is the same case still: we are as much afraid of doubting. We must be sure to say, 'It cannot be' and 'It is demonstrable,' for, otherwise, 'Who knows?' and not to know is to yield!

Thus we will needs know everything and be at the pains of examining nothing. Of all philosophy, therefore, how absolutely the most disagreeable must that appear which goes upon no established hypothesis nor presents us with any flattering scheme, talks only of probabilities, suspense of judgment, inquiry, search and caution not to be imposed on or deceived?[F] This is that academic discipline in which formerly the youth were trained, when not only horsemanship and military arts had their public places of exercise, but philosophy too had its wrestlers in repute.[4] Reason and wit had their academy and underwent this trial, not in a formal way apart from the world but openly among the better sort and as an exercise of the genteeler kind. This the greatest men were not ashamed to practise in the intervals of public affairs in the highest stations and employments and at the latest hour of their lives. Hence that way of dialogue and patience of debate and reasoning, of which we have scarce a resemblance left in any of our conversations at this season of the world.

Consider then, Palemon, what our picture is like to prove and how it will appear, especially in the light you have unluckily chosen to set it. For who would thus have confronted philosophy with the gaiety, wit and humour of the

---

E   Archimedes, *c.* 287–212 BC, was the greatest mathematician of the ancient world. His understanding of simple machines, including the lever, led him to claim that he could move the earth if he had a place to stand.

F   On Shaftesbury's relation to scepticism, see Introduction, p. xiv.

3   See p. 407.

4   See p. 148.

age? If this, however, can be for your credit, I am content. The project is your own. It is you who have matched philosophy thus unequally. Therefore, leaving you to answer for the success, I begin this inauspicious work, which my ill stars and you have assigned me and in which I hardly dare ask succour of the Muses, as poetical as I am obliged to show myself in this enterprise.

Section 2

'O wretched state of mankind! Hapless nature, thus to have erred in thy chief workmanship! Whence sprang this fatal weakness? What chance or destiny shall we accuse? Or shall we mind the poets when they sing thy tragedy, Prometheus, who with thy stolen celestial fire, mixed with vile clay, didst mock heaven's countenance and, in abusive likeness of the immortals, madest the compound, man, that wretched mortal, ill to himself and cause of ill to all?'[G]

What say you, Palemon, to this rant, now upon second thoughts? Or have you forgot it was just in such a romantic strain that you broke out against humankind upon a day when everything looked pleasing and the kind itself, I thought, never appeared fairer or made a better show?

But it was not the whole creation you thus quarrelled with nor were you so out of conceit with all beauty. The verdure of the field, the distant prospects, the gilded horizon and purple sky formed by a setting sun, had charms in abundance and were able to make impression on you. Here, Palemon, you allowed me to admire as much as I pleased when, at the same instant, you would not bear my talking to you of those nearer beauties of our own kind, which I thought more natural for men at our age to admire. Your severity however could not silence me upon this subject. I continued to plead the cause of the fair and advance their charms above all those other beauties of nature. And when you took advantage from this opposition to show how little there was of nature and how much of art in what I admired, I made the best apology I could and, fighting for beauty, kept the field as long as there was one fair one present.

Considering how your genius stood inclined to poetry, I wondered most to find you on a sudden grown so out of conceit with our modern poets and *galante*[H] writers, whom I quoted to you as better authorities than any ancient in behalf of the fair sex and their prerogative. But this you treated slightly. You acknowledged it to be true indeed, what had been observed by some late wits, that gallantry was of a modern growth.[I] And well it might be so, you thought, without dishonour to the ancients, who understood truth and nature too well to admit so ridiculous an invention.

[G] On Prometheus, see p. 93n.
[H] Gallant, gentlemanly and, especially, attentive to ladies.
[I] This point was made by, among others, Charles de Marguetel de Saint Denis, Sieur de Saint-Evremond, in his essay on Petronius, published in 1664, and developed by Charles Perrault in his *Parallèle des anciens et des modernes*, which appeared between 1688 and 1697.

It was in vain, therefore, that I held up this shield in my defence. I did my cause no service when, in behalf of the fair, I pleaded all the fine things which are usually said in this romantic way to their advantage. You attacked the very fortress of gallantry, ridiculed the point of honour with all those nice sentiments and ceremonials belonging to it. You damned even our favourite novels, those dear, sweet, natural pieces, written most of them by the fair sex themselves. In short, this whole order and scheme of wit you condemned absolutely as false, monstrous and Gothic, quite out of the way of nature, and sprung from the mere dregs of chivalry or knight-errantry, a thing which in itself you preferred as of a better taste than that which reigns at present in its stead. For at a time when this mystery of gallantry carried along with it the notion of doughty knighthood, when the fair were made witnesses and, in a manner, parties to feats of arms, entered into all the points of war and combat and were won by dint of lance and manly prowess, it was not altogether absurd, you thought, on such a foundation as this to pay them homage and adoration, make them the standard of wit and manners and bring mankind under their laws. But in a country where no she-saints were worshipped by any authority from religion, it was as impertinent and senseless as it was profane to deify the sex, raise them to a capacity above what nature had allowed and treat them with a respect which, in the natural way of love, they themselves were the aptest to complain of.

Indeed, as for the moral part, it was wonderful, you said, to observe the licentiousness which this foppish, courtly humour had established in the world. What such a flattering way of address to all the sex in common could mean, you knew not, unless it were to render them wholly common indeed, and make each fair one apprehend that the public had a right to her and that beauty was too communicative and divine a thing to be made a property and confined to one at once.

Meanwhile our company began to leave us. The *beau monde*, whom you had been thus severely censuring, drew off apace, for it grew late. I took notice that the approaching objects of the night were the more agreeable to you for the solitude they introduced and that the moon and planets which began now to appear were in reality the only proper company for a man in your humour. For now you began to talk with much satisfaction of natural things and of all orders of beauties, man only excepted. Never did I hear a finer description than you made of the order of the heavenly luminaries, the circles of the planets and their attendant satellites. And you who would allow nothing to those fair earthly luminaries in the circles which just now we moved in, you, Palemon, who seemed to overlook the pride of that theatre, began now to look out with ravishment on this other and triumph in the new philosophical scene of worlds unknown. Here, when you had pretty well spent the first fire of your imagination, I would have got you to reason more calmly with me upon that other part of the creation, your own kind, to which, I told you, you discovered so much aversion as would make one believe you a complete Timon or man-hater.

'Can you then, O Philocles,' said you in a high strain and with a moving air of passion, 'can you believe me of that character or can you think it of me in earnest that, being man and conscious of my nature, I should have yet so little of humanity as not to feel the affections of a man? Or, feeling what is natural towards my kind, that I should hold their interest light and be indifferently affected with what affects or seriously concerns them? Am I so ill a lover of my country? Or is it that you find me indeed so ill a friend? For what are all relations else? What are the ties of private friendship if that to mankind be not obliging? Can there be yet a bond in nature if that be none? O Philocles! Believe me when I say I feel it one and fully prove its power within me. Think not that I would willingly break my chain nor count me so degenerate or unnatural as, while I hold this form and wear a human heart, I should throw off love, compassion, kindness, and not befriend mankind.——But oh! What treacheries! What disorders! And how corrupt is all!——Did you not observe even now, when all this space was filled with goodly rows of company, how peaceful all appeared.——What charms there are in public companies! What harmony in courts and courtly places! How pleased is every face! How courteous and humane the general carriage and behaviour!——What creature capable of reflection, if he thus saw us mankind and saw no more, would not believe our earth a very heaven? What foreigner – the inhabitant, suppose, of some near planet – when he had travelled hither and surveyed this outward face of things, would think of what lay hid beneath the mask?——But let him stay a while. Allow him leisure till he has gained a nearer view and, following our dissolved assemblies to their particular recesses, he has the power of seeing them in this new aspect.——Here he may behold those great men of the Ministry, who not an hour ago in public appeared such friends, now plotting craftily each other's ruin, with the ruin of the state itself, a sacrifice to their ambition. Here he may see too those of a softer kind who knowing not ambition follow only love. Yet, Philocles, who would think it?'

At these words, you may remember, I discovered the lightness of my temper and laughed aloud, which I could hardly hope you would have pardoned had I not freely told you the true reason. It was not for want of being affected with what you spoke. I only imagined a more particular cause had provoked you when, having passed over the ambitious, you were coming full-charged against the people of a softer passion. At first I looked on you as deeply in the spleen, but now I concluded you in love and so unhappily engaged as to have reason to complain of infidelity. 'This', thought I, 'has moved Palemon thus. Hence the sad world! Here was that corruption and those disorders he lamented!'

After I had begged pardon for my rude mirth, which had the good fortune however to make some change in your humour, we fell naturally into cool reasoning about the nature and cause of ill in general: through what contingency, what chance, by what fatal necessity, what will or what permission it came upon the world or, being come once, should still subsist. This inquiry,[5] which with slight reasoners is easily got over, stuck hard, I found, with one of your close judgment and penetration. And this insensibly led us into a nice criticism of nature, whom you sharply arraigned for many absurdities you thought her guilty of in relation to mankind and his peculiar state.

Fain would I have persuaded you to think with more equality of nature and to proportion her defects a little better. My notion was that the grievance lay not altogether in one part, as you placed it, but that everything had its share of inconvenience. Pleasure and pain, beauty and deformity, good and ill, seemed to me everywhere interwoven, and one with another made, I thought, a pretty mixture, agreeable enough in the main. It was the same, I fancied, as in some of those rich stuffs where the flowers and ground were oddly put together with such irregular work and contrary colours as looked ill in the pattern but mighty natural and well in the piece.

But you were still upon extremes. Nothing would serve to excuse the faults or blemishes of this part of the creation, mankind, even though all besides were fair without a blemish. The very storms and tempests had their beauty in your account, those alone excepted which arose in human breasts. It was only for this turbulent race of mortals you offered to accuse nature. And I now found why you had been so transported with the story of Prometheus.[J] You wanted such an operator as this for mankind, and you were tempted to wish the story could have been confirmed in modern divinity: that clearing the supreme powers of any concern or hand in the ill workmanship, you might have the liberty of inveighing against it without profaneness.

This however, I told you, was but a slight evasion of the religious poets among the ancients. It was easy to answer every objection by a Prometheus, as, 'Why had mankind originally so much folly and perverseness? Why so much pride, such ambition and strange appetites? Why so many plagues and curses entailed on him and his posterity?' Prometheus was the cause. The plastic artist, with his unlucky hand, solved all. 'It was his contrivance,' they said, 'and he was to answer for it.' They reckoned it a fair game if they could gain a single remove and put the evil cause farther off. If the people asked a question, they told them a tale and sent them away satisfied. None besides a few philosophers would be such busybodies, they thought, as to look beyond or ask a second question.

And in reality, continued I, it is not to be imagined how serviceable a tale

---

[J] On Prometheus, see p. 93n.

[5] 'An Inquiry Concerning Virtue': see the beginning.

is to amuse others besides mere children and how much easier the generality of men are paid in this paper coin than in sterling reason. We ought not to laugh so readily at the Indian philosophers who, to satisfy their people how this huge frame of the world is supported, tell them it is by an elephant. 'And the elephant how?' A shrewd question but which by no means should be answered. It is here only that our Indian philosophers are to blame. They should be contented with the elephant and go no farther. But they have a tortoise in reserve, whose back, they think, is broad enough. So the tortoise must bear the new load, and thus the matter stands worse than before.

The heathen story of Prometheus was, I told you, much the same with this Indian one, only the heathen mythologists were so wise as not to go beyond the first remove. A single Prometheus was enough to take the weight from Jove. They fairly made Jove a bystander. He resolved, it seems, to be neuter and see what would come of this notable experiment, how the dangerous man-moulder would proceed and what would be the event of his tampering. Excellent account to satisfy the heathen vulgar! But how, think you, would a philosopher digest this? 'For the gods', he would say presently, 'either could have hindered Prometheus' creation or they could not. If they could, they were answerable for the consequences. If they could not, they were no longer gods, being thus limited and controlled. And whether Prometheus were a name for chance, destiny, a plastic nature[K] or an evil daemon, whatever was designed by it, it was still the same breach of omnipotence.'

That such a hazardous affair as this of creation should have been undertaken by those who had not perfect foresight as well as command, you owned was neither wise nor just. But you stood to foresight. You allowed the consequences to have been understood by the creating powers when they undertook their work and you denied that it would have been better for them to have omitted it, though they knew what would be the event.

'It was better still that the project should be executed, whatever might become of mankind or how hard soever such a creation was like to fall on the generality of this miserable race. For it was impossible', you thought, 'that Heaven should have acted otherwise than for the best. So that even from this misery and ill of man there was undoubtedly some good arising, something which over-balanced all and made full amends.'

This was a confession I wondered indeed how I came to draw from you, and soon afterwards I found you somewhat uneasy under it. For here I took up your own part against you and, setting all those villainies and corruptions of humankind in the same light you had done just before, I put it upon you to tell where possibly could be the advantage or good arising hence or what excellence or beauty could redound from those tragical pictures you yourself had

---

[K] A moulding or creative agent: see p. 93n.

240

drawn so well after the life. Whether it must not be a very strong philosophical faith which should persuade one that those dismal parts you set to view
were only the necessary shades of a fine piece, to be reckoned among the beauties of the creation, or whether possibly you might look upon that maxim as
very fit for heaven, which I was sure you did not approve at all in mankind,
'to do ill that good might follow'.

This, I said, made me think of the manner of our modern Prometheuses,
the mountebanks, who performed such wonders of many kinds here on our
earthly stages. They could create diseases and make mischief in order to heal
and to restore. But should we assign such a practice as this to Heaven? Should
we dare to make such empirics of the gods and such a patient of poor nature?

'Was this a reason for nature's sickliness? Or how else came she (poor innocent!) to fall sick or run astray? Had she been originally healthy or created
sound at first, she had still continued so. It was no credit to the gods to leave
her destitute or with a flaw which would cost dear the mending and make them
sufferers for their own work.'

I was going to bring Homer to witness for the many troubles of Jove, the
death of Sarpedon and the frequent crosses Heaven met with from the fatal
sisters.[L] But this discourse, I saw, displeased you. I had by this time plainly
discovered my inclination to scepticism. And here not only religion was
objected to me, but I was reproached too on the account of that gallantry which
I had some time before defended. Both were joined together in the charge you
made against me when you saw I adhered to nothing, but was now as ready to
declaim against the fair as I had been before to plead their cause and defend
the moral of lovers. This, you said, was my constant way in all debates: I was
as well pleased with the reason on one side as on the other; I never troubled
myself about the success of the argument but laughed still whatever way it
went and, even when I convinced others, never seemed as if I was convinced
myself.

I owned to you, Palemon, there was truth enough in your charge. For above
all things I loved ease and, of all philosophers, those who reasoned most at
their ease and were never angry or disturbed, as those called sceptics, you
owned, never were. I looked upon this kind of philosophy as the prettiest,
agreeablest, roving exercise of the mind possible to be imagined. The other
kind, I thought, was painful and laborious: 'to keep always in the limits of one
path, to drive always at a point and hold precisely to what men at a venture

---

[L] Among other forms, fate in Greek mythology took that of three sisters, assigning a length of
life, spinning the thread of life and cutting the thread at the appointed time. Though close to
Zeus (or Jove – a Roman name), they often seemed to act independently of his will, as Homer
repeatedly showed. When, in Book XVI of the *Iliad*, Sarpedon, a Trojan ally and son of Zeus,
was about to meet his fate, Zeus considered intervening until reminded by his wife Hera how
such a move would violate the order of the universe.

called "the truth", a point, in all appearance, very unfixed and hard to ascertain'.

Besides, my way hurt nobody. I was always the first to comply on any occasion and, for matters of religion, was farther from profaneness and erroneous doctrine than anyone. I could never have the sufficiency to shock my spiritual and learned superiors. I was the farthest from leaning to my own understanding nor was I one who exalted reason above faith or insisted much upon what the dogmatical men call 'demonstration' and dare oppose to the sacred mysteries of religion. And to show you, continued I, how impossible it is for the men of our sort ever to err from the catholic and established faith, pray consider that, whereas others pretend to see with their own eyes what is properest and best for them in religion, we, for our parts, pretend not to see with any other than those of our spiritual guides. Neither do we presume to judge those guides ourselves but submit to them as they are appointed us by our just superiors. In short, you who are rationalists and walk by reason in everything pretend to know all things while you believe little or nothing. We, for our parts, know nothing and believe all.ᴹ

Here I ended and, in return, you only asked me coldly 'whether with that fine scepticism of mine I made no more distinction between sincerity and insincerity in actions than I did between truth and falsehood, right and wrong, in arguments?'

I durst not ask what your question drove at. I was afraid I saw it too plainly and that, by this loose way of talking which I had learnt in some fashionable conversations of the world, I had given you occasion to suspect me of the worst sort of scepticism, such as spared nothing but overthrew all principles, moral and divine.

'Forgive me,' said I, 'good Palemon! You are offended, I see, and not without cause. But what if I should endeavour to compensate my sceptical misbehaviour by using a known sceptic privilege and asserting strenuously the cause I have hitherto opposed? Do not imagine that I dare aspire so high as to defend revealed religion or the holy mysteries of the Christian faith. I am unworthy of such a task and should profane the subject. It is of mere philosophy I speak, and my fancy is only to try what I can muster up thence to make head against the chief arguments of atheism and re-establish what I have offered to loosen in the system of theism.'

'Your project', said you, 'bids fair to reconcile me to your character, which I was beginning to mistrust. For as averse as I am to the cause of theism or name of "deist" when taken in a sense exclusive of revelation, I consider still that, in strictness, the root of all is theism and that, to be a settled Christian,

---

ᴹ The accompaniment of Philocles' scepticism was fideism, the assertion that, since all religious knowledge depended on revelation, the believer should submit unquestioningly to those authorities to whom the interpretation of revelation was entrusted.

it is necessary to be first of all a good theist. For theism can only be opposed to polytheism or atheism.[6] Nor have I patience to hear the name of deist, the highest of all names, decried and set in opposition to Christianity, as if our religion was a kind of magic, which depended not on the belief of a single supreme being or as if the firm and rational belief of such a being on philosophical grounds was an improper qualification for believing anything further. Excellent presumption for those who naturally incline to the disbelief of revelation or who through vanity affect a freedom of this kind!

But let me hear', continued you, 'whether in good earnest and thorough sincerity you intend to advance anything in favour of that opinion which is fundamental to all religion or whether you design only to divert yourself with the subject as you have done hitherto? Whatever your thoughts are, Philocles, I am resolved to force them from you. You can no longer plead the unsuitableness of the time or place to such grave subjects. The gaudy scene is over with the day. Our company have long since quitted the field, and the solemn majesty of such a night as this may justly suit with the profoundest meditation or most serious discourse.'

Thus, Palemon, you continued to urge me till by necessity I was drawn into the following vein of philosophical enthusiasm.

Section 3
'You shall find then', said I, taking a grave air, 'that it is possible for me to be serious and that it is probable I am growing so for good and all. Your over-seriousness a while since, at such an unseasonable time, may have driven me perhaps into a contrary extreme by opposition to your melancholy humour. But I have now a better idea of that melancholy you discovered and, notwithstanding the humorous turn you were pleased to give it, I am persuaded it has a different foundation from any of those fantastical causes I then assigned to it. Love, doubtless, is at the bottom but a nobler love than such as common beauties inspire.'

Here, in my turn, I began to raise my voice and imitate the solemn way you had been teaching me. 'Knowing as you are,' continued I, 'well-knowing and experienced in all the degrees and orders of beauty, in all the mysterious charms of the particular forms, you rise to what is more general and, with a larger heart and mind more comprehensive, you generously seek that which is highest in the kind. Not captivated by the lineaments of a fair face or the well-drawn proportions of a human body, you view the life itself and embrace rather the mind which adds the lustre and renders chiefly amiable.

Nor is the enjoyment of such a single beauty sufficient to satisfy such an aspiring soul. It seeks how to combine more beauties and by what coalition of

[6] As above, p. 166n.

these to form a beautiful society. It views communities, friendships, relations, duties and considers by what harmony of particular minds the general harmony is composed and commonweal established.

Nor satisfied even with public good in one community of men, it frames itself a nobler object and with enlarged affection seeks the good of mankind. It dwells with pleasure amid that reason and those orders on which this fair correspondence and goodly interest is established. Laws, constitutions, civil and religious rites (whatever civilizes or polishes rude mankind!), the sciences and arts, philosophy, morals, virtue, the flourishing state of human affairs and the perfection of human nature – these are its delightful prospects, and this the charm of beauty which attracts it.

Still ardent in this pursuit (such is its love of order and perfection), it rests not here nor satisfies itself with the beauty of a part but, extending further its communicative bounty, seeks the good of all and affects the interest and prosperity of the whole. True to its native world and higher country, it is here it seeks order and perfection, wishing the best and hoping still to find a just and wise administration.

And since all hope of this were vain and idle if no universal mind presided, since without such a supreme intelligence and providential care the distracted universe must be condemned to suffer infinite calamities, it is here the generous mind labours to discover that healing cause by which the interest of the whole is securely established, the beauty of things and the universal order happily sustained.

This, Palemon, is the labour of your soul, and this its melancholy when, unsuccessfully pursuing the supreme beauty, it meets with darkening clouds which intercept its sight. Monsters arise, not those from Libyan deserts, but from the heart of man more fertile, and, with their horrid aspect, cast an unseemly reflection upon nature. She, helpless (as she is thought) and working thus absurdly, is contemned, the government of the world arraigned, and Deity made void.

Much is alleged in answer to show why nature errs and how she came thus impotent and erring from an unerring hand. But I deny she errs and, when she seems most ignorant or perverse in her productions, I assert her even then as wise and provident as in her goodliest works. For it is not then that men complain of the world's order or abhor the face of things, when they see various interests mixed and interfering – natures subordinate of different kinds opposed one to another and in their different operations submitted the higher to the lower. It is on the contrary from this order of inferior and superior things that we admire the world's beauty, founded thus on contrarieties, while from such various and disagreeing principles a universal concord is established.[7]

[7] See what is cited in the notes on p. 450 from the ancient author of *On the Cosmos*.

Thus, in the several orders of terrestrial forms a resignation is required, a sacrifice and mutual yielding of natures one to another. The vegetables by their death sustain the animals, and animal bodies dissolved enrich the earth and raise again the vegetable world. The numerous insects are reduced by the superior kinds of birds and beasts, and these again are checked by man, who in his turn submits to other natures and resigns his form a sacrifice in common to the rest of things. And, if in natures so little exalted or pre-eminent above each other, the sacrifice of interests can appear so just, how much more reasonably may all inferior natures be subjected to the superior nature of the world, that world, Palemon, which even now transported you, when the sun's fainting light gave way to these bright constellations and left you this wide system to contemplate!

Here are those laws which ought not nor can submit to anything below. The central powers, which hold the lasting orbs in their just poise and movement, must not be controlled to save a fleeting form and rescue from the precipice a puny animal, whose brittle frame, however protected, must of itself so soon dissolve. The ambient air, the inward vapours, the impending meteors or whatever else is nutrimental or preservative of this earth must operate in a natural course, and other constitutions must submit to the good habit and constitution of the all-sustaining globe.

Let us not therefore wonder if, by earthquakes, storms, pestilential blasts, nether or upper fires or floods, the animal kinds are often afflicted and whole species perhaps involved at once in common ruin; but much less let us account it strange if, either by outward shock or some interior wound from hostile matter, particular animals are deformed even in their first conception, when the disease invades the seats of generation and seminal parts are injured and obstructed in their accurate labours. It is then alone that monstrous shapes are seen, nature still working as before and not perversely or erroneously, not faintly or with feeble endeavours, but overpowered by a superior rival and by another nature's justly conquering force.

Nor need we wonder if the interior form, the soul and temper, partakes of this occasional deformity and sympathizes often with its close partner. Considering the strictness of this relation, who can wonder, if from a body originally impure, corrupt, distorted, a like soul arises?[N] Who is there can wonder either at the sicknesses of sense or the depravity of minds enclosed in such frail bodies and dependent on such pervertible organs?

Here then is that solution you require and hence those seeming blemishes cast upon nature. Nor is there anything in this beside what is natural and good. It is good which is predominant, and every corruptible and mortal nature by

---

[N] This sentence did not appear in the second edition of *Characteristics* although it did appear in the first edition and there is no manuscript warrant for its elimination in the second.

its mortality and corruption yields only to some better, and all in common to that best and highest nature which is incorruptible and immortal.'

I scarcely had ended these words before you broke out in admiration, asking what had befallen me that of a sudden I had thus changed my character and entered into thoughts which must certainly, you supposed, have some foundation in me, since I could express them with such seeming affection as I had done.

'O!,' said I, 'Palemon! That it had been my fortune to have met you the other day just at my return out of the country from a friend whose conversation had in one day or two made such an impression on me that I should have suited you to a miracle. You would have thought indeed that I had been cured of my scepticism and levity, so as never to have rallied more at that wild rate on any subject, much less on these which are so serious.'

'Truly,' said you, 'I could wish I had met you rather at that time or that those good and serious impressions of your friend had without interruption lasted with you till this moment.'

'Whatever they were,' I told you, Palemon, 'I had not so lost them neither as not easily, you saw, to revive them on occasion, were I not afraid.'

'Afraid!,' said you. 'For whose sake, good Philocles, I entreat you? For mine or your own?'

'For both,' replied I. 'For though I was like to be perfectly cured of my scepticism, it was by what I thought worse, downright enthusiasm. You never knew a more agreeable enthusiast!'

'Were he my friend,' said you, 'I should hardly treat him in so free a manner, nor should I, perhaps, judge that to be enthusiasm which you so freely term so. I have a strong suspicion that you injure him. Nor can I be satisfied till I hear further of that serious conversation for which you tax him as enthusiastic.'

'I must confess', said I, 'he had nothing of that savage air of the vulgar enthusiastic kind. All was serene, soft and harmonious. The manner of it was more after the pleasing transports of those ancient poets you are often charmed with than after the fierce unsociable way of modern zealots, those starched, gruff gentlemen who guard religion as bullies do a mistress, and give us the while a very indifferent opinion of their lady's merit and their own wit, by adoring what they neither allow to be inspected by others nor care themselves to examine in a fair light. But here, I will answer for it, there was nothing of disguise or paint. All was fair, open and genuine as nature herself. It was nature he was in love with. It was nature he sung. And, if anyone might be said to have a natural mistress, my friend certainly might, whose heart was thus engaged. But love, I found, was everywhere the same. And though the object here was very fine and the passion it created very noble, yet liberty, I thought, was finer than all. And I, who never cared to engage in other love of the least continuance, was the more afraid, I told you, of this which had such a power with my poor friend as to make him appear the perfectest enthusiast in the world, ill humour only excepted. For this was singular in him, that, though he had all of the enthusiast, he had nothing of the bigot. He heard everything with mildness and delight and bore with me when I treated all his thoughts as visionary and when, sceptic-like, I unravelled all his systems.'

Here was that character and description which so highly pleased you that you would hardly suffer me to come to a conclusion. It was impossible, I found, to give you satisfaction without reciting the main of what passed in those two days between my friend and me in our country retirement. Again and again I bid you beware: you knew not the danger of this philosophical passion, nor considered what you might possibly draw upon yourself and make me the author of. I was far enough engaged already, and you were pushing me further at your own hazard.

All I could say made not the least impression on you. But rather than proceed any further this night, I engaged, for your sake, to turn writer and draw up the memoirs of those two philosophical days, beginning with what had passed this last day between ourselves, as I have accordingly done, you see, by way of introduction to my story.

By this time, being got late to town, some hours after the latest of our company, you set me down at my own lodging, and thus we bade good-night.

Part II

Section 1
Philocles to Palemon
After such a day as yesterday I might well have thought it hard, when I awaked the next morning, to find myself under positive engagements of proceeding in the same philosophical way without intermission and upon harder terms than ever. For it was no longer the agreeable part of a companion which I had now to bear. Your conversation, Palemon, which had hitherto supported me, was at an end. I was now alone, confined to my closet, obliged to meditate by myself and reduced to the hard circumstances of an author and historian in the most difficult subject.

But here, methought, propitious Heaven in some manner assisted me. For if dreams were, as Homer teaches, sent from the throne of Jove, I might conclude I had a favourable one of the true sort towards the morning light, which, as I recollected myself, gave me a clear and perfect idea of what I desired so earnestly to bring back to my memory.

I found myself transported to a distant country, which presented a pompous rural scene. It was a mountain not far from the sea, its brow adorned with ancient wood and at its foot a river and well-inhabited plain, beyond which the sea appearing, closed the prospect.

No sooner had I considered the place than I discerned it to be the very same where I had talked with Theocles the second day I was with him in the country.[O] I looked about to see if I could find my friend and, calling 'Theocles!,' I awoke. But so powerful was the impression of my dream and so perfect the idea raised in me of the person, words, and manner of my friend that I could now fancy myself philosophically inspired, as that Roman sage by his Egeria, and invited on this occasion to try my historical muse.[8] For justly might I hope for such assistance in behalf of Theocles, who so loved the Muses, and was I thought no less beloved by them.

To return therefore to that original rural scene and that heroic genius, the companion and guide of my first thoughts in these profounder subjects, I found him the first morning with his beloved Mantuan Muse,[P] roving in the fields, where, as I had been informed at his house, he was gone out, after his usual way, to read. The moment he saw me, his book vanished, and he came with friendly haste to meet me. After we had embraced, I discovered my curiosity to know what he was reading and asked 'if it were of a secret kind, to which I could not be admitted'.

On this he showed me his poet and, looking pleasantly, 'Now tell me truly,' said he, 'Philocles, did you not expect some more mysterious book than this?'

I owned I did, considering his character, which I took to be of so contemplative a kind.

'And do you think', said he, 'that without being contemplative one can truly relish these diviner poets?'

'Indeed,' said I, 'I never thought there was any need of growing contemplative or retiring from the world to read Virgil or Horace.'

'You have named two', said he, 'who can hardly be thought so very like, though they were friends and equally good poets. Yet joining them as you are pleased to do, I would willingly learn from you whether in your opinion there

---

[O] The setting for these philosophical discussions was an idealized pastoral landscape in the Arcadian tradition. Arcadia, a province in the Greek Peloponnesus, was turned in mythology into a fertile paradise occupied by nature spirits, both satyrs and nymphs, and by refined shepherds and shepherdesses. It inspired allegorical and idealized landscape painting by Claude Lorrain and Nicolas Poussin, which Shaftesbury admired and appears here to be imitating. See p. 296 for another evocation of Arcadia.

[P] Virgil, who was born in the vicinity of Mantua in north-central Italy. On Virgil, see Introduction, p. xxii.

[8] Numa. [A philosopher, Numa was called by the Romans to succeed Romulus as their second king at the end of the eighth century BC. He was said to have consorted with and received advice from Egeria, a water deity.]

be any disposition so fitted for reading them as that in which they wrote themselves. In this, I am sure, they both joined heartily: to love retirement, when, for the sake of such a life and habit as you call contemplative, they were willing to sacrifice the highest advantages, pleasures and favour of a court. But I will venture to say more in favour of retirement: that not only the best authors but the best company require this seasoning. Society itself cannot be rightly enjoyed without some abstinence and separate thought. All grows insipid, dull and tiresome without the help of some intervals of retirement. Say, Philocles, whether you yourself have not often found it so? Do you think those lovers understand the interests of their loves who by their good will would never be parted for a moment? Or would they be discreet friends, think you, who would choose to live together on such terms? What relish then must the world have, that common world of mixed and undistinguished company, without a little solitude, without stepping now and then aside out of the road and beaten track of life, that tedious circle of noise and show, which forces wearied mankind to seek relief from every poor diversion?'

'By your rule,' said I, 'Theocles, there should be no such thing as happiness or good in life since every enjoyment wears out so soon and, growing painful, is diverted by some other thing, and that again by some other, and so on. I am sure, if solitude serves as a remedy or diversion to anything in the world, there is nothing which may not serve as diversion to solitude, which wants it more than anything besides. And thus there can be no good which is regular or constant. Happiness is a thing out of the way, and only to be found in wandering.'

'O Philocles,' replied he, 'I rejoice to find you in the pursuit of happiness and good, however you may wander. Nay, though you doubt whether there be that thing, yet, if you reason, it is sufficient. There is hope still. But see how you have unawares engaged yourself! For if you have destroyed all good, because, in all you can think of, there is nothing will constantly hold so, then you have set it as a maxim, and very justly in my opinion, that "nothing can be good but what is constant".'

'I own', said I, 'that all I know of worldly satisfaction is inconstant. The things which give it are never at a stay, and the good itself, whatever it be, depends no less on humour than on fortune. For that which chance may often spare, time will not. Age, change of temper, other thoughts, a different passion, new engagements, a new turn of life or conversation – the least of these are fatal and alone sufficient to destroy enjoyment. Though the object be the same, the relish changes and the short-lived good expires. But I should wonder much if you could tell me anything in life which was not of as changeable a nature and subject to the same common fate of satiety and disgust.'

'I find then', replied he, 'that the current notion of "good" is not sufficient to satisfy you. You can afford to scepticize where no one else will so much as hesitate. For almost every one philosophizes dogmatically on this head. All are positive in this, that *our real good is pleasure.*[Q]

'If they would inform us "which"', said I, 'or "what sort", and ascertain once the very species and distinct kind, such as must constantly remain the same and equally eligible at all times, I should then perhaps be better satisfied. But when will and pleasure are synonymous, when everything which pleases us is called pleasure[9] and we never choose or prefer but as we please, it is trifling to say, "Pleasure is our good." For this has as little meaning as to say, "We choose what we think eligible" and "We are pleased with what delights or pleases us." The question is, "Whether we are rightly pleased and choose as we should do?" For as highly pleased as children are with baubles or with whatever affects their tender senses, we cannot in our hearts sincerely admire their enjoyment or imagine them possessors of any extraordinary good. Yet are their senses, we know, as keen and susceptible of pleasure as our own. The same reflection is of force as to mere animals, who, in respect of the liveliness and delicacy of sensation, have many of them the advantage of us. And as for some low and sordid pleasures of humankind, should they be ever so lastingly enjoyed and in the highest credit with their enjoyers, I should never afford them the name of happiness or good.'

'Would you then appeal', said he, 'from the immediate feeling and experience of one who is pleased and satisfied with what he enjoys?'

'Most certainly I should appeal,' said I, continuing the same zeal which Theocles had stirred in me against those dogmatizers on pleasure. 'For is there that sordid creature on earth who does not prize his own enjoyment? Does not the forwardest, the most rancorous distempered creature do as much? Is not malice and cruelty of the highest relish with some natures? Is not a hoggish life the height of some men's wishes? You would not ask me surely to enumerate the several species of sensations which men of certain tastes have adopted and owned for their chief pleasure and delight. For with some men even diseases have been thought valuable and worth the cherishing, merely for the pleasure found in allaying the ardour of an irritating sensation. And to these absurd epicures those other are near akin who by studied provocatives raise unnatural thirst and appetite and, to make way for fresh repletion, prepare emetics as the last dessert, the sooner to renew the feast. It is said, I know, proverbially, that "tastes are different and must not be disputed".[R] And I remember some such motto as this placed once on a device, which was found

---

[Q] Shaftesbury here associated modern moral doctrine with Epicurean principles although modern hedonism or libertinism was far from Epicurus' goal of imperturbability. See Introduction, p. xxvi.

[R] The proverb is usually rendered, *De gustibus non disputandum*, 'There is no arguing about tastes.'

[9] See pp. 138, 423.

suitable to the notion. A fly was represented feeding on a certain lump. The food, however vile, was natural to the animal. There was no absurdity in the case. But should you show me a brutish or a barbarous man thus taken up and solaced in his pleasure, should you show me a sot in his solitary debauch or a tyrant in the exercise of his cruelty with this motto over him, to forbid my appeal, I should hardly be brought to think the better of his enjoyment. Nor can I possibly suppose that a mere sordid wretch, with a base, abject soul and the best fortune in the world, was ever capable of any real enjoyment.'

'By this zeal,' replied Theocles, 'which you have shown in the refuting a wrong hypothesis, one would imagine you had in reality some notion of a right [one] and began to think that there might possibly be such a thing at last as good.'

'That there is something nearer to good and more like it than another, I am free', said I, 'to own. But what real good is I am still to seek and must therefore wait till you can better inform me. This I only know, that either all pleasure is good or only some. If all, then every kind of sensuality must be precious and desirable. If some only, then we are to seek what kind and discover, if we can, what it is which distinguishes between one pleasure and another and makes one indifferent, sorry, mean, another valuable and worthy. And, by this stamp, this character, if there be any such, we must define good, and not by pleasure itself, which may be very great and yet very contemptible. Nor can anyone truly judge the value of any immediate sensation otherwise than by judging first of the situation of his own mind. For that which we esteem a happiness in one situation of mind is otherwise thought of in another. Which situation therefore is the justest must be considered: how to gain that point of sight whence probably we may best discern and how to place ourselves in that unbiassed state in which we are fittest to pronounce.'

'O Philocles,' replied he, 'if this be unfeignedly your sentiment, if it be possible you should have the fortitude to withhold your assent in this affair,[10] and go in search of what the meanest of mankind think they already know so certainly, it is from a nobler turn of thought than what you have observed in any of the modern sceptics you have conversed with. For if I mistake not, there are hardly anywhere at this day a sort of people more peremptory or who deliberate less on the choice of good. They who pretend to such a scrutiny of other evidences are the readiest to take the evidence of the greatest deceivers in the world, their own passions. Having gained, as they think, a liberty from some seeming constraints of religion, they suppose they employ this liberty to perfection by following the first motion of their will and assenting to the first dictate or report of any prepossessing fancy,[11] any foremost opinion or conceit of

[10] See p. 38.
[11] See p. 143ff.

good. So that their privilege is only that of being perpetually amused and their liberty that of being imposed on in their most important choice. I think one may say with assurance that "the greatest of fools is he who imposes on himself, and in his greatest concern thinks certainly he knows that which he has least studied, and of which he is most profoundly ignorant". He who is ignorant but knows his ignorance is far wiser. And to do justice to these fashionable men of wit, they are not all of them, indeed, so insensible as not to perceive something of their own blindness and absurdity. For often when they seriously reflect on their past pursuits and engagements they freely own that "for what remains of life they know not whether they shall be of a piece with themselves or whether their fancy, humour or passion will not hereafter lead them to a quite different choice in pleasure and to a disapprobation of all they ever enjoyed before". – Comfortable reflection!

To bring the satisfactions of the mind', continued he, 'and the enjoyments of reason and judgment under the denomination of pleasure is only a collusion and a plain receding from the common notion of the word. They deal not fairly with us who in their philosophical hour admit that for pleasure which at an ordinary time and in the common practice of life is so little taken for such. The mathematician who labours at his problem, the bookish man who toils, the artist who endures voluntarily the greatest hardships and fatigues – none of these are said "to follow pleasure". Nor will the men of pleasure by any means admit them to be of their number. The satisfactions which are purely mental and depend only on the motion of a thought must in all likelihood be too refined for the apprehensions of our modern epicures, who are so taken up with pleasure of a more substantial kind. They who are full of the idea of such a sensible solid good can have but a slender fancy for the mere spiritual and intellectual sort. But it is this latter they set up and magnify upon occasion to save the ignominy which may redound to them from the former. This done, the latter may take its chance: its use is presently at an end. For it is observable that, when the men of this sort have recommended the enjoyments of the mind under the title of pleasure, when they have thus dignified the word and included in it whatever is mentally good or excellent, they can afterwards suffer it contentedly to slide down again into its own genuine and vulgar sense, whence they raised it only to serve a turn. When pleasure is called in question and attacked, then reason and virtue are called in to her aid and made principal parts of her constitution. A complicated form appears and comprehends straight all which is generous, honest and beautiful in human life. But when the attack is over and the objection once solved, the spectre vanishes. Pleasure returns again to her former shape. She may even be pleasure still and have as little concern with dry, sober reason as in the nature of the thing and according to common understanding she really has. For, if this rational sort of enjoyment be admitted into the notion of good, how is it possible to admit withal that kind of sensation which in effect is rather opposite to this enjoyment? It is certain that in respect of the mind and its enjoyments, the eagerness and irritation of mere pleasure is as disturbing as the importunity and vexation of pain. If either throws the mind off its bias and deprives it of the satisfaction it takes in its natural exercise and employment, the mind in this case must be sufferer as well by one as by the other. If neither does this, there is no harm on either side . . .'

'By the way,' said I, interrupting him, 'as sincere as I am in questioning whether pleasure be really good, I am not such a sceptic as to doubt whether pain be really ill.'

'Whatever is grievous', replied he, 'can be no other than ill. But what is grievous to one is not so much as troublesome to another, let sportsmen, soldiers and others of the hardy kinds be witness. Nay, that what is pain to one is pleasure to another, and so alternately, we very well know, since men vary in their apprehension of these sensations and on many occasions confound one with the other. Has not even nature herself in some respects, as it were, blended them together and, as a wise man said once, "joined the extremity of one so nicely to the other that it absolutely runs into it and is indistinguishable"?'

'In fine then,' said I, 'if pleasure and pain be thus convertible and mixed, if, according to your account, "that which is now pleasure, by being strained a little too far, runs into pain, and pain, when carried far, creates again the highest pleasure by mere cessation and a kind of natural succession; if some pleasures to some are pains, and some pains to others are pleasures", all this, if I mistake not, makes still for my opinion and shows that there is nothing you can assign which can really stand as good. For if pleasure be not good, nothing is. And if pain be ill, as I must necessarily take for granted, we have a shrewd chance on the ill side indeed, but none at all on the better. So that we may fairly doubt "whether life itself be not mere misery", since gainers by it we can never be; losers we may sufficiently and are like to be every hour of our lives. Accordingly, what our English poetess says of good should be just and proper: "It is good not to be born." And thus for anything of good which can be expected in life, we may even "beg pardon of nature and return her present on her hands without waiting for her call". For what should hinder us or what are we the better for living?'

'The query', said he, 'is pertinent. But why such dispatch if the case be doubtful? This surely, my good Philocles, is a plain transgression of your sceptical bounds. We must be sufficiently dogmatical to come to this determination. It is a deciding as well concerning death as life, "what possibly may be hereafter and what not?". Now to be assured that we can never be concerned in anything hereafter, we must understand perfectly what it is which concerns or engages us in anything present. We must truly know ourselves and in what this self of ours consists. We must determine against pre-existence and give a better reason for our having never been concerned in anything before our birth than merely "because we remember not nor are conscious". For in many things we have been concerned to purpose, of which we have now no memory or consciousness remaining. And thus we may happen to be again and again to perpetuity, for any reason we can show to the contrary. All is revolution in us. We are no more the self-same matter or system of matter from one day to another. What succession there may be hereafter we know not since even now we live by succession and only perish and are renewed. It is in vain we flatter ourselves with the assurance of our interest's ending with a certain shape or form. What interested us at first in it, we know not, any more than how we have since held on and continue still concerned in such an assemblage of fleeting particles. Where besides or in what else we may have to do, perchance, in time to come, we know as little nor can tell how chance or providence hereafter may dispose of us. And if providence be in the case, we have still more reason to consider how we undertake to be our own disposers. It must needs become a sceptic above all men to hesitate in matters of exchange. And though he acknowledges no present good or enjoyment in life, he must be sure, however, of bettering his condition before he attempts to alter it. But, as yet, Philocles, even this point remains undetermined between us, "whether in this present life there be not such a thing as real good".'

'Be you therefore,' said I, 'my instructor, sagacious Theocles, and inform me "what that good is, or where, which can afford contentment and satisfaction always alike without variation or diminution". For though on some occasions and in some subjects, the mind may possibly be so bent and the passion so wrought up that for the time no bodily sufferance or pain can alter it, yet this is what can seldom happen and is unlikely to last long since, without any pain or inconvenience, the passion in a little time does its own work, the mind relaxes with its bent and the temper wearied with repetition finds no more enjoyment but runs to something new.'

'Hear then!,' said Theocles. 'For though I pretend not to tell you at once the nature of this which I call good, yet I am content to show you something of it in yourself, which you will acknowledge to be naturally more fixed and constant than anything you have hitherto thought on. Tell me, my friend, if ever you were weary of doing good to those you loved? Say when you ever found it unpleasing to serve a friend? Or whether, when you first proved this generous pleasure, you did not feel it less than at this present, after so long experience? Believe me, Philocles, this pleasure is more debauching than any other. Never did any soul do good, but it came readier to do the same again with more enjoyment. Never was love or gratitude or bounty practised but with increasing joy, which made the practiser still more in love with the fair act. Answer me, Philocles, you who are such a judge of beauty and have so good a taste of pleasure: Is there anything you admire so fair as friendship, or anything so charming as a generous action? What would it be, therefore, if all life were in reality but one continued friendship and could be made one such entire act? Here surely would be that fixed and constant good you sought. Or would you look for anything beyond?'

'Perhaps not,' said I. 'But I can never, surely, go beyond this to seek for a chimera, if this good of yours be not thoroughly chimerical. For though a poet may possibly work up such a single action, so as to hold a play out, I can conceive but very faintly how this high strain of friendship can be so managed as to fill a life. Nor can I imagine where the object lies of such a sublime, heroic passion.'

'Can any friendship', said he, 'be so heroic as that towards mankind? Do you think the love of friends in general and of one's country to be nothing, or that particular friendship can well subsist without such an enlarged affection and sense of obligation to society? Say, if possible, you are a friend but hate your country. Say, you are true to the interest of a companion but false to that of society. Can you believe yourself? Or will you lay the name aside and refuse to be called the friend since you renounce the man?'

'That there is something', said I, 'due to mankind is what I think will not be disputed by one who claims the name of friend. Hardly indeed could I allow the name of man to one who never could call or be called "friend". But he who justly proves himself a friend is man enough nor is he wanting to society. A single friendship may acquit him. He has deserved a friend and is man's friend, though not in strictness or according to your high moral sense, the friend of mankind. For, to say truth as to this sort of friendship, it may by wiser heads be esteemed perhaps more than ordinarily manly and even heroic, as you assert it, but, for my part, I see so very little worth in mankind and have so indifferent an opinion of the public that I can propose little satisfaction to myself in loving either.'

'Do you, then, take bounty and gratitude to be among the acts of friendship and good-nature?'

'Undoubtedly, for they are the chief.'

'Suppose then that the obliged person discovers in the obliger several failings. Does this exclude the gratitude of the former?'

'Not in the least.'

'Or does it make the exercise of gratitude less pleasing?'

'I think rather the contrary. For when deprived of other means of making a return, I might rejoice still in that sure way of showing my gratitude to my benefactor by bearing his failings as a friend.'

'And, as to bounty, tell me, I beseech you: is it to those only who are deserving that we should do good? Is it only to a good neighbour or relation, a good father, child, or brother? Or does nature, reason and humanity better teach us to do good still to a father because a father and to a child because a child and so to every relation in human life?'

'I think', said I, 'this last is rightest.'

'O Philocles,' replied he, 'consider then what it was you said when you objected against the love of mankind because of human frailty and seemed to scorn the public because of its misfortunes. See if this sentiment be consistent with that humanity which elsewhere you own and practise. For where can generosity exist if not here? Where can we ever exert friendship if not in this chief subject? To what should we be true or grateful in the world if not to mankind and that society to which we are so deeply indebted? What are the faults or blemishes which can excuse such an omission or, in a grateful mind, can ever lessen the satisfaction of making a grateful, kind return? Can you then out of good breeding merely, and from a temper natural to you, rejoice to show civility, courteousness, obligingness, seek objects of compassion, and be pleased with every occurrence where you have power to do some service even to people unknown? Can you delight in such adventures abroad in foreign countries or, in the case of strangers here at home, to help, assist, relieve all who require it, in the most hospitable, kind and friendly manner? And can your country or, what is more, your kind require less kindness from you or deserve less to be considered than even one of these chance creatures? O Philocles! How little do you know the extent and power of good nature and to what an heroic pitch a soul may rise which knows the thorough force of it and, distributing it rightly, frames in itself an equal, just and universal friendship!'

Just as he had ended these words, a servant came to us in the field to give notice of some company who were come to dine with us and waited our coming in. So we walked homewards. I told Theocles, going along, that I feared I should never make a good friend or lover after his way. As for a plain natural love of one single person in either sex, I could compass it, I thought, well enough, but this complex, universal sort was beyond my reach. I could love the individual but not the species. This was too mysterious, too metaphysical an object for me. In short, I could love nothing of which I had not some sensible, material image.

'How!,' replied Theocles. 'Can you never love except in this manner when yet I know that you admired and loved a friend long before you knew his person? Or was Palemon's character of no force when it engaged you in that long correspondence which preceded your late personal acquaintance?'

'The fact,' said I, 'I must of necessity own to you. And now, methinks, I understand your mystery and perceive how I must prepare for it. For, in the same manner as when I first began to love Palemon, I was forced to form a kind of material object and had always such a certain image of him ready drawn in my mind whenever I thought of him, so I must endeavour to order it in the case before us, if possibly by your help I can raise any such image or spectre as may represent this odd being you would have me love.'

'Methinks', said he, 'you might have the same indulgence for nature or mankind as for the people of old Rome, whom, notwithstanding their blemishes, I have known you in love with, many ways, particularly under the representation of a beautiful youth called "the genius of the people".[S] For I remember that, viewing once some pieces of antiquity where the people were thus represented, you allowed them to be no disagreeable object.'

'Indeed,' replied I, 'were it possible for me to stamp upon my mind such a figure as you speak of, whether it stood for mankind or nature, it might probably have its effect, and I might become perhaps a lover after your way, but, more especially, if you could so order it as to make things reciprocal between us and bring me to fancy of this genius that it could be "sensible of my love and capable of a return". For without this I should make but an ill lover, though of the perfectest beauty in the world.'

'It is enough,' said Theocles, 'I accept the terms and, if you promise to love, I will endeavour to show you that beauty which I count the perfectest and most deserving of love and which will not fail of a return. Tomorrow, when the eastern sun (as poets describe) with his first beams adorns the front of yonder hill, there, if you are content to wander with me in the woods you see, we will pursue those loves of ours by favour of the sylvan nymphs, and, invoking first the genius of the place,[T] we will try to obtain at least some faint and distant view of the sovereign genius and first beauty. This if you can come once to contemplate, I will answer for it that all those forbidding features and deformities, whether of nature or mankind, will vanish in an instant and leave you that love I could wish.

But now, enough! Let us to our company and change this conversation for some other more suitable to our friends and table.'

Section 2

You see here, Palemon, what a foundation is laid for the enthusiasms I told you of and which, in my opinion (I told you too) were the more dangerous, because so very odd and out of the way. But curiosity had seized you, I perceived, as it had done me before. For, after this first conversation, I must own, I longed for nothing so much as the next day and the appointed morning walk in the woods.

We had only a friend or two at dinner with us and for a good while we

---

[S] Roman sculptors often represented personifications of localities (*genius loci*) or classes of society (*genius populi romani*) as youthful male figures, naked or draped.

[T] Or *genius loci* in Latin, as in Virgil, *Aeneid* 5.95 and 7.136: the attendant god or spirit of a place or, figuratively, the associations of a place or the inspirations to which it gives rise.

discoursed of news and indifferent things, till I, who had my head still running upon those other subjects, gladly laid hold of something dropped by chance concerning friendship and said that 'for my own part, truly, though I once thought I had known friendship and really counted myself a good friend during my whole life, yet I was now persuaded to believe myself no better than a learner, since Theocles had almost convinced me that to be a friend to any one in particular, it was necessary to be first a friend to mankind. But how to qualify myself for such a friendship was, methought, no little difficulty.'

'Indeed,' said Theocles, 'you have given us a very indifferent character of yourself in saying so. If you had spoken thus of the friendship of any great man at court or perhaps of a court itself and had complained "how hard it was for you to succeed or make interest with such as governed there", we should have concluded in your behalf that there were such terms to be complied with as were unworthy of you. But "to deserve well of the public" and "to be justly styled the friend of mankind" requires no more than to be good and virtuous, terms which for one's own sake one would naturally covet.'

'How comes it then', said I, 'that even these good terms themselves are so ill accepted and hardly ever taken (if I may so express it) except on further terms? For virtue by itself is thought but an ill bargain, and I know few, even of the religious and devout, who take up with it any otherwise than as children do with physic, where the rod and sweetmeat are the potent motives.'

'They are children indeed,' replied Theocles, 'and should be treated so, who need any force or persuasion to do what conduces to their health and good. But where, I beseech you, are those forbidding circumstances which should make virtue go down so hardly? Is it not, among other things, that you think yourself by this means precluded the fine tables and costly eating of our modern epicures and that perhaps you fear the being reduced to eat always as ill as now, upon a plain dish or two and no more?'

This, I protested, was injuriously supposed of me. For I wished never to eat otherwise than I now did at his table, which, by the way, had more resemblance, I thought, of Epicurus' than those which nowadays preposterously passed under his name. For, if his opinion might be taken, the highest pleasures in the world were owing to temperance and moderate use.

'If then the merest studier of pleasure,' answered Theocles, 'even Epicurus himself, made that favourable report of temperance, so different from his modern disciples, if he could boldly say that "with such fare as a mean garden afforded, he could vie even with the gods for happiness", how shall we say of this part of virtue that it needs be taken upon terms?[U] If the immediate practice of temperance be thus harmless, are its consequences injurious? Does it

---

[U] According to Aelian, *Miscellany* 4.13, Epicurus said that he rivalled Zeus in happiness so long as he had bread and water.

take from the vigour of the mind, consume the body and render both the one and the other less apt to their proper exercises, "the enjoyments of reason or sense or the employments and offices of civil life"? Or is it that a man's circumstances are the worse for it, as he stands towards his friends or mankind? Is a gentleman in this sense to be pitied "as one burdensome to himself and others, one whom all men will naturally shun as an ill friend and a corrupter of society and good manners"? Shall we consider our gentleman in a public trust and see whether he is like to succeed best with this restraining quality, or whether he may be more relied on, and thought more incorrupt, if his appetites are high and his relish strong towards that which we call pleasure? Shall we consider him as a soldier in a campaign or siege and advise with ourselves how we might be best defended if we had occasion for such a one's service? "Which officer would make the best for the soldiers, which soldier for the officers, or which army for their country?" What think you of our gentleman for a fellow-traveller? Would he, as a temperate man, be an ill choice? Would it indeed be more eligible and delightful "to have a companion who, in any shift or necessity, would prove the most ravenous and eager to provide in the first place for himself and his own exquisite sensations"? I know not what to say where beauty is concerned. Perhaps the amorous *galants*[V] and exquisite refiners on this sort of pleasure may have so refined their minds and tempers that, notwithstanding their accustomed indulgence, they can upon occasion renounce their enjoyment rather than violate honour, faith or justice. And, thus at last there will be little virtue or worth ascribed to this patient, sober character. "The dull, temperate man is no fitter to be trusted than the elegant, luxurious one. Innocence, youth and fortune may be as well committed to the care of this latter gentleman. He would prove as good an executor, as good a trustee, as good a guardian, as he would a friend. The family which entrusted him would be secure, and no dishonour in any likelihood would happen from the honest man of pleasure."'

The seriousness with which Theocles spoke this made it the more pleasant and set our other company upon saying a great many good things on the same subject in commendation of a temperate life. So that, our dinner by this time being ended and the wine, according to custom, placed before us, I found still we were in no likelihood of proceeding to a debauch. Everyone drank only as he fancied, in no order or proportion and with no regard to circular healths or pledges – a manner which the sociable men of another scheme of morals would have censured no doubt as a heinous irregularity and corruption of good fellowship.[W]

[V] Gallants, ladies' men.

[W] Healths and pledges were toasts to the honour of someone present at a gathering or of an admired personage elsewhere. Such rituals of drinking originated in upper-class circles, radiating down the social scale. According to Peter Clark, the 1660–1750 period saw the zenith of toasting (*The English Alehouse: A Social History 1200–1830* (Harlow, Essex: Longman, 1983)).

'I own', said I, 'I am far from thinking temperance so disagreeable a character. As for this part of virtue, I think there is no need of taking it on any other terms to recommend it than the mere advantage of being saved from intemperance and from the desire of things unnecessary.'

'How', said Theocles, 'are you thus far advanced? And can you carry this temperance so far as to estates and honours by opposing it to avarice and ambition? Nay, then truly you may be said to have fairly embarked yourself in this cause. You have passed the channel and are more than half-seas over. There remains no further scruple in the case of virtue unless you will declare yourself a coward or conclude it a happiness to be born one. For, if you can be temperate withal towards life and think it not so great a business whether it be of fewer or more years but, satisfied with what you have lived, can rise a thankful guest from a full, liberal entertainment, is not this the sum of all, the finishing stroke and very accomplishment of virtue? In this temper of mind, what is there can hinder us from forming for ourselves as heroic a character as we please? What is there, either good, generous or great, which does not naturally flow from such a modest temperance? Let us once gain this simple, plain-looked virtue and see whether the more shining virtues will not follow. See what that country of the mind will produce when, by the wholesome laws of this legislatress, it has obtained its liberty! You, Philocles, who are such an admirer of civil liberty and can represent it to yourself with a thousand several graces and advantages, can you imagine no grace or beauty in that original, native liberty which sets us free from so many inborn tyrannies, gives us the privilege of ourselves and makes us our own and independent? A sort of property which, methinks, is as material to us to the full as that which secures us our lands or revenues.

I should think', said he, carrying on his humour, 'that one might draw the picture of this moral dame to as much advantage as that of her political sister, whom you admire, as described to us, "in her Amazon-dress, with a free, manly air becoming her; her guards the laws, with their written tables, like bucklers, surrounding her; riches, traffic and plenty, with the cornucopia, serving as her attendants; and in her train the arts and sciences, like children, playing". The rest of the piece is easy to imagine: "her triumph over tyranny and lawless rule of lust and passion". (But what a triumph would her sister's be! What monsters of savage passions would there appear subdued!) "There fierce ambition, lust, uproar, misrule, with all the fiends which rage in human breasts, would be securely chained. And, when fortune herself, the queen of flatteries, with that prince of terrors, death, were at the chariot wheels as captives, how natural would it be to see fortitude, magnanimity, justice, honour, and all that generous band attend as the companions of our inmate Lady Liberty! She, like some new-born goddess, would grace her mother's chariot and own her birth from humble temperance, that nursing mother of the virtues, who like the parent of the gods, old reverend Cybele, would properly appear drawn by reined lions, patient of the bit, and on her head a turret-like attire, the image of defensive power and strength of mind." [X]

By this picture, Theocles, I found, had given entertainment to the company, who, from this rough draft of his, fell to designing upon the same subject after the ancient manner till Prodicus and Cebes and all the ancients were exhausted. [Y]

'Gentlemen,' said I, 'the descriptions you have been making are, no doubt, the finest in the world, but, after all, when you have made virtue as glorious and triumphant as you please, I will bring you an authentic picture of another kind, where we shall see this triumph in reverse: "Virtue herself a captive in her turn and by a proud conqueror triumphed over, degraded, spoiled of all her honours and defaced, so as to retain hardly one single feature of real beauty." '

I offered to go on further but could not, being so violently decried by my two fellow guests, who protested they would never be brought to own so detestable a picture. And one of them, a formal sort of gentleman somewhat advanced in years, looking earnestly upon me, said, in an angry tone, that he had hitherto, indeed, conceived some hopes of me, notwithstanding he observed my freedom of thought and heard me quoted for such a passionate lover of liberty, but he was sorry to find that my principle of liberty extended in fine to 'a liberty from all principles', so he expressed himself, 'and none', he thought, 'beside a libertine in principle would approve of such a picture of virtue as only an atheist could have the impudence to make'.

Theocles the while sat silent, though he saw I minded not my antagonists but kept my eye fixed steadily on himself, expecting to hear what he would

---

[X] The 'pictures' of moral and political liberty drew on the iconography of Libertas, a personified deity at Rome, and informed the engraved frontispiece for Volume II (containing 'The Moralists') of the second edition of *Characteristics*: see Felix Paknadel, 'Shaftesbury's Illustrations of *Characteristics*', *Journal of the Warburg and Courtauld Institutes* 37 (1974): 290–312. Cybele, an Anatolian fertility goddess imported into Greece and then Rome, was sometimes said to be the wife of the Greek Cronos or the Roman Saturn, father of Zeus. Cybele was often represented in the company of lions, sometimes being drawn by them in a chariot.

[Y] Prodicus was a sophist and contemporary of Socrates. In Xenophon's *Memorabilia*, Socrates repeated Prodicus' account of the incident known as 'Hercules at the Crossroads' or 'The Choice (or Judgment) of Hercules', in which the young hero chose between the rival claims of virtue and pleasure (or vice). Frequently repeated and given graphic representation over the centuries, the incident was the subject of Shaftesbury's *Notion of the Historical Draught or Tablature of the Judgment of Hercules*, first published in French in 1712 and in English in 1713, and of the painting on the subject, commissioned by Shaftesbury, by Paolo de Mattheis. Cebes of Thebes was a pupil of Socrates to whom the dialogue, *The Picture of Cebes*, was often ascribed. (The dialogue actually dated from the first century AD.) In the dialogue, a painting – a kind of topographical allegory – was explicated to unfold Socratic meanings, such as the identity of knowledge and virtue and the primacy of character in education. In his planned companion volume to *Characteristics* concerning the visual arts, Shaftesbury intended to include both *A Notion of the Historical Draught* and a new commentary on *The Picture of Cebes*.

say. At last, fetching a deep sigh, 'O Philocles,' said he, 'how well you are master of that cause you have taken on you to defend! How well you know the way to gain advantage to the worst of causes from the imprudent management of those who defend the best! I dare not, for my own share, affirm to you, as my worthy friends have done, that "it is the atheist alone can lay this load on virtue and picture her thus disgracefully". No. There are other over-officious and less suspected hands which do her perhaps more injury though with a better colour.

That virtue should, with any show of reason, be made a victim,' continued he, turning himself to his guests, 'must have appeared strange to you, no doubt, to hear asserted with such assurance as has been done by Philocles. You could conceive no tolerable ground for such a spectacle. In this "reversed triumph" you expected perhaps to see some foreign conqueror exalted, as either vice itself or pleasure, wit, spurious philosophy or some false image of truth or nature. Little were you aware that the cruel enemy opposed to virtue should be religion itself! But you will call to mind that even innocently, and without any treacherous design, virtue is often treated so by those who would magnify to the utmost the corruption of man's heart and, in exposing, as they pretend, the falsehood of human virtue, think to extol religion. How many religious authors, how many sacred orators, turn all their edge this way and strike at moral virtue as a kind of step-dame or rival to religion! "Morality must not be named; nature has no pretence; reason is an enemy; common justice, folly; and virtue, misery. Who would not be vicious had he his choice? Who would forbear but because he must? Or who would value virtue but for hereafter?"'[12]

'Truly,' said the old gentleman, interrupting him, 'if this be the triumph of religion, it is such as her greatest enemy, I believe, would scarce deny her, and I must still be of opinion (with Philocles' leave) that it is no great sign of tenderness for religion to be so zealous in honouring her at the cost of virtue.'

'Perhaps so,' said I. 'Yet that there are many such zealots in the world you will acknowledge. And that there is a certain harmony between this zeal and what you call atheism, Theocles, you hear, has allowed. But let us hear him out, if perhaps he will be so free as to discover to us what he thinks of the generality of our religious writers and their method of encountering their common enemy, the atheist. This is a subject which possibly may need a better clearing. For it is notorious that the chief opposers of atheism write upon contrary principles to one another, so as in a manner to confute themselves. Some of them hold zealously for virtue, and are realists in the point. Others, one may say, are only nominal moralists by making virtue nothing in itself, a creature of will only or a mere name of fashion.[z] It is the same in natural philosophy:

[z] On Shaftesbury's hostility to nominalism, see Introduction, p. xxviii.

[12] See p. 469.

some take one hypothesis and some another. I should be glad to discover once the true foundation, and distinguish those who effectually refute their other antagonists as well as the atheists, and rightly assert the joint cause of virtue and religion.'

Here, Palemon, I had my wish. For, by degrees, I engaged Theocles to discover himself fully upon these subjects, which served as a prelude to those we were to engage in the next morning, for the approach of which I so impatiently longed. If his speculations proved of a rational kind, this previous discourse, I knew, would help me to comprehend them; if only pleasing fancies, this would help me, however, to please myself the better with them.

Here then began his criticism of authors, which grew by degrees into a continued discourse. So that, had this been at a university, Theocles might very well have passed for some grave divinity professor or teacher of ethics, reading an afternoon lecture to his pupils.

Section 3

'It would be undoubtedly', said he, 'a happy cause which could have the benefit of such managers as should never give their adversaries any handle of advantage against it. I could wish that in the cause of religion we had reason to boast as much. But since it is not impossible to write ill even in the best of causes, I am inclined to think this great one of religion may have run at least an equal hazard with any other, since they who write in defence of it are apt generally to use so much the less caution as they are more exempt from the fear of censure or criticism in their own person. Their adversary is well secured and silenced to their hand. They may safely provoke him to a field where he cannot appear openly or as a professed antagonist. His weapons are private and can often reach the cause without offence to its maintainers, while no direct attack robs them of their imaginary victory. They conquer for themselves and expect to be approved still for their zeal, however the cause itself may have suffered in their hands.'

'Perhaps then,' said I, interrupting him, 'it may be true enough what was said once by a person who seemed zealous for religion, that "none writ well against the atheists beside the clerk who drew the warrant for their execution".'

'If this were the true writing,' replied he, 'there would be an end of all dispute or reasoning in the case. For where force is necessary, reason has nothing to do. But, on the other hand, if reason be needful, force in the meanwhile must be laid aside, for there is no enforcement of reason but by reason. And therefore, if atheists are to be reasoned with at all, they are to be reasoned with like other men, since there is no other way in nature to convince them.'

'This I own', said I, 'seems rational and just, but I am afraid that most of the devout people will be found ready to abandon the patient for the more concise method. And, though force without reason may be thought somewhat hard, yet your other way of reason without force, I am apt to think, would meet with fewer admirers.'

'But perhaps,' replied Theocles, 'it is a mere sound which troubles us. The word or name of "atheist" may possibly occasion some disturbance, by being made to describe two characters so very different as his who absolutely denies and his who only doubts. Now he who doubts may possibly lament his own unhappiness and wish to be convinced. He who denies is daringly presumptuous and sets up an opinion against the interest of mankind and being of society. It is easily seen that one of these persons may bear a due respect to the magistrate and laws, though not the other, who being obnoxious to them is therefore punishable. But how the former is punishable by man will be hard to say, unless the magistrate had dominion over minds as well as over actions and behaviour and had power to exercise an inquisition within the inmost bosoms and secret thoughts of men.'

'I apprehend you,' said I. 'And by your account, as there are two sorts of people who are called atheists, so there are two ways of writing against them, which may be fitly used apart but not so well jointly. You would set aside mere menaces and separate the philosopher's work from the magistrate's, taking it for granted that the more discreet and sober part of unbelievers, who come not under the dispatching pen of the magistrate, can be affected only by the more deliberate and gentle one of philosophy. Now the language of the magistrate, I must confess, has little in common with that of philosophy. Nothing can be more unbecoming the magisterial authority than a philosophical style, and nothing can be more unphilosophical than a magisterial one. A mixture of these must needs spoil both. And therefore, in the cause before us, if anyone besides the magistrate can be said to write well, it is he (according to your account) who writes as becomes philosophy, with freedom of debate and fairness towards his adversary.'

'Allow it,' replied he. 'For what can be more equitable?'

'Nothing. But will the world be of the same opinion? And may this method of writing be justly practised in it?'

'Undoubtedly it may. And for a proof we have many instances in antiquity to produce. The freedom taken in this philosophical way was never esteemed injurious to religion or prejudicial to the vulgar, since we find it to have been a practice both in writing and converse among the great men of a virtuous and religious people and that even those magistrates who officiated at the altars and were the guardians of the public worship were sharers in these free debates.'

'Forgive me, Theocles,' said I, 'if I presume to say that still this reaches not the case before us. We are to consider Christian times, such as are now present. You know the common fate of those who dare to appear fair authors. What was that pious and learned man's case who wrote *The Intellectual System of the Universe?*[AA] I confess it was pleasant enough to consider that, though the whole world were no less satisfied with his capacity and learning than with his sincerity in the cause of deity, yet was he accused of giving the upper hand to the atheists for having only stated their reasons and those of their adversaries fairly together. And among other writings of this kind you may remember how a certain fair *Inquiry* (as you called it) was received and what offence was taken at it.'[BB]

'I am sorry,' said Theocles, 'it proved so. But now indeed you have found a way which may, perhaps, force me to discourse at large with you on this head by entering the lists in defence of a friend unjustly censured for this philosophical liberty.'

I confessed to Theocles and the company that this had really been my aim and that, for this reason alone, I made myself the accuser of this author, whom I here actually charged, as I did all those other moderate calm writers, with no less than profaneness for reasoning so unconcernedly and patiently, without the least show of zeal or passion, upon the subject of a deity and a future state.

'And I, on the other side,' replied Theocles, 'am rather for this patient way of reasoning and will endeavour to clear my friend of this imputation, if you can have patience enough to hear me out in an affair of such a compass.'

We all answered for ourselves, and he began thus:

'Of the many writers engaged in the defence of religion, it seems to me that the greatest part are employed either in supporting the truth of the Christian faith in general, or in refuting such particular doctrines as are esteemed innovations in the Christian church. There are not, it is thought, many persons in the world who are loose in the very grounds and principles of all religion and, to such as these we find, indeed, there are not many writers who purposely apply themselves. They may think it a mean labour and scarce becoming them to argue sedately with such as are almost universally treated with detestation and horror. But as we are required by our religion to have charity for all men, so we cannot surely avoid having a real concern for those whom we apprehend to be under the worst of errors and whom we find by experience to be with the greatest difficulty reclaimed. Neither ought they perhaps in prudence to be treated with so little regard whose number, however small, is thought to be rather increasing, and this, too, among the people of no despicable rank.[CC] So

---

[AA] On the response to Ralph Cudworth's *True Intellectual System of the Universe*, published in 1678, see John Redwood, *Reason, Ridicule and Religion: The Age of Enlightenment in England* (Cambridge, MA: Harvard University Press, 1976), pp. 50–60. On Shaftesbury's relation to Cudworth, see Introduction, p. xxix.

[BB] A reference to Shaftesbury's own *Inquiry Concerning Virtue* as it was first published in 1699. This version elicited one known response, Robert Day's *Free Thoughts in Defence of a Future State* (1700).

[CC] On the problem of atheism in contemporary debate, see Redwood, *Reason, Ridicule and Religion*, pp. 29–48.

that it may well deserve some consideration, whether in our age and country the same remedies may serve which have hitherto been tried, or whether some other may not be preferred, as being suitable to times of less strictness in matters of religion and places less subject to authority.

This might be enough to put an author upon thinking of such a way of reasoning with these deluded persons, as in his opinion might be more effectual for their benefit, than the repeated exclamations and invectives with which most of the arguments used against them are commonly accompanied. Nor was it so absurd to imagine that a quite different method might be attempted, by which a writer might offer reason to these men with so much more favour and advantage as he appeared unprepossessed and willing to examine everything with the greatest unconcern and indifference. For to such persons as these it is to be feared it will always appear that what was never questioned was never proved and that whatever subject had not, at some time or other, been examined with perfect indifference, was never rightly examined nor could rightly be believed. And, in a treatise of this kind, offered as an essay or inquiry only, they would be far from finding that impartiality and indifference which is requisite if, instead of a readiness to comply with whatever consequences such an examination as this and the course of reasoning brought forth, the author should show a previous inclination to the consequences only on one side and an abhorrence of any conclusion on the other.

Others, therefore, in different circumstances may perhaps have found it necessary and becoming their character to show all manner of detestation both of the persons and principles of these men. Our author, on the contrary, whose character exceeds not that of a layman, endeavours to show civility and favour by keeping the fairest measures he possibly can with the men of this sort, allowing them all he is able and arguing with a perfect indifference, even on the subject of a deity. He offers to conclude nothing positive himself but leaves it to others to draw conclusions from his principles, having this one chief aim and intention: how, in the first place, to reconcile these persons to the principles of virtue that, by this means, a way might be laid open to religion by removing those greatest, if not only obstacles to it, which arise from the vices and passions of men.

It is upon this account he endeavours chiefly to establish virtue on principles by which he is able to argue with those who are not as yet induced to own a god or future state. If he cannot do thus much, he reckons he does nothing. For how can supreme goodness be intelligible to those who know not what goodness itself is? Or how can virtue be understood to deserve reward when as yet its merit and excellence is unknown? We begin surely at the wrong end when we would prove merit by favour and order by a deity.

This our friend seeks to redress. For being, in respect of *virtue*, what you lately called a realist, he endeavours to show that *it is really something in itself and in the nature of things, not arbitrary or factitious (if I may so speak), not constituted from without or dependent on custom, fancy or will, not even on the supreme will itself, which can no way govern it but, being necessarily good, is governed by it and ever uniform with it.* And, notwithstanding he has thus made virtue his chief subject and in some measure independent on religion, yet I fancy he may possibly appear at last as high a divine as he is a moralist.

I would not willingly advance it as a rule that those who make only a name of virtue make no more of deity and cannot without affectation defend the principles of religion; but this I will venture to assert, that *whoever sincerely defends virtue and is a realist in morality must of necessity, in a manner, by the same scheme of reasoning, prove as very a realist in divinity.*

All affectation but chiefly in philosophy, I must own, I think unpardonable. And you, Philocles, who can give no quarter to ill reasoning nor endure any unsound or inconsistent hypothesis, you will be so ingenuous, I dare say, as to reject our modern deism and challenge those who assume a name to which their philosophy can never in the least entitle them.

Commend me to honest Epicurus, who raises his deities aloft in the imaginary spaces and, setting them apart out of the universe and nature of things, makes nothing of them beyond a word.[DD] This is ingenuous and plain dealing, for this everyone who philosophizes may easily understand.

The same ingenuity belongs to those philosophers whom you, Philocles, seem inclined to favour. When a sceptic questions "whether a real theology can be raised out of philosophy alone without the help of revelation", he does no more than pay a handsome compliment to authority and the received religion. He can impose on no one who reasons deeply, since whoever does so will easily conceive that at this rate theology must have no foundation at all. For revelation itself, we know, is founded on the acknowledgment of a divine existence, and it is the province of philosophy alone to prove what revelation only supposes.

I look on it therefore as a most unfair way for those who would be builders and undertake this proving part to lay such a foundation as is insufficient to bear the structure. Supplanting and undermining may in other cases be fair war, but in philosophical disputes it is not allowable to work underground or, as in sieges, by the sap. Nothing can be more unbecoming than to talk magisterially and in venerable terms of "a supreme nature", "an infinite being", and "a deity" when all the while a providence is never meant nor anything like order or the government of a mind admitted. For, when these are understood and real divinity acknowledged, the notion is not dry and barren, but such

---

[DD] Though Epicurus had a materialist conception of the gods, he did place them at a tremendous remove from human life and in a state of bliss that made them oblivious to human vicissitudes. On Epicurus, see Introduction, p. xxvi.

consequences are necessarily drawn from it as must set us in action and find employment for our strongest affections. All the duties of religion evidently follow hence, and no exception remains against any of those great maxims which revelation has established.

Now whether our friend be unfeignedly and sincerely of this latter sort of real theologists, you will learn best from the consequences of his hypothesis. You will observe whether, instead of ending in mere speculation, it leads to practice, and you will then surely be satisfied when you see such a structure raised as, with the generality of the world, must pass at least for high religion and, with some in all likelihood, for no less than enthusiasm.

For I appeal to you, Philocles, whether there be anything in divinity which you think has more the air of enthusiasm than that notion of divine love such as separates from everything worldly, sensual or meanly interested? A love which is simple, pure and unmixed, which has no other object than merely the excellency of that being itself nor admits of any other thought of happiness than in its single fruition. Now I dare presume you will take it as a substantial proof of my friend's being far enough from irreligion if it be shown that he has espoused this notion, and thinks of making out this high point of divinity from arguments familiar even to those who oppose religion.

According therefore to his hypothesis, he would in the first place, by way of prevention, declare to you that, though the disinterested love of God were the most excellent principle, yet he knew very well that, by the indiscreet zeal of some devout, well-meaning people, it had been stretched too far, perhaps even to extravagance and enthusiasm, as formerly among the mystics of the ancient church, whom these of latter days have followed. On the other hand, that there were those who in opposition to this devout mystic way and, as professed enemies to what they call enthusiasm, had so far exploded everything of this ecstatic kind, as in a manner to have given up devotion, and in reality had left so little of zeal, affection or warmth in what they call their rational religion as to make them much suspected of their sincerity in any. For, though it be natural enough (he would tell you) for a mere political writer to ground his great argument for religion on the necessity of such a belief as that of a future reward and punishment, yet, if you will take his opinion, it is a very ill token of sincerity in religion, and in the Christian religion more especially, to reduce it to such a philosophy as will allow no room to that other principle of love, but treats all of that kind as enthusiasm for so much as aiming at what is called disinterestedness, or teaching the love of God or virtue for God or virtue's sake.

Here, then, we have two sorts of people, according to my friend's account, who in these opposite extremes expose religion to the insults of its adversaries. For as, on one hand, it will be found difficult to defend the notion of that high-raised love, espoused with so much warmth by those devout mystics, so, on the other hand, it will be found as hard a task, upon the principles of these cooler men, to guard religion from the imputation of mercenariness and a slavish spirit. For how shall one deny that to serve God by compulsion, or for interest merely, is servile and mercenary? Is it not evident that the only true and liberal service, paid either to that supreme being or to any other superior, is that which proceeds from an esteem or love of the person served, a sense of duty or gratitude, and a love of the dutiful and grateful part as good and amiable in itself? And where is the injury to religion from such a concession as this? Or what detraction is it from the belief of an after-reward or punishment to own that the service caused by it is not equal to that which is voluntary and with inclination, but is rather disingenuous and of the slavish kind? Is it not still for the good of mankind and of the world that obedience to the rule of right should some way or other be paid, if not in the better way yet at least in this imperfect one? And is it not to be shown that, although this service of fear be allowed ever so low or base, yet, religion still being a discipline and progress of the soul towards perfection, the motive of reward and punishment is primary and of the highest moment with us till, being capable of more sublime instruction, we are led from this servile state to the generous service of affection and love?

To this it is that in our friend's opinion we ought all of us to aspire, so as to endeavour that the excellence of the object, not the reward or punishment, should be our motive, but that where, through the corruption of our nature, the former of these motives is found insufficient to excite to virtue, there the latter should be brought in aid and on no account be undervalued or neglected.

Now this being once established, how can religion be any longer subject to the imputation of mercenariness? But thus we know religion is often charged. "Godliness", say they, "is great gain, nor is God devoutly served for naught." Is this therefore a reproach? Is it confessed there may be a better service, a more generous love? Enough, there needs no more. On this foundation our friend presumes it easy to defend religion, and even that devoutest part, which is esteemed so great a paradox of faith. For, if there be in nature such a service as that of affection and love, there remains then only to consider of the object whether there be really that supreme one we suppose; for, if there be divine excellence in things, if there be in nature a supreme mind or deity, we have then an object consummate and comprehensive of all which is good or excellent. And this object, of all others, must of necessity be the most amiable, the most engaging and of highest satisfaction and enjoyment. Now that there is such a principal object as this in the world, the world alone (if I may say so) by its wise and perfect order must evince. This order, if indeed perfect, excludes all real ill. And that it really does so is what our author so earnestly maintains by solving the best he can those untoward phenomena and ill signs, taken from the course of providence in the seemingly unequal lot of virtue in this world.

It is true, though the appearances hold ever so strongly against virtue and in favour of vice, the objection which arises hence against a deity may be easily removed, and all set right again on the supposal of a future state. This to a Christian, or one already convinced of so great a point, is sufficient to clear every dark cloud of providence. For he needs not be over-and-above solicitous as to the fate of virtue in this world who is secure of hereafter. But the case is otherwise as to the people we are here to encounter. They are at a loss for providence and seek to find it in the world. The aggravation of the appearing disorders in worldly affairs and the blackest representation of society and human nature will hardly help them to this view. It will be difficult for them to read providence in such characters. From so uncomely a face of things below, they will presume to think unfavourably of all above. By the effects they see, they will be inclined to judge the cause and, by the fate of virtue, to determine of a providence. But being once convinced of order and a providence as to things present, they may soon, perhaps, be satisfied even of a future state. For, if virtue be to itself no small reward and vice in a great measure its own punishment, we have a solid ground to go upon. The plain foundations of a distributive justice and due order in this world may lead us to conceive a further building. We apprehend a larger scheme and easily resolve ourselves why things were not completed in this state, but their accomplishment reserved rather to some further period. For had the good and virtuous of mankind been wholly prosperous in this life, had goodness never met with opposition nor merit ever lain under a cloud, where had been the trial, victory or crown of virtue? Where had the virtues had their theatre or whence their names? Where had been temperance or self-denial? Where patience, meekness, magnanimity? Whence have these their being? What merit except from hardship? What virtue without a conflict and the encounter of such enemies as arise both within and from abroad?

But, as many as are the difficulties which virtue has to encounter in this world, her force is yet superior. Exposed as she is here, she is not however abandoned or left miserable. She has enough to raise her above pity though not above our wishes and, as happy as we see her here, we have room for further hopes in her behalf. Her present portion is sufficient to show providence already engaged on her side. And, since there is such provision for her here, such happiness and such advantages even in this life, how probable must it appear that this providential care is extended yet further to a succeeding life and perfected hereafter?

This is what, in our friend's opinion, may be said in behalf of a future state to those who question revelation. It is this must render revelation probable and secure that first step to it, the belief of a deity and providence. A providence must be proved from what we see of order in things present. We must contend for order and, in this part chiefly, where virtue is concerned, all must not be referred to a hereafter. For a disordered state, in which all present care of things is given up, vice uncontrolled and virtue neglected, represents a very chaos and reduces us to the beloved atoms, chance and confusion of the atheists.

What therefore can be worse done in the cause of a deity than to magnify disorder and exaggerate, as some zealous people do, the misfortunes of virtue so far as to render it an unhappy choice with respect to this world? They err widely who propose to turn men to the thoughts of a better world by making them think so ill of this. For to declaim in this manner against virtue to those of a looser faith will make them the less believe a deity but not the more a future state. Nor can it be thought sincerely that any man, by having the most elevated opinion of virtue and of the happiness it creates, was ever the less inclined to the belief of a future state. On the contrary, it will ever be found that, as they who are favourers of vice are always the least willing to hear of a future existence, so they who are in love with virtue are the readiest to embrace that opinion which renders it so illustrious and makes its cause triumphant.

Thus it was that among the ancients the great motive which inclined so many of the wisest to the belief of this doctrine, unrevealed to them, was purely the love of virtue in the persons of those great men, the founders and preservers of societies, the legislators, patriots, deliverers, heroes, whose virtues they were desirous should live and be immortalized. Nor is there at this day anything capable of making this belief more engaging among the good and virtuous than the love of friendship, which creates in them a desire not to be wholly separated by death but that they may enjoy the same blessed society hereafter. How is it possible, then, that an author should, for exalting virtue merely, be deemed an enemy to a future state? How can our friend be judged false to religion for defending a principle on which the very notion of God and goodness depends? For this he says only, and this is the sum of all, that, by building a future state on the ruins of virtue, religion in general and the cause of a deity is betrayed, and by making rewards and punishments the principal motives to duty, the Christian religion in particular is overthrown, and its greatest principle, that of love, rejected and exposed.

Upon the whole then, we may justly as well as charitably conclude that it is truly our author's design, in applying himself with so much fairness to the men of looser principles, to lead them into such an apprehension of the constitution of mankind and of human affairs as might form in them a notion of order in things, and draw hence an acknowledgment of that wisdom, goodness and beauty, which is supreme, that, being thus far become proselytes, they might be prepared for that divine love which our religion would teach them, when once they should embrace its precepts and form themselves to its sacred character.

Thus,' continued he, 'I have made my friend's apology, which may have shown him to you perhaps a good moralist and, I hope, no enemy to religion. But if you find still that the divine has not appeared so much in his character as I promised, I can never think of satisfying you in any ordinary way of conversation. Should I offer to go further, I might be engaged deeply in spiritual affairs and be forced to make some new model of a sermon upon his system of divinity. However, I am in hopes, now that in good earnest matters are come well-nigh to preaching, you will acquit me for what I have already performed.'

Section 4

Just as he had made an end of speaking came in some visitants, who took us up the remaining part of the afternoon in other discourses. But these being over and our strangers gone (all except the old gentleman and his friend, who had dined with us), we began anew with Theocles by laying claim to his sermon and entreating him again and again to let us hear him at large in his theological way.

This, he complained, was persecuting him 'as you have seen company', said he, 'often persecute a reputed singer, not out of any fancy for the music, but to satisfy a malicious sort of curiosity, which ends commonly in censure and dislike'.

However it might be, we told him we were resolved to persist. And I assured our companions that, if they would second me heartily in the manner I intended to press him, we should easily get the better.

'In revenge then,' said he, 'I will comply on this condition, that, since I am to sustain the part of the divine and preacher, it shall be at Philocles' cost, who shall bear the part of the infidel and stand for the person preached to.'

'Truly,' said the old gentleman, 'the part you have proposed for him is so natural and suitable that, I doubt not, he will be able to act it without the least pain. I could wish rather that you had spared yourself the trouble of putting him thus in mind of his proper character. He would have been apt enough of his own accord to interrupt your discourse by his perpetual cavils. Therefore, since we have now had entertainment enough by way of dialogue, I desire the law of sermon may be strictly observed and that there be no answering to whatever is argued or advanced.'

I consented to all the terms and told Theocles I would stand his mark willingly. And, besides, if I really were that infidel he was to suppose me, I should count it no unhappiness since I was sure of being so thoroughly convinced by him if he would vouchsafe to undertake me.

Theocles then proposed we should walk out, the evening being fine and the free air suiting better, as he thought, with such discourses than a chamber.

Accordingly we took our evening walk in the fields from whence the laborious hinds were now retiring. We fell naturally into the praises of a country life and discoursed a while of husbandry and the nature of the soil. Our friends began to admire some of the plants which grew here to great perfection. And it being my fortune as having acquired a little insight into the nature of simples[EE] to say something they mightily approved upon this subject, Theocles immediately turning about to me: 'O my ingenious friend!,' said he, 'whose reason in other respects must be allowed so clear and happy, how is it possible that with such insight and accurate judgment in the particulars of natural beings and operations, you should no better judge of the structure of things in general and of the order and frame of nature? Who better than yourself can show the structure of each plant and animal body, declare the office of every part and organ and tell the uses, ends and advantages to which they serve? How therefore should you prove so ill a naturalist in this whole, and understand so little the anatomy of the world and nature, as not to discern the same relation of parts, the same consistency and uniformity in the universe!

Some men perhaps there are of so confused a thought and so irregularly formed within themselves that it is no more than natural for them to find fault and imagine a thousand inconsistencies and defects in this wider constitution. It was not, we may presume, the absolute aim or interest of the universal nature to render every private one infallible and without defect. It was not its intention to leave us without some pattern of imperfection, such as we perceive in minds like these, perplexed with froward[FF] thought. But you, my friend, are master of a nobler mind. You are conscious of better order within and can see workmanship and exactness in yourself and other innumerable parts of the creation. Can you answer it to yourself, allowing thus much not to allow all? Can you induce yourself ever to believe or think that, where there are parts so variously united and conspiring fitly within themselves, the whole itself should have neither union nor coherence and, where inferior and private natures are often found so perfect, the universal one should want perfection and be esteemed like whatsoever can be thought of, most monstrous, rude and imperfect?

Strange! That there should be in nature the idea of an order and perfection which nature herself wants! That beings which arise from nature should be so perfect as to discover imperfection in her constitution and be wise enough to correct that wisdom by which they were made!

Nothing surely is more strongly imprinted on our minds or more closely interwoven with our souls than the idea or sense of order and proportion. Hence all the force of numbers and those powerful arts founded on their management and use! What a difference there is between harmony and discord, cadency and convulsion! What a difference between composed and orderly motion and that which is ungoverned and accidental, between the regular and uniform pile of

[EE] Herbs with medicinal properties.
[FF] Perverse or unwieldy.

273

some noble architect and a heap of sand or stones, between an organized body and a mist or cloud driven by the wind!

Now, as this difference is immediately perceived by a plain internal sensation, so there is withal in reason this account of it: that whatever things have order, the same have unity of design and concur in one, are parts constituent of one whole or are, in themselves, entire systems. Such is a tree with all its branches, an animal with all its members, an edifice with all its exterior and interior ornaments. What else is even a tune or symphony or any excellent piece of music than a certain system of proportioned sounds?

Now in this which we call the universe, whatever the perfection may be of any particular systems or whatever single parts may have proportion, unity or form within themselves, yet, if they are not united all in general in one system but are, in respect of one another, as the driven sands or clouds or breaking waves, then, there being no coherence in the whole, there can be inferred no order, no proportion and consequently no project or design. But, if none of these parts are independent but all apparently united, then is the whole a system complete, according to one simple, consistent and uniform design.[13]

Here then is our main subject insisted on, that neither man nor any other animal, though ever so complete a system of parts as to all within, can be allowed in the same manner complete as to all without, but must be considered as having a further relation abroad to the system of his kind. So even this system of his kind to the animal system, this to the world, our earth, and this again to the bigger world and to the universe.

All things in this world are united. For as the branch is united with the tree, so is the tree as immediately with the earth, air and water which feed it. As much as the fertile mould is fitted to the tree, as much as the strong and upright trunk of the oak or elm is fitted to the twining branches of the vine or ivy, so much are the very leaves, the seeds and fruits of these trees fitted to the various animals: these again to one another and to the elements where they live and to which they are as appendices, in a manner fitted and joined, as either by wings for the air, fins for the water, feet for the earth and by other correspondent inward parts of a more curious frame and texture. Thus, in con-

---

[13] See John Locke, *Essay Concerning Human Understanding* 4.6.11. *And to my mind those men of old, embracing something greater in spirit, seem to have seen much more than the sharpness of our intellects is able to perceive. They said that all these things which are above and below are one and have been bonded by a single force and by a single agreement of nature. For there is no kind of thing which can sustain existence on its own if torn away from its other parts; nor can the other parts, if deprived of it, preserve their own force and eternity*: Cicero, *On the Orator* 3.5.20. *All this that you see, from which divine and human are comprised, is one; we are the limbs of a great body*: Seneca, *Epistles* 95.52. *Our fellowship is like the arching of stones which would fall were they not obstructing one another; thus, it is actually upheld*: Seneca, *Epistles* 95.53. *Is there an abode of god if not earth and sea and air and heaven and virtue? Why do we seek the gods beyond? Whatever you see, by whatever you are stirred, is Jupiter*: Lucan, *Civil War* 9.578–80.

templating all on earth, we must of necessity view all in one as holding to one common stock. Thus too in the system of the bigger world. See there the mutual dependency of things, the relation of one to another, of the sun to this inhabited earth and of the earth and other planets to the sun, the order, union and coherence of the whole! And know, my ingenious friend, that by this survey you will be obliged to own the universal system and coherent scheme of things to be established on abundant proof, capable of convincing any fair and just contemplator of the works of nature. For scarce would anyone, till he had well surveyed this universal scene, believe a union thus evidently demonstrable, by such numerous and powerful instances of mutual correspondency and relation, from the minutest ranks and orders of beings to the remotest spheres.

Now, in this mighty union, if there be such relations of parts one to another as are not easily discovered, if on this account the end and use of things does not everywhere appear, there is no wonder since it is no more indeed than what must happen of necessity. Nor could supreme wisdom have otherwise ordered it. For in an infinity of things thus relative, a mind which sees not infinitely can see nothing fully and, since each particular has relation to all in general, it can know no perfect or true relation of anything in a world not perfectly and fully known.

The same may be considered in any dissected animal, plant or flower where he who is no anatomist nor versed in natural history sees that the many parts have a relation to the whole, for thus much even a slight view affords. But he who like you, my friend, is curious in the works of nature and has been let into a knowledge of the animal and vegetable world, he alone can readily declare the just relation of all these parts to one another and the several uses to which they serve.

But, if you would willingly enter further into this thought and consider how much we ought not only to be satisfied with this our view of things but even to admire its clearness, imagine only some person entirely a stranger to navigation and ignorant of the nature of the sea or waters. How great his astonishment would be, when finding himself on board some vessel, anchoring at sea, remote from all land prospect, while it was yet a calm, he viewed the ponderous machine firm and motionless in the midst of the smooth ocean and considered its foundations beneath, together with its cordage, masts and sails above. How easily would he see the whole one regular structure, all things depending on one another, the uses of the rooms below, the lodgments and conveniences of men and stores? But being ignorant of the intent or design of all above, would he pronounce the masts and cordage to be useless and cumbersome and, for this reason, condemn the frame and despise the architect? O my friend! Let us not thus betray our ignorance, but consider where we are and in what a universe. Think of the many parts of the vast machine in which we have so little insight and of which it is impossible we should know the ends and uses, when, instead of seeing to the highest pendants, we see only some lower deck and are in this dark case of flesh, confined even to the hold and meanest station of the vessel.

Now having recognized this uniform consistent fabric and owned the universal system, we must of consequence acknowledge a universal mind, which no ingenious man can be tempted to disown except through the imagination of disorder in the universe, its seat. For can it be supposed of anyone in the world, that being in some desert far from men and hearing there a perfect symphony of music or seeing an exact pile of regular architecture arising gradually from the earth in all its orders and proportions, he should be persuaded that at the bottom there was no design accompanying this, no secret spring of thought, no active mind? Would he, because he saw no hand, deny the handiwork and suppose that each of these complete and perfect systems were framed and thus united in just symmetry and conspiring order, either by the accidental blowing of the winds or rolling of the sands?

What is it then should so disturb our views of nature as to destroy that unity of design and order of a mind, which otherwise would be so apparent? All we can see either of the heavens or earth demonstrates order and perfection so as to afford the noblest subjects of contemplation to minds, like yours, enriched with sciences and learning. All is delightful, amiable, rejoicing, except with relation to man only and his circumstances, which seem unequal. Here the calamity and ill arises and hence the ruin of this goodly frame. All perishes on this account, and the whole order of the universe, elsewhere so firm, entire and immovable, is here overthrown and lost by this one view, in which we refer all things to ourselves, submitting the interest of the whole to the good and interest of so small a part.

But how is it you complain of the unequal state of man and of the few advantages allowed him above the beasts? What can a creature claim, so little differing from them or whose merit appears so little above them except in wisdom and virtue, to which so few conform? Man may be virtuous and, by being so, is happy. His merit is reward. By virtue he deserves, and in virtue only can meet his happiness deserved. But, if even virtue itself be unprovided for and vice, more prosperous, be the better choice, if this, as you suppose, be in the nature of things, then is all order in reality inverted and supreme wisdom lost, imperfection and irregularity being, after this manner, undoubtedly too apparent in the moral world.

Have you then, before you pronounced this sentence, considered of the state of virtue and vice with respect to this life merely, so as to say with assurance when and how far, in what particulars and how circumstantiated, the one or the other is good or ill? You who are skilled in other fabrics and compositions, both of art and nature, have you considered of the fabric of the mind, the constitution of the soul, the connection and frame of all its passions and affections, to know accordingly the order and symmetry of the part and how it either improves or suffers, what its force is when naturally preserved in its sound state and what becomes of it when corrupted and abused? Till this, my friend, be well examined and understood, how shall we judge either of the force of virtue or power of vice, or in what manner either of these may work to our happiness or undoing?

Here, therefore, is that inquiry we should first make. But who is there can afford to make it as he ought? If happily we are born of a good nature, if a liberal education has formed in us a generous temper and disposition, well-regulated appetites and worthy inclinations, it is well for us, and so indeed we esteem it. But who is there endeavours to give these to himself or to advance his portion of happiness in this kind? Who thinks of improving or so much as of preserving his share in a world where it must of necessity run so great a hazard and where we know an honest nature is so easily corrupted? All other things relating to us are preserved with care and have some art or economy belonging to them. This which is nearest related to us and on which our happiness depends is alone committed to chance, and temper is the only thing ungoverned while it governs all the rest.

Thus we inquire concerning what is good and suitable to our appetites, but what appetites are good and suitable to us is no part of our examination. We inquire what is according to interest, policy, fashion, vogue, but it seems wholly strange and out of the way to inquire what is according to nature. The balance of Europe, of trade, of power, is strictly sought after, while few have heard of the balance of their passions or thought of holding these scales even. Few are acquainted with this province or knowing in these affairs. But were we more so (as this inquiry would make us), we should then see beauty and decorum here as well as elsewhere in nature, and the order of the moral world would equal that of the natural. By this, the beauty of virtue would appear and hence, as has been shown, the supreme and sovereign beauty, the original of all which is good or amiable.

But lest I should appear at last too like an enthusiast, I choose to express my sense and conclude this philosophical sermon in the words of one of those ancient philologists, whom you are used to esteem. "For divinity itself", says he, "is surely beauteous, and of all beauties the brightest, though not a beauteous body but that from whence the beauty of bodies is derived, not a beauteous plain but that from whence the plain looks beautiful. The river's beauty, the sea's, the heaven's and heavenly constellations' all flow from hence as from a source eternal and incorruptible. As beings partake of this, they are fair and flourishing and happy; as they are lost to this, they are deformed, perished and lost." 'GG

GG Maximus Tyrius, *Orations* II.II.

When Theocles had thus spoken, he was formally complimented by our two companions. I was going to add something in the same way, but he presently stopped me by saying he should be scandalized if, instead of commending him, I did not, according to my character, choose rather to criticize some part or other of his long discourse.

'If it must be so then,' replied I, 'in the first place, give me leave to wonder that, instead of the many arguments commonly brought for proof of a deity, you make use only of one single one to build on. I expected to have heard from you, in customary form, of a first cause, a first being and a beginning of motion, how clear the idea was of an immaterial substance, and how plainly it appeared that, at some time or other, matter must have been created. But, as to all this, you are silent. As for what is said of "a material unthinking substance being never able to have produced an immaterial thinking one", I readily grant it but on the condition that this great maxim of "nothing being ever made from nothing" may hold as well on my side as my adversary's.[IIII] And then, I suppose, that, while the world endures, he will be at a loss how to assign a beginning to matter or how to suggest a possibility of annihilating it. The spiritual men may, as long as they please, represent to us in the most eloquent manner that "matter considered in a thousand different shapes, joined and disjoined, varied and modified to eternity, can never, of itself, afford one single thought, never occasion or give rise to anything like sense or knowledge". Their argument will hold good against a Democritus, an Epicurus or any of the elder or latter atomists. But it will be turned on them by an examining Academist, and, when the two substances are fairly set asunder and considered apart as different kinds, it will be as strong sense and as good argument to say as well of the immaterial kind "that, do with it as you please, modify it a thousand ways, purify it, exalt it, sublime it, torture it ever so much or rack it, as they say, with thinking, you will never be able to produce or force the contrary substance out of it". The poor dregs of sorry matter can no more be made out of the simple pure substance of immaterial thought than the high spirits of thought or reason can be extracted from the gross substance of heavy matter. So let the dogmatists make of this argument what they can.

But for your part,' continued I, 'as you have stated the question, it is not about what was first or foremost but what is instant and now in being. "For if deity be now really extant, if by any good token it appears that there is at this present a universal mind, it will easily be yielded there ever was one." This is your argument. You go, if I may say so, upon *fact* and would prove that things *actually are* in such a state and condition, which, if they really were, there would indeed be no dispute left. Your *union* is your main support. Yet how is

---

[IIII] This maxim can be found in Persius, *Satires* 3.84, in Marcus Aurelius, *Meditations* 4.4, and, according to Diogenes Laertius in *Lives of Eminent Philosophers* 9.57, in Diogenes of Apollonia.

it you prove this? What demonstration have you given? What have you so much as offered at, beyond bare probability? So far are you from demonstrating anything that, if this uniting scheme be the chief argument for deity, as you tacitly allow, you seem rather to have demonstrated that "the case itself is incapable of demonstration". For "how", say you, "can a narrow mind see all things?" And yet, if in reality it sees not all, it had as good see nothing. The demonstrable part is still as far behind. For grant that this all, which lies within our view or knowledge, is orderly and united, as you suppose, this mighty all is a mere point still, a very nothing compared to what remains. "It is only a separate by-world", we'll say, "of which perhaps there are, in the wide waste, millions besides, as horrid and deformed as this of ours is regular and proportioned. In length of time, amid the infinite hurry and shock of beings, this single odd world, by accident, might have been struck out and cast into some form (as, among infinite chances, what is there which may not happen?). But for the rest of matter, it is of a different hue. Old Father Chaos, as the poets call him, in these wild spaces reigns absolute and upholds his realms of darkness. He presses hard upon our frontier and one day, belike, shall by a furious inroad recover his lost right, conquer his rebel state, and reunite us to primitive discord and confusion."

This, Theocles!,' said I, concluding my discourse, 'is all I dare offer in opposition to your philosophy. I imagined, indeed, you might have given me more scope, but you have retrenched yourself in narrower bounds so that, to tell you truth, I look upon your theology to be hardly so fair or open as that of our divines in general. They are strict, it is true, as to names but allow a greater latitude in things. Hardly indeed can they bear a home-charge, a downright questioning of deity, but in return they give always fair play against nature and allow her to be challenged for her failings. She may freely err and we as freely censure. Deity, they think, is not accountable for her; only she for herself. But you are straiter and more precise in this point. You have unnecessarily brought nature into the controversy and taken upon you to defend her honour so highly that I know not whether it may be safe for me to question her.'

'Let not this trouble you,' replied Theocles, 'but be free to censure nature, whatever may be the consequence. It is only my hypothesis can suffer. If I defend it ill, my friends need not be scandalized. They are fortified, no doubt, with stronger arguments for a deity and can well employ those metaphysical weapons, of whose edge you seem so little apprehensive. I leave them to dispute this ground with you whenever they think fit. For my own arguments, if they can be supposed to make any part of this defence, they may be looked upon only as distant lines or outworks, which may easily perhaps be won, but without any danger to the body of the place.'

'Notwithstanding, then,' said I, 'that you are willing I should attack nature in form, I choose to spare her in all other subjects, except man only. How comes it, I entreat you, that, in this noblest of creatures and worthiest her care, she should appear so very weak and impotent while, in mere brutes and the irrational species, she acts with so much strength and exerts such hardy vigour? Why is she spent so soon in feeble man, who is found more subject to diseases and of fewer years than many of the wild creatures? They range secure and proof against all the injuries of seasons and weather, want no help from art but live in careless ease, discharged of labour and freed from the cumbersome baggage of a necessitous human life. In infancy more helpful, vigorous in age, with senses quicker, and more natural sagacity, they pursue their interests, joys, recreations, and cheaply purchase both their food and maintenance, clothed and armed by nature herself, who provides them both a couch and mansion. So has nature ordered for the rest of creatures. Such is their hardiness, robustness, vigour. Why not the same for man? . . .'

'And do you stop thus short', said Theocles, 'in your expostulation? Methinks it were as easy to proceed, now you are in the way, and, instead of laying claim to some few advantages of other creatures, you might as well stand for all and complain that "man, for his part, should be anything less than a consummation of all advantages and privileges which nature can afford". Ask not merely "why man is naked, why unhoofed, why slower footed than the beasts?" Ask "why he has not wings also for the air, fins for the water and so on that he might take possession of each element and reign in all?"'

'Not so,' said I, 'neither. This would be to rate him high indeed! As if he were, by nature, lord of all, which is more than I could willingly allow.'

'It is enough', replied he, 'that this is yielded. For, if we allow once a subordination in his case, if nature herself be not for man but man for nature, then must man, by his good leave, submit to the elements of nature and not the elements to him. Few of these are at all fitted to him, and none perfectly. If he be left in air, he falls headlong, for wings were not assigned him. In water he soon sinks. In fire he consumes. Within earth he suffocates . . .'

'As for what dominion he may naturally have in other elements,' said I, 'my concern truly is not very great in his behalf since by art he can even exceed the advantages nature has given to other creatures. But for the air, methinks it had been wonderfully obliging in nature to have allowed him wings.'

'And what would he have gained by it?,' replied Theocles. 'For consider what an alteration of form must have ensued. Observe in one of those winged creatures whether the whole structure be not made subservient to this purpose and all other advantages sacrificed to this single operation. The anatomy of the creature shows it, in a manner, to be all wing, its chief bulk being composed of two exorbitant muscles which exhaust the strength of all the other and engross, if I may say so, the whole economy of the frame. It is thus the aerial racers are able to perform so rapid and strong a motion, beyond comparison with any other kind and far exceeding their little share of strength elsewhere

– these parts of theirs being made in such superior proportion as in a manner to starve their companions. And in man's architecture, of so different an order, were the flying engines to be affixed, must not the other members suffer and the multiplied parts starve one another? What think you of the brain in this partition? Is it not like to prove a starveling? Or would you have it be maintained at the same high rate and draw the chief nourishment to itself from all the rest? . . .'

'I understand you, Theocles,' said I, interrupting him. 'The brain certainly is a great starver where it abounds, and the thinking people of the world, the philosophers and virtuosi especially, must be contented, I find, with a moderate share of bodily advantages for the sake of what they call parts and capacity in another sense. The parts, it seems, of one kind agree ill in their economy with the parts of the other. But, to make this even on both sides, let us turn the tables and the case, I suppose, will stand the same with the Milos of the age, the men of bodily prowess and dexterity.[II] For, not to mention a vulgar sort, such as wrestlers, vaulters, racers, hunters, what shall we say of our fine-bred gentlemen, our riders, fencers, dancers, tennis players and such like? It is the body surely is the starver here and, if the brain were such a terrible devourer in the other way, the body and bodily parts seem to have their reprisals in this rank of men.'

'If then', said he, 'the case stands thus between man and man, how must it stand between man and a quite different creature? If the balance be so nice that the least thing breaks it, even in creatures of the same frame and order, of what fatal effect must it be to change the order itself and make some essential alteration in the frame? Consider therefore how it is we censure nature in these and such-like cases. "Why", says one, "was I not made by nature strong as a horse? Why not hardy and robust as this brute creature or nimble and active as that other?" And yet, when uncommon strength, agility and feats of body are subjoined, even in our own species, see what befalls! So that, for a person thus in love with an athletic Milonean constitution, it were better, methinks, and more modest in him to change the expostulation and ask, "Why was I not made in good earnest a very brute?" For that would be more suitable.'

'I am apt, indeed,' said I, 'to think that the excellence of man lies somewhat different from that of a brute and that, such among us as are more truly men, should naturally aspire to manly qualities and leave the brute his own. But nature, I see, has done well to mortify us in this particular by furnishing us with such slight stuff, and in such a tender frame, as is indeed wonderfully commodious to support that man-excellence of thought and reason, but

---

[II] Milo of Croton was a celebrated athlete of the later sixth century BC, a frequent victor at the Olympic and Pythian games.

wretchedly scanty and ineffectual for other purposes – as if it were her very design to hinder us from aspiring ridiculously to what was misbecoming our character.'

'I see', said Theocles, 'you are not one of those timorous arguers who tremble at every objection raised against their opinion or belief and are so intent in upholding their own side of the argument that they are unable to make the least concession on the other. Your wit allows you to divert yourself with whatever occurs in the debate, and you can pleasantly improve even what your antagonist brings as a support to his own hypothesis. This, indeed, is a fairer sort of practice than what is common nowadays. But it is no more than suitable to your character. And were I not afraid of speaking with an air of compliment in the midst of a philosophical debate, I should tell you, perhaps, what I thought of the becoming manner of your scepticism in opposition to a kind of bigot-sceptics, who forfeit their right to the philosophic character and retain hardly so much as that of the gentleman or good companion.

But to our argument.

Such then', continued he, 'is the admirable distribution of nature, her adapting and adjusting not only the stuff or matter to the shape and form, and even the shape itself and form to the circumstance, place, element or region, but also the affections, appetites, sensations, mutually to each other, as well as to the matter, form, action and all besides: all managed for the best with perfect frugality and just reserve, profuse to none but bountiful to all, never employing in one thing more than enough but with exact economy retrenching the superfluous and adding force to what is principal in every thing. And is not *thought* and *reason* principal in man? Would he have no reserve for these, no saving for this part of his engine? Or would he have the same stuff or matter, the same instruments or organs, serve alike for different purposes, and an ounce be equivalent to a pound?

It cannot be. What wonders, then, can he expect from a few ounces of blood in such a narrow vessel, fitted for so small a district of nature? Will he not rather think highly of that nature which has thus managed his portion for him to best advantage with this happy reserve (happy indeed for him, if he knows and uses it!), by which he has so much a better use of organs than any other creature, by which he holds his reason, is a man and not a beast?'

'But beasts', said I, 'have instincts which man has not.'[14]

'True,' said he. 'They have indeed perceptions, sensations, and pre-sensations, if I may use the expression, which man, for his part, has not in any proportionable degree.[15] Their females, newly pregnant and before they have borne young, have a clear prospect or pre-sensation of their state which is to

[14] See pp. 198–200, 213, 429ff.
[15] See p. 326.

follow, know what to provide and how, in what manner and at what time. How many things do they preponderate? How many at once comprehend? The seasons of the year, the country, climate, place, aspect, situation, the basis of their building, the materials, architecture, the diet and treatment of their offspring, in short, the whole economy of their nursery, and all this as perfectly at first and when inexperienced as at any time of their life afterwards. And, "Why not this", say you, "in human kind?" Nay, rather, on the contrary, I ask, "Why this? Where was the occasion or use? Where the necessity? Why this sagacity for men? Have they not what is better in another kind? Have they not reason and discourse? Does not this instruct them? What need then of the other? Where would be the prudent management at this rate? Where the reserve?"

The young of most other kinds', continued he, 'are instantly helpful to themselves, sensible, vigorous, know to shun danger and seek their good. A human infant is of all the most helpless, weak, infirm. And wherefore should it not have been thus ordered? Where is the loss in such a species? Or what is man the worse for this defect, amid such large supplies? Does not this defect engage him the more strongly to society and force him to own that he is purposely, and not by accident, made rational and sociable and can no otherwise increase or subsist than in that social intercourse and community which is his natural state? Is not both conjugal affection and natural affection to parents, duty to magistrates, love of a common city, community or country, with the other duties and social parts of life, deduced from hence and founded in these very wants? What can be happier than such a deficiency as is the occasion of so much good? What better than a want so abundantly made up and answered by so many enjoyments? Now if there are still to be found among mankind such as even in the midst of these wants seem not ashamed to affect a right of independency and deny themselves to be by nature sociable, where would their shame have been, had nature otherwise supplied these wants? What duty or obligation had been ever thought of? What respect or reverence of parents, magistrates, their country or their kind? Would not their full and self-sufficient state more strongly have determined them to throw off nature and deny the ends and author of their creation?'

While Theocles argued thus concerning nature, the old gentleman, my adversary, expressed great satisfaction in hearing me, as he thought, refuted and my opinions exposed. For he would needs believe these to be strongly my opinions which I had only started as objections in the discourse. He endeavoured to reinforce the argument by many particulars from the common topics of the schoolmen and civilians.[JJ] He added, withal, that it was better for me to

---

[JJ] The old gentleman, being old-fashioned, resorts to arguments from scholastics ('schoolmen') and scholars of the Roman civil, as opposed to the Church's canon or English common, law ('civilians').

declare my sentiments openly, for he was sure I had strongly imbibed that principle, that the state of nature was a state of war.[16]

'That it was no state of government or public rule,' replied I, 'you yourself allow.'

'I do so.'

'Was it then a state of fellowship or society?'

'No, for, when men entered first into society, they passed from the state of nature into that new one which is founded upon compact.'

'And was that former state a tolerable one?'

'Had it been absolutely intolerable, there had never been any such. Nor could we properly call that a state, which could not stand or endure for the least time.'

'If man, therefore, could endure to live without society and if it be true that he actually lived so when in the state of nature, how can it be said that he is by nature sociable?'

The old gentleman seemed a little disturbed at my question, but, having recovered himself, he said in answer, that 'man indeed, from his own natural inclination, might not, perhaps, have been moved to associate, but rather from some particular circumstances'.

'His nature then', said I, 'was not so very good, it seems, since, having no natural affection or friendly inclination belonging to him, he was forced into a social state against his will, and this, not from any necessity in respect of outward things (for you have allowed him a tolerable subsistence), but in probability from such inconveniences as arose chiefly from himself and his own malignant temper and principles. And indeed it was no wonder if creatures who were naturally thus unsociable should be as naturally mischievous and troublesome. If, according to their nature, they could live out of society with so little affection for one another's company, it is not likely that upon occasion they would spare one another's persons. If they were so sullen as not to meet for love, it is more than probable they would fight for interest. And thus from your own reasoning it appears that "the state of nature must in all likelihood have been little different from a state of war".'

He was going to answer me with some sharpness, as by his looks appeared, when Theocles, interposing, desired that, as he had occasioned this dispute, he might be allowed to try if he could end it by setting the question in a fairer light.

'You see', said he to the old gentleman, 'what artifice Philocles made use of when he engaged you to allow that the state of nature and that of society were

---

[16] See p. 51. [The state of nature was a common supposition of the natural law tradition. The degeneration of the state of nature into a state of war was posited by both Hobbes, *Leviathan* 1.13, and Locke, *Second Treatise of Government* 3.]

perfectly distinct. But let us question him now in his turn and see whether he can demonstrate to us that there can be naturally any human state which is not social.'

'What is it then', said the old gentleman, 'which we call "the state of nature"?'

'Not that imperfect rude condition of mankind,' said Theocles, 'which some imagine but which, if it ever were in nature, could never have been of the least continuance or any way tolerable or sufficient for the support of the human race. Such a condition cannot indeed so properly be called a state. For what if, speaking of an infant just coming into the world and in the moment of the birth, I should fancy to call this a state, would it be proper?'

'Hardly so, I confess.'

'Just such a state, therefore, was that which we suppose of man before yet he entered into society and became in truth a human creature. It was the rough draft of man, the essay or first effort of nature, a species in the birth, a kind as yet unformed, not in its natural state, but under violence and still restless till it attained its natural perfection.

And thus,' said Theocles addressing still more particularly to the old gentleman, 'the case must necessarily stand, even on the supposal that there was ever such a condition or state of men, when as yet they were unassociated, unacquainted and consequently without any language or form of art. But that it was their natural state to live thus separately can never without absurdity be allowed. For sooner may you divest the creature of any other feeling or affection than that towards society and his likeness. Allowing you, however, the power of divesting him at pleasure, allowing you to reduce even whole parts and members of his present frame, would you transform him thus and call him still a man? Yet better might you do this indeed than you could strip him of his natural affections, separate him from all his kind and, enclosing him like some solitary insect in a shell, declare him still a man. So might you call the human egg or embryo the man. The bug which breeds the butterfly is more properly a fly, though without wings, than this imaginary creature is a man. For, though his outward shape were human, his passions, appetites and organs must be wholly different. His whole inward make must be reversed to fit him for such a recluse economy and separate subsistence.

To explain this a little further,' continued he, 'let us examine this pretended state of nature, how and on what foundation it must stand. For either man must have been from eternity or not. If from eternity, there could be no primitive or original state, no state of nature other than we see at present before our eyes. If not from eternity, he arose either all at once (and consequently he was at the very first as he is now) or by degrees, through several stages and conditions, to that in which he is at length settled and has continued for so many generations.

For instance, let us suppose he sprang, as the old poets feigned, from a big-bellied oak, and then belike he might resemble more a mandrake than a man.[KK] Let us suppose him at first with little more of life than is discovered in that plant which they call the sensitive. But when the mother-oak had been some time delivered and the false birth by some odd accident or device was wrought into form, the members were then fully displayed, and the organs of sense began to unfold themselves. Here sprang an ear. There peeped an eye. Perhaps a tail too came in company. For what superfluities nature may have been charged with at first is difficult to determine. They dropped off, it seems, in time and happily have left things at last in a good posture, and (to a wonder!) just as they should be.

This surely is the lowest view of the original affairs of humankind. For if a providence and not chance gave man his being, our argument for his social nature must surely be the stronger. But admitting his rise to be, as we have described and as a certain sort of philosophers would needs have it,[LL] nature has then had no intention at all, no meaning or design in this whole matter. So how anything can be called natural in the case, how any state can be called a state of nature or according to nature, one more than another, I know not.

Let us go on, however, and on their hypothesis consider which state we may best call nature's own. She has by accident, through many changes and chances, raised a creature which, springing at first from rude seeds of matter, proceeded till it became what now it is and arrived where for many generations it has been at a stay. In this long procession (for I allow it any length whatever), I ask, "Where was it that this state of nature could begin?" The creature must have endured many changes, and each change, while he was thus growing up, was as natural one as another. So that either there must be reckoned a hundred different states of nature or, if one, it can be only that in which nature was perfect and her growth complete. Here where she rested and attained her end, here must be her state, or nowhere.

Could she then rest, think you, in that desolate state before society? Could she maintain and propagate the species, such as it now is, without fellowship or community? Show it us in fact anywhere among any of our own kind. For, as for creatures which may much resemble us in outward form, if they differ yet in the least part of their constitution, if their inwards are of a different texture, if their skin and pores are otherwise formed or hardened, if they have other excrescences of body, another temper, other natural inseparable habits or affections, they are not truly of our kind. If, on the other hand, their con-

---

[KK] The mandrake is a plant with a forked root, said to resemble the human form and fabled to emit a shriek when pulled from the ground.

[LL] That is, the Epicureans. Cf. Lucretius, *On the Nature of Things* 5.416.

stitution be as ours, their natural parts or inward faculties as strong and their bodily frame as weak as ours, if they have memory and senses and affections and a use of organs as ours, it is evident they can no more by their good will abstain from society than they can possibly preserve themselves without it.

And here, my friends, we ought to remember what we discoursed a while since and was advanced by Philocles himself concerning the weakness of human bodies[17] and the necessitous state of man in respect of all other creatures: "his long and helpless infancy, his feeble and defenceless make, by which he is more fitted to be a prey himself than live by prey on others". Yet it is impossible for him to subsist like any of those grazing kinds. He must have better provision and choicer food than the raw herbage, a better couch and covering than the bare earth or open sky. How many conveniences of other kinds does he stand in need of? What union and strict society is required between the sexes to preserve and nurse their growing offspring? This kind of society will not, surely, be denied to man, which to every beast of prey is known proper and natural. And can we allow this social part to man and go no further? Is it possible he should pair and live in love and fellowship with his partner and offspring and remain still wholly wild and speechless and without those arts of storing, building and other economy as natural to him, surely, as to the beaver or to the ant or bee? Where, therefore, should he break off from this society if once begun? For that it began thus, as early as generation, and grew into a household and economy, is plain. Must not this have grown soon into a tribe, and this tribe into a nation? Or, though it remained a tribe only, was not this still a society for mutual defence and common interest? *In short, if generation be natural, if natural affection and the care and nurture of the offspring be natural, things standing as they do with man and the creature being of that form and constitution he now is, it follows that society must be also natural to him and that out of society and community he never did, nor ever can, subsist.*

To conclude,' said he, addressing still to the two companions, 'I will venture to add a word in behalf of Philocles: that, since the learned have such a fancy for this notion and love to talk of this imaginary state of nature, I think it is even charity to speak as ill of it as we possibly can. Let it be a state of war, rapine and injustice. Since it is unsocial, let it even be as uncomfortable and as frightful as it is possible. To speak well of it is to render it inviting and tempt men to turn hermits. Let it, at least, be looked on as many degrees worse than the worst government in being. The greater dread we have of anarchy, the better countrymen we shall prove and value more the laws and constitution under which we live and by which we are protected from the outrageous violences of such an unnatural state. In this I agree heartily with those transformers of human nature who, considering it abstractedly and apart from

[17] See pp. 279–80.

government or society, represent it under monstrous visages of dragons, leviathans and I know not what devouring creatures. They would have done well, however, to have expressed themselves more properly in their great maxim. For to say in disparagement of man that "he is to man a wolf"[MM] appears somewhat absurd, when one considers that wolves are to wolves very kind and loving creatures. The sexes strictly join in the care and nurture of the young, and this union is continued still between them. They howl to one another to bring company, whether to hunt or invade their prey or assemble on the discovery of a good carcase. Even the swinish kinds want not common affection and run in herds to the assistance of their distressed fellows. The meaning, therefore, of this famous sentence (if it has any meaning at all) must be, that "man is naturally to man as a wolf is to a tamer creature", as, for instance, to a sheep. But this will be as little to the purpose as to tell us that "there are different species or characters of men, that all have not this wolfish nature, but that one half at least are naturally innocent and mild".[18] And thus the sentence comes to nothing. For without belying nature and contradicting what is evident from natural history, fact and the plain course of things, it is impossible to assent to this ill-natured proposition when we have even done our best to make tolerable sense of it.

But such is mankind! And even here human nature shows itself, such as it is, not perfect or absolutely successful though rightly tending and moved by proper and just principles. It is here, therefore, in philosophy as in the common conversations of the world. As fond as men are of company and as little able to enjoy any happiness out of it, they are yet strangely addicted to the way of satire. And in the same manner as a malicious censure, craftily worded and pronounced with assurance, is apt to pass with mankind for shrewd wit, so a virulent maxim in bold expressions, though without any justness of thought, is readily received for true philosophy.'

Section 5
In these discourses the evening ended and, night advancing, we returned home from our walk. At supper and afterwards for the rest of that night, Theocles said little. The discourse was now managed chiefly by the two companions, who turned it upon a new sort of philosophy, such as you will excuse me, good Palemon, if I pass over with more haste.

There was much said and with great learning on the nature of spirits and apparitions, of which the most astonishing accounts were the most ravishing with our friends, who endeavoured to exceed one another in this admirable

----

[MM] Erasmus, *Adagia* [Adages] 1.1.70, a shortened version of a line in Plautus, *Asinaria* 2.495.

[18] See pp. 41–2, 55.

way and performed to a miracle in raising one another's amazement. Nothing was so charming with them as that which was disagreeing and odd, nothing so soothing as that which moved horror. In short, whatever was rational, plain and easy bore no relish, and nothing came amiss which was cross to nature, out of sort and order, and in no proportion or harmony with the rest of things. Monstrous births, prodigies, enchantments, elementary wars and convulsions were our chief entertainment. One would have thought that, in a kind of rivalship between providence and nature, the latter lady was made to appear as homely as possible that her deformities might recommend and set off the beauties of the former. For, to do our friends justice, I must own I thought their intention to be sincerely religious.[NN] But this was not a face of religion I was like to be enamoured with. It was not from hence I feared being made enthusiastic or superstitious. If ever I became so, I found it would rather be after Theocles' manner. The monuments and churchyards were not such powerful scenes with me as the mountains, the plains, the solemn woods and groves, of whose inhabitants I chose much rather to hear than of the other. And I was readier to fancy truth in those poetical fictions which Theocles made use of than in any of his friends' ghastly stories, so pompously set off, after the usual way, in a lofty tone of authority and with an assuming air of truth.

You may imagine, Palemon, that my scepticism, with which you so often reproach me, could not well forsake me here nor could it fail to give disturbance to our companions, especially to the grave gentleman who had clashed with me some time before.[19] He bore with me a while till having lost all patience.

'One must certainly', said he, 'be master of no small share of assurance to hold out against the common opinion of the world and deny things which are known by the report of the most considerable part of mankind.'

'This', said I, 'is far from being my case. You have never yet heard me deny anything, though I have questioned many. If I suspend my judgment, it is because I have less sufficiency than others. There are people, I know, who have so great a regard to every fancy of their own, that they can believe their very dreams. But I, who could never pay any such deference to my sleeping fancies, am apt sometimes to question even my waking thoughts and examine whether these are not dreams too, since men have a faculty of dreaming sometimes with their eyes open. You will own it is no small pleasure with mankind to make their dreams pass for realities and that the love of truth is, in earnest,

[NN] On the intellectual climates in which magical and religious beliefs were entwined and then unravelled, see Keith Thomas, *Religion and the Decline of Magic* (New York: Charles Scribner's Sons, 1971), especially pp. 641–68.

[19] See pp. 369–70, 440–1, 471–2, 472ff.

not half so prevalent as this passion for novelty and surprise, joined with a desire of making impression and being admired. However, I am so charitable still as to think there is more of innocent delusion than voluntary imposture in the world and that they who have most imposed on mankind have been happy in a certain faculty of imposing first upon themselves, by which they have a kind of salvo for their consciences and are so much the more successful as they can act their part more naturally and to the life. Nor is it to be esteemed a riddle that men's dreams should sometimes have the good fortune of passing with them for truth, when we consider that in some cases that which was never so much as dreamt of, or related as truth, comes afterwards to be believed by one who has often told it.'

'So that the greatest impostor in the world', replied he, 'at this rate may be allowed sincere.'

'As to the main of his imposture,' said I, 'perhaps he may, notwithstanding some pious frauds made use of between whiles in behalf of a belief thought good and wholesome. And so very natural do I take this to be that, in all religions except the true, I look upon the greatest zeal to be accompanied with the strongest inclination to deceive. For the design and end being the truth, it is not customary to hesitate or be scrupulous about the choice of means. Whether this be true or no, I appeal to the experience of the last age, in which it will not be difficult to find very remarkable examples where imposture and zeal, bigotry and hypocrisy, have lived together in one and the same character.'[oo]

'Let this be as it will,' replied he, 'I am sorry, upon the whole, to find you of such an incredulous temper.'

'It is just', said I, 'that you should pity me as a sufferer for losing that pleasure which I see others enjoy. For what stronger pleasure is there with mankind or what do they earlier learn or longer retain than the love of hearing and relating things strange and incredible? How wonderful a thing is the love of wondering and of raising wonder! It is the delight of children to hear tales they shiver at and the vice of old age to abound in strange stories of times past. We come into the world wondering at everything and, when our wonder about common things is over, we seek something new to wonder at. Our last scene is to tell wonders of our own to all who will believe them. And amid all this, it is well if truth comes off but moderately tainted.'

'It is well,' replied he, 'if with this moderate faith of yours you can believe any miracles whatever.'

'No matter', said I, 'how incredulous I am of modern miracles, if I have a

---

[oo] The era of Civil War and Interregnum in England from 1642 to 1660 had raised questions, which continued to be pondered over at least the next half of a century, about the relation between religious profession and behaviour. The enthusiast and the hypocrite became stock characters in ideology and analysis.

right faith in those of former times by paying the deference due to sacred writ.[PP] It is here I am so much warned against credulity and enjoined never to believe even the greatest miracles which may be wrought in opposition to what has been already taught me. And this injunction I am so well fitted to comply with that I can safely engage to keep still in the same faith and promise never to believe amiss.'

'But is this a promise which can well be made?'

'If not, and that my belief indeed does not absolutely depend upon myself, how am I accountable for it? I may be justly punished for actions in which my will is free, but with what justice can I be challenged for my belief, if in this I am not at my liberty? If credulity and incredulity are defects only in the judgment and the best-meaning person in the world may err on either side, while a much worse man, by having better parts, may judge far better of the evidence of things, how can you punish him who errs, unless you would punish weakness and say it is just for men to suffer for their unhappiness and not their fault?'

'I am apt to think', said he, 'that very few of those who are punished for their incredulity can be said to be sufferers for their weakness.'

'Taking it for granted then', replied I, 'that simplicity and weakness is more the character of the credulous than of the unbelieving; yet I see not but that even this way still we are as liable to suffer by our weakness as, in the contrary case, by an over-refined wit. For if we cannot command our own belief, how are we secure against those false prophets and their deluding miracles of which we have such warning given us? How are we safe from heresy and false religion? Credulity being that which delivers us up to all impostures of this sort and which actually at this day holds the pagan and Mahometan world in error and blind superstition. Either, therefore, there is no punishment due to wrong belief because we cannot believe as we will ourselves or, if we can, why should we not promise never to believe amiss? Now in respect of miracles to come, the surest way never to believe amiss is never to believe at all. For being satisfied of the truth of our religion by past miracles so as to need no other to confirm us, the belief of new may often do us harm but can never do us good. Therefore, as the truest mark of a believing Christian is to seek after no sign or miracle to come, so the safest station in Christianity is his who can be moved by nothing of this kind and is thus miracle-proof. For if the miracle be on the side of his faith, it is superfluous and he needs it not; if against his faith, let it

---

[PP] The status of miracles had been discussed from at least the middle of the seventeenth century. While conservative clerics defended their reality and persistence and radicals denied their possibility, mainstream religious thought, accommodating rationalism and science, sought more complex views. The notion that miracles had been confined to the Apostolic Age can be found in the writings of John Tillotson and Robert South. See R. M. Burns, *The Great Debate on Miracles from Joseph Glanvill to David Hume* (Lewisburg, PA: Bucknell University Press, 1981).

be as great as possible, he will never regard it in the least or believe it any other than imposture though coming from an angel. So that, with all that incredulity for which you reproach me so severely, I take myself to be still the better and more orthodox Christian. At least I am more sure of continuing so than you, who with your credulity may be imposed upon by such as are far short of angels. For, having this preparatory disposition, it is odds you may come in time to believe miracles in any of the different sects who, we know, all pretend to them. I am persuaded, therefore, that the best maxim to go by is that common one, that "miracles are ceased". And I am ready to defend this opinion of mine to be the most probable in itself as well as most suitable to Christianity.'

This question, upon further debate, happened to divide our two companions. For the elderly gentleman, my antagonist, maintained that 'the giving up of miracles for the time present would be of great advantage to the atheists'. The younger gentleman, his companion, questioned 'whether the allowing them might not be of as great advantage to the enthusiasts and sectaries against the national church, this of the two being the greatest danger', he thought, 'both to religion and the state'. He was resolved, therefore, for the future to be as cautious in examining these modern miracles as he had before been eager in seeking them. He told us very pleasantly what an adventurer he had been of that kind and on how many parties he had been engaged with a sort of people who were always on the hot scent of some new prodigy or apparition, some upstart revelation or prophecy. This, he thought, was true fanaticism errant. He had enough of this visionary chase and would ramble no more in blind corners of the world as he had been formerly accustomed in ghostly company of spirit hunters, witch finders, and layers-out for hellish stories and diabolical transactions. There was no need, he thought, of such intelligences from hell to prove the power of heaven and being of a God. And now at last he began to see the ridicule of laying such a stress on these matters, as if a providence depended on them and religion were at stake when any of these wild feats were questioned. He was sensible there were many good Christians who made themselves strong partisans in this cause, though he could not avoid wondering at it, now he began to consider and look back.

'The heathens,' he said, 'who wanted Scripture, might have recourse to miracles, and providence perhaps had allowed them their oracles and prodigies as an imperfect kind of revelation. The Jews too, for their hard heart and harder understanding, had this allowance, when stubbornly they asked for signs and wonders. But Christians, for their parts, had a far better and truer revelation: they had their plainer oracles, a more rational law and clearer Scripture, carrying its own force and withal so well attested as to admit of no dispute. And were I', continued he, 'to assign the exact time when miracles probably might first have ceased, I should be tempted to fancy it was when sacred writ took place and was completed.'

'This is fancy indeed,' replied the grave gentleman, 'and a very dangerous one to that Scripture you pretend is of itself so well attested. The attestation of men dead and gone in behalf of miracles past and at an end can never surely be of equal force with miracles present, and, of these, I maintain, there are never wanting a number sufficient in the world to warrant a divine existence. If there were no miracles nowadays, the world would be apt to think there never were any. The present must answer for the credibility of the past. This is "God witnessing for himself", not "men for God". For who shall witness for men, if in the case of religion they have no testimony from heaven in their behalf?'

'What it is may make the report of men credible', said the younger gentleman, 'is another question. But for mere miracles, it seems to me, they cannot be properly said "to witness either for God or men". For who shall witness for the miracles themselves and what, though they are ever so certain? What security have we that they are not acted by daemons? What proof that they are not wrought by magic? In short, what trust is there to anything above or below, if the signs are only of power and not of goodness?'

'And are you so far improved then,' replied the severe companion, 'under your new sceptical master,' pointing to me, 'that you can thus readily discard all miracles as useless?'

The young gentleman, I saw, was somewhat daunted with this rough usage of his friend, who was going on still with his invective. 'Nay then,' said I, interposing, 'it is I who am to answer for this young gentleman, whom you make to be my disciple. And since his modesty, I see, will not allow him to pursue what he has so handsomely begun, I will endeavour it myself, if he will give me leave.'

The young gentleman assented and I went on, representing his fair intention of establishing in the first place a rational and just foundation for our faith, so as to vindicate it from the reproach of having no immediate miracles to support it.

'He would have done this', I said, 'undoubtedly by showing how good proof we had already for our sacred oracles from the testimony of the dead, whose characters and lives might answer for them as to the truth of what they reported to us from God. This, however, was by no means "witnessing for God", as the zealous gentleman had hastily expressed himself, for this was above the reach either of men or miracles. Nor could God witness for himself or assert his being any other way to men than "by revealing himself to their reason, appealing to their judgment and submitting his ways to their censure and cool deliberation". The contemplation of the universe, its laws and government, was', I averred, 'the only means which could establish the sound belief of a deity. For what, though innumerable miracles from every part assailed the sense and gave the trembling soul no respite, what, though the sky should suddenly open and all kinds of prodigies appear, voices be heard or characters read, what would this evince more than that there were certain powers could do all this? But what powers, whether one or more, whether superior or subaltern, mortal or immortal, wise or foolish, just or unjust, good or bad?——this would still remain a mystery as would the true intention, the infallibility or certainty of whatever those powers asserted. Their word could not be taken in their own case. They might silence men indeed but not convince them since power can never serve as proof for goodness, and goodness is the only pledge of truth.[20] By goodness alone trust is created. By goodness superior powers may win belief. They must allow their works to be examined, their actions criticized, and thus, thus only, they may be confided in when by repeated marks their benevolence is proved and their character of sincerity and truth established. To whom therefore the laws of this universe and its government appear just and uniform, to him they speak the government of one Just One; to him they reveal and witness a God; and, laying in him the foundation of this first faith, they fit him for a subsequent one.[21] He can then hearken to historical revelation and is then fitted, and not till then, for the reception of any message or miraculous notice from above, where he knows beforehand all is just and true. But this no power of miracles, nor any power besides his reason can make him know or apprehend.

But now,' continued I, 'since I have been thus long the defendant only, I am resolved to take up offensive arms and be aggressor in my turn, provided Theocles be not angry with me for borrowing ground from his hypothesis.'

'Whatever you borrow of his,' replied my antagonist, 'you are pretty sure of spoiling it and, as it passes through your hands, you had best beware lest you seem rather to reflect on him than me.'

'I'll venture it,' said I, 'while I maintain that most of those maxims you build upon are fit only to betray your own cause. For, while you are labouring to unhinge nature, while you are searching heaven and earth for prodigies and studying how to "miraculize" everything, you bring confusion on the world, you break its uniformity and destroy that admirable simplicity of order from whence the one infinite and perfect principle is known. Perpetual strifes, convulsions, violences, breach of laws, variation and unsteadiness of order show either no control or several uncontrolled and unsubordinate powers in nature. We have before our eyes either the chaos and atoms of the atheists or the magic and daemons of the polytheists. Yet is this tumultuous system of the universe

---

[20] See pp. 44, 387. [On the similarity of this position to that of Pierre Bayle, see Stanley Grean, *Shaftesbury's Philosophy of Religion and Ethics: A Study in Enthusiasm* (Athens, OH: Ohio University Press, 1967), p. 54.]

[21] See pp. 133, 267–8.

asserted with the highest zeal by some who would maintain a deity. This is that face of things and these the features by which they represent divinity. Hither the eyes of our more inquisitive and ingenuous youth are turned with care lest they see anything otherwise than in this perplexed and amazing view. As if atheism were the most natural inference which could be drawn from a regular and orderly state of things! But, after all this mangling and disfigurement of nature, if it happens (as oft it does) that the amazed disciple, coming to himself and searching leisurely into nature's ways, finds more of order, uniformity and constancy in things than he suspected, he is, of course, driven into atheism, and this merely by the impressions he received from that preposterous system which taught him to seek for deity in confusion and to discover providence in an irregular disjointed world.'

'And when you,' replied he, 'with your newly espoused system, have brought all things to be as uniform, plain, regular and simple as you could wish, I suppose you will send your disciple to seek for deity in mechanism, that is to say, in some exquisite system of self-governed matter.^{QQ} For what else is it you naturalists make of the world than a mere machine?'

'Nothing else,' replied I, 'if to the machine you allow a mind. For in this case it is not a self-governed but a God-governed machine.'

'And what are the tokens', said he, 'which should convince us? What signs should this dumb machine give of its being thus governed?'

'The present', replied I, 'are sufficient. It cannot possibly give stronger signs of life and steady thought. Compare our own machines with this great one and see whether by their order, management and motions they betoken either so perfect a life or so consummate an intelligence. The one is regular, steady, permanent; the other are irregular, variable, inconstant. In one there are the marks of wisdom and determination; in the other, of whimsy and conceit. In one there appears judgment; in the other, fancy only. In one, will; in the other, caprice. In one, truth, certainty, knowledge; in the other, error, folly, and madness.

But to be convinced there is something above which thinks and acts, we want, it seems, the latter of these signs, as supposing there can be no thought or intelligence beside what is like our own. We sicken and grow weary with the orderly and regular course of things. Periods and stated laws and revolutions, just and proportionable, work not upon us nor win our admiration. We must have riddles, prodigies, matter for surprise and horror! By harmony, order and concord, we are made atheists. By irregularity and discord, we are convinced of deity! The world is mere accident if it proceed in course but an effect of wisdom if it runs mad!'

Thus I took upon me the part of a sound theist while I endeavoured to refute

---

^{QQ} Shaftesbury had little patience with mechanical metaphors or explanations. This, again, is aimed at both ancient atomism and more modern mechanical pictures of the cosmos.

my antagonist and show that his principles favoured atheism. The zealous gentleman took high offence and we continued debating warmly till late at night. But Theocles was moderator, and we retired at last to our repose, all calm and friendly. However, I was not a little rejoiced to hear that our companions were to go away early the next morning and leave Theocles to me alone.

For now, Palemon, that morning was approaching for which I so much longed. What your longing may prove I may have reason to fear. You have had enough, one would think, to turn the edge of your curiosity in this kind. Can it be imagined that, after the recital of two such days already past, you can with patience hear of another yet to come, more philosophical than either?

But you have made me promise and now, whatever it cost, take it you must, as follows.

Part III

Section 1
Philocles to Palemon
It was yet deep night, as I imagined, when I waked with the noise of people up in the house. I called to know the matter and was told that Theocles had a little before parted with his friends, after which he went out to take his morning walk but would return, they thought, pretty soon, for so he had left word and that nobody in the meantime should disturb my rest.

This was disturbance sufficient when I heard it. I presently got up and, finding it light enough to see the hill, which was at a little distance from the house, I soon got thither and, at the foot of it, overtook Theocles, to whom I complained of his unkindness. For I was not certainly, I told him, so effeminate and weak a friend as to deserve that he should treat me like a woman. Nor had I shown such an aversion to his manners or conversation as to be thought fitter for the dull luxury of a soft bed and ease than for business, recreation or study with an early friend. He had no other way, therefore, of making me amends than by allowing me henceforward to be a party with him in his serious thoughts, as he saw I was resolved to be in his hours and exercises of this sort.

'You have forgot then', said Theocles, 'the assignation you had yesterday with the silvan nymphs at this place and hour?'[RR]

'No, truly,' said I, 'for, as you see, I am come punctually to the place appointed. But I never expected you should have come hither without me.'

'Nay then,' said Theocles, 'there's hope you may in time become a lover with me, for you already begin to show jealousy. How little did I think these nymphs could raise that passion in you?'

[RR] On this Arcadian imagery, see p. 248n.

'Truly,' said I, 'for the nymphs you mention, I know little of them as yet. My jealousy and love regard you only. I was afraid you had a mind to escape me; but, now that I am again in possession of you, I want no nymph to make me happy here, unless it were perhaps to join forces against you in the manner your beloved poet makes the nymph Aegle join with his two youths in forcing the god Silenus to sing to them.'[SS]

'I dare trust your gallantry', replied Theocles, 'that, if you had such fair company as you speak of, you would otherwise bestow your time than in an adventure of philosophy. But do you expect I should imitate the poet's god you mentioned and sing "the rise of things from atoms, the birth of order from confusion and the origin of union, harmony and concord from the sole powers of chaos and blind chance"?[TT] The song indeed was fitted to the god. For what could better suit his jolly character than such a drunken creation, which he loved often to celebrate by acting it to the life? But even this song was too harmonious for the night's debauch. Well has our poet made it of the morning when the god was fresh, for hardly should we be brought ever to believe that such harmonious numbers could arise from a mere chaos of the mind. But we must hear our poet speaking in the mouth of some soberer demi-god or hero. He then presents us with a different principle of things and in a more proper order of precedency gives thought the upper hand. He makes mind originally to have governed body, not body mind; for this had been a chaos everlasting and must have kept all things in a chaos state to this day and for ever, had it ever been. But:

> The active mind, infused through all the space,
> Unites and mingles with the mighty mass;
> Hence men and beasts . . .[UU]

Here, Philocles, we shall find our sovereign genius, if we can charm the genius of the place[VV] (more chaste and sober than your Silenus) to inspire us with a truer song of nature, teach us some celestial hymn and make us feel divinity present in these solemn places of retreat.'

'Haste then, I conjure you,' said I, 'good Theocles, and stop not one moment for any ceremony or rite. For well I see, methinks, that without any such preparation some divinity has approached us and already moves in you. We are come

---

[SS] Like a satyr, a silenus was a woodland spirit, cunning yet wild and often depicted with some bestial features. As an individual, Silenus was shown as an old man with horse ears. Possessed of secret knowledge, he was repeatedly captured in order to reveal it. In Virgil's *Eclogues* 6.13ff, two shepherds capture Silenus with the aid of Aegle, a female water spirit. In exchange for freedom, he sings them mythological songs.

[TT] Virgil, *Eclogues* 6.31–40. Shaftesbury's version of Silenus' creation story was cast in Epicurean language.

[UU] Virgil, *Aeneid* 6.726–8.

[VV] On the genius of the place, see p. 257n.

to the sacred groves of the Hamadryads, which formerly were said to render oracles.[WW] We are on the most beautiful part of the hill, and the sun, now ready to rise, draws off the curtain of night and shows us the open scene of nature in the plains below. Begin! For now I know you are full of those divine thoughts which meet you ever in this solitude. Give them but voice and accents. You may be still as much alone as you are used and take no more notice of me than if I were absent.'

Just as I had said this, he turned away his eyes from me, musing a while by himself and, soon afterwards, stretching out his hand, as pointing to the objects round him, he began:

'Ye fields and woods, my refuge from the toilsome world of business, receive me in your quiet sanctuaries and favour my retreat and thoughtful solitude.——Ye verdant plains, how gladly I salute ye!——Hail all ye blissful mansions! Known seats! Delightful prospects! Majestic beauties of this earth and all ye rural powers and graces!——Blessed be ye chaste abodes of happiest mortals, who here in peaceful innocence enjoy a life unenvied, though divine, while with its blessed tranquillity it affords a happy leisure and retreat for man, who, made for contemplation and to search his own and other natures, may here best meditate the cause of things and, placed amid the various scenes of nature, may nearer view her works.

O glorious nature! Supremely fair and sovereignly good! All-loving and all-lovely, all-divine! Whose looks are so becoming and of such infinite grace, whose study brings such wisdom and whose contemplation such delight, whose every single work affords an ampler scene and is a nobler spectacle than all which ever art presented!——O mighty nature! Wise substitute of Providence! Empowered creatress! Or thou empowering deity, supreme creator! Thee I invoke and thee alone adore. To thee this solitude, this place, these rural meditations are sacred while thus inspired with harmony of thought, though unconfined by words and in loose numbers, I sing of nature's order in created beings and celebrate the beauties which resolve in thee, the source and principle of all beauty and perfection.

Thy being is boundless, unsearchable, impenetrable. In thy immensity all thought is lost, fancy gives over its flight and wearied imagination spends itself in vain, finding no coast nor limit of this ocean, nor, in the widest tract through which it soars, one point yet nearer the circumference than the first centre whence it parted.——Thus having oft essayed, thus sallied forth into the wide expanse, when I return again within myself, struck with the sense of this so

---

[WW] The nymphs, or female nature spirits, who were the life spirits of trees and sometimes specifically oaks. The oracle of Dodona was an oak whose rustling leaves were interpreted for divine messages.

narrow being and of the fullness of that immense one, I dare no more behold the amazing depths nor sound the abyss of deity.——

Yet since by thee, O sovereign mind, I have been formed such as I am, intelligent and rational, since the peculiar dignity of my nature is to know and contemplate thee, permit that with due freedom I exert those faculties with which thou hast adorned me. Bear with my venturous and bold approach. And since nor vain curiosity, nor fond conceit, nor love of aught save thee alone inspires me with such thoughts as these, be thou my assistant and guide me in this pursuit, while I venture thus to tread the labyrinth of wide nature and endeavour to trace thee in thy works . . .'

Here he stopped short and, starting, as out of a dream, 'Now, Philocles,' said he, 'inform me: how have I appeared to you in my fit? Seemed it a sensible kind of madness, like those transports which are permitted to our poets? Or was it downright raving?'

'I only wish,' said I, 'that you had been a little stronger in your transport, to have proceeded as you began, without ever minding me. For I was beginning to see wonders in that nature you taught me and was coming to know the hand of your Divine Artificer. But if you stop here, I shall lose the enjoyment of the pleasing vision. And already I begin to find a thousand difficulties in fancying such a universal genius as you describe.'

'Why,' said he, 'is there any difficulty in fancying the universe to be one entire thing? Can one otherwise think of it by what is visible than that all hangs together as of a piece?'

'Grant it. And what follows?'

'Only this: that, if it may indeed be said of the world that "it is simply one", there should be something belonging to it which makes it one.'

'As how?'

'No otherwise than as you may observe in everything. For to instance in what we see before us, I know you look upon the trees of this vast wood to be different from one another, and this tall oak, the noblest of the company, as it is by itself a different thing from all its fellows of the wood, so, with its own wood of numerous spreading branches (which seem so many different trees), it is still, I suppose, one and the selfsame tree. Now should you, as a mere caviller and not as a fair sceptic, tell me that, if a figure of wax or any other matter were cast in the exact shape and colours of this tree and tempered, if possible, to the same kind of substance, it might therefore possibly be a real tree of the same kind or species, I would have done with you and reason no longer. But, if you questioned me fairly, and desired I should satisfy you what I thought it was which made this oneness or sameness in the tree or any other plant, or by what it differed from the waxen figure or from any such figure accidentally made, either in the clouds or on the sand by the seashore, I should tell you that neither the wax nor sand nor cloud thus pieced together by our hand or fancy had any real relation within themselves, or had any nature by which they corresponded any more in that near situation of parts than if scattered ever so far asunder. But this I should affirm: that wherever there was such a sympathizing of parts as we saw here in our real tree, wherever there was such a plain concurrence in one common end and to the support, nourishment and propagation of so fair a form, we could not be mistaken in saying there was a peculiar nature belonging to this form and common to it with others of the same kind. By virtue of this, our tree is a real tree, lives, flourishes, and is still one and the same even when by vegetation and change of substance not one particle in it remains the same.'

'At this rate indeed,' said I, 'you have found a way to make very adorable places of these sylvan habitations. For, besides the living genius of each place, the woods too, which by your account are animated, have their Hamadryads, no doubt, and the springs and rivulets their nymphs in store belonging to them, and these too, by what I can apprehend, of immaterial and immortal substances.'

'We injure them then', replied Theocles, 'to say "they belong to these trees" and not rather "these trees to them". But, as for their immortality, let them look to it themselves. I only know that both theirs and all other natures must for their duration depend alone on that nature on which the world depends, and that every genius else must be subordinate to that one good genius, whom I would willingly persuade you to think belonging to this world, according to our present way of speaking.

Leaving, therefore, these trees', continued he, 'to personate themselves the best they can, let us examine this thing of personality between you and me and consider how you, Philocles, are you, and I am myself. For that there is a sympathy of parts in these figures of ours other than in those of marble formed by Phidias or Praxiteles, sense, I believe, will teach us.[XX] And yet that our own marble or stuff (whatever it be of which we are composed) wears out in seven, or at the longest in twice seven years, the meanest anatomist can tell us. Now where, I beseech you, will that same one be found at last, supposing it to lie in the stuff itself or any part of it? For when that is wholly spent and not one particle of it left, we are ourselves still as much as before.'

'What you philosophers are,' replied I, 'may be hard perhaps to determine, but, for the rest of mankind, I dare affirm that few are so long themselves as half seven years. It is good fortune if a man be one and the same only for a day or two. A year makes more revolutions than can be numbered.'

[XX] Phidias was an Athenian sculptor, active from about 475 to 430 BC and responsible for many works and designs in the great building programme in mid-fifth century BC Athens. Praxiteles was a celebrated Athenian sculptor active about a century later.

'True,' said he. 'But, though this may happen to a man and chiefly to one whose contrary vices set him at odds so often with himself, yet when he comes to suffer or be punished for those vices, he finds himself, if I mistake not, still one and the same. And you, Philocles, who, though you disown philosophy, are yet so true a proselyte to Pyrrhonism,[YY] should you at last, feeling the power of the Genius I preach, be wrought upon to own the divine hypothesis and, from this new turn of thought, admit a total change in all your principles and opinions, yet would you be still the selfsame Philocles, though better yet, if you will take my judgment, than the present one, as much as I love and value him. You see, therefore, there is a strange simplicity in this "you" and "me", that in reality they should be still one and the same, when neither one atom of body, one passion nor one thought remains the same. And, for that poor endeavour of making out this sameness or identity of being from some self-same matter or particle of matter, supposed to remain with us when all besides is changed, this is by so much the more contemptible as that matter itself is not really capable of such simplicity. For I dare answer, you will allow this "you" and "me" to be each of us simply and individually one better than you can allow the same to anything of mere matter, unless, quitting your inclination for scepticism, you fall so in love with the notion of an atom as to find it full as intelligible and certain to you as that "you" are "yourself".

But whatever', continued Theocles, 'be supposed of uncompounded matter (a thing at best pretty difficult to conceive), yet being compounded and put together in a certain number of such parts as unite and conspire in these frames of ours and others like them, if it can present us with so many innumerable instances of particular forms, who share this simple principle, by which they are really one, live, act and have a nature or genius peculiar to themselves and provident for their own welfare, how shall we at the same time overlook this in the whole and deny the great and general One of the world? How can we be so unnatural as to disown divine nature, our common parent, and refuse to recognize the universal and sovereign Genius?'

'Sovereigns', said I, 'require no notice to be taken of them when they pass incognito nor any homage where they appear not in due form. We may even have reason to presume they should be displeased with us for being too officious in endeavouring to discover them when they keep themselves either wholly invisible or in very dark disguise. As for the notice we take of these invisible powers in the common way of our religion, we have our visible sovereigns to answer for us. Our lawful superiors teach us what we are to own and to perform in worship. And we are dutiful in complying with them and

---

[YY] Pyrrhonism was the most radical and thorough-going scepticism, named for Pyrrho of Elis, *c.* 360 – *c.* 270 BC, who aimed at freeing the mind of disturbance by admitting the impossibility of any certain knowledge. For Shaftesbury's relation to scepticism, see Introduction, p. xiv.

following their example. But in a philosophical way I find no warrant for our being such earnest recognizers of a controverted title. However it be, you must allow one at least to understand the controversy and know the nature of these powers described. May one not inquire what substances they are of, whether material or immaterial?'

'May one not on the other hand', replied Theocles, 'inquire as well: what substance, or which of these two substances, you count your real and proper self? Or would you rather be no substance but choose to call yourself a mode or accident?'

'Truly,' said I, 'as accidental as my life may be or as random that humour is which governs it, I know nothing, after all, so real and substantial as myself. Therefore, if there be that thing you call a substance, I take for granted I am one. But for anything further relating to this question, you know my sceptic principles – I determine neither way.'

'Allow me then,' replied he, 'good Philocles, the same privilege of scepticism in this respect, since it concerns not the affair before us, which way we determine or whether we come to any determination at all in this point. For be the difficulty ever so great, it stands the same, you may perceive, against your own being as against that which I am pretending to convince you of. You may raise what objections you please on either hand, and your dilemma may be of notable force against the manner of such a supreme being's existence. But after you have done all, you will bring the same dilemma home to you and be at a loss still about yourself. When you have argued ever so long upon these metaphysical points of mode and substance, and have philosophically concluded from the difficulties of each hypothesis that "there cannot be in nature such a universal One as this", you must conclude from the same reasons that "there cannot be any such particular one as yourself". But that there is actually such a one as this latter, your own mind, it is hoped, may satisfy you. And of this mind it is enough to say that it is something which acts upon a body and has something passive under it and subject to it, that it has not only body or mere matter for its subject but in some respect even itself too and what proceeds from it, that it superintends and manages its own imaginations, appearances, fancies, correcting, working and modelling these as it finds good and adorning and accomplishing the best it can this composite order of body and understanding. Such a mind and governing part I know there is somewhere in the world. Let Pyrrho, by the help of such another, contradict me if he pleases. We have our several understandings and thoughts, however we came by them. Each understands and thinks the best he can for his own purpose: he for himself; I for another self. And who, I beseech you, for the whole?——No one? Nothing at all?——The world, perhaps, you suppose to be mere body, a mass of modified matter. The bodies of men are part therefore of this body. The imaginations, sensations, apprehensions of men are included in this body and inherent in it, produced out of it and resumed again into it, though the body, it seems, never dreams of it! The world itself is never the wiser for all the wit and wisdom it breeds! It has no apprehension at all of what it is doing, no thought kept to itself for its own proper use or purpose, not a single imagination or reflection by which to discover or be conscious of the manifold imaginations and inventions which it sets afoot and deals abroad with such an open hand! The goodly bulk, so prolific, kind and yielding for every one else, has nothing left at last for its own share, having unhappily lavished all away!

By what chance? I would fain understand. How or by what necessity? Who gives the law? Who orders and distributes thus?

"Nature," say you.

And what is nature? Is it sense? Is it a person? Has she reason or understanding?

"No."

Who then understands for her or is interested or concerned in her behalf?

"No one, not a soul. But everyone for himself."

Come on then. Let us hear further. Is not this nature still a self? Or tell me, I beseech you: How are you one? By what token? Or by virtue of what?

"By a principle which joins certain parts and which thinks and acts consonantly for the use and purpose of those parts."

Say, therefore: What is your whole system a part of? Or is it, indeed, no part, but a whole, by itself, absolute, independent and unrelated to anything besides? If it be indeed a part and really related, to what else, I beseech you, than to the whole of nature? Is there then such a uniting principle in nature? If so, how are you then a self and nature not so? How have you something to understand and act for you and nature, who gave this understanding, nothing at all to understand for her, advise her or help her out – poor being! – on any occasion, whatever necessity she may be in? Has the world such ill fortune in the main? Are there so many particular understanding active principles everywhere? And is there nothing at last which thinks, acts or understands for all? Nothing which administers or looks after all?

"No," says one of a modern hypothesis, "for the world was from eternity as you see it and is no more than barely what you see: matter modified; a lump in motion, with here and there a thought or scattered portion of dissoluble intelligence."

"No", says one of an ancienter hypothesis, "for the world was once without any intelligence or thought at all: mere matter, chaos and a play of atoms, till thought, by chance, came into play and made up a harmony which was never designed or thought of."

Admirable conceit! Believe it who can. For my own share (Thank Providence!), I have a mind in my possession which serves, such as it is, to

303

keep my body and its affections, my passions, appetites, imaginations, fancies and the rest in tolerable harmony and order. But the order of the universe, I am persuaded still, is much the better of the two. Let Epicurus, if he please, think his the better and, believing no genius or wisdom above his own, inform us by what chance it was dealt him and how atoms came to be so wise.

In fine,' continued Theocles, raising his voice and action, 'being thus, even by scepticism itself, convinced the more still of my own being and of this self of mine that it is a real self drawn out and copied from another principal and original self, the great one of the world, I endeavour to be really one with it and conformable to it as far as I am able. I consider that, as there is one general mass, one body of the whole, so to this body there is an order, to this order a mind, that to this general mind each particular one must have relation as being of like substance (as much as we can understand of substance), alike active upon body, original to motion and order, alike simple, uncompounded, individual, of like energy, effect and operation, and more like still if it cooperates with it to general good and strives to will according to the best of wills. So that it cannot surely but seem natural that the particular mind should seek its happiness in conformity with the general one and endeavour to resemble it in its highest simplicity and excellence.'

'Therefore, now,' said I, 'good Theocles, be once again the enthusiast, and let me hear anew that divine song with which I was lately charmed. I am already got over my qualm and begin better than ever to fancy such a nature as you speak of insomuch that I find myself mightily in its interest and concerned that all should go happily and well with it, though, at the rate it often runs, I can scarce help being in some pain on its account.'

'Fear not, my friend,' replied he. 'For know that every particular nature certainly and constantly produces what is good to itself unless something foreign disturbs or hinders it, either by overpowering and corrupting it within or by violence from without. Thus nature in the patient struggles to the last and strives to throw off the distemper. Thus, even in these plants we see round us, every particular nature thrives and attains its perfection, if nothing from without obstructs it nor anything foreign has already impaired or wounded it, and, even in this case, it does its utmost still to redeem itself. What are all weaknesses, distortions, sicknesses, imperfect births and the seeming contradictions and perversities of nature other than of this sort? And how ignorant must one be of all natural causes and operations to think that any of these disorders happen by a miscarriage of the particular nature and not by the force of some foreign nature which overpowers it? If, therefore, every particular nature be thus constantly and unerringly true to itself, and certain to produce only what is good for itself and conducing to its own right state, shall not the general one, the nature of the whole, do full as much? Shall that alone miscarry or fail? Or is there anything foreign which should at any time do violence upon it or force it out of its natural way? If not, then all it produces is to its own advantage and good, the good of all in general, and what is for the good of all in general is just and good.'

'It is so,' said I, 'I confess.'

'Then you ought to rest satisfied,' replied he, 'and not only so, but be pleased and rejoice at what happens, knowing whence it comes and to what perfection it contributes.'

'Bless me!,' said I, 'Theocles, into what a superstition are you like to lead me! I thought it heretofore the mark of a superstitious mind to search for Providence in the common accidents of life and ascribe to the divine power those common disasters and calamities which nature has entailed on mankind. But now I find I must place all in general to one account and, viewing things through a kind of magical glass, I am to see the worst of ills transformed to good and admire equally whatever comes from one and the same perfect hand. But no matter, I can surmount all. Go on, Theocles, and let me advise you in my own behalf that, since you have rekindled me, you do not by delaying give me time to cool again.'

'I would have you know,' replied he, 'I scorn to take the advantage of a warm fit and be beholden to temper or imagination for gaining me your assent. Therefore, before I go yet a step farther, I am resolved to enter again into cool reason with you and ask if you admit for proof what I advanced yesterday upon that head, of a universal union, coherence or sympathizing of things?'

'By force of probability,' said I, 'you overcame me. Being convinced of a consent and correspondence in all we saw of things, I considered it as unreasonable not to allow the same throughout.'

'Unreasonable indeed!,' replied he. 'For, in the infinite residue, were there no principle of union, it would seem next to impossible that things within our sphere should be consistent and keep their order. For what was infinite would be predominant.'

'It seems so.'

'Tell me then,' said he, 'after this union owned, how you can refuse to allow the name of demonstration to the remaining arguments, which establish the government of a perfect mind.'

'Your solutions', said I, 'of the ill appearances are not perfect enough to pass for demonstration. And whatever seems vicious or imperfect in the creation puts a stop to further conclusions till the thing be solved.'

'Did you not then', said he, 'agree with me when I averred that the appearances must of necessity stand as they are and things seem altogether as imperfect, even on the concession of a perfect supreme mind existent?'

'I did so.'

'And is not the same reason good still, namely, that in an infinity of things, mutually relative, a mind which sees not infinitely can see nothing fully and must therefore frequently see that as imperfect which in itself is really perfect?'

'The reason is still good.'

'Are the appearances, then, any objection to our hypothesis?'

'None, while they remain appearances only.'

'Can you then prove them to be any more? For if you cannot, you prove nothing. And that it lies on you to prove you plainly see, since the appearances do not only agree with the hypothesis but are a necessary consequence from it. To bid me prove, therefore, in this case is in a manner the same as to bid me be infinite. For nothing beside what is infinite can see infinite connections.'

'The presumption, I must confess,' said I, 'by this reckoning is wholly on your side. Yet still this is only presumption.'

'Take demonstration then,' said he, 'if you can endure I should reason thus abstractedly and drily. The appearances of ill, you say, are not necessarily that ill they represent to us.'

'I own it.'

'Therefore, what they represent may possibly be good.'

'It may.'

'And therefore there may possibly be no real ill in things, but all may be perfectly concurrent to one interest, the interest of that universal One.'

'It may be so.'

'Why, then, if it may be so (be not surprised), it follows that it must be so, on the account of that great unit and simple self-principle, which you have granted in the whole. For whatever is possible in the whole the nature or mind of the whole will put in execution for the whole's good. And, if it be possible to exclude ill, it will exclude it. Therefore, since, notwithstanding the appearances, it is possible that ill may actually be excluded, count upon it that actually it is excluded. For nothing merely passive can oppose this universally active principle. If anything active oppose it, it is another principle.'

'I allow it.'

'It is impossible. For, were there in nature two or more principles, either they must agree or not. If they agree not, all must be confusion till one be predominant. If they agree, there must be some natural reason for their agreement, and this natural reason cannot be from chance but from some particular design, contrivance or thought, which brings us up again to one principle and makes the other two to be subordinate. And thus, when we have compared each of the three opinions, namely, that there is no designing active principle, that there is more than one, or that finally there is but one, we shall perceive that the only consistent opinion is the last. And since one or other of these opinions must of necessity be true, what can we determine other than that the last is, and must be so, demonstrably (if it be demonstration that in three opinions, one of which must necessarily be true, two being plainly absurd, the third must be the truth).'

'Enough,' said I, 'Theocles. My doubts are vanished. Malice and chance – vain phantoms! – have yielded to that all-prevalent wisdom which you have established. You are conqueror in the cool way of reason and may with honour now grow warm again in your poetic vein. Return therefore, I entreat you, once more to that perfection of being and address yourself to it as before on our approaches to these sylvan scenes where first it seemed to inspire you. I shall now no longer be in danger of imagining either magic or superstition in the case since you invoke no other power than that single One which seems so natural.'

'Thus I continue then,' said Theocles, 'addressing myself as you would have me, to that guardian deity and inspirer whom we are to imagine present here, but not here only. For –

O mighty Genius! Sole animating and inspiring power! Author and subject of these thoughts! Thy influence is universal, and in all things thou art inmost. From thee depend their secret springs of action. Thou movest them with an irresistible unwearied force, by sacred and inviolable laws, framed for the good of each particular being, as best may suit with the perfection, life and vigour of the whole. The vital principle is widely shared and infinitely varied, dispersed throughout, nowhere extinct. All lives and, by succession, still revives. The temporary beings quit their borrowed forms and yield their elementary substance to newcomers. Called in their several turns to life, they view the light and, viewing, pass, that others too may be spectators of the goodly scene and greater numbers still enjoy the privilege of nature. Munificent and great, she imparts herself to most and makes the subjects of her bounty infinite. Nought stays her hastening hand. No time nor substance is lost or unimproved. New forms arise and, when the old dissolve, the matter whence they were composed is not left useless but wrought with equal management and art, even in corruption, nature's seeming waste and vile abhorrence. The abject state appears merely as the way or passage to some better. But could we nearly view it and with indifference, remote from the antipathy of sense, we then perhaps should highest raise our admiration, convinced that even the way itself was equal to the end. Nor can we judge less favourably of that consummate art exhibited through all the works of nature, since our weak eyes, helped by mechanic art, discover in these works a hidden scene of wonders, worlds within worlds of infinite minuteness, though as to art still equal to the greatest and pregnant with more wonders than the most discerning sense, joined with the greatest art or the acutest reason, can penetrate or unfold.

But it is in vain for us to search the bulky mass of matter, seeking to know its nature, how great the whole itself or even how small its parts.

If, knowing only some of the rules of motion, we seek to trace it further, it is in vain we follow it into the bodies it has reached. Our tardy apprehensions fail us and can reach nothing beyond the body itself, through which it is diffused. Wonderful being (if we may call it so), which bodies never receive except from others which lose it, nor ever lose, unless by imparting it to others. Even without change of place it has its force, and bodies big with motion labour to move, yet stir not, while they express an energy beyond our comprehension.

In vain, too, we pursue that phantom time, too small and yet too mighty for our grasp, when, shrinking to a narrow point, it escapes our hold or mocks our scanty thought by swelling to eternity, an object unproportioned to our capacity, as is thy being, O thou ancient cause, older than time, yet young with fresh eternity!

In vain we try to fathom the abyss of space, the seat of thy extensive being, of which no place is empty, no void which is not full.

In vain we labour to understand that principle of sense and thought, which seeming in us to depend so much on motion, yet differs so much from it and from matter itself as not to suffer us to conceive how thought can more result from this than this arise from thought. But thought we own pre-eminent, and confess the reallest of beings, the only existence of which we are made sure by being conscious. All else may be only dream and shadow. All which even sense suggests may be deceitful. The sense itself remains still, reason subsists, and thought maintains its eldership of being. Thus are we in a manner conscious of that original and eternally existent thought whence we derive our own. And thus the assurance we have of the existence of beings above our sense and of thee, the great exemplar of thy works, comes from thee, the all true and perfect, who hast thus communicated thyself more immediately to us, so as in some manner to inhabit within our souls, thou who art original soul, diffusive, vital in all, inspiriting the whole.

All nature's wonders serve to excite and perfect this idea of their author. It is here he suffers us to see and even converse with him in a manner suitable to our frailty. How glorious is it to contemplate him in this noblest of his works apparent to us, the system of the bigger world!'

Here I must own, it was no small comfort to me to find that, as our meditation turned, we were likely to get clear of an entangling abstruse philosophy. I was in hopes Theocles, as he proceeded, might stick closer to nature since he was now come upon the borders of our world. And here I would willingly have welcomed him, had I thought it safe at present to venture the least interruption.

'Besides the neighbouring planets,' continued he in his rapturous strain, 'what multitudes of fixed stars did we see sparkle not an hour ago in the clear night, which yet had hardly yielded to the day? How many others are discovered by the help of art? Yet how many remain still beyond the reach of our discovery! Crowded as they seem, their distance from each other is as unmeasurable by art as is the distance between them and us. Whence we are naturally taught the immensity of that being who, through these immense spaces, has disposed such an infinity of bodies, belonging each (as we may well presume) to systems as complete as our own world, since even the smallest spark of this bright galaxy may vie with this our sun, which, shining now full out, gives us new life, exalts our spirits and makes us feel divinity more present.

Prodigious orb! Bright source of vital heat and spring of day!——Soft flame, yet how intense, how active! How diffusive and how vast a substance yet how collected thus within itself and in a glowing mass confined to the centre of this planetary world!——Mighty being! Brightest image and representative of the Almighty! Supreme of the corporeal world! Unperishing in grace and of undecaying youth! Fair, beautiful and hardly mortal creature! By what secret ways dost thou receive the supplies which maintain thee still in such unwearied vigour and unexhausted glory, notwithstanding those eternally emitted streams and that continual expense of vital treasures which enlighten and invigorate the surrounding worlds?

Around him all the planets, with this our earth, single or with attendants, continually move, seeking to receive the blessing of his light and lively warmth! Towards him they seem to tend with prone descent, as to their centre, but happily controlled still by another impulse, they keep their heavenly order and, in just numbers and exactest measure, go the eternal rounds.

But, O thou who art the author and modifier of these various motions! O sovereign and sole mover, by whose high art the rolling spheres are governed and these stupendous bodies of our world hold their unrelenting courses! O wise economist and powerful chief, whom all the elements and powers of nature serve! How hast thou animated these moving worlds? What spirit or soul infused? What bias fixed? Or how encompassed them in liquid ether, driving them as with the breath of living winds, thy active and unwearied ministers in this intricate and mighty work?

Thus powerfully are the systems held entire and kept from fatal interfering. Thus is our ponderous globe directed in its annual course, daily revolving on its own centre, while the obsequious moon with double labour, monthly surrounding this our bigger orb, attends the motion of her sister planet and pays in common her circular homage to the sun.

Yet is this mansion globe, this man container, of a much narrower compass even than other its fellow wanderers of our system. How narrow then must it appear compared with the capacious system of its own sun? And how narrow, or as nothing, in respect of those innumerable systems of other suns? Yet how immense a body it seems compared with ours of human form, a borrowed remnant of its variable and oft-converted surface, though animated with a sublime celestial spirit by which we have relation and tendency to Thee our heavenly sire, centre of souls, to whom these spirits of ours by nature tend, as earthly bodies to their proper centre.——O did they tend as unerringly and constantly!——But thou alone composest the disorders of the corporeal world and, from the restless and fighting elements, raisest that peaceful concord and conspiring beauty of the ever-flourishing creation. Even so canst thou convert these jarring motions of intelligent beings and, in due time and manner, cause them to find their rest, making them contribute to the good and perfection of the universe, thy all-good and perfect work.'

Here again he broke off, looking on me as if he expected I should speak, which, when he found plainly I would not but continued still in a posture of musing thought, 'Why Philocles,' said he, with an air of wonder, 'what can this mean that you should suffer me thus to run on without the least interruption? Have you at once given over your scrupulous philosophy to let me range thus at pleasure through these aerial spaces and imaginary regions where my capricious fancy or easy faith has led me? I would have you to consider better and know, my Philocles, that I had never trusted myself with you in this vein of enthusiasm, had I not relied on you to govern it a little better.'

'I find, then,' said I, rousing myself from my musing posture, 'you expect I should serve you in the same capacity as that musician, whom an ancient orator made use of at his elbow, to strike such moving notes as raised him when he was perceived to sink and calmed him again when his impetuous spirit was transported in too high a strain.'

'You imagine right,' replied Theocles, 'and therefore I am resolved not to go on till you have promised to pull me by the sleeve when I grow extravagant.'

'Be it so,' said I. 'You have my promise.'

'But if, instead of rising in my transports, I should grow flat and tiresome, what lyre or instrument would you employ to raise me?'

The danger, I told him, could hardly be supposed to lie on this hand. His vein was a plentiful one, and his enthusiasm in no likelihood of failing him. His subject, too, as well as his numbers, would bear him out. And with the advantage of the rural scene around us, his numbered prose, I thought, supplied the room of the best pastoral song. For, in the manner I was now wrought up, it was as agreeable to me to hear him, in this kind of passion, invoke his stars and elements, as to hear one of those amorous shepherds complaining to his flock and making the woods and rocks resound the name of her whom he adored.

'Begin therefore,' continued I, still pressing him, 'begin anew and lead me boldly through your elements. Wherever there is danger, be it on either hand, I promise to give you warning when I perceive it.'

'Let us begin, then,' said he, 'with this our element of earth, which yonder we see cultivated with such care by the early swains now working in the plain below.

Unhappy restless men who first disdained these peaceful labours, gentle rural tasks, performed with such delight! What pride or what ambition bred this scorn? Hence all those fatal evils of your race, enormous luxury, despising homely fare, ranges through seas and lands, rifles the globe, and men, ingenious to their misery, work out for themselves the means of heavier labour, anxious cares, and sorrow. Not satisfied to turn and manure for their use the wholesome and beneficial mould of this their earth, they dig yet deeper and, seeking out imaginary wealth, they search its very entrails.

Here, led by curiosity, we find minerals of different natures which, by their simplicity, discover no less of the divine art than the most compounded of nature's works. Some are found capable of surprising changes, others as durable, and hard to be destroyed or changed by fire or utmost art. So various are the subjects of our contemplation that even the study of these inglorious parts of nature in the nether world is able itself alone to yield large matter and employment for the busiest spirits of men, who in the labour of these experiments can willingly consume their lives.——But the noisome poisonous steams which the earth breathes from these dark caverns, where she conceals her treasures, suffer not prying mortals to live long in this search.

How comfortable is it to those who come out hence alive to breathe a purer air, to see the rejoicing light of day and tread the fertile ground! How gladly they contemplate the surface of the earth, their habitation heated and enlivened by the sun and tempered by the fresh air of fanning breezes! These exercise the resty plants and scour the unactive globe. And when the sun draws hence thick clouded steams and vapours, it is only to digest and exalt the unwholesome particles and commit them to the sprightly air, which, soon imparting its quick and vital spirit, renders them again with improvement to the earth in gentle breathings or in rich dews and fruitful showers. The same air, moving about the mighty mass, enters its pores, impregnating the whole. And both the sun and air conspiring, so animate this mother earth that, though ever breeding, her vigour is as great, her beauty as fresh and her looks as charming as if she newly came out of the forming hands of her creator.

How beautiful is the water among the inferior earthly works! Heavy, liquid and transparent, without the springing vigour and expansive force of air but not without activity. Stubborn and unyielding when compressed, but placidly avoiding force and bending every way with ready fluency! Insinuating, it dissolves the lumpish earth, frees the entangled bodies, procures their intercourse and summons to the field the keen terrestrial particles whose happy strifes, soon ending in strict union, produce the various forms which we behold. How vast are the abysses of the sea, where this soft element is stored and whence the sun and winds extracting raise it into clouds! These, soon converted into rain, water the thirsty ground and supply afresh the springs and rivers, the comfort of the neighbouring plains and sweet refreshment of all animals.

But whither shall we trace the sources of the light or in what ocean comprehend the luminous matter so wide diffused through the immense spaces which it fills? What seats shall we assign to that fierce element of fire, too active to be confined within the compass of the sun and not excluded even the bowels of the heavy earth? The air itself submits to it and serves as its inferior instrument. Even this our sun, with all those numerous suns, the glittering host of heaven, seem to receive from hence the vast supplies which keep them ever in their splendid state. The invisible ethereal substance, penetrating both liquid and solid bodies, is diffused throughout the universe. It cherishes the cold dull massy globe and warms it to its centre. It forms the minerals, gives life and growth to vegetables, kindles a soft, invisible and vital flame in the breasts of living creatures, frames, animates and nurses all the various forms, sparing as well as employing for their use, those sulphurous and combustible matters of which they are composed. Benign and gentle amid all, it still maintains this happy peace and concord, according to its stated and peculiar laws. But these once broken, the acquitted being takes its course unruled. It runs impetuous through the fatal breach and, breaking into visible and fierce flames, passes triumphant over the yielding forms, converting all into itself and dissolving now those systems which itself before had formed. It is thus . . .'

Here Theocles stopped on a sudden when, as he imagined, I was putting my hand out to lay hold on his sleeve.

'O Philocles,' said he, 'it is well remembered. I was growing too warm, I find, as well I might indeed in this hot element. And here perhaps I might have talked yet more mysteriously, had you been one who could think otherwise than in the common way of the soft flames of love. You might, perhaps, have heard wonders in this kind: how all things had their being hence and how their noblest end was to be here wrapped up, consumed and lost. But in these high flights I might possibly have gone near to burn my wings.'

'Indeed,' said I, 'you might well expect the fate of Icarus for your high soaring.[ZZ] But this, indeed, was not what I feared. For you were got above danger and, with that devouring element on your side, had mastered not only the sun himself but everything which stood in your way. I was afraid it might, in the issue, run to what they tell us of a universal conflagration, in which I knew not how it might go, possibly, with our Genius.'

'I am glad,' said he, 'Philocles, to find this grown such a concern with you. But you may rest secure here, if the case you meant were that periodical conflagration talked of by some philosophers.[AAA] For there the Genius would of necessity be all in all. And, in those intervals of creation, when no form nor

---

[ZZ] In Greek legend, Icarus was the son of Daedalus, an inventive craftsman, who, after the two were imprisoned by King Minos on Crete, constructed artificial wings for their escape. Daedalus made it to Sicily, but Icarus flew too close to the sun so that the wax of the wings melted and he drowned in the Aegean Sea.

[AAA] Such a belief was mistakenly attributed by the stoics to Heraclitus, an Ionian philosopher who wrote about 500 BC.

species existed anywhere out of the divine mind, all then was deity, all was that One, collected thus within itself and subsisting (as they imagined) rather in a more simple and perfect manner than when multiplied in more ways and becoming productive, it unfolded itself in the various map of nature and this fair visible world.'

'But for my part,' said I, interrupting him, 'who can much better see divinity unfolded than in that involved and solitary state before creation, I could wish you would go a little further with me in the map of nature, especially if, descending from your lofty flights, you would be content to pitch upon this humble spot of earth, where I could better accompany you, wherever you led me.'

'But you,' replied he, 'who would confine me to this heavy earth, must yet allow me the same wings of fancy. How else shall I fly with you through different climates, from pole to pole and from the frigid to the torrid zone?'

'O,' said I, 'for this purpose I will allow you the Pegasus of the poets or that winged griffin which an Italian poet of the moderns gave to one of his heroes, yet on this condition, that you take no such extravagant flight, as his was, to the moon but keep closely to this orb of earth.'[BBB]

'Since you will have it so,' replied Theocles, 'let us try first on the darkest and most imperfect parts of our map, and see how you can endure the prospect.

How oblique and faintly looks the sun on yonder climates, far removed from him! How tedious are the winters there! How deep the horrors of the night and how uncomfortable even the light of day! The freezing winds employ their fiercest breath yet are not spent with blowing. The sea, which elsewhere is scarce confined within its limits, lies here immured in walls of crystal. The snow covers the hills and almost fills the lowest valleys. How wide and deep it lies, incumbent over the plains, hiding the sluggish rivers, the shrubs and trees, the dens of beasts and mansions of distressed and feeble men!——See where they lie confined, hardly secure against the raging cold or the attacks of the wild beasts, now masters of the wasted field and forced by hunger out of the naked woods!——Yet not disheartened, such is the force of human breasts, but thus provided for by art and prudence, the kind compensating gifts of heaven, men and their herds may wait for a release. For at length the sun, approaching, melts the snow, sets longing men at liberty and affords them means and time to make provision against the next return of cold. It breaks the icy fetters of the main, where vast sea monsters pierce through floating islands, with arms which can withstand the crystal rock, while others, who of themselves seem great as islands, are by their bulk alone armed against all but

---

[BBB] In Greek mythology, Pegasus was a winged horse who carried Zeus's thunderbolt. In Ludovico Ariosto's epic, *Orlando Furioso* (1516), a hippogriffin, part horse and part eagle, conveyed Astolfo to the moon (Book 34).

man, whose superiority over creatures of such stupendous size and force should make him mindful of his privilege of reason and force him humbly to adore the great composer of these wondrous frames and author of his own superior wisdom.

But leaving these dull climates, so little favoured by the sun, for those happier regions, on which he looks more kindly, making perpetual summer, how great an alteration do we find? His purer light confounds weak-sighted mortals, pierced by his scorching beams. Scarce can they tread the glowing ground. The air they breathe cannot enough abate the fire which burns within their panting breasts. Their bodies melt. Overcome and fainting, they seek the shade and wait the cool refreshments of the night. Yet oft the bounteous creator bestows other refreshments. He casts a veil of clouds before them and raises gentle gales favoured by which the men and beasts pursue their labours, and plants refreshed by dews and showers can gladly bear the warmest sunbeams.

And here the varying scene opens to new wonders. We see a country rich with gems but richer with the fragrant spices it affords. How gravely move the largest of land creatures on the banks of this fair river! How ponderous are their arms and vast their strength, with courage and a sense superior to the other beasts! Yet are they tamed, we see, by mankind and brought even to fight their battles rather as allies and confederates than as slaves.——But let us turn our eyes towards these smaller and more curious objects, the numerous and devouring insects on the trees in these wide plains. How shining, strong and lasting are the subtle threads spun from their artful mouths! Who, beside the all-wise, has taught them to compose the beautiful soft shells, in which, recluse and buried yet still alive, they undergo such a surprising change when not destroyed by men, who clothe and adorn themselves with the labours and lives of these weak creatures and are proud of wearing such inglorious spoils? How sumptuously apparelled, gay and splendid are all the various insects which feed on the other plants of this warm region! How beautiful the plants themselves in all their various growths, from the triumphant palm down to the humble moss!

Now may we see that happy country where precious gums and balsams flow from trees and nature yields her most delicious fruits. How tame and tractable, how patient of labour and of thirst, are those large creatures who, lifting up their lofty heads, go led and loaden through these dry and barren places! Their shape and temper show them framed by nature to submit to man and fitted for his service, who from hence ought to be more sensible of his wants and of the divine bounty thus supplying them.

But see, not far from us, that fertilest of lands, watered and fed by a friendly generous stream which, before it enters the sea, divides itself into many branches to dispense more equally the rich and nitrous manure it bestows so kindly and in due time on the adjacent plains.——Fair image of that fruitful and exuberant nature who, with a flood of bounty, blesses all things and, parent-like, out of her many breasts sends the nutritious draught in various streams to her rejoicing offspring!——Innumerable are the dubious forms and unknown species which drink the slimy current, whether they are such as, leaving the scorched deserts, satiate here their ardent thirst and promiscuously engendering, beget a monstrous race or whether, as it is said, by the sun's genial heat, active on the fermenting ooze, new forms are generated and issue from the river's fertile bed.——See there the noted tyrant of the flood and terror of its borders when, suddenly displaying his horrid form, the amphibious ravager invades the land, quitting his watery den, and, from the deep emerging with hideous rush, sweeps over the trembling plain. The natives from afar behold with wonder the enormous bulk sprung from so small an egg. With horror they relate the monster's nature, cruel and deceitful – how he with dire hypocrisy and false tears beguiles the simple-hearted and, inspiring tenderness and kind compassion, kills with pious fraud.——Sad emblem of that spiritual plague, dire superstition! Native of this soil, where first religion grew unsociable and, among different worshippers, bred mutual hatred and abhorrence of each other's temples.[22] The infection spreads, and nations now profane one to another war fiercer and, in religion's cause, forget humanity while savage zeal, with meek and pious semblance, works dreadful massacre and, for heaven's sake (horrid pretence!) makes desolate the earth.——

Here let us leave these monsters (glad if we could here confine them) and, detesting the dire prolific soil, fly to the vast deserts of these parts. All ghastly and hideous as they appear, they want not their peculiar beauties. The wildness pleases. We seem to live alone with nature. We view her in her inmost recesses, and contemplate her with more delight in these original wilds than in the artificial labyrinths and feigned wildernesses of the palace. The objects of the place, the scaly serpents, the savage beasts and poisonous insects, how terrible soever or how contrary to human nature, are beauteous in themselves and fit to raise our thoughts in admiration of that divine wisdom, so far superior to our short views. Unable to declare the use or service of all things in this universe, we are yet assured of the perfection of all and of the justice of that economy to which all things are subservient and in respect of which things seemingly deformed are amiable, disorder becomes regular, corruption wholesome and poisons, such as these we have seen, prove healing and beneficial.

But, behold! Through a vast tract of sky before us, the mighty Atlas rears his lofty head, covered with snow above the clouds.[CCC] Beneath the mountain's

---

[CCC] The great mountain range that bends across the north-western corner of Africa.

[22] See pp. 364–5 [for further discussion of Egypt and the history of priestcraft and superstition].

foot, the rocky country rises into hills, a proper basis of the ponderous mass above, where huge embodied rocks lie piled on one another and seem to prop the high arch of heaven.——See with what trembling steps poor mankind tread the narrow brink of the deep precipices, from whence with giddy horror they look down, mistrusting even the ground which bears them, while they hear the hollow sound of torrents underneath and see the ruin of the impending rock, with falling trees which hang with their roots upwards and seem to draw more ruin after them. Here thoughtless men, seized with the newness of such objects, become thoughtful and willingly contemplate the incessant changes of this earth's surface. They see, as in one instant, the revolutions of past ages, the fleeting forms of things and the decay even of this our globe, whose youth and first formation they consider while the apparent spoil and irreparable breaches of the wasted mountain show them the world itself only as a noble ruin and make them think of its approaching period.——But here, mid-way the mountain, a spacious border of thick wood harbours our wearied travellers, who now are come among the evergreen and lofty pines, the firs and noble cedars, whose towering heads seem endless in the sky, the rest of the trees appearing only as shrubs beside them. And here a different horror seizes our sheltered travellers when they see the day diminished by the deep shades of the vast wood, which, closing thick above, spreads darkness and eternal night below. The faint and gloomy light looks horrid as the shade itself, and the profound stillness of these places imposes silence upon men, struck with the hoarse echoings of every sound within the spacious caverns of the wood. Here space astonishes. Silence itself seems pregnant while an unknown force works on the mind and dubious objects move the wakeful sense. Mysterious voices are either heard or fancied, and various forms of deity seem to present themselves and appear more manifest in these sacred sylvan scenes, such as of old gave rise to temples and favoured the religion of the ancient world. Even we ourselves, who in plain characters may read divinity from so many bright parts of earth, choose rather these obscurer places to spell out that mysterious being, which to our weak eyes appears at best under a veil of cloud.'

Here he paused a while and began to cast about his eyes, which before seemed fixed. He looked more calmly, with an open countenance and free air, by which, and other tokens, I could easily find we were come to an end of our descriptions and that, whether I would or no, Theocles was now resolved to take his leave of the sublime, the morning being spent and the forenoon by this time well advanced.

Section 2

'Methinks, Philocles,' said he, changing to a familiar voice, 'we had better leave these unsociable places whither our fancy has transported us and return to ourselves here again in our more conversable woods and temperate climates. Here no fierce heats nor colds annoy us; no precipices nor cataracts amaze us. Nor need we here be afraid of our own voices while we hear the notes of such a cheerful choir and find the echoes rather agreeable and inviting us to talk.'

'I confess,' said I, 'those foreign nymphs, if there were any belonging to those miraculous woods, were much too awful beauties to please me. I found our familiar home nymphs a great deal more to my humour. Yet, for all this, I cannot help being concerned for your breaking off just when we were got half the world over and wanted only to take America in our way home. Indeed, as for Europe, I could excuse your making any great tour there because of the little variety it would afford us. Besides that, it would be hard to see it in any view without meeting still that politic face of affairs which would too much disturb us in our philosophical flights. But, for the western tract, I cannot imagine why you should neglect such noble subjects as are there, unless perhaps the gold and silver, to which I find you such a bitter enemy, frighted you from a mother-soil so full of it. If these countries had been as bare of those metals as old Sparta,[DDD] we might have heard more perhaps of the Perus and Mexicos than of all Asia and Africa. We might have had creatures, plants, woods, mountains, rivers, beyond any of those we have passed. How sorry am I to lose the noble Amazon! How sorry . . .'

Here, as I would have proceeded, I saw so significant a smile on Theocles' face that it stopped me, out of curiosity, to ask him his thought.

'Nothing,' said he, 'nothing but this very subject itself. Go on. I see you'll finish it for me. The spirit of this sort of prophecy has seized you. And Philocles, the cold indifferent Philocles, is become a pursuer of the same mysterious beauty.'

'It is true,' said I, 'Theocles. I own it. Your genius, the genius of the place and the Great Genius have at last prevailed. I shall no longer resist the passion growing in me for things of a natural kind, where neither art nor the conceit or caprice of man has spoiled their genuine order by breaking in upon that primitive state. Even the rude rocks, the mossy caverns, the irregular unwrought grottos and broken falls of waters, with all the horrid graces of the wilderness itself, as representing nature more, will be the more engaging and appear with a magnificence beyond the formal mockery of princely gardens.——But tell me, I entreat you: how comes it that, excepting a few philosophers of your sort, the only people who are enamoured in this way and seek the woods, the rivers or seashores, are your poor vulgar lovers?'

'Say not this', replied he, 'of lovers only. For is it not the same with poets and all those other students in nature and the arts which copy after her? In

---

[DDD] Shaftesbury repeated the received opinion, based on Xenophon, Plutarch and others, that the Spartans were forbidden the use of gold and silver as money. Modern scholarly opinion does not agree: see H. Michell, *Sparta* (London: Cambridge University Press, 1952), pp. 298–307.

short, is not this the real case of all who are lovers either of the Muses or the Graces?'

'However,' said I, 'all those who are deep in this romantic way are looked upon, you know, as a people either plainly out of their wits or overrun with melancholy and enthusiasm.[23] We always endeavour to recall them from these solitary places. And I must own that often, when I have found my fancy run this way, I have checked myself, not knowing what it was possessed me when I was passionately struck with objects of this kind.'

'No wonder', replied he, 'if we are at a loss when we pursue the shadow for the substance. For, if we may trust to what our reasoning has taught us, whatever in nature is beautiful or charming is only the faint shadow of that first beauty. So that every real love depending on the mind and being only the contemplation of beauty, either as it really is in itself or as it appears imperfectly in the objects which strike the sense, how can the rational mind rest here or be satisfied with the absurd enjoyment which reaches the sense alone?'

'From this time forward then,' said I, 'I shall no more have reason to fear those beauties which strike a sort of melancholy, like the places we have named or like these solemn groves. No more shall I avoid the moving accents of soft music or fly from the enchanting features of the fairest human face.'

'If you are already', replied he, 'such a proficient in this new love that you are sure never to admire the representative beauty except for the sake of the original nor aim at other enjoyment than of the rational kind, you may then be confident.'

'I am so and presume accordingly to answer for myself. However, I should not be ill satisfied if you explained yourself a little better as to this mistake of mine you seem to fear.'

'Would it be any help to tell you that the absurdity lay in seeking the enjoyment elsewhere than in the subject loved?'

'The matter, I must confess, is still mysterious.'

'Imagine then, good Philocles, if being taken with the beauty of the ocean, which you see yonder at a distance, it should come into your head to seek how to command it and, like some mighty admiral, ride master of the sea. Would not the fancy be a little absurd?'

'Absurd enough, in conscience. The next thing I should do, it is likely, upon this frenzy would be to hire some bark and go in nuptial ceremony, Venetian-like, to wed the gulf, which I might call perhaps as properly my own.'[EEE]

[EEE] The doge, the chief magistrate of the Venetian Republic, annually led a fleet of boats into the Adriatic where he cast a consecrated ring into the sea and renewed the union of Venice and the sea with the words, *Desponsamus te, mare*, 'We wed thee, sea.' The state galley was called Bucentaur, *bucintoro*, which derives from 'golden bark'.

[23] See *Letter of Enthusiasm* towards the end. See also pp. 191, 351–2.

'Let who will call it theirs,' replied Theocles, 'you will own the enjoyment of this kind to be very different from that which should naturally follow from the contemplation of the ocean's beauty. The bridegroom-doge who, in his stately Bucentaur, floats on the bosom of his Thetis has less possession than the poor shepherd who, from a hanging rock or point of some high promontory, stretched at his ease, forgets his feeding flocks while he admires her beauty.

But to come nearer home and make the question still more familiar. Suppose, my Philocles, that, viewing such a tract of country as this delicious vale we see beneath us, you should, for the enjoyment of the prospect, require the property or possession of the land.'

'The covetous fancy', replied I, 'would be as absurd altogether as that other ambitious one.'

'O Philocles!,' said he, 'may I bring this yet a little nearer and will you follow me once more? Suppose that, being charmed as you seem to be with the beauty of those trees under whose shade we rest, you should long for nothing so much as to taste some delicious fruit of theirs and, having obtained of nature some certain relish by which these acorns or berries of the wood became as palatable as the figs or peaches of the garden, you should afterwards, as oft as you revisited these groves, seek hence the enjoyment of them by satiating yourself in these new delights.'

'The fancy of this kind', replied I, 'would be sordidly luxurious and as absurd, in my opinion, as either of the former.'

'Can you not then on this occasion', said he, 'call to mind some other forms of a fair kind among us, where the admiration of beauty is apt to lead to as irregular a consequence?'

'I feared,' said I, 'indeed, where this would end and was apprehensive you would force me at last to think of certain powerful forms in humankind which draw after them a set of eager desires, wishes and hopes, no way suitable, I must confess, to your rational and refined contemplation of beauty. The proportions of this living architecture, as wonderful as they are, inspire nothing of a studious or contemplative kind. The more they are viewed, the further they are from satisfying by mere view. Let that which satisfies be ever so disproportionable an effect or ever so foreign to its cause, censure it as you please, you must allow, however, that it is natural. So that you, Theocles, for aught I see, are become the accuser of nature by condemning a natural enjoyment.'

'Far be it from us both', said he, 'to condemn a joy which is from nature. But when we spoke of the enjoyment of these woods and prospects, we understood by it a far different kind from that of the inferior creatures, who, rifling in these places, find here their choicest food. Yet we too live by tasteful food and feel those other joys of sense in common with them. But it was not here, my Philocles, that we had agreed to place our good nor consequently our enjoyment. We who were rational and had minds, methought, should place it rather in those minds, which were indeed abused and cheated of their real good when drawn to seek absurdly the enjoyment of it in the object of sense and not in those objects they might properly call their own, in which kind, as I remember, we comprehended all which was truly fair, generous or good.'

'So that beauty', said I, 'and good with you, Theocles, I perceive, are still one and the same.'[24]

'It is so,' said he. 'And thus are we returned again to the subject of our yesterday's morning conversation. Whether I have made good my promise to you in showing the true good, I know not.[25] But so, doubtless, I should have done with good success had I been able in my poetic ecstasies or by any other efforts to have led you into some deep view of nature and the sovereign genius. We then had proved the force of divine beauty and formed in ourselves an object capable and worthy of real enjoyment.'

'O Theocles!,' said I, 'well do I remember now the terms in which you engaged me that morning when you bespoke my love of this mysterious beauty. You have indeed made good your part of the condition and may now claim me for a proselyte. If there be any seeming extravagance in the case, I must comfort myself the best I can and consider that all sound love and admiration is enthusiasm.[26] The transports of poets, the sublime of orators, the rapture of musicians, the high strains of the virtuosi – all mere enthusiasm! Even learning itself, the love of arts and curiosities, the spirit of travellers and adventurers, gallantry, war, heroism – all, all enthusiasm! It is enough; I am content to be this new enthusiast in a way unknown to me before.'

'And I', replied Theocles, 'am content you should call this love of ours "enthusiasm", allowing it the privilege of its fellow passions. For is there a fair and plausible enthusiasm, a reasonable ecstasy and transport allowed to other subjects, such as architecture, painting, music, and shall it be exploded here? Are there senses by which all those other graces and perfections are perceived, and none by which this higher perfection and grace is comprehended? Is it so preposterous to bring that enthusiasm hither and transfer it from those secondary and scanty objects to this original and comprehensive one? Observe how the case stands in all those other subjects of art or science. What difficulty to be in any degree knowing! How long before a true taste is gained! How many things shocking, how many offensive at first, which afterwards are known and acknowledged the highest beauties! For it is not instantly we acquire the sense by which these beauties are discoverable. Labour and pains are required and time to cultivate a natural genius ever so apt or forward. But who is there

[24] See pp. 254–5.
[25] See p. 257.
[26] See pp. 27–8.

once thinks of cultivating this soil or of improving any sense or faculty which nature may have given of this kind? And is it a wonder we should be dull then, as we are, confounded and at a loss in these affairs, blind as to this higher scene, these nobler representations? Which way should we come to understand better, which way be knowing in these beauties? Is study, science or learning necessary to understand all beauties else? And, for the sovereign beauty, is there no skill or science required? In painting there are shades and masterly strokes which the vulgar understand not but find fault with; in architecture there is the rustic; in music the chromatic kind and skilful mixture of dissonancies: and is there nothing which answers to this in the whole?'

'I must confess,' said I, 'I have hitherto been one of those vulgar who could never relish the shades, the rustic or the dissonancies you talk of. I have never dreamt of such masterpieces in nature. It was my way to censure freely on the first view. But I perceive I am now obliged to go far in the pursuit of beauty, which lies very absconded and deep, and, if so, I am well assured that my enjoyments hitherto have been very shallow. I have dwelt, it seems, all this while upon the surface and enjoyed only a kind of slight superficial beauties, having never gone in search of beauty itself but of what I fancied such. Like the rest of the unthinking world, I took for granted that what I liked was beautiful and what I rejoiced in was my good. I never scrupled loving what I fancied and, aiming only at the enjoyment of what I loved, I never troubled myself with examining what the subjects were nor ever hesitated about their choice.'

'Begin then,' said he, 'and choose. See what the subjects are and which you would prefer, which honour with your admiration, love and esteem. For by these again you will be honoured in your turn. Such, Philocles, as is the worth of these companions, such will your worth be found. As there is emptiness or fullness here, so will there be in your enjoyment. See therefore where fullness is and where emptiness. See in what subject resides the chief excellence, where beauty reigns, where it is entire, perfect, absolute, where broken, imperfect, short. View these terrestrial beauties and whatever has the appearance of excellence and is able to attract. See that which either really is or stands as in the room of fair, beautiful and good. "A mass of metal, a tract of land, a number of slaves, a pile of stones, a human body of certain lineaments and proportions": is this the highest of the kind? Is beauty founded then in body only and not in action, life or operation?'

'Hold! hold!,' said I, 'good Theocles, you take this in too high a key above my reach. If you would have me accompany you, pray lower this strain a little and talk in a more familiar way.'

'Thus then,' said he, smiling, 'whatever passion you may have for other beauties, I know, good Philocles, you are no such admirer of wealth in any kind as to allow much beauty to it, especially in a rude heap or mass. But in medals, coins, embossed work, statues and well-fabricated pieces, of whatever sort, you can discover beauty and admire the kind.'

'True,' said I, 'but not for the metal's sake.'

'It is not then the metal or matter which is beautiful with you?'

'No.'

'But the art.'

'Certainly.'

'The art then is the beauty.'

'Right.'

'And the art is that which beautifies.'

'The same.'

'So that the beautifying, not the beautified, is the really beautiful.'

'It seems so.'

'For that which is beautified is beautiful only by the accession of something beautifying, and, by the recess or withdrawing of the same, it ceases to be beautiful.'

'Be it.'

'In respect of bodies therefore, beauty comes and goes.'

'So we see.'

'Nor is the body itself any cause either of its coming or staying.'

'None.'

'So that there is no principle of beauty in body.'

'None at all.'

'For body can no way be the cause of beauty to itself.'

'No way.'

'Nor govern nor regulate itself.'

'Nor yet this.'

'Nor mean nor intend itself.'

'Nor this neither.'

'Must not that, therefore, which means and intends for it, regulates and orders it, be the principle of beauty to it?'

'Of necessity.'

'And what must that be?'

'Mind, I suppose, for what can it be else?'

'Here then', said he, 'is all I would have explained to you before: that *the beautiful, the fair, the comely, were never in the matter but in the art and design, never in body itself but in the form or forming power*. Does not the beautiful form confess this and speak the beauty of the design whenever it strikes you? What is it but the design which strikes? What is it you admire but mind or the effect of mind? It is mind alone which forms. All which is void of mind is horrid, and matter formless is deformity itself.'

'Of all forms then,' said I, 'those, according to your scheme, are the most amiable and in the first order of beauty which have a power of making other forms themselves. From whence methinks they may be styled *the forming forms*. So far I can easily concur with you and gladly give the advantage to the human form, above those other beauties of man's formation. The palaces, equipages and estates shall never in my account be brought in competition with the original living forms of flesh and blood. And for the other, the dead forms of nature, the metals and stones, however precious and dazzling, I am resolved to resist their splendour and make abject things of them, even in their highest pride, when they pretend to set off human beauty and are officiously brought in aid of the fair.'

'Do you not see then', replied Theocles, 'that you have established three degrees or orders of beauty?'

'As how?'

'Why, first, *the dead forms*, as you properly have called them, which bear a fashion and are formed, whether by man or nature, but have no forming power, no action or intelligence.'

'Right.'

'Next, and as the second kind, *the forms which form*, that is, which have intelligence, action and operation.'

'Right still.'

'Here therefore is double beauty. For here is both the form, the effect of mind, and mind itself. The first kind low and despicable in respect of this other, from whence the dead form receives its lustre and force of beauty. For what is a mere body, though a human one and ever so exactly fashioned, if inward form be wanting and the mind be monstrous or imperfect, as in an idiot or savage?'

'This too I can apprehend,' said I, 'but where is the third order?'

'Have patience,' replied he, 'and see first whether you have discovered the whole force of this second beauty. How else should you understand the force of love or have the power of enjoyment? Tell me, I beseech you, when first you named these "the forming forms", did you think of no other productions of theirs besides the dead kinds, such as the palaces, the coins, the brazen or the marble figures of men? Or did you think of something nearer life?'

'I could easily', said I, 'have added that these forms of ours had a virtue of producing other living forms like themselves. But this virtue of theirs, I thought, was from another form above them and could not properly be called their virtue or art if in reality there was a superior art or something artist-like which guided their hand and made tools of them in this specious work.'

'Happily thought!,' said he. 'You have prevented a censure which I hardly imagined you could escape. And here you have unawares discovered *that third order of beauty, which forms not only such as we call mere forms but even the forms which form*. For we ourselves are notable architects in matter and can show lifeless bodies brought into form and fashioned by our own hands, but that which fashions even minds themselves contains in itself all the beauties fashioned by those minds and is consequently the principle, source and fountain of all beauty.'

'It seems so.'

'Therefore, whatever beauty appears in our second order of forms or whatever is derived or produced from thence, all this is eminently, principally and originally in this last order of supreme and sovereign beauty.'

'True.'

'Thus architecture, music and all which is of human invention resolves itself into this last order.'

'Right,' said I, 'and thus all the enthusiasms of other kinds resolve themselves into ours. The fashionable kinds borrow from us and are nothing without us. We have undoubtedly the honour of being originals.'

'Now therefore say again', replied Theocles, 'whether are those fabrics of architecture, sculpture and the rest of that sort the greatest beauties which man forms or are there greater and better?'

'None which I know,' replied I.

'Think, think again,' said he, 'and, setting aside those productions which just now you excepted against as masterpieces of another hand, think what there are which more immediately proceed from us and may more truly be termed our issue.'

'I am barren,' said I, 'for this time you must be plainer yet in helping me to conceive.'

'How can I help you?', replied he. 'Would you have me be conscious for you of that which is immediately your own and is solely in and from yourself?'

'You mean my sentiments,' said I.

'Certainly,' replied he, 'and, together with your sentiments, your resolutions, principles, determinations, actions – whatsoever is handsome and noble in the kind, whatever flows from your good understanding, sense, knowledge and will, whatever is engendered in your heart, good Philocles, or derives itself from your parent-mind, which, unlike to other parents, is never spent or exhausted but gains strength and vigour by producing. So you, my friend, have proved it by many a work, not suffering that fertile part to remain idle and inactive. Hence those good parts which from a natural genius you have raised by due improvement. And here, as I cannot but admire the pregnant genius and parent-beauty, so am I satisfied of the offspring, that it is and will be ever beautiful.'

I took the compliment and wished, I told him, the case were really as he imagined that I might justly merit his esteem and love. My study therefore should be to grow beautiful in his way of beauty, and, from this time forward, I would do all I could to propagate that lovely race of mental children, happily sprung from such a high enjoyment and from a union with what was fairest and best.

'But it is you, Theocles,' continued I, 'must help my labouring mind and be as it were the midwife to those conceptions, which else, I fear, will prove abortive.'

'You do well', replied he, 'to give me the midwife's part only, for the mind, conceiving of itself, can only be, as you say, assisted in the birth. Its pregnancy is from its nature. Nor could it ever have been thus impregnated by any other mind than that which formed it at the beginning and which, as we have already proved, is original to all mental as well as other beauty.'

'Do you maintain then', said I, 'that these mental children, the notions and principles of fair, just and honest, with the rest of these ideas, are innate?'[FFF]

'Anatomists', said he, 'tell us that the eggs, which are principles in body, are innate, being formed already in the foetus before the birth. But when it is, whether before or at or after the birth or at what time after, that either these or other principles, organs of sensation or sensations themselves are first formed in us, is a matter doubtless of curious speculation but of no great importance. The question is whether the principles spoken of are from art or nature? If from nature purely, it is no matter for the time, nor would I contend with you though you should deny life itself to be innate, as imagining it followed rather than preceded the moment of birth. But this I am certain of, that life and the sensations which accompany life, come when they will, are from mere nature and nothing else. Therefore, if you dislike the word "innate", let us change it, if you will, for "instinct", and call instinct that which nature teaches, exclusive of art, culture or discipline.'

'Content,' said I.

'Leaving then', replied he, 'those admirable speculations to the virtuosi, the anatomists and school divines, we may safely aver, with all their consents, that the several organs, particularly those of generation, are formed by nature. Whether is there also from nature, think you, any instinct for the after use of them? Or whether must learning and experience imprint this use?'

'It is imprinted', said I, 'enough in conscience. The impression or instinct is so strong in the case that it would be absurdity not to think it natural, as well in our own species as in other creatures, among whom, as you have already taught me, not only the mere engendering of the young but the various and almost infinite means and methods of providing for them are all foreknown. For thus much we may indeed discern in the preparatory labours and arts of

[FFF] In *An Essay Concerning Human Understanding*, Book I, John Locke attacked the notion of innate ideas as it had been set forth primarily by the Cambridge Platonists. In characteristic fashion, Shaftesbury was dismissive of the technical side of the debate. See G. A. J. Rogers, 'Locke, Newton and the Cambridge Platonists', *Journal of the History of Ideas* 40 (1979): 191–205.

these wild creatures, which demonstrate their anticipating fancies, pre-conceptions or pre-sensations, if I may use a word you taught me yesterday.'[27]

'I allow your expression', said Theocles, 'and will endeavour to show you that the same pre-conceptions, of a higher degree, have place in humankind.'

'Do so,' said I, 'I entreat you, for so far am I from finding in myself these pre-conceptions of fair and beautiful, in your sense, that methinks, till now of late, I have hardly known of anything like them in nature.'

'How then', said he, 'would you have known that outward fair and beautiful of humankind if such an object, a fair fleshly one, in all its beauty had for the first time appeared to you, by yourself, this morning in these groves? Or do you think perhaps you should have been unmoved and have found no difference between this form and any other if first you had not been instructed?'

'I have hardly any right', replied I, 'to plead this last opinion after what I have owned just before.'

'Well then,' said he, 'that I may appear to take no advantage against you, I quit the dazzling form which carries such a force of complicated beauties, and am contented to consider separately each of those simple beauties which taken all together create this wonderful effect. For you will allow, without doubt, that, in respect of bodies, whatever is commonly said of the inexpressible, the unintelligible, the "I-know-not-what" of beauty, there can lie no mystery here but what plainly belongs either to figure, colour, motion or sound. Omitting therefore the three latter and their dependent charms, let us view the charm in what is simplest of all, mere figure. Nor need we go so high as sculpture, architecture or the designs of those who from this study of beauty have raised such delightful arts. It is enough if we consider the simplest of figures, as either a round ball, a cube or die. Why is even an infant pleased with the first view of these proportions? Why is the sphere or globe, the cylinder and obelisk, preferred and the irregular figures, in respect of these, rejected and despised?'

'I am ready', replied I, 'to own there is in certain figures a natural beauty, which the eye finds as soon as the object is presented to it.'[28]

'Is there then', said he, 'a natural beauty of figures and is there not as natural a one of actions? No sooner the eye opens upon figures, the ear to sounds, than straight the beautiful results and grace and harmony are known and acknowledged. No sooner are actions viewed, no sooner the human affections and passions discerned (and they are most of them as soon discerned as felt) than straight an inward eye distinguishes and sees the fair and shapely, the amiable and admirable, apart from the deformed, the foul, the odious or the despicable. How is it possible therefore not to own that as these distinctions

---

[27] See p. 282.
[28] See p. 172.

have their foundation in nature, the discernment itself is natural and from nature alone?'

'If this', I told him, 'were as he represented it, there could never, I thought, be any disagreement among men concerning actions and behaviour as which was base, which worthy, which handsome and which deformed. But now we found perpetual variance among mankind, whose differences were chiefly founded on this disagreement in opinion, the one affirming, the other denying, that this or that was fit or decent.'

'Even by this then,' replied he, 'it appears there is fitness and decency in actions since the fit and decent is in this controversy ever presupposed. And while men are at odds about the subjects, the thing itself is universally agreed. For neither is there agreement in judgments about other beauties. It is controverted, "Which is the finest pile? the loveliest shape or face?"; but without controversy it is allowed "there is a beauty of each kind". This no one goes about to teach, nor is it learned by any but confessed by all. All own the standard, rule and measure, but, in applying it to things, disorder arises, ignorance prevails, interest and passion breed disturbance. Nor can it otherwise happen in the affairs of life, while that which interests and engages men as good, is thought different from that which they admire and praise as honest.

But with us, Philocles, it is better settled, since for our parts we have already decreed that *beauty and good are still the same*.'[29]

'I remember', said I, 'what you forced me to acknowledge more than once before. And now, good Theocles, that I am become so willing a disciple, I want not so much to be convinced, methinks, as to be confirmed and strengthened. And I hope this last work may prove your easiest task.'

'Not unless you help in it yourself,' replied Theocles, 'for this is necessary as well as becoming. It had been indeed shameful for you to have yielded without making good resistance. To help oneself to be convinced is to prevent reason and bespeak error and delusion. But, upon fair conviction, to give our heart up to the evident side and reinforce the impression, this is to help reason heartily. And thus we may be said honestly to persuade ourselves.'

'Show me then how I may best persuade myself.'

'Have courage, Philocles,' said he, raising his voice. 'Be not offended that I say, "Have courage!" It is cowardice alone betrays us. For whence can false shame be except from cowardice? To be ashamed of what one is sure can never be shameful must needs be from the want of resolution. We seek the right and wrong in things; we examine what is honourable, what shameful; and, having at last determined, we dare not stand to our own judgment and are ashamed to own there is really a shameful and an honourable. "Hear me," says one who pretends to value Philocles and be valued by him. "There can be no such thing

[29] See pp. 254–5, 257, 320.

as real valuableness or worth; nothing in itself estimable or amiable, odious or shameful. All is opinion.[GGG] It is opinion which makes beauty and unmakes it. The graceful or ungraceful in things, the decorum and its contrary, the amiable and unamiable, vice, virtue, honour, shame, all this is founded in opinion only. Opinion is the law and measure. Nor has opinion any rule besides mere chance, which varies it as custom varies and makes now this, now that, to be thought worthy, according to the reign of fashion and the ascendant power of education."

What shall we say to such a one? How represent to him his absurdity and extravagance? Will he desist the sooner? Or shall we ask, "What shame?", of one who acknowledges no shameful?

Yet he derides and cries, "Ridiculous!"

By what right, what title? For thus, if I were Philocles, would I defend myself: "Am I ridiculous? As how? What is ridiculous? Everything? Or nothing?"

Ridiculous indeed!

But something, then, something there is ridiculous, and the notion, it seems, is right, of a shameful and ridiculous in things.

How then shall we apply the notion? For this being wrong applied cannot itself but be ridiculous. Or will he who cries shame refuse to acknowledge any in his turn? Does he not blush nor seem discountenanced on any occasion? If he does, the case is very distinct from that of mere grief or fear. The disorder he feels is from a sense of what is shameful and odious in itself, not of what is hurtful or dangerous in its consequences. For the greatest danger in the world can never breed shame, nor can the opinion of all the world compel us to it, where our own opinion is not a party. We may be afraid of appearing impudent and may therefore feign a modesty. But we can never really blush for anything beside what we think truly shameful, and what we should still blush for were we ever so secure as to our interest, and out of the reach of all inconvenience which could happen to us from the thing we were ashamed of.

Thus,' continued he, 'should I be able by anticipation to defend myself and, looking narrowly into men's lives and that which influenced them on all occasions, I should have testimony enough to make me say within myself, "Let who will be my adversary in this opinion, I shall find him some way or other prepossessed with that of which he would endeavour to dispossess me." Has he gratitude or resentment, pride or shame? Whichever way it be, he acknowl-

[GGG] On the early modern recognition that opinion reigns in human affairs, see J. A. W. Gunn, *Beyond Liberty and Property* (Kingston and Montreal: McGill-Queen's University Press, 1983), pp. 260–7.

edges a sense of just and unjust, worthy and mean. If he be grateful or expects gratitude, I ask, "Why, and on what account?" If he be angry, if he indulges revenge, I ask, "How? And in what case? Revenged of what? Of a stone or madman?" Who is so mad? "But for what? For a chance hurt? An accident against thought or intention?" Who is so unjust? Therefore, there is just and unjust and, belonging to it, a natural presumption or anticipation on which the resentment or anger is founded. For what else should make the wickedest of mankind often prefer the interest of their revenge to all other interests and even to life itself, except only a sense of wrong, natural to all men, and a desire to prosecute that wrong at any rate? Not for their own sakes, since they sacrifice their very being to it, but out of hatred to the imagined wrong and from a certain love of justice, which even in unjust men is by this example shown to be beyond the love of life itself.

Thus, as to pride, I ask, "Why proud? Why conceited? And of what? Does any one who has pride think meanly or indifferently of himself?"

No, but honourably.

And how this if there be no real honour or dignity presupposed? For self-valuation supposes self-worth and, in a person conscious of real worth, is either no pride or a just and noble one. In the same manner, self-contempt supposes a self-meanness or defectiveness and may be either a just modesty or unjust humility. But this is certain that whoever is proud must be proud of something. And we know that men of thorough pride will be proud even in the meanest circumstances and when there is no visible subject for them to be proud of. But they descry a merit in themselves which others cannot, and it is this merit they admire. No matter whether it be really in them, as they imagine, it is a worth still, an honour or merit which they admire and would do, wherever they saw it, in any subject besides. For then it is, then only, that they are humbled, when they see in a more eminent degree in others what they respect and admire so much in themselves.

And, thus, as long as I find men either angry or revengeful, proud or ashamed, I am safe. For they conceive an honourable and dishonourable, a foul and fair, as well as I. No matter where they place it or how they are mistaken in it, this hinders not my being satisfied that the thing is, and is universally, acknowledged, that it is of nature's impression, naturally conceived and by no art or counter-nature to be eradicated or destroyed.

And now, what say you, Philocles,' continued he, 'to this defence I have been making for you? It is grounded, as you see, on the supposition of your being deeply engaged in this philosophical cause. But perhaps you have yet many difficulties to get over before you can so far take part with beauty as to make this to be your good.'

'I have no difficulty so great', said I, 'as not to be easily removed. My inclinations lead me strongly this way, for I am ready enough to yield there is no real good beside the enjoyment of beauty.'

'And I am as ready', replied Theocles, 'to yield there is no real enjoyment of beauty beside what is good.'

'Excellent! But upon reflection I fear I am little beholden to you for your concession.'

'As how?'

'Because, should I offer to contend for any enjoyment of beauty out of your mental way, you would, I doubt, call such enjoyment of mine absurd as you did once before.'

'Undoubtedly I should. For what is it should enjoy or be capable of enjoyment except mind? Or shall we say, "Body enjoys"?'

'By the help of sense, perhaps; not otherwise.'

'Is beauty, then, the object of sense? Say how? Which way? For otherwise the help of sense is nothing in the case. And, if body be of itself incapable and sense no help to it to apprehend or enjoy beauty, there remains only the mind which is capable either to apprehend or to enjoy.'

'True,' said I, 'but show me, then, why beauty may not be the object of the sense?'

'Show me first, I entreat you, why, where or in what you fancy it may be so?'

'Is it not beauty which first excites the sense and feeds it afterwards in the passion we call love?'

'Say, in the same manner, that it is beauty first excites the sense and feeds it afterwards in the passion we call hunger.——You will not say it. The thought, I perceive, displeases you. As great as the pleasure is of good eating, you disdain to apply the notion of beauty to the good dishes which create it. You would hardly have applauded the preposterous fancy of some luxurious Romans of old, who could relish a fricassee the better for hearing it was composed of birds which wore a beautiful feather or had sung deliciously. Instead of being incited by such a historical account of meats, you would be apt, I believe, to have less appetite the more you searched their origin and descended into the kitchen science to learn the several forms and changes they had undergone before they were served at this elegant voluptuous table. But, though the kitchen forms be ever so disgraceful, you will allow that the materials of the kitchen, such, for instance, as the garden furnishes, are really fair and beautiful in their kind. Nor will you deny beauty to the wild field or to these flowers which grow around us on this verdant couch. And yet, as lovely as are these forms of nature, the shining grass or silvered moss, the flowery thyme, wild rose or honeysuckle, it is not their beauty allures the neighbouring herds, delights the browsing fawn or kid and spreads the joy we see amidst the feeding flocks. It is not the form rejoices but that which is beneath the form. It is savouriness attracts, hunger impels, and thirst better allayed by the clear brook than the thick puddle, makes the fair nymph to be preferred, whose form is otherwise slighted. For never can the form be of real force where it is uncontemplated, unjudged of, unexamined and stands only as the accidental note or token of what appeases provoked sense and satisfies the brutish part. Are you persuaded of this, good Philocles, or, rather than not give brutes the advantage of enjoyment, will you allow them also a mind and rational part?'

'Not so,' I told him.

'If brutes, therefore,' said he, 'be incapable of knowing and enjoying beauty as being brutes and having sense only (the brutish part) for their own share, it follows that neither can man by the same sense or brutish part conceive or enjoy beauty, but all the beauty and good he enjoys is in a nobler way and by the help of what is noblest, his mind and reason. Here lies his dignity and highest interest, here his capacity toward good and happiness. His ability or incompetency, his power of enjoyment or his impotence, is founded in this alone. As this is sound, fair, noble, worthy, so are its subjects, acts and employments. For as the riotous mind, captive to sense, can never enter in competition or contend for beauty with the virtuous mind of reason's culture, so neither can the objects which allure the former compare with those which attract and charm the latter. And when each gratifies itself in the enjoyment and possession of its object, how evidently fairer are the acts which join the latter pair and give a soul the enjoyment of what is generous and good? This at least, Philocles, you will surely allow, that, when you place a joy elsewhere than in the mind, the enjoyment itself will be no beautiful subject nor of any graceful or agreeable appearance. But when you think how friendship is enjoyed, how honour, gratitude, candour, benignity and all internal beauty, how all the social pleasures, society itself and all which constitutes the worth and happiness of mankind, you will here surely allow beauty in the act and think it worthy to be viewed and passed in review often by the glad mind, happily conscious of the generous part and of its own advancement and growth in beauty.

Thus, Philocles,' continued he after a short pause, 'thus have I presumed to treat of beauty before so great a judge and such a skilful admirer as yourself. For, taking rise from nature's beauty which transported me, I gladly ventured further in the chase and have accompanied you in search of beauty, as it relates to us, and makes our highest good in its sincere and natural enjoyment. And if we have not idly spent our hours nor ranged in vain through these deserted regions, it should appear from our strict search that there is nothing so divine as beauty, which, belonging not to body nor having any principle or existence except in mind and reason, is alone discovered and acquired by this diviner part, when it inspects itself, the only object worthy of itself. For whatever is void of mind is void and darkness to the mind's eye. This languishes and grows dim whenever detained on foreign subjects, but thrives and attains its natural vigour when employed in contemplation of what is like itself. It is thus *the improving mind*, slightly surveying other objects and passing over bodies and the common forms (where only a shadow of beauty rests), ambitiously presses onward to its source and views the original of form and order in that which is intelligent. And thus, O Philocles, may we improve and become artists in the kind, learning to know ourselves and what that is which, by improving, we may be sure to advance our worth and real self-interest. For neither is this knowledge acquired by contemplation of bodies or the outward forms, the view of pageantries, the study of estates and honours, nor is he to be esteemed that self-improving artist who makes a fortune out of these; but he, he only, is the wise and able man who, with a slight regard to these things, applies himself to cultivate another soil, builds in a different matter from that of stone or marble and, having righter models in his eye, becomes in truth *the architect of his own life and fortune* by laying within himself the lasting and sure foundations of order, peace and concord.

But now it is time to think of returning home. The morning is far spent. Come! Let us away and leave these uncommon subjects till we retire again to these remote and unfrequented places.'

At these words, Theocles, mending his pace and going down the hill, left me at a good distance till he heard me calling earnestly after him. Having joined him once again, I begged he would stay a little longer or, if he were resolved so soon to leave both the woods and that philosophy which he confined to them, that he would let me, however, part with them more gradually and leave the best impression on me he could against my next return. For, as much convinced as I was and as great a convert to his doctrine, my danger still, I owned to him, was very great, and I foresaw that when the charm of these places and his company was ceased, I should be apt to relapse and weakly yield to that too powerful charm, the world.

'Tell me,' continued I, 'how is it possible to hold out against it and withstand the general opinion of mankind, who have so different a notion of that which we call good? Say truth now, Theocles: can anything be more odd or dissonant from the common voice of the world than what we have determined in this matter?'

'Whom shall we follow, then?,' replied he. 'Whose judgment or opinion shall we take concerning what is good, what contrary? If all or any part of mankind are consonant with themselves and can agree in this, I am content to leave philosophy and follow them. If otherwise, why should we not adhere to what we have chosen?

Let us, then, in another view consider how this matter stands.'

Section 3

We then walked gently homewards (it being almost noon), and he continued his discourse.

'One man', said he, 'affects the hero, esteems it the highest advantage of life to have seen war and been in action in the field. Another laughs at this humour, counts it all extravagance and folly, prizes his own wit and prudence and would take it for a disgrace to be thought adventurous. One person is assiduous and indefatigable in advancing himself to the character of a man of business. Another, on the contrary, thinks this impertinent, values not fame or a character in the world and, by his good will, would always be in a debauch and never live out of the stews or taverns, where he enjoys, as he thinks, his highest good. One values wealth as a means only to indulge his palate and to eat finely. Another loathes this and affects popularity and a name. One admires music and paintings, cabinet curiosities and indoor ornaments. Another admires gardens, architecture and the pomp of buildings. Another, who has no *gusto* of either sort, believes all those they call virtuosi to be half-distracted.[HHH] One looks upon all expense to be madness and thinks only wealth itself to be good. One games, another dresses and studies an equipage, another is full of heraldry, points of honour, a family and a blood. One recommends gallantry and intrigue; another, ordinary good fellowship; another, buffoonery, satire and the common wit; another, sports and the country; another, a court; another, travelling and the sight of foreign parts; another, poetry and the fashionable learning.——All these go different ways. All censure one another and are despicable in one another's eyes. By fits too they are as despicable in their own and as often out of conceit with themselves as their humour changes and their passion turns from one thing to another.——What is it, then, I should be concerned for? Whose censure do I fear or by whom, after all, shall I be guided?

If I ask, "Are riches good when only heaped up and unemployed?", one answers, "They are." The rest deny.

"How is it, then, they are to be employed in order to be good?" All disagree. All tell me different things.

"Since, therefore, riches are not of themselves good (as most of you declare) and since there is no agreement among you which way they become good, why may not I hold it for my opinion that they are neither good in themselves nor directly any cause or means of good?"

If there be those who wholly despise fame and if, among those who covet it, he who desires it for one thing despises it for another, he who seeks it with some men despises it with others, why may not I say that "neither do I know how any fame can be called a good"?

[HHH] *Gusto* is Italian for 'taste'. For virtuosi, see p. 62n.

If, of those who covet pleasure, they who admire it in one kind are superior to it in another, why may not I say that "neither do I know which of these pleasures, or how pleasure itself, can be called good"?

If, among those who covet life ever so earnestly, that life which to one is eligible and amiable is to another despicable and vile, why may not I say that "neither do I know how life itself can of itself be thought a good"?

In the meantime, this I know certainly, that the necessary consequence of esteeming these things highly is to be a slave and consequently miserable. But perhaps, Philocles, you are not yet enough acquainted with this odd kind of reasoning?'

'More', said I, 'than I believe you can easily imagine. I perceived the goodly lady, your celebrated beauty, was about to appear anew, and I easily knew again that fair face of liberty, which I had seen but once in the picture you drew yesterday of that moral dame.[30] I can assure you I think of her as highly as possible and find that without her help to raise one above these seemingly essential goods, and make one more easy and indifferent towards life and towards a fortune, it will be the hardest thing in the world to enjoy either. Solicitude, cares and anxiety will be multiplied and, in this unhappy dependency, it is necessary to make court and be not a little servile. To flatter the great, to bear insults, to stoop and fawn and abjectly resign one's sense and manhood – all this must courageously be endured and carried off with as free an air and good countenance as possible by one who studies greatness of this sort, who knows the general way of courts and how to fix unsteady fortune. I need not mention the envyings, the mistrusts and jealousies . . .'

'No, truly,' said he, interrupting me, 'neither need you. But finding you so sensible, as I do, of this unhappy state and of its inward sores (whatever may be its outward looks), how is it possible but you must find the happiness of that other contrary state? Can you not call to mind what we resolved concerning nature? Can anything be more desirable than to follow her? Or is it not by this freedom from our passions and low interests that we are reconciled to the goodly order of the universe, that we harmonize with nature and live in friendship both with God and man?

Let us compare', continued he, 'the advantages of each state and set their goods one against another: on one side, those which we found were uncertainly so and depended both on fortune, age, circumstances and humour; on the other side, those which, being certain themselves, are founded on the contempt of those others so uncertain. Is manly liberty, generosity, magnanimity, not a good? May we not esteem as happiness that self-enjoyment which arises from a consistency of life and manners, a harmony of affections, a freedom from the reproach of shame or guilt and a consciousness of worth and merit with all

[30] See pp. 260, 424, 468.

334

mankind, our society, country and friends, all which is founded in virtue only? A mind subordinate to reason, a temper humanized and fitted to all natural affections, an exercise of friendship uninterrupted, a thorough candour, benignity and good nature, with constant security, tranquillity, equanimity, if I may use such philosophical terms – are not these ever and at all seasons good? Is it of these one can at any time nauseate and grow weary? Are there any particular ages, seasons, places, circumstances, which must accompany these to make them agreeable? Are these variable and inconstant? Do these, by being ardently beloved or sought, occasion any disturbance or misery? Can these be at any time overvalued? Or, to say more yet, can these be ever taken from us or can we ever be hindered in the enjoyment of them unless by ourselves? How can we better praise the goodness of Providence than in this, that it has placed our happiness and good in things we can bestow upon ourselves?'

'If this be so,' said I, 'I see no reason we have to accuse Providence on any account. But men, I fear, will hardly be brought to this good temper while their fancy is so strong, as it naturally is, towards those other movable goods. And, in short, if we may depend on what is said commonly, "All good is merely as we fancy it. It is conceit which makes it. All is opinion and fancy only."'

'Wherefore, then,' said he, 'do we act at any time? Why choose, or why prefer one thing to another? You will tell me, I suppose, it is because we fancy it or fancy good in it. Are we therefore to follow every present fancy, opinion or imagination of good? If so, then we must follow that at one time which we decline at another, approve at one time what we disapprove at another and be at perpetual variance with ourselves. But, if we are not to follow all fancy or opinion alike, if it be allowed that, of fancies, some are true, some false, then we are to examine every fancy, and there is some rule or other by which to judge and determine. It was the fancy of one man to set fire to a beautiful temple in order to obtain immortal memory or fame. It was the fancy of another man to conquer the world for the same reason or what was very like it.[III] If this were really the man's good, why do we wonder at him? If the fancy were wrong, say plainly in what it was so or why the subject was not good to him as he fancied? Either, therefore, that is every man's good which he fancies and because he fancies it and is not content without it or, otherwise, there is that in which the nature of man is satisfied and which alone must be his good. If that in which the nature of man is satisfied and can rest contented be alone his good, then he is a fool who follows that with earnestness as his good which a man can be without and yet be satisfied and contented. In the same manner is he a fool who flies that earnestly as his ill which a man may endure and yet be

---

[III] Erostratus, or Eratostratus, set fire to the Temple of Diana at Ephesus in order to secure a place in history for his name. This event occurred on the night that Alexander the Great, the man who conquered the world, was born.

easy and contented. Now a man may possibly not have burnt a temple, as Erostratus, and yet may be contented. Or, though he may not have conquered the world, as Alexander, yet he may be easy and contented, as he may still without any of those advantages of power, riches or renown, if his fancy hinders not. In short, we shall find that, without any one of those which are commonly called goods, a man may be contented, as, on the contrary, he may possess them all and still be discontented and not a jot the happier. If so, it follows that *happiness is from within, not from without*. A good fancy is the main. And thus you see I agree with you that opinion is all in all.[31]

But what is this, Philocles, which has seized you? You seem of a sudden grown deeply thoughtful.'

'To tell you truth,' said I, 'I was considering what would become of me if after all I should, by your means, turn philosopher.'

'The change, truly, would be somewhat extraordinary,' replied Theocles. 'But be not concerned. The danger is not so great. And experience shows us every day that, for talking or writing philosophy, people are not at all the nearer being philosophers.'

'But', said I, 'the very name is a kind of reproach. The word "idiot" stood formerly as the opposite to "philosopher", but nowadays it means nothing more commonly than the philosopher himself.'

'Yet, in effect,' replied he, 'what else is it we all do in general than philosophize? If philosophy be, as we take it, *the study of happiness*, must not everyone, in some manner or other, either skilfully or unskilfully philosophize? Is not every deliberation concerning our main interest, every correction of our taste, every choice and preference in life to be reckoned of this kind? For if happiness be not allowed to be from self and from within, then either is it from outward things alone or from self and outward things together. If from outward things alone, show it us in fact that all men are happy in proportion to these and that no one who possesses them is ever miserable by his own fault.'

'But this, it seems, hardly any one will pretend to evince. All own the contrary.'

'Therefore, if happiness be partly from self, partly from outward things, then each must be considered and a certain value set on the concerns of an inward kind and which depend on self alone. If so, and that I consider how and in what these are to be preferred, when and on what occasion they are in season or out of season, when properly to take place, when to yield, what is this after all but to philosophize?'

'Yet even this, still, is enough to put one out of the ordinary way of thinking and give one an unhappy turn for business and the world.'

'Right! For this also is to be considered and well weighed. And therefore

---

[31] See pp. 137, 143, 144–5, 421–2, 423.

this still is philosophy, to inquire where and in what respect one may be most a loser, which are the greatest gains, the most profitable exchanges, since everything in this world goes by exchange. Nothing is had for nothing. Favour requires courtship; interest is made by solicitation; honours are acquired with hazard; riches with pains; learning and accomplishments by study and application. Security, rest, indolence are to be had at other prices. They may be thought, perhaps, to come easy. For what hardship is there? Where is the harm? It is only to abate of fame and fortune. It is only to waive the point of honour and share somewhat less of interest. If this be easy, all is well. Some patience, you see, is necessary in the case. Privacy must be endured, even obscurity and contempt.——Such are the conditions. And thus everything has its condition. Power and preferments are to be had at one rate, pleasures at another, liberty and honesty at another. A good mind must be paid for as other things.

But we had best beware lest, perhaps, we pay too dear for it. Let us be assured we have a good bargain.

Come on then. Let us account. "What is a mind worth? What allowance may one handsomely make for it? Or what may one well afford it for?"

If I part with it or abate of it, it is not for nothing. Some value I must needs set upon my liberty, some upon my inward character. Something there is in what we call worth, something in sincerity and a sound heart. Orderly affections, generous thoughts and a commanding reason are fair possessions, not slightly to be given up.

I am to consider first "what may be their equivalent? Whether I shall find my account in letting these inward concerns run as they please, or whether I shall not be better secured against fortune by adjusting matters at home, rather than by making interest abroad and acquiring first one great friend, then another, to add still more and more to my estate or quality?"

For where am I to take up?

Begin and set the bounds.

Let me hear positively "how far I am to go and why no further?" What is a moderate fortune, a competency and those other degrees commonly talked of? Where is my anger to stop, or how high may I suffer it to rise? How far may I engage in love? How far give way to ambition? How far to other appetites? Or am I to let all loose? Are the passions to take their swing and no application to be given to them, but all to the outward things they aim at? Or, if any application be requisite, say plainly "how much to one and how much to the other?" How far are the appetites to be minded and how far outward things? Give us the measure and rule. See whether this be not to philosophize? And whether willingly or unwillingly, knowingly or unknowingly, directly or indirectly, every one does not as much?

"Where, then, is the difference? Which manner is the best?"

Here lies the question. This is what I would have you weigh and examine.

"But the examination", say you, "is troublesome, and I had better be without it."

Who tells you thus? Your reason, you say, whose force, of necessity, you must yield to.

Tell me, therefore, have you fitly cultivated that reason of yours, polished it, bestowed the necessary pains on it and exercised it on this subject? Or is it like to determine full as well when unexercised as when thoroughly exercised or ever so expert? Consider, pray, in mathematics, whose is the better reason of the two, and fitter to be relied on, the practiser's or his who is unpractised? Whose in the way of war, of policy or civil affairs? Whose in merchandise, law, physic? And in morality and life, I ask still, whose? May he not, perhaps, be allowed the best judge of living who studies life and endeavours to form it by some rule? Or is he indeed to be esteemed most knowing in the matter who slightly examines it and who accidentally and unknowingly philosophizes?

Thus, Philocles,' said he, concluding his discourse, 'thus is philosophy established. For everyone, of necessity, must reason concerning his own happiness, *what his good is and what his ill*. The question is only, "Who reasons best?" For even he who rejects this reasoning or deliberating part does it from a certain reason, and from a persuasion that this is best.'

By this time we found ourselves insensibly got home. Our philosophy ended, and we returned to the common affairs of life.

Miscellaneous Reflections on the Preceding Treatises and Other Critical Subjects

Of course, favourable only to virtue and her friends.[1]

Miscellany I

Chapter 1

Of the nature, rise and establishment of miscellanies. The subject of these which follow. Intention of the writer.

Peace be with the soul of that charitable and courteous author who, for the common benefit of his fellow authors, introduced the ingenious way of miscellaneous writing! It must be owned that, since this happy method was established, the harvest of wit has been more plentiful, and the labourers more in number than heretofore. It is well known to the able practitioners in the writing art that, as easy as it is to conceive wit, it is the hardest thing imaginable to be delivered of it upon certain terms. Nothing could be more severe or rigid than the conditions formerly prescribed to writers when criticism took place, and regularity and order were thought essential in a treatise. The notion of a genuine work, a legitimate and just piece, has certainly been the occasion of great timidity and backwardness among the adventurers in wit, and the imposition of such strict laws and rules of composition has sat heavy on the free spirits and forward geniuses of mankind. It was a yoke, it seems, which our forefathers bore, but which, for our parts, we have generously thrown off. In effect, the invidious distinctions of bastardy and legitimacy being at length removed, the natural and lawful issue of the brain comes with like advantage into the world, and wit, mere wit, is well received without examination of the kind or censure of the form.

This the miscellaneous manner of writing, it must be owned, has happily

---

[1] Horace, *Satires* 2.1.70.

339

effected. It has rendered almost every soil productive. It has disclosed those various seeds of wit which lay suppressed in many a bosom, and has reared numberless conceits and curious fancies which the natural rudeness and asperity of their native soil would have withheld, or at least not have permitted to rise above the ground. From every field, from every hedge or hillock, we now gather as delicious fruits and fragrant flowers as of old from the richest and best cultivated gardens. Miserable were those ancient planters who, understanding not how to conform themselves to the rude taste of unpolished mankind, made it so difficult a task to serve the world with intellectual entertainments and furnish out the repasts of literature and science.

There was certainly a time when the name of author stood for something considerable in the world. To succeed happily in such a labour as that of writing a treatise or a poem was taken as a sure mark of understanding and good sense. The task was painful, but, it seems, it was honourable. How the case happened in process of time to be so much reversed is hard to say. The primitive authors, perhaps being few in number and highly respected for their art, fell under the weight of envy. Being sensible of their misfortune in this respect and being excited, as it is probable, by the example of some popular genius, they quitted their regular schemes and accurate forms of workmanship in favour of those wits who could not possibly be received as authors upon such difficult terms. It was necessary, it seems, that the bottom of wit should be enlarged. It was advisable that more hands should be taken into the work. And nothing could better serve this popular purpose than the way of miscellany or common essay, in which the most confused head, if fraught with a little invention and provided with commonplace-book learning, might exert itself to as much advantage as the most orderly and well-settled judgment.

To explain the better how this revolution in letters has been effected, it may not perhaps be indecent should we offer to compare our writing artists to the manufacturers in stuff or silk. For among these it is esteemed a principal piece of skill to frame a pattern or plan of workmanship in which the several colours are agreebly disposed, with such proportionable adjustment of the various figures and devices as may, in the whole, create a kind of harmony to the eye. According to this method, each piece must be in reality an original. For to copy what has gone before can be of no use. The fraud would easily be perceived. On the other side, to work originally and in a manner create each time anew must be a matter of pressing weight and fitted to the strength and capacity of none besides the choicest workmen.

A manner therefore is invented to confound this simplicity and conformity of design. Patchwork is substituted. Cuttings and shreds of learning, with various fragments and points of wit, are drawn together and tacked in any fantastic form. If they chance to cast a lustre and spread a sort of sprightly glare, the miscellany is approved and the complex form and texture of the work admired. The eye, which before was to be won by regularity and had kept true to measure and strict proportion, is by this means pleasingly drawn aside to commit a kind of debauch and amuse itself in gaudy colours and disfigured shapes of things. Custom, in the meanwhile, has not only tolerated this licentiousness but rendered it even commendable and brought it into the highest repute. The wild and whimsical, under the name of the odd and pretty, succeed in the room of the graceful and the beautiful. Justness and accuracy of thought are set aside as too constraining and of too painful an aspect to be endured in the agreeable and more easy commerce of gallantry and modern wit.

Now, since it has been thought convenient in these latter ages to distinguish the provinces of wit and wisdom and set apart the agreeable from the useful, it is evident there could be nothing devised more suitable to the distinct and separate interest of the former of these provinces than this complex manner of performance which we call 'miscellany'. For whatever is capricious and odd is sure to create diversion to those who look no further. And where there is nothing like nature, there is no room for the troublesome part of thought or contemplation. It is the perfection of certain grotesque painters to keep as far from nature as possible.[A] To find a likeness in their works is to find the greatest fault imaginable. A natural connection is a slur. A coherence, a design, a meaning is against their purpose and destroys the very spirit and genius of their workmanship.

I remember formerly, when I was a spectator in the French theatre,[B] I found it the custom at the end of every grave and solemn tragedy to introduce a comic farce or miscellany which they called the 'little piece'. We have indeed a method still more extraordinary upon our own stage. For we think it agreeable and just to mix the 'little piece' or farce with the main plot or fable through every act. This perhaps may be the rather chosen, because our tragedy is so much deeper and bloodier than that of the French, and therefore needs more immediate refreshment from the elegant way of drollery and burlesque wit, which, being thus closely interwoven with its opposite, makes that most accomplished kind of theatrical miscellany, called by our poets a tragicomedy.

I could go further perhaps and demonstrate from the writings of many of our grave divines, the speeches of our senators, and other principal models of

---

[A] Elsewhere, Shaftesbury took up the question of the grotesque in art or ryparography, a term for 'painting of sordid subjects' borrowed from Pliny, *Natural History* 35.37.112. See Benjamin Rand, ed., *Second Characters or the Language of Forms by the Right Honourable Anthony, Earl of Shaftesbury* (originally published 1914; reprint, New York: Greenwood Press, Publishers, 1969), pp. 134–7, where he names Adriaen Brouwer, *c.* 1605–38, and other 'masters Flemish, not worthy of being mentioned'.

[B] As Lord Ashley, Shaftesbury had visited Paris on his Grand Tour, arriving there in November 1687 and staying through August 1688. He was sixteen years old.

our national erudition, that the miscellaneous manner is at present in the highest esteem. But since my chief intention in the following sheets is to descant cursorily upon some late pieces of a British author, I will presume that what I have said already on this head is sufficient and that it will not be judged improper or absurd in me, as I proceed, to take advantage of this miscellaneous taste, which now evidently prevails. According to this method, while I serve as critic or interpreter to this new writer, I may the better correct his phlegm and give him more of the fashionable air and manner of the world, especially in what relates to the subject and manner of his two last pieces, which are contained in his second volume.^{C} For these, being of the more regular and formal kind, may easily be oppressive to the airy reader, and may therefore with the same assurance as tragedy claim the necessary relief of the 'little piece' or farce above-mentioned.

Nor ought the title of a miscellaneous writer to be denied me on the account that I have grounded my miscellanies upon a certain set of treatises already published. Grounds and foundations are of no moment in a kind of work which, according to modern establishment, has properly neither top nor bottom, beginning nor end. Besides, I shall no way confine myself to the precise contents of these treatises, but, like my fellow miscellanarians, shall take occasion to vary often from my proposed subject and make what deviations or excursions I shall think fit, as I proceed in my random essays.

Chapter 2

Of controversial writings: answers, replies. Polemic divinity, or the writing Church Militant. Philosophers and bear garden. Authors paired and matched. The matchmakers. Football. A dialogue between our author and his bookseller.

Among the many improvements daily made in the art of writing, there is none perhaps which can be said to have attained a greater height than that of controversy, or the method of answer and refutation. It is true, indeed, that anciently the wits of men were for the most part taken up in other employment. If authors wrote ill, they were despised; if well, they were by some party or other espoused. For parties there would necessarily be, and sects of every kind, in learning and philosophy. Everyone sided with whom he liked and, having the liberty of hearing each side speak for itself, stood in no need of express 'warning pieces' against pretended sophistry or dangerous reasoning. Particular answers to single treatises were thought to be of little use. And it was esteemed no compliment to a reader to help him so carefully in the judg-

^{C} In the original three-volume editions of *Characteristics*, published by John Darby, the second volume contained 'An Inquiry Concerning Virtue or Merit' and 'The Moralists'.

ment of every piece which came abroad. Whatever sects there were in those days, the zeal of party causes ran not so high as to give the reader a taste of those personal reproaches which might pass in a debate between the different party men.

Thus matters stood of old when as yet the method of writing controversy was not raised into an art, nor the feuds of contending authors become the chief amusement of the learned world. But we have at present so high a relish of this kind that the writings of the learned are never truly gustful till they are come to what we may properly enough call their due ripeness and have begot a fray. When the answer and reply is once formed, our curiosity is excited: we begin then, for the first time, to whet our attention and apply our ear.

For example, let a zealous divine and flaming champion of our faith, when inclined to show himself in print, make choice of some tremendous mystery of religion, opposed heretofore by some damnable heresiarch. Having vehemently refuted him, the divine turns himself towards the orthodox opinion and supports the true belief with the highest eloquence and profoundest erudition. He shall, notwithstanding this, remain perhaps in deep obscurity, to the great affliction of his bookseller and the regret of all who bear a just veneration for Church history and the ancient purity of the Christian faith.

But let it so happen that, in this prosecution of his deceased adversary, our doctor raises up some living antagonist who, on the same foot of orthodoxy with himself, pretends to arraign his expositions and refute the refuter upon every article he has advanced. From this moment, the writing gathers life, the public listens, the bookseller takes heart, and, when issue is well joined, the repartees grown smart, and the contention vigorous between the learned parties, a ring is made and readers gather in abundance. Every one takes party and encourages his own side. 'This shall be my champion!' 'This man for my money!' 'Well hit, on our side!' 'Again, a good stroke!' 'There he was even with him!' 'Have at him the next bout!' 'Excellent sport!' And when the combatants are for a while drawn off and each retired with his own companions, what praises and congratulations! What applauses of the supposed victor! And how honourably is he saluted by his favourers and complimented even to the disturbance of his modesty!

'Nay, but gentlemen! Good gentlemen! Do you really think thus? Are you sincere with me? Have I treated my adversary as he deserves?'

'Never was man so mauled. Why, you have killed him downright.'

'O sirs! You flatter me.'

'He can never rise more.'

'Think ye so indeed?'

'Or, if he should, it would be a pleasure to see how you would handle him.'

These are the triumphs. This is what sets sharp. This gives the author his edge and excites the reader's attention, when the trumpets are thus sounded to the crowd and a kind of amphitheatrical entertainment exhibited to the multitude by these gladiatorian penmen.

The author of the preceding treatises, being by profession a nice inspector into the ridicule of things, must in all probability have raised to himself some such views as those which hindered him from engaging in the way of controversy. For when, by accident, the first of these treatises, a private letter and, in the writer's esteem, little worthy of the public's notice,[2] came to be read abroad in copies, and afterwards in print, the smartest answers which came out against it could not, it seems, move our author to form any reply. All he was heard to say in return was that 'he thought whoever had taken upon him to publish a book in answer to that casual piece had certainly made either a very high compliment to the author or a very ill one to the public'.[D]

It must be owned that, when a writer of any kind is so considerable as to deserve the labour and pains of some shrewd heads to refute him in public, he may, in the quality of an author, be justly congratulated on that occasion. It is supposed necessarily that he must have written with some kind of ability or wit. But if his original performance be in truth no better than ordinary, his answerer's task must certainly be very mean. He must be very indifferently employed who would take upon him to answer nonsense in form, ridicule what is of itself a jest, and put it upon the world to read a second book for the sake of the impertinencies of a former.

Taking it, however, for granted that a sorry treatise may be the foundation of a considerable answer, a reply still must certainly be ridiculous, whichever way we take it. For either the author, in his original piece, has been truly refuted or not. If refuted, why does he defend? If not refuted, why trouble himself? What has the public to do with his private quarrels or his adversary's impertinence? Or, supposing the world, out of curiosity, may delight to see a pedant exposed by a man of better wit, and a controversy thus unequally carried on between two such opposite parties, how long is this diversion likely to hold good? And what will become of these polemic writings a few years hence? What has already become of those mighty controversies with which some of the most eminent authors amused the world within the memory of the youngest scholar? An original work or two may perhaps remain; but, for the subsequent defences, the answers, rejoinders and replications, they have been long since paying their attendance to the pastry cooks. Mankind perhaps were heated at that time when first those matters were debated, but they are now cool again. They laughed; they carried on the humour; they blew the coals; they teased and set on maliciously to create themselves diversion. But the jest is now over.

[D] For the responses to *A Letter Concerning Enthusiasm*, see Introduction, p. xii.

[2] *A Letter Concerning Enthusiasm.*

No one so much as inquires where the wit was, or where possibly the sting should lie, of those notable reflections and satirical hints which were once found so pungent and gave the readers such high delight. Notable philosophers and divines, who can be contented to make sport and write in learned Billingsgate[E] to divert the coffeehouse and entertain the assemblies at booksellers' shops or the more airy stalls of inferior book retailers!

It must be allowed that, in this respect, controversial writing is not so wholly unprofitable and that, for book merchants of whatever kind or degree, they undoubtedly receive no small advantage from a right improvement of a learned scuffle. Nothing revives them more or makes a quicker trade than a pair of substantial divines or grave philosophers, well matched and soundly backed, till, by long worrying one another, they are grown out of breath and have almost lost their force of biting. 'So have I known a crafty glazier, in time of frost, procure a football to draw into the street the emulous chiefs of the robust youth. The tumid bladder bounds at every kick, bursts the withstanding casements, the chassis,[F] lanterns and all the brittle vitreous ware. The noise of blows and outcries fills the whole neighbourhood, and ruins of glass cover the stony pavements, till the bloated battering engine, subdued by force of foot and fist and yielding up its breath at many a fatal cranny, becomes lank and harmless, sinks in its flight and can no longer uphold the spirit of the contending parties.'

This our author supposes to have been the occasion of his being so often and zealously complimented by his amanuensis (for so he calls his bookseller or printer) on the fame of his first piece.[3] The obliging craftsman has at times presented him with many a handsome book, set off with titles of *Remarks*, *Reflections* and the like, which, as he assured him, were answers to his small treatise.

'Here, Sir,' says he, 'You have a considerable hand has undertaken you! This, Sir, is a Reverend. This a Right Reverend. This a noted author. Will you not reply, Sir? Oh my word, Sir, the world is in expectation.'

'Pity they should be disappointed!'

'A dozen sheets, Sir, would be sufficient! You might dispatch it presently.'

'Think you so?'

'I have my paper ready, and a good letter. Take my word for it. You shall see, Sir!'

'Enough. But hark ye, Mr. A——, my worthy engineer and manager of the war of letters! Before you prepare your artillery or engage me in acts of hos-

---

[E] Foul, abusive, obscene and/or blasphemous language, supposed to characterize the speech of the women of London's fish market, Billingsgate.

[F] Window-frame.

[3] See p. 136.

tility, let me hear, I entreat you, whether or no my adversary be taken notice of. Wait for his second edition and, if by next year or a year or two after, it be known in good company that there is such a book in being, I shall then perhaps think it time to consider of a reply.'

Chapter 3

Of A Letter Concerning Enthusiasm. *Foreign critics. Of letters in general and of the epistolary style. Addresses to great men. Authors and horsemanship. The modern amble. Further explanation of the miscellaneous manner.*

As resolute as our author may have shown himself in refusing to take notice of the smart writings published against him by certain zealots of his own country, he could not, it seems, but out of curiosity observe what the foreign and more impartial critics might object to his small treatise, which he was surprised to hear had been translated into foreign languages soon after it had been published here at home. The first censure of this kind which came to our author's sight was that of the Paris *Journal des Sçavans*.[4] Considering how little favourable the author of the *Letter* had shown himself towards the Romish Church and policy of France, it must be owned those journalists have treated him with sufficient candour, though they failed not to take what advantages they well could against the writing and particularly arraigned it for the want of order and method.[5]

The Protestant writers, such as live in a free country and can deliver their sentiments without constraint, have certainly done our author more honour than he ever presumed to think he could deserve.[6] His translator, indeed, who had done him the previous honour of introducing him to the acquaintance of the foreign world, represents, particularly by the turn given to the latter end of the *Letter*, that the writer of it was, as to his condition and rank, little bet-

---

[4] For 25 March 1709. [*Le journal des sçavans* (The journal of the learned) published a review of the French translation of the *Letter*, *Lettre sur l'entousiasme* (published at the Hague by Thomas Johnson, 1709) in the twelfth number of its 1709 edition, pp. 177–81.]

[5] *In this work, his ideas seem to occupy only such positions as chance assigned them* (p. 181).

[6] *Bibliothèque choisie* 19 (1709): 427. *Histoire des ouvrages des sçavans* (October–December 1708): 514. *Nouvelles de la république des lettres* (March 1710): 345–52. [*Bibliothèque choisie* (Select library) was produced by Jean Le Clerc at Amsterdam. Volume 19 (pp. 427–38) contained a review of the French translations of the *Letter* and *Sensus Communis* and of the first English edition of *The Moralists*. *Histoire des ouvrages des sçavans* (History of the works of the learned) was edited by Henri Basnage de Beauval and published at Rotterdam by Reinier Leers. The review of the *Letter* appeared in the number for October–December 1708. *Nouvelles de la république des lettres* (News of the republic of letters) was edited by Jacques Bernard and published at Amsterdam by Pierre Mortier. It reviewed the French translation of *Sensus Communis* in the March 1710 number. On the learned journals and their role in intellectual communication, see Anne Goldgar, *Impolite Learning: Conduct and Community in the Republic of Letters, 1680–1750* (New Haven and London: Yale University Press, 1995), pp. 54–114.]

ter than an inferior dependant on the noble Lord^G to whom he had addressed himself. And in reality the original has so much of that air that I wonder not, if what the author left ambiguous, the translator has determined to the side of clientship and dependency.^H

But whatever may have been the circumstance or character of our author himself, that of his great friend ought in justice to have been considered by those former critics above-mentioned. So much, at least, should have been taken notice of, that there was a real great man characterized and suitable measures of address and style preserved. But they who would neither observe this, nor apprehend the letter itself to be real, were insufficient critics and unqualified to judge of the turn or humour of a piece which they had never considered in a proper light.

It has become indeed so common a practice among authors to feign a correspondency and give the title of a private letter to a piece addressed solely to the public that it would not be strange to see other journalists and critics, as well as the gentlemen of Paris, pass over such particularities as things of form. This prejudice, however, could not misguide a chief critic of the Protestant side, when, mentioning this *Letter Concerning Enthusiasm*, he speaks of it as a real letter, such as in truth it was, not a precise and formal treatise designed for public view.⁷

It will be owned surely, by those who have learned to judge of elegancy and wit by the help merely of modern languages, that we could have little relish of the best letters of a Balzac or Voiture, were we wholly ignorant of the characters of the principal persons to whom those letters were actually written.^I But much less could we find pleasure in this reading should we take it into our heads that both the personages and correspondency itself were merely fictitious. Let the best of Tully's epistles be read in such a narrow view as this, and they will certainly prove very insipid. If a real Brutus, a real Atticus, be not supposed, there will be no real Cicero.^J The elegant writer will disappear,

---

G   John Baron Somers.
H   While the original *Letter* was subscribed, 'My Lord, Your Lordship's, &c', the French translation was subscribed, more fulsomely, 'Milord, your very humble, very obedient and very loyal servant.'
I   Jean Louis Guez de Balzac, 1594–1654, and Vincent Voiture, 1598–1648, were French writers whose literary reputations derived from letters they wrote to contemporaries in and around the French royal court and in literary circles.
J   Cicero (Marcus Tullius Cicero, 106–43 BC), Roman statesman, orator and philosopher, had an extensive correspondence; most of his letters were written to relatives and intimate friends such as Titus Pomponius Atticus, 109–32 BC, and Marcus Junius Brutus, 85–42 BC.

7   *Those who read it could see in general that the author did not intend there a clear plan to treat his material methodically, since this is a letter and not a treatise: Bibliothèque choisie* 19 (1709): 428. If in this joint edition, with other works, the *Letter* be made to pass under that general name of 'treatise', it is the bookseller must account for it. For the author's part, he considers it as no other than what it originally was.

as will the vast labour and art with which this eloquent Roman wrote those letters to his illustrious friends. There was no kind of composition in which this great author prided or pleased himself more than in this, where he endeavoured to throw off the mien of the philosopher and orator, while in effect he employed both his rhetoric and philosophy with the greatest force. They who can read an epistle or satire of Horace, in somewhat better than a mere scholastic relish, will comprehend that the concealment of order and method in this manner of writing makes the chief beauty of the work. They will own that, unless a reader be in some measure apprised of the characters of an Augustus, a Maecenas, a Florus or a Trebatius, there will be little relish in those satires or epistles addressed in particular to the courtiers, ministers and great men of the times.[K] Even the satiric or miscellaneous manner of the polite ancients required as much order as the most regular pieces. But the art was to destroy every such token or appearance, give an extemporary air to what was written, and make the effect of art be felt without discovering the artifice. There needs no further explanation on this head. Our author himself has said enough in his *Advice to an Author*, particularly where he treats of the simple style, in contradistinction to the learned, the formal or methodic.[8]

It is a different case indeed when the title of 'epistle' is improperly given to such works as were never written in any other view than that of being made public, or to serve as exercises or specimens of the wit of their composer. Such were those infinite numbers of Greek and Latin epistles, written by the ancient sophists, grammarians or rhetoricians, where we find the real character of the epistle, the genuine style and manners of the corresponding parties, sometimes imitated but, at other times, not so much as aimed at, nor any measures of historical truth preserved. Such perhaps we may esteem even the letters of a Seneca to his friend Lucilius.[9] Or supposing that philosophical courtier had

---

[K] Horace, though of humble origins, advanced through his acquaintance of Virgil and Varius to the patronage of Maecenas and the Augustan court (see Introduction, p. xxii). Gaius Trebatius Testa was a Roman jurist, a contemporary of Augustus and friend of Cicero and Horace. Julius Florus was a soldier and friend of Horace who addressed two letters to him.

[8] See pp. 105, 115–16.

[9] It is not the person, character or genius, but the style and manner of this great man which we presume to censure. We acknowledge his noble sentiments and worthy actions. We own the patriot and good minister, but we reject the writer. He was the first of any note or worth who gave credit to that false style and manner here spoken of. He might on this account be called in reality the corrupter of Roman eloquence. This indeed could not but naturally and of itself become relaxed and dissolute after such a relaxation and dissolution of manners, consequent to the change of government and to the horrid luxury and effeminacy of the Roman Court, even before the time of a Claudius or a Nero. There was no more possibility of making a stand for language than for liberty. As the world now stood, the highest glory which could be attained by mortal man was to be mitigator or moderator of that universal tyranny already established. To this I must add that, in every city, principality or smaller nation, where single will prevails and Court power, instead of laws or constitutions, guides the state, it is of the highest diffi-

really such a correspondency and, at several times, had sent so many fair epistles, honestly signed and sealed, to his country friend at a distance, it appears, however, by the epistles themselves, in their proper order (if they may be said to have any), that, after a few attempts at the beginning, the author by degrees loses sight of his correspondent and takes the world in general for his reader or disciple. He falls into the random way of miscellaneous writing, says everywhere great and noble things, in and out of the way, accidentally as words lead him (for with these he plays perpetually), with infinite wit but with little or no coherence, without a shape or body to his work, without a real beginning, a middle or an end.[10] Of a hundred and twenty-four epistles, you may, if you please, make five hundred or half a score. A great one, for instance, you may divide into five or six. A little one you may tack to another, and that to another, and so on. The unity of the writing will be the same, the life and spirit full as well preserved. It is not only whole letters or pages you may change and manage thus at pleasure; every period, every sentence almost, is independent and may be taken asunder, transposed, postponed, anticipated or set in any new order, as you fancy.

This is the manner of writing so much admired and imitated in our age that

---

culty for the best minister to procure a just or even a tolerable administration. Where such a minister is found who can but moderately influence the petty tyranny, he deserves considerable applause and honour. But in the case we have mentioned, where a universal monarchy was actually established and the interest of a whole world concerned, he surely must have been esteemed a guardian angel who, as a prime minister, could for several years turn the very worst of courts, and worst conditioned of all princes, to the fatherly care and just government of mankind. Such a minister was Seneca under an Agrippina and a Nero. And such he was acknowledged by the ancient and never-sparing satirists, who could not forbear to celebrate withal his generosity and friendship in a private life: *Nobody asks for what Seneca used to send his ordinary friends, what good Piso, what Cotta used to bestow: for once upon a time the glory of giving was held to be greater than titles and offices* (Juvenal, *Satires* 5.108–11); *Who would be so lost as to hesitate to prefer Seneca to Nero?* (Juvenal, *Satires* 8.211–12). This remark is what I have been tempted to make by the way on the character of this Roman author, more mistaken (if I am not very much so myself) than any other so generally studied. As for the philosophic character or function imputed to him, it was foreign and no way proper or peculiar to one who never assumed so much as that of sophist or pensionary teacher of philosophy. He was far wide of any such order or profession. There is great difference between a courtier who takes a fancy for philosophy and a philosopher who should take a fancy for a court. Now Seneca was born a courtier, being son of a Court rhetor, himself bred in the same manner and taken into favour for his wit and genius, his admired style and eloquence, not for his learning in the books of philosophy and the ancients. For this indeed was not very profound in him. In short, he was a man of wonderful wit, fluency of thought and language, an able minister and honest courtier. And what has been delivered down to his prejudice is by the common enemy of all the free and generous Romans, that apish shallow historian and Court flatterer, Dion Cassius, of a low age, when barbarism (as may be easily seen in his own work) came on apace and the very traces and features of virtue, science and knowledge were wearing out of the world. [Dion Cassius occupied high imperial office in the early decades of the third century AD. His discussion of Seneca appeared in his ambitious *Roman History* 61–2. For Seneca, see Introduction, p. xxii.]

[10] See pp. 67, 448n.

we have scarce the idea of any other model. We know little, indeed, of the difference between one model or character of writing and another. All runs to the same tune and beats exactly one and the same measure. Nothing, one would think, could be more tedious than this uniform pace. The common amble or canterbury[1] is not, I am persuaded, more tiresome to a good rider than this seesaw of essay writers is to an able reader. The just composer of a legitimate piece is like an able traveller, who exactly measures his journey, considers his ground, premeditates his stages and intervals of relaxation and intention to the very conclusion of his undertaking, that he happily arrives where he first proposed when he set out. He is not presently upon the spur or in his full career but walks his steed leisurely out of his stable, settles himself in his stirrups and, when fair road and season offer, puts on perhaps to a round trot, thence into a gallop and, after a while, takes up. As down or meadow or shady lane present themselves, he accordingly suits his pace, favours his palfrey, and is sure not to bring him puffing and in a heat into his last inn. But the post way has become highly fashionable with modern authors. The very same stroke sets you out and brings you in. Nothing stays or interrupts. Hill or valley, rough or smooth, thick or thin – no difference, no variation. When an author sits down to write, he knows no other business he has than to be witty and take care that his periods be well turned or, as they commonly say, run smooth. In this manner he doubts not to gain the character of 'bright'. When he has written as many pages as he likes or as his run of fancy would permit, he then perhaps considers what name he had best give to his new writing, whether he should call it *Letter*, *Essay*, *Miscellany* or anything else. The bookseller perhaps is to determine this at last, when all, besides the preface, epistle dedicatory and title page, is dispatched. *Uncertain whether to make a stool or a statue of Priapus . . . a god then I became!*[11]

[1] The modern word 'canter', for a slow gallop, is a contraction of 'Canterbury pace', an allusion to the slow rate at which pilgrims rode towards the shrine of St Thomas à Becket at Canterbury.

[11] Horace, *Satires* 1.8.2–3.

Miscellany II

Chapter 1

Review of enthusiasm. Its defence, praise. Use in business as well as pleasure. Operation by fear, love. Modifications of enthusiasm: magnanimity; heroic virtue; honour; public zeal; religion; superstition; persecution; martyrdom. Energy of the ecstatic devotion in the tender sex. Account of ancient priesthood. Religious war. Reference to a succeeding chapter.

Whether, in fact, there be any real enchantment, any influence of stars, any power of daemons or of foreign natures over our own minds, is thought questionable by many. Some there are who assert the negative, and endeavour to solve the appearances of this kind by the natural operation of our passions and the common course of outward things. For my own part, I cannot but at this present apprehend a kind of enchantment or magic in that which we call 'enthusiasm', since I find that, having touched slightly on this subject, I cannot so easily part with it at pleasure.

After having made some cursory reflections on our author's *Letter*,[1] I thought I might have sufficiently acquitted myself on this head till, passing to his next treatise, I found myself still further engaged. I perceived plainly that I had as yet scarce entered into our author's humour or felt anything of that passion which, as he informs us, is so easily communicable and naturally engaging. But what I had passed over in my first reflections I found naturally rising in me upon second thoughts. So that by experience I proved it true what our author says, that 'we all of us know something of this principle'.[2] And now that I find I have in reality so much of it imparted to me, I may with better reason be pardoned if, after our author's example, I am led to write on such subjects as these with caution, at different reprises[A] and not singly in one breath.

I have heard indeed that the very reading of treatises and accounts of melancholy has been apt to generate that passion in the over-diligent and attentive reader. And this perhaps may have been the reason why our author himself, as he seems to intimate towards the conclusion of his first *Letter*,[3] cared not in reality to grapple closely with his subject or give us at once the precise definition of enthusiasm. This, however, we may, with our author, presume to infer from the coolest of all studies, even from criticism itself, of which we have been lately treating, that 'there is a power in numbers, harmony, proportion

---

[A] A repeated passage or occasion.

[1] That is, *A Letter Concerning Enthusiasm*, above.

[2] See p. 28.

[3] See p. 28.

and beauty of every kind, which naturally captivates the heart and raises the imagination to an opinion or conceit of something majestic and divine'.[4]

Whatever this subject may be in itself, we cannot help being transported with the thought of it. It inspires us with something more than ordinary and raises us above ourselves. Without this imagination or conceit, the world would be but a dull circumstance, and life a sorry pastime. Scarce could we be said to live. The animal functions might in their course be carried on, but nothing further sought for or regarded. The gallant sentiments, the elegant fancies, the *belles passions*,[B] which have, all of them, this beauty in view, would be set aside and leave us probably no other employment than that of satisfying our coarsest appetites at the cheapest rate in order to the attainment of a supine state of indolence and inactivity.

Slender would be the enjoyments of the lover, the ambitious man, the warrior or the virtuoso, as our author has elsewhere intimated,[5] if, in the beauties which they admire and passionately pursue, there were no reference or regard to any higher majesty or grandeur than what simply results from the particular objects of their pursuit. I know not, in reality, what we should do to find a seasoning to most of our pleasures in life, were it not for the taste or relish which is owing to this particular passion, and the conceit or imagination which supports it. Without this, we could not so much as admire a poem or a picture, a garden or a palace, a charming shape or a fair face. Love itself would appear the lowest thing in nature when thus anticipated and treated according to the anti-enthusiastic poet's method: *And to cast off collected fluid upon every body*.[6]

How heroism or magnanimity must stand in this hypothesis is easy to imagine. The Muses themselves must make a very indifferent figure in this philosophical draught. Even the prince of poets would prove a most insipid writer if he were thus reduced.[7] Nor could there, according to this scheme, be yet a place of honour left even for our Latin poet, the great disciple of this un-polite philosophy, who dares with so little equity employ the Muses' art in favour of such a system.[8] But, in spite of his philosophy, he everywhere gives way to admiration and rapturous views of nature. He is transported with the several beauties of the world, even while he arraigns the order of it and destroys the

---

[B]   The tender passions.

[4]   See pp. 191, 203, 320.

[5]   See p. 320.

[6]   Lucretius, *Of the Nature of Things* 4.1065.

[7]   *No part in Homer is without divinity nor lacking a lord nor empty of rulership but all is full of names of gods and words of gods and craft of gods*: Maximus Tyrius, *Orations* 26.8. [Shaftesbury identified this as Oration 16.]

[8]   Namely, Lucretius, as above, p. 26.

principle of beauty from whence, in ancient languages, the world itself was named.[9]

This is what our author advances when, in behalf of enthusiasm, he quotes its formal enemies and shows that they are as capable of it as its greatest confessors and assertors. So far is he from degrading enthusiasm or disclaiming it in himself that he looks on this passion, simply considered, as the most natural, and its object as the justest, in the world. Even virtue itself he takes to be no other than a noble enthusiasm justly directed and regulated by that high standard which he supposes in the nature of things.

He seems to assert that there are certain moral species or appearances so striking and of such force over our natures that, when they present themselves, they bear down all contrary opinion or conceit, all opposite passion, sensation or mere bodily affection.[10] Of this kind he makes virtue itself to be the chief since, of all views or contemplations, this, in his account, is the most naturally and strongly affecting. The exalted part of love is only borrowed hence. That of pure friendship is its immediate self. He who yields his life a sacrifice to his prince or country, the lover who for his paramour performs as much, the heroic, the amorous, the religious martyrs who draw their views, whether visionary or real, from this pattern and exemplar of divinity – all these, according to our author's sentiment, are alike actuated by this passion and prove themselves in effect so many different enthusiasts.

Nor is thorough honesty, in his hypothesis, any other than zeal or passion moving strongly upon the species or view of the decorum and sublime of actions. Others may pursue different forms and fix their eye on different species, as all men do on one or other.[11] The real honest man, however plain or simple he appears, has that highest species, honesty itself, in view, and, instead of outward forms or symmetries, is struck with that of inward character, the harmony and numbers of the heart and beauty of the affections, which form the manners and conduct of a truly social life.[12]

It is indeed peculiar to the genius of that cool philosophy, above-described, that, as it denies the order or harmony of things in general, so, by a just consequence and truth of reasoning, it rejects the habit of admiring or being charmed with whatever is called beautiful in particular.[13] According to the regimen prescribed by this philosophy, it must be acknowledged that the evils of

---

[9] κόσμος, *mundus* [universe]. From whence that expostulation, *Can a cosmic order be set within you but in the universe no order?*: Marcus Aurelius, *Meditations* 4.27. And that other allusion to the same word, *You might truly call the whole an order but not a disorder*, Aristotle, *On the Cosmos* 6 [399a.14]. [Although Peripatetic in substance, the work was written several centuries after Aristotle.] See p. 450n.

[10] See pp. 64–5, 201, 202–4.

[11] See p. 333.

[12] The *honestum*, τὸ καλόν [honourable], *pulchrum*, πρέπον [morally beautiful]. See pp. 415–17.

[13] See pp. 25, 54–6, 352.

love, ambition, vanity, luxury, with other disturbances derived from the florid, high and elegant ideas of things, must in appearance be set in a fair way of being radically cured.

It need not be thought surprising that religion itself should in the account of these philosophers be reckoned among those vices and disturbances which it concerns us after this manner to extirpate. If the idea of majesty and beauty in other inferior subjects be in reality distracting, it must chiefly prove so in that principal subject, the basis and foundation of this conceit. Now if the subject itself be not in nature, neither the idea nor the passion grounded on it can be properly esteemed natural, and thus all admiration ceases and enthusiasm is at an end. But if there be naturally such a passion, it is evident that religion itself is of the kind and must be therefore natural to man.

We can admire nothing profoundly without a certain religious veneration. And because this borders so much on fear and raises a certain tremor or horror of like appearance, it is easy to give that turn to the affection and represent all enthusiasm and religious ecstasy as the product or mere effect of fear: *Fear first created gods in the world.*[C] But the original passion, as appears plainly, is of another kind and, in effect, is so confessed by those who are the greatest opposers of religion and who, as our author observes, have shown themselves sufficiently convinced that, 'although these ideas of divinity and beauty were vain, they were yet in a manner innate or such as men were really born to and could hardly by any means avoid'.[14]

Now as all affections have their excess and require judgment and discretion to moderate and govern them, so this high and noble affection, which raises man to action and is his guide in business as well as pleasure, requires a steady rein and strict hand over it. All moralists, worthy of any name, have recognized the passion, though among these the wisest have prescribed restraint, pressed moderation and, to all tyros in philosophy, forbid the forward use of admiration, rapture or ecstasy, even in the subjects they esteemed the highest and most divine. They knew very well that the first motion, appetite and ardour of the youth in general towards philosophy and knowledge depended chiefly on this turn of temper.[15] Yet, were they well apprised, withal, that in the progress of this study, as well as in the affairs of life, the florid ideas and exalted fancy of this kind became the fuel of many incendiary passions and that, in religious concerns particularly, the habit of admiration and contemplative delight would, by over-indulgence, too easily mount into high fanaticism or degenerate into abject superstition.

[C] Statius, *Thebaid* 3.661.

[14] See p. 25.

[15] So the Stagirite, *Through wonder, men both now and originally began to philosophize*: Aristotle, *Metaphysics* 1.2.10. See p. 424n. [Stagirus in Chalcidice was Aristotle's birthplace.]

Upon the whole, therefore, according to our author, enthusiasm is in itself a very natural honest passion, and has properly nothing for its object but what is good and honest.[16] It is apt indeed, he confesses, to run astray. And by modern example we know, perhaps yet better than by any ancient, that in religion the enthusiasm which works by love is subject to many strange irregularities, and that which works by fear to many monstrous and horrible superstitions. Mystics and fanatics are known to abound as well in our reformed as in the Romish churches. The pretended floods of grace, poured into the bosoms of the quietists, pietists and those who favour the ecstatic way of devotion, raise such transports as by their own proselytes are confessed to have something strangely agreeable and in common with what ordinary lovers are used to feel. And it has been remarked by many that the female saints have been the greatest improvers of this soft part of religion. What truth there may be in the related operations of this pretended grace and amorous zeal, or in the accounts of what has usually passed between the saints of each sex in these devout ecstasies, I shall leave the reader to examine, supposing he will find credible accounts sufficient to convince him of the dangerous progress of enthusiasm in this amorous lineage.

There are many branches indeed more vulgar, as that of fear, melancholy, consternation, suspicion, despair. And when the passion turns more towards the astonishing and frightful than the amiable and delightful side, it creates rather what we call *superstition* than *enthusiasm*. I must confess, withal, that what we commonly style zeal in matters of religion is seldom without a mixture of both these extravagancies. The ecstatic motions of love and admiration are seldom unaccompanied with the horrors and consternations of a lower sort of devotion. These paroxysms of zeal are in reality as the hot and cold fits of an ague, and depend on the different and occasional views or aspects of the divinity, according as the worshipper is guided from without or affected from within by his particular constitution.[17] Seldom are those aspects so determinate and fixed as to excite constantly one and the same spirit of devotion. In religions, therefore, which hold most of love, there is generally room left for terrors of the deepest kind. Nor is there any religion so diabolical as, in its representation of divinity, to leave no room for admiration and esteem. Whatever personage or spectre of divinity is worshipped, a certain esteem and love is generally affected by his worshippers. Or if, in the devotion paid him, there be in truth no real or absolute esteem, there is however a certain astonishing delight or ravishment excited.

This passion is experienced in common by every worshipper of the zealot kind. The motion, when unguided and left wholly to itself, is in its nature

[16] τὸ καλὸν καὶ ἀγαθόν [the beautiful and the good].
[17] See p. 393.

turbulent and incentive. It disjoints the natural frame and relaxes the ordinary tone or tenor of the mind. In this disposition the reins are let loose to all passion which arises, and the mind, as far as it is able to act or think in such a state, approves the riot and justifies the wild effects by the supposed sacredness of the cause. Every dream and frenzy is made *inspiration*; every affection, *zeal*. And in this persuasion, the zealots, no longer self-governed but set adrift to the wide sea of passion, can in one and the same spirit of devotion exert the opposite passions of love and hatred, unite affectionately and abhor furiously, curse, bless, sing, mourn, exult, tremble, caress, assassinate, inflict and suffer martyrdom, with a thousand other the most vehement efforts of variable and contrary affections.[18]

The common heathen religion, especially in its latter age, when adorned with the most beautiful temples and rendered more illustrious by the munificence of the Roman Senate and succeeding emperors, ran wholly into pomp and was supported chiefly by that sort of enthusiasm which is raised from the external objects of grandeur, majesty and what we call 'august'.[19] On the other side, the Egyptian or Syrian religions, which lay more in mystery and concealed rites, having less dependence on the magistrate and less of that decorum of art, politeness and magnificence, ran into a more pusillanimous, frivolous, and mean kind of superstition: 'The observation of days, the forbearance of meats and the contention about traditions, seniority of laws and priority of godships.'[20] *Hence there is a height of frenzy at large on both sides, because each place hates the neighbours' divinities, since it believes that only those which it itself worships should be held as gods.*[21]

History, withal, informs us of a certain establishment in Egypt which was very extraordinary and must needs have had a very uncommon effect, no way advantageous to that nation in particular or to the general society of mankind.

---

[18] A passage of history comes to my mind, as it is cited by an eminent divine of our own Church, with regard to that spirit of martyrdom, which furnishes, it seems, such solid matter for the opinion and faith of many zealots. The story, in the words of our divine and with his own reflections on it, is as follows: 'Two Franciscans offered themselves to the fire to prove Savonarola to be a heretic, but a certain Jacobin offered himself to the fire to prove that Savonarola had true revelations and was no heretic. In the meantime Savonarola preached, but made no such confident offer, nor dared he venture at that new kind of fire-ordeal. And put case that all four had passed through the fire and died in the flames, what would that have proved? Had he been a heretic or no heretic, the more or the less, for the confidence of these zealous idiots? If we mark it, a great many arguments, whereon many sects rely, are no better probation than this comes to.' Bishop [Jeremy] Taylor in his dedicatory discourse, before his *Discourse of the Liberty of Prophesying* [London (1647), p. 39]. See pp. 14–15. [On Taylor, see p. 47n above.]

[19] See pp. 377–8.

[20] See pp. 314–15.

[21] Juvenal, *Satires* 15.35–8.

We know very well that nothing is more injurious to the police[D] or municipal constitution of any city or colony than the forcing of a particular trade; nothing more dangerous than the over-peopling any manufacture or multiplying the traders or dealers of whatever vocation beyond their natural proportion and the public demand. Now it happened of old, in this motherland of superstition, that the sons of certain artists were by law obliged always to follow the same calling with their fathers.[22] Thus the son of a priest was always a priest by birth, as was the whole lineage after him without interruption. Nor was it a custom with this nation, as with others, to have only one single priest or priestess to a temple, but, as the number of gods and temples was infinite, so was that of the priests.[23] The religious foundations were without restriction and, to one single worship or temple, as many of the holy order might be retainers as could raise a maintenance from the office.

Whatever happened to other races or professions, that of the priest, in all likelihood, must by this regulation have propagated the most of any. It is a tempting circumstance to have so easy a mastery over the world, to subdue by wit instead of force, to practise on the passions and triumph over the judgment of mankind, to influence private families and public councils, conquer conquerors, control the magistrate himself, and govern without the envy which attends all other government or superiority. No wonder if such a profession was apt to multiply, especially when we consider the easy living and security of the professors, their exemption from all labour and hazard, the supposed

---

[D] Public administration.

[22] *There are seven tribes of Egyptians: and of these one is called priests, another, warriors . . . nor is it permitted for these to practise any craft but they practise only activities for war, inheriting this role in childhood from the father*: Herodotus, *History* 2.164, 166. *No single man is the priest of each of the gods but many men . . . and, whenever one dies, his son takes his place*: Herodotus, *History* 2.37.

[23] *Since the whole country is divided into three parts, the order of priests claims the first portion for itself; it enjoys great power with the inhabitants both because of its piety towards the gods and because their learning allows men of this kind to apply much knowledge. From their revenues, they administer all sacrifices throughout Egypt, they look after their servants, and they defray the cost of their own needs. For the Egyptians consider that it is not right to change the honours paid to the gods, but that they should always be conducted by the same men in the same fashion and that those who look to the communal good of all should not lack the necessities of life. For in looking to the general good in the most important matters, they are always in the company of the king; and in some matters they share his power; in others, they appear as kings, leaders and teachers. By astrology and inspection of sacrificial victims, they foretell the future, and, from the writings of sacred books, they read out records of what is instructive. For it is not the case, as with Greeks, that just one man or woman performs the office of a single priesthood but several perform the sacrifices and honours for the gods, and they bequeath this same way of life to their children. Moreover, these priests are exempt from all taxes and, after the king, hold the first positions of honour and power*: Diodorus Siculus, *Compilation of History* 1.73.1–5. [Shaftesbury quoted a Latin translation here, which is the basis for this translation.]

sacredness of their character and their free possession of wealth, grandeur, estates and women.

There was no need to invest such a body as this with rich lands and ample territories, as it happened in Egypt. The generation or tribe, being once set apart as sacred, would without further encouragement be able, no doubt, in process of time to establish themselves a plentiful and growing fund or religious land bank. It was a sufficient donative to have had only that single privilege from the law, that 'they might retain what they could get', and that 'it might be lawful for their order to receive such estates by voluntary contribution, as could never afterwards be converted to other uses'.[24]

Now if, besides the method of propagation by descent, other methods of increase were allowed in this order of men, if volunteers were also admitted at pleasure without any stint or confinement to a certain number, it is not difficult to imagine how enormous the growth would be of such a science or profession, thus recognized by the magistrate, thus invested with lands and power and thus entitled to whatever extent of riches or possession could be acquired by practice and influence over the superstitious part of mankind.

There were, besides, in Egypt some natural causes of superstition, beyond those which were common to other regions. This nation might well abound in prodigies when even their country and soil itself was a kind of prodigy in nature. Their solitary idle life while shut up in their houses by the regular inundations of the Nile, the unwholesome vapours arising from the new mud and slimy relicts of their river exposed to the hot suns, their various meteors and phenomena with the long vacancy they had to observe and comment on them, the necessity, withal, which, on the account of their navigation and the measure of their yearly drowned lands, compelled them to promote the studies of astronomy and other sciences, of which their priesthood could make good advantages – all these may be reckoned perhaps as additional causes of the immense growth of superstition and the enormous increase of the priesthood in this fertile land.

It will, however, as I conceive, be found unquestionably true, according to political arithmetic, in every nation whatsoever, that *the quantity of superstition (if I may so speak) will in proportion nearly answer the number of priests, diviners, soothsayers, prophets, or such who gain their livelihood or receive advantages by officiating in religious affairs.* For if these dealers are numerous, they will force a trade. And as the liberal hand of the magistrate can easily raise swarms of this kind where they are already but in a moderate proportion, so, where through any other cause the number of these, increasing still by degrees, is suffered to grow beyond a certain measure, they will soon raise such a ferment in men's minds as will at least compel the magistrate, however sensible of the grievance, to be cautious in proceeding to a reform.

We may observe in other necessary professions raised on the infirmities and

<hr />

[24] See p. 372.

defects of mankind, as, for instance, in law and physic, that, with the least help from the bounty or beneficence of the magistrate, the number of the professors and the subject matter of the profession is found over and above increasing. New difficulties are started, new subjects of contention. Deeds and instruments of law grow more numerous and prolix; hypotheses, methods, regimens, more various; and the *materia medica*,[E] more extensive and abundant. What, in process of time, must therefore naturally have happened in the case of religion among the Egyptians may easily be gathered.

Nor is it strange that we should find the property[25] and power of the Egyptian priesthood in ancient days arrived to such a height as in a manner to have swallowed up the state and monarchy. A worse accident befell the Persian crown, of which the hierarchy, having got absolute possession, had once a fair chance for universal empire. Now that the Persian or Babylonian hierarchy was much after the model of the Egyptian, though different perhaps in rites and ceremonies, we may well judge not only from the history of the Magi,[26] but from what is recorded of ancient colonies sent long before by the Egyptians into Chaldea and the adjacent countries.[27] And whether the Ethiopian model was from that of Egypt, or the Egyptian from that of Ethiopia (for each nation had its pretence),[28] we know, by remarkable effects, that the Ethiopian empire was once in the same condition, the state having been wholly swallowed in the exorbitant power of their landed hierarchy.[29] So true it is, that 'dominion must

---

, [E] Healing substances used in the practice of medicine.

[25] Which was one third. *But since Isis wished to induce, by profit, the priests to make those acts of worship (of Osiris, of course, her deceased husband), she granted to them a third of the land so that its revenues could be used upon sacred offices and services for the gods*: Diodorus Siculus, *Compilation of History* 1.21.7. A remarkable effect of female superstition! See also the passage of the same historian, cited above, p. 357n.

[26] See pp. 40–1. Herodotus gives us the history at length in his third book.

[27] Diodorus Siculus, *Compilation of History* 1.28, 81.

[28] Herodotus, *History* 2.30, 104, 110, and Diodorus Siculus, *Compilation of History* 3.3.

[29] *The priests (this order has a very powerful authority), who in Meroe (the city and principal island of the Ethiopians) attend to the worship and honour of the gods, send word to the king, whenever it occurs to them and order him to relinquish his life. For they say that this is declared by the oracles of the gods and it is not right for anything which the immortal gods have commended to be disregarded by any mortal* [Diodorus Siculus, *Compilation of History* 3.6.1–2]. So much for their kings. For, as to subjects, the manner was related a little before: *One of the lictors is sent to the defendant bearing the sign of death. And he, when he has seen this, goes home and inflicts death upon himself* [Diodorus Siculus, *Compilation of History* 3.5.2]. This the people of our days would call passive obedience and priestcraft, with a witness. But our historian proceeds, *And in previous times the kings, mastered not by arms or force but by the bewitching quality of pure superstition, obeyed the priests, until Ergamenes, king of the Ethiopians (in the reign of the second Ptolemy), who was familiar with Greek education and philosophy, dared for the first time to spurn those instructions. For, with a spirit which befitted a king, he went with a troop of soldiers into the forbidden place, where there was the golden temple of the Ethiopians. He slaughtered all those priests, abolished the old custom and inaugurated rites to his own liking*: Diodorus Siculus, *Compilation of History* 3.6.3–4.

naturally follow property'.^F Nor is it possible, as I conceive, for any state or monarchy to withstand the encroachments of a growing hierarchy, founded on the model of these Egyptian and Asiatic priesthoods. No superstition will ever be wanting among the ignorant and vulgar while the able and crafty have a power to gain inheritances and possessions by working on this human weakness. This is a fund which, by these allowances, will prove inexhaustible. New modes of worship, new miracles, new heroes, saints, divinities (which serve as new occasions for sacred donatives), will be easily supplied on the part of the religious orders, while the civil magistrate authorizes the accumulative donation and neither restrains the number or possessions of the sacred body.

We find, withal, that, in the early days of this ancient priestly nation of whom we have been speaking, it was thought expedient also, for the increase of devotion, to enlarge their system of deity and, either by mystical genealogy, consecration or canonization, to multiply their revealed objects of worship and raise new personages of divinity in their religion. They proceeded, it seems, in process of time, to increase the number of their gods so far that at last they became in a manner numberless.[30] What odd shapes, species and forms of deity were in latter times exhibited is well known. Scarce an animal or plant but was adopted into some share of divinity. *O nation of sanctity, for whom these divinities grow in gardens!*[31]

No wonder if, by a nation so abounding in religious orders, spiritual conquests were sought in foreign countries, colonies led abroad, and missionaries detached on expeditions in this prosperous service.[32] It was thus a zealot people – influenced of old by their very region and climate and who through a long tract of time, under a peculiar policy, had been raised both by art and nature to an immense growth in religious science and mystery – came by degrees to spread their variety of rites and ceremonies, their distinguishing marks of separate worships and secret communities, through the distant world but chiefly through their neighbouring and dependent countries.

We understand from history that, even when the Egyptian state was least powerful in arms, it was still respected for its religion and mysteries. It drew

---

^F This was an idea associated with James Harrington. He wrote in the Preliminaries of *Oceana*: 'Dominion is property real or personal; that is to say in lands, or in money and goods.' See J. G. A. Pocock, ed., *The Political Works of James Harrington* (Cambridge: Cambridge University Press, 1977), p. 163.

[30] *As they themselves say, it is 17,000 years to when Amasis was king from when the twelve gods came out of the eight gods*: Herodotus, *History* 2.43.

[31] Juvenal, *Satires* 15.10.

[32] *The Egyptians say that very many colonies out of Egypt had been scattered over the world. Belus, who is considered the son of Neptune and Libya, led colonists to Babylon. He established a settlement by the Euphrates and introduced priests who, after the fashion of the Egyptians, were exempt from public obligations and taxes. These the Babylonians call the Chaldeans. They watch the stars after the example of priests, scientists, and astrologers in Egypt*: Diodorus Siculus, *Compilation of History* 1.28.1. Also 1.81.6.

strangers from all parts to behold its wonders. And the fertility of its soil forced the adjacent people and wandering nations who lived dispersed in single tribes to visit them, court their alliance and solicit a trade and commerce with them on whatsoever terms. The strangers, no doubt, might well receive religious rites and doctrines from those to whom they owed their maintenance and bread.

Before the time that Israel was constrained to go down to Egypt and sue for maintenance to these powerful dynasties or lowland states, the holy patriarch Abraham himself had been necessitated to this compliance on the same account.[33] He applied in the same manner to the Egyptian court. He was at first well received and handsomely presented, but afterwards ill-used and out of favour with the prince, yet suffered to depart the kingdom and retire with his effects without any attempt of recalling him again by force, as it happened in the case of his posterity. It is certain that, if this holy patriarch, who first instituted the sacred rite of circumcision within his own family or tribe, had no regard to any policy or religion of the Egyptians, yet he had formerly been a guest and inhabitant in Egypt (where historians mention this to have been a national rite)[34] long before he had received any divine notice or revelation concerning this affair.[35] Nor was it in religion merely that this reverend guest was said to have derived knowledge and learning from the Egyptians. It was from this parent-country of occult sciences that he was presumed, together with other wisdom, to have learned that of judicial astrology, as his successors did afterwards other prophetical and miraculous arts, proper to the Magi or priesthood of this land.[36]

One cannot indeed but observe, in after times, the strange adherence and servile dependency of the whole Hebrew race on the Egyptian nation. It appears that, though they were of old abused in the person of their grand patriarch, though afterwards held in bondage and treated as the most abject slaves, though twice expelled or necessitated to save themselves by flight out of this oppressive region, yet, in the very instant of their last retreat, while they were yet on

---

[33] Genesis 12.10ff.

[34] *Abraham, when he entered Egypt, had not yet been circumcised nor over the course of more than twenty years after return . . . His descendants were circumcised both before the entrance and while they lingered in Egypt. After departure, however, they were not circumcised until the life of Moses. 'And Joshua made him sharp knives, and circumcised the children of Israel at the hill of the foreskins . . . And the Lord said to Joshua, this day have I rolled away the reproach of Egypt from off you' (Joshua, 5.3,9). As for the Egyptians, so for the Jews, not to be circumcised was disgraceful. Among the Egyptians, the ritual of circumcision was very old and had been instituted in the very beginning. They wish to use the customs of no other men (Herodotus 2.91). 'Others leave the genitals as they were except for all those who have learned from the Egyptians; but the Egyptians practise circumcision' (Herodotus 2.36):* John Marsham, *Chronicus Canon Aegypticus, Ebraicus, Graecus et Disquisitiones* [A master scheme of Egyptian, Hebrew and Greek chronology, with investigations] (London, 1672), p. 72.

[35] Genesis 17.9–14.

[36] According to Julius Firmicus Maternus in Marsham, *Chronicus Canon*, pp. 451–3.

their march, conducted by visible divinity, supplied and fed from Heaven and supported by continual miracles, they notwithstanding inclined so strongly to the manners, the religion, rites, diet, customs, laws and constitutions of their tyrannical masters that it was with the utmost difficulty they could be withheld from returning again into the same subjection.[37] Nor could their great captains and legislators prevent their relapsing perpetually into the same worship to which they had been so long accustomed.[38]

How far the divine providence might have indulged the stubborn habit and stupid humour of this people, by *giving them laws* (as the Prophet says) *which he himself approved not*, I have no intention to examine.[39] This only I pretend to infer from what has been advanced, that 'the manners, opinions, rites and customs of the Egyptians had, in the earliest times and from generation to generation, strongly influenced the Hebrew people, their guests and subjects, and had undoubtedly gained a powerful ascendancy over their natures'.

How extravagant soever the multitude of the Egyptian superstitions may appear, it is certain that their doctrine and wisdom were in high repute, since it is taken notice of in Holy Scripture as no small advantage even to Moses

[37] It can scarce be said in reality, from what appears in Holy Writ, that their retreat was voluntary. And for the historians of other nations, they have presumed to assert that this people was actually expelled Egypt on account of their leprosy, to which the Jewish laws appear to have so great a reference. Thus: *Most authors agree that, when a pestilence arose throughout Egypt and disfigured bodies, King Occhoris went to the oracle of Ammon to seek a cleansing of his kingdom and was instructed to remove to other lands that class of men as hateful to the gods. Thus, when that mob was sought out and gathered . . . , Moses alone warned, etc.*: Tacitus, *Histories* 5.3; *When the Egyptians were suffering from skin diseases, they were advised by an oracular response and drove Moses out, along with the sick, from the boundaries of Egypt, so that the pestilence should not spread to more. Made therefore leader of the exiles, he secretly made off with the holy things of the Egyptians. When the Egyptians sought to recover these by arms, they were forced by storms to return home*: Marcus Junianus Justinus, *Epitome of Trogus Pompeius* 36.2.12–13. And in Marsham we find this remarkable citation from Manetho: *That King Amenophis aspired to become spectator of the gods just as Horus an earlier king. He received the oracular response that he would see the gods if he cleansed the country of lepers and impure men*: Marsham, *Chronicus Canon*, p. 52.

[38] See what is cited above, p. 361, in the notes from Marsham, of the Jews returning to circumcision under Joshua after a generation's intermission. This being approved by God for the reason given, that 'it was taking from them the reproach of the Egyptians, or what rendered them odious and impious in the eyes of that people'. Compare with this the passage concerning Moses himself, Exodus 4.18, 25, 26 (together with Acts 7.30, 34), where in regard to the Egyptians, to whom he was now returning when fourscore years of age, he appears to have circumcised his children and taken off this national reproach, Zipporah, his wife, nevertheless, reproaching him with the bloodiness of the deed, to which she appears to have been a party only through necessity and in fear rather of her husband than of God.

[39] Ezekiel 20.25. Acts 15.10. Of these Egyptian institutions received among the Jews, see our Spencer: *When toleration of certain ancient mores prevailed with great force, effecting the conciliation of the minds of the Hebrews to the law and worship of God, and, as a result of the reforms of Moses, toleration removed all ill will, it then came about that God incorporated some observances that had been customary from antiquity into the number of His own rites, and that the law that Moses gave bore some appearance of the worship that had been earlier accepted . . . Surely, given the nature of the Israelites and what had been done to them, after their recent exodus from Egypt, it was, as it*

himself that 'he had imbibed the wisdom of this nation', which, as is well known, lay chiefly among their priests and Magi.[40]

Before the time that the great Hebrew legislator received his education among these sages, a Hebrew slave, who came a youth into the Egyptian court, had already grown so powerful in this kind of wisdom as to outdo the chief diviners, prognosticators and interpreters of Egypt.[41] He raised himself to be chief minister to a prince who, following his advice, obtained in a manner the whole property and consequently the absolute dominion of that land. But to what height of power the established priesthood was arrived even at that time may be conjectured hence: that the Crown, to speak in a modern style, offered not to meddle with the Church lands and that in this great revolution nothing was attempted so much as by way of purchase or exchange in prejudice of this landed clergy,[42] the prime minister himself having joined his interest with theirs and entered by marriage into their alliance.[43] And in this he was followed by the great founder of the Hebrew state. For he also matched himself with the priesthood of some of the neighbouring nations[44] and traders[45] into Egypt, long

---

were, necessary for God (may it be right to speak in human terms) to grant them usage of some old observances and to reconcile those arrangements with their character and capacity. For the people had been conditioned by the delicate mores of Egypt, and strengthened in them by usage of many years . . . The Hebrews were not only accustomed to the mores of Egypt but they were also stubborn . . . Just as there are dispositions peculiar to the people of each region and place and particular mores, so nature moulded the nation of Hebrews more than other inhabitants of the world to a disposition that was morose, difficult and stubborn to the point of disrepute . . . Since therefore the Hebrews of old had such harsh and fierce manners, the condition of the people dictated that God should concede them some observances that had the durability of long usage, and instituted 'obligatory service befitting their weakness' (as Theodoretus says) . . . The Hebrews were a superstitious nation and destitute of almost all literature. How deeply they were immersed in the superstitions of nations can be understood from their laws, which were imposed on the people as though remedies for superstition. Superstition is an obstinate beast, especially if it has absorbed fresh ferocity and obstinacy from the dark corners of igno-rance. It is easily to be believed that the Israelites, recently freed from the house of slavery, had no experience of the more humane arts and had tasted scarce else beyond the bricks and garlic of Egypt. When therefore God had to deal with a people so barbarous and so heavily committed to superstition, it was almost necessary that he do something for their infirmity and bind them to himself by some guile (not arguments). No animal is more morose than the superstitious, and especially the naively so, or needing to be handled by a greater art: John Spencer, *De Legibus Hebraeorum Ritualibus et Earum Rationibus* [On the ritual laws of the Hebrews and their explanations] (Cambridge, 1685), pp. 627–9.

[40] *And Moses was learned in all the wisdom of the Egyptians and was mighty in words and in deeds*: Acts 7.22. Also, Exodus 7.11, 22, 8.7. Marcus Junianus Justinus, *Epitome of Trogus Pompeius* 36.2.

[41] Genesis 39ff. *Joseph was the youngest of the brothers and they, fearing his outstanding character, secretly caught him and sold him to travelling merchants. Brought by them into Egypt, after he had understood the arts of magic there with his clever nature, he soon became very dear to the king him-self*: Marcus Junianus Justinus, *Epitome of Trogus Pompeius* 36.2.6–7.

[42] Genesis 47.22, 26.

[43] Genesis 41.45.

[44] Exodus 3.1, 18.1ff.

[45] Such were the Midianites, Genesis 37.28, 36.

before his establishment of the Hebrew religion and commonwealth. Nor had he perfected his model till he consulted the foreign priest, his father-in-law, to whose advice he paid such remarkable deference.[46]

But to resume the subject of our speculation concerning the wide diffusion of the priestly science or function, it appears from what has been said that, notwithstanding the Egyptian priesthood was by ancient establishment hereditary, the skill of divining, soothsaying and magic was communicated to others besides their national sacred body, and that the wisdom of the magicians, their power of miracles, their interpretation of dreams and visions and their art of administering in divine affairs were entrusted even to foreigners who resided among them.

It appears withal, from these considerations, how apt the religious profession was to spread itself widely in this region of the world, and what efforts would naturally be made by the more necessitous of these unlimited professors towards a fortune or maintenance for themselves and their successors.

Common arithmetic will, in this case, demonstrate to us that, as the proportion of so many laymen to each priest grew every day less and less, so the wants and necessities of each priest must grow more and more. The magistrate too, who, according to this Egyptian regulation, had resigned his title or share of right in sacred things, could no longer govern as he pleased in these affairs or check the growing number of these professors. The spiritual generations were left to prey on others and, like fish of prey, even on themselves when destitute of other capture and confined within too narrow limits. What method, therefore, was there left to heighten the zeal of worshippers and augment their liberality, but to foment their emulation, prefer worship to worship, faith to faith and turn the spirit of enthusiasm to the side of sacred horror, religious antipathy and mutual discord between worshippers?

Thus provinces and nations were divided by the most contrary rites and customs which could be devised in order to create the strongest aversion possible between creatures of a like species. For when all other animosities are allayed and anger of the fiercest kind appeased, the religious hatred, we find, continues still, as it began, without provocation or voluntary offence. The presumed misbeliever and blasphemer, as one rejected and abhorred of God, is, through a pious imitation, abhorred by the adverse worshipper whose enmity must naturally increase as his religious zeal increases.

From hence the opposition rose of temple against temple, proselyte against proselyte. The most zealous worship of one god was best expressed, as they conceived, by the open defiance of another. Surnames and titles of divinity passed as watchwords. He who had not the symbol nor could give the word

---

[46] Exodus 18.17–24. [Moses' father-in-law was Jethro, a Midianite priest.]

received the knock. 'Down with him, kill him, merit Heaven thereby,' as our poet has it in his American tragedy.[47]

Nor did philosophy, when introduced into religion, extinguish but rather inflame this zeal, as we may show perhaps in our following chapter more particularly, if we return again as is likely to this subject.[48] For this, we perceive, is of a kind apt enough to grow upon our hands. We shall here therefore observe only what is obvious to every student in sacred antiquities, that from the contentious learning and sophistry of the ancient schools (when true science, philosophy and arts were already deep in their decline)[49] religious problems of a like contentious form sprang up, and certain doctrinal tests were framed by which religious parties were engaged and listed against one another with more animosity than in any other cause or quarrel that had been ever known. Thus religious massacres began and were carried on, temples were demolished, holy utensils destroyed, the sacred pomp trodden underfoot, insulted, and the insulters in their turn exposed to the same treatment in their persons as well as in their worship. Thus madness and confusion were brought upon the world, like that chaos which the poet miraculously describes in the mouth of his mad hero, when, even in celestial places, disorder and blindness reigned – no dawn of light:

> No glimpse or starry spark,
> But Gods met Gods, and justled in the dark.[50]

Chapter 2

Judgment of divines and grave authors concerning enthusiasm. Reflections upon scepticism. A sceptic-Christian. Judgment of the inspired concerning their own inspirations. Knowledge and belief. History of religion resumed. Zeal offensive and defensive. A Church in danger. Persecution. Policy of the Church of Rome.

What I had to remark of my own concerning enthusiasm, I have thus dispatched. What others have remarked on the same subject, I may, as an apologist to another author, be allowed to cite, especially if I take notice only of what has been dropped very naturally by some of our most approved authors and ablest divines.

It has been thought an odd kind of temerity in our author to assert, that 'even atheism itself was not wholly exempt from enthusiasm', that 'there have been in reality enthusiastical atheists', and that 'even the spirit of martyrdom

---

[47] John Dryden, *The Indian Emperor* 5.2.9.
[48] See p. 373.
[49] See pp. 99–100, 156n, 373.
[50] John Dryden and Nathaniel Lee, *Oedipus* 4.1.625–6. [The quotation is not precise.]

could, upon occasion, exert itself as well in this cause as in any other'.[51] Now, besides what has been intimated in the preceding chapter and what in fact may be demonstrated from the examples of Vaninus[G] and other martyrs of a like principle, we may hear an excellent and learned divine, of highest authority at home and fame abroad, who, after having described an enthusiastical atheist and one atheistically inspired, says of this very sort of men that 'they are fanatics too, however that word seem to have a more peculiar respect to something of a deity, all atheists being that blind goddess Nature's fanatics'.[52]

And again, 'all atheists', says he, 'are possessed with a certain kind of madness, that may be called pneumatophobia, that makes them have an irrational but desperate abhorrence from spirits or incorporeal substances, they being acted also, at the same time, with an hylomania, whereby they madly dote upon matter and devoutly worship it as the only numen'.[53]

What the power of ecstasy is, whether through melancholy, wine, love or other natural causes, another learned divine of our church, in a discourse upon enthusiasm, sets forth, bringing an example from Aristotle 'of a Syracusean poet who never versified so well as when he was in his distracted fits'.[54] But, as to poets in general, compared with the religious enthusiasts, he says there

---

[G] Lucilio or, as he signed his works, Giulio Cesare, Vanini, 1585–1619, was an Italian freethinker who, after a life peregrinating through western Europe, was tried and burned in France as an atheist.

[51] Namely, in his *Letter Concerning Enthusiasm*.

[52] Ralph Cudworth, *The True Intellectual System of the Universe* (London, 1678), p. 134 [Book I, Chapter 3, Section 29].

[53] [Cudworth, *The True Intellectual System of the Universe*, p. 135, Book I, Chapter 3, Section 30.] The good doctor makes use here of a stroke of raillery against the over-frighted anti-superstitious gentlemen, with whom our author reasons at large in his second treatise (see pp. 40–1, and 42–3). It is indeed the nature of fear, as of all other passions, when excessive, to defeat its own end and prevent us in the execution of what we naturally propose to ourselves as our advantage. Superstition itself is but a certain kind of fear which, possessing us strongly with the apprehended wrath or displeasure of divine powers, hinders us from judging what those powers are in themselves or what conduct of ours may, with best reason, be thought suitable to such highly rational and superior natures. Now, if from the experience of many gross delusions of a superstitious kind the course of this fear begins to turn, it is natural for it to run with equal violence a contrary way. The extreme passion for religious objects passes into an aversion. And a certain horror and dread of imposture causes as great a disturbance as even imposture itself had done before. In such a situation as this, the mind may easily be blinded, as well in one respect as in the other. It is plain both these disorders carry something with them which discovers us to be in some manner beside our reason and out of the right use of judgment and understanding. For how can we be said to entrust or use our reason if in any case we fear to be convinced? How are we masters of ourselves when we have acquired the habit of bringing horror, aversion, favour, fondness or any other temper than that of mere indifference and impartiality, into the judgment of opinions and search of truth?

[54] Henry More, *Enthusiasmus Triumphatus; or a Brief Discourse of the Nature, Causes, Kinds and Cure of Enthusiasm*, originally published in *A Collection of Several Philosophical Writings of Dr. Henry More* (London, 1662), Section 11.

is this difference, that 'a poet is an enthusiast in jest, and an enthusiast is a poet in good earnest'.[55]

'It is a strong temptation', says the Doctor, 'with a melancholist, when he feels a storm of devotion and zeal come upon him like a mighty wind, his heart being full of affection, his head pregnant with clear and sensible representations and his mouth flowing and streaming with fit and powerful expressions such as would astonish an ordinary auditory [to hear],[56] it is, I say, a shrewd temptation to him to think it the very spirit of God that then moves supernaturally in him, whenas all that excess of zeal and affection and fluency of words is most palpably to be resolved into the power of melancholy, which is a kind of natural inebriation.'[57]

The learned doctor, with much pains afterwards and by help of the peripatetic philosophy, explains this enthusiastic inebriation, and shows in particular how the vapours and fumes of 'melancholy partake of the nature of wine'.[58]

One might conjecture from hence that the malicious opposers of early Christianity were not unversed in this philosophy, when they sophistically objected against the apparent force of the Divine Spirit speaking in diverse languages and attributed it 'to the power of new wine'.[59]

But our devout and zealous doctor seems to go yet further. For besides what he says of the enthusiastic power of fancy in atheists,[60] he calls melancholy 'a pertinacious and religious complexion' and asserts that 'there is not any true spiritual grace from God, but this mere natural constitution, according to the several tempers and workings of it, will not only resemble but sometimes seem to outstrip'.[61] And, after speaking of prophetical enthusiasm[62] and establishing, as our author does,[63] a legitimate and a bastard sort, he asserts and justifies the 'devotional enthusiasm', as he calls it, 'of holy and sincere souls' and ascribes this also to melancholy.[64]

He allows that 'the soul may sink so far into phantasms as not to recover the use of her free faculties, and that this enormous strength of imagination

---

[55] More, *Enthusiasmus Triumphatus*, Section 20.
[56] It appears from hence that, in the notion which this learned divine gives us of enthusiasm, he comprehends the social or popular genius of the passion, agreeably with what our author in his *Letter Concerning Enthusiasm* (pp. 10, 23) has said of the influence and power of the assembly or auditory itself, and of the communicative force and rapid progress of this ecstatic fervour, once kindled and set in action.
[57] More, *Enthusiasmus Triumphatus*, Section 16.
[58] More, *Enthusiasmus Triumphatus*, Sections 20, 22, 23, 26. [More's peripatetic support is frequent citation of the *Problemata*, Section 30, spuriously attributed to Aristotle.]
[59] Acts 2.13.
[60] More, *Enthusiasmus Triumphatus*, Section 1.
[61] More, *Enthusiasmus Triumphatus*, Section 15.
[62] More, *Enthusiasmus Triumphatus*, Sections 30 and 57.
[63] See p. 27.
[64] More, *Enthusiasmus Triumphatus*, Section 63.

does not only beget the belief of mad internal apprehensions, but is able to assure us of the presence of external objects which are not'. He adds that 'what custom and education do by degrees, distempered fancy may do in a shorter time'. And speaking of ecstasy and the power of melancholy in ecstatic fancies, he says that 'what the imagination then puts forth, of herself, is as clear as broad day, and the perception of the soul at least as strong and vigorous as at any time in beholding things awake'.[65]

From whence the doctor infers that 'the strength of perception is no sure ground of truth'.

Had any other than a reverend father of our church expressed himself in this manner, he must have been contented perhaps to bear a sufficient charge of scepticism.

It was a good fortune in my Lord Bacon's case that he should have escaped being called an atheist or a sceptic when, speaking in a solemn manner of the religious passion, the ground of superstition or enthusiasm (which he also terms a panic), he derives it from an imperfection in the creation, make or natural constitution of man.[66] How far the author of the *Letter Concerning Enthusiasm* differs from this author in his opinion, both of the end and foundation of this passion, may appear from what has been said above. And, in general, from what we read in the other succeeding treatises of our author, we may venture to say of him with assurance that 'he is as little a sceptic, according to the vulgar sense of that word, as he is Epicurean or atheist'. This may be proved sufficiently from his philosophy, and, for anything higher, it is what he nowhere presumes to treat, having forborne in particular to mention any holy mysteries of our religion or sacred article of our belief.

As for what relates to revelation in general, if I mistake not our author's meaning, he professes to believe, as far as is possible for anyone who himself had never experienced any divine communication, whether by dream, vision, apparition or other supernatural operation, nor was ever present as eyewitness of any sign, prodigy or miracle whatsoever.[67] Many of these, he observes, are

---

[65] More, *Enthusiasmus Triumphatus*, Section 28.
[66] *Nature has placed in all living things fear and fright, the protector of their life and essence, and they avoid and repel the assaults of evil things. But in truth the same nature does not know to keep to moderation but mixes fears that are always empty and idle with those that are salutary, and this happens to such an extent that all creatures, especially humans (if they could be seen within), are quite full of panicky terrors. And most of all, in the case of the common people, who struggle and are vexed immensely by superstition (which in truth is nothing else but panicky terror), this particularly occurs when times are hard and frightening and hostile*: Francis Bacon, *De Augmentis Scientiarum* [Of the advancement of learning] 2.13. The author of the *Letter*, I dare say, would have expected no quarter from his critics, had he expressed himself as this celebrated author here quoted, who by his *Nature* can mean nothing less than the universal dispensing nature, erring blindly in the very first design, contrivance or original frame of things, according to the opinion of Epicurus himself, whom this author immediately after cites with praise.
[67] See p. 471.

at this day pretendedly exhibited in the world with an endeavour of giving them the perfect air and exact resemblance of those recorded in Holy Writ.[68] He speaks indeed with contempt of the mockery of modern miracles and inspiration. And, as to all pretences to things of this kind in our present age, he seems inclined to look upon them as no better than mere imposture or delusion. But for what is recorded of ages heretofore, he seems to resign his judgment, with entire condescension, to his superiors. He pretends not to frame any certain or positive opinion of his own, notwithstanding his best searches into antiquity and the nature of religious record and tradition, but, on all occasions, submits most willingly and with full confidence and trust, to the opinions by law established.[69] And, if this be not sufficient to free him from the reproach of scepticism, he must, for anything I see, be content to undergo it.

To say truth, I have often wondered to find such a disturbance raised about the simple name of sceptic.[70] It is certain that, in its original and plain signification, the word imports no more than barely 'that state or frame of mind in which everyone remains on every subject of which he is not certain'. He who is certain, or presumes to say he knows, is in that particular, whether he be mistaken or in the right, a dogmatist. Between these two states or situations of mind, there can be no medium. For he who says that he believes for certain, or is assured of what he believes, either speaks ridiculously or says in effect that he believes strongly but is not sure. So that whoever is not conscious of revelation, nor has certain knowledge of any miracle or sign, can be no more than sceptic in the case, and the best Christian in the world, who, being destitute of the means of certainty, depends only on history and tradition for his belief in these particulars, is at best but a sceptic-Christian. He has no more than a nicely critical historical faith, subject to various speculations and a thousand different criticisms of languages and literature.[71]

This he will naturally find to be the case if he attempts to search into originals in order to be his own judge, and proceed on the bottom of his own discernment and understanding. If, on the other hand, he is no critic nor competently learned in these originals, it is plain he can have no original judgment of his own but must rely still on the opinion of those who have opportunity to examine such matters, and whom he takes to be the unbiassed and disinterested judges of these religious narratives. His faith is not in ancient facts or persons, nor in the ancient writ or primitive recorders, nor in the successive collators or conservators of these records, for of these he is unable to take cognizance. But his confidence and trust must be in those modern men, or societies

---

[68] See pp. 23–4, 288–9.
[69] See pp. 161–2, 382, 435, 471.
[70] See pp. 241, 289, 472–83. [On Shaftesbury and scepticism, see Introduction, p. xiv.]
[71] See pp. 67–8, 471–2, 472–5.

of men, to whom the public or he himself ascribes the judgment of these records and commits the determination of sacred writ and genuine story.

Let the person seem ever so positive or dogmatical in these high points of learning, he is yet in reality no dogmatist, nor can any way free himself from a certain kind of scepticism. He must know himself still capable of doubting, or, if, for fear of it, he strives to banish every opposite thought and resolves not so much as to deliberate on the case, this still will not acquit him. So far are we from being able to be sure when we have a mind, that indeed we can never be thoroughly sure, but then only when we cannot help it and find of necessity we must be so, whether we will or not. Even the highest implicit faith is in reality no more than a kind of passive scepticism, a resolution to examine, recollect, consider or hear as little as possible to the prejudice of that belief which, having once espoused, we are ever afterwards afraid to lose.

If I might be allowed to imitate our author in daring to touch now and then upon the characters of our divine worthies, I should, upon this subject of belief, observe how fair and generous the great Christian convert and learned apostle has shown himself in his sacred writings.[11] Notwithstanding he had himself an original testimony and revelation from Heaven on which he grounded his conversion, notwithstanding he had in his own person the experience of outward miracles and inward communications, he condescended still, on many occasions, to speak sceptically and with some hesitation and reserve as to the certainty of these divine exhibitions. In his account of some transactions of this kind, himself being the witness and speaking, as we may presume, of his own person and proper vision, he says only that 'he knew a man, whether in the body or out of it, he cannot tell. But such a one caught up to the third heaven he knew formerly', he says, 'above fourteen years before his then writing.'[72] And, when in another capacity the same inspired writer, giving precepts to his disciples, distinguishes what he writes by divine commission from what he delivers as his own judgment and private opinion, he condescends nevertheless to speak as one no way positive or master of any absolute criterion in the case.[73] And in several subsequent passages he expresses himself as under some kind of doubt how to judge or determine certainly, 'whether he writes by inspiration or otherwise'. He only 'thinks he has the spirit'. He 'is not sure' nor would have us to depend on him as positive or certain in a matter of so nice discernment.[74]

---

[11] St Paul.

[72] 2 Corinthians 12.2–4. [The verses in the King James version are: 'I knew a man in Christ above fourteen years ago (whether in the body, I cannot tell; or whether out of the body, I cannot tell: God knoweth), such an one caught up to the third heaven. And I knew such a man (whether in the body, or out of the body, I cannot tell: God knoweth).']

[73] 1 Corinthians 7.10, 12.

[74] 1 Corinthians 7.40. [The verse in the King James version is: 'But she is happier if she so abide, after my judgment: and I think also that I have the Spirit of God.']

The holy founders and inspired authors of our religion required not, it seems, so strict an assent or such implicit faith in behalf of their original writings and revelations as later uninspired doctors, without the help of divine testimony or any miracle on their side, have required in behalf of their own comments and interpretations. The earliest and worst of heretics, it is said, were those called Gnostics, who took their name from an audacious pretence to certain knowledge and comprehension of the greatest mysteries of faith.[1] If the most dangerous state of opinion was this dogmatical and presumptuous sort, the safest, in all likelihood, must be the sceptical and modest.

There is nothing more evident than that our holy religion, in its original constitution, was set so far apart from all philosophy or refined speculation that it seemed in a manner diametrically opposed to it. A man might have been not only a sceptic in all the controverted points of the academies or schools of learning, but even a perfect stranger to all of this kind and yet complete in his religion, faith and worship.

Among the polite heathens of the ancient world, these different provinces of religion and philosophy were upheld, we know, without the least interfering with each other. If in some barbarous nations the philosopher and priest were joined in one, it is observable that the mysteries, whatever they were, which sprang from this extraordinary conjunction were kept secret and undivulged. It was satisfaction enough to the priest-philosopher if the initiated party preserved his respect and veneration for the tradition and worship of the temple, by complying in every respect with the requisite performances and rites of worship. No account was afterwards taken of the philosophic faith of the proselyte or worshipper. His opinions were left to himself, and he might philosophize according to what foreign school or sect he fancied. Even among the Jews themselves, the Sadducee, a materialist and denier of the soul's immortality, was as well admitted as the Pharisee, who, from the schools of Pythagoras, Plato or other latter philosophers of Greece, had learned to reason upon immaterial substances and the natural immortality of souls.[J]

It is no astonishing reflection to observe how fast the world declined in wit and sense, in manhood, reason, science and in every art when once the Roman

---

[1]   Gnosticism was a syncretic religious movement of the second and third century AD which combined Christian components with others deemed heterodox by the contemporary church.

[J]   The Sadducees were a party among the ancient Hebrews during the Roman era associated with the high priesthood and aristocracy. They were conservative in their loyalty to the letter of the Old Testament. By contrast, the Pharisees drew their following from all segments of the population. They relied on both the letter of the Law and the oral tradition surrounding it. Their ideas included a belief in angels and ministering spirits and a notion of the resurrection of the body, both of which the Sadducees denied. The idea that Pharisaic thinking was shaped by Greek philosophy was an impression Shaftesbury probably took from the account by the Roman Jewish historian Flavius Josephus, who correlated distinctions among contemporary Jews with the schools of Greek philosophy.

Empire had prevailed and spread an universal tyranny and oppression over mankind.[75] Even the Romans themselves, after the early sweets of one peaceful and long reign,[K] began to groan under that yoke of which they had been themselves the imposers. How much more must other nations and mighty cities at a far distance have abhorred this tyranny, and detested their common servitude under a people who were themselves no better than mere slaves?

It may be looked upon, no doubt, as providential that, at this time and in these circumstances of the world, there should arise so high an expectation of a divine deliverer, and that, from the eastern parts and confines of Judea, the opinion should spread itself of such a deliverer to come, with strength from Heaven sufficient to break that Empire, which no earthly power remaining could be thought sufficient to encounter. Nothing could have better disposed the generality of mankind to receive the evangelical advice while they mistook the news, as many of the first Christians plainly did, and understood the promises of a messiah in this temporal sense, with respect to his second coming and sudden reign here upon earth.

Superstition, in the meanwhile, could not but naturally prevail as misery and ignorance increased.[76] The Roman emperors, as they grew more barbarous, grew so much the more superstitious. The lands and revenues as well as the numbers of the heathen priests grew daily. And when the season came that, by means of a convert-emperor,[L] the heathen church lands, with an increase of power, became transferred to the Christian clergy, it was no wonder if, by such riches and authority, they were in no small measure influenced and corrupted, as may be gathered even from the accounts given us of these matters by themselves.[77]

[K] The reign of Augustus.
[L] Constantine I.

[75] See pp. 99–100, 365.
[76] See pp. 61–2, 377
[77] How rich and vast these were, especially in the latter times of that empire, may be judged from what belonged to the single order of the Vestals and what we read of the revenues belonging to the temples of the sun (as in the time of the monster Heliogabalus) and of other donations by other emperors. But what may give us yet a greater idea of these riches is that in the latter heathen times, which grew more and more superstitious, the restraining laws or statutes of mortmain, by which men had formerly been withheld from giving away estates by will or otherwise to religious uses, were repealed, and the heathen church, left in this manner as a bottomless gulf and devouring receptacle of land and treasure. *By decree of the Senate and by the edicts of emperors, it was permitted to name as heirs Apollo of Didyma, Diana of Ephesus, the mother of the gods . . . (Ulpianus post Cod. Theodos. p. 92)* in Marsham, *Chronicus Canon*, p. 131. This answers not amiss to the modern practice and expression of 'making our soul our heir', giving to God what has been taken sometimes with freedom enough from man, and conveying estates in such a manner in this world as to make good interest of them in another. The reproach of the ancient satirist is at present out of doors. It is no affront to religion nowadays to compute its profits. And a man might well be accounted dull, who, in our present age, should ask the question, *Tell, pontiffs, what good gold does in a shrine?*: Persius, *Satires* 2.69. See pp. 376n, 377, 391.

When, together with this, the schools of the ancient philosophers, which had been long in their decline, came now to be dissolved and their sophistic teachers became ecclesiastical instructors, the unnatural union of religion and philosophy was completed, and the monstrous product of this match appeared soon in the world.[78] The odd exterior shapes of deities, temples and holy utensils, which by the Egyptian sects had been formerly set in battle against each other,[79] were now metamorphosed into philosophical forms and phantoms and, like flags and banners, displayed in hostile manner and borne offensively by one party against another. In former times, those barbarous nations above-mentioned were the sole warriors in these religious causes, but now the whole world became engaged when, instead of storks and crocodiles, other ensigns were erected, when sophistical chimeras, crabbed notions, bombastic phrases, solecisms, absurdities and a thousand monsters of a scholastic brood were set on foot and made the subject of vulgar animosity and dispute.

Here first began that spirit of bigotry, which broke out in a more raging manner than had been ever known before and was less capable of temper or moderation than any species, form or mixture of religion in the ancient world. Mysteries, which were heretofore treated with profound respect and lay unexposed to vulgar eyes, became public and prostitute, being enforced with terrors and urged with compulsion and violence on the unfitted capacities and apprehensions of mankind. The very Jewish traditions and cabbalistic learning underwent this fate. That which was naturally the subject of profound speculation and inquiry was made the necessary subject of a strict and absolute assent. The allegorical, mythological account of sacred things was wholly inverted, liberty of judgment and exposition taken away, no ground left for inquiry, search or meditation, no refuge from the dogmatical spirit let loose. Every quarter was taken up, every portion prepossessed. All was reduced to article and proposition.[80]

Thus a sort of philosophical enthusiasm overspread the world. And bigotry, a species of superstition hardly known before, took place in men's affections and armed them with a new jealousy against each other.[81] Barbarous terms and idioms were every day introduced, monstrous definitions invented and imposed, new schemes of faith erected from time to time, and hostilities, the fiercest imaginable, exercised on these occasions. So that the enthusiasm or zeal, which was usually shown by mankind in behalf of their particular worships and which for the most part had been hitherto defensive only, grew now to be universally of the offensive kind.

---

[78] See p. 365.
[79] See pp. 156n, 356, 358–9, 364.
[80] See pp. 365, 478–9n.
[81] Let anyone who considers distinctly the meaning and force of the word 'bigotry' endeavour to render it in either of the ancient languages and he will find how peculiar a passion it implies and how different from the mere affection of enthusiasm or superstition.

It may be expected of me perhaps that, being fallen thus from remote antiquity to later periods, I should speak on this occasion with more than ordinary exactness and regularity. It may be urged against me that I talk here as at random and without book, neglecting to produce my authorities or continue my quotations, according to the professed style and manner in which I began this present chapter. But, as there are many greater privileges by way of variation, interruption and digression allowed to us writers of miscellany, and especially to such as are commentators upon other authors, I shall be content to remain mysterious in this respect and explain myself no further than by a noted story, which seems to suit our author's purpose and the present argument.

It is observable from Holy Writ that the ancient Ephesian worshippers,[M] however zealous or enthusiastic they appeared, had only a defensive kind of zeal in behalf of their temple, whenever they thought in earnest it was brought in danger.[82] In the tumult which happened in that city near the time of the holy apostle's retreat,[83] we have a remarkable instance of what our author calls a religious panic. As little bigots as the people were and as far from any offensive zeal, yet, when their established church came to be called in question, we see in what a manner their zeal began to operate: 'All with one voice, about the space of two hours, cried out, saying, "Great is Diana of the Ephesians."'[84] At the same time this assembly was so confused that 'the greater part knew not wherefore they were come together'[85] and consequently could not understand why their church was 'in any danger'.[N] But the enthusiasm was got up, and a panic fear for the church had struck the multitude. It ran into a popular rage or epidemical frenzy and was communicated, as our author expresses it, 'by aspect or, as it were, by contact or sympathy'.[86]

[M] Ephesus was a city founded by Greeks on the west coast of Asia Minor near a holy place of the Anatolian goddess known to the Greeks as Artemis. A succession of temples occupied the site. By St Paul's time, the temple of Diana (whom the Romans identified with Artemis) was huge and served not only as a religious centre but as a treasury for deposits from kings and cities.

[N] The 'Church in Danger' was a watchword of the High Church party among the Tories during the reign of Anne.

[82] The magnificence and beauty of that temple is well known to all who have formed any idea of the ancient Grecian arts and workmanship. It seems to me to be remarkable in our learned and elegant apostle that, though an enemy to this mechanical spirit of religion in the Ephesians, yet, according to his known character, he accommodates himself to their humour and the natural turn of their enthusiasm by writing to his converts in a kind of architect style and almost with a perpetual allusion to building and to that majesty, order and beauty of which their temple was a masterpiece. *[Followers of Christ] are built upon the foundation of the apostles and prophets, Jesus Christ himself being the chief cornerstone; in whom all the building fitly framed together groweth unto an holy temple in the Lord: in whom ye also are builded together for an habitation of God through the Spirit*: Ephesians 2.20–2, and so 3.17–18 and 4.16, 29.

[83] Acts 19.23.

[84] Acts 19.28, 34.

[85] Acts 19.32.

[86] See p. 10.

It must be confessed that there was, besides these motives, a secret spring which forwarded this enthusiasm. For certain parties concerned, men of craft and strictly united in interest, had been secretly called together and told, 'Gentlemen! (or Sirs!) Ye know that by this mystery or craft we have our wealth. Ye see withal and have heard that not only here at Ephesus, but almost throughout all Asia, this Paul has persuaded and turned away many people by telling them, "They are no real gods who are figured or wrought with hands," so that not only this our craft is in danger but also the temple itself.'[87]

Nothing could be more moderate and wise, nothing more agreeable to that magisterial science or policy which our author recommends,[88] than the behaviour of the town clerk or recorder of the city, as he is represented on this occasion in Holy Writ. I must confess indeed he went pretty far in the use of this moderating art. He ventured to assure the people that 'everyone acquiesced in their ancient worship of the great goddess and in their tradition of the image which fell down from Jupiter', that 'these were facts undeniable', and that 'the new sect neither meant the pulling down of their church nor so much as offered to blaspheme or speak amiss of their goddess'.

This, no doubt, was stretching the point sufficiently, as may be understood by the event in after time. One might, perhaps, have suspected this recorder to have been himself a dissenter, or at least an occasional conformist, who could answer so roundly for the new sect and warrant the church in being secure of damage and out of all danger for the future. Meanwhile, the tumult was appeased; no harm befell the temple for that time. The new sect acquiesced in what had been spoken on their behalf. They allowed the apology of the recorder. Accordingly, the zeal of the heathen church, which was only defensive, gave way, and the new religionists were prosecuted no further.

Hitherto, it seems, the face of persecution had not openly shown itself in the wide world. It was sufficient security for every man that he gave no disturbance to what was publicly established. But when offensive zeal came to be discovered in one party, the rest became in a manner necessitated to be aggressors in their turn. They who observed or had once experienced this intolerating spirit could no longer tolerate on their part.[89] And they who had once

---

[87] Acts 19.24–7.

[88] See pp. 10–11.

[89] Thus the controversy stood before the time of the Emperor Julian, when blood had been so freely drawn and cruelties so frequently exchanged not only between Christian and heathen, but between Christian and Christian after the most barbarous manner. What the zeal was of many early Christians against the idolatry of the old heathen church, at that time the established one, may be comprehended by any person who is ever so slenderly versed in the history of those times. Nor can it be said indeed of us moderns that, in the quality of good Christians, as that character is generally understood, we are found either backward or scrupulous in assigning to perdition such wretches as we pronounce guilty of idolatry. The name 'idolater' is sufficient excuse for almost any kind of insult against the person, and much more against the worship of such a misbeliever. The very word 'Christian' is in common language used for 'man',

exerted it over others could expect no better quarter for themselves. So that nothing less than mutual extirpation became the aim and almost open profession of each religious society.

In this extremity, it might well perhaps have been esteemed the happiest wish for mankind that one of these contending parties of incompatible religionists should at last prevail over the rest, so as, by an universal and absolute power, to determine orthodoxy and make that opinion effectually catholic

---

in opposition to brute beast, without leaving so much as a middle place for the poor heathen or pagan who, as the greater beast of the two, is naturally doomed to massacre, and his gods and temples to fracture and demolishment. Nor are we masters of this passion even in our best humour. The French poets, we see, can with great success and general applause exhibit this primitive zeal even on the public stage: *Let us not waste any more time. The sacrifice is ready. Let us go and beg the interest of the true God. Let us trample underfoot this ludicrous thunderbolt with which an excessively credulous people arm a rotten piece of wood. Let us go to enlighten this fatal blindness. Let us go to break these gods of stone and metal. Let us give ourselves over to this heavenly enthusiasm and make God triumph in order that He may dispose of the rest*: Corneille, *Polyeucte* 2.6. I should scarce have mentioned this, but that it came into my mind how ill a construction some people have endeavoured to make of what our author, stating the case of heathen and Christian persecution in his *Letter Concerning Enthusiasm*, has said concerning the Emperor Julian. It was no more indeed than had been said of that virtuous and gallant Emperor by his greatest enemies, even by those who, to the shame of Christianity, boasted of his having been most insolently affronted on all occasions and even treacherously assassinated by one of his Christian soldiers. As for such authors as these, should I cite them in their proper invective style and saint-like phrase, they would make no very agreeable appearance, especially in miscellanies of the kind we have here undertaken. But a letter of that elegant and witty Emperor may not be improperly placed among our citations as a pattern of his humour and genius as well as of his principle and sentiments on this occasion.

Julian
'To the Bostrens'
'I should have thought, indeed, that the Galilean leaders would have esteemed themselves more indebted to me than to him who preceded me in the administration of the Empire. For in his time many of them suffered exile, persecution and imprisonment. Multitudes of those whom in their religion they term "heretics" were put to the sword, insomuch that, in Samosata, Cyzicum, Paphlagonia, Bithynia, Galatia and many other countries, whole towns were levelled with the earth. The just reverse of this has been observed in my time. The exiles have been recalled, and the proscribed restored to the lawful possession of their estates. But to that height of fury and distraction are this people arrived that, being no longer allowed the privilege to tyrannize over one another, or persecute either their own sectaries or the religious of the lawful church, they swell with rage and leave no stone unturned, no opportunity unemployed, of raising tumult and sedition, so little regard have they to true piety, so little obedience to our laws and constitutions, however humane and tolerating. For still do we determine and steadily resolve never to suffer one of them to be drawn involuntarily to our altars . . . As for the mere people, indeed, they appear driven to these riots and seditions by those among them whom they call clerics, who are now enraged to find themselves restrained in the use of their former power and intemperate rule . . . They can no longer act the magistrate or civil judge nor assume authority to make people's wills, supplant relations, possess themselves of other men's patrimonies, and by specious pretences transfer all into their own possession . . . For this reason, I have thought fit by this public edict to forewarn the people of this sort that they raise no more commotions, nor gather in a riotous manner about their seditious clerics in defiance of the magistrate, who has been insulted and in danger of being stoned by these incited rabbles. In their congregations they may, notwithstanding, assemble as they please and crowd about their leaders, performing worship, receiving doctrine and praying, according as they are by them taught

which in their particular judgment had the best right to that denomination.[90] And thus, by force of massacre and desolation, peace in worship and civil unity by help of the spiritual might be presumed in a fair way of being restored to mankind.

I shall conclude with observing how ably the Roman Christian and once catholic church, by the assistance of their converted emperors, proceeded in the establishment of their growing hierarchy.[91] They considered wisely the various superstitions and enthusiasms of mankind and proved the different kinds and force of each. All these seeming contrarieties of human passion they knew how to comprehend in their political model and subservient system of divinity. They knew how to make advantage both from the high speculations of philosophy and the grossest ideas of vulgar ignorance. They saw there was nothing more different than that enthusiasm which ran upon spirituals, according to the simpler views of the divine existence,[92] and that which ran upon external proportions, magnificence of structures, ceremonies, processions, choirs and those other harmonies which captivate the eye and ear.[93] On this account they even added to this latter kind and displayed religion in a yet more gorgeous habit of temples, statues, paintings, vestments, copes, mitres, purple and the cathedral pomp. With these arms they could subdue the victorious Goths and secure themselves an Attila when their Caesars failed them.[94]

and conducted, but, if with any tendency to sedition, let them beware how they hearken or give assent and remember it is at their peril, if by these means they are secretly wrought up to mutiny and insurrection . . . Live therefore in peace and quietness, neither spitefully opposing nor injuriously treating one another. You misguided people of the new way, beware, on your side! And you of the ancient and established church, injure not your neighbours and fellow-citizens, who are enthusiastically led away in ignorance and mistake rather than with design or malice! It is by discourse and reason, not by blows, insults or violence, that men are to be informed of truth and convinced of error. Again therefore, and again I enjoin and charge the zealous followers of the true religion, no way to injure, molest or affront the Galilean people.' [Shaftesbury identified this as Letter No. 52; in modern editions, it is No. 41.]

Thus the generous and mild Emperor, whom we may indeed call heathen but not so justly apostate, since, being at different times of his youth transferred to different schools or universities and bred under tutors of each religion, as well heathen as Christian, he happened, when of full age, to make his choice, though very unfortunately, in the former kind and adhered to the ancient religion of his country and forefathers. See the same Emperor's letters to Artabius, No. 7 [37], and to Hecebolius, No. 43 [40], and to the people of Alexandria, No. 10 [21]. See p. 14.

90 See pp. 482–3.
91 See pp. 61, 372.
92 See p. 268.
93 See p. 356.
94 When this victorious ravager was in full march to Rome, St Leo, the then pope, went out to meet him in solemn pomp. The Goth was struck with the appearance, obeyed the priest and retired instantly with his whole army in a panic fear, alleging that, among the rest of the pontifical train, he had seen one of an extraordinary form who threatened him with death if he did not instantly retire. Of this important encounter there are in St Peter's Church, in the Vatican, and elsewhere at Rome, many fine sculptures, paintings and representations, deservingly made in honour of the miracle. [For example, Raphael's fresco, the *Repulse of Attila*, in the Stanza of Heliodorus in the Vatican, painted in 1513.]

The truth is, it is but a vulgar species of enthusiasm which is moved chiefly by show and ceremony and wrought upon by chalices and candles, robes and figured dances. Yet this, we may believe, was looked upon as no slight ingredient of devotion in those days, since at this hour the manner is found to be of considerable efficacy with some of the devout among ourselves, who pass the least for superstitious and are reckoned in the number of the polite world. This the wise hierarchy duly preponderating, but being satisfied withal that there were other tempers and hearts which could not so easily be captivated by this exterior allurement, they assigned another part of religion to proselytes of another character and complexion, who were allowed to proceed on a quite different bottom by the inward way of contemplation and divine love.

They are indeed so far from being jealous of mere enthusiasm or the ecstatic manner of devotion that they allow their mystics to write and preach in the most rapturous and seraphic strains. They suffer them in a manner to supersede all external worship and triumph over outward forms till the refined religionists proceed so far as either expressly or seemingly to dissuade the practice of the vulgar and established ceremonial duties. And then, indeed, they check the supposed exorbitant enthusiasm which would prove dangerous to their hierarchal state.[95]

If modern visions, prophecies and dreams, charms, miracles, exorcisms and the rest of this kind be comprehended in that which we call fanaticism or superstition, to this spirit they allow a full career, while to ingenious writers they afford the liberty, on the other side, in a civil manner, to call in question these spiritual feats performed in monasteries, or up and down by their mendicant or itinerant priests and ghostly missionaries.

This is that ancient hierarchy which, in respect of its first foundation, its policy and the consistency of its whole frame and constitution, cannot but appear in some respect august and venerable, even in such as we do not usually esteem weak eyes. These are the spiritual conquerors who, like the first Caesars, from small beginnings established the foundations of an almost universal monarchy. No wonder if at this day the immediate view of this hierarchal residence, the city and court of Rome, be found to have an extraordinary effect on foreigners of other latter churches. No wonder if the amazed surveyors are for the future so apt either to conceive the horridest aversion to all

---

[95] Witness the case of Molinos and of the pious, worthy and ingenious Abbé Fénelon, now Archbishop of Cambrai. [Miguel de Molinos, *c*. 1640–97, was a Spanish priest who led the religious revival known as Quietism. His mystical doctrine did suggest that advanced practitioners could leave behind the Church's assistance. The Jesuits launched a campaign which led to his imprisonment and the condemnation of his doctrine. François de Salignac de la Mothe Fénelon, 1651–1715, was a French nobleman and writer who was already the archbishop of Cambrai as well as tutor to Louis XIV's eldest grandson when he was attracted to Quietism. His mystical writings were condemned in 1699, after which he was confined to his diocese.]

priestly government or, on the contrary, to admire it so far as even to wish a coalescence or reunion with this ancient mother church.

In reality, the exercise of power, however arbitrary or despotic, seems less intolerable under such a spiritual sovereignty, so extensive, ancient and of such a long succession, than under the petty tyrannies and mimical polities of some new pretenders.º The former may even persecute with a tolerable grace;[96] the latter, who would willingly derive their authority from the former and graft on their successive right, must necessarily make a very awkward figure. And while they strive to give themselves the same air of independency on the civil magistrate, while they affect the same authority in government, the same grandeur, magnificence and pomp in worship, they raise the highest ridicule in the eyes of those who have real discernment and can distinguish originals from copies: *O you mimics, you slavish herd!*[97]

Chapter 3

Of the force of humour in religion. Support of our author's argument in his Essay on the Freedom of Wit and Raillery. *Zeal discussed. Spiritual surgeons, executioners, carvers. Original of human sacrifice. Exhilaration of religion. Various aspects from outward causes.*

The celebrated wits of the miscellanarian race, the essay writers, casual discoursers, reflection coiners, meditation founders and others of the irregular kind of writers may plead it as their peculiar advantage that 'they follow the variety of nature'. And, in such a climate as ours, their plea, no doubt, may be very just. We islanders, famed for other mutabilities, are particularly noted for the variableness and inconstancy of our weather. And, if our taste in letters be found answerable to this temperature of our climate, it is certain a writer must, in our account, be the more valuable in his kind as he can agreeably surprise his reader by sudden changes and transports from one extreme to another.

Were it not for the known prevalency of this relish and the apparent deference paid those geniuses who are said to elevate and surprise, the author of these miscellanies might, in all probability, be afraid to entertain his reader with this multifarious, complex and desultory kind of reading. It is certain that, if we consider the beginning and process of our present work, we shall find sufficient variation in it. From a professed levity, we are lapsed into a sort of gravity unsuitable to our manner of setting out. We have steered an adventurous course and seem newly come out of a stormy and rough sea. It is time

---

º This is presumably a reference to recent Protestant establishments such as the Church of England.

[96] See p. 385.
[97] Horace, *Epistles* 1.19.19.

indeed we should enjoy a calm and, instead of expanding our sails before the swelling gusts, it befits us to retire under the lee shore and ply our oars in a smooth water.

It is the philosopher, the orator or the poet whom we may compare to some first-rate vessel which launches out into the wide sea and with a proud motion insults the encountering surges. We essay-writers are of the small craft or galley kind. We move chiefly by starts and bounds according as our motion is by frequent intervals renewed. We have no great adventure in view nor can tell certainly whither we are bound. We undertake no mighty voyage by help of stars or compass, but row from creek to creek, keep up a coasting trade and are fitted only for fair weather and the summer season.

Happy therefore it is for us in particular that, having finished our course of enthusiasm and pursued our author into his second treatise,[98] we are now at last obliged to turn towards pleasanter reflections and have such subjects in view as must naturally reduce us to a more familiar style. Wit and humour, the professed subject of the treatise now before us, will hardly bear to be examined in ponderous sentences and poised discourse. We might now perhaps do best to lay aside the gravity of strict argument and resume the way of chat, which, through aversion to a contrary formal manner, is generally relished with more than ordinary satisfaction. For excess of physic, we know, has often made men hate the name of 'wholesome'. And an abundancy of forced instruction and solemn counsel may have made men full as averse to anything which is delivered with an air of high wisdom and science, especially if it be so high as to be set above all human art of reasoning and even above reason itself in the account of its sublime dispensers.

However, since it may be objected to us by certain formalists of this sort that 'we can prove nothing duly without proving it in form', we may for once condescend to their demand, state our case formally and divide our subject into parts after the precise manner and according to just rule and method.

Our purpose, therefore, being to defend an author who has been charged as too presumptuous for introducing the way of wit and humour into religious searches, we shall endeavour to make appear:

first, that wit and humour are corroborative of religion and promotive of true faith;

second, that they are used as proper means of this kind by the holy founders of religion;

third, that, notwithstanding the dark complexion and sour humour of some religious teachers, we may be justly said to have, in the main, a witty and good-humoured religion.

Among the earliest acquaintance of my youth, I remember, in particular, a

[98] Namely, *Sensus Communis: An Essay on the Freedom of Wit and Humour.*

club of three or four merry gentlemen who had long kept company with one another and were seldom separate in any party of pleasure or diversion. They happened once to be upon a travelling adventure and came to a country where they were told for certain they should find the worst entertainment as well as the worst roads imaginable. One of the gentlemen, who seemed the least concerned for this disaster, said slightly and without any seeming design that 'the best expedient for them in this extremity would be to keep themselves in high humour and endeavour to commend everything which the place afforded'. The other gentlemen immediately took the hint, but, as it happened, kept silence, passed the subject over, and took no further notice of what had been proposed.

Being entered into the dismal country, in which they proceeded without the least complaint, it was remarkable that, if by great chance they came to any tolerable bit of road or any ordinary prospect, they failed not to say something or other in its praise and would light often on such pleasant fancies and representations as made the objects in reality agreeable.

When the greatest part of the day was thus spent and our gentlemen arrived where they intended to take their quarters, the first of them who made trial of the fare, or tasted either glass or dish, recommended it with such an air of assurance and in such lively expressions of approbation, that the others came instantly over to his opinion and confirmed his relish with many additional encomiums of their own.

Many ingenious reasons were given for the several odd tastes and looks of things which were presented to them at table. Some meats were 'wholesome'; others, 'of a high taste'; others, 'according to the manner of eating in this or that foreign country'. Every dish had the flavour of some celebrated receipt in cookery, and the wine and other liquors had, in their turn, the advantage of being treated in the same elegant strain. In short, our gentlemen ate and drank heartily and took up with their indifferent fare so well that it was apparent they had wrought upon themselves to believe they were tolerably well served.

Their servants, in the meantime, having laid no such plot as this against themselves, kept to their senses and stood it out that 'their masters had certainly lost theirs. For how else could they swallow so contentedly and take all for good which was set before them?'

Had I to deal with a malicious reader, he might perhaps pretend to infer from this story of my travelling friends, that I intended to represent it as an easy matter for people to persuade themselves into what opinion or belief they pleased. But it can never surely be thought that men of true judgment and understanding should set about such a task as that of perverting their own judgment and giving a wrong bias to their reason. They must easily foresee that an attempt of this kind, should it have the least success, would prove of far worse consequence to them than any perversion of their taste, appetite or ordinary senses.

I must confess it, however, to be my imagination that, where fit circumstances concur and many inviting occasions offer from the side of men's interest, their humour or their passion, it is no extraordinary case to see them enter into such a plot as this against their own understandings and endeavour by all possible means to persuade both themselves and others of what they think convenient and useful to believe.

If, in many particular cases where favour and affection prevail, it be found so easy a thing with us to impose upon ourselves, it cannot surely be very hard to do it where we take for granted our highest interest is concerned. Now it is certainly no small interest or concern with men to believe what is by authority established, since in the case of disbelief there can be here no choice left but either to live a hypocrite or be esteemed profane. Even where men are left to themselves and allowed the freedom of their choice, they are still forward enough in believing, and can officiously endeavour to persuade themselves of the truth of any flattering imposture.

Nor is it unusual to find men successful in this endeavour as, among other instances, may appear by the many religious faiths or opinions, however preposterous or contradictory, which, age after age, we know to have been raised on the foundation of miracles and pretended commissions from Heaven. These have been as generally espoused and passionately cherished as the greatest truths and most certain revelations. It is hardly to be supposed that such combinations should be formed and forgeries erected with such success and prevalency over the understandings of men, did not they themselves co-operate of their own accord towards the imposture and show that, 'by a good will and hearty desire of believing, they had in reality a considerable hand in the deceit'.

It is certain that, in a country where faith has for a long time gone by inheritance and opinions are entailed by law, there is little room left for the vulgar to alter their persuasion or deliberate on the choice of their religious belief. Whensoever a government thinks fit to concern itself with men's opinions and by its absolute authority impose any particular belief, there is none perhaps ever so ridiculous or monstrous in which it needs doubt of having good success. This we may see thoroughly effected in certain countries by a steady policy and sound application of punishment and reward, with the assistance of particular courts erected to this end, peculiar methods of justice, peculiar magistrates and officers, proper inquests and certain wholesome severities, not slightly administered and played with, as certain triflers propose, but duly and properly enforced, as is absolutely requisite to this end of strict conformity and unity in one and the same profession and manner of worship.

But should it happen to be the truth itself which was thus effectually propagated by the means we have described, the very nature of such means can, however, allow but little honour to the propagators and little merit to the disciples and believers. It is certain that Mahometism, paganism, Judaism or any other belief may stand as well as the truest upon this foundation. He who is now an orthodox Christian would, by virtue of such a discipline, have been infallibly as true a Mussulman or as errant a heretic, had his birth happened in another place.

For this reason there can be no rational belief but where comparison is allowed, examination permitted and a sincere toleration established. And, in this case, I will presume to say that, 'whatever belief is once espoused or countenanced by the magistrate, it will have a sufficient advantage without any help from force or menaces, on one hand, or extraordinary favour and partial treatment, on the other'. If the belief be in any measure consonant to truth and reason, it will find as much favour in the eyes of mankind as truth and reason need desire. Whatever difficulties there may be in any particular speculations or mysteries belonging to it, the better sort of men will endeavour to pass them over. They will believe, as our author says,[99] to the full stretch of their reason and add spurs to their faith in order to be the more sociable and conform the better with what their interest, in conjunction with their good humour, inclines them to receive as credible and observe as their religious duty and devotional task.

Here it is that good humour will naturally take place, and the hospitable disposition of our travelling friends above recited will easily transfer itself into religion and operate in the same manner with respect to the established faith, however miraculous or incomprehensible, under a tolerating, mild and gentle government.

Everyone knows, indeed, that by heresy is understood a stubbornness in the will, not a defect merely in the understanding. On this account, it is impossible that an honest and good-humoured man should be a schismatic or heretic, and affect to separate from his national worship on slight reason or without severe provocation.

To be pursued by petty inquisitors, to be threatened with punishment or penal laws, to be marked out as dangerous and suspected, to be railed at in high places with all the studied wit and art of calumny, are indeed sufficient provocations to ill humour and may force people to divide who at first had never any such intention. But the virtue of good humour in religion is such that it can even reconcile persons to a belief in which they were never bred, or to which they had conceived a former prejudice.

From these considerations, we cannot but of course conclude that there is nothing so ridiculous in respect of policy, or so wrong and odious in respect of common humanity, as a moderate and half-way persecution. It only frets the sore: it raises the ill humour of mankind, excites the keener spirits, moves indignation in beholders and sows the very seeds of schism in men's bosoms. A res-

---

[99] See p. 18.

olute and bold-faced persecution leaves no time or scope for these engendering distempers or gathering ill humours. It does the work at once, by extirpation, banishment or massacre, and, like a bold stroke in surgery, dispatches by one short amputation what a bungling hand would make worse and worse, to the perpetual sufferance and misery of the patient.

If there be on earth a proper way to render the most sacred truth suspected, it is by supporting it with threats and pretending to terrify people into the belief of it. This is a sort of daring mankind in a cause where they know themselves superior and out of reach. The weakest mortal finds within himself that, though he may be outwitted and deluded, he can never be forced in what relates to his opinion or assent. And there are few men so ignorant of human nature and of what they hold in common with their kind, as not to comprehend that, where great vehemence is expressed by anyone in what relates solely to another, it is seldom without some private interest of his own.

In common matters of dispute, the angry disputant makes the best cause to appear the worst. A clown once took a fancy to hear the Latin disputes of doctors at a university. He was asked what pleasure he could take in viewing such combatants when he could never know so much as which of the parties had the better. 'For that matter,' replied the clown, 'I a'n't such a fool neither but I can see who's the first that puts t'other into a passion.' Nature herself dictated this lesson to the clown, that he who had the better of the argument would be easy and well-humoured, but he who was unable to support his cause by reason would naturally lose his temper and grow violent.

Were two travellers agreed to tell their story separate in public, the one being a man of sincerity but positive and dogmatical, the other less sincere but easy and good-humoured, though it happened that the accounts of this latter gentleman were of the more miraculous sort, they would yet sooner gain belief and be more favourably received by mankind, than the strongly asserted relations and vehement narratives of the other fierce defender of the truth.

That good humour is a chief cause of compliance or acquiescence in matters of faith may be proved from the very spirit of those whom we commonly call critics. It is a known prevention against the gentlemen of this character that they are generally ill-humoured and splenetic. The world will needs have it that their spleen disturbs them. And I must confess I think the world in general to be so far right in this conceit that, though all critics perhaps are not necessarily splenetic, all splenetic people, whether naturally such or made so by ill usage, have a necessary propensity to criticism and satire. When men are easy in themselves, they let others remain so and can readily comply with what seems plausible and is thought conducing to the quiet or good correspondence of mankind. They study to raise no difficulties or doubts. And in religious affairs it is seldom that they are known forward to entertain ill thoughts or surmises while they are unmolested. But, if disturbed by groundless arraignments and suspicions, by unnecessary invectives and bitter declamations and by a contentious quarrelsome aspect of religion, they naturally turn critics and begin to question everything. The spirit of satire rises with the ill mood, and the chief passion of men thus diseased and thrown out of good humour is to find fault, censure, unravel, confound and leave nothing without exception and controversy.

These are the sceptics or scrupulists against whom there is such a clamour raised. It is evident in the meanwhile that the very clamour itself, joined with the usual menaces and show of force, is that which chiefly raises this sceptical spirit, and helps to multiply the number of these inquisitive and ill-humoured critics. Mere threats, without power of execution, are only exasperating and provocative. They who are masters of the carnal as well as spiritual weapon may apply each at their pleasure, and in what proportion they think necessary.[100] But where the magistrate resolves steadily to reserve his *fasces*[P] for his own proper province and keep the edge tools and deadly instruments out of other hands, it is in vain for spiritual pretenders to take such magisterial airs. It can then only become them to brandish such arms when they have strength enough to make the magistrate resign his office, and become provost or executioner in their service.

Should anyone who happens to read these lines perceive in himself a rising animosity against the author for asserting thus zealously the notion of a religious liberty and mutual toleration, it is wished that he would maturely deliberate on the cause of his disturbance and ill humour. Would he deign to look narrowly into himself, he would undoubtedly find that it is not zeal for religion or the truth which moves him on this occasion. For had he happened to be in a nation where he was no conformist, nor had any hope or expectation of obtaining the precedency for his own manner of worship, he would have found nothing preposterous in this our doctrine of indulgence. It is a fact indisputable that, whatever sect or religion is undermost, though it may have persecuted at any time before, yet as soon as it begins to suffer persecution in its turn, it recurs instantly to the principles of moderation and maintains this our plea for complacency, sociableness and good humour in religion. The mystery therefore of this animosity or rising indignation of my devout and zealous reader is only this: that, being devoted to the interest of a party already in possession or expectation of the temporal advantages annexed to a particular belief, he fails not, as a zealous party man, to look with jealousy on every unconformable opinion, and is sure to justify those means which he thinks proper to prevent its growth. He knows that, if in matters of religion anyone believes

---

[P]   The symbol of the power of the Roman magistracy, a bundle of rods from which protruded the blade of an axe bound within.

[100]   See p. 379.

amiss, it is at his own peril. If opinion damns, vice certainly does as much. Yet will our gentleman easily find, if he inquires the least into himself, that he has no such furious concern for the security of men's morals, nor any such violent resentment of their vices, when they are such as no way incommode him. And from hence it will be easy for him to infer that the passion he feels on this occasion is not from pure zeal, but private interest and worldly emulation.

Come we now, as authentic rhetoricians express themselves, to our second head, which we should again subdivide into firsts and seconds but that this manner of carving is of late days grown much out of fashion.

It was the custom of our ancestors, perhaps as long since as the days of our hospitable King Arthur, to have nothing served at table but what was entire and substantial. It was a whole boar or solid ox which made the feast. The figure of the animal was preserved entire, and the dissection made in form by the appointed carver, a man of might as well as profound craft and notable dexterity, who was seen erect, with goodly mien and action, displaying heads and members, dividing according to art and distributing his subject matter into proper parts, suitable to the stomachs of those he served. In latter days, it has become the fashion to eat with less ceremony and method. Everyone chooses to carve for himself. The learned manner of dissection is out of request, and a certain method of cookery has been introduced by which the anatomical science of the table is entirely set aside. Ragouts and fricassees are the reigning dishes, in which everything is so dismembered and thrown out of all order and form that no part of the mass can properly be divided or distinguished from another.

Fashion is indeed a powerful mistress and, by her single authority, has so far degraded the carving method and use of solids, even in discourse and writing, that our religious pastors themselves have many of them changed their manner of distributing to us their spiritual food. They have quitted their substantial service and uniform division into parts and underparts, and, in order to become fashionable, they have run into the more savoury way of learned ragout and medley. It is the unbred rustic orator alone who presents his clownish audience with a divisible discourse. The elegant Court divine exhorts in miscellany, and is ashamed to bring his twos and threes before a fashionable assembly.

Should I therefore, as a mere miscellanarian or essay writer, forgetting what I had premised, be found to drop a head and lose the connecting thread of my present discourse, the case perhaps would not be so preposterous. For fear, however, lest I should be charged for being worse than my word, I shall endeavour to satisfy my reader by pursuing my method proposed, if peradventure he can call to mind what that method was. Or, if he cannot, the matter is not so very important but he may safely pursue his reading without further trouble.

To proceed, therefore. Whatever means or methods may be employed at any time in maintaining or propagating a religious belief already current and established, it is evident that the first beginnings must have been founded in that natural complacency and good humour which inclines to trust and confidence in mankind. Terrors alone, though accompanied with miracles and prodigies of whatever kind, are not capable of raising that sincere faith and absolute reliance which is required in favour of the divinely authorized instructor and spiritual chief. The affection and love which procures a true adherence to the new religious foundation must depend either on a real or counterfeit goodness in the religious founder.[101] Whatever ambitious spirit may inspire him, whatever savage zeal or persecuting principle may lie in reserve ready to disclose itself when authority and power is once obtained, the first scene of doctrine, however, fails not to present us with the agreeable views of joy, love, meekness, gentleness and moderation.

In this respect, religion, according to the common practice in many sects, may be compared to that sort of courtship of which the fair sex are known often to complain. In the beginning of an amour, when these innocent charmers are first accosted, they hear of nothing but tender vows, submission, service, love. But soon afterwards, when, won by this appearance of gentleness and humility, they have resigned themselves and are no longer their own, they hear a different note and are taught to understand submission and service in a sense they little expected. Charity and brotherly love are very engaging sounds; but who would dream that out of abundant charity and brotherly love should come steel, fire, gibbets, rods, and such a sound and hearty application of these remedies as should at once advance the worldly greatness of religious pastors and the particular interest of private souls, for which they are so charitably concerned?

It has been observed by our author that 'the Jews were naturally a very cloudy people'.[102] That they had certainly in religion, as in everything else, the least good humour of any people in the world is very apparent. Had it been otherwise, their holy legislator and deliverer, who was declared the meekest man on earth[103] and who for many years together had, by the most popular and kind acts, endeavoured to gain their love and affection, would in all probability have treated them afterwards with more sweetness and been able with less blood and massacre to retain them in their religious duty.[104] This, however, we may observe, that, if the first Jewish princes and celebrated kings acted in reality according to the institutions of their great founder, not only music but even play and dance were of holy appointment and divine right. The first monarch of this nation, though of a melancholy complexion, joined music with his

---

[101] See pp. 44, 294.
[102] See pp. 16, 361–2.
[103] Numbers 12.3. [Moses.]
[104] Exodus 32.27; Numbers 16.41.

spiritual exercises, and even used it as a remedy under that dark enthusiasm or evil spirit,[105] which how far it might resemble that of prophecy, experienced by him[106] even after his apostasy, our author[107] pretends not to determine. It is certain that the successor of this prince was a hearty espouser of the merry devotion and, by his example, has shown it to have been fundamental in the religious constitution of his people. The famous entry or high dance[108] performed by him, after so conspicuous a manner, in the procession of the sacred coffer, shows that he was not ashamed of expressing any ecstasy of joy or playsome humour[109] which was practised by the meanest of the priests or people on such an occasion.[110]

Besides the many songs and hymns dispersed in Holy Writ, the *Book of Psalms* itself, *Job*, *Proverbs*, *Canticles*[Q] and other entire volumes of the sacred collection, which are plainly poetry and full of humorous images and jocular wit, may sufficiently show how readily the inspired authors had recourse to humour and diversion as a proper means to promote religion and strengthen the established faith.

When the affairs of the Jewish nation grew desperate and everything seemed tending to a total conquest and captivity, the style of their holy writers and prophets might well vary from that of earlier days in the rise and vigour of their commonwealth or during the first splendour of their monarchy, when the princes themselves prophesied and potent kings were of the number of the sacred penmen. This still we may be assured of, that, however melancholy or ill-humoured any of the prophets may appear at any time, it was not that kind of spirit which God was wont to encourage in them. Witness the case of the prophet Jonah, whose character is so naturally described in Holy Writ.

Pettish as this prophet was, unlike a man and resembling rather some refractory boyish pupil, it may be said that God, as a kind tutor, was pleased to

---

Q Song of Songs.

[105] 1 Samuel 18.10, 19.9. [Saul.]
[106] 1 Samuel 19.23, 24.
[107] See p. 23.
[108] 2 Samuel 6.5, 14, 16. [David.]
[109] 2 Samuel 6.21–2.
[110] Though this dance was not performed quite naked, the dancers, it seems, were so slightly clothed that, in respect of modesty, they might as well have worn nothing, their nakedness appearing still by means of their high caperings, leaps and violent attitudes which were proper to this dance. The reader, if he be curious, may examine what relation this religious ecstasy and naked dance had to the naked and processional prophecy (1 Samuel 19.23, 24), where prince, priest and people prophesied in conjunction, the prince himself being both of the itinerant and naked party. It appears that, even before he was yet advanced to the throne, he had been seized with this prophesying spirit – errant, processional and saltant [leaping] – attended, as we find, with a sort of martial dance performed in troops or companies, with pipe and tabret [a small percussive instrument, drum- or tambourine-like] accompanying the march, together with psaltery, harp, cornets, timbrels and other variety of music. See 1 Samuel 10.5, 19.23, 24, 2 Samuel 6.5, and see p. 23.

humour him, bear with his anger and, in a lusory manner, expose his childish forwardness and show him to himself.

'Arise,' said his gracious Lord, 'and go to Nineveh.'[111] 'No such matter', says our prophet to himself, but away over sea for Tarshish. He fairly plays the truant, like an arch schoolboy, hoping to hide out of the way. But his tutor had good eyes and a long reach. He overtook him at sea, where a storm was ready prepared for his exercise and a fish's belly for his lodging. The renegade found himself in harder durance than any at land. He was sufficiently mortified. He grew good, prayed, moralized and spoke mightily against lying vanities.[112]

Again the prophet is taken into favour and bid go to Nineveh to foretell destruction.[113] He foretells it. Nineveh repents, God pardons and the prophet is angry.

'Lord! Did I not foresee what this would come to? Was not this my saying when I was safe and quiet at home? What else should I have run away for? As if I knew not how little dependence there was on the resolution of those who are always so ready to forgive and repent of what they have determined. No! Strike me dead! Take my life this moment. It is better for me. If ever I prophesy again——'[114]

'And dost thou well then to be thus angry, Jonah? Consider with thyself. Come! Since thou wilt needs retire out of the city to see at a distance what will come of it, here, take a better fence than thy own booth against the hot sun which incommodes thee. Take this tall plant as a shady covering for thy head. Cool thyself and be delivered from thy grief.'[115]

When the Almighty had shown this indulgence to the prophet, he grew better-humoured and passed a tolerable night. But the next morning the worm came and an east wind, the arbour was nipped, the sun shone vehemently and the prophet's head was heated as before. Presently the ill mood returns, and the prophet is at the old pass. 'Better die than live at this rate. Death, death alone can satisfy me. Let me hear no longer of living. No! It is in vain to talk of it.'[116]

Again God expostulates but is taken up short and answered churlishly by the testy prophet. 'Angry he is, angry he ought to be, and angry he will be to his death.'[117] But the Almighty, with the utmost pity towards him in this melancholy and froward[R] temper, lays open the folly of it and exhorts to mildness

---

[R] Perverse or unreasonable.

[111] Jonah 1.2.
[112] Jonah 2.8.
[113] Jonah 3.
[114] Jonah 4.1, 2, 3.
[115] Jonah 4.4, 5, 6.
[116] Jonah 4.7, 8.
[117] Jonah 4.9.

and good humour in the most tender manner and under the most familiar and pleasant images, while He shows expressly more regard and tenderness to the very cattle and brute beasts than the prophet to his own humankind and to those very disciples whom by his preaching he had converted.[118]

In the ancienter parts of sacred story, where the beginning of things and origin of human race are represented to us, there are sufficient instances of this familiarity of style, this popular pleasant intercourse and manner of dialogue between God and man,[119] I might add even between man and beast,[120] and what is still more extraordinary, between God and Satan.[121]

Whatsoever of this kind may be allegorically understood, or in the way of parable or fable, this I am sure of, that the accounts, descriptions, narrations, expressions and phrases are in themselves many times exceedingly pleasant, entertaining and facetious. But fearing lest I might be misinterpreted should I offer to set these passages in their proper light (which, however, has been performed by undoubted good Christians and most learned and eminent divines of our own church),[122] I forbear to go any further into the examination or criticism of this sort.

As for our Saviour's style, it is not more vehement and majestic in his gravest animadversions or declamatory discourses than it is sharp, humorous and witty in his repartees, reflections, fabulous narrations or parables, similes, comparisons and other methods of milder censure and reproof. His exhortations to his disciples, his particular designation of their manners, the pleasant images under which he often couches his morals and prudential rules, even his miracles themselves, especially the first he ever wrought,[123] carry with them a certain festivity, alacrity and good humour so remarkable that I should look upon it as impossible not to be moved in a pleasant manner at their recital.

Now, if what I have here asserted in behalf of pleasantry and humour be found just and real in respect of the Jewish and Christian religions, I doubt not it will be yielded to me, in respect of the ancient heathen establishments, that the highest care was taken by their original founders and following reformers to exhilarate religion, and correct that melancholy and gloominess to which it is subject, according to those different modifications of enthusiasm above specified.[124]

---

[118] See the last verse of this prophet.
[119] Genesis 3.9ff.
[120] Numbers 22.28ff.
[121] Job 1 and 2; 2 Chronicles 18.18, 19.
[122] See Thomas Burnet, *Archaeologiae Philosophicae: Sive Doctrina Antiqua de Rerum Originibus* [Philosophical archaeologies, or the ancient doctrine concerning the origin of things] (London, 1692), Book II, Chapter 7, pp. 280ff.
[123] John 2.11. [The transformation of water into wine at the marriage in Cana.]
[124] Above, Chapters 1 and 2.

Our author, as I take it, has elsewhere shown that these founders were real musicians and improvers of poetry, music and the entertaining arts, which they in a manner incorporated with religion, not without good reason, as I am apt to imagine.[125] For to me it plainly appears that in the early times of all religions, when nations were yet barbarous and savage, there was ever an aptness or tendency towards the dark part of superstition, which among many other horrors produced that of human sacrifice. Something of this nature might possibly be deduced even from Holy Writ.[126] And in other histories we are informed of it more at large.

Everyone knows how great a part of the old heathen worship consisted in play, poetry and dance. And though some of the more melancholy and superstitious votaries might approach the shrines of their divinities with mean grimaces, crouchings and other fawning actions, betraying the low thoughts they had of the divine nature, yet it is well known that in those times the illiberal sycophantic manner of devotion[127] was by the wiser sort contemned and oft suspected as knavish and indirect.[128]

How different an air and aspect the good and virtuous were presumed to carry with them to the temple, let Plutarch singly, instead of many others, witness in his excellent treatise of superstition[129] and in another against the

---

[125] See pp. 106–7.

[126] Genesis 22 [Abraham's sacrifice of Isaac] and Judges 11.30ff [Jephthah's sacrifice of his daughter]. These places relating to Abraham and Jephthah are cited only with respect to the notion which these primitive warriors may be said to have entertained concerning this horrid enormity, so common among the inhabitants of Palestine and other neighbouring nations. It appears that even the elder of these Hebrew princes was under no extreme surprise on this trying revelation. Nor did he think of expostulating in the least on this occasion when at another time he could be so importunate for the pardon of an inhospitable, murderous, impious and incestuous city (Genesis 18.23). See John Marsham's citations in *Chronicus Canon*, pp. 76, 77: *Accordingly it is more satisfactory to conclude that this temptation of Abraham was no innovation; it was not recently devised but was contrived in accordance with the ancient mores of Canaanites.* See the learned [Louis] Cappel's dissertation upon Jephthah [in *Commentarii et Notae Criticae in Vetus Testamentum*, 'Commentaries and Critical Notes on the New Testament' (Amsterdam, 1689), pp. 422–4]: *In following the injunction of this vow* (Leviticus 27.28,29*), Jephtha expressly seems to have sacrificed his daughter, that is to say, effected her death, and so discharged the vow which he had himself sworn* (Judges 11.39*).*

[127] See p. 19.

[128] *You make no greedy merchant's prayer, etc. Not just anybody is ready to remove the murmuring and lowly whisperings from the temples . . . What do you think about Jupiter? Before whom would you care to prefer him? . . . What is your price for the ears of the gods? . . . O souls bent to the earth and empty of heavenly things! What profit in unleashing our mores upon the temples and basing our thoughts of goods for the gods on this corrupt flesh!*: Persius, *Satires* 2.3, 6–7, 18–19, 29–30, 61–3. *It is not for me, if the mast bellow in African gales, to scurry off to wretched prayers*: Horace, *Odes* 3.29.57–9. See pp. 61, 372n.

[129] 'O wretched Greeks', says he, speaking to his then declining countrymen, 'who in a way of superstition run so easily into the relish of barbarous nations and bring into religion that frightful mien of sordid and vilifying devotion, ill-favoured humiliation and contrition, abject looks and countenances, consternations, prostrations, disfigurations and, in the act of worship,

Epicurean atheism,[130] where it will plainly enough appear what a share good humour had in that which the politer ancients esteemed as piety and true religion.

But now, methinks, I have been sufficiently grave and serious in defence of what is directly contrary to seriousness and gravity. I have very solemnly

---

distortions, constrained and painful postures of the body, wry faces, beggarly tones, mumpings, grimaces, cringings and the rest of this kind . . . A shame indeed to us Grecians! . . . For to us, we know, it is prescribed from of old, by our peculiar laws concerning music and the public choruses, that we should perform in the handsomest manner and with a just and manly countenance, avoiding those grimaces and contortions of which some singers contract a habit. And shall we not in the more immediate worship of the Deity preserve this liberal air and manly appearance? Or, on the contrary, while we are nicely observant of other forms and decencies in the temple, shall we neglect this greater decency in voice, words and manners and, with vile cries, fawnings and prostitute behaviour, betray the natural dignity and majesty of that divine religion and national worship delivered down to us by our forefathers and purged from everything of a barbarous and savage kind?' [Plutarch, *Superstition* 4 [*Moralia* 166]].

What Plutarch mentions here of the 'just countenance' or 'liberal air', the στόμα δίϰαιον, of the musical performer is agreeably illustrated in his *Alcibiades* [2.4–6, *Parallel Lives*]. It was that heroic youth who, as appears by this historian, first gave occasion to the Athenians of the higher rank wholly to abandon the use of flutes, which had before been highly in favour with them. The reason given was 'the illiberal air which attended such performers and the unmanly disfiguration of their looks and countenance which this piping work produced'. As for the real figure or plight of the superstitious mind, our author thus describes it: 'Gladly would the poor comfortless mind by whiles keep festival and rejoice; but, such as its religion is, there can be no free mirth or joy belonging to it. Public thanksgivings are but private mournings. Sighs and sorrows accompany its praises. Fears and horrors corrupt its best affections. When it assumes the outward ornaments of best apparel for the temple, it even then strikes melancholy and appears in paleness and ghastly looks. While it worships, it trembles. It sends up vows in faint and feeble voices, with eager hopes, desires and passions, discoverable in the whole disorder of the outward frame, and, in the main, it evinces plainly by practice, that the notion of Pythagoras was but vain, who dared assert that "we were then in the best state and carried our most becoming looks with us, when we approached the gods". For then, above all other seasons, are the superstitious found in the most abject miserable state of mind and with the meanest presence and behaviour, approaching the sacred shrines of the divine powers in the same manner as they would the dens of bears or lions, the caves of basilisks or dragons, or other hideous recesses of wild beasts or raging monsters. To me therefore it appears wonderful that we should arraign atheism as impious while superstition escapes the charge. Shall he who holds there are no divine powers be esteemed impious and shall not he be esteemed far more impious who holds the divine beings such in their nature as the superstitious believe and represent? For my own part, I had rather men should say of me . . .' [Plutarch, *Superstition* 9–10 [*Moralia* 169D–F]]. See p. 21n. Nothing can be more remarkable than what our author says again a little below: 'The atheist believes there is no deity; the religionist or superstitious believer wishes there were none. If he believes, it is against his will: mistrust he dares not, nor call his thought in question. But could he with security, at once, throw off that oppressive fear, which like the rock of Tantalus impends and presses over him, he would with equal joy spurn his enslaving thought and embrace the atheist's state and opinion as his happiest deliverance. Atheists are free of superstition, but the superstitious are ever willing atheists, though impotent in their thought and unable to believe of the divine being as they gladly would' [Plutarch, *Superstition* 11 [*Moralia* 170F]]. See pp. 19, 21.

[130] Where speaking of religion, as it stood in the heathen church and in his own time, he confesses that 'as to the vulgar disposition there was no remedy. Many even of the better sort would be found, of course, to intermix with their veneration and esteem something of terror or fear in

pleaded for gaiety and good humour. I have declaimed against pedantry in learned language and opposed formality in form. I now find myself somewhat impatient to get loose from the constraint of method, and I pretend lawfully to exercise the privilege which I have asserted of rambling from subject to subject, from style to style, in my miscellaneous manner according to my present profession and character.

I may, in the meanwhile, be censured probably for passing over my third head. But the methodical reader, if he be scrupulous about it, may content himself with looking back, and, if possibly he can pick it out of my second, he will forgive this anticipation in a writing which is governed less by form than humour. I had indeed resolved with myself to make a large collection of passages from our most eminent and learned divines in order to have set forth this latter head of my chapter and, by better authority than my own, to have evinced that *we had in the main a good-humoured religion*. But, after considering a little while, I came to this short issue with myself, that it was better not to cite at all than to cite partially. Now, if I cited fairly what was said as well on the melancholy as the cheerful side of our religion, the matter, I found, would be pretty doubtfully balanced, and the result at last would be this: that, generally speaking, as often as a divine was in good humour, we should find religion the sweetest and best-humoured thing in nature, but at other times, and that pretty often, we should find a very different face of matters.

Thus are we alternately exalted and humbled, cheered and dejected, according as our spiritual director is himself influenced,[131] and this, peradventure for our edification and advantage, that by these contrarieties and changes we may be rendered more supple and compliant. If we are very low and down, we are taken up. If we are up and high, we are taken down. This is discipline. This is authority and command. Did religion carry constantly one and the same face, and were it always represented to us alike in every respect, we might perhaps

---

their religious worship, which might give it perhaps the character of superstition; but that this evil was a thousand times over-balanced by the satisfaction, hope, joy and delight which attended religious worship. This', says he, 'is plain and evident from the most demonstrable testimonies, for neither the societies or public meetings in the temples, nor the festivals themselves, nor any other diverting parties, sights or entertainments, are more delightful or rejoicing than what we ourselves behold and act in the divine worship and in the holy sacrifices and mysteries which belong to it. Our disposition and temper is not, on this occasion, as if we were in the presence of worldly potentates, dread sovereigns and despotic princes. Nor are we here found meanly humbling ourselves, crouching in fear and awe and full of anxiety and confusion as would be natural to us in such a case. But where the divinity is esteemed the nearest and most immediately present, there horrors and amazements are the furthest banished; there the heart, we find, gives freest way to pleasure, to entertainment, to play, mirth, humour and diversion, and this even to an excess.' [Plutarch, *That Epicurus Actually Makes a Pleasant Life Impossible* 21 [*Moralia* 1101D–F]].

131 See p. 355.

be overbold and make acquaintance with it in too familiar a manner. We might think ourselves fully knowing in it and assured of its true character and genius. From whence perhaps we might become more refractory towards the ghostly teachers of it, and be apt to submit ourselves the less to those who by appointment and authority represent it to us in such lights as they esteem most proper and convenient.

I shall therefore not only conclude abruptly but even sceptically on this my last head, referring my reader to what has been said already on my preceding heads for the bare probability of *our having in the main a witty and good-humoured religion.*

This, however, I may presume to assert, that there are undoubtedly some countenances or aspects of our religion which are humorous and pleasant in themselves, and that the sadder representations of it are many times so over-sad and dismal, that they are apt to excite a very contrary passion to what is intended by the representers.

Miscellany III

Chapter 1

Further remarks on the author of the treatises. His order and design. His remarks on the succession of wit and progress of letters and philosophy. Of words, relations, affections. Countrymen and country. Old England. Patriots of the soil. Virtuosi and philosophers. A taste.

Having already asserted my privilege, as a miscellaneous or essay writer of the modern establishment, to write on every subject and in every method as I fancy, to use order or lay it aside as I think fit, and to treat of order and method in other works, though free perhaps and unconfined as to my own, I shall presume, in this place, to consider the present method and order of my author's treatises as in this joint edition they are ranged.

Notwithstanding the high airs of scepticism which our author assumes in his first piece, I cannot, after all, but imagine that even there he proves himself at the bottom a real dogmatist and shows plainly that he has his private opinion, belief or faith, as strong as any devotee or religionist of them all. Though he affects perhaps to strike at other hypotheses and schemes, he has something of his own still in reserve and holds a certain plan or system peculiar to himself, or such at least in which he has at present but few companions or followers.

On this account I look upon his management to have been much after the rate of some ambitious architect who, being called perhaps to prop a roof, redress a leaning wall or add to some particular apartment, is not contented with this small specimen of his mastership but, pretending to demonstrate the unserviceableness and inconvenience of the old fabric, forms the design of a new building and longs to show his skill in the principal parts of architecture and mechanics.

It is certain that in matters of learning and philosophy the practice of pulling down is far pleasanter and affords more entertainment than that of building and setting up. Many have succeeded to a miracle in the first who have miserably fallen in the latter of these attempts. We may find a thousand engineers who can sap, undermine and blow up with admirable dexterity for one single one who can build a fort or lay the platform of a citadel. And though compassion in real war may make the ruinous practice less delightful, it is certain that, in the literate warring-world, the springing of mines, the blowing up of towers, bastions and ramparts of philosophy with systems, hypotheses, opinions and doctrines into the air, is a spectacle of all other the most naturally rejoicing.

Our author, we suppose, might have done well to consider this. We have fairly conducted him through his first and second letter and have brought him, as we see here, into his third piece. He has hitherto, methinks, kept up his sapping method and unravelling humour with tolerable good grace. He has given only some few and very slender hints of going further or attempting to erect any scheme or model which may discover his pretence to a real architect-capacity.[1] Even in this his third piece, he carries with him the same sceptical mien, and what he offers by way of project or hypothesis is very faint, hardly spoken aloud but muttered to himself in a kind of dubious whisper or feigned soliloquy. What he discovers of form and method is indeed so accompanied with the random miscellaneous air that it may pass for raillery rather than good earnest. It is in his following treatise[2] that he discovers himself openly as a plain dogmatist, a formalist and man of method, with his hypothesis tacked to him and his opinions so close sticking as would force one to call to mind the figure of some precise and strait-laced professor in a university.

What may be justly pleaded in his behalf, when we come in company with him to inquire into such solemn and profound subjects, seems very doubtful. Meanwhile, as his affairs stand hitherto in this his treatise of advice, I shall be contented to yoke with him and proceed, in my miscellaneous manner, to give my advice also to men of note, whether they are authors or politicians, virtuosi or fine gentlemen, comprehending him, the said author, as one of the number of the advised and myself too, if occasion be, after his own example of self-admonition and private address.

But first, as to our author's dissertation in this third treatise, where his reflections upon authors in general and the rise and progress of arts make the inlet or introduction to his philosophy,[3] we may observe that it is not without some appearance of reason that he has advanced this method. It must be acknowledged that, though in the earliest times there may have been divine men of a transcending genius who have given laws both in religion and government to the great advantage and improvement of mankind, yet philosophy itself, as a science and known profession worthy of that name, cannot with any probability be supposed to have risen, as our author shows, till other arts had been raised and, in a certain proportion, advanced before it. As this was of the greatest dignity and weight, so it came last into form. It was long clearing itself from the affected dress of sophists or enthusiastic air of poets, and appeared late in its genuine, simple and just beauty.

---

[1] Namely, in the *Letter Concerning Enthusiasm*, pp. 21–3, 25 at the end, and 27–8 concerning the previous knowledge. So again *Sensus Communis*, pp. 38–9, 54. And again *Soliloquy*, pp. 131–3, where the *Inquiry Concerning Virtue* is proposed and the system and genealogy of the affections previously treated, with an apology (p. 139) for the examining practice and seeming pedantry of the method. And afterwards the apology for the *Inquiry* in *The Moralists*, pp. 264–5. Concerning this series and dependency of these joint treatises, see more particularly below, pp. 419–20, 458–9.

[2] Namely, *An Inquiry Concerning Virtue*.

[3] See p. 106ff.

The reader perhaps may justly excuse our author for having in this place so overloaded his margin with those weighty authorities and ancient citations,[4] when he knows that there are many grave professors in humanity and letters among the moderns who are puzzled in this search, and write both repugnantly to one another and to the plain and natural evidence of the case. The real lineage and succession of wit is indeed plainly founded in nature, as our author has endeavoured to make appear both from history and fact. The Greek nation, as it is original to us in respect to these polite arts and sciences, so it was in reality original to itself. For whether the Egyptians, Phoenicians, Thracians or barbarians of any kind may have hit fortunately on this or that particular invention, either in agriculture, building, navigation or letters, whichever may have introduced this rite of worship, this title of a deity, this or that instrument of music, this or that festival, game or dance (for on this matter there are high debates among the learned), it is evident, beyond a doubt, that the arts and sciences were formed in Greece itself. It was there that music, poetry and the rest came to receive some kind of shape and be distinguished into their several orders and degrees. Whatever flourished or was raised to any degree of correctness or real perfection in the kind was by means of Greece alone, and in the hands of that sole polite, most civilized and accomplished nation.[A]

Nor can this appear strange when we consider the fortunate constitution of that people. For though composed of different nations, distinct in laws and governments, divided by seas and continents, dispersed in distant islands, yet, being originally of the same extract, united by one single language and animated by that social, public and free spirit which, notwithstanding the animosity of their several warring states, induced them to erect such heroic congresses and powers as those which constituted the Amphictionian councils, the Olympic, Isthmian and other games,[B] they could not but naturally polish and refine each other. It was thus they brought their beautiful and comprehensive language to a just standard, leaving only such variety in the dialects as rendered their poetry, in particular, so much the more agreeable. The standard was in the same proportion carried into other arts. The secretion was made; the several species found and set apart; the performers and masters in

[A] The tradition of this sort of foundationalist Hellenism is treated extensively in the first volume of Martin Bernal, *Black Athena: The Afroasiatic Roots of Classical Civilization* (New Brunswick, NJ: Rutgers University Press, 1987).

[B] The Amphictionic League comprised twelve peoples in central Greece. Its council, with representatives from the twelve, maintained the cult at several important temples and engaged as well in a certain amount of pan-Hellenic legislation and mediation. Festivals also brought the independent city-states of ancient Greece together on a regular schedule. While the festivals originally were occasions for worship, games and other activities were added. Among the most important of these gatherings were the Olympic games, held every four years at Olympia in honour of Zeus, and the Isthmian games, held every two years at Corinth in honour of Poseidon.

[4] See pp. 109–14.

every kind honoured and admired; and, last of all, even critics themselves acknowledged and received as masters over all the rest. From music, poetry, rhetoric, down to the simple prose of history, through all the plastic arts of sculpture, statuary, painting, architecture and the rest, everything muse-like, graceful and exquisite was rewarded with the highest honours and carried on with the utmost ardour and emulation. Thus Greece, though she exported arts to other nations, had properly for her own share no import of the kind. The utmost which could be named would amount to no more than raw materials of a rude and barbarous form. And thus the nation was evidently original in art and, with them, every noble study and science was, as the great master, so often cited by our author, says of certain kinds of poetry, *self-formed*,[5] wrought out of nature and drawn from the necessary operation and course of things, working, as it were, of their own accord and proper inclination. Now, according to this natural growth of arts peculiar to Greece, it would necessarily happen that at the beginning, when the force of language came to be first proved, when the admiring world made their first judgment and essayed their taste in the elegancies of this sort, the lofty, the sublime, the astonishing and amazing would be the most in fashion and preferred. Metaphorical speech, multiplicity of figures and high-sounding words would naturally prevail. Though in the commonwealth itself and in the affairs of government men were used originally to plain and direct speech, yet, when speaking became an art and was taught by sophists and other pretended masters, the high poetic and the figurative way began to prevail, even at the Bar and in the public assemblies, insomuch that the grand master, in the above-cited part of his *Rhetoric*, where he extols the tragic poet Euripides, upbraids the rhetoricians of his own age, who retained that very bombastic style, which even poets, and those too of the tragic kind, had already thrown off, or at least considerably mitigated.[6] But the taste of Greece was now polishing. A better judgment was soon formed when a Demosthenes[c] was heard and had found success. The people themselves, as our author has shown, came now to reform their comedy and familiar manner, after tragedy and the higher style had been brought to its perfection under the last hand of an Euripides. And now in all the principal works of ingenuity and art, simplicity and nature began chiefly to be sought, and this was the taste

[c] Demosthenes, 384–322 BC, one of the greatest of Athenian orators.

[5] αὐτοσχεδιαστική [Shaftesbury here stretched the meaning of a term referring to the improvised and extemporaneous]. See p. 109 [for the citation from Aristotle's *Poetics*]. It is in this sense of the natural production and self-formation of the arts, in this free state of ancient Greece, that the same great master uses this word a little before, in the same chapter of his *Poetics*, 4.7, speaking in general of the poets: *Proceeding a little at a time, they generated poetry out of their improvisations*. And presently after, 4.18: *And after speaking came along, nature itself found the suitable metre*.

[6] See p. 110n. [Euripides was one of the most celebrated writers of tragedy in ancient Greece. He lived through most of the fifth century BC.]

which lasted through so many ages till the ruin of all things under a universal monarch.[D]

If the reader should peradventure be led by his curiosity to seek some kind of comparison between this ancient growth of taste and that which we have experienced in modern days and within our own nation, he may look back to the speeches of our ancestors in Parliament. He will find them, generally speaking, to have been very short and plain, but coarse and what we properly call homespun, till learning came in vogue and science was known among us. When our princes and senators became scholars, they spoke scholastically. And the pedantic style was prevalent from the first dawn of letters, about the age of the Reformation, till long afterwards. Witness the best written discourses, the admired speeches, orations or sermons, through several reigns, down to these latter, which we compute within the present age. It will undoubtedly be found that till very late days the fashion of speaking and the turn of wit was after the figurative and florid manner. Nothing was so acceptable as the high-sounding phrase, the far-fetched comparison, the capricious point and play of words, and nothing so despicable as what was merely of the plain or natural kind. So that it must either be confessed that, in respect of the preceding age, we are fallen very low in taste or that, if we are in reality improved, the natural and simple manner which conceals and covers art is the most truly artful and of the genteelest, truest and best studied taste, as has above been treated more at large.[7]

Now, therefore, as to our author's philosophy itself, as it lies concealed in this treatise[8] but more professed and formal in his next,[9] we shall proceed gradually according to his own method, since it becomes not one who has undertaken the part of his airy assistant and humorous paraphrast to enter suddenly without good preparation into his dry reasonings and moral researches about the social passions and natural affections, of which he is such a punctilious examiner.

Of all human affections, the noblest and most becoming human nature is that of love to one's country. This, perhaps, will easily be allowed by all men who have really a country and are of the number of those who may be called a people, as enjoying the happiness of a real constitution and polity by which

---

[D] Alexander III of Macedonia, the Great, 356–323 BC, who consolidated his father's victories over the Greeks before setting out for his conquests in Asia.

[7] See pp. 115–16, 347–8. [The changes in rhetorical style noted here by Shaftesbury are interpreted diversely in modern scholarship: for example, George Williamson, *The Senecan Amble* (Chicago: University of Chicago Press, 1951), Robert Adolph, *The Rise of Modern Prose Style* (Cambridge, MA, and London: MIT Press, 1968), Roger Pooley, *English Prose of the Seventeenth Century, 1590–1700* (London and New York: Longman, 1992).]

[8] Namely, *Soliloquy*.

[9] Namely, *An Inquiry Concerning Virtue*.

they are free and independent.[10] There are few such countrymen or freemen so degenerate as directly to discountenance or condemn this passion of love to their community and national brotherhood. The indirect manner of opposing this principle is the most usual. We hear it commonly as a complaint that 'there is little of this love extant in the world'. From whence it is hastily concluded that 'there is little or nothing of friendly or social affection inherent in our nature or proper to our species'. It is however apparent that there is scarce a creature of humankind who is not possessed at least of some inferior degree or meaner sort of this natural affection to a country. *Native ground draws all with indefinable sweetness.*[11]

It is a wretched aspect of humanity which we figure to ourselves when we would endeavour to resolve the very essence and foundation of this generous passion into a relation to mere clay and dust, exclusively of anything sensible, intelligent or moral. It is, I must own, on certain relations or respective proportions that all natural affection does in some measure depend.[12] And in this view it cannot, I confess, be denied that we have each of us a certain relation to the mere earth itself, the very mould or surface of that planet in which, with other animals of various sorts, we (poor reptiles!) were also bred and nourished. But had it happened to one of us British men to have been born at sea, could we not therefore properly be called British men? Could we be allowed countrymen of no sort, as having no distinct relation to any certain soil or region, no original neighbourhood but with the watery inhabitants and sea monsters? Surely, if we were born of lawful parents, lawfully employed and under the protection of law, wherever they might be then detained, to whatever colonies sent or whithersoever driven by any accident, or in expeditions or adventures in the public service or that of mankind, we should still find we had a home and country ready to lay claim to us. We should be obliged still to consider ourselves as fellow-citizens and might be allowed to love our country or nation as honestly and heartily as the most inland inhabitant or native of the soil. Our political and social capacity would undoubtedly come in view and be acknowledged full as natural and essential in our species as the parental and filial kind, which gives rise to what we peculiarly call *natural affection*. Or, supposing that both our birth and parents had been unknown and that in this respect we were in a manner younger brothers in society to the rest of mankind, yet from our nurture and education we should surely espouse some country or other and, joyfully

---

[10] A multitude held together by force, though under one and the same head, is not properly united. Nor does such a body make a people. It is the social league, confederacy and mutual consent, founded in some common good or interest, which joins the members of a community and makes a people one. Absolute power annuls the public. And where there is no public or constitution, there is in reality no mother country or nation. See pp. 49–50.

[11] Ovid, *Epistles from Pontus* 1.3.35.

[12] *Proprieties are measured according to relationships* [Epictetus, *Enchiridion* 30].

embracing the protection of a magistracy, should of necessity and by force of nature join ourselves to the general society of mankind, and those in particular with whom we had entered into a nearer communication of benefits and closer sympathy of affections. It may therefore be esteemed no better than a mean subterfuge of narrow minds, to assign this natural passion for society and a country to such a relation as that of a mere fungus or common excrescence to its parent-mould or nursing dunghill.

The relation of countryman, if it be allowed anything at all, must imply something moral and social. The notion itself presupposes a naturally civil and political state of mankind, and has reference to that particular part of society to which we owe our chief advantages as men and rational creatures, such as are *naturally* and *necessarily* united for each other's happiness and support and for the highest of all happinesses and enjoyments, 'the intercourse of minds, the free use of our reason and the exercise of mutual love and friendship'.[13]

An ingenious physician among the moderns, having in view the natural dependency of the vegetable and animal kinds on their common mother earth, and observing that both the one and the other draw from her their continual sustenance (some rooted and fixed down to their first abodes, others unconfined and wandering from place to place to suck their nourishment), he accordingly, as I remember, styles this latter animal race, 'her released sons', *filios terrae emancipatos*. Now if this be our only way of reckoning for mankind, we may call ourselves indeed the sons of earth at large, but not of any particular soil or district. The division of climates and regions is fantastic and artificial, much more the limits of particular countries, cities or provinces. Our *natale solum*, or mother earth, must by this account be the real globe itself which bears us and in respect of which we must allow the common animals, and even the plants of all degrees, to claim an equal brotherhood with us under this common parent.

According to this calculation, we must of necessity carry our relation as far as to the whole material world or universe, where alone it can prove complete. But for the particular district or tract of earth, which in a vulgar sense we call our country, however bounded or geographically divided, we can never, at this rate, frame any accountable relation to it, nor consequently assign any natural or proper affection towards it.

If unhappily a man had been born either at an inn or in some dirty village, he would hardly, I think, circumscribe himself so narrowly as to accept a denomination or character from those nearest appendices or local circumstances of his nativity. So far should one be from making the hamlet or parish to be characteristical in the case, that hardly would the shire itself or county, how-

[13] See pp. 51, 310ff.

ever rich or flourishing, be taken into the honorary term or appellation of one's country.

'What, then, shall we presume to call our country? Is it England itself? But what of Scotland? Is it therefore Britain? But what of the other islands, the northern Orcades and the southern Jersey and Guernsey? What of the Plantations and poor Ireland?' Behold, here, a very dubious circumscription!

But what, after all, if there be a conquest or captivity in the case? a migration? a national secession or abandonment of our native seats for some other soil or climate? This has happened, we know, to our forefathers. And as great and powerful a people as we have been of late, and have ever shown ourselves under the influence of free councils and a tolerable ministry, should we relapse again into slavish principles or be administered long under such heads as, having no thought of liberty for themselves, can have much less for Europe or their neighbours, we may at last feel a war at home, become the seat of it and, in the end, a conquest. We might then gladly embrace the hard condition of our predecessors and exchange our beloved native soil for that of some remote and uninhabited part of the world. Now, should this possibly be our fate, should some considerable colony or body be formed afterwards out of our remains or meet as it were by miracle in some distant climate, would there be for the future no Englishman remaining? No common bond of alliance and friendship by which we could still call countrymen as before? How came we, I pray, by our ancient name of Englishmen? Did it not travel with us over land and sea? Did we not indeed bring it with us heretofore from as far as the remoter parts of Germany to this island?

I must confess I have been apt sometimes to be very angry with our language for having denied us the use of the word *patria* and afforded us no other name to express our native community than that of 'country', which already bore two different significations abstracted from mankind or society.[14] Reigning words are many times of such force as to influence us considerably in our apprehension of things. Whether it be from any such cause as this, I know not, but certain it is that, in the idea of a civil state or nation, we Englishmen are apt to mix somewhat more than ordinary gross and earthy. No people who owed so much to a constitution and so little to a soil or climate were ever known so indifferent towards one and so passionately fond of the other. One would imagine from the common discourse of our countrymen that the finest lands near the Euphrates, the Babylonian or Persian paradises, the rich plains of Egypt, the Grecian Tempe, the Roman Campania, Lombardy, Provence, the Spanish Andalusia, or the most delicious tracts in the Eastern or Western Indies were contemptible countries in respect of Old England.

---

[14] *Rus* and *regio* [in Latin]; in French *campagne* and *pays*. [*Rus* and *campagne* convey the idea of countryside; *regio* and *pays* convey the idea of a geographical area. The Latin *patria* connotes the idea of homeland, the object of patriotic feeling.]

Now, by the good leave of these worthy patriots of the soil, I must take the liberty to say I think Old England to have been in every respect a very indifferent country and that Late England, of an age or two old, even since Queen Bess's days, is indeed very much mended for the better. We were, in the beginning of her grandfather's reign,[E] under a sort of Polish nobility and had no other liberties than what were in common to us with the then fashionable monarchies and Gothic lordships of Europe.[F] For religion, indeed, we were highly famed above all nations by being the most subject to our ecclesiastics at home and the best tributaries and servants to the Holy See abroad.[G]

I must go further yet and own that I think Late England, since the Revolution, to be better still than Old England by many a degree, and that in the main we make somewhat a better figure in Europe than we did a few reigns before. But, however our people may of late have flourished, our name or credit have risen, our trade and navigation, our manufactures or our husbandry been improved, it is certain that our region, climate and soil is in its own nature still one and the same. And to whatever politeness we may suppose ourselves already arrived, we must confess that we are the latest barbarous, the last civilized or polished people of Europe. We must allow that our first conquest by the Romans brought us out of a state hardly equal to the Indian tribes, and that our last conquest by the Normans brought us only into the capacity of receiving arts and civil accomplishments from abroad. They came to us by degrees from remote distances, at second or third hand, from other Courts, states, academies and foreign nurseries of wit and manners.

Notwithstanding this, we have as overweening an opinion of ourselves as if we had a claim to be original and earth-born. As often as we have changed masters and mixed races with our several successive conquerors, we still pretend to be as legitimate and genuine possessors of our soil as the ancient Athenians accounted themselves to have been of theirs. It is remarkable, however, in that truly ancient, wise and witty people, that, as fine territories and noble countries as they possessed, as indisputable masters and superiors as they were in all science, wit, politeness and manners, they were yet so far from a conceited, selfish and ridiculous contempt of others that they were even, in a

---

[E] That is, in the era of Henry VII who ruled from 1485 to 1507.

[F] In republican literature, Poland, with its king highly dependent on a landed nobility, was often valued as an instance of a Gothic constitution, in which monarchal and aristocratic principles were balanced and liberty thus preserved. However, by Shaftesbury's era, critics of the republican tradition were suggesting that a society with little commerce, such as Poland, would lack both liberty and culture. See J. G. A. Pocock, *The Machiavellian Moment* (Princeton: Princeton University Press, 1975), pp. 423–61.

[G] This is presumably a reference to Peter's Pence, an annual donation, said to indicate special loyalty to the Pope, although the sum, which had remained constant over the course of the Middle Ages, was hardly a significant charge at the time of the Reformation. Also, at a moment of royal weakness, John had recognized the Pope as overlord in secular as well as spiritual matters – a submission ignored by John himself as soon as he was able and by his successors.

contrary extreme, 'admirers of whatever was in the least degree ingenious or curious in foreign nations'. Their great men were constant travellers. Their legislators and philosophers made their voyages into Egypt, passed into Chaldea and Persia and failed not to visit most of the dispersed Grecian governments and colonies through the islands of the Aegean, in Italy and on the coasts of Asia and Africa. It was mentioned as a prodigy, in the case of a great philosopher, though known to have been always poor, that 'he should never have travelled nor had ever gone out of Athens for his improvement'.[11] How modest a reflection in those who were themselves Athenians!

For our part, we neither care that foreigners should travel to us, nor any of ours should travel into foreign countries.[15] Our best policy and breeding is, it seems, 'to look abroad as little as possible, contract our views within the narrowest compass and despise all knowledge, learning or manners which are not of a home growth'. For hardly will the ancients themselves be regarded by those who have so resolute a contempt of what the politest moderns of any nation besides their own may have advanced in the way of literature, politeness or philosophy.

This disposition of our countrymen, from whatever causes it may possibly be derived, is, I fear, a very prepossessing circumstance against our author, whose design is to advance something new, or at least something different, from what is commonly current in philosophy and morals. To support this design of his, he seems intent chiefly on this single point, *to discover how we may to best advantage form within ourselves what in the polite world is called a relish or good taste.*

He begins, it is true, as near home as possible and sends us to the narrowest of all conversations, that of soliloquy or self-discourse. But this correspondence, according to his computation, is wholly impracticable without a previous

---

[11] Socrates as described by Diogenes Laertius, *Lives of Eminent Philosophers* 2.22.

[15] An ill token of our being thoroughly civilized, since in the judgment of the polite and wise this inhospitable disposition was ever reckoned among the principal marks of barbarism. So Strabo, *Geography* 17.1.19, from other preceding authors [Eratosthenes, in particular]: *The expulsion of foreigners is common habit of all barbarians.* The Ζεὺς Ξένιος [Zeus in his aspect as guarantor of the protocols of hospitality] of the ancients was one of the solemn characters of divinity: the peculiar attribute of the supreme deity, benign to mankind and recommending universal love, mutual kindness and benignity between the remotest and most unlike of human race. Thus their divine poet, in harmony with their sacred oracles, which were known frequently to confirm this doctrine: *Stranger, it is not right for me, even if a man worse than you were to come, to disrespect a stranger, for all strangers come from Zeus* (Homer, *Odyssey* 14.56–8). Again, *Nor does any other mortal mingle in our midst. But this is some wretched wanderer that comes here; we must now comfort him; for all strangers come from Zeus* (Homer, *Odyssey* 6.205–8). And again: *Wealthy in livelihood, and he was dear to men: dwelling by the road, he offered hospitality to all* (Homer, *Iliad* 6.14–15). See also Homer, *Odyssey* 3.34ff, 3.67ff, 4.30ff, 4.60. Such was ancient heathen charity and pious duty towards the whole of mankind, both those of different nations and different worships. See pp. 226–7.

commerce with the world, and the larger this commerce is, the more practicable and improving the other, he thinks, is likely to prove. The sources of this improving art of self-correspondence he derives from the highest politeness and elegance of ancient dialogue and debate in matters of wit, knowledge and ingenuity. And nothing, according to our author, can so well revive this self-corresponding practice as the same search and study of the highest politeness in modern conversation. For this, we must necessarily be at the pains of going farther abroad than the province we call home. And by this account it appears that our author has little hopes of being either relished or comprehended by any other of his countrymen than those who delight in the open and free commerce of the world, and are rejoiced to gather views and receive light from every quarter in order to judge the best of what is perfect, and according to a just standard and true taste in every kind.

It may be proper for us to remark, in favour of our author, that the sort of ridicule or raillery which is apt to fall upon philosophers is of the same kind with that which falls commonly on the virtuosi or refined wits of the age. In this latter general denomination we include the real fine gentlemen, the lovers of art and ingenuity, such as have seen the world and informed themselves of the manners and customs of the several nations of Europe, searched into their antiquities and records, considered their police,[1] laws and constitutions, observed the situation, strength and ornaments of their cities, their principal arts, studies and amusements, their architecture, sculpture, painting, music and their taste in poetry, learning, language and conversation.

Hitherto there can lie no ridicule nor the least scope for satiric wit or raillery. But when we push this virtuoso character a little further and lead our polished gentleman into more nice researches, when from the view of mankind and their affairs, our speculative genius and minute examiner of nature's works, proceeds with equal or perhaps superior zeal in the contemplation of the insect life, the conveniencies, habitations and economy of a race of shellfish, when he has erected a cabinet in due form and made it the real pattern of his mind, replete with the same trash and trumpery of correspondent empty notions and chimerical conceits, he then indeed becomes the subject of sufficient raillery and is made the jest of common conversations.[J]

A worse thing than this happens commonly to these inferior virtuosi. In seeking so earnestly for rarities they fall in love with rarity for rareness' sake. Now the greatest rarities in the world are monsters. So that the study and relish of these gentlemen, thus assiduously employed, becomes at last in reality monstrous, and their whole delight is found to consist in selecting and contemplating whatever is most monstrous, disagreeing, out of the way and to the least purpose of anything in nature.

[1]   Public administration.
[J]   For virtuoso, see p. 62n.

In philosophy, matters answer exactly to this virtuoso scheme. Let us suppose a man who, having this resolution merely, how to employ his understanding to the best purpose, considers *who or what he is, whence he arose or had his being, to what end he was designed, and to what course of action he is by his natural frame and constitution destined*, should he descend on this account into himself and examine his inward powers and faculties, or should he ascend beyond his own immediate species, city or community to discover and recognize his higher polity or community, that common and universal one of which he is born a member, nothing surely of this kind could reasonably draw upon him the least contempt or mockery. On the contrary, the finest gentleman must after all be considered but as an idiot who, talking much of the knowledge of the world and mankind, has never so much as thought of the study or knowledge of himself or of the nature and government of that real public and world from whence he holds his being: *what we are and the lives we are born to live.*[16] 'Where are we?', 'Under what roof?', 'Or on board what vessel?', 'Whither bound?', 'On what business?', 'Under whose pilotship, government or protection?' are questions which every sensible man would naturally ask if he were on a sudden transported into a new scene of life. It is admirable, indeed, to consider that a man should have been long come into a world, carried his reason and sense about with him, and yet have never seriously asked himself this single question, 'Where am I or what?', but, on the contrary, should proceed regularly to every other study and inquiry, postponing this alone as the least considerable or leaving the examination of it to others commissioned, as he supposes, to understand and think for him upon this head. To be bubbled or put upon by any sham advices in this affair is, it seems, of no consequence! We take care to examine accurately, by our own judgment, the affairs of other people and the concerns of the world which least belong to us. But what relates more immediately to ourselves and is our chief self-interest, we charitably leave to others to examine for us and readily take up with the first comers, on whose honesty and good faith it is presumed we may safely rely.

Here, methinks, the ridicule turns more against the philosophy-haters than the virtuosi or philosophers. While philosophy is taken, as in its prime sense it ought, for *mastership in life and manners*, it is like to make no ill figure in the world, whatever impertinencies may reign or however extravagant the times may prove. But let us view philosophy, like mere virtuosoship, in its usual career, and we shall find the ridicule rising full as strongly against the professors of the higher as the lower kind. Cockleshell abounds with each. Many things exterior and without ourselves, of no relation to our real interests or to those of society and mankind, are diligently investigated; nature's remotest operations, deepest mysteries and most difficult phenomena discussed and

[16] Persius, *Satires* 3.67.

whimsically explained; hypotheses and fantastic systems erected; a universe anatomized and, by some notable scheme, so solved and reduced as to appear an easy knack or secret to those who have the clue.[17] Creation itself can, upon occasion, be exhibited – transmutations, projections and other philosophical arcana, such as in the corporeal world can accomplish all things – while, in the intellectual, a set frame of metaphysical phrases and distinctions can serve to solve whatever difficulties may be propounded either in logic, ethics or any real science of whatever kind.

It appears from hence that the defects of philosophy and those of virtuoso-ship are of the same nature. Nothing can be more dangerous than a wrong choice or misapplication in these affairs. But as ridiculous as these studies are rendered by their senseless managers, it appears, however, that each of them are, in their nature, essential to the character of a fine gentleman and man of sense.

To philosophize, in a just signification, is but to carry good breeding a step higher. For the accomplishment of breeding is to learn whatever is decent in company or beautiful in arts, and the sum of philosophy is to learn what is just in society and beautiful in nature and the order of the world.

It is not wit merely but a temper which must form the well-bred man. In the same manner, it is not a head merely but a heart and resolution which must complete the real philosopher. Both characters aim at what is excellent, aspire to a just taste and carry in view the model of what is beautiful and becoming. Accordingly, the respective conduct and distinct manners of each party are regulated: the one according to the perfectest ease and good entertainment of company, the other according to the strictest interest of mankind and society; the one according to a man's rank and quality in his private station, the other according to his rank and dignity in nature.

Whether each of these offices or social parts are in themselves as convenient as becoming, is the great question which must some way be decided. The well-bred man has already decided this in his own case and declared on the side of what is handsome, for, whatever he practises in this kind, he accounts no more than what he owes purely to himself, without regard to any further advantage.[18] The pretender to philosophy who either knows not how to determine this affair or, if he has determined, knows not how to pursue his point with constancy and firmness, remains in respect of philosophy what a clown or coxcomb is in respect of breeding and behaviour. Thus, according to our author, the taste of beauty and the relish of what is decent, just and amiable perfects the character of the gentleman and the philosopher. And the study of such a taste or relish will, as we suppose, be ever the great employment and concern of him who

---

[17] See pp. 232, 235.
[18] See p. 60.

covets as well to be wise and good as agreeable and polite. *My care and curiosity is for what is true and what is right, and here wholly my being lies.*[19]

Chapter 2

Explanation of a taste continued. Ridiculers of it. Their wit and sincerity. Application of the taste to affairs of government and politics. Imaginary characters in the State. Young nobility and gentry. Pursuit of beauty. Preparation for philosophy.

By this time, surely, I must have proved myself sufficiently engaged in the project and design of our self-discoursing author whose defence I have undertaken. His pretension, as plainly appears in this third treatise, is to recommend morals on the same foot with what in a lower sense is called manners and to advance philosophy, as harsh a subject as it may appear, on the very foundation of what is called agreeable and polite.[20] And it is in this method and management that, as his interpreter or paraphrast, I have proposed to imitate and accompany him as far as my miscellaneous character will permit.

Our joint endeavour, therefore, must appear this: to show that nothing which is found charming or delightful in the polite world, nothing which is adopted as pleasure or entertainment of whatever kind can any way be accounted for, supported or established without the pre-establishment or supposition of a certain taste. Now a taste or judgment, it is supposed, can hardly come ready formed with us into the world. Whatever principles or materials of this kind we may possibly bring with us, whatever good faculties, senses or anticipating sensations and imaginations may be of nature's growth and arise properly of themselves without our art, promotion or assistance, the general idea which is formed of all this management and the clear notion we attain of what is preferable and principal in all these subjects of choice and estimation will not, as I imagine, by any person be taken for innate. Use, practice and culture must precede the understanding and wit of such an advanced size and growth as this. A legitimate and just taste can neither be begotten, made, conceived or produced without the antecedent labour and pains of criticism.

For this reason we presume not only to defend the cause of critics but to declare open war against those indolent supine authors, performers, readers, auditors, actors or spectators who, making their humour alone the rule of what is beautiful and agreeable, and having no account to give of such their humour or odd fancy, reject the criticizing or examining art, by which alone they are able to discover the true beauty and worth of every object.

According to that affected ridicule which these insipid remarkers pretend to

---

[19] Horace, *Epistles* 1.1.11.
[20] See p. 150.

throw upon just critics, the enjoyment of all real arts or natural beauties would be entirely lost; even in behaviour and manners we should at this rate become in time as barbarous as in our pleasures and diversions. I would presume it, however, of these critic-haters, that they are not yet so uncivilized or void of all social sense as to maintain that 'the most barbarous life or brutish pleasure is as desirable as the most polished or refined'.

For my own part, when I have heard sometimes men of reputed ability join in with that effeminate plaintive tone of invective against critics, I have really thought they had it in their fancy to keep down the growing geniuses of the youth, their rivals, by turning them aside from that examination and search on which all good performance as well as good judgment depends. I have seen many a time a well-bred man, who had himself a real good taste, give way, with a malicious complaisance, to the humour of a company where, in favour chiefly of the tender sex, this soft languishing contempt of critics and their labours has been the subject set afoot. 'Wretched creatures!', says one, 'Impertinent things, these critics, as ye call them! As if one could not know what was agreeable or pretty without their help. It is fine, indeed, that one should not be allowed to fancy for oneself. Now, should a thousand critics tell me that Mr. A–'s new play was not the wittiest in the world, I would not mind them one bit.'

This our real man of wit hears patiently and adds, perhaps of his own, that 'he thinks it truly somewhat hard, in what relates to people's diversion and entertainment, that they should be obliged to choose what pleased others and not themselves'. Soon after this he goes himself to the play, finds one of his effeminate companions commending or admiring at a wrong place. He turns to the next person who sits by him and asks privately 'what he thinks of his companion's relish'.

Such is the malice of the world! They who by pains and industry have acquired a real taste in arts rejoice in their advantage over others, who have either none at all or such as renders them ridiculous. At an auction of books or pictures, you shall hear these gentlemen persuading everyone 'to bid for what he fancies'. But at the same time they would be soundly mortified themselves if, by such as they esteemed good judges, they should be found to have purchased by a wrong fancy or ill taste. The same gentleman who commends his neighbour for ordering his garden or apartment as his humour leads him takes care his own should be so ordered as the best judgments would advise. Being once a judge himself, or but tolerably knowing in these affairs, his aim is not to change the being of things and bring truth and nature to his humour, but, leaving nature and truth just as he found them, to accommodate his humour and fancy to their standard. Would he do this in a yet higher case, he might in reality become as wise and great a man as he is already a refined and polished gentleman. By one of these tastes, he understands how to lay out his garden, model his house, fancy his equipage, appoint his table; by the other, he learns of what value these amusements are in life and of what importance to a man's freedom, happiness and self-employment. For if he would try effectually to acquire the real science or taste of life, he would certainly discover that a right mind and generous affection had more beauty and charm than all other symmetries in the world besides and that a grain of honesty and native worth was of more value than all the adventitious ornaments, estates or preferments for the sake of which some of the better sort so often turn knaves, forsaking their principles and quitting their honour and freedom for a mean, timorous, shifting state of gaudy servitude.

A little better taste (were it a very little) in the affair of life itself would, if I mistake not, mend the manners and secure the happiness of some of our noble countrymen, who come with high advantage and a worthy character into the public. But before they have long engaged in it, their worth unhappily becomes venal. Equipages, titles, precedencies, staffs, ribbons and other such glittering ware are taken in exchange for inward merit, honour and a character.

This they may account perhaps a shrewd bargain. But there will be found very untoward abatements in it when the matter comes to be experienced. They may have descended in reality from ever so glorious ancestors, patriots and sufferers for their nation's liberty and welfare; they may have made their entrance into the world upon this bottom of anticipated fame and honour; they may have been advanced on this account to dignities which they were thought to have deserved. But, when induced to change their honest measures and sacrifice their cause and friends to an imaginary private interest, they will soon find, by experience, that they have lost the relish and taste of life and, for insipid, wretched honours of a deceitful kind, have unhappily exchanged an amiable and sweet honour, of a sincere and lasting relish and good savour. They may, after this, act farces as they think fit, and hear qualities and virtues assigned to them under the titles of 'Graces', 'Excellencies', 'Honours', and the rest of this mock praise and mimical appellation. They may even with serious looks be told of honour and worth, their principle and their country, but they know better within themselves and have occasion to find that after all the world too knows better, and that their few friends and admirers have either a very shallow wit or a very profound hypocrisy.

It is not in one party alone that these purchases and sales of honour are carried on. I can represent to myself a noted patriot and reputed pillar of the religious part of our constitution who, having by many and long services and a steady conduct gained the reputation of thorough zeal with his own party and of sincerity and honour with his very enemies, on a sudden (the time being come that the fulness of his reward was set before him) submits complacently to the proposed bargain and sells himself for what he is worth, in a vile, detestable old age, to which he has reserved the infamy of betraying both his friends and country.[K]

I can imagine, on the other side, one of a contrary party, a noted friend to liberty in Church and State, an abhorrer of the slavish dependency on Courts and of the narrow principles of bigots. Such a one, after many public services of note, I can see wrought upon by degrees to seek Court preferment, and this too under a patriot character. But having perhaps tried this way with less success, he is obliged to change his character and become a royal flatterer, a courtier against his nature, submitting himself and suing, insomuch the meaner degree, as his inherent principles are well known at Court and to his newly adopted party, to whom he feigns himself a proselyte.[L]

The greater the genius or character is of such a person, the greater is his slavery and heavier his load. Better had it been that he had never discovered such a zeal for public good or signalized himself in that party which can with least grace make sacrifices of national interests to a Crown or to the private will, appetite or pleasure of a prince. For supposing such a genius as this had been to act his part of courtship in some foreign and absolute Court, how much less infamous would his part have proved? How much less slavish amid a people who were all slaves? Had he peradventure been one of that forlorn begging troop of gentry extant in Denmark or Sweden since the time that those nations lost their liberties,[M] had he lived out of a free nation and happily balanced constitution, had he been either conscious of no talent in the affairs of government or of no opportunity to exert any such to the advantage of mankind – where had been the mighty shame if perhaps he had employed some of his abilities in flattering like others and paying the necessary homage required for safety's sake and self-preservation in absolute and despotic governments? The taste perhaps, in strictness, might still be wrong, even in this hard circumstance, but how inexcusable in a quite contrary one! For let us suppose our courtier not only an Englishman, but of the rank and stem of those old English patriots who were wont to curb the licentiousness of our Court, arraign its flatterers and purge away those poisons from the ear of princes, let us suppose him of a competent fortune and moderate appetites without any apparent luxury or lavishment in his manners, what shall we, after this, bring in excuse, or as an apology, for such a choice as his? How shall we explain this preposterous relish, this odd preference of subtlety and indirectness to true wisdom, open honesty and uprightness?

[K] The picture of the High Church Tory corrupted by office.
[L] The picture of the Country Whig corrupted by office.
[M] Shaftesbury's friend of many years, Robert Molesworth, had written the basic work on the decline of Scandinavian liberty, from the standpoint of Country Whiggism, *An Account of Denmark* (1694).

It is easier, I confess, to give account of this corruption of taste in some noble youth of a more sumptuous, gay fancy, supposing him born truly great and of honourable descent, with a generous free mind as well as ample fortune. Even these circumstances themselves may be the very causes perhaps of his being thus ensnared. The elegance of his fancy in outward things may have made him overlook the worth of inward character and proportion, and the love of grandeur and magnificence, wrong turned, may have possessed his imagination over-strongly with such things as frontispieces, parterres, equipages, trim varlets in parti-coloured clothes and others in gentlemen's apparel.[21] Magnanimous exhibitions of honour and generosity! 'In town, a palace and suitable furniture! In the country, the same, with the addition of such edifices and gardens as were unknown to our ancestors and are unnatural to such a climate as Great Britain!'

Meanwhile the year runs on, but the year's income answers not its expense. For: 'Which of these articles can be retrenched? Which way take up after having thus set out?' A princely fancy has begot all this, and a princely slavery and Court dependence must maintain it.

The young gentleman is now led into a chase in which he will have slender capture, though toil sufficient. He is himself taken. Nor will he so easily get out of that labyrinth to which he chose to commit his steps, rather than to the more direct and plainer paths in which he trod before. 'Farewell that generous, proud spirit, which was wont to speak only what it approved, commend only whom it thought worthy and act only what it thought right! Favourites must be now observed; little engines of power attended on and loathsomely caressed; an honest man dreaded; and every free tongue or pen abhorred as dangerous and reproachful.' For till our gentleman is become wholly prostitute and shameless, till he is brought to laugh at public virtue and the very notion of common good, till he has openly renounced all principles of honour and honesty, he must in good policy avoid those to whom he lies so much exposed and shun that commerce and familiarity which was once his chief delight.

Such is the sacrifice made to a wrong pride and ignorant self-esteem by one whose inward character must necessarily, after this manner, become as mean and abject as his outward behaviour insolent and intolerable.

There are another sort of suitors to power and traffickers of inward worth and liberty for outward gain, whom one would be naturally drawn to compassionate. They are themselves of a humane, compassionate and friendly nature, well-wishers to their country and mankind. They could, perhaps, even embrace poverty contentedly rather than submit to anything diminutive either of their inward freedom or national liberty. But what they can bear in their own per-

[21] See p. 64.

sons, they cannot bring themselves to bear in the persons of such as are to come after them. Here the best and noblest of affections are borne down by the excess of the next best, those of tenderness for relations and near friends.

Such captives as these would disdain, however, to devote themselves to any prince or ministry whose ends were wholly tyrannical and irreconcilable with the true interest of their nation. In other cases of a less degeneracy, they may bow down perhaps in the temple of Rimmon,[N] support the weight of their supine lords and prop the steps and ruining credit of their corrupt patrons.

This is drudgery sufficient for such honest natures, such as by hard fate alone could have been made dishonest. But as for pride or insolence on the account of their outward advancement and seeming elevation, they are so far from anything resembling it that one may often observe what is very contrary in these fairer characters of men. For though perhaps they were known somewhat rigid and severe before, you see them now grown in reality submissive and obliging. Though in conversation formerly dogmatical and overbearing on the points of state and government, they are now the patientest to hear, the least forward to dictate and the readiest to embrace any entertaining subject of discourse rather than that of the public and their own personal advancement.

Nothing is so near virtue as this behaviour, and nothing so remote from it; nothing so sure a token of the most profligate manners as the contrary. In a free government, it is so much the interest of everyone in place, who profits by the public, to demean himself with modesty and submission, that to appear immediately the more insolent and haughty on such an advancement is the mark only of a contemptible genius and of a want of true understanding, even in the narrow sense of interest and private good.

Thus, we see, after all, that it is not merely what we call *principle* but a *taste* which governs men. They may think for certain, 'This is right or that wrong'; they may believe, 'This a crime or that a sin', 'This punishable by man or that by God'; yet, if the savour of things lies cross to honesty, if the fancy be florid and the appetite high towards the subaltern beauties and lower order of worldly symmetries and proportions, the conduct will infallibly turn this latter way.

Even conscience, I fear, such as is owing to religious discipline, will make but a slight figure where this taste is set amiss. Among the vulgar, perhaps, it may do wonders. A devil and a hell may prevail where a jail and gallows are thought insufficient. But such is the nature of the liberal, polished and refined part of mankind, so far are they from the mere simplicity of babes and sucklings that, instead of applying the notion of a future reward or punishment to their immediate behaviour in society, they are apt much rather, through the

---

[N] In 2 Kings 5, the Syrian general Naaman is cured of leprosy through the intervention of the prophet Elisha. Though Naaman submits himself to the power of the God of Israel, he asks pardon for continuing to accompany his lord, the king of Syria, to worship in the Temple of Rimmon, a principal Assyrian god.

whole course of their lives, to show evidently that they look on the pious narrations to be indeed no better than children's tales or the amusement of the mere vulgar: *That there are shades of the dead and kingdoms below the earth . . . not even boys believe, except those who are not yet paying to bathe.*[22]

Something therefore should, methinks, be further thought of, in behalf of our generous youths, towards the correcting of their taste or relish in the concerns of life. For this at last is what will influence. And in this respect the youth alone are to be regarded. Some hopes there may be still conceived of these. The rest are confirmed and hardened in their way. A middle-aged knave, however devout or orthodox, is but a common wonder; an old one is no wonder at all; but a young one is still (thank heaven!) somewhat extraordinary. And I can never enough admire what was said once by a worthy man at the first appearance of one of these young able prostitutes, that 'he even trembled at the sight to find nature capable of being turned so soon and that he boded greater calamity to his country from this single example of young villainy than from the practices and arts of all the old knaves in being'.

Let us therefore proceed in this view, addressing ourselves to the grown youth of our polite world. Let the appeal be to these whose relish is retrievable and whose taste may yet be formed in morals as it seems to be already in exterior manners and behaviour.

That there is really *a standard* of this latter kind will immediately and on the first view be acknowledged. The contest is only, 'Which is right, which the unaffected carriage and just demeanour and which the affected and false?' Scarce is there anyone who pretends not to know and to decide what is well-bred and handsome. There are few so affectedly clownish as absolutely to disown good breeding and renounce the notion of a beauty in outward manners and deportment. With such as these, wherever they should be found, I must confess I could scarce be tempted to bestow the least pains or labour towards convincing them of a beauty in inward sentiments and principles.

Whoever has any impression of what we call gentility or politeness is already so acquainted with the decorum and grace of things that he will readily confess a pleasure and enjoyment in the very survey and contemplation of this kind. Now if in the way of polite pleasure the study and love of beauty be essential, the study and love of symmetry and order, on which beauty depends, must also be essential in the same respect.

It is impossible we can advance the least in any relish or taste of outward symmetry and order, without acknowledging that the proportionate and regular state is the truly prosperous and natural in every subject. The same features which make deformity create incommodiousness and disease. And the same shapes and proportions which make beauty afford advantage by adapting

---

[22] Juvenal, *Satires* 2.149.

to activity and use. Even in the imitative or designing arts, to which our author so often refers, the truth or beauty of every figure or statue is measured from the perfection of nature in her just adapting of every limb and proportion to the activity, strength, dexterity, life and vigour of the particular species or animal designed.

Thus beauty and truth are plainly joined with the notion of utility and convenience,[23] even in the apprehension of every ingenious artist, the architect, the statuary or the painter.[24] It is the same in the physician's way. Natural health is the just proportion, truth and regular course of things in a constitution. It is the inward beauty of the body. And when the harmony and just measures of the rising pulses, the circulating humours and the moving airs or spirits are disturbed or lost, deformity enters and, with it, calamity and ruin.

Should not this, one would imagine, be still the same case and hold equally as to the mind? Is there nothing there which tends to disturbance and dissolution? Is there no natural tenor, tone or order of the passions or affections? No beauty or deformity in this moral kind? Or allowing that there really is, must it not, of consequence, in the same manner imply health or sickliness, prosperity or disaster? Will it not be found in this respect, above all, that what is beautiful is harmonious and proportionable, what is harmonious and proportionable is true, and what is at once both beautiful and true is, of consequence, agreeable and good?[25]

---

[23] See p. 65.

[24] *In Greek works no one has put dentils below a mutule ... So, if what, according to reality, ought to be positioned above rafters and beams is set below in likenesses, the scheme of the work will be faulty. Moreover, the ancients disapproved of and did not practise this ... Accordingly, they did not think that what cannot happen in reality could have a clear scheme, when done in likenesses. For they adapted everything appropriately and by conventions truly derived from nature to the perfections of their works, and they approved things the explanations for which could have a justification in reality. Therefore, they bequeathed symmetries and proportions of every single type as established by those beginnings*: Vitruvius, *On Architecture* 4.2.5–6, whose commentator [Gulielmus] Philander may be also read on this place [in the 1586 Lyons edition of his Vitruvius, p. 136, an edition owned by Shaftesbury]. See pp. 93, 149–52, 156–8, 448–9.

[25] This is the *honestum* [the honourable], the *pulchrum*, τὸ καλόν [the morally beautiful] on which our author lays the stress of virtue and the merits of this cause, as well in his other treatises as in this of *Soliloquy* here commented. This beauty the Roman orator, in his rhetorical way and in the majesty of style, could express no otherwise than as 'a mystery': *We understand, therefore, the honourable to be such that, when all utility is removed and when there are no rewards or benefits, it can justly be praised in and for itself. As to its nature, it cannot be understood so much by a definition of the sort I have employed (although that has some force) as much as by the common judgment of all and the pursuits and actions of all the best people; they do very many things for the simple reason that it is proper, that it is right, that is honourable, even if they see that no advantage will follow* [Cicero, *On Ends* 2.14.45]. Our author, on the other side, having little of the orator and less of the constraint of formality belonging to some graver characters, can be more familiar on this occasion and, accordingly, descending without the least scruple into whatever style or humour, he refuses to make the least difficulty or mystery of this matter. He pretends, on this head, to claim the assent not only of orators, poets and the higher virtuosi, but even of the beaux themselves and such as go no farther than the dancing master to seek for grace and

Where then is this beauty or harmony to be found? How is this symmetry to be discovered and applied? Is it any other art than that of philosophy or the study of inward numbers and proportions, which can exhibit this in life? If no other, who then can possibly have a taste of this kind without being beholden to philosophy? Who can admire the outward beauties and not recur instantly to the inward, which are the most real and essential, the most naturally affecting and of the highest pleasure as well as profit and advantage?

---

beauty. He pretends, we see, to fetch this natural idea from as familiar amusements as dress, equipage, the tiring room or toyshop. And thus, in his proper manner of soliloquy or self-discourse, we may imagine him running on, beginning perhaps with some particular scheme or fancied scale of beauty, which, according to his philosophy, he strives to erect by distinguishing, sorting and dividing into things *animate*, *inanimate* and *mixed*.

As thus:

In *the inanimate*: beginning from those regular figures and symmetries, with which children are delighted, and proceeding gradually to the proportions of architecture and the other arts. The same in respect of sounds and music. From beautiful stones, rocks, minerals, to vegetables, woods, aggregate parts of the world, seas, rivers, mountains, vales. The globe. Celestial bodies and their order. The higher architecture of nature. Nature herself considered as inanimate and passive.

In *the animate*: from animals and their several kinds, tempers, sagacities, to men. And from single persons of men, their private characters, understandings, geniuses, dispositions, manners, to public societies, communities or commonwealths. From flocks, herds and other natural assemblages or groups of living creatures to human intelligences and correspondencies or whatever is higher in the kind. The correspondence, union and harmony of nature herself, considered as animate and intelligent.

In *the mixed*: as in a single person (a body and a mind), the union and harmony of this kind, which constitutes the real person, and the friendship, love or whatever other affection is formed on such an object. A household, a city or nation, with certain lands, buildings and other appendices or local ornaments, which jointly form that agreeable idea of home, family, country.

'And what of this?', says an airy spark, no friend to meditation or deep thought. 'What means this catalogue or scale, as you are pleased to call it?'

'Only, Sir, to satisfy myself that I am not alone or single in a certain fancy I have of a thing called beauty, that I have almost the whole world for my companions, and that each of us admirers and earnest pursuers of beauty (such as in a manner we all are), if peradventure we take not a certain sagacity along with us, we must err widely, range extravagantly, and run ever upon a false scent. We may, in the sportsman's phrase, have many hares afoot but shall stick to no real game nor be fortunate in any capture which may content us.

See with what ardour and vehemence the young man, neglecting his proper race and fellow creatures and forgetting what is decent, handsome or becoming in human affairs, pursues these species in those common objects of his affection, a horse, a hound, a hawk! What doting on these beauties! What admiration of the kind itself! And, of the particular animal, what care and, in a manner, idolatry and consecration, when the beast beloved is (as often happens) even set apart from use and only kept to gaze on and feed the enamoured fancy with highest delight! See in another youth, not so forgetful of human kind, but remembering it still in a wrong way! a φιλόκαλος [lover of beauty] of another sort, a Chaerea. *How refined a spectator of beauties!* [Terence, *The Eunuch* 3.5.18]. See as to other beauties, where there is no possession, no enjoyment or reward, but barely seeing and admiring, as in the virtuoso passion, the love of painting and the designing arts of every kind, so often observed. How fares it with our princely genius, our grandee who assembles all these beauties and, within the bounds of his sumptuous palace, encloses all these graces of a thousand kinds? What pains, study, science! Behold the disposition and order of these finer sorts of apartments, gardens, villas! The kind of harmony to the eye from the various shapes and colours agreeably mixed and ranged in lines, inter-

In so short a compass does that learning and knowledge lie on which manners and life depend. It is we ourselves create and form our taste. If we resolve to have it just, it is in our power. We may esteem and resolve, approve and disapprove, as we would wish. For who would not rejoice to be always equal and consonant to himself and have constantly that opinion of things which is natural and proportionable? But who dares search opinion to the bottom or call in question his early and prepossessing taste? Who is so just to himself as to recall his fancy from the power of fashion and education to that of reason? Could we, however, be thus courageous, we should soon settle in ourselves such an opinion of good as would secure to us an invariable, agreeable and just taste in life and manners.

Thus have I endeavoured to tread in my author's steps and prepare the reader for the serious and downright philosophy, which, even in this last commented treatise,[26] our author keeps still as a mystery and dares not formally profess. His pretence has been to advise authors and polish styles, but his aim

---

crossing without confusion and fortunately coincident. A parterre, cypresses, groves, wildernesses. Statues, here and there, of virtue, fortitude, temperance. Heroes' busts, philosophers' heads, with suitable mottoes and inscriptions. Solemn representations of things deeply natural. Caves, grottoes, rocks. Urns and obelisks in retired places and disposed at proper distances and points of sight, with all those symmetries which silently express a reigning order, peace, harmony and beauty! But what is there answerable to this in the minds of the possessors? What possession of propriety is theirs? What constancy or security of enjoyment? What peace, what harmony within?'

Thus our monologist, or self-discoursing author, in his usual strain, when incited to the search of beauty and the decorum by vulgar admiration and the universal acknowledgment of the species in outward things and in the meaner and subordinate subjects. By this inferior species, it seems, our strict inspector disdains to be allured and, refusing to be captivated by anything less than the superior, original and genuine kind, he walks at leisure, without emotion, in deep philosophical reserve, through all these pompous scenes, passes unconcernedly by those Court pageants, the illustrious and much envied potentates of the place, overlooks the rich, the great and even the fair, feeling no other astonishment than what is accidentally raised in him by the view of these impostures and of this specious snare. For here he observes those gentlemen chiefly to be caught and fastest held, who are the highest ridiculers of such reflections as his own and who in the very height of this ridicule prove themselves the impotent contemners of a species which, whether they will or no, they ardently pursue, some in a face and certain regular lines or features, others in a palace and apartments, others in an equipage and dress.

O Effeminacy! Effeminacy! Who would imagine this could be the vice of such as appear no inconsiderable men? But person is a subject of flattery which reaches beyond the bloom of youth. The experienced senator and aged general can in our days dispense with a toilet and take his outward form into a very extraordinary adjustment and regulation. All embellishments are affected, besides the true. And thus, led by example, while we run in search of elegancy and neatness, pursuing beauty, and adding, as we imagine, more lustre and value to our own person, we grow, in our real character and truer self, deformed and monstrous, servile and abject, stooping to the lowest terms of courtship and sacrificing all internal proportion, all intrinsic and real beauty and worth for the sake of things which carry scarce a shadow of the kind. See pp. 64–5, 150, 317–19.

[26] *Soliloquy.*

has been to correct manners and regulate lives. He has affected soliloquy, as pretending only to censure himself, but he has taken occasion to bring others into his company and make bold with personages and characters of no inferior rank. He has given scope enough to raillery and humour and has entrenched very largely on the province of us miscellanarian writers. But the reader is now about to see him in a new aspect, a formal and professed philosopher, a system-writer, a dogmatist and expounder.[27] *You have a defendant who is confessing.*[o]

So to his philosophy I commit him. Though, according as my genius and present disposition will permit, I intend still to accompany him at a distance, keep him in sight and convoy him, the best I am able, through the dangerous seas he is about to pass.

[o] A legal expression for the surest route to conviction.

[27] In *An Inquiry Concerning Virtue.*

Miscellany IV

Chapter 1

Connection and union of the subject-treatises. Philosophy in form. Metaphysics.
Egoity. Identity. Moral footing. Proof and discipline of the fancies. Settlement
or opinion. Anatomy of the mind. A fable.

We have already, in the beginning of our preceding miscellany, taken notice
of our author's plan and the connection and dependency of his joint tracts,
comprehended in two preceding volumes.[1] We are now, in our commentator
capacity, arrived at length to his second volume, to which the three pieces of
his first appear preparatory. That they were really so designed, the advertisement to the first edition of his *Soliloquy* is a sufficient proof. He took occasion
there, in a line or two, under the name of his printer, or (as he otherwise calls
him) his amanuensis, to prepare us for a more elaborate and methodical piece
which was to follow.[A] We have the system now before us. Nor need we wonder, such as it is, that it came so hardly into the world and that our author has
been delivered of it with so much difficulty and after so long a time. His amanuensis and he were not, it seems, heretofore upon such good terms of correspondence. Otherwise such an unshapen foetus or false birth as that of which
our author in his title-page complains had not formerly appeared abroad.[2] Nor
had it ever risen again in its more decent form but for the accidental publication of our author's first letter,[3] which, by a necessary train of consequences,
occasioned the revival of this abortive piece and gave usherance to its companions.

It will appear, therefore, in this joint edition of our author's five treatises
that the three former are preparatory to the fourth, on which we are now
entered, and the fifth, with which he concludes, a kind of apology for this
revived treatise concerning virtue and religion.

As for his apology, particularly in what relates to revealed religion and a
world to come, I commit the reader to the disputant divines and gentlemen
whom our author has introduced in that concluding piece of dialogue writing
or rhapsodical philosophy. Meanwhile we have here no other part left us than

---

[A] 'You may ... be assur'd, as well as you possibly can be, upon my testimony, that the following piece, with which I present you, is only a preliminary discourse to a more elaborate treatise and that, if this taste I have given you of the genius of my author be found pleasing, I shall
further oblige you and myself by publishing the entire work in a very short time': 'The Printer
to the Reader', *Soliloquy* (London, 1710), p. iv.

[1] See pp. 395–6, 458–9.

[2] Namely, *An Inquiry Concerning Virtue.* [The title-page of the *Inquiry* in the John Darby editions of *Characteristics* included the words, 'formerly printed from an imperfect copy, now corrected and published entire'.]

[3] Namely, *A Letter Concerning Enthusiasm.*

to enter into the dry philosophy and rigid manner of our author, without any excursions into various literature, without help from the comic or tragic muse or from the flowers of poetry or rhetoric.

Such is our present pattern and strict moral task, which our more humorous reader, foreknowing, may immediately, if he pleases, turn over, skipping (as is usual in many grave works) a chapter or two as he proceeds. We shall, to make amends, endeavour afterwards, in our following miscellany, to entertain him again with more cheerful fare, and afford him a dessert to rectify his palate and leave his mouth at last in good relish.

To the patient and grave reader, therefore, who in order to moralize can afford to retire into his closet as to some religious or devout exercise, we presume thus to offer a few reflections in the support of our author's profound inquiry. And, accordingly, we are to imagine our author speaking as follows.

How little regard soever may be shown to that moral speculation or inquiry which we call the study of ourselves, it must, in strictness, be yielded that all knowledge whatsoever depends upon this previous one: 'And that we can in reality be assured of nothing till we are first assured of what we are ourselves.' For by this alone we can know what certainty and assurance is.

That there is something undoubtedly which thinks, our very doubt itself and scrupulous thought evinces. But in what subject that thought resides, and how that subject is continued one and the same so as to answer constantly to the supposed train of thoughts or reflections which seem to run so harmoniously through a long course of life, with the same relation still to one single and self-same person, this is not a matter so easily or hastily decided by those who are nice self-examiners or searchers after truth and certainty.

It will not, in this respect, be sufficient for us to use the seeming logic of a famous modern and say, 'We think; therefore we are,'[4] which is a notably invented saying, after the model of that like philosophical proposition, that 'What is, is.' Miraculously argued! 'If I am, I am.' Nothing more certain! For the Ego or I, being established in the first part of the proposition, the *ergo*, no doubt, must hold it good in the latter. But the question is, 'What constitutes the "we" or "I"?', and 'Whether the "I" of this instant be the same with that of any instant preceding or to come?' For we have nothing but memory to warrant us, and memory may be false. We may believe we have thought and reflected thus or thus, but we may be mistaken. We may be conscious of that as truth which perhaps was no more than dream, and we may be conscious of that as a past dream which perhaps was never before so much as dreamt of.

This is what metaphysicians mean when they say 'that identity can be proved only by consciousness, but that consciousness, withal, may be as well false as

---

[4] Monsieur [René] Descartes [in *Discours de la méthode pour bien conduire sa raison et chercher la vérité dans les sciences* (Discourse on the method for guiding one's reason and searching for truth in the sciences), Part IV].

real in respect of what is past'. So that the same successional 'we' or 'I' must remain still, on this account, undecided.

To the force of this reasoning, I confess, I must so far submit as to declare that, for my own part, I take my being upon trust. Let others philosophize as they are able: I shall admire their strength when, upon this topic, they have refuted what able metaphysicians object and Pyrrhonists plead in their own behalf.[B]

Meanwhile, there is no impediment, hindrance or suspension of action on account of these wonderfully refined speculations. Argument and debate go on still. Conduct is settled. Rules and measures are given out and received. Nor do we scruple to act as resolutely upon the mere supposition that we are, as if we had effectually proved it a thousand times to the full satisfaction of our metaphysical or Pyrrhonian antagonist.

This to me appears sufficient ground for a moralist. Nor do I ask more when I undertake to prove the reality of virtue and morals.

If it be certain that *I am*, it is certain and demonstrable *who and what I ought to be*, even on my own account and for the sake of my own private happiness and success. For thus I take the liberty to proceed.

The affections of which I am conscious are either grief or joy, desire or aversion. For whatever mere sensation I may experience, if it amounts to neither of these, it is indifferent and no way affects me.

That which causes joy and satisfaction when present causes grief and disturbance when absent, and that which causes grief and disturbance when present does, when absent, by the same necessity occasion joy and satisfaction.

Thus love, which implies desire with hope of good, must afford occasion to grief and disturbance when it acquires not what it earnestly seeks. And hatred, which implies aversion and fear of ill, must, in the same manner, occasion grief and calamity when that which it earnestly shunned, or would have escaped, remains present or is altogether unavoidable.

That which being present can never leave the mind at rest, but must of necessity cause aversion, is its ill. But that which can be sustained without any necessary abhorrence or aversion is not its ill, but remains indifferent in its own nature, the ill being in the affection only, which wants redress.

In the same manner, that which being absent can never leave the mind at rest, or without disturbance and regret, is of necessity its good. But that which can be absent without any present or future disturbance to the mind is not its good, but remains indifferent in its own nature. From whence it must follow that the affection towards it, as supposed good, is an ill affection and creative only of disturbance and disease. So that the affections of love and hatred, liking and dislike, on which the happiness or prosperity of the person so much

[B] On Pyrrhonism, see p. 301n.

depends, being influenced and governed by opinion, the highest good or happiness must depend on right opinion and the highest misery be derived from wrong.

To explain this, I consider, for instance, the fancy or imagination I have of death, according as I find this subject naturally passing in my mind. To this fancy, perhaps, I find united an opinion or apprehension of evil and calamity. Now the more my apprehension of this evil increases, the greater I find my disturbance proves not only at the approach of the supposed evil, but at the very distant thought of it. Besides that, the thought itself will of necessity so much the oftener recur as the aversion or fear is violent and increasing.

From this supposed evil, I must, however, fly with so much the more earnestness as the opinion of the evil increases. Now if the increase of the aversion can be no cause of the decrease or diminution of the evil itself but rather the contrary, then the increase of the aversion must necessarily prove the increase of disappointment and disturbance. And so, on the other hand, the diminution or decrease of the aversion, if this may any way be effected, must of necessity prove the diminution of inward disturbance and the better establishment of inward quiet and satisfaction.

Again, I consider with myself that I have the imagination of something beautiful, great and becoming in things.[5] This imagination I apply perhaps to such subjects as plate, jewels, apartments, coronets, patents of honour, titles or precedencies. I must therefore naturally seek these not as mere conveniencies, means or helps in life (for as such my passion could not be so excessive towards them) but as excellent in themselves, necessarily attractive of my admiration and directly and immediately causing my happiness and giving me satisfaction. Now if the passion raised on this opinion (call it avarice, pride, vanity or ambition) be indeed incapable of any real satisfaction, even under the most successful course of fortune, and then too, attended with perpetual fears of disappointment and loss, how can the mind be other than miserable when possessed by it? But, if instead of forming thus the opinion of good, if instead of placing worth or excellence in these outward subjects, we place it where it is truest, in the affections or sentiments, in the governing part and inward character, we have then the full enjoyment of it within our power: the imagination or opinion remains steady and irreversible, and the love, desire and appetite is answered without apprehension of loss or disappointment.

Here, therefore, arises work and employment for us within, *to regulate fancy*

---

[5] Of the necessary being and prevalency of some such imagination or sense (natural and common to all men, irresistible, of original growth in the mind, the guide of our affections, and the ground of our admiration, contempt, shame, honour, disdain and other natural and unavoidable impressions), see pp. 64, 149–50, 172–3, 317–18, 329, 333, 351–3, 415n.

and rectify opinions, on which all depends.[6] For if our loves, desires, hatreds and aversions are left to themselves, we are necessarily exposed to endless vexation and calamity, but, if these are found capable of amendment or in any measure flexible or variable by opinion, we ought, methinks, to make trial, at least, how far we might by this means acquire felicity and content.

Accordingly, if we find it evident, on one hand, that by indulging any wrong appetite (as either debauch, malice or revenge) the opinion of the false good increases and the appetite, which is a real ill, grows so much the stronger, we may be as fully assured, on the other hand, that, by restraining this affection and nourishing a contrary sort in opposition to it, we cannot fail to diminish what is ill and increase what is properly our happiness and good.

On this account, a man may reasonably conclude that *it becomes him, by working upon his own mind, to withdraw the fancy or opinion of good or ill from that to which justly and by necessity it is not joined, and apply it with the strongest resolution to that with which it naturally agrees.* For if the fancy or opinion of good be joined to what is not durable nor in my power either to acquire or to retain, the more such an opinion prevails, the more I must be subject to disappointment and distress. But if there be that to which, whenever I apply the opinion or fancy of good, I find the fancy more consistent and the good more durable, solid and within my power and command, then the more such an opinion prevails in me, the more satisfaction and happiness I must experience.

Now, if I join the opinion of good to the possessions of the mind, if it be in the affections themselves that I place my highest joy and in those objects, whatever they are, of inward worth and beauty (such as honesty, faith, integrity, friendship, honour), it is evident I can never possibly, in this respect, rejoice amiss or indulge myself too far in the enjoyment. The greater my indulgence is, the less I have reason to fear either reverse or disappointment.

This, I know, is far contrary in another regimen of life. The tutorage of fancy and pleasure and the easy philosophy of taking that for good which pleases me, or which I fancy merely, will in time give me uneasiness sufficient.[7] It is plain, from what has been debated, that the less fanciful I am in what relates to my content and happiness, the more powerful and absolute I must be in self-enjoyment and the possession of my good. And since it is fancy merely which gives the force of good, or power of passing as such, to things of chance and outward dependency, it is evident that the more I take from fancy in this

---

[6] *Apprehension [ὑπόληψις] is everything, and this is up to you. Therefore, remove the apprehension when you wish, and there is a great calm as though you were rounding the headland, and all is still and the bay is still:* Marcus Aurelius, Meditations 12.22. *The soul is like the basin of water. Fancies [φαντασίαι] are like the ray of light that strikes upon the water. Thus, when the water is disturbed, the ray seems too to be disturbed; but it is not. And so when anyone is agitated, it is not the arts and the virtues that are confounded but the spirit in which they exist. And when this steadies, they do as well:* Epictetus, Discourses 3.3.20–2. See pp. 83, 132–3, 144–6, 336.

[7] See pp. 138, 250.

respect, the more I confer upon myself. As I am less led or betrayed by fancy to an esteem of what depends on others, I am the more fixed in the esteem of what depends on myself alone. And if I have once gained the taste of liberty, I shall easily understand the force of this reasoning and know both my true self and interest.[8]

The method, therefore, required in this my inward economy, is to make those fancies themselves the objects of my aversion which justly deserve it, by being the cause of a wrong estimation and measure of good and ill and, consequently, the cause of my unhappiness and disturbance.

Accordingly, as the learned masters in this science advise, we are to begin rather by the averse than by the prone and forward disposition.[9] We are to work rather by the weaning than the engaging passions since, if we give way chiefly to inclination, by loving, applauding and admiring what is great and good, we may possibly, it seems, in some high objects of that kind, be so amused and ecstasied as to lose ourselves and miss our proper mark for want of a steady and settled aim. But being more sure and infallible in what relates to our ill, we should begin, they tell us, by applying our aversion on that side and raising our indignation against those meannesses of opinion and sentiment which are the causes of our subjection and perplexity.

Thus, the covetous fancy, if considered as the cause of misery and conse-

---

[8] See pp. 334, 468.

[9] *Therefore, give up aversion of all things which are not in your power and transfer it to those things in our power which are contrary to nature*: Epictetus, *Enchiridion* 2. *You must give up desire completely, transfer your aversion exclusively to things that are the business of moral purpose [προαιρετικά]*: Epictetus, *Discourses* 3.22.13. This subdued or moderated admiration or zeal in the highest subjects of virtue and divinity, the philosopher calls *commensurate and composed desire*; the contrary disposition, *the irrational and impetuous* [Epictetus, *Discourses* 4.1.84]. The reason why this over-forward ardour and pursuit of high subjects runs naturally into enthusiasm and disorder is shown in what succeeds the first of the passages here cited, namely, *of the things that are in our power, insofar as it would be good to desire them, not a single thing is within your grasp* [Epictetus, *Enchiridion* 2]. And hence the repeated injunction, *refrain at some time altogether from desire, so that at some time you may actually desire with good reason. If you do desire with good reason, whenever you have some good in yourself, you will be desiring well* [Epictetus, *Discourses* 3.13.21]. To this Horace, in one of his latest epistles of the deeply philosophical kind, alludes: *Let the wise man carry the name of madman, the just man of the unjust, if he seeks virtue itself beyond what is sufficient* [1.6.15–16]. And in the beginning of the epistle: *To admire nothing, Numicius, is pretty much the only thing and alone able to make and keep a man happy* [1.6.1–2]. For though these first lines (as many other of Horace's on the subject of philosophy) have the air of the Epicurean discipline and Lucretian style, yet, by the whole taken together, it appears evidently on what system of ancient philosophy this epistle was formed. Nor was this prohibition of the wondering or admiring habit in early students peculiar to one kind of philosophy alone. It was common to many, however the reason and account of it might differ in one sect from the other. The Pythagoreans sufficiently checked their tyros by silencing them so long on their first courtship to philosophy. And though admiration, in the Peripatetic sense, as above mentioned, may be justly called the inclining principle or first motive to philosophy, yet this mistress, when once espoused, teaches us to admire after a different manner from what we did before. See pp. 21, 354.

quently detested as a real ill, must of necessity abate, and the ambitious fancy, if opposed in the same manner with resolution by better thought, must resign itself and leave the mind free and disencumbered in the pursuit of its better objects.

Nor is the case different in the passion of cowardice or fear of death. For if we leave this passion to itself or to certain tutors to manage for us, it may lead us to the most anxious and tormenting state of life. But if it be opposed by sounder opinion and a just estimation of things, it must diminish of course, and the natural result of such a practice must be the rescue of the mind from numberless fears and miseries of other kinds.

Thus at last a mind, by knowing itself and its own proper powers and virtues, becomes free and independent. It sees its hindrances and obstructions and finds they are wholly from itself and from opinions wrong conceived. The more it conquers in this respect (be it in the least particular), the more it is its own master, feels its own natural liberty and congratulates with itself on its own advancement and prosperity.

Whether some who are called philosophers have so applied their meditations as to understand anything of this language, I know not. But well I am assured that many an honest and free-hearted fellow, among the vulgar rank of people, has naturally some kind of feeling or apprehension of this self-enjoyment when, refusing to act for lucre or outward profit, the thing which from his soul he abhors and thinks below him, he goes on, with harder labour but more content, in his direct plain path. He is secure within, free of what the world calls policy or design and sings, according to the old ballad: 'My mind to me a kingdom is.'C Which in Latin we may translate: *And I wrap myself in my virtue, and I court honest poverty without a dowry.*[10]

But I forget, it seems, that I am now speaking in the person of our grave inquirer. I should consider I have no right to vary from the pattern he has set and that, while I accompany him in this particular treatise, I ought not to make the least escape out of the high road of demonstration into the diverting paths of poetry or humour.

As grave however as morals are presumed in their own nature, I look upon it as an essential matter in their delivery to take now and then the natural air of pleasantry. The first morals which were ever delivered in the world were in parables, tales or fables. And the latter and most consummate distributors of morals, in the very politest times, were great tale-tellers and retainers to honest Aesop.D

C   The line is the first in a poem by Sir Edward Dyer, *c.* 1540–1607, an English courtier and poet.
D   The legendary sixth-century BC figure to whom Greek fables had been ascribed by the end of the fifth century BC.

[10]   Horace, *Odes* 3.29.54–6.

After all the regular demonstrations and deductions of our grave author, I dare say it would be a high relief and satisfaction to his reader to hear an apologue or fable well told, and with such humour as to need no sententious moral at the end to make the application.

As an experiment in this case, let us at this instant imagine our grave inquirer taking pains to show us, at full length, the unnatural and unhappy excursions, rovings or expeditions of our ungoverned fancies and opinions over a world of riches, honours and other ebbing and flowing goods. He performs this, we will suppose, with great sagacity to the full measure and scope of our attention. Meanwhile, as full or satiated as we might find ourselves of serious and solid demonstration, it is odds but we might find vacancy still sufficient to receive instruction by another method. And I dare answer for success should a merrier moralist of the Aesopean school present himself and, hearing of this chase described by our philosopher, beg leave to represent it to the life by a homely cur or two of his master's ordinary breed.

'Two of this race,' he would tell us, 'having been daintily bred and in high thoughts of what they called pleasure and good living, travelled once in quest of game and rarities till they came by accident to the seaside. They saw there, at a distance from the shore, some floating pieces of a wreck, which they took a fancy to believe some wonderful rich dainty, richer than ambergris or the richest product of the ocean. They could prove it by their appetite and longing to be no less than "quintessence of the main", "ambrosial substance", "the repast of marine deities surpassing all which earth afforded". By these rhetorical arguments, after long reasoning with one another in this florid vein, they proceeded from one extravagance of fancy to another till they came at last to this issue. Being unaccustomed to swimming, they would not, it seems, in prudence, venture so far out of their depth as was necessary to reach their imagined prize, but, being stout drinkers, they thought with themselves they might compass to drink all which lay in their way, even the sea itself, and that by this method they might shortly bring their goods safe to dry land. To work therefore they went and drank till they were both burst.'

For my own part, I am fully satisfied that there are more sea-drinkers than one or two to be found among the principal personages of mankind and that, if these dogs of ours were silly curs, many who pass for wise in our own race are little wiser and may properly enough be said to have the sea to drink.

It is pretty evident that they who live in the highest sphere of human affairs have a very uncertain view of the thing called happiness or good. It lies out at sea, far distant, in the offing, where those gentlemen ken it but very imperfectly, and the means they employ in order to come up with it are very wide of the matter and far short of their proposed end. 'First a general acquaintance. Visits, levees. Attendance upon the great and little. Popularity. A place in Parliament. Then another at Court. Then intrigue, corruption, prostitution.

Then a higher place. Then a title. Then a remove. A new minister! Factions at Court. Shipwreck of ministries. The new, the old. Engage with one, piece up with t'other. Bargains, losses, after-games, retrievals.' Is not this the sea to drink? *But if riches could render you prudent, if less desirous and fearful, then surely you would blush if there were alive upon the earth anyone more greedy than you.*[11] But lest I should be tempted to fall into a manner I have been obliged to disclaim in this part of my miscellaneous performance, I shall here set a period to this discourse and renew my attempt of serious reflection and grave thought by taking up my clue in a fresh chapter.

Chapter 2

Passage from Terra Incognita[E] *to the visible world. Mistress-ship of nature. Animal confederacy, degrees, subordination. Master-animal man. Privilege of his birth. Serious countenance of the author.*

As heavily as it went with us in the deep philosophical part of our preceding chapter, and as necessarily engaged as we still are to prosecute the same serious inquiry and search into those dark sources, it is hoped that our remaining philosophy may flow in a more easy vein, and the second running be found somewhat clearer than the first. However it be, we may at least congratulate with ourselves for having thus briefly passed over that metaphysical part to which we have paid sufficient deference. Nor shall we scruple to declare our opinion that *it is in a manner necessary for one who would usefully philosophize, to have a knowledge in this part of philosophy sufficient to satisfy him that there is no knowledge or wisdom to be learnt from it.* For this truth nothing besides experience and study will be able fully to convince him.

When we are even past these empty regions and shadows of philosophy, it will still perhaps appear an uncomfortable kind of travelling through those other invisible ideal worlds such as the study of morals, we see, engages us to visit. Men must acquire a very peculiar and strong habit of turning their eye inwards in order to explore the interior regions and recesses of the mind, the hollow caverns of deep thought, the private seats of fancy, and the wastes and wildernesses as well as the more fruitful and cultivated tracts of the obscure climate.

But what can one do? Or how dispense with these darker disquisitions and moonlight voyages when we have to deal with a sort of moon-blind wits who, though very acute and able in their kind, may be said to renounce daylight and extinguish in a manner the bright visible outward world, by allowing us to know nothing beside what we can prove by strict and formal demonstration?

It is therefore to satisfy such rigid inquirers as these, that we have been

E   Unknown land.

11   Horace, *Epistles* 2.2.155–7.

necessitated to proceed by the inward way, and that in our preceding chapter we have built only on such foundations as are taken from our very perceptions, fancies, appearances, affections and opinions themselves, without regard to anything of an exterior world and even on the supposition that there is no such world in being.

Such has been our late dry task. No wonder if it carries, indeed, a meagre and raw appearance. It may be looked on in philosophy as worse than a mere Egyptian imposition.[F] For to make brick without straw or stubble is perhaps an easier labour than to prove morals without a world, and establish a conduct of life without the supposition of anything living or extant besides our immediate fancy and world of imagination.

But having finished this mysterious work, we come now to open day and sunshine and, as a poet perhaps might express himself, we are now ready to quit 'the dubious labyrinths, and Pyrrhonian cells of a Cimmerian darkness'. We are henceforward to trust our eyes and take for real the whole creation and the fair forms which lie before us. We are to believe the anatomy of our own body and, in proportionable order, the shapes, forms, habits and constitutions of other animal races. Without demurring on the profound modern hypothesis of animal insensibility,[G] we are to believe firmly and resolutely that other creatures have their sense and feeling, their mere passions and affections, as well as ourselves. And in this manner we proceed accordingly, on our author's scheme, to inquire what is truly natural to each creature and whether that which is natural to each and is its perfection be not withal its happiness or good.

To deny there is anything properly natural, after the concessions already made, would be undoubtedly very preposterous and absurd. Nature and the outward world being owned existent, the rest must of necessity follow. The anatomy of bodies, the order of the spheres, the proper mechanisms of a thousand kinds and the infinite ends and suitable means established in the general constitution and order of things – all this being once admitted and allowed to pass as certain and unquestionable, it is as vain afterwards to except against the phrase of 'natural' and 'unnatural' and question the propriety of this speech applied to the particular forms and beings in the world, as it would be to except against the common appellations of vigour and decay in plants, health or sickness in bodies, sobriety or distraction in minds, prosperity or degeneracy in any variable part of the known creation.

We may, perhaps, for humour's sake or, after the known way of disputant hostility, in the support of any odd hypothesis, pretend to deny this 'natural' and 'unnatural' in things. It is evident, however, that, though our humour or

[F] Exodus 5 where Pharaoh commanded that the enslaved Hebrews no longer be provided straw with which to make bricks.
[G] Descartes, applying his mechanical views to living organisms, asserted that animals were highly complicated machines and, thus, insensible automata.

taste be by such affectation ever so much depraved, we cannot resist our natural anticipation in behalf of nature, according to whose supposed standard we perpetually approve and disapprove and to whom in all natural appearances, all moral actions (whatever we contemplate, whatever we have in debate), we inevitably appeal and pay our constant homage with the most apparent zeal and passion.[12]

It is here, above all other places, that we say, with strict justice, *should you drive off nature with a pitchfork, nevertheless she will always hurry back.*[13]

The airy gentlemen, who have never had it in their thoughts to study nature in their own species but, being taken with other loves, have applied their parts and genius to the same study in a horse, a dog, a gamecock, a hawk or any other animal of that degree, know very well that to each species there belongs a several humour, temper and turn of inward disposition, as real and peculiar as the figure and outward shape which is with so much curiosity beheld and admired.[14] If there be anything ever so little amiss or wrong in the inward

---

[12] See what is said above on the word *sensus communis* in that second treatise, pp. 48–51, 64–5, 150, 156–8, 282–3, 325–6, concerning the natural ideas and the preconceptions or presensations of this kind, the προλήψεις, of which a learned critic and master in all philosophy, modern and ancient, takes notice in his lately published volume of Socratic dialogues, where he adds this reflection, with respect to some philosophical notions much in vogue among us of late here in England: *We shall add in passing that the Socratic doctrine, which we set forth, can be of great use, if it is properly weighed, in settling the controversy among learned men that arose a few years before, especially in Britain, concerning innate ideas, which you could call ἐμφύτους ἐννοίας. Although, if we speak accurately, there are no notions fixed in our souls by nature, none the less nobody has denied that the faculties of our souls have so been made by nature that, as soon as we begin to use reason, we begin to distinguish in some way what is true from what is false, what is bad from what is good. The appearance of truth is always pleasing to us; on the other hand, the appearance of mendacity is displeasing. We prefer what is honourable to what is base and dishonourable; on account of seeds planted within us, which finally come forth into the light of day, we are able to reason, and they produce fruit more abundant the better we reason and are aided by more exact instruction,* Jean Le Clerc, *Silvae Philologicae* [Groves of philology] 2.8 in Le Clerc's edition of Aeschines, *Socratici Dialogi Tres* (Amsterdam, 1711), p. 176. They seem indeed to be but weak philosophers, though able sophists and artful confounders of words and notions, who would refute nature and common sense. But nature will be able still to shift for herself and get the better of those schemes, which need no other force against them than that of Horace's single verse: *The wolf attacks with tooth, the bull with horn: how can this be, unless it is innately ordained?* [*Satires* 2.1.52–3]. An ass, as an English author says, never butts with his ears, though a creature born to an armed forehead exercises his butting faculty long before his horns are come to him. And perhaps, if the philosopher would accordingly examine himself and consider his natural passions, he would find there were such belonged to him, as nature had premeditated in his behalf and for which she had furnished him with ideas, long before any particular practice or experience of his own. Nor would he need be scandalized with the comparison of a goat or boar or other of Horace's premeditating animals, who have more natural wit, it seems, than our philosopher, if we may judge of him by his own hypothesis, which denies the same implanted sense and natural ideas to his own kind: *Tomorrow a kid will be bestowed upon you with horns budding on its brow, marking it for love and battles* [*Odes* 3.13.3–5] and *of a boar practising its sideways strike* [*Odes* 3.22.7].

[13] Horace, *Epistles* 1.10.24.

[14] See pp. 198–201, 213, 282–3.

frame, the humour or temper of the creature, it is readily called vicious and, when more than ordinarily wrong, unnatural. The humours of the creatures, in order to their redress, are attentively observed, sometimes indulged and flattered, at other times controlled and checked with proper severities. In short, their affections, passions, appetites and antipathies are as duly regarded as those in humankind under the strictest discipline of education. Such is *the sense of inward proportion and regularity of affections*, even in our noble youths themselves, who in this respect are often known expert and able masters of education, though not so susceptible of discipline and culture in their own case, after those early indulgences to which their greatness has entitled them.

As little favourable, however, as these sportly gentlemen are presumed to show themselves towards the care or culture of their own species, as remote as their contemplations are thought to lie from nature and philosophy, they confirm plainly and establish our philosophical foundation of the natural ranks, orders, interior and exterior proportions of the several distinct species and forms of animal beings.

Ask one of these gentlemen, unawares, when solicitously careful and busied in the great concerns of his stable or kennel 'whether his hound or greyhound bitch who eats her puppies is as natural as the other who nurses them?', and he will think you frantic.

Ask him again, 'whether he thinks the unnatural creature who acts thus, or the natural one who does otherwise, is best in its kind and enjoys itself the most?' And he will be inclined to think still as strangely of you.

Or, if perhaps he esteems you worthy of better information, he will tell you that 'his best-bred creatures and of the truest race are ever the noblest and most generous in their natures', that 'it is this chiefly which makes the difference between the horse of good blood and the errant jade of a base breed, between the gamecock and the dunghill craven, between the true hawk and the mere kite or buzzard, and between the right mastiff, hound or spaniel and the very mongrel'. He might, withal, tell you perhaps with a masterly air in this brute science 'that the timorous, poor-spirited, lazy and gluttonous of his dogs were those whom he either suspected to be of a spurious race, or who had been by some accident spoiled in their nursing and management, for that this was not natural to them; that in every kind they were still the miserablest creatures who were thus spoiled and that, having each of them their proper chase or business, if they lay resty and out of their game, chambered and idle, they were the same as if taken out of their element; that the saddest curs in the world were those who took the kitchen chimney and dripping-pan for their delight; and that the only happy dog (were one to be a dog oneself) was he who in his proper sport and exercise, his natural pursuit and game, endured all hardships and had so much delight in exercise and in the field as to forget home and his reward'.

Thus the natural habits and affections of the inferior creatures are known and their unnatural and degenerate part discovered. Depravity and corruption is acknowledged as real in their affections as when anything is misshapen, wrong or monstrous in their outward make. And notwithstanding much of this inward depravity is discoverable in the creatures tamed by man and, for his service or pleasure merely, turned from their natural course into a contrary life and habit, notwithstanding that, by this means, the creatures who naturally herd with one another lose their associating humour and they who naturally pair and are constant to each other lose their kind of conjugal alliance and affection, yet, when released from human servitude and returned again to their natural wilds and rural liberty, they instantly resume their natural and regular habits, such as are conducing to the increase and prosperity of their own species.

Well it is perhaps for mankind that, though there are so many animals who naturally herd for company's sake and mutual affection, there are so few who for conveniency and by necessity are obliged to a strict union and kind of confederate state. The creatures who, according to the economy of their kind, are obliged to make themselves habitations of defence against the seasons and other incidents, they who in some parts of the year are deprived of all subsistence and are therefore necessitated to accumulate in another and to provide withal for the safety of their collected stores, are by their nature indeed as strictly joined, and with as proper affections towards their public and community, as the looser kind, of a more easy subsistence and support, are united in what relates merely to their offspring and the propagation of their species. Of these thoroughly associating and confederate animals, there are none I have ever heard of who in bulk or strength exceed the beaver. The major part of these political animals and creatures of a joint stock are as inconsiderable as the race of ants or bees. But, had nature assigned such an economy as this to so puissant an animal, for instance, as the elephant and made him withal as prolific as those smaller creatures commonly are, it might have gone hard perhaps with mankind; and a single animal who, by his proper might and prowess, has often decided the fate of the greatest battles which have been fought by the human race, should he have grown up into a society with a genius for architecture and mechanics, proportionable to what we observe in those smaller creatures, we should, with all our invented machines, have found it hard to dispute with him the dominion of the continent.

Were we in a disinterested view, or with somewhat less selfishness than ordinary, to consider the economies, parts, interests, conditions and terms of life, which nature has distributed and assigned to the several species of creatures round us, we should not be apt to think ourselves so hardly dealt with. But whether our lot in this respect be just or equal is not the question with us at present. It is enough that we know there is certainly an assignment and distribution, that each economy or part so distributed is in itself uniform, fixed and invariable, and that, if anything in the creature be accidentally impaired,

431

if anything in the inward form, the disposition, temper or affections, be contrary or unsuitable to the distinct economy or part, the creature is wretched and unnatural.

The social or natural affections, which our author considers as essential to the health, wholeness or integrity of the particular creature, are such as contribute to the welfare and prosperity of that whole or species, to which he is by nature joined. All the affections of this kind our author comprehends in that single name of *natural*. But as the design or end of nature in each animal system is exhibited chiefly in the support and propagation of the particular species, it happens, of consequence, that those affections of earliest alliance and mutual kindness between the parent and the offspring are known more particularly by the name of *natural affection*.[15] However, since it is evident that all defect or depravity of affection which counterworks or opposes the original constitution and economy of the creature is unnatural, it follows that, *in creatures who by their particular economy are fitted to the strictest society and rule of common good, the most unnatural of all affections are those which separate from this community and the most truly natural, generous and noble are those which tend towards public service and the interest of the society at large.*

This is the main problem which our author in more philosophical terms demonstrates in this treatise:[16] that, for a creature whose natural end is society, to operate as is by nature appointed him towards the good of such his society or whole is in reality to pursue his own natural and proper good; and that to operate contrariwise, or by such affections as sever from that common good or public interest, is in reality to work towards his own natural and proper ill. Now, if man, as has been proved, be justly ranked in the number of those creatures whose economy is according to a joint stock and public weal, if it be understood, withal, that the only state of his affections which answers rightly to this public weal is the regular, orderly or virtuous state, it necessarily follows that *virtue is his natural good, and vice his misery and ill.*

As for that further consideration, whether nature has orderly and justly distributed the several economies or parts and whether the defects, failures or calamities of particular systems are to the advantage of all in general and contribute to the perfection of the one common and universal system, we must refer to our author's profounder speculation in this his *Inquiry* and in his following philosophic dialogue. But, if what he advances in this respect be real, or at least the most probable by far of any scheme or representation which can be made of the universal nature and cause of things, it will follow that, since man has been so constituted, by means of his rational part, as to be conscious of this his more immediate relation to the universal system and principle of

---

[15] στοργή, for which we have no particular name in our language.
[16] Namely, *An Inquiry Concerning Virtue.*

order and intelligence, *he is not only by nature sociable within the limits of his own species or kind but in a yet more generous and extensive manner. He is not only born to virtue, friendship, honesty and faith but to religion, piety, adoration and a generous surrender of his mind to whatever happens from that supreme cause or order of things, which he acknowledges entirely just and perfect.*[17]

These are our author's formal and grave sentiments, which, if they were not truly his and sincerely espoused by him as the real result of his best judgment and understanding, he would be guilty of a more than common degree of imposture. For, according to his own rule,[18] an affected gravity and feigned seriousness carried on through any subject in such a manner as to leave no insight into the fiction or intended raillery is in truth no raillery or wit at all, but a gross, immoral and illiberal way of abuse, foreign to the character of a good writer, a gentleman or man of worth.

But since we have thus acquitted ourselves of that serious part, of which our reader was beforehand well apprised, let him now expect us again in our original miscellaneous manner and capacity. It is here, as has been explained to him, that raillery and humour are permitted, and flights, sallies and excursions of every kind are found agreeable and requisite. Without this, there might be less safety found, perhaps, in thinking. Every light reflection might run us up to the dangerous state of meditation. And, in reality, profound thinking is many times the cause of shallow thoughts. To prevent this contemplative habit and character, of which we see so little good effect in the world, we have reason perhaps to be fond of the diverting manner in writing and discourse, especially if the subject be of a solemn kind. There is more need in this case to interrupt the long-spun thread of reasoning and bring into the mind, by many different glances and broken views, what cannot so easily be introduced by one steady bent or continued stretch of sight.

[17] See pp. 190–1.
[18] See p. 31.

Miscellany V

Chapter 1

Ceremonial adjusted between author and reader. Affectation of precedency in the former. Various claims to inspiration. Bards, prophets, Sibylline scripture. Written oracles in verse and prose. Common interest of ancient letters and Christianity. State of wit, elegance and correctness. Poetic truth. Preparation for criticism on our author in his concluding treatise.

Of all the artificial relations formed between mankind, the most capricious and variable is that of author and reader. Our author, for his part, has declared his opinion of this where he gives his advice to modern authors.[1] And though he supposes that every author in form is, in respect of the particular matter he explains, superior in understanding to his reader, yet he allows not that any author should assume the upper hand or pretend to withdraw himself from that necessary subjection to foreign judgment and criticism, which must determine the place of honour on the reader's side.

It is evident that an author's art and labour are for his reader's sake alone. It is to his reader he makes his application, if not openly and avowedly, yet at least with implicit courtship. Poets indeed, and especially those of a modern kind, have a peculiar manner of treating this affair with a high hand. They pretend to set themselves above mankind. 'Their pens are sacred, their style and utterance divine.' They write often as in a language foreign to humankind and would disdain to be reminded of those poor elements of speech, their alphabet and grammar.

But here inferior mortals presume often to intercept their flight and remind them of their fallible and human part. Had those first poets who began this pretence to inspiration been taught a manner of communicating their rapturous thoughts and high ideas by some other medium than that of style and language, the case might have stood otherwise. But the inspiring divinity or Muse having, in the explanation of herself, submitted her wit and sense to the mechanic rules of human arbitrary composition, she must in consequence and by necessity submit herself to human arbitration and the judgment of the literate world. And thus the reader is still superior and keeps the upper hand.

It is indeed no small absurdity to assert a work or treatise, written in human language, to be above human criticism or censure. For if the art of writing be from the grammatical rules of human invention and determination, if even these rules are formed on casual practice and various use, there can be no scripture but what must of necessity be subject to the reader's narrow scrutiny and strict judgment, unless a language and grammar, different from any of human

[1] Namely, in *Soliloquy*.

structure, were delivered down from Heaven and miraculously accommodated to human service and capacity.

It is no otherwise in the grammatical art of characters and 'painted speech' than in the art of painting itself. I have seen, in certain Christian churches, an ancient piece or two, affirmed, on the solemn faith of priestly tradition, 'to have been angelically and divinely wrought by a supernatural hand and sacred pencil'. Had the piece happened to be of a hand like Raphael's, I could have found nothing certain to oppose to this tradition.[A] But having observed the whole style and manner of the pretended heavenly workmanship to be so indifferent as to vary in many particulars from the truth of art, I presumed within myself to beg pardon of the tradition and assert confidently that, 'if the pencil had been Heaven-guided, it could never have been so lame in its performance', it being a mere contradiction to all divine and moral truth that a celestial hand, submitting itself to the rudiments of a human art, should sin against the art itself and express falsehood and error instead of justness and proportion.

It may be alleged, perhaps, that 'there are however certain authors in the world who, though of themselves they neither boldly claim the privilege of divine inspiration nor carry indeed the least resemblance of perfection in their style or composition, yet subdue the reader, gain the ascendant over his thought and judgment and force from him a certain implicit veneration and esteem'.

To this, I can only answer that, 'if there be neither spell nor enchantment in the case, this can plainly be no other than mere enthusiasm', except, perhaps, where the supreme powers have given their sanction to any religious record or pious writ. And, in this case, indeed, it becomes immoral and profane in anyone to deny absolutely or dispute the sacred authority of the least line or syllable contained in it. But, should the record, instead of being single, short and uniform, appear to be multifarious, voluminous and of the most difficult interpretation, it would be somewhat hard, if not wholly impracticable in the magistrate, to suffer this record to be universally current, and at the same time prevent its being variously apprehended and descanted on by the several differing geniuses and contrary judgments of mankind.

It is remarkable that, in the politest of all nations,[B] the writings looked upon as most sacred were those of their great poets, whose works indeed were truly divine in respect of art and the perfection of their frame and composition. But there was yet more divinity ascribed to them than what is comprehended in this latter sense.[2] The notions of vulgar religion

---

[A] For Shaftesbury, Raphael (Raffaello Sanzio, 1483–1520) was one of the few modern painters of distinction.

[B] That is, classical Greece.

[2] See p. 404n.

were built on their miraculous narrations. The wiser and better sort themselves paid a regard to them in this respect, though they interpreted them indeed more allegorically. Even the philosophers who criticized them with most severity were not their least admirers, when they ascribed[3] to them that divine inspiration or sublime enthusiasm, of which our author has largely treated elsewhere.[4]

It would, indeed, ill become any pretender to divine writing to publish his work under a character of divinity if, after all his endeavours, he came short of a consummate and just performance. In this respect the Cumean Sibyl was not so indiscreet or frantic as she might appear, perhaps, by writing her prophetic warnings and pretended inspirations upon joint leaves, which, immediately after their elaborate superscription, were torn in pieces and scattered by the wind. *You will behold a raving prophetess who, in the depths of her grotto, sings the fates and entrusts her marks and meanings to leaves. Whatever verses the maid has written down upon leaves, she sets in order and secludes in her cave. They remain undisturbed in their places and do not shift from their position. Yet these same verses, when the hinge turns and a breath of wind has stirred them and the doorway has disturbed the delicate foliage, she never cares to capture as they fly about the craggy cave, nor to restore their places, nor to put the verses together; people go away without advice and hate the abode of the sibyl.*[5] It was impossible to disprove the divinity of such writings while they could be perused only in fragments. Had the sister priestess of Delphos, who delivered herself in audible plain metre, been found at any time to have transgressed the rule of verse, it would have been difficult in those days to father the lame poetry upon Apollo himself. But where the invention of the leaves prevented the reading of a single line entire, whatever interpretations might have been made of this fragile and volatile scripture, no imperfection could be charged on the original text itself.[C]

What those volumes may have been which the disdainful Sibyl or prophetess committed to the flames, or what the remainder was which the Roman prince received and consecrated,[D] I will not pretend to judge, though it has been admitted for truth by the ancient Christian fathers, that these writings were so far sacred and divine as to have prophesied of the birth of our religious founder, and bore testimony to that Holy Writ which has preserved

[C] On the Sibyls, see p. 24n. Here Shaftesbury contrasted the practice of the Cumaean Sibyl, whose messages were inscribed on palm leaves, with that of the Delphic oracle, whose utterances were interpreted by an assistant and delivered in verse.

[D] Aulus Gellius, in *Attic Nights*, 1.19, recorded that an old woman offered to sell nine Sybilline books to the last Roman king, Tarquin the Proud, and that, before the negotiations were over, six had been burnt.

[3] See pp. 27–8.
[4] In *A Letter Concerning Enthusiasm* and *Miscellany* II, Chapters 1 and 2.
[5] Virgil, *Aeneid* 3:443–52.

his memory and is justly held in the highest degree sacred among Christians.[6]

The policy, however, of old Rome was such as not absolutely to rest the authority of their religion on any composition of literature. The Sibylline volumes were kept safely locked and inspected only by such as were ordained or deputed for that purpose. And in this policy the new Rome has followed their example in scrupling to annex the supreme authority and sacred character of infallibility to Scripture itself, and in refusing to submit that Scripture to public judgment, or to any eye or ear but what they qualify for the inspection of such sacred mysteries.

The Mahometan clergy seem to have a different policy. They boldly rest the foundation of their religion on a book: such a one as, according to their pretension, is not only perfect but inimitable. Were a real man of letters and a just critic permitted to examine this scripture by the known rules of art, he would soon perhaps refute this plea. But so barbarous is the accompanying policy and temper of these Eastern religionists that they discourage and in effect extinguish all true learning, science and the politer arts, in company with the ancient authors and languages, which they set aside, and, by this infallible method, leave their sacred writ the sole standard of literate performance. For being compared to nothing beside itself, or what is of an inferior kind, it must undoubtedly be thought incomparable.

It will be yielded, surely, to the honour of the Christian world that their faith, especially that of the Protestant churches, stands on a more generous foundation. They not only allow comparison of authors but are content to derive their proofs of the validity of their sacred record and revelation even from those authors called profane, as being well apprised, according to the maxim of our divine master, that, 'in what we bear witness only to ourselves, our witness cannot be established as a truth'.[7] So that, there being at present no immediate testimony of miracle or sign in behalf of Holy Writ, and there being in its own particular composition or style nothing miraculous or self-convincing, if the collateral testimony of other ancient records, historians and foreign authors were destroyed or wholly lost, there would be less argument or plea remaining against that natural suspicion of those who are called sceptical, that 'the holy records themselves were no other than the pure invention or artificial compilement of an interested party in behalf of the richest corporation and most profitable monopoly which could be erected in the world'.

---

[6]   *Three books, called Sibylline, were deposited in a shrine. The Board of Fifteen come to them as though to an oracle, when the immortal gods have to be consulted in the public interest*: Aulus Gellius, *Attic Nights* 1.19.10–11. Also, Pliny, *Natural History* 13.17.88. But of this first Sibylline scripture and of other canonized books and additional sacred writ among the Romans, see what Dionysius Halicarnasseus cites (from Varro's *Roman Theologics*) in his *Roman Antiquities* 4.62.

[7]   John 5.31.

Thus, in reality, the interest of our pious clergy is necessarily joined with that of ancient letters and polite learning. By this they perpetually refute the crafty arguments of those objectors. When they abandon this, they resign their cause. When they strike at it, they strike even at the root and foundation of our holy faith and weaken that pillar on which the whole fabric of our religion depends.

It belongs to mere enthusiasts and fanatics to plead the sufficiency of a reiterate translated text, derived to them through so many channels and subjected to so many variations, of which they are wholly ignorant. Yet, would they persuade us, it seems, that from hence alone they can recognize the Divine Spirit and receive it in themselves, unsubject, as they imagine, to any rule and superior to what they themselves often call the dead letter and unprofitable science. This, anyone may see, is building castles in the air and demolishing them again at pleasure, as the exercise of an aerial fancy or heated imagination.

But the judicious divines of the established Christian churches have sufficiently condemned this manner. They are far from resting their religion on the common aspect or obvious form of their vulgar Bible, as it presents itself in the printed copy or modern version. Neither do they in the original itself represent it to us as a very masterpiece of writing, or as absolutely perfect in the purity and justness either of style or composition. They allow the holy authors to have written according to their best faculties and the strength of their natural genius: 'A shepherd, like a shepherd, and a prince, like a prince; a man of reading and advanced in letters, like a proficient in the kind; and a man of meaner capacity and reading, like one of the ordinary sort, in his own common idiom and imperfect manner of narration.'

It is the substance only of the narrative and the principal facts confirming the authority of the revelation which our divines think themselves concerned to prove according to the best evidence of which the matter itself is capable. And while the sacred authors themselves allude not only to the annals and histories of the heathen world but even to the philosophical works, the regular poems,[8] the very plays and comedies[9] of the learned and polite ancients, it must be owned that, as those ancient writings are impaired or lost, not only the light

---

[8] Aratus in Acts 17.28 and Epimenides in Titus 1.12. For so the holy apostle deigned to speak of a heathen poet, a physiologist and divine, who prophesied of events, wrought miracles and was received as an inspired writer and author of revelations in the chief cities and states of Greece. [Acts quoted *Phaenomena* 5, an astronomical poem by Aratus, *c.* 315 – *c.* 239 BC, a Greek poet at the Macedonian court: 'For in him we live and move and and have our being; as certain also of your own poets have said, for we are also his offspring.' In the epistle to Titus, Paul did not name Epimenides, a semi-legendary religious leader from Crete; but a century later Clement of Alexandria asserted that Paul was referring to the Cretan when he wrote, 'One of themselves, even one of their own prophets, said, "The Cretans are always liars, evil beasts, slow bellies."']

[9] Menander in 1 Corinthians 15.33. ['Be not deceived: evil communications corrupt good manners.' Paul quoted a surviving line from Menander's *Thais* (218K).]

and clearness of Holy Writ but even the evidence itself of its main facts must in proportion be diminished and brought in question. So ill advised were those devout churchmen heretofore who, in the height of zeal, did their utmost to destroy all footsteps of heathen literature and consequently all further use of learning or antiquity.[10]

---

[10] Even in the sixth century the famed Gregory, Bishop of Rome, who is so highly celebrated for having planted the Christian religion by his missionary monks in our English nation of heathen Saxons, was so far from being a cultivator or supporter of arts or letters that he carried on a kind of general massacre upon every product of human wit. His own words in a letter to one of the French bishops, a man of the highest consideration and merit (as a noted modern critic and satirical genius of that nation acknowledges), are as follows: *Something has come to our attention which we cannot mention without shame, that your fraternity is expounding grammar to some. We have been so upset at this, and we have viewed it with such great contempt, we turned what has been reported into groaning and sadness, because the praises of Christ do not belong in a single mouth with praises of Jupiter . . . Hence, if afterwards the information that has been brought to us proves to be false, and it is the case that you have not devoted your attentions to trifles and secular literature, we give thanks to our God who did not allow your heart to be stained with blasphemous praises of wickednesses*: Gregory I (the Great), 'Epistles' 9.48, *Opera* [Works] (Paris, 1533), p. 444. And in his dedication, or first preface, to his 'Morals', after some very insipid rhetoric and figurative dialect, employed against the study and art of speech, he has another fling at the classic authors and discipline, betraying his inveterate hatred to ancient learning as well as the natural effect of this zealot-passion in his own barbarity, both of style and manners. His words are: *Hence I have scorned observing the art of eloquence, which the teachings of an alien education are introducing. For just as the tenor of this letter attests, I do not avoid a clash of m-sounds; I do not steer clear of a mingling of barbarisms; I spurn careful attention to positionings and changings of prepositions and inflections, because I am most firmly of the opinion that it is unworthy for me to constrain the words of the heavenly oracle beneath the rubrics of Donatus* [sig. hh 5 recto]. That he carried this savage zeal of his so far as to destroy (what in him lay) the whole body of learning, with all the classic authors then in being, was generally believed. And (what was yet more notorious and unnatural in a Roman pontiff) the destruction of the statues, sculptures and finest pieces of antiquity in Rome was charged on him by his successor in the See, as, besides [Bartholomaeus Sacchi de] Platina [in *Historia de vitis pontificum romanorum* (History of the lives of the Roman popes) (Venice, 1479)], another writer of his life, without the least apology, confesses. See in the above-cited edition of St Gregory's works, at the beginning, namely *Vita Divi Gregorii* [Life of St Gregory] by Joannes Laziardus [sig. gg 8 recto]. It is no wonder, therefore, if other writers have given account of that sally of the prelate's zeal against the books and learning of the ancients, for which the reason alleged was very extraordinary, that 'the Holy Scriptures would be the better relished and receive a considerable advantage by the destruction of these rivals'. It seems they had no very high idea of the Holy Scriptures when they supposed them such losers by a comparison. However, it was thought advisable by other Fathers (who had a like view) to frame new pieces of literature after the model of these condemned ancients. Hence those ridiculous attempts of new heroic poems, new epics and dramatics, new Homers, Euripideses, Menanders, which were with so much pains and so little effect industriously set afoot by the zealous priesthood, when ignorance prevailed and the hierarchal dominion was so universal. But though their power had well nigh compassed the destruction of those great originals, they were far from being able to procure any reception for their puny imitations. The mock works have lain in their deserved obscurity, as will all other attempts of that kind, concerning which our author has already given his opinion: see pp. 159–61. But as to the ill policy as well as barbarity of this zealot enmity against the works of the ancients, a foreign Protestant divine and most learned defender of religion, making the best excuse he can for the Greek Fathers and endeavouring to clear them from this general charge of havoc and massacre committed upon science and erudition, has these words: *If it is the case, here is still a*

But happily the zeal of this kind is now left as proper only to those despised and ignorant modern enthusiasts we have described. The Roman Church itself is so recovered from this primitive fanaticism that their great men, and even their pontiffs, are found ready to give their helping hand and confer their bounty liberally towards the advancement of all ancient and polite learning.[11] They justly observe that their very traditions stand in need of some collateral proof. The conservation of these other ancient and disinterested authors they wisely judge essential to the credibility of those principal facts on which the whole religious history and tradition depend.

It would indeed be in vain for us to bring a Pontius Pilate into our Creed, and recite what happened under him in Judea, if we knew not under whom he himself governed, whose authority he had or what character he bore in that remote country and amid a foreign people.[E] In the same manner, it would be in vain for a Roman pontiff to derive his title to spiritual sovereignty from the seat, influence, power and donation of the Roman Caesars and their successors if it appeared not by any history or collateral testimony who the first Caesars were and how they came possessed of that universal power and long residence of dominion.

My reader, doubtless, by this time must begin to wonder through what labyrinth of speculation and odd texture of capricious reflections I am offering to conduct him. But he will not, I presume, be altogether displeased with me when I give him to understand that, being now come into my last miscellany and being sensible of the little courtship I have paid him, comparatively with what is practised in that kind by other modern authors, I am willing, by way of compensation, to express my loyalty or homage towards him and show by

---

new reason for disdaining the patriarchs of Constantinople, who were nothing less than good men in other respects. But I have difficulty believing it because there remain for us poets infinitely more obscene than those who are lost. No one doubts that Aristophanes was much more obscene than Menander was. Plutarch is a good witness of this in the comparison he made of these two poets. However, it could have happened that some ecclesiastical enemies of belles lettres dealt with things as Laonicus Chalcondyles says, without thinking that, in preserving all of Greek antiquity, they would preserve the language of their predecessors and an infinity of facts that would serve very much for the understanding and confirmation of sacred history and even of the Christian religion. These men should at least have preserved the ancient histories of the Oriental peoples, such as the Chaldeans, the Tyrians and the Egyptians; they acted more out of ignorance and negligence than out of reason, Bibliothèque choisie 14 (1708): 132–3. [These remarks by Jean Le Clerc appeared in a review of a 1707 work by Petrus Alcyonius, who discussed the destruction of ancient literary texts by Orthodox clergy at Constantinople.]

[11] Such a one is the present prince, Clement XI, an encourager of all arts and sciences. [Clement XI, Giovanni Francesco Albani, 1649–1721, was pope from 1700 to 1721.]

[E] Pontius Pilate, Roman governor of Judaea from AD 26 to 36 under the Emperor Tiberius, had difficulty managing the Jewish population who dominated the area. Jesus, after being condemned by the high Jewish court, was brought before Pilate, who used his authority to impose capital punishment, in this case, crucifixion.

my natural sentiments and principles what particular deference and high respect I think to be his due.

The issue therefore of this long deduction is, in the first place, with due compliments in my capacity of author, and in the name of all modest workmen willingly joining with me in this representation, to congratulate our English reader on the establishment of what is so advantageous to himself – I mean that mutual relation between him and ourselves, which naturally turns so much to his advantage and makes us to be in reality the subservient party. And, in this respect, it is to be hoped he will long enjoy his just superiority and privilege over his humble servants who compose and labour for his sake. The relation in all likelihood must still continue and be improved. Our common religion and Christianity, founded on letters and Scripture, promises thus much. Nor is this hope likely to fail us while readers are really allowed *the liberty to read*, that is to say, *to examine, construe and remark with understanding.* Learning and science must of necessity flourish while the language of the wisest and most learned of nations is acknowledged to contain the principal and essential part of our holy revelation.[F] And criticism, examinations, judgments, literate labours and inquiries must still be in repute and practice while ancient authors, so necessary to the support of the sacred volumes, are in request and afford employment of such infinite extent to us moderns, of whatever degree, who are desirous to signalize ourselves by any achievement in letters and be considered as the investigators of knowledge and politeness.

I may undoubtedly, by virtue of my preceding argument in behalf of criticism, be allowed, without suspicion of flattery or mere courtship, to assert the reader's privilege above the author and assign to him, as I have done, the upper hand and place of honour. As to fact, we know for certain that the greatest of philosophers, the very founder of philosophy itself, was no author.[G] Nor did the divine author and founder of our religion condescend to be an author in this other respect.[H] He who could best have given us the history of his own life, with the entire sermons and divine discourses which he made in public, was pleased to leave it to others 'to take in hand'.[12] As there were many, it

---

[F]   Greek was the language in which most of the New Testament was originally written.
[G]   Socrates.
[H]   Jesus.

[12] So Luke 1.1–4: '(1) Forasmuch as many have taken in hand to set forth in order a declaration (exposition or narrative) of those things which are most surely believed among (or were fulfilled in or among) us, (2) Even as they delivered them unto us, which from the beginning were eyewitnesses and ministers of the word, (3) It seemed good to me also, having had perfect understanding of all things from the very first (or having looked back and searched accurately into all matters from the beginning or highest time) to write unto thee in order, most excellent Theophilus, (4) That thou mightest know the certainty (or validity, sound discussion) of those things wherein thou hast been instructed (or catechized).' Whether the words πεπληροφορημένων ἐν ἡμῖν in the first verse should be rendered 'believed among' or 'fulfilled

seems, long afterwards, who did and undertook accordingly 'to write in order, and as seemed good to them, for the better information of particular persons, what was then believed among the initiated or catechized from tradition and early instruction in their youth, or what had been transmitted by report from such as were the presumed auditors and eye-witnesses of those things in former time'.

Whether those sacred books ascribed to the divine legislator of the Jews and which treat of his death, burial and succession[13] as well as of his life and actions, are strictly to be understood as coming from the immediate pen of that holy founder or rather from some other inspired hand, guided by the same influencing spirit, I will not presume so much as to examine or inquire. But in general we find that, both as to public concerns in religion and in philosophy, the great and eminent actors were of a rank superior to the writing worthies. The great Athenian legislator, though noted as a poetical genius, cannot be esteemed an author for the sake of some few verses he may occasionally have made.[1] Nor was the great Spartan founder a poet himself, though author or redeemer (if I may so express it) to the greatest and best of poets, who owed in a manner his form and being to the accurate searches and collections of that great patron.[J] The politicians and civil sages, who were fitted in all respects for the great scene of business, could not, it seems, be well taken out of it to attend the slender and minute affairs of letters and scholastic science.

It is true, indeed, that, without a capacity for action and a knowledge of the world and mankind, there can be no author naturally qualified to write with dignity or execute any noble or great design. But there are many who, with

---

in' or 'among us' may depend on the different reading of the original. For in some copies the ἐν next following is left out. However, the exact interpreters or verbal translators render it 'fulfilled': see Benedictus Arias Montanus' polyglot edition of the Old and New Testaments, published by Christopher Plantin, Antwerp, 1584. In verse 4, the word 'certainty', ἀσφάλειαν, is interpreted ἀκρίβειαν, 'validity', 'soundness', 'good foundation', from the sense of the preceding verse. See the late edition [of the Greek New Testament] of our learned Dr [John] Mill, as improved by Ludolph Kuster, Rotterdam, 1710, p. 122. For the word 'catechized', κατηχήθης (the last of the fourth verse), Robertus Constantinus has this explanation of it: *It was the custom for theologians of old in Egypt to transmit their sacred rites to posterity only orally as though handing them down. Among the Christians, those who were candidates for baptism received the secret rite of the Christian faith by word of mouth, without texts. This is what Paul and Luke call* κατηχεῖν. *Hence those who were instructed were called catechumens, those who instructed, catechists* [*Lexicon Graecolatinum*, 2nd edition (Geneva, 1592), II, p. 67].

13 Deuteronomy 34.5–7ff. [The five 'books of Moses', the Hebrew *Torah* or, in Greek, the Pentateuch.]

1   On Solon, the Athenian lawgiver of the late seventh and early sixth centuries BC, as poet, see Plutarch, *Solon* 3.3, *Parallel Lives*.

J   According to Plutarch, Lycurgus, the legendary Spartan legislator, encountered Homer's writings when on his youthful travels in Ionia in Asia Minor and was responsible for transcribing and ordering them and making them known among the rest of the Greeks: *Lycurgus* 4.4, *Parallel Lives*.

the highest capacity for business, are by their fortune denied the privilege of that higher sphere. As there are others who, having once moved in it, have been afterwards, by many impediments and obstructions, necessitated to retire and exert their genius in this lower degree.[K]

It is to some catastrophe of this kind that we owe the noblest historians (even the two princes and fathers of history)[L] as well as the greatest philosophical writers, the founder of the Academy[M] and others, who were also noble in respect of their birth and fitted for the highest stations in the public, but discouraged from engaging in it on account of some misfortunes experienced either in their own persons or that of their near friends.

It is to the early banishment and long retirement of a heroic youth out of his native country that we owe an original system of works, the politest, wisest, usefullest, and, to those who can understand the divineness of a just simplicity, the most amiable and even the most elevating and exalting of all uninspired and merely human authors.[14]

To this fortune we owe some of the greatest of the ancient poets. It was this chance which produced the muse of an exalted Grecian lyric[15] and of his follower Horace,[16] whose character, though easy to be gathered from history and his own works, is little observed by any of his commentators: the general idea conceived of him being drawn chiefly from his precarious and low circumstances at Court, after the forfeiture of his estate under the usurpation and conquest of an Octavius and the ministry of a Maecenas, not from his better condition and nobler employments in earlier days, under the favour and friendship of greater and better men, while the Roman state and liberty subsisted. For of this change he himself, as great a courtier as he seemed afterwards, gives sufficient intimation.[17]

[K] Sensitive to the fact that his own participation in the world of political action was limited, Shaftesbury insisted on the civic importance of his thinking and writing. Though retired at Naples at the end of his life, he wrote: 'Whatever my studies or amusements are, I endeavour still to turn them towards the interests of virtue and liberty in general' (Shaftesbury to Benjamin Furley, 22 March 1712, PRO 30/24/21/200).

[L] Herodotus and Thucydides.

[M] Plato.

[14] *The most agreeable and graceful Xenophon*, as Athenaeus calls him, *The Deipnosophists* 11.504c. See p. 114.

[15] *And you, Alcaeus, sounding more fully with golden music the harshnesses of seafaring, of flight, the harshnesses of war*: Horace, *Odes* 2.13.26–8.

[16] *Come tell, my lyre, a Latin song though first you were tuned by the citizen of Lesbos who, if fierce in war . . .* : Horace, *Odes* 1.32.3–6.

[17] *But harsh times dislodged me from a pleasant place and, though inexperienced, the swell of civil war bore me into arms that would be no answer to the might of Caesar Augustus. As soon as Philippi gave me my discharge, brought low with wings clipped and without the resources of paternal house and estate, the audacity of poverty drove me to be a poet*: Horace, *Epistles* 2.2.46–52. Also: *But once, because a Roman legion obeyed me as an officer*: Horace, *Satires* 1.6.47–8. Namely, under Brutus. Whence again that natural boast: *That I pleased [placuisse] the first men of this city in war and*

Let authors therefore know themselves and, though conscious of worth, virtue and a genius, such as may justly place them above flattery or mean courtship to their reader, yet let them reflect that, as authors merely, they are but of the second rank of men. And let the reader withal consider, that *when he unworthily resigns the place of honour and surrenders his taste or judgment to an author of ever so great a name or venerable antiquity and not to reason and truth, at whatever hazard, he not only betrays himself but withal the common cause of author and reader, the interest of letters and knowledge and the chief liberty, privilege and prerogative of the rational part of mankind.*

It is related in the history of the Cappadocians that, being offered their liberty by the Romans and permitted to govern themselves by their own laws and constitutions, they were much terrified at the proposal and, as if some sore harm had been intended them, humbly made it their request that 'they might be governed by arbitrary power, and that an absolute governor might without delay be appointed over them at the discretion of the Romans'.[N] For such was their disposition towards mere slavery and subjection that they dared not pretend so much as to choose their own master. So essential they thought slavery and so divine a thing the right of mastership, that they dared not be so free even as to presume to give themselves that blessing, which they chose to leave rather to providence, fortune or a conqueror to bestow upon them. They dared not make a king but would rather take one from their powerful neighbours.

---

peace *[belli domique]*: Horace, *Epistles* 1.20.23. And again: *Envy will be reluctant to admit that I have ever lived [vixisse] with great men [magni]*: Horace, *Satires* 2.1.76–7. Where the *vixisse* shows plainly whom he principally meant by his *magni*, his early patrons and great men in the State, his apology and defence here (as well as in his fourth and sixth satires of his first book and his second epistle of his second and elsewhere) being supported still by the open and bold assertion of his good education (equal to the highest senators and under the best masters), his employments at home and abroad, and his early commerce and familiarity with former great men, before these his new friendships and this latter Court acquaintance, which was now envied him by his adversaries. *Now, because I live on terms of intimacy with you, Maecenas, but once, because a Roman legion obeyed me as an officer*: *Satires* 1.6.47–8. The reproach now was with respect to a Maecenas or Augustus. It was the same formerly with respect to a Brutus and those who were then the principal and leading men. The complaint or murmur against him on account of his being an upstart or favourite under a Maecenas and Augustus could not be answered by a *vixisse* relating to the same persons, any more than his *placuisse* joined with his *belli domique* could relate to those under whom he never went to war nor would ever consent to bear any honours. For so he himself distinguishes (to Maecenas): *[this instance is different from that] because, although someone may rightly perhaps begrudge me honour, it would not be so to begrudge too the fact that you are my friend*: *Satires* 1.6.49–50. He was formerly an actor and in the ministry of affairs, now only a friend to a minister, himself still a private and retired man. That he refused Augustus' offer of the secretaryship is well known. But in these circumstances, the politeness as well as artifice of Horace is admirable in making futurity or posterity to be the speaking party in both those places, where he suggests his intimacy and favour with the great, that there might in some measure be room left (though in strictness there was scarce any) for an Octavius and a Maecenas to be included. See p. 121n.

N Strabo, *Geography* 12.2.11.

Had they been necessitated to come to an election, the horror of such a use of liberty in government would perhaps have determined them to choose blindfold or leave it to the decision of the commonest lot, cast of die, cross or pile or whatever it were which might best enable them to clear themselves of the heinous charge of using the least foresight, choice or prudence in such an affair.

I should think it a great misfortune were my reader of the number of those who, in a kind of Cappadocian spirit, could easily be terrified with the proposal of giving him his liberty and making him his own judge. My endeavour, I must confess, has been to show him his just prerogative in this respect and to give him the sharpest eye over his author, invite him to criticize honestly without favour or affection and with the utmost bent of his parts and judgment. On this account it may be objected to me, perhaps, that 'I am not a little vain and presumptuous in my own as well as in my author's behalf, who can thus, as it were, challenge my reader to a trial of his keenest wit'.

But to this I answer that, should I have the good fortune to raise the masterly spirit of just criticism in my readers and exalt them ever so little above the lazy, timorous, over-modest or resigned state in which the generality of them remain, though by this very spirit I myself might possibly meet my doom, I should, however, abundantly congratulate with myself on these my low flights, be proud of having plumed the arrows of better wits and furnished artillery or ammunition of any kind to those powers to which I myself had fallen a victim. *I shall perform the role of a whetstone.*[18]

I could reconcile my ambition in this respect to what I call my loyalty to the reader, and say of his elevation in criticism and judgment what a Roman princess said of her son's advancement to empire: *Let him murder me so long as he has power.*[19]

Had I been a Spanish Cervantes and, with success equal to that comic author, had destroyed the reigning taste of Gothic or Moorish chivalry,[O] I could afterwards contentedly have seen my burlesque work itself despised and set aside, when it had wrought its intended effect and destroyed those giants and monsters of the brain against which it was originally designed. Without regard, therefore, to the prevailing relish or taste which, in my own person, I may unhappily experience, when these my miscellaneous works are leisurely examined, I shall proceed still in my endeavour to refine my reader's palate, whetting and sharpening it the best I can for use and practice in the lower subjects, that by this exercise it may acquire the greater keenness and be of so much the

---

[O] Miguel de Cervantes Saavedra, 1547–1616, Spanish novelist, playwright and poet wrote his masterwork, *Don Quixote*, with the expressed intent of ridiculing the extravagances and absurdities of contemporary romances in the chivalric vein.

[18] Horace, *The Art of Poetry* 304.

[19] Tacitus, *Annals* 14.9. [With foresight, Agrippina of her son, the future emperor, Nero, who did arrange her demise.]

better effect in subjects of a higher kind, which relate to his chief happiness, his liberty and manhood.

Supposing me therefore a mere comic humorist in respect of those inferior subjects, which, after the manner of my familiar prose satire, I presume to criticize, may not I be allowed to ask 'whether there remains not still among us noble Britons something of that original barbarous and Gothic relish not wholly purged away, when, even at this hour, romances and gallantries of like sort, together with works as monstrous of other kinds, are current and in vogue, even with the people who constitute our reputed polite world'? Need I on this account refer again to our author, where he treats in general of the style and manner of our modern authors, from the divine to the comedian?[20] What person is there of the least judgment or understanding who cannot easily, and without the help of a divine or rigid moralist,[P] observe the lame condition of our English stage, which nevertheless is found the rendezvous and chief entertainment of our best company, and from whence in all probability our youth will continue to draw their notion of manners and their taste of life more directly and naturally than from the rehearsals and declamations of a graver theatre?

Let those whose business it is advance, as they best can, the benefit of that sacred oratory, which we have lately seen and are still like to see employed to various purposes and further designs than that of instructing us in religion or manners. Let them in that high scene endeavour to refine our taste and judgment in sacred matters. It is the good critic's task to amend our common stage, nor ought this dramatic performance to be decried or sentenced by those critics of a higher sphere. The practice and art is honest in itself. Our foundations are well laid. And, in the main, our English stage, as has been remarked,[21] is capable of the highest improvement, as well from the present genius of our nation as from the rich ore of our early poets in this kind. But faults are easier imitated than beauties.

We find, indeed, our theatre become of late the subject of a growing criticism. We hear it openly complained that 'in our newer plays as well as in our older, in comedy as well as tragedy, the stage presents a proper scene of uproar: duels fought; swords drawn, many of a side; wounds given and sometimes dressed too; the surgeon called and the patient probed and tented upon the spot'; that 'in our tragedy nothing is so common as wheels, racks and gibbets

---

[P] As a critic of the contemporary stage, Shaftesbury found himself in uncomfortable agreement with Jeremy Collier, who initiated a public debate about the moral influence of the theatre with his *Short View of the Immorality and Profaneness of the English Stage* (1698). Collier, 1650–1726, was an Anglican clergyman who refused to take the oath of allegiance to William and Mary in 1689 (a non-juror) and remained loyal to the deposed James II (a Jacobite).

[20] Namely, in *Soliloquy*.
[21] See pp. 97–8, 100, 116–17, 123–4.

properly adorned, executions decently performed, headless bodies and bodiless heads exposed to view, battles fought, murders committed, and the dead carried off in great numbers'. Such is our politeness!

Nor are these plays, on this account, the less frequented by either of the sexes, which inclines me to favour the conceit our author has suggested concerning the mutual correspondence and relation between our royal theatre and popular circus or bear-garden.[22] For in the former of these assemblies, it is undeniable that at least the two upper regions or galleries contain such spectators as indifferently frequent each place of sport. So that it is no wonder we hear such applause resounded on the victories of an Almanzor,[Q] when the same parties had possibly no later than the day before bestowed their applause as freely on the victorious butcher, the hero of another stage, where amid various frays, bestial and human blood, promiscuous wounds and slaughter, one sex are observed as frequent and as pleased spectators as the other, and sometimes not spectators only, but actors in the gladiatorian parts. These congregations, which we may be apt to call heathenish (though in reality never known among the politer heathens), are in our Christian nation unconcernedly allowed and tolerated as no way injurious to religious interests, whatever effect they may be found to have on national manners, humanity and civil life.[23] Of such indulgencies as these we hear no complaints. Nor are any assemblies, though of the most barbarous and enormous kind, so offensive, it seems, to men of zeal as religious assemblies of a different fashion or habit from their own.

I am sorry to say that, though in the many parts of poetry our attempts have been high and noble, yet in general the taste of wit and letters lies much upon a level with what relates to our stage.

I can readily allow to our British genius what was allowed to the Roman heretofore: *A nature sublime and sharp: for his spirit is sufficient for tragedy and his daring brings success.*[24] But then I must add too that the excessive indulgence and favour shown to our authors, on account of what their mere genius and flowing vein afford, has rendered them intolerably supine, conceited and admirers of themselves. The public having once suffered them to take the ascendant, they become, like flattered princes, impatient of contradiction or advice. They think it a disgrace to be criticized, even by a friend, or to reform at his desire what they themselves are fully convinced is negligent and uncorrect. *But he fears the eraser and considers it beneath him in his writings.*[25]

[Q] The protagonist of John Dryden's heroic drama in two parts, *The Conquest of Granada*, published in 1672.

[22] See pp. 121–2.
[23] See p. 121.
[24] Horace, *Epistles* 2.1.165–6.
[25] Horace, *Epistles* 2.1.167.

The *limae labor*[26] is the great grievance with our countrymen. An English author would be all genius. He would reap the fruits of art but without study, pains or application. He thinks it necessary, indeed, lest his learning should be called in question, to show the world that he errs knowingly against the rules of art. And for this reason, whatever piece he publishes at any time, he seldom fails, in some prefixed apology, to speak in such a manner of criticism and art as may confound the ordinary reader and prevent him from taking up a part which, should he once assume, would prove fatal to the impotent and mean performance.

It were to be wished that, when once our authors had considered of a model or plan and attained the knowledge of a whole and parts,[27] when from this beginning they had proceeded to morals and the knowledge of what is called poetic manners and truth,[28] when they had learned to reject false thought,

[26] Horace, *The Art of Poetry* 291. [The labour of refining.]

[27] *A whole is that which has a beginning and a middle and an end. A beginning is that which does not of necessity follow something else, but after it something else naturally exists or develops. An end is the opposite, that which naturally exists after something else either by necessity or as a general rule, but nothing else comes after this. A middle is that which comes after something else, and another thing comes after it*: Aristotle, *Poetics* 7.3–6. And in the following chapter, *A unitary plot is not, as some believe, a matter of being concerned with a single individual*: Aristotle, *Poetics* 8.1. *Finally then let it be what you want so long as it is simple and single*: Horace, *The Art of Poetry* 23. See pp. 66–7. It is an infallible proof of the want of just integrity in every writing, from the epopee or heroic poem down to the familiar epistle or slightest essay, either in verse or prose, if every several part or portion fits not its proper place so exactly that the least transposition would be impracticable. Whatever is episodic, though perhaps it be a whole and in itself entire, yet being inserted as a part in a work of greater length, it must appear only in its due place. And that place alone can be called its due one which alone befits it. If there be any passage in the middle or end which might have stood in the beginning, or any in the beginning which might have stood as well in the middle or end, there is properly in such a piece neither beginning, middle nor end. It is a mere rhapsody, not a work. And the more it assumes the air or appearance of a real work, the more ridiculous it becomes. See pp. 66–7, 349.

[28] *I shall bid the learned imitator to look to the example of life and character and thence to draw true voices*: Horace, *The Art of Poetry* 317–18. The chief of ancient critics, we know, extols Homer above all things for understanding how 'to lie in perfection', as the passage shows which we have cited above [Aristotle, *Poetics* 24.18]: see p. 154. His lies, according to that master's opinion and the judgment of many of the gravest and most venerable writers, were in themselves the justest moral truths and exhibitive of the best doctrine and instruction in life and manners.

It may be asked, perhaps, 'How comes the poet, then, to draw no single pattern of the kind, no perfect character, in either of his heroic pieces?'

I answer that, should he attempt to do it, he would as a poet be preposterous and false. It is not the possible but the probable and likely which must be the poet's guide in manners. By this he wins attention and moves the conscious reader or spectator, who judges best from within, by what he naturally feels and experiences in his own heart. The perfection of virtue is from long art and management, self-control and, as it were, force on nature. But the common auditor or spectator, who seeks pleasure only and loves to engage his passion by view of other passion and emotion, comprehends little of the restraints, allays and corrections which form this new and artificial creature. For such indeed is *the truly virtuous man*, whose art, though ever so natural in itself or justly founded in reason and nature, is an improvement far beyond the

embarrassing and mixed metaphors, the ridiculous point in comedy, and the false sublime and bombast in heroic, they would at last have some regard to numbers, harmony and an ear[29] and correct, as far as possible, the harsh sounds of our language, in poetry at least, if not in prose.

----

common stamp or known character of humankind. And thus the completely virtuous and perfect character is unpoetical and false. Effects must not appear where causes must necessarily remain unknown and incomprehensible. A hero without passion is in poetry as absurd as a hero without life or action. Now if passion be allowed, passionate action must ensue. The same heroic genius and seeming magnanimity which transport us when beheld are naturally transporting in the lives and manners of the great who are described to us. And thus the able designer, who feigns in behalf of truth and draws his characters after the moral rule, fails not to discover nature's propensity and assigns to these high spirits their proper exorbitancy and inclination to exceed in that tone or species of passion, which constitutes the eminent or shining part of each poetical character. The passion of an Achilles is towards that glory which is acquired by arms and personal valour. In favour of this character, we forgive the generous youth his excess of ardour in the field and his resentment when injured and provoked in council and by his allies. The passion of an Ulysses is towards that glory which is acquired by prudence, wisdom and ability in affairs. It is in favour of this character that we forgive him his subtle, crafty and deceitful air, since the intriguing spirit, the over-reaching manner and over-refinement of art and policy are as naturally incident to the experienced and thorough politician as sudden resentment, indiscreet and rash behaviour to the open undesigning character of a warlike youth. The gigantic force and military toil of an Ajax would not be so easily credible or engaging but for the honest simplicity of his nature and the heaviness of his parts and genius. For, strength of body being so often noted by us as unattended with equal parts and strength of mind, when we see this natural effect expressed and find our secret and malicious kind of reasoning confirmed on this hand, we yield to any hyperbole of our poet on the other. He has afterwards his full scope and liberty of enlarging and exceeding in the peculiar virtue and excellence of his hero. He may lie splendidly, raise wonder and be as astonishing as he pleases. Everything will be allowed him in return for this frank allowance. Thus the tongue of a Nestor may work prodigies while the accompanying allays of a rhetorical fluency and aged experience are kept in view. An Agamemnon may be admired as a noble and wise chief while a certain princely haughtiness, a stiffness and stately carriage natural to the character, are represented in his person and noted in their ill effects. For thus the excesses of every character are by the poet redressed. And the misfortunes naturally attending such excesses being justly applied, our passions, while in the strongest manner engaged and moved, are in the wholesomest and most effectual manner corrected and purged. Were a man to form himself by one single pattern or original, however perfect, he would himself be a mere copy. But while he draws from various models, he is original, natural and unaffected. We see in outward carriage and behaviour how ridiculous anyone becomes who imitates another, be he ever so graceful. They are mean spirits who love to copy merely. Nothing is agreeable or natural but what is original. Our manners, like our faces, though ever so beautiful, must differ in their beauty. An over-regularity is next to a deformity. And in a poem (whether epic or dramatic) a complete and perfect character is the greatest monster and, of all poetic fictions, not only the least engaging but the least moral and improving. Thus much by way of remark upon poetical truth and the just fiction or artful lying of the able poet, according to the judgment of the master-critic. What Horace expresses of the same lying virtue is of an easier sense and needs no explanation. *And so does he make fictions, so does he blend false with true; so that the middle does not clash with the beginning, the end with the middle*: Horace, *The Art of Poetry* 151–2. The same may be observed not only in heroic draughts, but in the inferior characters of comedy: *How like himself each is!* (Terence, *Phormio*, 3.2). See pp. 5, 65–6, 150, 156–7n.

[29]   See p. 97.

But so much are our British poets taken up in seeking out that monstrous ornament which we call rhyme,[30] that it is no wonder if other ornaments and real graces are unthought of and left unattempted. However, since in some parts of poetry, especially in the dramatic, we have been so happy as to triumph over this barbarous taste, it is unaccountable that our poets, who from this privilege ought to undertake some further refinements, should remain still upon the same level as before. It is a shame to our authors that, in their elegant style and metred prose, there should not be found a peculiar grace and harmony resulting from a more natural and easy disengagement of their periods, and from a careful avoiding the encounter of the shocking consonants and jarring sounds to which our language is so unfortunately subject.

They have of late, it is true, reformed in some measure the gouty joints and darning work of 'whereuntos', 'wherebys', 'thereofs', 'therewiths' and the rest of this kind, by which complicated periods are so curiously strung or hooked on, one to another, after the long-spun manner of the Bar or pulpit. But to take into consideration no real accent or cadency of words, no sound or measure of syllables, to put together, at one time, a set of compounds of the longest Greek or Latin termination, and at another to let whole verses, and those too of our heroic and longest sort, pass currently in monosyllables, is, methinks, no slender negligence. If single verses, at the head or in the most emphatical places of the most considerable works, can admit of such a structure and pass for truly harmonious and poetical in this negligent form, I see no reason why

---

[30] The reader, if curious in these matters, may see Isaac Vossius, *De poematum cantu et viribus rhythmi* [On the melody of poems and the powers of rhythm (Oxford, 1673)] and what he says withal of ancient music and the degrees by which they surpass us moderns (as has been demonstrated by late mathematicians of our nation), contrary to a ridiculous notion some have had that, because in this, as in all other arts, the ancients studied simplicity and affected it as the highest perfection in their performances, they were therefore ignorant of parts and symphony. Against this, Isaac Vossius, among other authors, cites the ancient Peripatetic *On the Cosmos* at the beginning of his fifth chapter, to which he might have added another passage in Chapter 6. The suitableness of this ancient author's thought to what has been often advanced in the philosophical parts of these volumes, concerning the universal symmetry or union of the whole, may make it excusable if we add here the two passages together, in their inimitable original. *Perhaps nature desires opposites too and to bring about harmony from these, not from things that are alike, just as, doubtless, she has guided the male to the female and not each to its own kind, and joined together the first unanimity by means of opposites, not identicals. And art seems to do this too in imitating nature. For painting, in its combination of lights and darks, yellows and reds, makes the images harmonize with their originals. Music in mixing high and low sounds, and long and short, together makes a single harmony out of different sounds. And grammar, in blending vowels and consonants, accomplishes all its art out of them. This is just what was said by Heraclitus the Murky: 'combinations are whole and not whole, similarity and dissimilarity, consonance and dissonanance; and out of all one, and out of one all':* Aristotle, *On the Cosmos* 5. *A single harmony of all things singing together and dancing across heaven both comes out of one thing and ends in one thing. You would call the universe a cosmic order and not a disorder. Just as when in a chorus, when the leader commences, all the chorus of men and sometimes too of women join in the singing, creating a single harmonious mixture out of their different low and high sounds, and so too is it under God's conducting of the universe*: Aristotle, *On the Cosmos* 6. See pp. 244, 415–17n.

more verses than one or two of the same formation should not be as well admitted, or why an uninterrupted succession of these well-strung monosyllables might not be allowed to clatter after one another, like the hammers of a paper mill, without any breach of music or prejudice to the harmony of our language. But if persons who have gone no farther than a smith's anvil to gain an ear are yet likely, on fair trial, to find a plain defect in these ten-monosyllable heroics, it would follow, methinks, that even a prose author, who attempts to write politely, should endeavour to confine himself within those bounds, which can never without breach of harmony be exceeded in any just metre or agreeable pronunciation.[R]

Thus have I ventured to arraign the authority of those self-privileged writers who would exempt themselves from criticism, and save their ill-acquired reputation, by the decrial of an art on which the cause and interest of wit and letters absolutely depend. Be it they themselves or their great patrons in their behalf, who would thus arbitrarily support the credit of ill writings, the attempt, I hope, will prove unsuccessful. Be they moderns or ancients, foreigners or natives, ponderous and austere writers or airy and of the humorous kind, whoever takes refuge here or seeks protection hence, whoever joins his party or interest to this cause, it appears from the very fact and endeavour alone that there is just ground to suspect some insufficiency or imposture at the bottom. And on this account the reader, if he be wise, will the rather redouble his application and industry to examine the merit of his assuming author. If, as reader and judge, he dare once assert that liberty to which we have shown him justly entitled, he will not easily be threatened or ridiculed out of the use of his examining capacity and native privilege of criticism.

It was to this art, so well understood and practised heretofore, that the wise ancients owed whatever was consummate and perfect in their productions. It is to the same art we owe the recovery of letters in these latter ages. To this alone we must ascribe the recognition of ancient manuscripts, the discovery of what is spurious, and the discernment of whatever is genuine of those venerable remains, which have passed through such dark periods of ignorance and raised us to the improvements we now make in every science. It is to this art that even the sacred authors themselves owe their highest purity and correctness. So sacred ought the art itself to be esteemed, when from its supplies alone is formed that judicious and learned strength by which the defenders of our holy religion are able so successfully to refute the heathens, Jews, sectarians, heretics and other enemies or opposers of our primitive and ancient faith.

But having thus, after our author's example, asserted the use of criticism in all literate works, from the main frame or plan of every writing down to the

---

[R] In revising the first edition of *Characteristics* for the second, Shaftesbury frequently made note of such monosyllabic excess in his own prose and altered the words accordingly.

minutest particle, we may now proceed to exercise this art upon our author himself and, by his own rules, examine him in this his last treatise, reserving still to ourselves the same privilege of variation and excursion into other subjects, the same episodic liberty and right of wandering which we have maintained in the preceding chapters.

Chapter 2

Generation and succession of our national and modern wit. Manners of the proprietors. Corporation and joint stock. Statute against criticism. A coffeehouse committee. Mr Bayes. Other Bayeses in divinity. Censure of our author's dialogue piece and of the manner of dialogue writing used by reverend wits.

According to the common course of practice in our age, we seldom see the character of writer and that of critic united in the same person. There is, I know, a certain species of authors who subsist wholly by the criticizing or commenting practice upon others and can appear in no other form besides what this employment authorizes them to assume. They have no original character or first part, but wait for something which may be called 'a work' in order to graft upon it and come in for shares at second hand.

The penmen of this capacity and degree are, from their function and employment, distinguished by the title of Answerers. For it happens in the world that there are readers of a genius and size just fitted to these answering authors. These, if they teach them nothing else, will teach them, they think, to criticize. And though the new practising critics are of a sort unlikely ever to understand any original book or writing, they can understand or at least remember and quote the subsequent reflections, flouts and jeers which may accidentally be made on such a piece. Wherever a gentleman of this sort happens at any time to be in company, you shall no sooner hear a new book spoken of than it will be asked, 'Who has answered it?' or 'When is there an answer to come out?' Now the answer, as our gentleman knows, must needs be newer than the book, and the newer a thing is, the more fashionable still and the genteeler the subject of discourse. For this the bookseller knows how to fit our gentleman to a nicety, for he has commonly an answer ready bespoke, and perhaps finished, by the time his new book comes abroad. And it is odds but our fashionable gentleman, who takes both together, may read the latter first and drop the other for good and all.

But of these answering wits and the manner of rejoinders and reiterate replies, we have said what is sufficient in a former miscellany.[31] We need only remark in general that *it is necessary a writing critic should understand how to write*. And though every writer is not bound to show himself in the capacity

---

[31] See *Miscellany* I, Chapter 2.

of critic, every writing critic is bound to show himself capable of being a writer. For if he be apparently impotent in this latter kind, he is to be denied all title or character in the other.

To censure merely what another person writes, to twitch, snap, snub up or banter, to torture sentences and phrases, turn a few expressions into ridicule or write what is nowadays called *An Answer* to any piece, is not sufficient to constitute what is properly esteemed a writer or author in due form. For this reason, though there are many Answerers seen abroad, there are few or no critics or satirists. But whatever may be the state of controversy in our religious or politic concerns, it is certain that, in the mere literate world, affairs are managed with a better understanding between the principal parties concerned. The writers or authors in possession have an easier time than any ministry or religious party which is uppermost. They have found a way, by decrying all criticism in general, to get rid of their dissenters and prevent all pretences to further reformation in their state. The critic is made to appear distinct and of another species, wholly different from the writer. None who have a genius for writing and can perform with any success are presumed so ill-natured or illiberal as to endeavour to signalize themselves in criticism.

It is not difficult, however, to imagine why this practical difference between writer and critic has been so generally established among us as to make the provinces seem wholly distinct and irreconcilable. The forward wits who, without waiting their due time or performing their requisite studies, start up in the world as authors, having with little pains or judgment, and by the strength of fancy merely, acquired a name with mankind, can on no account afterwards submit to a decrial or disparagement of those raw works to which they owed their early character and distinction. Ill would it fare with them, indeed, if on these tenacious terms they should venture upon criticism or offer to move that spirit which would infallibly give such disturbance to their established title.

Now we may consider that in our nation, and especially in our present age, while wars, debates and public convulsions turn our minds so wholly upon business and affairs, the better geniuses being in a manner necessarily involved in the active sphere, on which the general eye of mankind is so strongly fixed, there must remain in the theatre of wit a sufficient vacancy of place, and the quality of actors upon that stage must of consequence be very easily attainable and at a low price of ingenuity or understanding.

The persons, therefore, who are in possession of the prime parts in this deserted theatre, being suffered to maintain their ranks and stations in full ease, have naturally a good agreement and understanding with their fellow wits. Being indebted to the times for this happiness, that with so little industry or capacity they have been able to serve the nation with wit and supply the place of real dispensers and ministers of the Muses' treasures, they must necessarily, as they have any love for themselves or fatherly affection for their works, conspire with one another to preserve their common interest of indolence and justify their remissness, uncorrectness, insipidness and downright ignorance of all literate art or just poetic beauty. *Great is the concord among the effeminate.*[32]

For this reason you see them mutually courteous and benevolent, gracious and obliging beyond measure, complimenting one another interchangeably at the head of their works, in recommendatory verses or in separate panegyrics, essays and fragments of poetry, such as in the miscellaneous collections (our yearly retail of wit) we see curiously compacted and accommodated to the relish of the world. Here the *tyrocinium*[S] of geniuses is annually displayed. Here, if you think fit, you may make acquaintance with the young offspring of wits as they come up gradually under the old, with due courtship and homage paid to those high predecessors of fame in hope of being one day admitted, by turn, into the noble order and made wits by patent and authority.

This is the young fry which you may see busily surrounding the grown poet or chief playhouse author at a coffeehouse. They are his guards, ready to take up arms for him, if by some presumptuous critic he is at any time attacked. They are indeed the very shadows of their immediate predecessor, and represent the same features with some small alteration perhaps for the worse. They are sure to aim at nothing above or beyond their master, and would on no account give him the least jealousy of their aspiring to any degree or order of writing above him. From hence that harmony and reciprocal esteem, which, on such a bottom as this, cannot fail of being perfectly well established among our poets, the age, meanwhile, being after this manner hopefully provided and secure of a constant and like succession of meritorious wits in every kind!

If by chance a man of sense, unapprised of the authority of these high powers, should venture to accost the gentlemen of this fraternity at some coffeehouse committee, while they were taken up in mutual admiration and the usual praise of their national and co-temporary wits, it is possible he might be treated with some civility while he inquired, for satisfaction's sake, into the beauties of those particular works so unanimously extolled. But should he presume to ask in general, 'Why is our epic or dramatic, our essay or common prose, no better executed?' or 'Why in particular does such or such a reputed wit write so incorrectly and with so little regard to justness of thought or language?', the answer would presently be given that 'we Englishmen are not tied up to such rigid rules as those of the ancient Grecian or modern French critics'.

'Be it so, gentlemen! It is your good pleasure. Nor ought anyone to dispute it with you. You are masters, no doubt, in your own country. But, gentlemen, the question here is not what your authority may be over your own writers. You may have them of what fashion or size of wit you please, and allow them

---

[S] Apprenticeship.

[32] Juvenal, *Satires* 2.47.

to entertain you at the rate you think sufficient and satisfactory. But can you, by your good pleasure or the approbation of your highest patrons, make that to be either wit or sense which would otherwise have been bombast and contradiction? If your poets are still Mr Bayeses[T] and your prose authors Sir Rogers,[U] without offering at a better manner, must it follow that the manner itself is good or the wit genuine?[33] What say you, gentlemen, to this new piece? Let us examine these lines which you call "shining", this string of sentences which you call "clever", this pile of metaphors which you call "sublime"! Are you unwilling, gentlemen, to stand the test? Do you despise the examination?

Sir! Since you are pleased to take this liberty with us, may we presume to ask you a question?'

'Oh, gentlemen! As many as you please: I shall be highly honoured.'

'Why then, pray Sir! Inform us whether you have ever written?'

'Very often, gentlemen, especially on a post night.'

'But have you written, for instance, Sir, a play, a song, an essay or a paper, as, by way of eminence, the current pieces of our weekly wits are generally styled?'

[T] Mr Bayes was the caricature of John Dryden in *The Rehearsal*, first published in 1672, by George Villiers, second Duke of Buckingham. See Shaftesbury's subsequent note 33. Dryden, 1631–1700, was appointed Poet Laureate in 1670 and gave literary expression to a Tory worldview; he pilloried the first Earl of Shaftesbury, and mocked the second, in his poetic attack on the Exclusion-era Whigs, *Absalom and Achitophel* (1681).

[U] Sir Roger L'Estrange, 1616–1704, was a Tory ideologue who had the reputation of being a great prose writer. Both Dryden and L'Estrange were great enemies of the first Earl of Shaftesbury and targeted him in their writings.

[33] To see the incorrigibleness of our poets in their pedantic manner, their vanity, defiance of criticism, their rhodomontade and poetical bravado, we need only turn to our famous Poet Laureate, the very Mr Bayes himself, in one of his latest and most valued pieces, written many years after the ingenious author of *The Rehearsal* had drawn his picture. 'I have been listening', says our poet in his preface to *Don Sebastian* [first produced in 1689 and published in 1690], 'what objections had been made against the conduct of the play, but found them all so trivial that, if I should name them, a true critic would imagine that I played booty [that is, acted falsely with an ulterior aim] . . . Some are pleased to say the writing is dull. But *he is of age; ask him: he shall speak for himself* [John 9.21]. Others, that the double poison is unnatural. Let the common received opinion, and Ausonius's famous epigram [*Epigrams* 3], answer that. Lastly, a more ignorant sort of creatures than either of the former maintain that the character of Dorax is not only unnatural but inconsistent with itself. Let them read the play and think again . . . A longer reply is what those cavillers deserve not. But I will give them and their fellows to understand that the Earl of Dorset was pleased to read the tragedy twice over before it was acted, and did me the favour to send me word that I had written beyond any of my former plays and that he was displeased anything should be cut away. If I have not reason to prefer his single judgment to a whole faction, let the world be judge, for the opposition is the same with that of Lucan's hero against an army, *a man against an army* [*Pharsalia* 6.191–2]. I think I may modestly conclude . . .'. Thus he goes on to the very end in the self-same strain. Who, after this, can ever say of *The Rehearsal* author that his picture of our poet was over-charged or the national humour wrong described? [See the text and commentary on Dryden's preface in H. T. Swedenberg, Jr, general editor, *The Works of John Dryden* (Berkeley: University of California Press, 1956–), XV, pp. 70–1, 416–17.]

'Something of this kind I may perhaps, gentlemen, have attempted, though without publishing my work. But pray, gentlemen, what is my writing or not writing to the question in hand?'

'Only this, Sir, and you may fairly take our words for it: that whenever you publish you will find the Town against you. Your piece will infallibly be condemned.'

'So let it. But for what reason, gentlemen? I am sure you never saw the piece.'

'No, Sir. But you are a critic. And we know by certain experience that, when a critic writes according to rule and method, he is sure never to hit the English taste. Did not Mr. Rymer,[V] who criticized our English tragedy, write a sorry one of his own?'

'If he did, gentlemen, it was his own fault, not to know his genius better. But is his criticism the less just on this account? If a musician performs his part well in the hardest symphonies, he must necessarily know the notes and understand the rules of harmony and music. But must a man, therefore, who has an ear and has studied the rules of music, of necessity have a voice or hand? Can no one possibly judge a fiddle but who is himself a fiddler? Can no one judge a picture but who is himself a layer of colours?'

Thus far our rational gentleman perhaps might venture before his coffee-house audience. Had I been at his elbow to prompt him as a friend, I should hardly have thought fit to remind him of anything further. On the contrary, I should have rather taken him aside to inform him of this cabal and established corporation of wit, of their declared aversion to criticism, and of their known laws and statutes in that case made and provided. I should have told him, in short, that learned arguments would be misspent on such as these and that he would find little success, though he should ever so plainly demonstrate to the gentlemen of this size of wit and understanding that 'the greatest masters of art, in every kind of writing, were eminent in the critical practice'. But that they really were so, witness, among the ancients, their greatest philosophers,[34] whose critical pieces lie intermixed with their profound philosophical works and other politer tracts ornamentally writ for public use.[35] Witness, in history and rhetoric, Isocrates, Dionysius Halicarnasseus, Plutarch and the corrupt

---

[V] Inspired by the classical rules of unity found in Aristotle, Thomas Rymer, 1641–1713, criticized the English stage, notably the achievements of Shakespeare, in a number of works including *The Tragedies of the Last Age Considered* (1678) and *A Short View of Tragedy* (1693). His own tragedy, *Edgar, or the English Monarch*, was never performed. He had more success as the Historiographer Royal from 1692, producing *Foedera*, a large printed collection of diplomatic documents that began appearing in 1704.

[34] Namely, Plato, Aristotle. See in particular the *Phaedrus* of the former, where an entire piece of the orator Lysias is criticized in form.

[35] The distinction of treatises was into the ἀκροαματικοί [the esoteric] and ἐξωτερικοί [the exoteric].

456

Lucian himself, the only one perhaps of these authors whom our gentlemen may, in some modern translation, have looked into with any curiosity or delight. To these, among the Romans, we may add Cicero, Varro, Horace, Quintilian, Pliny and many more.

Among the moderns, a Boileau and a Corneille are sufficient precedents in the case before us.[W] They applied their criticism with just severity, even to their own works. This indeed is a manner hardly practicable with the poets of our own nation. It would be unreasonable to expect of them that they should bring such measures in use as, being applied to their works, would discover them to be wholly deformed and disproportionable. It is no wonder, therefore, if we have so little of this critical genius extant to guide us in our taste. It is no wonder if what is generally current in this kind lies in a manner buried and in disguise under burlesque, as particularly in the witty comedy of a noble author of this last age.[36] To the shame, however, of our professed wits and enterprisers in the higher spheres of poetry, it may be observed that they have not wanted good advice and instruction of the graver kind from as high a hand in respect of quality and character, since one of the justest of our modern poems, and so confessed even by our poets themselves, is a short criticism, an art of poetry, by which, if they themselves were to be judged, they must in general appear no better than mere bunglers and void of all true sense and knowledge in their art.[X] But if in reality both critic and poet, confessing the justice of these rules of art, can afterwards in practice condemn and approve, perform and judge in a quite different manner from what they acknowledge just and true, it plainly shows that, though perhaps we are not indigent in wit, we want what is of more consequence and can alone raise wit to any dignity or worth, even plain honesty, manners and a sense of that moral truth on which (as has been often expressed in these volumes) poetic truth and beauty must naturally depend.[37] *He who has learnt the obligation due to fatherland and friends, the love that should be for parent, brother and guest, duty for a senator and a judge . . . he assuredly knows how to render what is appropriate for each character.*[38]

As for this species of morality which distinguishes the civil offices of life and describes each becoming personage or character in this scene, so necessary it is for the poet and polite author to be apprised of it that even the divine himself may with juster pretence be exempted from the knowledge of this sort. The composer of religious discourses has the advantage of that higher scene of mystery which is above the level of human commerce. It is not so much his

---

[W] For Boileau and Corneille, see p. 98n.

[X] *An Essay upon Poetry*, by John Sheffield, Marquess of Normanby and later first Duke of Buckingham and Normanby (1648–1721). The poem first appeared in 1682.

[36] *The Rehearsal.* See pp. 116, 455n.

[37] See pp. 93, 124–5, 150, 448–9.

[38] Horace, *The Art of Poetry* 312–16.

concern or business to be agreeable. And often when he would endeavour it, he becomes more than ordinarily displeasing. His theatre and that of the polite world are very different insomuch that, in a reverend author or declaimer of this sort, we naturally excuse the ignorance of ordinary decorum in what relates to the affairs of our inferior temporal world. But for the poet or genteel writer, who is of this world merely, it is a different case. He must be perfect in this moral science. We can easily bear the loss of indifferent poetry or essay. A good bargain it were, could we get rid of every moderate performance in this kind. But were we obliged to hear only excellent sermons and to read nothing in the way of devotion which was not well written, it might possibly go hard with many Christian people, who are at present such attentive auditors and readers.[Y] Established pastors have a right to be indifferent. But voluntary discoursers and attempters in wit or poetry are as intolerable, when they are indifferent, as either fiddlers or painters: *Because the dinner could be conducted without him.*[39] Other Bayeses and poetasters may be lawfully baited, though we patiently submit to our Bayeses in divinity.

Had the author of our subject treatises considered thoroughly of these literate affairs and found how the interest of wit stood at present in our nation, he would have had so much regard surely to his own interest as never to have written but either in the single capacity of mere critic or that of author in form.[40] If he had resolved never to produce a regular or legitimate piece, he might pretty safely have written on still after the rate of his first volume and mixed manner. He might have been as critical, as satirical or as full of raillery as he had pleased. But to come afterwards as a grave actor upon the stage and expose himself to criticism in his turn by giving us a work or two in form, after the regular manner of composition, as we see in his second volume, this I think was no extraordinary proof of his judgment or ability in what related to his own credit and advantage.

One of these formal pieces (the *Inquiry*, already examined) we have found to be wholly after the manner which in one of his critical pieces he calls 'the methodic'. But his next piece (*The Moralists*, which we have now before us) must, according to his own rules, be reckoned as an undertaking of greater weight.[41] It is not only, at the bottom, as systematical, didactic and preceptive as that other piece of formal structure, but it assumes withal another garb and more fashionable turn of wit. It conceals what is scholastical under the appearance of a polite work. It aspires to dialogue and carries with it not only those

[Y]   For other remarks by Shaftesbury on sermons, see his introduction to *Select Sermons of Dr. Whichcote* (1698), for which see Introduction, p. xxix.

[39]   Horace, *The Art of Poetry* 376.
[40]   See pp. 396–419.
[41]   See pp. 87, 115–16.

poetic features of the pieces anciently called mimes,^z but it attempts to unite the several personages and characters in one action or story, within a determinate compass of time, regularly divided and drawn into different and proportioned scenes, and this, too, with variety of style – the simple, comic, rhetorical and even the poetic or sublime, such as is the aptest to run into enthusiasm and extravagance. So much is our author, by virtue of this piece, a poet in due form, and by a more apparent claim than if he had written a play or dramatic piece in as regular a manner, at least, as any known at present on our stage.[42]

It appears, indeed, that, as high as our author in his critical capacity would pretend to carry the refined manner and accurate simplicity of the ancients, he dares not, in his own model and principal performance, attempt to unite his philosophy in one solid and uniform body nor carry on his argument in one continued chain or thread. Here our author's timorousness is visible. In the very plan or model of his work, he is apparently put to a hard shift to contrive how, or with what probability, he might introduce men of any note or fashion reasoning expressly and purposely, without play or trifling, for two or three hours together on mere philosophy and morals.[43] He finds these subjects, as he confesses, so wide of common conversation and, by long custom, so appropriated to the school, the university chair or pulpit, that he thinks it hardly safe or practicable to treat of them elsewhere or in a different tone. He is forced

---

^z See p. 87n.

[42] That he is conscious of this, we may gather from that line or two of advertisement, which stands at the beginning of his first edition [*The Moralists* (London, 1710), pp. iii–iv]. 'As for the characters and incidents, they are neither wholly feigned', says he, 'nor wholly true, but, according to the liberty allowed in the way of dialogue, the principal matters are founded upon truth, and the rest as near resembling as may be. It is a sceptic recites, and the hero of the piece passes for an enthusiast. If a perfect character be wanting, it is the same case here as with the poets in some of their best pieces. And this surely is a sufficient warrant for the author of a philosophical romance.' Thus our author himself, who, to conceal, however, his strict imitation of the ancient poetic dialogue, has prefixed an auxiliary title to his work and given it the surname of *Rhapsody*, as if it were merely of that essay or mixed kind of works, which come abroad with an affected air of negligence and irregularity. But whatever our author may have affected in his title page, it was so little his intention to write after that model of incoherent workmanship that it appears to be sorely against his will if this dialogue piece of his has not the just character and correct form of those ancient poems described. He would gladly have constituted one single action and time, suitable to the just simplicity of those dramatic works. And this, one would think, was easy enough for him to have done. He needed only to have brought his first speakers immediately into action and saved the narrative or recitative part of Philocles to Palemon by producing them as speaking personages upon his stage. The scene all along might have been the park. From the early evening to the late hour of night, that the two gallants withdrew to their Town apartments, there was sufficient time for the narrator Philocles to have recited the whole transaction of the second and third part, which would have stood throughout as it now does; only at the conclusion, when the narrative or recitative part had ceased, the simple and direct dialogue would have again returned to grace the exit. By this means the temporal as well as local unity of the piece had been preserved. Nor had our author been necessitated to commit that anachronism of making his first part in order to be last in time.

[43] See pp. 90–1.

therefore to raise particular machines and constrain his principal characters in order to carry a better face and bear himself out against the appearance of pedantry. Thus, his gentleman-philosopher Theocles, before he enters into his real character, becomes a feigned preacher. And even when his real character comes on, he hardly dares stand it out, but, to deal the better with his sceptic friend, he falls again to personating and takes up the humour of the poet and enthusiast. Palemon, the man of quality who is first introduced as speaker in the piece, must, for fashion's sake, appear in love and under a kind of melancholy produced by some misadventures in the world. How else should he be supposed so serious? Philocles, his friend, an airy gentleman of the world and a thorough *railleur*,[AA] must have a home charge upon him and feel the anger of his grave friend before he can be supposed grave enough to enter into a philosophical discourse. A quarter of an hour's reading must serve to represent an hour or two's debate. And a new scene presenting itself, ever and anon, must give refreshment, it seems, to the faint reader and remind him of the characters and business going on.

It is in the same view that we miscellanarian authors, being fearful of the natural lassitude and satiety of our indolent reader, have prudently betaken ourselves to the ways of chapters and contents, that, as the reader proceeds, by frequent intervals of repose contrived on purpose for him, he may from time to time be advertised of what is yet to come and be tempted thus to renew his application.

Thus, in our modern plays, we see, almost in every other leaf, descriptions or illustrations of the action, not in the poem itself or in the mouth of the actors, but by the poet, in his own person, in order, as appears, to help out a defect of the text by a kind of marginal note or comment, which renders these pieces of a mixed kind between the narrative and dramatic.[BB] It is in this fashionable style, or manner of dumb show, that the reader finds the action of the piece more amazingly expressed than he possibly could by the lines of the drama itself, where the parties alone are suffered to be speakers.

It is out of the same regard to ease, both in respect of writer and reader, that we see long characters and descriptions at the head of most dramatic pieces, to inform us of the relations, kindred, interest and designs of the *dramatis personae*,[CC] this being of the highest importance to the reader, that he may the better understand the plot and find out the principal characters and incidents

---

[AA] That is, one who engages in raillery or good-humoured ridicule.

[BB] According to a manuscript note (III, 289) in Shaftesbury's copy of the 1711 edition (see Note on the text): 'I was going once to set down an example (as you may find a hundred in our modern tragedy) as thus: "Such a one stabs such a one, while such a one snatches the dagger and immediately stabs such a one; whereupon such a one runs at such a one", and so on. But I thought this would be below me to cite, in any after-note. Everyone who reads our English drama with any attention and judgment will very easily call to mind these indexes and marginal descriptions, which serve to help out the lame action.'

[CC] The characters of the play.

of the piece, which otherwise could not possibly discover themselves as they are read in their due order. And to do justice to our play-readers, they seldom fail to humour our poets in this respect and read over the characters with strict application, as a sort of grammar or key, before they enter on the piece itself. I know not whether they would do so much for any philosophical piece in the world. Our author seems very much to question it, and has therefore made that part easy enough, which relates to the distinction of his characters, by making use of the narrative manner – though he had done as well, perhaps, not to have gone out of the natural plain way on this account. For with those to whom such philosophical subjects are agreeable, it could be thought no laborious task to give the same attention to characters in dialogue as is given at the first entrance by every reader to the easiest play, composed of fewest and plainest personages. But for those who read these subjects with mere supineness and indifference, they will as much begrudge the pains of attending to the characters, thus particularly pointed out, as if they had only been discernible by inference and deduction from the mouth of the speaking parties themselves.

More reasons are given by our author himself for his avoiding the direct way of dialogue, which at present lies so low and is used only now and then in our party pamphlets or new-fashioned theological essays.[44] For, of late, it seems, the manner has been introduced into Church controversy, with an attempt of raillery and humour, as a more successful method of dealing with heresy and infidelity. The burlesque divinity grows mightily in vogue. And the cried-up answers to heterodox discourses are generally such as are written in drollery or with resemblance of the facetious and humorous language of conversation.

Joy to the reverend authors who can afford to be thus gay and condescend to correct us in this lay wit. The advances they make, in behalf of piety and manners, by such a popular style are doubtless found upon experience to be very considerable. As these reformers are nicely qualified to hit the air of breeding and gentility, they will in time, no doubt, refine their manner and improve this jocular method, to the edification of the polite world, who have been so long seduced by the way of raillery and wit. They may do wonders by their comic muse and may thus, perhaps, find means to laugh gentlemen into their religion, who have unfortunately been laughed out of it. For what reason is there to suppose that orthodoxy should not be able to laugh as agreeably and with as much refinedness as heresy or infidelity?

At present, it must be owned, the characters or personages employed by our new orthodox dialogists carry with them little proportion or coherence and, in this respect, may be said to suit perfectly with that figurative metaphorical style

[44] See pp. 233–4.

and rhetorical manner in which their logic and arguments are generally couched. Nothing can be more complex or multiform than their moral drafts or sketches of humanity. These, indeed, are so far from representing any particular man or order of men that they scarce resemble anything of the kind. It is by their names only that these characters are figured. Though they bear different titles and are set up to maintain contrary points, they are found, at the bottom, to be all of the same side and, notwithstanding their seeming variance, to co-operate in the most officious manner with the author towards the display of his own proper wit and the establishment of his private opinion and maxims. They are indeed his very legitimate and obsequious puppets, as like real men in voice, action and manners as those wooden or wire engines of the lower stage. Philotheus and Philatheus, Philautus and Philalethes are of one and the same order: just tallies to one another, questioning and answering in concert and with such a sort of alternative as is known in a vulgar play, where one person lies down blindfold and presents himself, as fair as may be, to another who, by favour of the company or the assistance of his good fortune, deals his companion many a sound blow, without being once challenged or brought into his turn of lying down.

There is the same curious mixture of chance and elegant vicissitude in the style of these mock personages of our new theological drama, with this difference only, that, after the poor phantom or shadow of an adversary has said as little for his cause as can be imagined, and given as many opens and advantages as could be desired, he lies down for good and all and passively submits to the killing strokes of his unmerciful conqueror.

Hardly, as I conceive, will it be objected to our moralist, the author of the philosophic dialogue above, that the personages who sustain the sceptical or objecting parts are overtame and tractable in their disposition. Did I perceive any such foul dealing in his piece, I should scarce think it worthy of the criticism here bestowed. For, in this sort of writing, where personages are exhibited and natural conversation set in view, if characters are neither tolerably preserved nor manners with any just similitude described, there remains nothing but what is too gross and monstrous for criticism or examination.

It will be alleged, perhaps, in answer to what is here advanced, that, 'should a dialogue be wrought up to the exactness of these rules, it ought to be condemned as the worse piece for affording the infidel or sceptic such good quarter and giving him the full advantage of his argument and wit'.

But to this I reply that either dialogue should never be attempted or, if it be, the parties should appear natural and such as they really are. If we paint at all, we should endeavour to paint like life and draw creatures as they are knowable in their proper shapes and better features, not in metamorphosis, not mangled, lame, distorted, awkward forms and impotent chimeras. Atheists have their sense and wits as other men, or why is atheism so often challenged in those of the better rank, why charged so often to the account of wit and subtle reasoning?

Were I to advise these authors, towards whom I am extremely well-affected on account of their good-humoured zeal and the seeming sociableness of their religion, I should say to them, 'Gentlemen! Be not so cautious of furnishing your representative sceptic with too good arguments or too shrewd a turn of wit or humour. Be not so fearful of giving quarter. Allow your adversary his full reason, his ingenuity, sense and art. Trust to the chief character or hero of your piece. Make him as dazzling bright as you are able. He will undoubtedly overcome the utmost force of his opponent and dispel the darkness or cloud which the adversary may unluckily have raised. But if, when you have fairly wrought up your antagonist to his due strength and cognizable proportion, your chief character cannot afterwards prove a match for him or shine with a superior brightness, whose fault is it? The subject's? This, I hope, you will never allow. Whose, therefore, beside your own? Beware then, and consider well your strength and mastership in this manner of writing, and in the qualifying practice of the polite world, before you attempt these accurate and refined limnings or portraitures of mankind or offer to bring gentlemen on the stage. For if real gentlemen, seduced, as you pretend, and made erroneous in their religion or philosophy, discover not the least feature of their real faces in your looking-glass, nor know themselves in the least by your description, they will hardly be apt to think they are refuted. How wittily soever your comedy may be wrought up, they will scarce apprehend any of that wit to fall upon themselves. They may laugh indeed at the diversion you are pleased to give them, but the laugh perhaps may be different from what you intend. They may smile secretly to see themselves thus encountered when they find, at last, your authority laid by and your scholastic weapons quitted in favour of this weak attempt to master them by their own arms and proper ability.'

Thus we have performed our critical task and tried our strength both on our author and those of his order, who attempt to write in dialogue after the active dramatic, mimical or personating way, according to which a writer is properly poetical.[45]

What remains, we shall examine in our succeeding and last chapter.

---

[45] See p. 87.

Chapter 3

Of extent or latitude of thought. Freethinkers. Their cause and character. Dishonesty, a half-thought. Short-thinking, cause of vice and bigotry. Agreement of slavery and superstition. Liberty, civil, moral, spiritual. Freethinking divines. Representatives incognito. Ambassadors from the moon. Effectual determination of Christian controversy and religious belief.

Being now come to the conclusion of my work, after having defended the cause of critics in general and employed what strength I had in that science upon our adventurous author in particular, I may, according to equity and with the better grace, attempt a line or two in defence of that freedom of thought which our author has used, particularly in one of the personages of his last dialogue treatise.[DD]

There is good reason to suppose that, however equally framed or near alike the race of mankind may appear in other respects, they are not always equal thinkers, or of a like ability in the management of this natural talent, which we call *thought*. The race, on this account, may therefore justly be distinguished, as they often are, by the appellation of the thinking and the unthinking sort. The mere unthinking are such as have not yet arrived to that happy thought by which they should observe how necessary thinking is, and how fatal the want of it must prove to them. The thinking part of mankind, on the other side, having discovered the assiduity and industry requisite to right thinking and being already commenced thinkers upon this foundation, are, in the progress of the affair, convinced of the necessity of thinking to good purpose and carrying the work to a thorough issue. They know that, if they refrain or stop once upon this road, they had done as well never to have set out. They are not so supine as to be withheld by mere laziness when nothing lies in the way to interrupt the free course and progress of their thought.

Some obstacles, it is true, may on this occasion be pretended. Spectres may come across, and shadows of reason rise up against reason itself. But if men have once heartily espoused the reasoning or thinking habit, they will not easily be induced to lay the practice down; they will not at an instant be arrested or made to stand and yield themselves when they come to such a certain boundary, landmark, post or pillar, erected here or there (for what reason may probably be guessed) with the inscription of a *ne plus ultra*.[EE]

It is not, indeed, any authority on earth, as we are well assured, can stop us on this road, unless we please to make the arrest or restriction of our own accord. It is our own thought which must restrain our thinking. And whether

---

[DD] Namely, Philocles.

[EE] A point beyond which one cannot go. Literally, 'not farther beyond', which was said to be inscribed on the Pillars of Hercules at the Strait of Gibraltar, warning ships against leaving the Mediterranean Sea for the ocean beyond.

the restraining thought be just, how shall we ever judge without examining it freely and out of all constraint? How shall we be sure that we have justly quitted reason as too high and dangerous, too aspiring or presumptive, if, through fear of any kind or submitting to mere command, we quit our very examining thought and in the moment stop short so as to put an end to further thinking on the matter? Is there much difference between this case and that of the obedient beasts of burden who stop precisely at their appointed inn or at whatever point the charioteer or governor of the reins thinks fit to give the signal for a halt?

I cannot but from hence conclude that, of all species of creatures said commonly to have brains, the most insipid, wretched and preposterous are those whom, in just propriety, of speech we call 'half-thinkers'.

I have often known pretenders to wit break out into admiration on the sight of some raw, heedless, unthinking gentleman, declaring on this occasion that they esteemed it the happiest case in the world 'never to think or trouble one's head with study or consideration'. This I have always looked upon as one of the highest airs of distinction which the self-admiring wits are used to give themselves in public company. Now the echo or antiphony, which these elegant exclaimers hope, by this reflection, to draw necessarily from their audience, is that 'they themselves are over-freighted with this merchandise of thought, and have not only enough for ballast but such a cargo over and above as is enough to sink them by its weight'. I am apt, however, to imagine of these gentlemen that it was never their over-thinking which oppressed them and that, if their thought had ever really become oppressive to them, they might thank themselves for having under-thought or reasoned short, so as to rest satisfied with a very superficial search into matters of the first and highest importance.

If, for example, they overlooked the chief enjoyments of life, which are founded in honesty and a good mind, if they presumed mere life to be fully worth what its tenacious lovers are pleased to rate it at, if they thought public distinction, fame, power, an estate or title to be of the same value as is vulgarly conceived or as they concluded on a first thought without further scepticism or after-deliberation, it is no wonder, if being in time become such mature dogmatists and well-practised dealers in the affairs of what they call a settlement or fortune, they are so hardly put to it to find ease or rest within themselves.

These are the deeply-loaded and over-pensive gentlemen who, esteeming it the truest wit to pursue what they call their interest, wonder to find they are still as little at ease when they have succeeded as when they first attempted to advance.

There can never be less self-enjoyment than in these supposed wise characters, these selfish computers of happiness and private good, whose pursuits of interest, whether for this world or another, are attended with the same steady vein of cunning and low thought, sordid deliberations, perverse and crooked fancies, ill dispositions and false relishes of life and manners. The most negligent, undesigning, thoughtless rake has not only more of sociableness, ease, tranquillity and freedom from worldly cares but, in reality, more of worth, virtue and merit than such grave plodders and thoughtful gentlemen as these.

If it happens, therefore, that these graver, more circumspect and deeply interested gentlemen have, for their soul's sake and through a careful provision for hereafter, engaged in certain speculations of religion, their taste of virtue and relish of life is not the more improved on this account. The thoughts they have on these new subjects of divinity are so biassed and perplexed by those half-thoughts and raw imaginations of interest and worldly affairs, that they are still disabled in the rational pursuit of happiness and good, and, being necessitated thus to remain 'short thinkers', they have the power to go no further than they are led by those to whom, under such disturbances and perplexities, they apply themselves for cure and comfort.[FF]

It has been the main scope and principal end of these volumes to assert the reality of a beauty and charm in moral as well as natural subjects, and to demonstrate the reasonableness of a proportionate taste and determinate choice in life and manners. The standard of this kind and the noted character of moral truth appear so firmly established in nature itself, and so widely displayed through the intelligent world, that there is no genius, mind or thinking principle which, if I may say so, is not really conscious in the case. Even the most refractory and obstinate understandings are by certain reprises or returns of thought on every occasion convinced of this existence and necessitated, in common with others, to acknowledge the actual right and wrong.

It is evident that, whensoever the mind, influenced by passion or humour, consents to any action, measure or rule of life contrary to this governing standard and primary measure of intelligence, it can only be through a weak thought, a scantiness of judgment and a defect in the application of that unavoidable impression and first natural rule of honesty and worth, against which whatever is advanced will be of no other moment than to render a life distracted, incoherent, full of irresolution, repentance and self-disapprobation.

Thus every immorality and enormity of life can only happen from a partial and narrow view of happiness and good. Whatever takes from the largeness or freedom of thought must of necessity detract from that first relish or taste on which virtue and worth depend.

For instance, when the eye or appetite is eagerly fixed on treasure and the monied bliss of bags and coffers, it is plain there is a kind of fascination in the

---

[FF] According to a manuscript note (III, 302) in Shaftesbury's copy of the 1711 edition (see Note on the text): 'It is a tender place. I dare go no further in clearing it, if it be still obscure; as, I think, it will hardly appear to be at present.'

case. The sight is instantly diverted from all other views of excellence or worth. And here, even the vulgar, as well as the more liberal part of mankind, discover the contracted genius and acknowledge the narrowness of such a mind.

In luxury and intemperance we easily apprehend how far thought is oppressed, and the mind debarred from just reflection, and from the free examination and censure of its own opinions or maxims, on which the conduct of a life is formed.

Even in that complicated good of vulgar kind, which we commonly call *interest*, in which we comprehend both pleasure, riches, power and other exterior advantages, we may discern how a fascinated sight contracts a genius and, by shortening the view even of that very interest which it seeks, betrays the knave and necessitates the ablest and wittiest proselyte of the kind to expose himself on every emergency and sudden turn.

But above all other enslaving vices and restrainers of reason and just thought, the most evidently ruinous and fatal to the understanding is that of *superstition, bigotry* and *vulgar enthusiasm*. This passion, not contented like other vices to deceive and tacitly supplant our reason, professes open war, holds up the intended chains and fetters and declares its resolution to enslave.

The artificial managers of this human frailty declaim against free thought and latitude of understanding. To go beyond those bounds of thinking which they have prescribed is by them declared a sacrilege. To them, freedom of mind, a mastery of sense and a liberty in thought and action imply debauch, corruption and depravity.

In consequence of their moral maxims and political establishments, they can indeed advance no better notion of human happiness and enjoyment than that which is in every respect the most opposite to liberty. It is to them doubtless that we owe the opprobriousness and abuse of those naturally honest appellations of free livers, freethinkers, latitudinarians or whatever other character implies a largeness of mind and generous use of understanding. Fain would they confound licentiousness in morals with liberty in thought and action and make the libertine, who has the least mastery of himself, resemble his direct opposite. For such indeed is the man of resolute purpose and immovable adherence to reason against everything which passion, prepossession, craft or fashion can advance in favour of anything else. But here, it seems, the grievance lies. It is thought dangerous for us to be over-rational or too much masters of ourselves in what we draw by just conclusions from reason only. Seldom therefore do these expositors ever fail of bringing the thought of liberty into disgrace. Even at the expense of virtue and of that very idea of goodness on which they build the mysteries of their profitable science, they derogate from morals and reverse all true philosophy: they refine on selfishness and explode generosity, promote a slavish obedience in the room of voluntary duty and free service, exalt blind ignorance for devotion, recommend low thought, decry reason, extol voluptuousness,[46] wilfulness, vindictiveness, arbitrariness, vainglory and even deify those weak passions which are the disgrace rather than ornament of human nature.[47]

But so far is it from the nature of liberty to indulge such passions as these,[48] that whoever acts at any time under the power of any single one may be said to have already provided for himself an absolute master. And he who lives under the power of a whole race, since it is scarce possible to obey one without the other, must of necessity undergo the worst of servitudes, under the most capricious and domineering lords.

That this is no paradox even the writers for entertainment can inform us, however others may moralize who discourse or write (as they pretend) for profit and instruction. The poets even of the wanton sort give ample testimony of this slavery and wretchedness of vice. They may extol voluptuousness to the skies and point their wit as sharply as they are able against a virtuous state. But when they come afterwards to pay the necessary tribute to their commanding pleasures, we hear their pathetic moans and find the inward discord and calamity of their lives. Their example is the best of precepts since they conceal nothing, are sincere and speak their passion out aloud. And it is in this that the very worst of poets may justly be preferred to the generality of modern philosophers or other formal writers of a yet more specious name. The Muses' pupils never fail to express their passions and write just as they feel. It is not, indeed, in their nature to do otherwise while they indulge their vein and are under the power of that natural enthusiasm which leads them to what is highest in their performance. They follow nature. They move chiefly as she moves in them, without thought of disguising her free motions and genuine operations, for the sake of any scheme or hypothesis which they have formed at leisure and in particular narrow views. On this account, though at one time they quarrel perhaps with virtue for restraining them in their forbidden loves, they can at another time make her sufficient amends, when with indignation they complain that 'merit is neglected, and their worthless rival preferred before them'.[49] *Does the pure nature of a poor man have no power against lucre?*[50] And thus even in common elegiac, in song, ode or epigram consecrated to pleasure itself, we may often read the dolorous confession in behalf of virtue and see at the bottom how the case stands: *For at last voices of truth are summoned forth from the depth of the heart.*[51] The airy poets in these fits can, as freely as the tragedian, condole with virtue, and bemoan the case of suffering merit:

---

[46] See pp. 262, 469.
[47] See p. 20.
[48] See pp. 260-1, 334.
[49] See p. 65.
[50] Horace, *Epode* 11.11–12.
[51] Lucretius, *On the Nature of Things* 3.57–8.

The oppressor's wrong, the proud man's contumely [. . .],
The insolence of office, and the spurns
That patient merit of the unworthy takes.[GG]

The poetic chiefs may give what reason they think fit for their humour of representing our mad appetites, especially that of love, under the shape of urchins and wanton boys, scarce out of their state of infancy. The original design and moral of this fiction, I am persuaded, was to show us how little there was of great and heroic in the government of these pretenders, how truly weak and childish they were in themselves and how much lower than mere children we then became when we submitted ourselves to their blind tutorage. There was no fear lest in this fiction the boyish nature should be misconstrued as innocent and gentle. The storms of passion, so well known in every kind, kept the tyrannic quality of this wanton race sufficiently in view. Nor could the poetical description fail to bring to mind their mischievous and malignant play. But when the image of imperious threatening and absolute command was joined to that of ignorance, puerility and folly, the notion was completed of that wretched slavish state which modern libertines, in conjunction with some of a graver character, admire and represent as the most eligible of any. 'Happy condition!', says one. 'Happy life, that of the indulged passions! Might we pursue it! Miserable condition! Miserable life, that of reason and virtue, which we are bid pursue!'[52]

It is the same, it seems, with men in morals as in politics. When they have been unhappily born and bred to slavery, they are so far from being sensible of their slavish course of life, or of that ill usage, indignity and misery they sustain, that they even admire their own condition and, being used to think short and carry their views no farther than those bounds which were early prescribed to them, they look upon tyranny as a natural case and think mankind in a sort of dangerous and degenerate state when under the power of laws and in the possession of a free government.

We may by these reflections come easily to apprehend what men they were who first brought reason and free thought under disgrace and made the noblest of characters, that of a free thinker, to become invidious. It is no wonder if the same interpreters would have those also to be esteemed free in their lives and masters of good living who are the least masters of themselves and the most impotent in passion and humour of all their fellow creatures. But far be it, and far surely will it ever be, from any worthy genius to be consenting to such a treacherous language and abuse of words. For my own part, I thoroughly confide in the good powers of reason, that liberty and freedom shall never by

[GG] William Shakespeare, *Hamlet* 3.1.71–4.

[52] See p. 262.

any artifice or delusion be made to pass with me as frightful sounds or as reproachful or invidious in any sense.

I can no more allow that to be free living, where unlimited passion and unexamined fancy govern, than I can allow that to be a free government where the mere people govern and not the laws. For no people in a civil state can possibly be free, when they are otherwise governed than by such laws as they themselves have constituted or to which they have freely given consent. Now, to be released from these, so as to govern themselves by each day's will or fancy, and to vary on every turn the rule and measure of government, without respect to any ancient constitutions or establishments or to the stated and fixed rules of equity and justice, is as certain slavery as it is violence, distraction and misery, such as in the issue must prove the establishment of an irretrievable state of tyranny and absolute dominion.

In the determinations of life and in the choice and government of actions, he alone is free who has within himself no hindrance or control in acting what he himself, by his best judgment and most deliberate choice, approves. Could vice agree possibly with itself or could the vicious any way reconcile the various judgments of their inward counsellors, they might with justice perhaps assert their liberty and independency. But while they are necessitated to follow least what, in their sedate hours, they most approve, while they are passively assigned and made over from one possessor to another in contrary extremes and to different ends and purposes, of which they are themselves wholly ignorant,[53] it is evident that the more they turn their eyes (as many times they are obliged) towards virtue and a free life, the more they must confess their misery and subjection.[54] They discern their own captivity, but not with force and resolution sufficient to redeem themselves and become their own. Such is the real tragic state, as the old tragedian[55] represents it: *I see and I approve the better, I follow the worse.*[56] And thus the highest spirits and most refractory wills contribute to the lowest servitude and most submissive state. Reason and virtue alone can bestow liberty. Vice is unworthy and unhappy on this account only, that it is slavish and debasing.

Thus have we pleaded the cause of liberty in general and vindicated withal our author's particular freedom in taking the person of a sceptic, as he has done

---

[53] *Are you following this one or that? You must submit to your masters in turn with wavering allegiance*: Persius, *Satires* 5.155–6. See pp. 127–8, 138, 144–5.

[54] *Great Father of the Gods, may it be your wish to punish savage tyrants, when dreadful lust, tinged with fiery poison, has stirred their nature, by no other means than this, that they look upon virtue and pine away at her abandonment*: Persius, *Satires* 3.35–8.

[55] *And I do know the wickednesses I shall dare; but my passion is mightier than my reasonings*: Euripides, *Medea* 4.1078–9.

[56] Ovid, *Metamorphoses* 7.21.

in this last treatise, on which we have so largely paraphrased.[57] We may now perhaps, in compliance with general custom, justly presume to add something in defence of the same kind of freedom we ourselves have assumed in these latter miscellaneous comments, since it would doubtless be very unreasonable and unjust for those who had so freely played the critic to expect anything less than the same free treatment and thorough criticism in return.

As for the style or language used in these comments, it is very different, we find, and varies in proportion with the author commented and with the different characters and persons frequently introduced in the original treatises. So that there will undoubtedly be scope sufficient for censure and correction.

As for the observations on antiquity, we have in most passages, except the very common and obvious, produced our vouchers and authorities in our own behalf. What may be thought of our judgment or sense in the application of these authorities, and in the deductions and reasonings we have formed from such learned topics, must be submitted to the opinion of the wise and learned.

In morals, of which the very force lies in a love of discipline and in a willingness to redress and rectify false thought and erring views, we cannot but patiently wait redress and amicable censure from the sole competent judges, the wise and good, whose interest it has been our whole endeavour to advance.

The only subject on which we are perfectly secure and without fear of any just censure or reproach is that of faith and orthodox belief. For, in the first place, it will appear that, through a profound respect and religious veneration, we have forborne so much as to name any of the sacred and solemn mysteries of revelation.[58] And, in the next place, as we can with confidence declare that we have never in any writing, public or private, attempted such high researches, nor have ever in practice acquitted ourselves otherwise than as just conformists to the lawful church, so we may, in a proper sense, be said faithfully and dutifully to embrace those holy mysteries, even in their minutest particulars and without the least exception on account of their amazing depth. And, though we are sensible that it would be no small hardship to deprive others of a liberty of examining and searching, with due modesty and submission, into the nature of those subjects, yet, as for ourselves, who have not the least scruple whatsoever, we pray not any such grace or favour in our behalf, being fully assured of our own steady orthodoxy, resignation and entire submission to the truly Christian and catholic doctrines of our Holy Church as by law established.

It is true, indeed, that, as to critical learning and the examination of

---

[57] Namely, *The Moralists* recited in the person of a sceptic, under the name of Philocles. See pp. 241–3.

[58] See pp. 368-9.

originals, texts, glosses, various readings, styles, compositions, manuscripts, compilements, editions, publications and other circumstances, such as are common to the sacred books with all other writings and literature, this we have confidently asserted to be a just and lawful study.[59] We have even represented this species of criticism as necessary to the preservation and purity of Scripture, that sacred Scripture which has been so miraculously preserved in its successive copies and transcriptions under the eye, as we must needs suppose, of holy and learned critics through so many dark ages of Christianity to these latter times, in which learning has been happily revived.

But if this critical liberty raises any jealousy against us, we shall beg leave of our offended reader to lay before him our case at the very worst: that, if on such a naked exposition it be found criminal, we may be absolutely condemned; if otherwise, acquitted, and with the same favour indulged as others in the same circumstances have been before us.

On this occasion, therefore, we may be allowed to borrow something from the form or manner of our dialogue author and represent a conversation of the same free nature as that recited by him in his night scene,[60] where the supposed sceptic or freethinker delivers his thoughts and reigns in the discourse.

It was in a more considerable company and before a more numerous audience that, not long since, a gentleman of some rank, one who was generally esteemed to carry a sufficient caution and reserve in religious subjects of discourse as well as an apparent deference to religion and, in particular, to the national and established church, having been provoked by an impertinent attack of a certain violent bigoted party, was drawn into an open and free vindication not only of freethinking but free professing and discoursing in matters relating to religion and faith.

Some of the company, it seems, after having made bold with him as to what they fancied to be his principle, began to urge 'the necessity of reducing men to one profession and belief'. And several gentlemen, even of those who passed for moderate in their way, seemed so far to give in to this zealot opinion as to agree, that, 'notwithstanding the right method was not yet found, it was highly requisite that some way should be thought on to reconcile differences in opinion since, so long as this variety should last, religion, they thought, could never be successfully advanced'.

To this, our gentleman at first answered coldly, 'What was impossible to be done, could not', he thought, 'be properly pursued as necessary to be done.' But the raillery being ill taken, he was forced at last to defend himself the best he could upon this point, that 'variety of opinion was not to be cured' and that 'it was impossible all should be of one mind'.

[59] See pp. 67–8.
[60] See pp. 288–90.

'I well know', said he, 'that many pious men, seeing the inconveniences which the disunion of persuasions and opinions accidentally produces, have thought themselves obliged to stop this inundation of mischiefs and have made attempts accordingly. Some have endeavoured to unite these fractions by propounding such a guide as they were all bound to follow, hoping that the unity of a guide would have produced unity of minds. But who this guide should be, after all, became such a question that it was made part of that fire itself which was to be extinguished. Others thought of a rule. This was to be the effectual means of union! This was to do the work or nothing could! But supposing all the world had been agreed on this rule, yet the interpretation of it was so full of variety that this also became part of the disease.'

The company, upon this preamble of our gentleman, pressed harder upon him than before, objecting the authority of Holy Scripture against him and affirming this to be of itself a sufficient guide and rule. They urged again and again that known saying of a famed controversial divine of our Church against the divines of another, that 'the Scripture, the Scripture was the religion of Protestants'.[61]

To this, our gentleman at first replied only by desiring them to explain their word, 'Scripture', and by inquiring into the original of this collection of ancienter and later tracts, which in general they comprehended under that title: whether it were the apocryphal Scripture or the more canonical? the full or the half-authorized? the doubtful or the certain? the controverted or uncontroverted? the singly read or that of various reading? the text of these manuscripts or of those? the transcripts, copies, titles, catalogues of this Church and nation or of that other? of this sect and party or of another? of those in one age called orthodox and in possession of power or of those who in another overthrew their predecessors' authority and in their turn also assumed the guardianship and power of holy things? For how these sacred records were guarded in those ages might easily, he said, be imagined by anyone who had the least insight into the history of those times which we called primitive and those characters of men whom we styled Fathers of the Church.

'It must be confessed,' continued he, 'it was strange industry and unlucky diligence which was used, in this respect, by these ecclesiastical forefathers. Of all those heresies which gave them employment, we have absolutely no record or monument but what themselves who were adversaries have transmitted to us, and we know that adversaries, especially such who observe all opportunities to discredit both the persons and doctrines of their enemies, are not always the best recorders or witnesses of such transactions. We see it,' continued he in a very emphatical but somewhat embarrassed style, 'we see it

---

[61] William Chillingworth in *The Religion of Protestants a Safe Way to Salvation* (1637).

now in this very age, in the present distemperatures, that parties are no good registers of the actions of the adverse side, and, if we cannot be confident of the truth of a story now (now, I say, that it is possible for any man, especially for the interested adversary, to discover the imposture), it is far more unlikely that after-ages should know any other truth than such as serves the ends of the representers.'

Our gentleman, by these expressions, had already given considerable offence to his zealot auditors. They plied him faster with passionate reproaches than with arguments or rational answers. This, however, served only to animate him the more and made him proceed the more boldly with the same assumed formality and air of declamation in his general criticism of holy literature.

'There are', said he, 'innumerable places that contain, no doubt, great mysteries but so wrapped in clouds or hid in umbrages,[||||] so heightened with expressions or so covered with allegories and garments of rhetoric, so profound in the matter or so altered and made intricate in the manner, that they may seem to have been left as trials of our industry, and as occasions and opportunities for the exercise of mutual charity and toleration rather than as the repositories of faith and furniture of creeds. For, when there are found in the explications of these writings so many commentaries, so many senses and interpretations, so many volumes in all ages, and all like men's faces, no one exactly like another, either this difference is absolutely no fault at all or, if it be, it is excusable. There are, besides, so many thousands of copies that were written by persons of several interests and persuasions, such different understandings and tempers, such distinct abilities and weaknesses, that it is no wonder there is so great variety of readings: whole verses in one that are not in another; whole books admitted by one church or communion which are rejected by another; and whole stories and relations admitted by some Fathers and rejected by others. I consider, withal, that there have been many designs and views in expounding these writings, many senses in which they are expounded, and, when the grammatical sense is found out, we are many times never the nearer. Now, there being such variety of senses in Scripture and but few places so marked out as not to be capable of more than one, if men will write commentaries by fancy, what infallible criterion will be left to judge of the certain sense of such places as have been the matter of question? I consider again that there are indeed diverse places in these sacred volumes, containing in them mysteries and questions of great concernment, yet such is the fabric and constitution of the whole that there is no certain mark to determine whether the sense of these passages should be taken as literal or figurative. There is nothing in the nature of the

[||||] Shadows.

thing to determine the sense or meaning, but it must be gotten out as it can. And therefore it is unreasonably required that what is of itself ambiguous should be understood in its own prime sense and intention, under the pain of either a sin or an anathema. Very wise men, even the ancient Fathers, have expounded things allegorically when they should have expounded them literally. Others expound things literally when they should understand them in allegory. If such great spirits could be deceived in finding out what kind of senses were to be given to Scriptures, it may well be endured that we who sit at their feet should be subject at least to equal failure. If we follow any one translation or any one man's commentary, what rule or direction shall we have by which to choose that one aright? Or is there any one man that has translated perfectly or expounded infallibly? If we resolve to follow anyone as far only as we like or fancy, we shall then only do wrong or right by chance. If we resolve absolutely to follow anyone whithersoever he leads, we shall probably come at last where, if we have any eyes left, we shall see ourselves become sufficiently ridiculous.'

The reader may here, perhaps, by his natural sagacity, remark a certain air of studied discourse and declamation not so very proper or natural in the mouth of a mere gentleman, nor suitable to a company where alternate discourse is carried on in unconcerted measure and unpremeditated language. Something there was so very emphatical, withal, in the delivery of these words by the sceptical gentleman that some of the company, who were still more incensed against him for these expressions, began to charge him as a preacher of pernicious doctrines, one who attacked religion in form and carried his lessons or lectures about with him to repeat by rote, at any time, to the ignorant and vulgar, in order to seduce them.

'It is true, indeed,' said he, 'gentlemen, that what I have here ventured to repeat is addressed chiefly to those you call ignorant, such, I mean, as being otherwise engaged in the world, have had little time, perhaps, to bestow upon inquiries into divinity matters. As for you, gentlemen, in particular, who are so much displeased with my freedom, I am well assured you are in effect so able and knowing that the truth of every assertion I have advanced is sufficiently understood and acknowledged by you, however it may happen that, in your great wisdom, you think it proper to conceal these matters from such persons as you are pleased to style the vulgar.

It is true, withal, gentlemen,' continued he, 'I will confess to you that the words you have heard repeated are not my own. They are no other than what have been publicly and solemnly delivered even by one of the episcopal order, a celebrated churchman and one of the highest sort, as appears by his many devotional works, which carry the rites, ceremonies and pomp of worship with the honour and dignity of the priestly and episcopal order to the highest degree.[62] In effect, we see the reverend doctor's treatises standing, as it were, in the front of this order of authors and as the foremost of those good books used by the politest and most refined devotees of either sex. They maintain the principal place in the study of almost every elegant and high divine. They stand in folios and other volumes, adorned with variety of pictures, gildings and other decorations on the advanced shelves or glass cupboards of the ladies' closets. They are in use at all seasons and for all places, as well for church service as closet preparation and, in short, may vie with any devotional books in British Christendom. And, for the life and character of the man himself, I leave it to you, gentlemen, you, I mean, of the zealot kind, to except against it, if you think proper. It is your manner, I know, and what you never fail to have recourse to when any authority is produced against you. Personal reflection is

---

[62] The pious and learned Bishop [Jeremy] Taylor, in his treatise *Of the Liberty of Prophesying*, printed in Συμβολον Ήθικο-Πολεμικον *or a Collection of Polemical and Moral Discourses* [London, 1657]. The pages answering to the places above cited are 401, 402 (and in the epistle dedicatory, three or four leaves before), 438, 439–44, 451, 452. After which, in the succeeding page, he sums up his sense on this subject of sacred literature and the liberty of criticism and of private judgment and opinion in these matters, in the following words: 'since there are so many copies, with infinite varieties of reading, since a various interpunction, a parenthesis, a letter, an accent may much alter the sense, since some places have diverse literal senses, many have spiritual, mystical and allegorical meanings, since there are so many tropes, metonymies, ironies, hyperboles, proprieties and improprieties of language, whose understanding depends upon such circumstances, that it is almost impossible to know the proper interpretation, now that the knowledge of such circumstances and particular stories is irrecoverably ['irrevocably' in the original] lost, since there are some mysteries, which at the best advantage of expression are not easy to be apprehended and whose explication, by reason of our imperfections, must needs be dark, sometimes weak, sometimes unintelligible, and lastly, since those ordinary means of expounding Scripture, as searching the originals, conference of places, parity of reason and analogy of faith are all dubious, uncertain and very fallible, he that is the wisest and, by consequence, the likeliest to expound truest, in all probability of reason, will be very far from confidence, because every one of these, and many more, are like so many degrees of improbability and uncertainty, all depressing our certainty of finding out truth in such mysteries and amid so many difficulties. And, therefore, a wise man that considers this would not willingly be prescribed to by others . . ., for it is best every man should be left in that liberty, from which no man can justly take him, unless he could secure him from error' [p. 453].

The Reverend Prelate had but a few pages before acknowledged, indeed, that 'we have . . . an apostolical warrant' to 'contend earnestly for the faith. But then,' says the good bishop, very candidly and ingeniously, 'as these things recede farther from the foundation, our certainty is the less . . . and therefore it were very fit that our confidence should be according to our evidence, and our zeal according to our confidence' (p. 427).

He adds, 'All these disputes concerning tradition, councils, Fathers, etc., are not arguments against or besides reason, but contestations and pretences to the best arguments and the most certain satisfaction of our reason. But then all these coming into question submit themselves to reason, that is, to be judged by human understanding upon the best grounds and information it can receive. So that Scripture, tradition, councils and Fathers are the evidence in a question, but reason is the judge: that is, we being the persons that are to be persuaded, we must see that we be persuaded reasonably, and it is unreasonable to assent to a lesser evidence when a greater and clearer is propounded, but, of that, every man for himself is to take cognizance, if he be able to judge; if he be not, he is not bound under the tie of necessity to know anything of it' (p. 507). [On Taylor, see p. 46n.]

always seasonable and at hand on such an occasion, no matter what virtue, honesty or sanctity may lie in the character of the person cited, no matter though he be ever so much, in other respects, of your own party and devoted to your interest. If he has indiscreetly spoken some home truths or discovered some secret which strikes at the temporal interests of certain spiritual societies, he is quickly doomed to calumny and defamation.

I shall try this experiment, however, once more', continued our gentleman, 'and, as a conclusion to this discourse, will venture to produce to you a further authority of the same kind. You shall have it before you in the exact phrase and words of the great author in his theological capacity, since I have now no further occasion to conceal my citations and accommodate them to the more familiar style and language of conversation.

Our excellent Archbishop and late Father of our Church, when expressly treating that very subject of a rule in matters of belief, in opposition to Mr. S—— and Mr. R——, his Romish antagonists, shows plainly how great a shame it is for us Protestants at least, whatever the case may be with Romanists, to disallow difference of opinions and forbid private examination and search into matters of ancient record and Scriptural tradition, when at the same time we have no pretence to oral or verbal, no claim to any absolute superior judge or decisive judgment in the case, no polity, church or community, no particular man or number of men who are not, even by our own confession, plainly fallible and subject to error and mistake.[63]

"The Protestants", says his Grace, speaking in the person of Mr. S—— and the Romanists, "cannot know how many the books of Scripture ought to be, and which of the many controverted ones may be securely put in that catalogue, which not." "But I shall . . . tell him", replies his Grace, "that we know that just so many ought to be received as uncontroverted books, concerning which it cannot be shown there was ever any controversy." It was not incumbent perhaps on my lord Archbishop to help Mr. S—— so far in his objection as to add that, in reality, the burning, suppressing and interpolating method, so early in fashion and so tightly practised on the epistles, comments, histories and writings of the orthodox and heretics of old, made it impossible to say, with any kind of assurance, "what books, copies or transcripts those were concerning which there was never any controversy at all". This indeed would be a point not so easily to be demonstrated. But his Grace proceeds in

---

[63] Namely, Archbishop [John] Tillotson in his *Rule of Faith*, p. 677. [Shaftesbury's page references here were to the version of this work found in *The Works of the Most Reverend Dr. John Tillotson*, 5th edition (London, 1707). The work was first published in 1666: it was a response to *Sure Footing in Christianity* by John Sergeant, a Catholic controversialist. These passages are from Part II, Section 3. Tillotson, 1630–94, was associated with a latitudinarian view of Christianity. Well read in classic Christian literature, he had been a London preacher and had many associations with the Whigs. Favoured by King William III and Queen Mary II, he became Archbishop of Canterbury in 1691.]

showing the weakness of the Romish pillar, tradition. "For it must either", says he, "acknowledge some books to have been controverted or not. If not, why doth he make a supposition of controverted books? If oral tradition acknowledges some books to have been controverted, then it cannot assure us that they have not been controverted, nor consequently that they ought to be received as never having been controverted, but only as such, concerning which those Churches who did once raise a controversy about them, have been since satisfied that they are canonical[64] . . . Where is then the infallibility of oral tradition? How does the living voice of the present Church assure us that what books are now received by her were ever received by her? And, if it cannot do this but the matter must come to be tried by the best records of former ages (which the Protestants are willing to have the catalogue tried by), then it seems the Protestants have a better way to know what books are canonical than is the infallible way of oral tradition. And so long as it is better, no matter though it be not called infallible."[II]

Thus the free and generous Archbishop. For, indeed, what greater generosity is there than in owning truth frankly and openly, even where the greatest advantages may be taken by an adversary? Accordingly, our worthy Archbishop speaking again immediately in the person of his adversary: "The Protestants", says he, "cannot know that the very original, or a perfectly true copy of these books, hath been preserved." "Nor is it necessary", replies the Archbishop, "that they should know either of these. It is sufficient that they know that those copies which they have are not materially corrupted . . . But how do the Church of Rome know that they have perfectly true copies of the Scriptures in the original languages? They do not pretend to know this. The learned men of that Church acknowledge the various readings as well as we, and do not pretend to know otherwise than by probable conjecture (as we also may do) which of those readings is the true one."[65]

[II] P. 677.

[64] His Grace subjoins immediately: 'The traditionary Church now receives the *Epistle to the Hebrews* as canonical. I ask, do they receive it as ever delivered for such? That they must, if they receive it from oral tradition, which conveys things to them under this notion as ever delivered. And yet St Jerome, speaking not as a speculator but a testifier, says expressly of it that "the custom of the Latin Church doth not receive it among the canonical Scriptures". What saith Mr S—— to this? It is clear from this testimony that the Roman Church in St Jerome's time did not acknowledge this epistle for canonical, and it is as plain that the present Roman Church doth receive it for canonical' [p. 677].

[65] P. 678. The reader perhaps may find it worthwhile to read after this what the Archbishop represents (pp. 716–18 [Part III, Section 7]) of the plausible introduction of the grossest article of belief in the times when the habit of making creeds came in fashion. And accordingly it may be understood of what effect the dogmatizing practice in divinity has ever been. 'We will suppose, then, that about the time when universal ignorance and the genuine daughter of it (call her Devotion or Superstition) had overspread the world, and the generality of people were strongly inclined to believe strange things, and even the greatest contradictions were recom-

And thus', continued our lay gentleman, 'I have finished my quotations, which I have been necessitated to bring in my own defence to prove to you that I have asserted nothing on this head of religion, faith or the sacred mysteries which has not been justified and confirmed by the most celebrated churchmen and respected divines. You may now proceed in your invectives, bestowing as free language of that kind as your charity and breeding will permit. And you, reverend sirs, who have assumed a character which sets you above that of the mere gentleman and releases you from those decorums and constraining measures of behaviour to which we of an inferior sort are bound, you may liberally deal your religious compliments and salutations in what dialect you think fit, since, for my own part, neither the names of heterodox, schismatic, heretic, sceptic, nor even infidel or atheist itself will in the least scandalize me while the sentence comes only from your mouths. On the contrary, I rather strive with myself to suppress whatever vanity might naturally arise in me from such favour bestowed. For whatever may in the bottom be intended me by such a treatment, it is impossible for me to term it other than favour, since there are certain enmities which it will be ever esteemed a real honour to have merited.

If, contrary to the rule and measure of conversation, I have drawn the company's attention towards me thus long, without affording them an intermission during my recital, they will, I hope, excuse me, the rather because they heard the other recitals and were witnesses to the heavy charge and personal reflection which, without any real provocation, was made upon me in public by these zealot gentlemen, to whom I have thus replied. And, notwithstanding they may,

---

mended to them under the notion of mysteries, being told by their priests and guides that the more contradictious anything is to reason, the greater merit there is in believing it, I say, let us suppose that, in this state of things, one or more of the most eminent then in the Church, either out of design or out of superstitious ignorance and mistake of the sense of our Saviour's words used in the consecration of the Sacrament, should advance this new doctrine, that the words of consecration, etc.... Such a doctrine as this was very likely to be advanced by the ambitious clergy of that time as a probable means to draw in the people to a greater veneration of them ... Nor was such a doctrine less likely to take and prevail among the people in an age prodigiously ignorant and strongly inclined to superstition and thereby well prepared to receive the grossest absurdities under the notion of mysteries ... Now supposing such a doctrine as this, so fitted to the humour and temper of the age, to be once asserted either by chance or out of design, it would take like wildfire, especially if, by some one or more who bore sway in the Church, it were but recommended with convenient gravity and solemnity ... And for the contradictions contained in this doctrine, it was but telling the people then, as they do in effect now, that contradictions ought to be no scruple in the way of faith, that the more impossible anything is, it is the fitter to be believed, that it is not praiseworthy to believe plain possibilities, but this is the gallantry and heroical power of faith, this is the way to oblige God Almighty forever to us, to believe flat and downright contradictions ... The more absurd and unreasonable anything is, it is for that very reason the more proper matter for an article of faith. And if any of these innovations be objected against as contrary to former belief and practice, it is but putting forth a lusty act of faith and believing another contradiction, that though they be contrary yet they are the same.' See above p. 373.

after such breaches of charity as are usual with them, presume me equally out of charity on my own side, I will take upon me, however, to give them this good advice at parting: that, since they have of late been so elated by some seeming advantages and a prosperity which they are ill fitted to bear, they would at least beware of accumulating too hastily those high characters, appellations, titles and ensigns of power, which may be tokens, perhaps, of what they expect hereafter, but which, as yet, do not answer the real power and authority bestowed on them. The garb and countenance will be more graceful when the thing itself is secured to them and in their actual possession. Meanwhile, the anticipation of high titles, honours and nominal dignities beyond the common style and ancient usage, though it may be highly fashionable at present, may not prove beneficial or advantageous in the end.

I would, in particular, advise my elegant antagonists of this zealot kind that, among the many titles they assume to themselves, they would be rather more sparing in that high one of ambassador till such time as they have just means and foundation to join that of plenipotentiary together with it. For, as matters stand hitherto in our British world, neither their commission from the sovereign, nor that which they pretend from Heaven, amounts to any absolute or determining power.

The first holy messengers, for that I take to be the highest apostolic name, brought with them their proper testimonials in their lives, their manners and behaviour, as well as in powerful works, miracles and signs from Heaven. And, though, indeed, it might well be esteemed a miracle in the kind, should our present messengers go about to represent their predecessors in any part of their demeanour or conversation, yet there are further miracles remaining for them to perform before they can in modesty plead the apostolic or messenger authority. For though, in the torrent of a sublime and figurative style, a holy apostle may have made use, perhaps, of such a phrase as that of embassy or ambassador to express the dignity of his errand, it were to be wished that some who were never sent of any errand or message at all from God himself would use a modester title to express their voluntary negotiation between us and Heaven.

I must confess, for my own part, that I think the notion of an embassy from thence to be at best somewhat high strained in the metaphorical way of speech. But certain I am that, if there be any such residentship or agentship now established, it is not immediately from God himself, but through the magistrate and by the prince or sovereign power here on earth, that these gentlemen agents are appointed, distinguished and set over us. They have undoubtedly legal charter and character, legal titles and precedencies, legal habits, coats of arms, colours, badges.[66] But they may do well to consider that a thousand badges or liveries bestowed by men merely can never be sufficient to entitle them to the

[66] See p. 161.

same authority as theirs who bore the immediate testimony and miraculous signs of power from above. For in this case there was need only of eyes and ordinary senses to distinguish the commission and acknowledge the embassy or message as divine.

But, allowing it ever so certain a truth that there has been a thousand or near two thousand years' succession in this commission of embassy, where shall we find this commission to have lain? How has it been supplied still or renewed? How often dormant? How often divided, even in one and the same species of claimants? What party are they among moderns who, by virtue of any immediate testimonial from Heaven, are thus entitled? Where are the letters patent? The credentials? For these should in the nature of the thing be open, visible and apparent.

A certain Indian of the train of the ambassador princes sent to us lately from some of those pagan nations, being engaged one Sunday in visiting our churches and happening to ask his interpreter "who the eminent persons were whom he observed haranguing so long with such authority from a high place?", was answered, "They were ambassadors from the Almighty or, according to the Indian language, from the sun." Whether the Indian took this seriously or in raillery did not appear. But, having afterwards called in, as he went along, at the chapels of some of his brother ambassadors of the Romish religion and at some other Christian dissenting congregations, where matters, as he perceived, were transacted with greater privacy and inferior state, he asked "whether these also were ambassadors from the same place". He was answered that "they had indeed been heretofore of the embassy and had possession of the same chief places he had seen, but they were now succeeded there by others". "If those, therefore," replied the Indian, "were ambassadors from the sun, these, I take for granted, are from the moon."

Supposing, indeed, one had been no pagan but a good Christian, conversant in the original Holy Scriptures but unacquainted with the rites, titles, habits and ceremonials, of which there is no mention in those writings, might one not have inquired, with humble submission, into this affair? Might one not have softly and at a distance applied for information concerning this high embassy and, addressing perhaps to some inferior officer or liveryman of the train, asked modestly, "How and whence they came? Whose equipage they appeared in? At whose charges they were entertained? And by whose suffrage or command appointed and authorized? Is it true, pray sirs!, that their Excellencies of the present establishment are the sole commissioned? Or are there as many real commissioners as there are pretenders? If so, there can be no great danger for us, whichever way we apply ourselves. We have ample choice and may adhere to which commission we like best. If there be only one single true one, we have then, it seems, good reason to look about us, search narrowly into the affair, be scrupulous in our choice and, as the current physic bills admonish us, beware of counterfeits, since there are so many of these abroad with earthly powers and temporal commissions to back their spiritual pretences."

It is to be feared, in good earnest, that the discernment of this kind will prove pretty difficult, especially amid this universal contention, embroil and fury of religious challengers, these high defiances of contrary believers, this zealous opposition of commission to commission and this din of hell, anathemas and damnations raised everywhere by one religious party against another.

So far are the pretendedly commissioned parties from producing their commission openly, or proving it from the original record or court rolls of Heaven, that they deny us inspection into these very records they plead and refuse to submit their title to human judgment or examination.

A poet of our nation insinuates indeed in their behalf that they are fair enough in this respect. For when the murmuring people, speaking by their chosen orator or spokesman to the priests, says to them,

> With ease you take what we provide with care,
> And we who your legation must maintain
> Find all your tribe in the commission are,
> And none but Heaven could send so large a train,

the apologist, afterwards excusing this boldness of the people and soothing the incensed priests with fairer words, says to them, on a foot of moderation, which he presumes to be their character,

> You with such temper their intemperance bear,
> To show your solid science does rely
> So on itself as you no trial fear:
> For arts are weak that are of sceptics shy.[67]

The poet, it seems, never dreamt of a time when the very countenance of moderation should be out of fashion with the gentlemen of this order, and the word itself exploded as unworthy of their profession. And, indeed, so far are they at present from bearing with any sceptic or inquirer, ever so modest or discreet, that to hear an argument on a contrary side to theirs or read whatever may be written in answer to their particular assertions is made the highest crime. While they have among themselves such differences and sharp debates about their heavenly commission and are even in one and the same community or establishment divided into different sects and headships, they will allow no particular survey or inspection into the foundations of their controverted title. They would have us inferior passive mortals, amazed as we are and beholding with astonishment from afar these tremendous subjects of dispute, wait blindfold

---

[67] William Davenant, *Gondibert* 2.1.53 and 58. [See David F. Gladish, ed., *Sir William Davenant's Gondibert* (Oxford: Clarendon Press, 1971), p. 122.]

the event and final decision of the controversy. Nor is it enough that we are merely passive. It is required of us that, in the midst of this irreconcilable debate concerning heavenly authorities and powers, we should be as confident of the veracity of some one as of the imposture and cheat of all the other pretenders and that, believing firmly there is still a real commission at the bottom, we should endure the misery of these conflicts and engage on one side or the other, as we happen to have our birth or education, till by fire and sword, execution, massacre and a kind of depopulation of this earth, it be determined at last among us which is the true commission, exclusive of all others and superior to the rest.'[68]

Here our secular gentleman, who in the latter end of his discourse had already made several motions and gestures which betokened a retreat, made his final bow in form and quitted the place and company for that time, till, as he told his auditors, he had another opportunity and fresh leisure to hear, in his turn, whatever his antagonists might anew object to him in a manner more favourable and moderate or, if they so approved, in the same temper and with the same zeal as they had done before.

[68] See pp. 376–7.

Index

Cambridge Texts in the History of Philosophy

Titles published in the series thus far

Arnauld and Nicole *Logic or the Art of Thinking* (edited by Jill Vance Buroker)

Boyle *A Free Enquiry into the Vulgarly Received Notion of Nature* (edited by Edward B. Davis and Michael Hunter)

Bruno *Cause, Principle and Unity* and *Essays on Magic* (edited by Richard Blackwell and Robert de Lucca with an introduction by Alfonso Ingegno)

Clarke *A Demonstration of the Being and Attributes of God and Other Writings* (edited by Ezio Vailati)

Conway *The Principles of the Most Ancient and Modern Philosophy* (edited by Allison P. Coudert and Taylor Corse)

Cudworth *A Treatise Concerning Eternal and Immutable Morality* with *A Treatise of Freewill* (edited by Sarah Hutton)

Descartes *Meditations on First Philosophy*, with selections from the *Objections and Replies* (edited by John Cottingham)

Descartes *The World and Other Writings* (edited by Stephen Gaukroger)

Hobbes and Bramhall on Liberty and Necessity (edited by Vere Chappell)

Humboldt *On Language* (edited by Michael Losonsky, translated by Peter Heath)

Kant *Critique of Practical Reason* (edited by Mary Gregor with an introduction by Andrews Reath)

Kant *Groundwork of the Metaphysics of Morals* (edited by Mary Gregor with an introduction by Christine M. Korsgaard)

Kant *The Metaphysics of Morals* (edited by Mary Gregor with an introduction by Roger Sullivan)

Kant *Prolegomena to any Future Metaphysics* (edited by Gary Hatfield)

Kant *Religion within the Boundaries of Mere Reason and Other Writings* (edited by Allen Wood and George di Giovanni with an introduction by Robert Merrihew Adams)

La Mettrie *Machine Man and Other Writings* (edited by Ann Thomson)

Leibniz *New Essays on Human Understanding* (edited by Peter Remnant and Jonathan Bennett)

Malebranche *Dialogues on Metaphysics and on Religion* (edited by Nicholas Jolley and David Scott)

Malebranche *The Search after Truth* (edited by Thomas M. Lennon and Paul J. Olscamp)

Melanchthon *Orations on Philosophy and Education* (edited by Sachiko Kusukawa, translated by Christine Salazar)

Mendelssohn *Philosophical Writings* (edited by Daniel O. Dahlstrom)

Nietzsche *The Birth of Tragedy and Other Writings* (edited by Raymond Geuss and Ronald Speirs)

Printed in the United Kingdom
by Lightning Source UK Ltd.
104246UKS00001B/152